CHILDREN'S HEARINGS IN SCOTLAND

CHILDREN'S HEARINGS IN SCOTLAND

THIRD EDITION

By

Kenneth McK. Norrie, LL.B., Ph.D., F.R.S.E.
Professor of Law at the University of Strathclyde

SWEET & MAXWELL

 THOMSON REUTERS

Published in 2013 by W. Green, 21 Alva Street,
Edinburgh EH2 4PS
Part of Thomson Reuters (Professional) UK Limited
(Registered in England & Wales, Company No 1679046. Registered
Office and address for service: Aldgate House, 33 Aldgate High Street,
London EC3N 1DL)

http://www.wgreen.co.uk

Typeset by LBJ Typesetting Ltd, Kingsclere
Printed in Great Britain by Ashford Colour Press Ltd

No natural forests were destroyed to make this product;
Only farmed timber was used and replanted

A CIP catalogue record for this book
is available from the British Library

ISBN 978-0-414-01809-9

Thomson Reuters and the Thomson Reuters logo are
trademarks of Thomson Reuters.

PREFACE

When, in July 2008, the Scottish Government published its Consultation Document, *Strengthening for the Future: A Consultation on the Reform of the Children's Hearing System*, it was thought (I thought) that many valuable changes to the Children (Scotland) Act 1995 were being considered. Structurally, the most important of these proposals was to replace the 32 local authority children's panels with a single, national, children's panel, though that in itself would lead to terminological rather than substantive changes in the law. In addition, however, a number of alterations to the law as contained in the 1995 Act were presaged as a result of the increasing requirements for human rights compatibility—and not only those identified by the courts. A new edition of the present book would clearly be required, though if truth be told I had assumed that the 1995 Act (of which I remain inordinately fond) would survive more or less intact, if with substantial amendment to Chapter 2 of Part 2 thereof. In the event, the decision was made to replace the relevant sections of the 1995 Act with a wholly new, self-contained, statute and that decision was given effect to by the passing of the Children's Hearings (Scotland) Act 2011. A more radical revision of the present book became necessary. It was with some relief, as an author, that the originally announced commencement date for the 2011 Act (September 2012) was postponed as those much more directly involved with implementing the changes than I was came to understand just how fundamental the changes were (at practical, structural and technical levels). The associated rules and regulations, and court rules, took some time to draft, to be consulted upon, to redraft, and to become publicly available, and the preparation of the present text involved fits and starts, dashed expectations and some blind alleys. Much of the secondary legislation was finalised only at the last moment and in some places necessitated a rethinking of the entire structure of this book. I hope nevertheless that the book's final appearance reflects the aims of the Scottish Parliament while at the same time providing useful guidance to all professional participants in the children's hearing system including, not least, members of the new national children's panel themselves. Though this is a legal textbook, it has always been written with the members of Scotland's largest quasi-judicial tribunal primarily in mind.

The first edition of this book appeared in 1997, shortly after Part 2 of the Children (Scotland) Act 1995 came into force. The second edition followed eight years later in 2005. The major differences between the first two editions reflected the profound constitutional developments embodied in the Scotland Act 1998 and the Human Rights Act 1998. Another eight years has passed since the publication of the second edition, and this third edition takes full account (of course) of the Children's Hearings (Scotland) Act 2011 and the associated rules and regulations. This Act came into force on June 24, 2013, and that is the date as at which I have attempted to state the law.

Kenneth McK. Norrie
Howwood, June 2013

CONTENTS

**CHAPTER FOUR: REPORTERS' DUTIES PRIOR TO
THE HEARING** **57**

**CHAPTER FIVE: PRE-HEARING PANELS AND
DEEMED RELEVANT PERSONS** **77**

TABLE OF CASES

TABLE OF STATUTES

Scottish Statutes

TABLE OF STATUTORY INSTRUMENTS

TABLE OF CONVENTIONS

CHAPTER ONE

INTRODUCTION

HISTORY

The children's hearing system is unique to Scotland. Its genesis is found in the **1–01** Report of the Kilbrandon Committee,[1] which was appointed in 1961 to consider the provisions of the law of Scotland relating to the treatment of "juvenile delinquents and juveniles in need of care and protection or beyond parental control" and, in particular, the powers and procedures of the tribunals who deal with such juveniles. The Committee reported in 1964 and suggested a radical restructuring of the procedures for dealing with children with problems, a class which it defined widely. Its proposals, with some modifications, were accepted by the Government of the day[2] and enacted in the Social Work (Scotland) Act 1968, which came into effect on April 15, 1971. For over 25 years thereafter, Part 3 of the 1968 Act was, together with the subsidiary legislation passed under it, the basic source of the law of Scotland in respect of child care and protection and juvenile justice. Though the system by and large worked well and attracted many supporters at home and admirers abroad, there were invariably certain difficulties with the operation of such a new and innovative system. In the late 1980s and early 1990s the system was subjected to rigorous scrutiny on various fronts, and a number of different reports about aspects of its operation were published.[3] In addition, a number of high profile cases, which were disastrous for the individuals concerned, brought some of the operational difficulties to the public attention. An increasing public awareness of the need for the highest calibre of provision for children, enhanced in part by the UK's ratification of the UN Convention on the Rights of the Child, gave children's needs a higher political profile than they had ever had before. In 1995, Part 3 of the 1968 Act was repealed, and re-enacted with modifications as Chapter 3 of Part 2 of the Children (Scotland) Act 1995, which was at least partly designed to rectify the flaws previously identified. The changes introduced by the 1995 Act, though important, were not fundamental and the basic philosophy behind the

[1] *Report on Children and Young Persons, Scotland*, Cmnd.2306 (1964). The Report, together with a Foreword by Lord Fraser of Carmyllie and an Introduction by Professor Fred Stone (one of the members of the Kilbrandon Committee), has more recently been published by HMSO in the *Children and Society Series*, ed S. Asquith: accessible at *www.scotland.gov.uk/Publications/2003/10/18259/26900* [Accessed September 19, 2013].

[2] See the White Paper *Social Work and the Community*, Cmnd.3065 (1966).

[3] See, for example, the *Report of the Inquiry into the Removal of Children From Orkney in February* 1991 (the Clyde Report, H.C. Papers 1992–1993, No.195), the *Report of the Inquiry into Child Care Policies in Fife* (the Kearney Report, H.C. Papers 1992–1993 No.191), *Reporters to the Children's Panel: Their Role, Function and Accountability* (the Finlayson Report, Scottish Office, 1992), *Review of Child Care Law in Scotland* (Scottish Office, 1990), and the White Paper, *Scotland's Children: Proposals for Child Care Policy and Law*, Cm.2286 (1993).

system remained as it was before. The system as governed by the 1995 Act and subsidiary legislation passed under it came into operation on April 1, 1997.

1–02   In 1998, the UK Parliament enacted the Human Rights Act 1998 and the Scotland Act 1998, both of which had profound effect on the constitutional structure within which the Scottish legal system, including of course children's hearings, operates. One important consequence, which has had great effect on the children's hearings system, is that it became possible to challenge existing statutory law and practice as being inconsistent with the European Convention on Human Rights. Acts of the Scottish Parliament can be struck down, and Acts of the UK Parliament are now susceptible to declarations of incompatibility; the courts, however, are strongly encouraged to avoid either of these outcomes by interpreting statutes in a way that achieves ECHR compatibility, even when this is clearly inconsistent with the intent with which the legislation was passed. The Scottish courts have used these powers, and thereby changed the design of central aspects of the children's hearing system, in particular in relation to legal representation and to the definition of the category of individuals who have a right to participate in hearings. Partly as a result of this change in legal thinking, partly because the system as a whole was becoming (at the very least in its terminology) dated, and partly to ensure the statutory framework was consistent with the objectives contained in its overall policy statement *Getting it Right for Every Child*[4] the Scottish Government published a Consultation Document on reform of the Children's Hearing system in 2008,[5] followed by a draft Bill in 2009 which led to a further period of consultation. The Children's Hearings (Scotland) Bill was presented to the Scottish Parliament in February 2010, passed in November 2010 and received Royal Assent as the Children's Hearing (Scotland) Act 2011 (asp 1) on January 6, 2011. This, together with the Children's Hearings (Scotland) Act 2011 (Rules of Procedure in Children's Hearings) Rules 2013,[6] contain most of the current law relating to children's hearings. The 2011 Act and the 2013 Rules were commenced on June 24, 2013.[7] References to statutory provisions are, throughout this book, to the Children's Hearings (Scotland) Act 2011 (unless otherwise stated).

1–03   A feature of this history, as noticeable as it is remarkable, is the commitment from across the political spectrum to the essential characteristics of the Scottish system for dealing with children who are at risk, either from their own actions or from the acts or neglects of others. The 1968 Act was passed by a UK Labour Government; the 1995 Act by a UK Conservative Government; and the 2011 Act by a Scottish Nationalist Government. These essential characteristics remain, without serious political challenge, at the heart of the system notwithstanding that the structures within which it operates today are very different from those envisaged by either the Kilbrandon Committee or the drafters of the 1968 Act. Both the structures and the approach to legal argument have evolved over the past half-century, but the philosophy underpinning the system has proved itself remarkably robust. This has provided a stability to the system, which the various legal developments might otherwise tend to obscure.

---

[4] Scottish Executive, *Getting it Right for Every Child: Proposals for Action*, June 2005.
[5] *Strengthening for the Future: A Consultation on the Reform of the Children's Hearing System*, July 2008.
[6] SSI 2013/194.
[7] Children's Hearings (Scotland) Act 2011 (Commencement No. 9) Order 2013 (SSI 2013/195).

PHILOSOPHY OF THE SYSTEM

The Kilbrandon Committee Report and each of the 1968, 1995 and 2011 Acts **1–04** are founded upon two basic premises which, taken together, provide the philosophical underpinning of the children's hearing system in Scotland.

First, it is assumed that a child who has committed an offence, though culpable, is just as much in need of protection, guidance, treatment and control as is the child against whom an offence has been committed.[8] The commission of an offence by a child calls, in other words, for a caring response rather than a punitive response, just as the abuse or the neglect of a child calls for a caring response: in both, "the true distinguishing factor, common to all children concerned, is their need for special measures of education and training, the normal upbringing process having, for whatever reason, fallen short".[9] The caring response to all such children is encapsulated in the welfare principle, which is today given effect by the rule in s.25(2) of the Children's Hearings (Scotland) Act 2011 that "The children's hearing . . . is to regard the need to safeguard and promote the welfare of the child throughout the child's childhood as the paramount consideration", is perhaps not so substantial an innovation as is sometimes thought. It is certainly not the feature of the children's hearing system that makes that system unique. Since at least 1937, Scottish courts dealing with offences committed by children have been obliged to have regard to the welfare of the child,[10] and many foreign systems of criminal justice contain a similar provision. The unusual feature lies in the fact that it is the same tribunal, operating under the same procedural rules and having the same disposals available, that deals with all children identified as being in need of help, whether because they have committed an offence or because they have been abused or neglected. Even more remarkable, perhaps, is the fact that Scotland retains this grasp on reality in the face of a near universal retreat from it elsewhere in the developed world.[11]

Secondly, it is recognised that a court of law, with its adversarial traditions, **1–05** procedures and atmosphere, may well be an appropriate forum to resolve disputes of fact but is a singularly inappropriate forum for determining, in a welfare context, what if any form of protection, guidance, treatment or control an individual child needs. The child's needs can best be determined by a relatively[12] informal but carefully structured discussion involving the child and the child's primary carers. Long before either the United Kingdom ratified art.12 of the UN Convention on the Rights of the Child[13] or the European Court of Human Rights started to emphasise the importance of participation in legal process, the children's hearing system was operating in Scotland with its central feature being a discussion with the child him or herself. The Kilbrandon Committee

---

[8] Kilbrandon Report, paras 12–15.

[9] Kilbrandon Report, para.15.

[10] Children and Young Persons (Scotland) Act 1937 s.49(1).

[11] See C. Hallett, "Ahead of the Game or Behind the Times? The Scottish Children's Hearing System in International Perspective" (2000) 14 Int. J Law Pol & Fam 31.

[12] Relative to a court setting, that is.

[13] Which provides as follows: "States parties shall assure to the child who is capable of forming his or her own views the right to express those views freely in all matters affecting the child, the views of the child being given due weight in accordance with the age and maturity of the child. For this purpose, the child shall in particular be provided the opportunity to be heard in any judicial and administrative proceedings affecting the child, either directly, or through a representative or an appropriate body, in a manner consistent with the procedural rules of national law".

recognised that a court of law is not an environment that is likely to encourage a child to take an active or a helpful part in such a discussion, and for that reason the determination of what, if any, measures of state intervention in a child's life should be effected lies with a lay tribunal, the children's hearing. This hearing is made up of three individuals whose only qualification beyond their training is their interest in, or knowledge of, the needs of children. They are locally recruited and serve, voluntarily and without payment, in their own local areas. A court will still be involved if there is a dispute of fact as to the existence or otherwise of circumstances that justify referring the child to a children's hearing, for a court system designed to test evidence is accepted as the appropriate forum to find out the truth. It is far less appropriate a forum to determine how to react in the light of the discovered truth. It is this dichotomy between the role of the court and the role of the children's hearing that provides the defining characteristic of Scotland's system: its "genius", in the words of Lord President Hope.[14]

1–06   In addition to these two fundamental principles there are several other indigenous features of the system which serve to enhance the operation of these principles. First, the child is not looked at in isolation and is, rather, regarded as a member of a family unit. This recognises that a child's problems usually stem from his or her home environment, or a failure in the normal upbringing processes, and can be effectively resolved only by effecting some change in that environment. So, though the children's hearing can impose compulsory supervision on a child but not on his or her parents, the parents do have an obligation to attend the hearing and have an obligation to co-operate with any social work involvement in the child's life that is deemed necessary. Secondly, each child is looked at as an individual.[15] There is no "tariff" for particular grounds of referral (as there might be in a criminal court) for it is the needs rather than the deeds of the individual child that is the primary consideration of the children's hearing. It follows from this that the hearing must have as much discretion as possible to structure whatever measures of supervision, whether orthodox or unorthodox, are deemed appropriate to meet the needs of the particular child who appears before the hearing. So any condition that the hearing considers necessary can be attached to the order that the hearing makes.[16] And the order has no fixed length (though it must be reviewed at stated intervals) and it can be either terminated or varied at any time to suit any change in circumstances. Thirdly, though the system contains some informality, that informality is seen only in the discussion of the case which lies at the heart of any children's hearing; other elements of the procedure are as formal and as mandatory as the procedure in a court of law. The children's hearing is a quasi-judicial tribunal that has many of the powers of a court and it must, therefore, for the protection of all those who appear before it, conform to the standards of procedural fairness required not only by natural justice but by international obligation—in particular art.6 of the European Convention on Human Rights. It is a fundamental misunderstanding to describe the whole procedure at a children's hearing as "informal". Fourthly, the breadth of investigation and discussion is not bound by artificial limits. Once the grounds in respect of which the child has been referred to a children's hearing have

---

[14] *Sloan v B*, 1991 S.L.T. 530 at 548E.
[15] Kilbrandon Report, para.79.
[16] Kilbrandon Report, para.157.

been accepted or established it is open to the hearing to explore any aspect of the child's life that affects his or her welfare.[17] While the grounds of referral must receive consideration, the outcome of the case depends upon what the hearing identifies as the child's needs having had regard to all the circumstances and not just those contained in the grounds that brought the child to the hearing. The hearing's powers of investigation are limited only by what might be relevant to the child's overall interests. Fifthly, the proceedings at a children's hearing are private and members of the public are not to be admitted. This principle is important not only because privacy will encourage a child to take part in the discussion, but also because children are less able than adults to cope with wide publicity of their personal affairs.[18] Deterrence of others plays no part in either the hearing's deliberations or its outcomes.

As well as the features mentioned above, which have characterised both the **1–07** structure and the operation of the children's hearing system since its inception, the influence of the European Convention on Human Rights (ECHR), particularly since its incorporation into domestic law by the Human Rights Act 1998, ensures that a number of other features are now central to the hearing system. Articles 6 (right to due process) and 8 (right to respect for family life) are particularly significant; underpinning both is a right to effective participation in any legal process that might interfere with a civil right. Both the reporter and the hearing itself are "public authorities" for the purposes of the 1998 Act and are obliged, therefore, to act in a manner consistent with the ECHR[19]: it follows that both the process by which the child is referred to a hearing and the process by which the outcome of the referral is decided must not infringe any ECHR requirement. The most important ECHR principles in this context are "participation" and "proportionality". The design of children's hearings has always aimed to ensure that the child and his or her primary carers can participate fully in the decision-making process but the ECHR imposes a positive obligation to make this a reality[20]—as well as imposing an obligation on the legislature to ensure that it defines the class of person entitled to participate sufficiently widely to ensure respect for family life.

Proportionality is seen most explicitly in art.8 (though the European Court of **1–08** Human Rights has pointed out on various occasions that the proportionality principle is "inherent in the whole Convention").[21] Article 8(1) provides that everyone is entitled to respect for their private and family life. Any action to refer a child to a children's hearing, and any order made by a children's hearing, is an interference with, or limitation to, the child's and the parent's free exercise of their family life. As such it requires to be justified by the principle in art.8(2) that there shall be no interference with a person's private and family life except when this is "necessary in a democratic society". The concept of "necessity" has been given a wide interpretation by the European Court of Human Rights. The Court requires that to be shown to be "necessary", the interference must be in accordance with the law, must pursue a legitimate aim, and the means adopted to achieve that aim must be "proportionate", that is to say the minimum that is

---

[17] Kilbrandon Report, para.77.

[18] See *X v BBC*, 2005 S.L.T. 796.

[19] Human Rights Act 1998 s.6.

[20] So, for example, the European Court required that papers available to the hearing members be shared, before the hearing, with the parents: *McMichael v UK* (1995) 20 E.H.R.R. 205.

[21] *Sporrong & Lönnroth v Sweden* (1982) 5 E.H.R.R. 35 at [57]; *Soering v United Kingdom* (1989) 11 E.H.R.R. 439 at [89].

necessary to achieve the aim.[22] It is not, for example, a proportionate response to a child's additional support needs in education to remove the child from his or her parents and prohibit contact[23]; it is not proportionate to remove a new-born child from its mother when its safety could be ensured by appropriate monitoring of the mother.[24] Within the children's hearing system there is seldom if ever any difficulty in identifying a legitimate aim: it is to protect or ensure or enhance the child's welfare. The more difficult issue is nearly always proving that the means adopted to achieve that aim are proportionate thereto in the sense of going no further than is necessary. To a large extent this principle reflects the minimum intervention principle now contained in s.28(2) of the Children's Hearings (Scotland) Act 2011,[25] but it is in fact more focused in that it requires a clear identification of an aim, which is legitimate, and a clear and effective link between that aim and the means chosen to achieve it. But in itself the introduction by the Human Rights Act 1998 of the proportionality test did not require a change of mindset for any of the active participants in the children's hearing system. The Kilbrandon Report itself recognised[26] that a welfare-based approach might in fact and in practice "represent an appreciable inroad into personal and family life" which in some cases would be unacceptable and therefore could not be taken. Nor, of course, did the requirement to ensure participation in the process require a change of mindset for panel members, though since the enactment of the Human Rights Act 1998 there has been an increased emphasis on the need to ensure *effective* participation and a recognition of the need to define entitlement to participate with ECHR considerations at the forefront of the mind.

1–09 The incorporation into domestic law of the art.6 right to a fair hearing, on the other hand, might be argued to have required a change of mindset within the hearing system. Prior to the coming into force of the Human Rights Act 1998, the child's interests were considered paramount, which was often (and wrongly) interpreted to mean that the child's interests were the concern of the hearing to the exclusion of all other considerations. Indeed Lord Justice-Clerk Ross may be found expressing the view that the child's welfare was more important than due process, and that procedural niceties must give way to the child's interests.[27] If this were ever truly the case it is certainly no longer so.[28] Article 6 protects everyone's right to a fair hearing in the determination of their civil rights. One of these civil rights is family autonomy, or freedom from state interference (itself protected by art.8). And this is a right that inheres in both child and parent. A system is not "fair" to one person if procedural niceties are

---

[22] See K. Norrie, "A Child's Right to be Looked After", Ch.7 in A. Cleland and E.E. Sutherland, *Children's Rights in Scotland*, 3rd edn (W. Green, 2009).

[23] *Kutzner v Germany* (2002) 35 E.H.R.R. 25.

[24] *P, C and S v United Kingdom* (2002) 35 E.H.R.R. 31. In *Haase v Germany* (2005) 40 E.H.R.R. 19 at [91] the Court said: "The taking of a new-born baby into public care at the moment of its birth is an extremely harsh measure. There must be extraordinarily compelling reasons before a baby can be physically removed from its mother, against her will, immediately after birth as a consequence of a procedure in which neither she nor her partner has been involved". See also *J & H, Petrs* [2013] CSOH 27 where it was held that a failure to ensure the participation of parents in the process at which a child protection order was made over a new-born baby was an infringement of art.8 in its procedural aspects. On CPOs, see below at Ch.15.

[25] See below, para.9–18.

[26] Kilbrandon Report, paras 79–80.

[27] *Kennedy v A*, 1986 S.L.T. 358 at 362A.

[28] *M v Authority Reporter*, 2011 G.W.D. 2–94, per Sheriff Principal Taylor at [34].

bypassed in order to favour another person, nor if their civil rights are ignored, nor if they are denied the means of effective participation in a system that might affect their rights. Basic principles of fairness must underpin the system if it is to survive ECHR challenge, and the right to a fair hearing inheres in the parents or relevant persons to the same extent as it inheres in the child: it follows that the hearing may no longer ignore or minimise the interests of the parents but is obliged to protect them to the same extent as it protects the interests of the child. So the change of mindset that was required by the Human Rights Act 1998 was for the hearing to operate in a way that balances sometimes competing interests, rather than simply holding the child's interests to be the paramount (by which was understood sole) consideration. The child's interests *are* paramount[29] but that does not prohibit the reporter or hearing from balancing them with the other considerations which they must also take into account.

LEGAL AID

Before the coming into force of the Children's Hearings (Scotland) Act 2011 no **1–10** form of legal aid or advice and assistance was available for the purposes of enabling a solicitor to represent a child or relevant person at a children's hearing though, in some circumstances, advice and assistance could be accessed for preparatory work before the hearing. Legal aid was, on the other hand, available for the associated court proceedings, including in particular applications to the sheriff for the establishment of grounds of referral and appeals from decisions of the children's hearing. One oddity in relation to legal aid in these proceedings was that it was the sheriff (rather than, as is now the norm, the Scottish Legal Aid Board) who assessed the criteria for eligibility to legal aid. Earlier editions of this book suggested that the lack of paid legal representation at children's hearings amounted to an infringement both of art.40 of the UN Convention[30] and of art.6 of the European Convention on Human Rights. When the matter was directly challenged, the Court of Session held that art.6 of the ECHR was indeed contravened by the failure, at least in certain circumstances, to provide paid legal representation to the child[31] and, subsequently, to the relevant person.[32] In the latter case, indeed, the Inner House described the absence of any statutory provision for legally aided attendance of solicitors at children's hearings as "an inbuilt systemic flaw in the legal aid scheme as it applied to the children's hearing system".[33] An interim scheme, outwith the legal aid scheme, to provide paid legal representation for children at hearings was established after the first of these cases, and extended after the second to include legal representation for relevant persons.[34] Legal representatives could be—in limited circumstances— appointed to the child or (latterly) the relevant person by the children's hearing

---

[29] Children's Hearings (Scotland) Act 2011 s.25(2).
[30] Children who are accused of a crime are to have legal assistance in preparing and presenting their defence.
[31] *S v Miller*, 2001 S.L.T. 531 and 1304.
[32] *K v Authority Reporter*, 2009 S.L.T. 1019.
[33] 2009 S.L.T. 1019 at [56].
[34] Children's Hearings (Legal Representation) (Scotland) Rules 2002 (SSI 2002/63), as amended by Children's Hearings (Legal Representation) (Scotland) Amendment Rules 2009 (SSI 2009/211).

itself,[35] and these legal representatives were funded by the local authority. That interim scheme was repealed and replaced by Pt 19 of the Children's Hearings (Scotland) Act 2011 and the Children's Legal Assistance (Scotland) Regulations 2013,[36] which amend the Legal Aid (Scotland) Act 1986 and associated legal assistance regulations so that the child and relevant person (and some others) may in appropriate circumstances access legal aid funds to pay for a solicitor (whether a duty solicitor or one selected by the individual him or herself).

1–11   As well as providing funding to solicitors who are registered[37] as competent to undertake children work, the 2011 Act renders the Scottish Legal Aid Board responsible for maintaining standards of representation, and it obliges the Board[38] to establish and maintain a register of solicitors and firms eligible to provide children's legal assistance; the Board must also maintain a Code of Practice and an associated scheme for quality assurance.[39] In this way the children's legal assistance provisions seek to ensure that legal representation at hearings is provided by solicitors with an appropriate level of knowledge and expertise in relation to children and the children's hearing system. Further normalising legal aid within the children's hearing system, responsibility for assessing eligibility for children's legal aid in sheriff court proceedings has been transferred from the sheriff to the Scottish Legal Aid Board. Children's legal assistance in relation to children's hearings, funded by the Scottish Legal Aid Board, takes five different forms, described below.[40]

Automatic legal aid

1–12   Any child appearing before certain types of children's hearing (or sheriff court) is entitled to legal aid to pay for a duty solicitor instructed by the child, without the satisfaction of any criteria relating either to the merits of the case or to the means of the child.[41] Children's legal aid is automatically available to allow a legal representative to appear on behalf of the child:

---

[35] See the second edition of this book, at pp.91–93.

[36] SSI 2013/200.

[37] In the Children's Legal Assistance Register, maintained by the Scottish Legal Aid Board.

[38] Legal Aid (Scotland) Act 1986 s.28M, as inserted by the Children's Hearings (Scotland) Act 2011 s.191.

[39] Legal Aid (Scotland) Act 1986 s.28N, as so inserted. The Code of Practice may be accessed from the website of the Scottish Legal Aid Board.

[40] Authoritative guidance on the operation of these forms of paid legal assistance is to be found in the *Children's Legal Assistance Handbook* published by the Scottish Legal Aid Board, accessible from their website.

[41] Neither the Legal Aid (Scotland) Act 1986 nor the Children's Hearings (Scotland) Act 2011 addresses the issue of the child's capacity to instruct a solicitor, and so the normal rule, found in s.2(4A) of the Age of Legal Capacity (Scotland) Act, 1991 applies: a person under the age of 16 years has legal capacity to instruct a solicitor in connection with any civil matter (which includes any children's hearing—including, it is submitted, a hearing at which the s.67 ground is that the child has committed a criminal offence) where that child has a general understanding of what it means to do so; and without prejudice to the generality of that rule a person aged 12 years or more is presumed to be of sufficient age and maturity to have such understanding. The test ought not to be interpreted restrictively in the context of children's hearings, and even less so in relation to automatic legal aid. Situations (c) and (d) in the text are unlikely to involve children too young to have a general understanding of what a solicitor is for, though situations (a) and (b) will often involve young infants from whom instruction simply cannot be taken. The application for legal aid itself may be made on the child's behalf by a relevant person, safeguarder or other representative (other than a solicitor): Children's Legal Assistance (Scotland) Regulations 2013 (SSI 2013/200) reg.8.

(a) before a sheriff hearing an application for variation or termination of a child protection order (CPO);

(b) at a children's hearing reviewing a CPO on the second working day after either the order was made or the child was taken to a place of safety;[42]

(c) at a children's hearing where a children's hearing or a pre-hearing panel has previously considered that it might be necessary to make a compulsory supervision order which includes as one of its measures a secure accommodation authorisation; and

(d) at a children's hearing held no later than the third day after the reporter has received notice that the child is being kept in a place of safety under the terms of s.43(4) of the Criminal Procedure (Scotland) Act 1995—that is to say when the child is being brought to a children's hearing after having been arrested and detained on suspicion of having committed a criminal offence.[43]

Automatic legal aid of this sort at these hearings is available for the child only.[44] If the child already has a solicitor of choice, that solicitor may be paid for by ABWOR, discussed below.[45] Subject to satisfaction of eligibility criteria other people (such as the relevant person) may be granted ABWOR (discussed below) for these hearings.

Children's Legal Aid

Children's legal aid may be provided to the child and relevant person **1–13** (including individuals deemed to be relevant persons) at all court proceedings under Pts 10 and 15 of the 2011 Act[46] (primarily applications to the sheriff for a grounds determination[47] and appeals[48]) on the Scottish Legal Aid Board being satisfied of specified conditions. As well, children's legal aid is available on the same conditions in applications to the sheriff to vary or terminate a CPO,[49] and to extend, further extend or vary an interim compulsory supervision order.[50] For the child the conditions are as follows:

(a) that it is in the best interests of the child that children's legal aid be made available;

(b) that it is reasonable in the particular circumstances of the case that the child should receive children's legal aid; and

---

[42] For second working day hearings, see below, paras 15–20—15–25.

[43] Legal Aid (Scotland) Act 1986 s.28C, as inserted by the Children's Hearings (Scotland) Act 2011 s.191.

[44] Payment is in accordance with the fees prescribed in relation to children's matters in Pt 1 of Sch.3 to the Advice and Assistance (Scotland) Regulations 1996: Civil Legal Aid (Scotland) (Fees) Regulations 1989, as amended by the Children's Legal Assistance (Fees) (Miscellaneous Amendments) (Scotland) Regulations 2013 (SSI 2013/144).

[45] See para.1–15.

[46] Children's Legal Assistance (Scotland) Regulations 2013 reg.6.

[47] For which see below, Ch.8.

[48] For which see below, Ch.14.

[49] For which see below, paras 15–26—15–32.

[50] For which see below, para. 10–07.

(c) that after consideration of the child's disposable income and disposable capital[51] the expenses of the case cannot be met without undue hardship to the child.[52]

For the relevant person, only conditions (b) and (c) above need be satisfied.[53] An individual who is appealing a decision that he or she is not or is no longer to be deemed to be a relevant person (or is responding to an appeal against a decision that he or she is or remains deemed to be a relevant person) is also eligible for children's legal aid in that appeal on satisfaction of conditions (b) and (c) above, and in addition the Scottish Legal Aid Board is satisfied that he or she has substantial grounds for making or responding to the appeal in question.[54] Finally, an individual who appeals against a decision relating to contact made by a hearing held under s.126 of the Children's Hearings (Scotland) Act 2011[55] is also entitled to receive children's legal aid for such an appeal on satisfying the Scottish Legal Aid Board of the following:

(a) that for the purpose of enabling the individual to participate effectively in the proceedings, it is necessary that the individual be represented by a solicitor or counsel[56];
(b) that it is reasonable in the particular circumstances of the case that the individual should receive children's legal aid; and
(c) that after consideration of the disposable income and disposable capital of the individual,[57] the expenses of the case cannot be met without undue hardship to the individual or the dependants of the individual.[58]

As well as assessing these conditions, the Scottish Legal Aid Board will apply a means test to the applicant.

Advice and assistance

1–14   Advice and assistance includes oral or written advice on the application of Scots law to any particular circumstances which have arisen, and assistance in the taking of any steps conducting or defending proceedings.[59] This has always been available to any individual whose legal position might be affected by the children's hearing process (including the child, relevant person, individuals claiming to be relevant persons and individuals whose contact rights might be affected by decisions of the children's hearing), and it has always been, and

---

[51] Disposable income and disposable capital are to be determined according to the rules in the Children's Legal Assistance (Scotland) Regulations 2013 (SSI 2013/200) regs 10–15 and Schs 1 and 2.

[52] Legal Aid (Scotland) Act 1986 s.28D(3), as inserted by the Children's Hearings (Scotland) Act 2011 s.191.

[53] Legal Aid (Scotland) Act 1986 s.28E(3), as so inserted.

[54] Legal Aid (Scotland) Act 1986 s.28F(2), as so inserted.

[55] For which see below, paras 13–41—13–44.

[56] Notice that the requirement is that *legal* representation must be shown to be necessary to enable effective participation.

[57] Determined as in fn.51 above.

[58] Children's Legal Assistance (Scotland) Regulations 2013 (SSI 2013/200) reg.5. The odd (and unique) reference to hardship of "dependants" is to be noted.

[59] For the full definition see s.6 of the Legal Aid (Scotland) Act 1986.

remains, means tested. The amendments to the legal aid provisions necessitated by the Children's Hearings (Scotland) Act 2011 have left this form of legal aid effectively untouched.[60]

ABWOR

Assistance by way of representation (which is a form of advice and assist- **1–15** ance) is governed by the Advice and Assistance (ABWOR) (Scotland) Regulations 2003,[61] which were substantially amended by the Children's Legal Assistance (Scotland) Regulations 2013. Regulation 3A of the 2003 Regulations provides that ABWOR will be available without satisfaction of any criteria to a child seeking assistance by way of representation in any circumstance in which automatic legal aid is available to the child and in applications to a sheriff for a CPO or a child assessment order; for other hearings[62] and pre-hearing panels[63]—and for relevant persons—ABWOR will be available if both a means test and a merits test have been satisfied (as determined by the solicitor involved and/or the Scottish Legal Aid Board). The merits test is that of "effective participation", as set out in reg.14 of the 2003 Regulations,[64] which is to be determined taking account of the following matters:

(a) the complexity of the case, including the existence and difficulty of any points of law in issue;
(b) the nature of the legal issues involved;
(c) the ability of the person to consider and challenge any document or information in the hearings or proceedings without the assistance of a solicitor; and
(d) the ability of the person to present his or her views in an effective manner without the assistance of a solicitor.

It is to be noted that what needs to be shown is that the assistance of a solicitor is required to ensure effective participation rather than, say, the assistance of an interpreter or signer.

Special urgency legal aid

The Children's Legal Assistance (Scotland) Regulations 2013 also provide **1–16** for legal aid to be made available for specially urgent work in any court proceedings that requires to be undertaken before an application for children's legal aid can be made or determined: the Scottish Legal Aid Board may provide legal aid if (a) it appears to the Board that it is reasonable in the particular circumstances of the case that the applicant should receive children's legal aid

---

[60] The Advice and Assistance (Scotland) Regulations 1996 (SI 1996/2447) have been amended no further than to reflect the fact that the governing Act is no longer the Children (Scotland) Act 1995 but is now the Children's Hearings (Scotland) Act 2011: see the Children's Legal Assistance (Scotland) Regulations 2013 (SSI 2013/200) reg.4.

[61] SSI 2003/179.

[62] Including s.126 hearings, for which see below, paras.13–41—13–44.

[63] ABWOR is available to any person who is entitled to attend a pre-hearing panel, including an individual seeking to be deemed to be a relevant person.

[64] As amended by the Children's Legal Assistance (Scotland) Regulations 2013 (SSI 2013/200) reg.3(5).

and (b) the Board is satisfied on application that participation in proceedings is required as a matter of special urgency to protect the applicant's position.[65] Where work has been carried out by a solicitor as a matter of special urgency but the application for children's legal aid is subsequently refused payments may nevertheless be made out of the legal aid fund for the urgently undertaken work so long as the Board is satisfied that the solicitor had reasonable grounds for believing, on the information available at the time the work was done, that the applicant would be eligible for children's legal aid and the work was actually, necessarily and reasonably done, due regard being had to economy.[66] Special urgency legal aid may not, however, be made available if an earlier application for children's legal aid by the applicant in relation to the same proceedings has been refused or abandoned, or where the Board has ceased to make legal aid available.[67]

Summary

1–17   It will be seen from the above that availability of state-funded legal advice, assistance and representation depends upon the type of hearing involved, and who is seeking legal aid. For work undertaken at some types of hearings there is neither a means nor a merits test; at other hearings there is one or both; sometimes it is for the solicitor to assess the test and sometimes the Scottish Legal Aid Board. A summary chart of the various types of hearing and the various tests to be satisfied,[68] is reproduced, with the kind permission of the Scottish Legal Aid Board, at the end of this chapter. I am grateful to both the drafter of this chart and the Board for making it available here.[69]

CONCLUSION

1–18   The children's hearing system continues to evolve, in light of better understandings and in response to political imperatives. Sometimes, such as with the extension of legal aid, just considered, the responses to changing understandings enhance the children's hearing system and clearly improve its operation. Sometimes, however, the responses to political imperatives fit uneasily into the underpinning philosophy of the system. For example in 2004 the Scottish Parliament, responding to public pressures to "do something" about the perceived problem of the unruly child, passed the Antisocial Behaviour etc.

---

[65] Children's Legal Assistance (Scotland) Regulations 2013 (SSI 2013/200) reg.18(1). This reflects the rules in the Civil Legal Aid (Scotland) Regulations 2002 (SSI 2002/494) and applies to all court proceedings for which children's legal aid is potentially available.

[66] Children's Legal Assistance (Scotland) Regulations 2013 (SSI 2013/200) reg.18(6) and (7). If the Board is not so satisfied it may still make payments by way of any contribution paid by a person for whom a solicitor has undertaken specially urgent work.

[67] Children's Legal Assistance (Scotland) Regulations 2013 (SSI 2013/200) reg.18(2). The rules in reg.18 are substantially similar to special urgency legal aid in other civil proceedings, governed by reg.18 of the Civil Legal Aid (Scotland) Regulations 2002 (SSI 2002/494). Guidance is provided on that latter provision in Pt 4, Ch. 6 of the *Civil Legal Aid Handbook*, published by the Scottish Legal Aid Board and available on its website, and on reg.18 of the 2013 Regulations in the *Children's Legal Assistance Handbook*, similarly available.

[68] Devised by Miss Elizabeth Cuschieri, Senior Solicitor at the Scottish Legal Aid Board.

[69] Though any errors in reproduction, presentation or indeed understanding, remain (of course) the author's responsibility.

(Scotland) Act 2004. The aim was to curb antisocial behaviour, primarily by the mechanism of antisocial behaviour orders granted by courts.[70] If a child is to be the subject of the order, the children's hearing will have a role to play. But that role is not informed by panel members' expertise in identifying the child's welfare: rather the purpose of the order is to protect others from actions of the child and this involves a small but dangerous shift in the focus of attention that panel members are asked to give in individual cases.[71] These orders are explicitly designed to deal with the deeds of the child and the needs of others. It was probably misconceived to involve children's hearings at all in the antisocial behaviour legislation.[72] The challenge remains therefore to ensure that legislators and policy-makers are fully aware of what it is that makes the hearing system successful, in order that that system can continue to build upon its experience as a means of identifying and addressing the issues of all children in need of state intervention in their lives in order to provide them with an appropriate level or protection, guidance, treatment or control.

---

[70] For a general examination of the 2004 Act, see T. Guthrie, *Antisocial Behaviour Legislation* (W. Green, 2005).

[71] See A. Cleland "The Antisocial Behaviour etc. (Scotland) Act 2004: Exposing the Punitive Fault Line Below the Children's Hearing System" (2005) Edin. L.R. 439.

[72] In fairness it should be noted that there are some very valuable provisions contained in the Antisocial Behaviour etc. (Scotland) Act 2004, particularly in the strengthening of local authorities' duties to give effect to the orders made by children's hearings and the introduction of mechanisms to enforce these duties: see further below, paras 13–34—13–36.

Legal Aid Overview

	Available To:	Proceedings Type:	Solicitor Test:	Board Test:
Advice & Assistance	Child / Relevant Person / Deemed Relevant Person / Non Deemed Relevant Person / S126 Individual / Other	Advice re a Children's Hearing or an associated court proceeding	Means / Merits	Means verification
Automatic	Child	Court Proceedings: 1. Variation or termination of a CPO Children's Hearing: 1. 2nd/working day hearing following CPO 2. Hearing to contemplate secure accommodation 3. Hearing following arrest/detention	None	Notification only
ABWOR	Child	Court Proceedings: 1. S35 Application for CAO 2. S38 Application for CPO 3. Variation or termination of a CPO Children's Hearing: 1. 2nd/working day hearing following CPO 2. Hearing to contemplate secure accommodation 3. Hearing following arrest/detention	None	Notification only
	Relevant Person / Deemed Relevant Person	Court Proceedings: 1. S35 Application for CAO 2. S38 Application for CPO 3. Variation or termination of a CPO Children's Hearing: 1. 2nd/working day hearing following CPO 2. Hearing to contemplate secure accommodation 3. Hearing following arrest/detention	Means / Merits	Means verification / Retrospective check of merits when account received
	Child / Relevant Person / Deemed Relevant Person	All other unspecified Children's Hearings / S79 (2) Pre-Hearing Panel	Means	Means verification / Merits
	S126 Individual	S126 Hearing only	Means	Means verification / Merits
	Non Deemed Relevant Person	S79 (2) Pre-Hearing Panel only / Children's hearing where S81 determination to be made	Means	Means verification / Merits
Legal Aid	Child / Relevant Person / Deemed Relevant Person	Proceedings under Part 10 or 15 of the 2011 Act (court proceedings arising from a pre-panel hearing or Children's hearing decision including appeals to the sheriff, Sheriff Principal and Court of Session)	None N.B. Submit Legal Aid application to the Board	Means / Merits
	Non Deemed Relevant Person	S160 appeal to the sheriff and S164 to the Sheriff Principal and Court of Session	None	Means / Merits
	S126 Individual	S161 appeal to sheriff and S165 appeal to the Sheriff Principal and Court of Session	None	Means / Merits

CHAPTER TWO

THE PERSONNEL OF THE CHILDREN'S HEARING SYSTEM

THE CHILDREN'S PANEL

Children's hearings are composed of three members of the Children's Panel,[1] **2–01** which is a national body made up of members of the public who have been appointed to the Panel by the National Convener of Children's Hearings Scotland.[2] The National Convener may delegate this function to area support teams.[3] Members of the Children's Panel hold office for three years but must thereafter be reappointed for a further three years unless the member declines reappointment or the National Convener is satisfied that the person is unfit to be a panel member by reason of inability, conduct, or failure without reasonable excuse to comply with the training requirements imposed by the National Convener.[4] On these same grounds, panel members may be removed from office at any time by the National Convener but, in an important protection of their independence, the National Convener may do so only with the consent of the Lord President of the Court of Session.[5]

The National Convener must endeavour to ensure that the Panel includes **2–02** persons from all local authority areas,[6] though there is no absolute requirement that panel members come from each of the 32 local authority areas in Scotland. A list of the names of each panel member must be published by the National Convener, together with information as to the local authority area in which the panel member lives or works and that list and information must be made available by the National Convener for public inspection.[7]

It is from this national Panel that members are chosen by the National **2–03** Convener or an area support team[8] to constitute particular children's hearings to deal with the cases of individual children. These hearings consist of three panel members, at least one of whom must be a woman and at least one of

---

[1] Children's Hearings (Scotland) Act 2011 s.5.
[2] 2011 Act s.4(1) and Sch.2 para 1.
[3] 2011 Act Sch.1 para.14(2)(a).
[4] 2011 Act Sch.2 para.1.
[5] 2011 Act Sch.2 para.1(6).
[6] 2011 Act s.4(2)(b).
[7] 2011 Act Sch.2 para.2.
[8] 2011 Act s.6 and Sch.1 para.14(1). A children's hearing may request that the National Convener select, where practicable, one of its members to be a member of the next hearing to be arranged in relation to the child: Children's Hearings (Scotland) Act 2013 (Rules of Procedure in Children's Hearings) Rules 2013 (SSI 2013/194) (hereinafter "2013 Rules") r.3.

whom must be a man.[9] It is to this lay tribunal[10] that the extensive decision-making powers over the lives of children and their families, described in the later chapters of this book, are given. Panel members are entitled to take time off work to sit on children's hearings.[11]

Role of the chairing member

2–04   One of the three members of the children's hearing will act as the chairing member of the hearing. Selection of the chairing member for any particular hearing lies with the National Convener, though in practice this function will be carried out by area support teams. If the chairing member has not been selected before the commencement of the hearing then the members themselves must, immediately before the beginning of the hearing, determine which of their number is to chair the hearing.[12] Every panel member is eligible to act as the chairing member and there is no special qualification required to do so, beyond membership of the Children's Panel and completion of training in the particular procedural responsibilities of chairing members. Though the chairing member of the hearing has no greater say in the disposal of the case than either of the other members, he or she does have various statutory functions to perform, in three broad areas: acting as master of procedure, giving information and explanations, and ensuring effective participation. How these functions are exercised will be discussed at the appropriate points later in this book, but for reference purposes it may be noted that the most important of the statutory functions of the chairing member are as listed below.

Master of procedure

2–05   • The procedure at any children's hearing or pre-hearing panel, except in so far as provided for under the 2011 Act or the 2013 Rules, is to be determined by the chairing member.[13]
    • It is the responsibility of the chairing member to take all reasonable steps to ensure that the number of persons present at a children's hearing at the same time is kept to a minimum.[14]

---

[9] 2011 Act s.6(3)(a). Problems created by the law's ambivalence to transgender individuals, previously resolved in practice by ensuring that a transgendered panel member sat with another man and another woman, have now diminished. The Gender Recognition Act 2004 allows for a transgendered individual to be recognised for all legal purposes in their new gender; and even before the granting under that Act of a Gender Recognition Certificate, the law will accept that a person has changed sex if they have done so for all social reasons and the policy behind the gender specific rule in question is satisfied by such recognition: *A v Chief Constable of West Yorkshire Police* [2004] UKHL 21. The end result of this is that for the purposes of satisfying the gender-specific requirements for the makeup of an individual children's hearing a panel member will be recognised in his or her new gender if either: (i) he or she has acquired a Gender Recognition Certificate under the 2004 Act to that effect; or (ii) he or she has been living in the new gender and presents to the world (including the child and family attending the hearing) as a member of that gender.

[10] Trained in accordance with the 2011 Act Sch.2 para.3. The National Convener must take reasonable steps to involve persons under the age of 25 in this training, and the training must include how best to elicit the views of the child.

[11] Employment Rights Act 1996 s.50(2)(b).

[12] 2013 Rules r.4(2).

[13] 2013 Rules r.7(1).

[14] 2011 Act s.78(4).

- The chairing member may permit the attendance at the hearing of any person who does not otherwise have a right to attend if the chairing member considers that the attendance of that person is necessary for a proper consideration of the matter before the children's hearing.[15]
- The chairing member must ask the person in respect of whom the hearing has been arranged to declare the person's age, but need not comply with that duty if he or she considers that the person would not be capable of understanding the question.[16]
- The chairing member makes a report of decisions and signs all orders and warrants.[17]

Giving information and explanations

- At the beginning of the hearing the chairing member must introduce **2–06** the members of the children's hearing to those attending the hearing, and explain the purpose of the hearing.[18]
- It is the duty of the chairing member of the children's hearing to explain to the child and each relevant person, at the opening of the grounds hearing, each of the section 67 grounds that are specified in the statement of grounds, and to ask them whether they accept that each ground applies in relation to the child.[19] The chairing member may, in order to comply with this duty, exclude any relevant person from the hearing during the explanation of the statement of grounds if satisfied that the presence of that person is preventing the hearing from obtaining the acceptance or denial of the grounds from any other person.[20]
- The chairing member must inform those present at the hearing of the substance of any relevant report or other relevant document.[21]
- If the children's hearing has decided to exclude a journalist the chairing member may, at the end of that exclusion, explain to the person, where appropriate to do so, the substance of what took place in his or her absence.[22] It would seem to be implicit in this that it is for the chairing member alone to determine whether it is appropriate to give this explanation though, as always, it is good practice for the chairing member to consult with the other members of the hearing.
- If the children's hearing has decided to exclude a relevant person or that person's representative the chairing member must, at the end of that exclusion, explain to the relevant person or representative what has taken place in his or her absence.[23]

---

[15] 2011 Act s.78(2) and (3).
[16] 2011 Act s.124(2) and (4).
[17] 2013 Rules rr.65(3), 67(3), 72(3), 77(5), 79(2), 82(1) and 83.
[18] 2013 Rules r.58(1)(a).
[19] 2011 Act s.90(1).
[20] 2013 Rules r.59(1). Note that exclusion is normally a matter for the hearing as a whole, but in this circumstance it rests with the chairing member alone, because the chairing member is responsible for obtaining the acceptance or denial of the grounds.
[21] 2013 Rules r.60(2)(a).
[22] 2011 Act s.78(6).
[23] 2011 Act ss.76(3) and 77(3).

- If the children's hearing has directed the reporter to apply to the sheriff for a determination on whether grounds not accepted are established, it is the duty of the chairing member to explain to the child and to the relevant person the purpose of the application, and to inform the child that he or she has an obligation to attend the hearing before the sheriff.[24] If the application to the sheriff is on the basis of lack of understanding the chairing member must fulfil this duty of explanation in so far as is reasonably practicable.[25]
- Once a decision has been made on how to dispose of the case, but before the conclusion of the hearing at which the decision is made, the chairing member must confirm the decision of the children's hearing and state the reason for that decision; the chairing member must also inform the child, relevant person and safeguarder of the right to appeal the children's hearing's decision.[26]
- The chairing member must inform the child of the availability of children's advocacy services, but need not comply with that duty if, taking account of the age and maturity of the child, the chairing member considers that it would not be appropriate to do so.[27]

Ensuring effective participation

2–07
- At the beginning of the hearing the chairing member must ask whether the child, relevant person and any safeguarder has received all relevant information and documents sent under the Rules, and confirm whether the child, relevant person and safeguarder has had the opportunity to review the information and documents and whether these have been understood.[28]
- The chairing member must ask the child whether the documents provided to the child accurately reflect any views expressed by the child, but need not comply with that duty if, taking account of the age and maturity of the child, the chairing member considers that it would not be appropriate to do so.[29] If the child responds by indicating that the documents do not accurately reflect the child's views the chairing member must endeavour to clarify the child's views on the relevant matter.[30]
- The chairing member must take all reasonable steps to obtain the views of the child, relevant person and safeguarder in relation to any relevant report, document or matter being considered by the hearing, and what, if any, measures would be in the best interests of the child; and may invite any other person present at the hearing (as the children's hearing considers appropriate) to express their views on or provide other information relevant to any matter or action being considered by the hearing.[31]

---

[24] 2011 Act s.93(4).
[25] 2011 Act s.94(4).
[26] 2013 Rules rr.61(3), 62(3), 63(3), 64(2), 66(4), 70(4), 73(4), 74(7) and 77(4).
[27] 2011 Act s.122. This provision was not brought into force with the rest of the 2011 Act on June 24, 2013.
[28] 2013 Rules r.58(1).
[29] 2011 Act s.121.
[30] 2013 Rules r.58(2).
[31] 2013 Rules rr.60(2), 66(2), 70(2), 72(2), 73(2), 74(5) and 75(2).

THE REPORTER

It is through the reporter that cases are referred to a children's hearing, and he **2–08** or she has various investigative functions in relation to children.[32] A child cannot be referred to a children's hearing except at the instance of the reporter. It is the reporter who draws up the statement of grounds upon which the referral is made, and the reporter who seeks to have the section 67 grounds that are not accepted or not understood established by proof in the sheriff court. It is tempting to regard the reporter in the way a prosecutor would be regarded in criminal process, but the analogy is not apt.[33] Though the reporter has a discretion whether or not to refer a case to a children's hearing (as a prosecutor has a discretion whether or not to bring a case to court), once he or she does so proceedings cannot be abandoned and the progression of the case thereafter lies in the hands of the hearing. The function of the reporter during the hearing is to keep a record of the proceedings at each children's hearing and pre-hearing panel.[34]

The Scottish Ministers are empowered to prescribe the qualifications of **2–09** reporters.[35] It is not a requirement that reporters be legally qualified, but if they are they are not to be regarded as practising solicitors for the purpose of being required to hold a practising certificate from the Law Society of Scotland.[36] Reporters are employed by the Scottish Children's Reporter Administration (SCRA)[37] and their functions are those delegated to them by the Principal Reporter.[38] No function of the Principal Reporter, however, may be delegated to a person who is employed by both SCRA and a local authority, except where consent is given in individual cases by SCRA.[39] SCRA is responsible for the terms and conditions of employment of reporters, including pensions.[40] Reporters must comply with any instructions or guidance given by the Principal Reporter.[41] If dismissed from office by SCRA, the Principal Reporter or any other specified employee of SCRA may appeal to the Scottish Ministers against such dismissal.[42] The term "Principal Reporter" is used throughout the

---

[32] See below, para.4–17.

[33] See the opinion of the Extra Division to this effect in *C v Miller*, 2003 S.L.T. 1379 at 1396C.

[34] 2013 Rules r.13. On the reporter's legal immunities, see Kearney *Children's Hearings and the Sheriff Court*, 2nd edn (Butterworths, 2000) at paras 2.07–2.10.

[35] 2011 Act Sch.3 para.8(4).

[36] *Miller v Council of the Law Society of Scotland*, 2000 S.L.T. 513. The reasoning was that in the reporter's professional activities there was no person who can appropriately be regarded as the reporter's "client". Doubts were raised but not resolved in *Miller* as to whether non-solicitor reporters have a right of audience before the sheriff principal: see the comments of Sheriff Principal Risk in *Templeton v E*, 1998 S.C.L.R. 672 and his decision in *Nassaris v The Children's Hearing Reporter* Unreported November 5, 1998 (Sheriffdom of Grampian, Highland and Island at Fort William). Section 19 of the 2011 Act now provides that Scottish Ministers may by regulations empower reporters to conduct proceedings before the sheriff or the sheriff principal, and prescribe qualifications or experience that must be acquired or training that must be undertaken before reporters can conduct such proceedings. This was done in the Children's Hearings (Scotland) Act 2011 (Rights of Audience of the Principal Reporter) Regulations 2012 (SSI 2012/335).

[37] 2011 Act Sch.3 para.11.

[38] 2011 Act Sch.3 para.10.

[39] 2011 Act Sch.3 para.10(4).

[40] 2011 Act Sch.3 para.11.

[41] Local Government etc. (Scotland) Act 1994 s.131(2).

[42] 2011 Act Sch.3 para.12. See Children's Hearings (Scotland) Act 2011 (Appeals Against Dismissal by SCRA) Regulations 2012 (SSI 2012/337).

Children's Hearings (Scotland) Act 2011 but r.2 of the 2013 Rules defines "reporter" to mean the Principal Reporter or any person carrying out a function on behalf of the Principal Reporter, having been delegated to do so by the Principal Reporter: the term "reporter" will therefore be used in this book to refer to these employees.

THE CHILD

2–10 The child is the central figure at a children's hearing, even when he or she is not present. For the purposes of the children's hearing system, a child is normally a person who is under 16 years of age,[43] but there are a number of circumstances in which a person over that age will be regarded as a "child" and so subject to the jurisdiction of the children's hearing.

(a) First, in relation to a person referred to a children's hearing on the basis of having failed to attend regularly at school, "child" means a person who is of school age.[44]

(b) Secondly, if the reporter after investigating information that he or she has received concerning the child has determined that the child might be in need of protection, guidance, treatment or control but (i) a compulsory supervision order has not yet been made or (ii) the child has not yet been notified that a hearing will not be held or (iii) the referral has not yet been discharged, the child will be regarded as a "child" for the purposes of the 2011 Act until the making of a compulsory supervision order or notification has been given that a hearing will not be held or the referral is discharged, notwithstanding that his or her 16th birthday occurs before then.[45] In other words, so long as the reporter has made the preliminary determination just mentioned before the child's 16th birthday, the referral to the hearing can be made even after the child becomes 16.

(c) Thirdly, whenever a person is subject to a compulsory supervision order on their 16th birthday, or a compulsory supervision order is made on or after their 16th birthday, the person remains a "child" for the purposes of the 2011 Act until the child's 18th birthday or, if earlier, the termination of the order.[46]

(d) Fourthly, where in a criminal court a person over 16 but under 18 has pled guilty to or been found guilty of an offence and the court has referred the case for disposal by the children's hearing, the person will be regarded as a "child" for the purposes of the 2011 Act until either the hearing or the sheriff discharges the referral, or the compulsory supervision order made in respect of the person is terminated, or the person becomes 18 years of age, whichever is earlier.[47]

---

[43] 2011 Act s.199(1).

[44] 2011 Act s.199(2). The specification of school leaving dates means that a child who attains 16 years of age during the school year remains "of school age" until the next following school leaving date.

[45] 2011 Act s.199(3)–(5).

[46] 2011 Act s.199(6) and (7).

[47] 2011 Act s.199(8) and (9).

Hearings always commence with inquiries being made as to the age of **2–11**
the person referred[48] and the person referred will be taken to be of the age worked
out on the basis of the person's most recent declaration, or as otherwise determined by a children's hearing[49]; if that age later turns out to be incorrect then
anything done by the hearing on the basis of the incorrect age remains valid.[50] If,
after proceedings have commenced on the basis that the person referred is a
child, it is determined that the person is not a child after all then the proceedings
must be terminated since the children's hearing will have no jurisdiction over
him or her.

As the central figure in the process, the child has a large variety of rights and **2–12**
powers under both the 2011 Act and the 2013 Rules, though the statutory
provisions seldom present them as "rights". Nevertheless, rights they are, and
the most important are as follows[51]:

- To receive notification of any application for a child protection
  order,[52] and of a referral to the children's hearing or a pre-hearing
  panel.[53]
- To have their views expressed in any document that is to be given to
  the members of the children's hearing or pre-hearing panel.[54]
- To require a pre-hearing panel to determine a "deemed relevant person"
  claim and to request a pre-hearing panel to consider the other matters
  open to it.[55]
- To attend any children's hearing or pre-hearing panel.
- To accept or deny the section 67 grounds.[56]
- To attend the sheriff court at which a grounds determination is
  sought.[57]
- To be represented at the sheriff court grounds determination.[58]
- To seek a review of the grounds determination[59] and to attend the
  sheriff court at that review.[60]
- To be accompanied at children's hearings by a representative who, if
  legally qualified, may be paid by the Scottish Legal Aid Board.[61]
- To express views at all hearings and to have these views taken into
  account.[62]

---

[48] 2011 Act s.124(2).
[49] 2011 Act s.124(6). In a different context, see *L v Angus Council*, 2012 S.L.T. 304, where
judicial review was sought of the immigration authorities' assessment of a young person's age.
[50] 2011 Act s.124(7).
[51] My thanks are due to Morag Driscoll of the Scottish Child Law Centre, who suggested that
this book could be improved with the addition of a list of children's rights within the children's
hearing system.
[52] 2011 Act s.43.
[53] 2013 Rules rr.22(2) and 45(2).
[54] 2013 Rules r.8.
[55] 2011 Act s.79(2).
[56] 2011 Act s.90.
[57] 2011 Act s.103(4).
[58] 2011 Act s.104(2).
[59] 2011 Act s.110.
[60] 2011 Act s.112(3).
[61] 2011 Act s.78(1)(b). On legal aid see above, paras 1–10—1–18.
[62] 2011 Act s.27.

- To appeal against any substantive decision[63] (that is to say one that disposes of the referral) and to ask for the decision to be suspended pending the appeal.[64]
- To require a review of a compulsory supervision order.[65]

RELEVANT PERSONS

2–13 Every person who, in relation to the child, is a "relevant person" has a duty to attend at all stages of any children's hearing; a right to accept the section 67 grounds stated by the reporter as applying in relation to the child, or to deny them and oblige the reporter to establish them by evidence before the sheriff; a right to appeal against a decision of the hearing to make, vary or terminate a compulsory supervision order in relation to the child; and a right to require a review of any such order. Until the 2011 Act came into force "relevant person status" was the only way in which any participation rights could be guaranteed, and today recognising that status is the means by which full participation in the children's hearing process from start to finish is ensured. Both the definition of "relevant person" and the means by which relevant person status could otherwise be acquired (if at all) were subject to much contentious litigation under the Children (Scotland) Act 1995 and the rules were restructured by the Children's Hearings (Scotland) Act 2011. The definition of "relevant person" contained in s.200 of the 2011 Act is noticeably more restricted than the definition in the 1995 Act, but a new procedure is created by ss.79–81 whereby a pre-hearing panel (or in some cases a children's hearing) may deem a person who is not within the s.200 definition to be a relevant person. That deeming procedure is discussed later.[66] The s.200 definition is discussed here.[67] For the purposes of the Children's Hearings (Scotland) Act 2011, s.200 provides that a "relevant person" is a person who falls into one or other of the following categories:

(a) A parent or guardian having parental responsibilities or parental rights in relation to the child under Part I of the Children (Scotland) Act 1995

2–14 This means: (i) the child's mother; (ii) the child's father if *either* married to the mother at the time of the child's conception or subsequently[68]; *or* registered as the child's father[69]; (iii) a woman who is parent of the child, where the child

---

[63] 2011 Act s.154.

[64] 2011 Act s.158.

[65] 2011 Act s.132.

[66] Below, paras 5–10—5–19.

[67] It does make a difference whether an individual is a relevant person by dint of the definition in s.200(1) or by being deemed a relevant person under s.81(3): not only does a procedure require to be followed to become a deemed relevant person, but that deeming can be removed by decision of the hearing: see below at paras 5–15 and 13–37—13–40.

[68] Children (Scotland) Act 1995 s.3(1)(b)(i). The marriage may be regular or irregular, valid, voidable or void (so long as, if void, it was believed in good faith by both parties to the marriage at the time it was entered into to be valid, whether as a result of error of law or error of fact).

[69] Children (Scotland) Act 1995 s.3(1)(b)(ii), as inserted by the Family Law (Scotland) Act 2006 s.23.

was born as a result of artificial conception, by virtue of being the civil partner of the mother[70]; or by virtue of being the unregistered partner of the mother and having agreed to become (and being registered as) the child's parent[71]; (iv) the father or other female parent who has entered into a registered agreement with the mother to share parental responsibilities and parental rights[72]; (iv) any parent not otherwise covered who has been awarded parental responsibilities and parental rights by a court under s.11(2)(b) of the 1995 Act and (v) any person appointed as the guardian to the child.[73] "Parent" includes persons presumed to be parent under s.5 of the Law Reform (Parent and Child) (Scotland) Act 1986, or deemed parent under s.35 or s.36 of the Human Fertilisation and Embryology Act 2008, or made parent either by means of a parental order under s.54 of the 2008 Act or by means of an adoption order made under s.28 or s.29 of the Adoption and Children (Scotland) Act 2007. It does not include any parent whose parental responsibilities and parental rights have been completely removed from them either under s.11(2)(a) of the Children (Scotland) Act 1995 or by virtue of the making of an adoption order or a permanence order under the Adoption and Children (Scotland) Act 2007. And it is explicitly provided[74] that a parent or guardian does not have parental responsibilities or rights—and therefore does not come within the definition of "relevant person"—merely by virtue of a contact order or a specific issue order under s.11(2)(d) or (e) of the 1995 Act. However, the Inner House of the Court of Session held, in relation to the equivalent definition in the 1995 Act (where that exclusion was not explicit but was held to be a necessary implication), that excluding from the definition a father who did not have parental responsibilities and parental rights but did have a contact order in his favour would be an interference in that father's ECHR right to a fair hearing: the contact order embodied a civil right and the fact that the hearing could make a compulsory supervision order interfering with the operation of the contact order meant that the hearing was obliged by art.6 to permit the father's full participation. In order to read this part of the 1995 definition of "relevant person" in a way that was compatible with art.6, the phrase "a parent having parental responsibilities or parental rights" required the addition of the words "or a right of contact in terms of a contact order under Pt 1" of the 1995 Act.[75] The issue became redundant, though only as far as parents are concerned, by the Children's Hearings (Review of Contact Directions and Definition of Relevant Persons) (Scotland) Order 2013, discussed under para.(g) below. Section 200(2) does not exclude other family members who have the responsibility and right of contact with the child in terms of an order made under s.11(2)(d) or (e) of the1995 Act and if they have an established family life with the child it is open to argument that—following *Authority Reporter v S*—they are relevant persons under the s.200 definition whether or not they can claim "deemed relevant person status" from a pre-hearing panel.

---

[70] Human Fertilisation and Embryology Act 2008 s.42.

[71] Human Fertilisation and Embryology Act 2008 s.43.

[72] Under ss.4 or 4A of the 1995 Act.

[73] By the court under s.11(2)(h) or by testamentary deed of a parent or guardian under s.7 of the 1995 Act.

[74] 2011 Act s.200(2).

[75] *Authority Reporter v S*, 2010 S.L.T. 765.

(b) A person in whom parental responsibilities or parental rights are vested by virtue of s.11(2)(b) of the Children (Scotland) Act 1995

2–15　　That is the section under which the court imposes on a person other than a parent parental responsibilities and gives them parental rights. Parents who acquire parental responsibilities and parental rights under s.11(2)(b) are covered by (a) above and this paragraph therefore covers any other person, such as a grandparent or sibling or other family member who acquires full parental responsibilities and parental rights. It is not limited to family members and might include, for example, long-term foster carers who obtain an order under s.11(2)(b) of the 1995 Act. "Person" as it appears in s.11 of the 1995 Act is limited to natural persons only[76] and so only natural persons can be considered relevant persons within the terms of this part of the definition. The paragraph refers to parental responsibilities "or" parental rights, which suggests that a person with one parental responsibility or parental right but not them all might be within the definition of relevant person, though the wording of s.11(2)(b) itself ("an order imposing ... such responsibilities *and* giving ... such rights") suggests the opposite. The solution is to adopt an expansive interpretation of the definition, following the guidance offered by Lord Hope in the Supreme Court decision of *Principal Reporter v K*[77]: if in doubt, include the person within the definition. It is suggested that, for example, a person who is appointed as the child's legal representative but who does not have the right to determine the child's residence ought to be regarded as a relevant person within the meaning of this paragraph, the responsibility and right of legal representation being as much a civil right as a right of contact, which now has its own protections through a s.126 hearing.[78] If that is so then art.6 of the ECHR requires the legal representative's[79] participation, which is ensured by reading the definition of "relevant person" in such a way as includes them. However, a person who acquires one or more parental responsibilities or parental rights by virtue of orders made under different paragraphs of s.11(2) will not come within this part of the definition of "relevant person" because the definition specifies only s.11(2)(b). So for example a person who acquires the right of contact with the child under s.11(2)(d), or the right to provide certain consents on behalf of the child under s.11(2)(e) (a "specific issue order") will not be covered here. Under the 1995 Act, the equivalent provision[80] was not limited to s.11(2)(b) and it had been held in the sheriff court that in order to ensure compatibility with art.6 of the ECHR the provision had to be read with the addition of words to include any person with a right of contact under a contact order (that is to say an order under s.11(2)(d)).[81] That interpretation is

---

[76] Children (Scotland) Act 1995 s.15(4).

[77] 2011 S.L.T. 271 at [69]. Lord Hope said, in relation to the unmarried father, that the case law on whether such persons have established family life with their children is sufficiently clear and consistent that "In a borderline case, it would be safer to include him and let others argue than to leave him out". The unmarried father is of course no longer an issue but the proposition has wider merits.

[78] For which, see below, paras 13–41—13–44.

[79] Note: "legal representative" in this context is the person with the responsibility and right to act in legal transactions on behalf of the child, traced to ss.1 and 2 of the Children (Scotland) Act 1995—it is *not* a legally qualified person who appears on behalf of the child at the hearing.

[80] Children (Scotland) Act 1995 s.93(2)(b)(b).

[81] *M, Appellant*, 2010 Fam. L.R. 152. This case involved a grandmother who had a contact order and was held to be entitled to be considered a relevant person.

probably not open to the present provision which is expressly limited to orders under s.11(2)(b)[82] and grandparents, siblings and others with contact orders under s.11(2)(d) will not be within the definition of "relevant person" (though their right to participate in hearings at which their civil rights might be interfered with is ensured by s.126 of the 2011 Act and associated regulations).[83]

(c) A person who has parental responsibilities or parental rights by virtue of the rule in s.11(12) of the Children (Scotland) Act 1995

This rule provides that when a child is required to reside with a person by **2–16** virtue of a residence order made under s.11(2)(c) of the 1995 Act, that person will acquire, as well as the right to have the child living with him or her, the responsibility to safeguard and promote the child's health, development and welfare, the responsibility to provide direction and guidance, the responsibility to act as the child's legal representative, together with the right to control, direct or guide the child's upbringing and the right to act as the child's legal representative. These responsibilities and rights flow from the residence order and are of such extent to justify the person in whom they are vested being considered a relevant person for the purposes of the children's hearing.

(d) A parent having parental responsibility for the child under Pt 1 of the Children Act 1989

This is the equivalent (though not exact) of a parent having parental respon- **2–17** sibilities and parental rights under s.3 of the Children (Scotland) Act 1995 and it ensures that a parent is a relevant person even when they trace their responsibilities and rights over the child to the English legislation.[84]

(e) A person having parental responsibility for the child by virtue of various other provisions in the English legislation

A person will have parental responsibility in the English sense, and so **2–18** become a relevant person within the context of the children's hearing system, if he or she has a residence order in his or her favour, or is a "special guardian" of the child (roughly equivalent to having a permanence order under the Adoption and Children (Scotland) Act 2007), or is a prospective adopter with whom the child has been placed.

(f) A person in whom parental responsibilities or parental rights are vested by virtue of a permanence order made under the Adoption and Children (Scotland) Act 2007

Not every permanence order will confer parental responsibilities or parental **2–19** rights on a person other than a local authority but the local authority will always acquire a range of responsibilities and rights (in particular and not least the right to determine the child's residence). There is nothing in the 2011 Act

---

[82] The interpretative stretching of words mandated by s.3 of the Human Rights Act 1998 does have limits and to say that "s.11(2)(b)" means "s.11(2)(b), (d) and (e)" is addition to the words and not interpretation of the words.
[83] See below, paras 13–41—13–44.
[84] cf. *D v Children's Reporter*, 2009 Fam. L.R. 88 (Sh Ct).

to suggest that "person" in this context is limited to natural person and it is open to question whether the local authority itself can be regarded as a relevant person. Reading this paragraph *noscitur a sociis* with the paragraphs that went before might suggest that only natural persons are intended by the whole definition to be relevant persons; on the other hand if the local authority is the only body that has parental responsibilities and parental rights in respect of the child[85] then it might be considered to be in the interests of the child that the system recognises the authority as a relevant person and therefore able, for example, to challenge the section 67 grounds or to appeal the hearing's decision. An interpretation that leads to any tribunal's decision being unappealable for want of anyone with title to appeal is, in general, to be avoided.

(g) A person who is a parent of the child other than a parent falling within the definition of relevant person contained in either paragraph (a) or (d) above, and other than a parent who previously had parental responsibilities and parental rights (or the equivalent in English law or Northern Irish law) but by virtue of a court order no longer has them[86]

2–20   The purpose of this catch-all paragraph is to bring within the definition of relevant person all parents not otherwise within the definition (other than those who have been deprived of their parental responsibilities and parental rights). So a parent who has lost all their parental responsibilities and parental rights by an order under s.11(2)(a) of the Children (Scotland) Act 1995, or under the terms of a permanence order made under s.81 of the Adoption and Children (Scotland) Act 2007, will not be a relevant person, but all other parents are. The loss of some parental responsibilities and parental rights would not, however, be sufficient to exclude a parent from the definition of relevant person and so if a parent is left with only the responsibility and right of contact he or she will remain a relevant person. Section 200(2) does not exclude such a parent from the definition of relevant person, for that merely provides that *for the purposes of paragraph (a)* of the definition a parent is not to be considered to have parental responsibilities and parental rights. A parent with the responsibility and right of contact is still a parent, and so within the definition of relevant person in paragraph (g) and not excluded through the loss of all the other parental responsibilities and rights.

SAFEGUARDERS

2–21   Safeguarders were introduced into the children's hearing system by s.66 of the Children Act 1975, coming into effect on June 30, 1985, with the insertion into the Social Work (Scotland) Act 1968 of a new s.34A thereof, which was replaced by s.41 of the Children (Scotland) Act 1995. Today, s.30 of the Children's Hearings (Scotland) Act 2011 provides that a children's hearing must consider whether to appoint a person to safeguard the interests of the child to whom the hearing relates and may make such an appointment at any

---

[85] And the mandatory provision in a permanence order will always require that the local authority has at least some of the parental responsibilities and parental rights.

[86] 2011 Act s.200(1)(g), as expanded by the Children's Hearings (Review of Contact Directions and Definition of Relevant Persons) Order 2013 (SSI 2013/193) art.3.

time when it is still deciding matters in relation to the child. A pre-hearing panel may also, where a safeguarder is not already in place, appoint a safeguarder for the child to whom the children's hearing which will follow relates.[87] In addition, and again where a safeguarder is not already in place, a sheriff may appoint a safeguarder for the child in proceedings for the establishment of the section 67 grounds, or their review, or on appeals from decisions of the hearing.[88] Any appointment as safeguarder is to be made from the national Safeguarders Panel created and regulated by the Scottish Ministers.[89] Only persons with key competencies and appropriate experience and who have undergone pre-appointment training may be appointed to the Safeguarders Panel; no-one may be appointed who is a member or employee of Children's Hearings Scotland or Scottish Children's Reporter Administration, or is a member of an area support team or of the children's panel, or is directly involved in the establishment, maintenance, operation or management of the Safeguarders Panel[90]—nor may any person who is barred from regulated work with children by virtue of the Protection of Vulnerable Groups (Scotland) Act 2007.[91] Appointment to the Panel is for three years and an existing appointee may be reappointed for between one and three years: the Scottish Ministers must reappoint a person unless they decline to be reappointed or the person is found to be unfit due to inability, conduct or failure without reasonable excuse to comply with training requirements.[92] The Scottish Ministers must endeavour to ensure that the Safeguarders Panel includes persons from all local authority areas in Scotland and they must monitor the performance of all members.[93] A person may be removed from the Safeguarders Panel at any point due to inability, conduct or failure without reasonable excuse to comply with training requirements or if they are barred from regulated work with children.[94]

The hearing may make the appointment at any time when it is "still deciding **2–22** matters in relation to the child".[95] This indicates that the appointment of a safeguarder is competent only when the children's hearing has not felt it appropriate, or has been unable, to make a dispositive decision, such as to make, vary or continue a compulsory supervision order, or to terminate the order or discharge the referral. The appointment is, therefore, designed to assist the hearing in deciding what the appropriate disposal should be. A sheriff, on the other hand, is not constrained to make the appointment only when he is

---

[87] 2011 Act s.82.

[88] 2011 Act s.31.

[89] Children's Hearings (Scotland) Act 2011 (Safeguarders Panel) Regulations 2012 (SSI 2012/54), made in exercise of the power in s.32(2) of the Children's Hearings (Scotland) Act 2011. Management and operation of the Safeguarders Panel, including selection of members, training and monitoring has been delegated to the charity Children 1st (previously the RSSPCC).

[90] Children's Hearings (Scotland) Act 2011 (Safeguarders Panel) Regulations (SSI 2012/54) reg.5.

[91] Children's Hearings (Scotland) Act 2011 (Safeguarders Panel) Regulations (SSI 2012/54) reg.6.

[92] Children's Hearings (Scotland) Act 2011 (Safeguarders Panel) Regulations (SSI 2012/54) reg.7. Training is governed by regs 8 and 9.

[93] Children's Hearings (Scotland) Act 2011 (Safeguarders Panel) Regulations (SSI 2012/54) reg.11.

[94] Children's Hearings (Scotland) Act 2011 (Safeguarders Panel) Regulations (SSI 2012/54) regs 6(b) and 7(5).

[95] 2011 Act s.30(2).

"still deciding matters in relation to the child" and it is unclear from the 2011 Act whether the sheriff has the power to appoint a safeguarder not only to assist him and inform proceedings at the sheriff court but also to assist any children's hearing that may be required as a result of the sheriff's decision. There is something uncomfortable in one tribunal (the sheriff) deciding that another tribunal (the children's hearing) needs help in coming to its decision, but that may be too narrow a view of why appointments of safeguarders are made. The safeguarder assists the tribunal, it is true, but their primary role is to assist the child and the sheriff may legitimately come to the view that the child's interests need to be safeguarded by an independent person in another tribunal. Confirmation of the sheriff's power to appoint a safeguarder to safeguard the interests of the child in proceedings before the children's hearing is found in the rules governing the termination of the appointment[96]: as we will see below, a safeguarder appointed by a sheriff while hearing either an application to establish grounds or an appeal under s.154 will last beyond the sheriff court proceedings and terminate only on the dispositive decision of the hearing (or final determination of an appeal against that dispositive decision).

2–23   Typically, a children's hearing will appoint a safeguarder when the section 67 grounds are sent by a grounds hearing to the sheriff for proof or when the hearing defers making a decision in order to allow for further investigation, or when a warrant to secure attendance has been granted or continued; the prehearing panel may appoint a safeguarder to assist the hearing which will follow that panel; the sheriff may appoint a safeguarder before hearing evidence of the existence of grounds of referral or before hearing an appeal (in order to assist the sheriff court proceedings), or at the end of the sheriff court proceedings in order that a safeguarder is in post to safeguard the interests of the child in any consequent children's hearing.

2–24   A children's hearing that appoints a safeguarder must record the appointment and give reasons for its decision: this will be a statement of why the hearing felt it necessary in the interests of the child to appoint a safeguarder.[97] This serves the useful purpose of indicating to the safeguarder the issues that the hearing considers he or she ought to address.[98] The safeguarder may call for any earlier safeguarders' reports held by the reporter in respect of the child.[99] The decision to appoint (or not appoint) a safeguarder is not appealable, though the failure to consider making an appointment might amount to a procedural irregularity which in some circumstances might found an appeal against the hearing's substantive decision.

---

[96] Children's Hearings (Scotland) Act 2011 (Safeguarders: Further Provision) Regulations 2012 (SSI 2012/336), discussed below, paras 2–29—2–32.

[97] 2011 Act s.30(3) and (4). Though in its terms, the obligation is limited to decisions to appoint, it is good practice for the hearing to state its reasons for not appointing a safeguarder, if for no other reason than to have on record that it has fulfilled its statutory duty under s.30(1) to give the matter consideration.

[98] It is of course for the safeguarder him or herself to decide what issues he or she will explore, but it is always helpful for the safeguarder to know what issues the hearing making the appointment considers it needs independently acquired information on.

[99] Children's Hearings (Scotland) Act 2011 (Safeguarders: Further Provision) Regulations 2012 (SSI 2012/336) reg.9. Any such report provided by the reporter must also be provided to the child, relevant person and the three members of the children's panel who will constitute the next children's hearing.

Role of the safeguarder

Section 30 of the 2011 Act does not specify the circumstances in which the **2–25** appointment of a safeguarder might be appropriate. Its predecessor, s.41 of the Children (Scotland) Act 1995, provided that an appointment of a safeguarder could be made when the hearing considered it necessary to safeguard the interests of the child in the proceedings; the predecessor to that provision, s.34A of the Social Work (Scotland) Act 1968, limited appointments of safeguarders to situations in which there was a conflict of interests between the relevant person and the child. Such conflict will still be a legitimate basis upon which to appoint a safeguarder under s.30 of the 2011 Act, as would a conflict of views between the family and the Social Work Department, or because this is the best way of allowing the child to express his or her view of the proceedings or to explain how the child sees the situation, or because it is felt that a safeguarder might be able to identify the real cause of the child's difficulties, or because it is felt that the child needs independent (though not necessarily legal) advice in the course of the proceedings. The complete lack of indication of the basis on which an appointment of safeguarder is made under s.30 other than the general application of the welfare principle in s.25, together with the non-appealability of the decision, suggests that the matter is completely at large for the hearing which may make the appointment whenever, and for whatever reason, it considers that it would be in the welfare of the child for a safeguarder to be appointed.

The functions of the safeguarder[100] are specified in s.33 of the 2011 Act, and **2–26** supplemented by regulations. Except where the children's hearing has directed the reporter to make an application to the sheriff to establish the section 67 grounds in respect of which the child has been referred to a children's hearing, the safeguarder must, on being appointed, prepare a report setting out anything that, in the safeguarder's opinion, is relevant to the consideration of the matter before the children's hearing.[101] In drawing up that report, the safeguarder must, in so far as practicable and taking account of the child's age and maturity, give the child the opportunity to express views and have regard to these views, and include these views (and an explanation of how they were obtained) in the report.[102] In addition, the safeguarder must: (a) so far as reasonably practicable, attend the children's hearing (which means all the hearings following the appointment until a dispositive decision is made); and (b) prepare any report that the safeguarder is required to prepare by a children's hearing.[103] The normal expectation is that the safeguarder will meet with the child, the child's family (and there is no point in limiting "family" in this context to "relevant

---

[100] The specified functions are clearly those of a safeguarder appointed for proceedings at a children's hearing or a pre-hearing panel. There is no equivalent provision setting out the functions of a safeguarder appointed by a sheriff for the purposes of sheriff court proceedings, other than reg.6 of the Children's Hearings (Scotland) Act 2011 (Safeguarders: Further Provision) Regulations 2012 (SSI 2012/336), which allows the sheriff to require the safeguarder to provide a report for the purpose of assisting the sheriff in determining an appeal under s.154 of the 2011 Act. Even without such a requirement, it is expected that the safeguarder will draw up a report containing his or her views on the interests of the child in the court proceedings.

[101] 2011 Act s.33(1)(a) and (2).

[102] Children's Hearings (Scotland) Act 2011 (Safeguarders: Further Provision) Regulations 2012 (SSI 2012/336) reg.7.

[103] 2011 Act s.33(1)(b) and (c).

persons") and any other significant person before drawing up his or her report.[104] It is not statutorily specified what should be in this report, except that it should deal with any matter specified by the children's hearing, and any matter that the safeguarder considers relevant. Though there is no statutory requirement to do so, the safeguarder may also legitimately make a recommendation as to what disposal available to the hearing would, in the opinion of the safeguarder, best serve the child's interests. The safeguarder's report must be given to the reporter within 35 days of the safeguarder being appointed, but if he or she has been unable to complete the report within that timescale, he or she must give the reporter an interim report, explaining the reasons for the production of an interim report, details of what investigation the safeguarder still has to make or the information he or she still has to obtain, and an estimate of the time it will take to complete the full report.[105] On receipt of the safeguarder's report or interim report the reporter must as soon as practicable thereafter arrange a children's hearing.[106] The safeguarder is entitled to be present throughout the duration of any hearing of the case until the disposal of that case,[107] and is entitled—indeed expected—to play an active role in the discussion of the case. The chairing member of the children's hearing is obliged to take all reasonable steps to obtain the views of any safeguarder in relation to any matter being considered by the hearing and what, if any, measures would be in the best interests of the child.[108] If the safeguarder has been able to produce only an interim report for the hearing's consideration, the hearing may defer making its decision on whether to make a compulsory supervision order, and set a further date up to a maximum of 35 days for the provision of a full report.[109] It would indeed be dangerous for a hearing to make (or vary) a compulsory supervision order on the basis of an interim report because, by definition, that is an incomplete report and the hearing would be making its decision, therefore, on less than complete information. It is not incompetent to do so but the hearing must be sure that it has enough information to adjudge that the missing information would not affect their decision: if the hearing does so the safeguarder's obligation to produce a full report falls.

2–27	The very fact that the safeguarder's role (other than in providing a report and attending and contributing to the hearing) is not delimited by statute means that the safeguarder is entitled to interpret his or her role in a wide sense. It may be appropriate, for example, for the safeguarder to do little more than to find out what the child thinks and to articulate the child's views on his or her behalf, on the ground that it is in the interests of the child to have his or her views properly presented. Or, the safeguarder might consider it appropriate to do little more than explain to the child the process that the child has found him or herself involved in—again it is in the interests of any child to be helped to a full awareness of a process which to many will be alien, baffling and

---

[104] The safeguarder must inform any person he or she interviews of what the role of the safeguarder is, and in particular must inform the child, relevant person or any other person that his or her role is to safeguard the interests of the child: Children's Hearings (Scotland) Act 2011 (Safeguarders: Further Provision) Regulations 2012 (SSI 2012/336) reg.8.

[105] 2013 Rules r.56(4) and (5).

[106] 2013 Rules r.57(1).

[107] 2011 Act s.78(1)(f).

[108] 2013 Rules rr.60(2), 66(2), 70(2), 72(2), 73(2), 74(5) and 75(2).

[109] 2013 Rules r.60(4).

frightening: knowledge empowers and for a safeguarder to adopt a purely educative, informative or advisory role will in some cases satisfactorily safeguard the child's interests.

To assist in the performance of the safeguarder's function, the reporter is **2–28** obliged to notify the safeguarder of the hearing and provide the same information or documents as are provided to the child, relevant persons and the members of the children's hearing.[110] After the hearing, the safeguarder is entitled to be given the same information about the hearing's decisions and its reasons, copies of any orders made or warrants granted, and notice of the right to appeal against the decision.[111] The safeguarder, like everyone else, is subject to the prohibition on publication of any information that is intended or likely to identify any child involved in the hearing or his or her address or school.[112]

Term of appointment

Regulations govern when appointments as safeguarder are terminated.[113] **2–29** The appointment by a children's hearing or a pre-hearing panel or a sheriff of a safeguarder ceases on the expiration of the time allowed for an appeal against the substantive decision in relation to which the safeguarder was appointed or, if an appeal is lodged, on the final determination of the appeal.[114] In other words, a safeguarder appointed by a children's hearing or pre-hearing panel ceases 21 days after the hearing's decision to make, vary or continue a compulsory supervision order or to discharge the referral; but the safeguarder will remain in post if an appeal to the sheriff is lodged, in which case the appointment will cease 28 days after the sheriff's decision in that appeal; but he or she will remain in post if an appeal to the sheriff principal or Court of Session is lodged, the appointment finally terminating at the moment the decision in that appeal is given.[115] Likewise, a safeguarder appointed by a sheriff, either at the hearing of an application by the reporter to establish grounds of referral or at an appeal against a hearing's decision to make, vary or continue a compulsory supervision order or to discharge the referral, will remain in office until the children's hearing has made its decision consequent upon the sheriff's finding (and time for appeal against the hearing's decision has passed or appeal is finally dealt with).

The same basic principle (with one qualification) applies to appointments of **2–30** safeguarders made by sheriffs in appeals other than those governed by s.154.[116] If the appointment was made in an appeal against a deemed relevant person

---

[110] 2013 Rules rr.22 and 26.

[111] 2013 Rules r.88.

[112] 2011 Act s.182. See further, below paras 6–42—6–46.

[113] 2011 Act s.34(2)(c).

[114] Children's Hearings (Scotland) Act 2011 (Safeguarders: Further Provision) Regulations 2012 (SSI 2012/336) reg.3(1) and (2). It is to be remembered that the safeguarder him or herself has a right of appeal against decisions of the children's hearings and of the sheriff or the sheriff principal: 2011 Act s.154(2)(c) and s.163(3)(c).

[115] This suffers an exception if the sheriff in upholding the appeal required the reporter to arrange a children's hearing (2011 Act s.156(3)(a)), in which case the appointment lasts until the expiry of the time for appeal, or the final determination of an appeal, against the dispositive decision of that hearing: Safeguarders: Further Provision Regulations 2012 reg.3(3) and (4).

[116] That is to say appeals other than against the dispositive decision of the children's hearing on whether to make, vary or continue a compulsory supervision order, or to discharge a referral.

determination,[117] that appointment will cease on the expiry of the time allowed for an appeal against the sheriff's decision (i.e. seven days) if no appeal is lodged but will continue if an appeal to the sheriff principal is timeously lodged; it subsequently ceases on the expiry of the time allowed for an appeal against the decision of the sheriff principal (i.e. 28 days) if no appeal from the sheriff principal is lodged but continues if an appeal to the Court of Session is timeously lodged and lasts until the disposal of the case by the sheriff after it has been remitted back to the sheriff for disposal.[118] If the appointment was made in an appeal against decisions (affecting contact or permanence orders) made in s.126 hearings,[119] that appointment will cease on the expiry of the time allowed for an appeal against the sheriff's decision (i.e. 21 days) if no appeal is lodged but will continue if an appeal to the sheriff principal is timeously lodged; it subsequently ceases on the expiry of the time allowed for an appeal against the decision of the sheriff principal (i.e. 28 days) if no appeal from the sheriff principal is lodged but continues if an appeal to the Court of Session is timeously lodged and lasts until the disposal of the case by the sheriff after it has been remitted back to the sheriff for disposal.[120] If the appeal in which the safeguarder is appointed by the sheriff is in respect of a decision to implement a secure accommodation authorisation,[121] the appointment ceases when the sheriff gives his decision in that appeal, unless the sheriff requires the reporter to arrange a children's hearing in which case the appointment ceases on the earliest occurrence of any of the events that terminate the appointment when a safeguarder is appointed in an appeal against a s.126 decision.[122] With all of these appointments the safeguarder is in post in order to assist the appeal process, and so (the qualification adverted to above) the appointment comes to an end when that process ends and (unlike a shrieval appointment in s.154 appeals) before the child's case returns to any children's hearing.

2–31   A safeguarder may also be appointed by a sheriff in a review requested by a local authority under s.166 of the 2011 Act where the local authority believes that it is not the "relevant local authority".[123] Here, the safeguarder's appointment last until the expiry of the time allowed to appeal against the sheriff's determination (i.e. 28 days) or if an appeal to the sheriff principal is made the final disposal of the review by the sheriff to whom the case is remitted by the sheriff principal having determined the appeal.[124]

2–32   It follows that the person who was appointed to safeguard the child's interests, and who attended the hearing that made a compulsory supervision order

---

[117] See below, para.14.37. Notice that the safeguarder has no right to appeal against such a decision.

[118] Children's Hearings (Scotland) Act 2011 (Safeguarders: Further Provision) Regulations 2012 (SSI 2012/336) reg.4(1).

[119] See below, para.14–38. Notice that the safeguarder has no right to appeal against such a decision.

[120] Children's Hearings (Scotland) Act 2011 (Safeguarders: Further Provision) Regulations 2012 (SSI 2012/336) reg.4(2).

[121] See below, paras 14–39—14–41. Notice that the safeguarder has no right to appeal against such a decision.

[122] Children's Hearings (Scotland) Act 2011 (Safeguarders: Further Provision) Regulations 2012 (SSI 2012/336) reg.4(3)–(5).

[123] See below, para.2–38.

[124] Children's Hearings (Scotland) Act 2011 (Safeguarders: Further Provision) Regulations 2012 (SSI 2012/336) reg.5.

over the child, has no right or duty to attend a hearing that is reviewing that order. Their appointment has terminated and they have no standing until reappointed to the office of safeguarder by the review hearing or a pre-hearing panel. There is no statutory means by which an appointment of a safeguarder to a particular child can be terminated early, and while this would normally be entirely unnecessary extreme cases, such as when an appointee abuses his or her position, are not beyond the realms of imagination. However, termination of membership of the Safeguarders Panel probably has the effect of terminating any particular appointment. A children's hearing may request that a particular individual be appointed as safeguarder, but they cannot require it. It has been held that there is no procedural irregularity if a hearing appoints separate safeguarders to two children in the same family and in the event only one safeguarder acts for both children.[125]

Fees and expenses of safeguarders

The fees of a person appointed as safeguarder, either by the sheriff or the children's hearing, are paid for by the Scottish Ministers, who may also pay expenses and allowances, as they think fit, to members and potential members of the Safeguarders Panel.[126] **2–33**

THE LOCAL AUTHORITY

While the local authority[127] itself has no standing to attend the children's hearing and is in no sense a party to the proceedings, it does nevertheless play a central role in the whole system. For one thing, there will nearly always be a local authority employee, in the form of a social worker, present.[128] Also, the local authority has various investigative duties in relation to children,[129] and must provide a social background report for every child whose case is referred to a children's hearing.[130] This report nearly always contains recommendations to the children's hearing, which are always to be given serious consideration by the hearing. **2–34**

Local authorities' duties to implement compulsory supervision order

In addition to the investigative and reporting duties mentioned above, the local authority specified in the compulsory supervision order or interim compulsory supervision order (known as the "implementation authority")[131] **2–35**

---

[125] *H v Kennedy*, 1999 S.C.L.R. 961. In *Catto v Pearson*, 1990 S.L.T. (Sh Ct) 77 a previous safeguarder who attended a review hearing and was treated as being still in post was held to be impliedly reappointed.

[126] Children's Hearings (Scotland) Act 2011 (Safeguarders Panel) Regulations 2012 (SSI 2012/54) reg.10. The rates of fees, expenses and allowances must be published by the Scottish Ministers.

[127] "Local authority" means "a council constituted under section 2 of the Local Government etc. (Scotland) Act 1994 (c.39), and 'area' in relation to a local authority, means the local government area for which the authority is constituted": Interpretation and Legislative Reform (Scotland) Act 2010 Sch.1.

[128] See further below, para.6–38.

[129] See below, paras 4–03—4–06.

[130] 2011 Act ss.60 and 66(4)–(6).

[131] 2011 Act ss.83(1)(b) and 86(1)(b).

has the duty to give effect to the order.[132] In particular, the implementation authority must comply with any requirements imposed on it in relation to the child,[133] and this may include the authority securing or facilitating the provision of services to the child of a kind that the authority does not itself provide.[134] A child who is subject to a compulsory supervision order or an interim compulsory supervision order is regarded as being "looked after" by the local authority,[135] with the result that the duties owed by the local authority under Ch.1 of Pt 2 of the Children (Scotland) Act 1995 are owed to the child.[136] The local authority is therefore expressly obliged, for example, to safeguard and promote the child's welfare, and to take such steps as appear to it to be both practicable and appropriate to promote regular contact between the child and any person with parental responsibilities.[137] Additionally, local authorities have specified duties[138] in relation to the after-care of children who ceased to be subject to a supervision requirement but who were "looked after" by them at the time they ceased to be of school age or subsequently. And local authorities, being "public authorities" for the purposes of the Human Rights Act 1998, are required to fulfil the requirements of the European Convention on Human Rights, such as the art.8 duty to respect family life (in practice, to ensure that contact between child and family is maintained, and indeed encouraged, until such time as that contact is found to be positively detrimental to the child).

2–36   The primary duty of the implementation authority, as we have seen, is to give effect to the compulsory supervision order or interim compulsory supervision order, including terms imposing requirements on the implementation authority itself. This duty is imposed on the local authority as a collective whole and not upon individual units or departments thereof. It follows that any measure contained within the order can be one which is the responsibility of any department, such as social services, education, health, housing, or even recreation and leisure. A measure directed towards the child may well impose a duty on a local authority to perform some action. Though social services departments within local authorities are likely to be most commonly involved, a child's needs may require to be met through the facilities provided by other departments, and there is no reason why the children's hearing cannot require that such other facilities be provided. It is no excuse for a failure to give effect to a compulsory supervision order that the services to be provided are the responsibility of some department other than the social work department. So, for example, a condition that the child reside in a residential establishment obliges the local authority to provide a place in that residential establishment; a condition that the child attend some group work project obliges the local

---

[132] 2011 Act s.144(1).

[133] Under the 2011 Act s.83(2)(i) one of the measures that may be included in a compulsory supervision order or an ICSO is "a requirement that the implementation authority carry out specified duties in relation to the child".

[134] 2011 Act s.144(2) and (3).

[135] Children (Scotland) Act 1995 s.17(6), as amended by the Children's Hearings (Scotland) Act 2011 Sch.5 para.2(4).

[136] See particularly the duties listed in s.17(1) and s.31, and the powers in s.26, of the Children (Scotland) Act 1995.

[137] Children (Scotland) Act 1995 s.17(1).

[138] Children (Scotland) Act 1995 ss.29 and 30.

authority to provide a place at that project; a condition that the child attend a named public school obliges the local authority to allow the child to attend that school. If, for whatever reason, the local authority, in any of its guises, cannot provide the service to the child, nor secure nor facilitate the provision of such a service from any other body, then they are obliged to seek a review of the compulsory supervision order and explain to the review hearing why the condition cannot be fulfilled: it is a breach of their statutory duty simply to fail to fulfil the condition in the expectation of giving an explanation at the next scheduled review hearing. The process for ensuring the local authority fulfils its obligations in terms of a compulsory supervision order are discussed later.[139]

In giving effect to a supervision requirement, the local authority may request **2–37** assistance in carrying out its functions from any other local authority or a health board, specifying the assistance that is required. On receipt of such a request for assistance, the other local authority or the health board must comply with the request, except where to do so would be incompatible with any of its own functions or would unduly prejudice the discharge of any of its own functions.[140] This allows local authorities to access, for example, medical or psychological services for the child even when they do not themselves directly provide these services, or to access particular specialist units provided only by a very few local authorities.

Challenging the designation as implementation authority

Every compulsory supervision order and interim compulsory supervision **2–38** order must specify the local authority which is to be responsible for giving effect to the measures included in the order[141] and this local authority is know as the implementation authority. The children's hearing making a compulsory supervision order or an interim compulsory supervision order does not have a free choice of which local authority to specify in the order, and it must specify the "relevant local authority", that is to say the local authority in whose area the child predominantly resides or, if the child does not predominantly reside in any local authority area the local authority with whose area the child has the closest connection.[142] Sometimes, however, the local authority will be of the view that it is not the relevant local authority under this definition and so has been wrongly designated as the implementation authority in the compulsory supervision order or interim compulsory supervision order. In that circumstance, the local authority may seek a review by the sheriff of the designation. The question for the sheriff will be whether the local authority specified in the order is the "relevant local authority", as defined in s.201. If the specified local

---

[139] Below, paras 13–34—13–36.

[140] 2011 Act s.183(3)–(6).

[141] 2011 Act s.83(1)(b) and s.86(1)(b).

[142] 2011 Act s.201. Notice that in determining where a child predominantly resides, no account is to be taken of any period of residence in a residential establishment or any other place or residence, or residence in any other place, prescribed by Scottish Ministers by regulations; and in determining the local authority area with which the child has the closest connection no account is to be taken of any connection with an area that relates to a period of residence in a residential establishment or any connection prescribed by Scottish Ministers by regulations: s.201(2).

authority is not the relevant local authority in this sense the sheriff must vary the order so that the duties it contains are transferred from the specified local authority to the local authority that is the relevant local authority[143]: that authority then becomes the implementation authority.

---

[143] 2011 Act s.166. Procedure is governed by the Act Sederunt (Child Care and Maintenance Rules) 1997 (SI 1997/291 (S 19)) rr.3.58A and 3.58B, as inserted by the Act of Sederunt (Children's Hearings (Scotland) Act 2011) (Miscellaneous Amendments) 2013 (SSI 2013/172) art.3 para.48. There is an appeal by the local authority from the sheriff's determination under s.166 to the sheriff principal under s.167(1) or by the child, relevant person, or a person representing either under s.167(2), by stated case (on a point of law or in respect of any procedural irregularity) before the expiry of the period of 28 days beginning with the day on which the determination or order was made. There is no further appeal.

CHAPTER THREE

THE SECTION 67 GROUNDS

INTRODUCTION

The question of whether a compulsory supervision order needs to be made in **3–01** respect of a particular child arises if, but only if, one or more of the grounds upon which a child can be referred to a children's hearing, listed in s.67(2) of the Children's Hearings (Scotland) Act 2011, apply in relation to that child. These grounds, known as "the section 67 grounds" will be regarded as applying when either: (i) the child and such relevant persons as attend the hearing accept that they apply[1]; (ii) the sheriff determines that one or more of the section 67 grounds are established[2]; (iii) a criminal court, having found a person guilty of certain offences, certifies that grounds of referral in respect of a particular child shall be treated as having been established[3]; or (iv) a child pleads guilty to or is found guilty of an offence by a criminal court which remits the case to a children's hearing for disposal.[4] It is competent for the reporter to refer a child on the basis of a number of different grounds and, indeed, the same statement of facts can often indicate the application of more than one of the section 67 grounds.[5] At least one of the section 67 grounds stated by the reporter in the "statement of grounds" that he or she is required to prepare[6] must be accepted or established or found to apply, and the hearing can move on to a determination of whether to make a compulsory supervision order whenever that is so, even if other grounds are not established to apply.

The effect of it being accepted, established or found that section 67 grounds **3–02** apply in relation to the child is two-fold. First, it raises the question of whether it is necessary for the protection, guidance, treatment or control of the child to make a compulsory supervision order. The fact that a section 67 ground applies is by no means conclusive of that necessity (though, conversely, the fact that no section 67 ground applies in relation to the child is conclusive of the lack of a need to make a compulsory supervision order over that child). Rather, the fact that one or more grounds apply merely raises the question, which can be answered either (in the negative) by the reporter exercising his or her discretion

---

[1] Children's Hearings (Scotland) Act 2011 s.91(1)(a). See further below, para.7–12.

[2] 2011 Act s.108 (on application by the reporter) or s.117 (on application by the child or relevant person for review of the establishment of the grounds).

[3] Criminal Procedure (Scotland) Act 1995 s.48. See further below, para.4–13.

[4] Criminal Procedure (Scotland) Act 1995 s.49. See further below, para.4–16.

[5] As a simple example, the child's defying of a parent's attempts to ensure that he or she goes to school can amount to grounds of referral based on school non-attendance and on being outwith parental control.

[6] 2011 Act s.89.

under s.68(1)(b) not to refer the child to a children's hearing[7] or (in the negative or in the affirmative) by the children's hearing arranged by the reporter under s.69(2). Secondly, the fact that one or more of the section 67 grounds apply in relation to the child confirms the jurisdiction of the children's hearing. If no section 67 ground applies in relation to a child the children's hearing has no jurisdiction to consider whether it is necessary to make a compulsory supervision order—though the referral itself does give the hearing jurisdiction to take interim steps, such as making an interim compulsory supervision order or granting a warrant to secure attendance.[8]

THE SECTION 67 GROUNDS

3–03 Section 67 sets out the grounds that the reporter must consider to apply in relation to a child before he or she is entitled to arrange a children's hearing for the purpose of deciding whether it is necessary that a compulsory supervision order be made in respect of the child. The grounds are as follows.

(a) The child is likely to suffer unnecessarily, or the health or development of the child is likely to be seriously impaired, due to a lack of parental care

3–04 "Parental care" is care provided by any person (whether a parent or not) who has the parental responsibility to safeguard and promote the child's health, development and welfare.[9] The reason for the lack of care is irrelevant, whether it is incapacity, indolence, indifference or malice towards the child, and the ground includes both practical inability (such as, for example, to provide suitable accommodation) and factual incapacity.[10] The important point is the effect that the lack of care has on the child rather than the reason for the lack of care. The test is an objective one, namely whether a reasonable person looking to the circumstances of the particular case would consider that the child is likely to be caused unnecessary suffering or serious impairment of health or development through lack of parental care.[11] This ground does not apply simply because it can be shown that some other person than the parent or some other mode of caring might (or even would) be better for the child.[12] Suffering, which may be physical or emotional, is "unnecessary" when it is avoidable through the exercise of proper care; an impairment of health or development is "serious" when it is not trivial or transient. A lack of parental care can be either a failure to

---

[7] See below, paras 4–20—4–22.

[8] 2011 Act s.93(5) and s.123(1).

[9] This will include guardians and others who have such responsibilities under the terms of a court order, such as an order under s.11(2)(b) of the Children (Scotland) Act 1995 or a permanence order under s.80 of the Adoption and Children (Scotland) Act 2007. It is, however, unlikely to include the care required to be shown by a de facto carer under the terms of s.5 of the Children (Scotland) Act 1995, though a parent who allows such a carer to fail in the responsibilities imposed by that section may thereby him or herself be guilty of a lack of parental care.

[10] *D v Kelly*, 1995 S.L.T. 1220 at 1223L. See also *Finlayson, Applicant*, 1989 S.C.L.R. 601.

[11] *M v McGregor*, 1982 S.L.T. 41, per Lord Justice-Clerk Wheatley at 43 (in relation to the very similarly worded ground in the Social Work (Scotland) Act 1968).

[12] *D v Kelly*, 1995 S.L.T. 1220; *H v Harkness*, 1998 S.L.T. 1431 at 1435J. This consists with E.C.H.R. jurisprudence: *Olsson v Sweden (No. 2)* (1994) 17 E.H.R.R. 134 at [72]; *K.A. v Finland* [2003] 1 F.L.R. 696, at [92]; *YC v United Kingdom* (2012) 55 E.H.R.R. 33 at [134].

protect the child from positive harm, such as abuse at the hands of others, or a failure to provide the child with such developmental stimulus as any rational parent would consider essential to the child's proper upbringing, such as for example by exhibiting a careless attitude towards education. It is not limited to neglect and a lack of parental care might well be constituted by active treatment of or behaviour towards the child. So it will cover failure to feed and clothe the child properly, maintaining a dirty and unhealthy living environment, allowing the child to wander the streets unsupervised late at night, allowing the child access to (or even providing) potentially harmful substances such as alcohol or pornography, failing to provide the emotional stability and social intercourse that is essential to the proper development of a child's character, allowing or even encouraging the child to enter into harmful relationships, acting in such a way as has the effect of lowering the child's self-esteem,[13] or any other act or omission, behaviour or attitude which the reasonable parent would not have done or failed to do, or would not have shown. The ground clearly includes ill-treatment short of a criminal offence. It must be likely that the deprivation of reasonable care will continue and will harm the child materially in the future: the test is an objective one and it is prospective.[14]

Either the likelihood of the child suffering or the likelihood that there will be **3–05** a lack of parental care raises the question of whether the making of a compulsory supervision order is necessary.[15] Likelihood of suffering might be when there is a substantial or real, and not remote, chance that the lack of parental care will cause suffering to the child. The English courts have held that "likelihood of harm" indicates "a real possibility of harm", as opposed to an assessment on the balance of probabilities that harm will be suffered.[16] The Court of Session said the following, in relation to the similarly worded ground in the Children (Scotland) Act 1995:

> "Obviously, what the statute is looking to is the likelihood of something happening in the future. We are prepared to accept that what is meant by the word 'likely' . . . is not 'probable' or 'more likely than not' but nevertheless that there is a significant or substantial risk of the events set out in the paragraph occurring in the future. In order to decide whether there is such a likelihood, it is necessary to consider in the first place events in the past and then to draw inferences by a process of inductive reasoning from those events and what else is known about the character of the person or persons involved in them, so that conclusions can if possible be drawn about what is likely to happen in the future. In short, it takes the form of a risk assessment, which must be based on evidence".[17]

Speculative injury is not sufficient, though the court accepts that it may be unrealistic to require precise specification of the harm that the child might

---

[13] As in *R v Grant*, 2000 S.L.T. 372.

[14] *D v Kelly*, 1995 S.L.T. 1220, per Lord Murray at 1224B.

[15] *McGregor v L*, 1981 S.L.T. 194; *M v McGregor*, 1982 S.L.T. 41.

[16] *Re H & Ors (Minors) (Sexual Abuse: Standard of Proof)* [1996] 1 All E.R. 1; *MA (Children) (Care Order: Likelihood of Significant Harm* [2009] EWCA Civ 853, per Ward L.J. at [52]. See also *L (A Child) (Care: Threshold Criteria)* [2007] 1 F.L.R. 2050.

[17] *M v McClafferty* [2008] Fam. L.R. 22 at [9]. See also *B v Authority Reporter*, 2011 S.L.T. (Sh Ct) 55; *Re B (A Child)* [2013] UKSC 33.

suffer.[18] In the context of a criminal charge it has been held (and there will be no difference in the present context) that being intoxicated while looking after a child does not in itself create a likelihood of injury (though if it renders the person incapable of caring for the child it will inevitably amount to a lack of care)[19]; rather, there must be some evidence to support an inference that suffering is likely to be caused such as, for example, the child needing fed or being left by an open fire and the parent being too intoxicated to notice the danger. Nor is the likelihood of suffering necessarily constituted by leaving even a very young child alone, though the length of time the child is left would be important, as would the circumstances and the potential sources of danger to which the child is thereby exposed.[20] The likelihood that the parents will show a lack of parental care can be proved from the parents' past actions, such as their treatment of their other children, at least when the circumstances suggest that they are likely to treat the referred child in the same way.[21] Past behaviour and attitudes are often a accurate predicter of future harm and so events in the past (involving a different child) may be used to establish this ground even when the referred child has never in fact been in the care of the relevant person, as when that child is removed into state care shortly after birth.[22] It is necessary, however, that a risk assessment be carried out in relation to the referred child, and risk to that child cannot simply be assumed from past improper conduct.[23]

3–06   If it is proved that the habits and mode of life of the parents are such as to yield the reasonable inference that they are unlikely to care for the child in a manner likely to prevent unnecessary suffering or serious impairment of his or her health or development, the ground applies.[24] A failure to provide or to consent to medical treatment considered necessary by sound medical opinion will constitute lack of parental care, even when the parents make their decision after careful consideration of the issue.[25] Parental good faith is nothing to the point: if their decision is not that which the reasonable parent would make, then they can be said to be showing a lack of parental care.[26] Character flaw that is likely to result in a harmful development of the child's personality has been held in England to "cross the threshold" for permanent removal of a child from otherwise loving parents' care[27] and, if such character flaw can be shown to be likely seriously to impair the child's development, in Scotland this ground might perhaps be said to apply if the character flaw results to a lack of the parental care that any child is entitled to.[28]

---

[18] *H v Harkness*, 1998 S.L.T. 1431, per Lord Coulsfield at 1435I.

[19] *H v Lees, D v Orr*, 1994 S.L.T. 908.

[20] *M v Normand*, 1995 S.L.T. 1284.

[21] *M v Scottish Children's Reporter for Renfrewshire*, 2009 Fam. L.R. 106.

[22] *McGregor v L*, 1981 S.L.T. 194. The European Court has, however, warned that removal of a new-born child can be justified only in extreme circumstances: *Haase v Germany* [2005] 40 E.H.R.R. 19 at [91].

[23] *M v McClafferty*, 2008 Fam. L.R. 22.

[24] *McGregor v L*, 1981 S.L.T. 194 at 196.

[25] *Finlayson, Applicant*, 1989 S.C.L.R. 601.

[26] *D v Kelly*, 1995 S.L.T. 1220.

[27] *Re B (A Child)* [2013] UKSC 33.

[28] But note the strong dissent by Lady Hale, whose views on any aspect of child law are not to be readily dismissed, even when expressed in dissent.

(b) The child is a child in respect of whom any of the offences mentioned in Schedule 1 to the Criminal Procedure (Scotland) Act 1995 has been committed

A child who has been the victim of any of the specified offences may be at **3–07** risk of being offended against again or may be in need of direction and guidance in coming to terms with his or her experiences. The specified offences (usually known as "Schedule 1 offences") are as follows:

(i)   any offence under Part I of the Criminal Law (Consolidation) (Scotland) Act 1995 (i.e. incest and related offences);

(ii)   any offence under s.18 (rape of a young child) or s.28 (having sexual intercourse with an older child) of the Sexual Offences (Scotland) Act 2009;

(iii)   any offence under s.19 (sexual assault of a young child by penetration) or s.29 (engaging in penetrative sexual activity with or towards an older child) of the 2009 Act;

(iv)   any offence under s.20 (sexual assault on a young child) or s.30 (engaging in sexual activity with or towards an older child) of the 2009 Act;

(v)   any offence under s.42 of the 2009 Act (sexual abuse of trust) towards a child under 17[29];

(vi)   any offence under ss.12,[30] 15,[31] 22[32] or 33[33] of the Children and Young Persons (Scotland) Act 1937;

(vii)   any offence under the Prohibition of Female Genital Mutilation (Scotland) Act 2005 where the mutilation has been committed or is proposed for a child under the age of 17 years;

(viii) any offence under ss.52 or 52A of the Civic Government (Scotland) Act 1982 in relation to an indecent photograph or pseudophotograph of a child under the age of 17 years;

(ix   any offence under ss. 1, 9, 10, 11 or 12 of the Protection of Children and Prevention of Sexual Offences (Scotland) Act 2005 in respect of a child under the age of 17 years (generally speaking, offences of grooming children for unlawful sexual activity, or involving children in prostitution or pornography);

(x)   any other offence involving bodily injury[34] to a child under the age of 17 years;

---

[29] Except where there is no family relationship between the child and the offender: Sexual Offences (Scotland) Act 2009 s.43(6).

[30] Cruelty (including neglect and assault) to person under 16. This provision may be used when the parent exceeds the bounds of legitimate chastisement: see for example *G v Templeton*, 1998 S.C.L.R. 180. It may not be used when the mens rea necessary for criminal assault cannot be established: *S v Authority Reporter*, 2012 S.L.T. (Sh Ct) 89 (but see *Dunn v McDonald*, 2013 S.L.T. (Sh Ct) 34).

[31] Causing or allowing person under 16 to be used for begging.

[32] Exposing child under seven to risk of burning.

[33] Causing or allowing person under 16 to take part in dangerous performance.

[34] "Bodily injury" requires physical injury or injury to the body of the child: *B v Kennedy*, 1987 S.L.T. 765; *F v Kennedy*, 1988 S.L.T. 404. Emotional injury is not covered here.

(xi)   any offence involving the use of lewd, indecent or libidinous practice or behaviour towards a child under the age of 17 years[35];

(xii)   any offence under ss.5 (coercing a person into being present during
a sexual activity), 6 (coercing a person into looking at a sexual
image), 7 (communicating indecently etc.), 8 (sexual exposure) or
9 (voyeurism) of the Sexual Offences (Scotland) Act 2009 towards
a child under the age of 17 years; and

(xiii) any offence under ss.21–26 or 31–37 of the 2009 Act (sexual
offences relating to children). Section 37 of the 2009 Act makes
consensual sexual conduct between older children an offence and,
where consensual, both older children are simultaneously the
offender and the victim of the Schedule 1 offence.[36]

It is of no significance to the existence of the ground who perpetrated the
offence, nor where the offence was perpetrated; these matters will, of course,
be highly relevant to the final disposal of the child's case. Proof of this ground,
despite being proof of a criminal offence, is on the civil standard,[37] and this
standard can be met even in the absence of a conviction: the issue at stake (with
this ground) is the harm to the child rather than how or by whom it was perpetrated. As such, there is no requirement that there be proved to have been a
conviction before it can be established that this ground exists. Nor is there any
requirement that the perpetrator be charged, or even identified.[38] Indeed, the
ground might exist even when a prosecution results in an acquittal.[39] The
elements of the crime must, however, all be shown to exist.[40] A conviction is
evidence of the commission of the offence,[41] but it must be established that the
child was a victim: the ground "is concerned with offences and not offenders".[42]
The hearing may, of course, take into account the identity of the offender (if
known to them) in their disposal of the referral, but the sheriff is not entitled to
make findings of fact beyond those necessary for the establishment of the
ground.[43]

3–08   Though this ground, in its terms, refers to the commission of certain offences,
it is not required that the actions which amount to the offences must have taken
place in Scotland and are therefore triable in a Scottish court. In *S v Kennedy*[44] it
was argued that since events which took place in Germany could not be tried as
offences in Scotland they could not therefore amount to a ground of referral that
the child was the victim of a schedule 1 offence. This argument was, however,

---

[35] For a discussion of the nature of this crime, see Gane, *Sexual Offences* (Butterworths, 1992),
pp.74–77; Gordon, *Criminal Law*, 3rd edn, by M.G.A. Christie (W. Green, 2001), para.36.09.

[36] Reporters would seem, therefore, to have the choice of referring the child under this ground
or the offence ground in s.67(2)(j). The difference is stark in the effects of being classified a "sex
offender" and so this ground rather than the offence ground should be used when the referral is
made primarily for protective reasons.

[37] *McGregor v D*, 1977 S.L.T. 182.

[38] *McGregor v K*, 1982 S.L.T. 293; *Kennedy v F*, 1985 S.L.T. 22.

[39] cf. *Kennedy v B*, 1992 S.C.L.R. 55.

[40] Thus in *S v Authority Reporter*, 2012 S.L.T. (Sh Ct) 89 the failure by the reporter to establish
the mens rea for assault resulted in the referral being discharged.

[41] Law Reform (Miscellaneous Provisions) (Scotland) Act 1968 s.10.

[42] *S v Kennedy*, 1987 S.L.T. 667, per Lord Justice-Clerk Ross at 669I.

[43] *S v Kennedy*, 1987 S.L.T. 667.

[44] 1996 S.L.T. 1087.

rejected on the basis that on a proper interpretation of the statute,[45] the ground of referral is established when there is proved to have been conduct amounting to any of the Schedule 1 offences rather than the commission of a triable Schedule 1 offence. The result was that it did not matter where the conduct took place. This interpretation is justified by the purpose of the statute, which is to provide protection for children at risk from conduct rather than to provide punishment for crimes against the law of Scotland. There is nothing anomalous about this result when it is remembered that the section 67 ground contained in this paragraph can be established (on the balance of probabilities) even in the face of an acquittal by a criminal court (because of a failure to prove the crime beyond reasonable doubt). The reference to schedule 1 is not a reference to particular crimes, but a means of identifying or characterising the conduct struck at.[46]

(c) The child has, or is likely to have, a close connection with a person who has committed a Schedule 1 offence

A person who commits a Schedule 1 offence, which are nearly all serious **3–09** offences against children, is nearly always, therefore, a risk to children,[47] and any child who has a close connection with such a person might require, for his or her protection, guidance, treatment or control, to be made subject to a compulsory supervision order in order to minimise or remove that risk. Of course such an order might not be necessary, but the very existence of the offence, together with the connection between the offender and the child, justifies the raising of the question, which the children's hearing must answer. "Close connection" means in this context (and in the context of paragraphs (f) and (g) below) that the child is a member of the same household as the Schedule 1 offender or, if not a member of the offender's household, has significant contact with the offender.[48] The meaning of "household" is discussed under paragraph (d) below; "significant contact" is intended to cover the situation where the source of potential danger does not live with the child but nevertheless is regularly present in the child's family circle—the typical example will be the boyfriend of the child's mother who lives apart from the mother and the child but who regularly visits. Given the purpose of the ground, and the words surrounding "significant contact", it is likely that the contact needs to be familial or personal, and not official or professional. "Significant" means regular, or at least frequent. This ground applies whenever a Schedule 1 offence has been committed, even when that offence was not committed against a child.[49] It will normally be essential to establish who the perpetrator is in order

---

[45] Then the Social Work (Scotland) Act 1968, but the principle applies with equivalent subsequent legislation.

[46] per Lord Murray at 1093H. This is very similar to the reasoning found in Lord Dunpark's dissenting judgment in *Merrin v S*, 1987 S.L.T. 193. cf. *Harris v E*, 1989 S.L.T. 42 in which a ground of referral was found established when the child was shown to be the victim of an offence which was not a scheduled offence at the time it was committed but had become a scheduled offence at the date of the referral.

[47] This is not always so, as the continually problematic s.37 of the Sexual Offences (Scotland) Act 2009 (listed in para.4B of Sch.1 to the Criminal Procedure (Scotland) Act 1995) shows: the 15 year old who had sex with another 15 year old may or may not constitute any form of risk to his or her siblings.

[48] 2011 Act s.67(3).

[49] Incest and related offences are still governed by Pt I of the Criminal Law (Consolidation) (Scotland) Act 1995 and can be committed against adults.

to establish that that person has a close connection with the child, though, rarely, it might be possible to establish that one of a number of adults in that position (for example by being members of the child's household) committed the offence without establishing precisely who. It is not, however, necessary that any charges have been laid against the perpetrator, and indeed the ground can be established even when a prosecution has been brought but has failed.[50] The burden of proof in establishing this ground is on the balance of probabilities (as it is for all the grounds except that in paragraph (j) below[51]). Proof of a conviction is sufficient evidence.[52]

(d) The child is, or is likely to become, a member of the same household as a child in respect of whom a Schedule 1 offence has been committed

3–10   If the adults in a household, one child of which was the victim of a Schedule 1 offence, were unable to protect that child, the question may legitimately be asked whether they will be able to protect other children in the same household and, consequently, if one child in a household has been the victim of a Schedule 1 offence all the children who are members of that household may be referred to a children's hearing for the purpose of answering the question, and for determining the appropriate response in case of a negative answer to the question. In addition, children who are likely to become members of that household may also be referred[53]: this might include, for example, a child born in a hospital who is likely, on leaving hospital, to become a member of a household in which one of the members was the victim of a scheduled offence. This is sometimes referred to as "the sibling ground" because it captures not the child who is the direct victim of a schedule 1 offence but that child's siblings and other children in that child's household.

3–11   This paragraph covers both the case where an adult member of the household constitutes the threat and where the threat comes from outside the household. In the former case there is likely to be, in addition, a ground under paragraph (c) above. As with the ground in paragraph (b) above, it is not necessary for the satisfaction of this condition that the perpetrator be identified, or that any criminal charge be laid against anyone. The question is simply whether the child referred under this paragraph is, or is likely to become, a member of the same household as a child victim of the offence. It is not necessary that the victim was him or herself referred to a children's hearing under paragraph (b) above. To establish this ground both the offence and membership of the household must be proved.[54] The identification of the victim of the offence will be a practical necessity, for otherwise membership of the victim's household would be impossible to prove. If a referral had previously been made of the victim of the offence under paragraph (b) and the sheriff found, after hearing evidence, that the ground was established, the production of a certified copy of the sheriff's interlocutor will be sufficient proof that that child was the victim of a scheduled

---

[50] *Kennedy v B*, 1992 S.C.L.R. 55.

[51] *Harris v F*, 1991 S.L.T. 242.

[52] Law Reform (Miscellaneous Provisions) (Scotland) Act 1968 s.10.

[53] This was an addition in 1995 to the predecessor ground as it appeared in s.32(2)(d) of the Social Work (Scotland) Act 1968. For a discussion of "likelihood" in this context, see *Templeton v E*, 1998 S.C.L.R. 672 (Sh Ct) at 678–679.

[54] *Ferguson v S*, 1992 S.C.L.R. 866.

offence,[55] and all that will need to be proved in relation to the child referred under the present paragraph is membership of the same household as that victim. If, on the other hand, the sheriff had found the ground under paragraph (b) to be not established in relation to the direct victim, it will be difficult for a reporter to argue that other children in the same household are properly referred under the present paragraph, but it would not, it is submitted, be incompetent to attempt to do so. The investigation of the child referred under this paragraph may well reveal information that was not available when the direct victim of the offence was referred under paragraph (b). It is open to a reporter to refer a child under this paragraph even after having taken the decision not to refer the direct victim of the offence under paragraph (b): though this would be unusual it might be appropriate, for example, if the victim is about to leave home or about to attain the age of 16 and is no longer in need of protection, guidance, treatment or control, while the child referred under this paragraph remains vulnerable. It is open to a relevant person to deny the existence of the ground under the present paragraph even when, at the referral of the direct victim under paragraph (b), he or she accepted the facts that now form the basis of the referral of another child. Their acceptance in the previous referral is not on its own sufficient proof before the sheriff that the present ground is established.[56]

There were a number of cases concerned with the meaning of "household" **3–12** as it appeared in the Social Work (Scotland) Act 1968 and the Children (Scotland) Act 1995,[57] and there is no intent that the word bears any different meaning in the Children's Hearings (Scotland) Act 2011. It has been accepted that persons may be members of the same "household" even when they live apart: the word refers more to a continuing relationship than to physical proximity. So in *McGregor v H*[58] the First Division held that a child was a member of the same household as another child even although the other child had been removed from the family home in terms of an order made by a children's hearing. Lord President Emslie said:

> "The word 'household' in s.32[59] is plainly intended to connote a family unit or something akin to a family unit—a group of persons, held together by a particular kind of tie who normally live together, even if individual members of the group may be temporarily separated from it . . . The test is membership of the household and not whether a child is . . . 'living' in the same household as the victim of a relevant offence".[60]

This dictum was applied in *Kennedy v R's Curator ad litem*,[61] in which a 13-year-old child had been subjected to lewd and indecent practices by her father and her one-and-a-half-year-old half sister was referred to the children's hearing, on the ground that she was a member of the same household as a

---

[55] *McGregor v H*, 1983 S.L.T. 626.

[56] *M v Kennedy*, 1995 S.L.T. 123; *M v Constanda*, 1999 S.L.T. 494.

[57] For a discussion, see Norrie, "The Meaning of 'Household' in Referrals to the Children's Hearing", 1993 S.L.T. (News) 192.

[58] 1983 S.L.T. 626.

[59] The 1968 predecessor of s.52 of the Children (Scotland) Act 1995 and of s.67 of the Children's Hearings (Scotland) Act 2011.

[60] 1983 S.L.T. 626 at 628.

[61] 1993 S.L.T. 295.

person who has committed a Schedule 1 offence.[62] Though the parents accepted this ground of referral, the hearing directed the reporter to make an application to the sheriff for the establishment of the ground, since the referred child was too young to understand. Shortly after the hearing, and before the case called before the sheriff, the child's mother removed herself and the child from the father and went to live with her own mother and claimed before the sheriff that the child was no longer a member of the same "household" as her father. That claim failed. Lord President Hope pointed out that, "the important question . . . is whether the ties of affection and regular contact which hold the parties together as a group of persons still continue. Since the criterion is that of relationship rather than locality, it is necessary to examine closely the reasons given for the suggestion that the relationship has broken down. A temporary separation will not do, especially as [the ground] looks to the future as well as the present state of affairs".[63] There must be more than a mere physical separation before a "household" comes to an end, otherwise the policy of the Act could be frustrated by determined parents. It follows that a separation will not destroy a "household" when it is due only to the intervention of the authorities[64] or to a fear that steps may be taken by the authorities which might result in a compulsory supervision order being made.[65]

3–13   A rather different aspect of the same point was raised in *A v Kennedy*,[66] in which a child had died aged two months as a result of being wilfully assaulted and ill-treated at his parents' home. Eight and a half years later the mother gave birth to another child and the reporter sought to refer this child to a children's hearing on the ground that the child was a member of the same household as a child who was the victim of a Schedule 1 offence. The parents disputed the ground of referral on the basis that the "household" into which the new baby had been born was different from that in which the previous child had lived.[67] They argued that the household had developed to such an extent that it could no longer be regarded as the same household: the previous child had died eight and a half years prior to the new baby entering the household, and an older sister, who had been removed after the death and sent to live with foster parents, had now returned to live with the parents under a supervision requirement (as compulsory supervision orders were then known). The parents argued that these substantial developments meant that the household into which the baby was born was different from that in which the previous child had lived. The Second Division disagreed and held that the "household" remained that which had existed when the baby died. Lord Justice-Clerk Ross pointed out that a household can continue even although there are changes in its membership. An older child may leave and a younger child may arrive, yet the "household" might remain intact. In *Cunningham v M*[68] Sheriff Principal Macphail summed up the authorities as follows:

---

[62] i.e. the ground now expanded into s.67(2)(c).

[63] 1993 S.L.T. 295 at 300A–B.

[64] As in *McGregor v H*, 1983 S.L.T. 626.

[65] 1993 S.L.T. 295, per Lord President Hope at 300B.

[66] 1993 S.L.T. 1188.

[67] The fact that the statute referred to a child who "is" a member of the same household as the child referred was not relied upon by counsel for the parents since the intention of the statute, as the Court put it, could clearly only be achieved by interpreting the word "is" to include "was".

[68] 2005 S.L.T. (Sh Ct) 73 at [26].

"The question whether people are members of the same household is a question of fact and degree; the concept of 'household' is of a group of persons and not the location in which they live; the fact that persons are living for the time being in separate houses is not decisive of the question whether they are members of the same household; the important question is whether ties of affection and regular contact which hold the parties together as a group still continue; the criterion is that of relationship rather than locality".[69]

So, a continuing relationship is important for the continuation of a household, but a relationship, even of blood and affection, will not in itself be sufficient. Nor will the mere fact that a person has parental responsibilities and parental rights in relation to the child, nor the fact that there exists between the two members of the asserted household "family life" within the meaning of art.6 ECHR.[70] There is no presumption that a daughter lives in the same household as her father.[71] "Household" involves more than simply a relationship and requires, it is submitted, some living together either presently, or in the past with the possibility of re-establishing the cohabitation. If the child is at risk from a merely visiting father another ground would have to be used to refer him or her to the children's hearing (such as, for example, the "exposure to persons whose conduct [is likely to be harmful]" ground in s.67(2)(e) about to be discussed or one of the "close connection" grounds in s.67(2)(c), (f) or (g)).

(e) The child is being, or is likely to be, exposed to persons whose conduct is (or has been) such that it is likely that (i) the child will be abused or harmed, or (ii) the child's health, safety or development will be seriously adversely affected

The nature of the conduct that founds this ground is governed by the harm **3–14** that is likely to befall the referred child. It might include conduct involving the person causing harm, whether deliberately, recklessly or negligently, to other children, or indicating a disposition of indifference to the welfare of children with whom the person comes into contact; it might be conduct in the past but only if that indicates a likelihood of harm to the child in the future: it might be active or passive conduct. The harm that is likely might be physical, emotional or developmental: exposure of the child to influences which subvert the generally accepted standards of society and thereby make the child less able to fit appropriately into society, such as endemic criminality or drug abuse is, it is submitted, seriously adverse to the child's development.[72] The purpose of this ground is to protect the child from people[73] whose conduct either directly or

---

[69] One, probably unintended, consequence of this focus on relationship may well be that a single mother with no close family cannot be a "household". So a single mother whose first child was permanently removed from the mother's care may not constitute a "household" when she gives birth to another child. But if the first child remains with the mother there would seem to exist a household into which the subsequent child is born.

[70] *Templeton v E*, 1998 S.C.L.R. 672 (Sh Ct).

[71] *Ferguson v S*, 1992 S.C.L.R. 866.

[72] cf. the English decision of the Supreme Court in *Re B (A Child)* [2013] UKSC 33.

[73] Though the statute uses the plural, unlike the grounds in paras (c), (f), (g) and (n), this should not be taken to mean that only abuse or harm from more than one person is captured by this ground: s.22 of the Interpretation and Legislative Reform (Scotland) Act 2010 provides that "words in the plural include the singular", and there is no necessary (or even sensible) implication that this should not be so in this context.

indirectly creates a risk of harm: if the child has already been harmed then another ground would be more appropriate. The commission by a parent of a criminal offence does not in itself indicate that the child's development is likely to be seriously adversely affected, but the fact that the parent is a habitual criminal may well do: in the latter but not (necessarily) in the former case the danger is real that the child, under the influence of the parents, will follow their lead and adopt their attitudes to the criminal law, to the child's obvious and long-term detriment. The risk need not have eventuated before this ground can be held to apply, for the essence of the ground is likelihood of harm rather than actual harm. "Exposure" to such a risk suggests that those responsible for caring for the child ought to have protected the child from contact with the person but failed to do so: the duty is to have taken such protective steps as the reasonable parent would have taken. However, there is no implication that parental failure is necessary for this ground: a child might be exposed to dangerous persons by friends or relatives who have no parental responsibility towards the child: it is exposure rather than parental failure that underlies this ground. Parental conduct (active or passive) is included though will usually be more appropriately dealt with under paragraph (a) above.[74] "Likely" exposure to a person whose conduct is such that it is likely to harm the child may—and it has been held in England that it does—include exposure to a person who has not been proved to have been the person who committed such conduct but who was one of those who might have done so.[75]

(f) The child has, or is likely to have, a close connection with a person who has carried out domestic abuse

3–15   Domestic abuse perpetrated against someone in the child's close circle will often, even when the child remains physically unharmed, have seriously detrimental emotional and developmental consequences, including distress at witnessing violence directed towards a parent, feelings of helplessness in the face of danger and, perhaps most invidiously, a growing acceptance of violence as an inevitable aspect of family life. Female children are especially at risk of being inured to the dangers of violent partners (taking the lesson that violence is an inescapable feature of domestic relationships); male children are especially at risk of replicating behaviour from a violent role-model: in either case, the upbringing and socialising of the child is being seriously derailed. In many respects the aim of a referral to the children's hearing on this ground is to break a cycle as well as to provide immediate protection.

3–16   "Close connection" has the same meaning as it has in paragraph (c) above, that is to say the child must either be a member of the person's household (as discussed in relation to paragraph (d) above) or, if not, have significant contact

---

[74] On the facts of *Re B (A Child)* [2013] UKSC 33, where serious character flaws in the parents meant that the child's emotional development was likely to be seriously adversely affected, it might be difficult to establish the lack of parental care necessary to found the ground in para.(a), but so long as such character flaws manifest themselves in conduct the ground in this paragraph may well be shown to apply.

[75] *Re J (Children) (Care Proceedings: Threshold Criteria)* [2013] 1 F.L.R. 1373. Here children were subject to care proceedings because their mother was the "possible" perpetrator of harm shown to have been suffered by a different child. The Supreme Court held that this was sufficient to "cross the threshold" justifying state action in the instant case.

with the person.[76] "Domestic abuse" is not defined in the Children's Hearings (Scotland) Act 2011, though as a concept it is easily recognised if a technical meaning is avoided and the protective aim of the legislation is kept in mind.[77] "Abuse" ought to be given as wide a meaning as it has in, for example, the Protection from Abuse (Scotland) Act 2001.[78] The phrase "domestic violence" as it appeared in English legislation was held by the Supreme Court to refer to "violence between people who are or were connected with one another in an intimate or familial way",[79] and "domestic abuse" ought, it is submitted, to be interpreted no less broadly. In particular, there is no justification within the context of a child protection system to limit "domestic abuse" to partner-abuse thereby excluding inter-generational abuse.[80] A child who witnesses a step-father (for example) abusing an elder (or indeed younger) sibling is a child who has a close connection with a person who has carried out domestic abuse, no less than the child who witnessed a step-father abusing the child's mother.

(g) The child has, or is likely to have, a close connection with a person who has committed an offence under Part 1, 4 or 5 of the Sexual Offences (Scotland) Act 2009

Not all of the offences in the 2009 Act are offences against children and not all, therefore, are Schedule 1 offences. Many are indeed Schedule 1 offences and if so the reporter will be able to refer the child to the children's hearing on both this ground and the ground in paragraph (c) above. Given that overlap, the primary importance of this ground is that it will provide protection to children against sex offenders whose offences were not against children: the commission of a sex offence raises the question whether it is necessary for the child's protection, guidance, treatment or control to make a compulsory supervision order, for sexual offences are peculiarly susceptible to repetition, and a propensity to commit offences of this nature heightens the risk, it may be assumed, of harm to children with whom the offender has significant contact. The hearing of course may find that the risk of actual harm to the child referred is not sufficient to make necessary a compulsory supervision order, but the offence itself justifies them investigating the matter. "Close connection" is defined as in paragraphs (c) and (f) above and, as with these grounds, the identify of the offender must be established. Part 4 of the 2009 Act includes the offence of an older child engaging in sexual activity with another older child,[81] with the result that this ground may be established in respect of a child whose 15-year-old sibling engaged in consensual sexual conduct with another 15 year old, but *not*

3–17

---

[76] 2011 Act s.67(3).

[77] *Yemshaw v London Borough Council of Hounslow* [2011] 1 All E.R. 912.

[78] "Abuse" there includes "violence, harassment, threatening conduct, and any other conduct giving rise, or likely to give rise, to physical or mental injury, fear, alarm or distress" (Protection from Abuse (Scotland) Act 2001 s.7); "conduct" is stated to include "speech; and presence in a specified place or area". ("Conduct" is similarly defined in the Protection from Harassment Act 1997 s.8A, as inserted by the Domestic Abuse (Scotland) Act 2011 s.1(2)).

[79] *Yemshaw v London Borough Council of Hounslow* [2011] 1 All E.R. 912, per Lady Hale at [20].

[80] The Domestic Abuse (Scotland) Act 2011 amends the Protection from Harassment Act 1997 to make special provision for harassment amounting to "domestic abuse" and defines that as abuse between spouses, civil partners, cohabitants or persons in an intimate personal relationship.

[81] Sexual Offences (Scotland) Act 2009 s.37. An "older child" is one who is over 13 and below 16 years old.

where the 15-year-old sibling engaged in consensual sexual conduct with a 16 year old. In the latter case the sibling is the victim while in the former case the sibling is (together with his or her partner) the offender—and it is to be remembered that the ground will exist even although the prosecuting authorities see no merit in prosecuting the sibling. When the sibling is the "victim" the ground in paragraph (d) may apply in respect of the referred child. In any case of consensual sexual activity the reporter should refer the child, or a sibling of the participant, only when there is a need for some practical protective step that the hearing system is able to provide.

(h) The child is being provided with accommodation by a local authority under s.25 of the Children (Scotland) Act 1995 and special measures are needed to support the child

3–18   Section 25 of the Children (Scotland) Act 1995 obliges local authorities to provide accommodation to any child: (i) in respect of whom no-one has parental responsibility; or (ii) who is lost or abandoned; or (iii) who was being cared for by a person who is now prevented, whether or not permanently and for whatever reason, from providing the child with suitable accommodation or care[82]; the local authority is also entitled, but not obliged, to provide accommodation for any child in their area if they consider that to do so would safeguard or promote the child's welfare.[83] The local authority has various duties in respect of any child who is being accommodated by it under these (and other) provisions. In carrying out these duties it sometimes happens that special measures are necessary properly to support the child, and if so the child can be referred to a children's hearing in order that the children's hearing can give consideration to such measures as are appropriate to provide the child with the necessary support. This might be because access to particular resources, such as specialist accommodation, is more readily available than otherwise when it is a condition or authorisation under a compulsory supervision order that the child is given such access. Or it might involve some form of restraining measure in the child's own interests or in the interests of those to whom the child poses a threat.

(i) A permanence order made under the Adoption and Children (Scotland) Act 2007 is in force in respect of the child and special measures are needed to support the child

3–19   For much the same reasons as discussed in paragraph (h) above, a child who is subject to a permanence order may need special measures of support. If so, the child may be referred to a children's hearing on this ground and the hearing may consider it necessary to make a compulsory supervision order to ensure, or perhaps to speed, the delivery of such special measures.

(j) The child has committed an offence

3–20   One of the abiding principles upon which the Kilbrandon Report was based is that the child who has committed a criminal offence is as much in need of

---

[82] Children (Scotland) Act 1995 s.25(1).
[83] Children (Scotland) Act 1995 s.25(2).

care and supervision as the child who is the victim of abuse or neglect. This principle was given statutory recognition in the Social Work (Scotland) Act 1968, was unaffected by the Children (Scotland) Act 1995, and remains central to the thinking behind the current legislation. That the child has committed a criminal offence is one of the most common grounds in respect of which children are referred to a children's hearing, though the consideration of and potential disposals applicable to a case brought on this ground are no different from cases brought on any other ground. The children's hearing considering the case will be less concerned with the question of the child's guilt than with the question of whether it is necessary for the child's protection, guidance, treatment or control to make a compulsory supervision order. The proceedings are not criminal proceedings since they are not concerned with prosecution and can lead to no conviction.[84] Nevertheless, this ground is slightly different from all the other grounds in two major respects. First, proof, if an application has been made to the sheriff to establish the ground, is on the criminal rather than the civil standard[85] and the rules of evidence applicable to criminal rather than civil cases will be applied.[86] And secondly, the ground is applicable only to children who are older than eight years of age, which is the age of criminal responsibility.[87] A factual basis that would justify a child over the age of eight being referred under this paragraph will, however, usually justify a referral under another paragraph of the child who is under eight. Paragraph (m) below is the most obvious ground for dealing with children under eight who act in a way that would amount to an offence, had they been over that age.

(k) The child has misused alcohol

The misuse of alcohol is a serious problem that can lead to long term health **3–21** difficulties (physical and psychological) for young people. Not all use of alcohol by a child will be "misuse", if responsible supervision and small amounts are involved. If, however, the child took alcohol without responsible adult supervision, or to such an extent as to become inebriated, then there is likely to have been a misuse. It must be the child who has misused the alcohol: it would not normally be considered to be a misuse by a young child to be plied with alcohol by an adult, and that circumstance will appropriately be dealt with as a lack of parental care. Consumption in certain premises of alcohol by a child or young person is a criminal offence in itself[88] and while that might found the ground in paragraph (j) above it is also likely to make this ground too applicable, for consuming alcohol in circumstances in which it is a crime to do so will invariably be considered a misuse of alcohol.

---

[84] per Lord President Emslie in *McGregor v T*, 1975 S.L.T. 76 at 81. See also *S v Miller*, 2001 S.L.T. 531.

[85] 2011 Act s.102(3). And the reporter cannot avoid this higher standard of proof by drawing up different grounds, such as exposure to moral danger, if the factual basis of the ground is the commission of an offence: *Constanda v M*, 1997 S.L.T. 1396.

[86] See below, para.8–24.

[87] Criminal Procedure (Scotland) Act 1995 s.41. See *Merrin v S*, 1987 S.L.T. 193. The Criminal Justice and Licensing (Scotland) Act 2010 raised the age of criminal prosecution to 12 (adding s.41A to the Criminal Procedure (Scotland) Act 1995) but left untouched the age at which a child can be referred to a children's hearing on the ground of having committed a criminal offence.

[88] Licensing (Scotland) Act 2005 s.102. See also the offence in s.108 of that Act: delivery of alcohol to a child.

(l) The child has misused a drug (whether or not a controlled drug within the meaning of the Misuse of Drugs Act 1971)

3–22   This ground is designed to give effect to art.33 of the UN Convention on the Rights of the Child, which obliges States to take all appropriate measures to protect children from the dangers of illicit use of drugs. Even without this paragraph[89] children who misuse drugs could be referred under another ground in any case, such as being beyond parental control, or in some circumstances lack of parental care. Drug abuse is, however, a significant threat to the well-being of some children and the existence of this separate ground serves to strengthen the concern rightly felt about the problem, as well as encouraging the hearing to focus on the real issue facing the child. Also, it may well be clearer as a ground in itself rather than evidence of another ground, and thus easier to establish. As with the ground in paragraph (k) above, there must be a "misuse".[90] A child may legitimately take a drug for medicinal purposes. The use by a child of drugs, for recreational or indeed any other reason than for medicinal purposes, will clearly amount to misuse. The ground is not established by the child being given drugs without consent by an adult (though that is likely to amount to another ground): as with ground (k) above it is the child's behaviour rather than the behaviour of any other person that is the focus of this ground.

(m) The child's conduct has had, or is likely to have, a serious adverse effect on the health, safety or development of the child or another person

3–23   The focus of this ground, like the ground in paragraph (j) above, is the child's own behaviour and, to differentiate it from paragraph (j), the behaviour (at least if the child is eight years of age or older) must be non-criminal.[91] The conduct that might found this ground may be either active or passive. Refusing to access or engage with the support mechanisms that the local authority or another body offers the child might well amount to conduct that has a serious adverse effect on the development of the child. For the child to place him or herself in situations of danger, such as associating with criminals and drug dealers or drug addicts may be captured by this ground. So may accepting a "joy ride" in a car stolen by another person, playing on railway lines or at the sides of busy roads, playing practical "jokes" on another that risk serious injury to another, or sending emotionally destructive texts, emails and social website messages to another child. The self-harming child will also come within this ground. The effect must in all cases be seriously adverse to either the child or the other person and so causing minor upset or risking minor injuries and bruises will not be sufficient to render this ground applicable.

---

[89] And there was no equivalent in s.32 of the Social Work (Scotland) Act 1968. The predecessor ground to this paragraph was introduced in s.52(2)(j) of the Children (Scotland) Act 1995.

[90] "Misuse" will frequently amount to an offence under the Misuse of Drugs Act 1971. Sheriff Kearney, *Children's Hearings and the Sheriff Court*, 2nd edn (Butterworths, 2000), para.46.22 suggests, on analogy with *Constanda v M*, 1997 S.L.T. 1396, that if the sole basis of the referral is that the child has committed an offence under the 1971 Act, reporters ought not to seek to avoid the higher standard of proof by relying on this ground rather than that contained in s.67(2)(j).

[91] cf. *Constanda v M*, 1997 S.L.T. 1396.

(n) The child is beyond the control of a relevant person

One of the major responsibilities that adults owe to children in their care is **3–24** the responsibility of providing them with control, in order that the child might learn how to fit in to the society of which he or she is a member. Appropriate control is an essential aspect of the growth and development of a child and if any person who has that responsibility is unable, for whatever reason, to exercise control the child shall be considered to be beyond the control of such a person; if that person is a "relevant person" as defined in s.200,[92] the ground of referral applies. It does not matter that the relevant person does not have full parental responsibilities or parental rights with which to exercise the control, for "control" in this context concerns what is reasonable to expect in the circumstances rather than what the law requires and permits. Nor does it matter why the relevant person is unable to exercise control, and it might be because of illness, incapacity or facility of the relevant person, instability or hyperactivity of the child, a breakdown of the relationship between the two, or for any other reason. In a change from the pre-2011 position, the ground applies whenever the child is beyond the control of one of the relevant persons, even when not beyond the control of another relevant person.[93] "Control" must, it is submitted, be interpreted in a manner appropriate to the particular child and its meaning and content will alter as the child grows up: the control required to be provided to a young child is very different from that to be afforded to a teenager who is nearing 16. Similarly, some children, due to their individual circumstances or due to their own (perhaps disturbed) personalities, will require greater control than others.[94] "Control" is to be interpreted according to the need of the particular child for protection, guidance, direction and advice. A child who defies the control appropriately sought to be exercised, and puts him or herself at risk thereby, is a child for whom it may be necessary, for his or her protection, guidance, treatment or control, to make a compulsory supervision order.

---

[92] Or, in relation to a child already in the system, has been deemed to be a relevant person under s.81. A person deemed to be a relevant person is to be treated as a relevant person for the purposes of various specified parts of the Act (s.81(4)) though s.67 is not within these parts. It is open to argument, therefore, that "relevant person" as it appears in s.67(2)(n) is limited to relevant persons as defined in s.200. It is, however, submitted that where a child's welfare is at issue the legislation should be interpreted expansively and the protection, guidance, treatment and control afforded by a compulsory supervision order should not be denied any child merely because the person who had the duty to control the child traces his or her relevant person status to s.81 rather than to s.200. Perhaps the problem is more apparent than real since the child will already be within the system (for otherwise there will not yet be a deemed relevant person), but a new ground often allows the issue to be focussed appropriately.

[93] The equivalent ground in the Children (Scotland) Act 1995 s.52(2)(a), was that the child was "beyond the control of *any* relevant person". Under the current law the ground would apply if the child were beyond the control of one relevant person but entirely controllable by another. Reporters are unlikely to refer the child to a hearing solely on the basis that one of several relevant persons cannot control the child although others can and do.

[94] As did the children in *D v Kelly*, 1995 S.L.T. 1220.

(o) The child has failed without reasonable excuse to attend school regularly

3–25   Parents have a duty to educate their children,[95] and children have a right to be educated.[96] Most children receive their education by attending school and their failure to do so regularly, without reasonable excuse, whether as a result of their own failure to go or their parents' failure to send them, raises the question of whether a compulsory supervision order is necessary in order to ensure that their right to education is not denied. The paragraph makes no specific exception for children who are educated by means other than attending school (which the law permits), but the providing to a child of an efficient education suitable to his or her age, ability and aptitude will clearly constitute a reasonable excuse for the child not attending school. In relation to the vast majority of children, who have attended a public school, non-attendance is easy to establish for an authorised record of attendance provided by the school will usually leave no room for argument.[97] Dispute is more likely to revolve around the question of whether the child has a reasonable excuse for non-attendance. Lack of reasonable excuse, being part of the ground of referral, probably requires to be proved by the reporter.[98] In practical terms, however, it is difficult to imagine a case in which the sheriff's decision would turn solely on the question of onus and if no, or no arguable, excuse is offered by the child or the relevant person the reporter, having proved failure to attend, will have shown all that is necessary to establish this ground. For the purposes of the parents' duty to secure the child's regular attendance at school under s.35 of the Education (Scotland) Act 1980, it is provided that there is a reasonable excuse for the parent's failure to ensure the child's attendance in the following circumstances:

(a) there is within two miles of the child's home, in the case of a child under eight, and within three miles in the case of any other child, measured in both cases by the nearest available route, no public or other school the managers of which are willing to receive the child and to provide him or her with free education, and either (i) no arrangements have been made by the education authority for enabling the child to attend an appropriate school, or for the provision of transport or the payment of travelling expenses, or (ii) any arrangements so made are such as to require the child to walk more than two miles (or three miles in the case of a child eight years of age or more) in the course of any journey between his or her home and school; or

---

[95] Education (Scotland) Act 1980 s.30.

[96] Standards in Scotland's Schools etc Act 2000 s.1. Article 2 of Protocol 1 of the European Convention on Human Rights, though expressed in terms of the parents' right to determine the child's education, has been held to include a direct right of the child to be educated according to the standards prevailing in the individual state. See *A v Headmaster and Governors of Lord Grey School* [2006] 2 A.C. 363, per Lord Bingham at [11]–[13], [24].

[97] Education (Scotland) Act 1980 s.86: the head teacher's certification of attendance is presumed accurate until the contrary is proved.

[98] In *Kennedy v Clark*, 1970 S.L.T. 260 it was held that a prosecutor does not need to prove lack of reasonable excuse when prosecuting a parent for not ensuring the child's regular attendance. But *O'Hagan v Rea*, 2001 S.L.T. (Sh Ct) 30 questioned whether that conclusion could stand in light of the Human Rights Act 1998.

(b) the child is being prevented by sickness from attending school or receiving education; or

(c) there are other circumstances which in the opinion of the education authority or the court afford a reasonable excuse.[99]

The existence of the circumstances in either (a) or (b) will almost certainly amount to reasonable excuse for the purpose of this paragraph; other than these, there will be few circumstances likely to be held to justify denying the child of his or her right to education.[100] It would not, it is submitted, be reasonable to keep a child off school in order to look after a sick parent[101] or to help with a disabled sibling, though the length of absence might sometimes be considered relevant. It will seldom, if ever, be reasonable for a child on his or her own initiative to stay away from school. An exclusion order issued due to the child's disruptive behaviour may not constitute a reasonable excuse for not attending school.[102]

By limiting the definition of "child" for the purpose of this ground to chil- **3–26** dren "of school age",[103] the ground is inapplicable to children who are outwith the ages of compulsory education (basically but not precisely, from 5 to 16).

Isolated absences may not prevent the child from having attended school **3–27** "regularly": the ground is designed to bring to a hearing children who are falling into a pattern of non-attendance and a single absence would not, it is submitted, satisfy this condition. However, reporters must strive to strike a difficult balance here, for sometimes isolated absences can be indicative of a real risk that they will become more frequent. There is little doubt that the earlier a potential school refuser is brought to a hearing the more likely it is that any compulsory supervision order made in respect of the child will be successful in returning the child to regular school attendance.

(p) The child has been,[104] is being, or is likely to be, subject to physical, emotional or other pressure to enter into a civil partnership, or is or is likely to become a member of the same household as such a child

The legal content of this ground is substantially similar (but not quite iden- **3–28** tical) to the ground considered below, which is vastly more likely to occur in practice.

---

[99] Education (Scotland) Act 1980 s.42. See *Skeen v Tunnah*, 1970 S.L.T. (Sh Ct) 66 and *R v Devon County Council, ex parte G* [1988] 3 W.L.R. 1386; J. Scott, *Education Law in Scotland* (W. Green, 2003), pp.203–206.

[100] s.42 of the Education (Scotland) Act 1980 is designed to avoid punishment of parents where this is not appropriate, but considerations relevant to that question are not necessarily relevant to the question of whether it is necessary, for the protection, guidance, treatment or control of the child, to make a compulsory supervision order.

[101] cf. *Jenkins v Howells* [1949] 2 K.B. 218.

[102] In *D v Kennedy*, 1988 S.L.T. 55 it was held that the ground of referral was not established when the child was excluded on the basis of an allegation of misconduct which was neither established in the evidence nor admitted by the child or parent. Though no concluded opinion was expressed by the court on what would be the case if misconduct was established, it would be sensible practice for reporters relying on this ground when the child has been excluded to lead evidence of the conduct that justified the child's exclusion.

[103] 2011 Act s.199(2).

[104] Words added to the 2011 Act s.67(2)(p) by the Children's Hearings (Scotland) Act 2011 (Modification of Primary Legislation) Order 2013 (SSI 2013/211) Sch.1 para.20(8).

(q) The child has been, is being or is likely to be forced into a marriage (that expression being construed in accordance with s.1 of the Forced Marriage etc. (Protection and Jurisdiction) (Scotland) Act 2011, or is or is likely to become, a member of the same household as such a child

3–29   Section 1(4) of the Forced Marriage etc. (Protection and Jurisdiction) (Scotland) Act 2011 provides that a person (A) is forced into marriage if another person (B) forces (A) to enter a marriage (whether with (B) or another person) without (A)'s full and free consent. "Force" for this purpose includes: (i) coercion by physical, verbal or psychological means, threatening conduct, harassment or other means; and (ii) knowingly to take advantage of a person's incapacity to consent to marriage or to understand the nature of marriage.[105] Being forced into a marriage is hugely destructive to a young person's self-esteem, as well as emphasising their separation from the generally accepted norms of Scottish society, however diverse that society is. It is a very real problem in certain sections of the community and it is right and proper that the state does more than simply declare any forced marriages that come to its attention to be invalid.[106] Some degree of protection is offered by the Forced Marriage etc. (Protection and Jurisdiction) (Scotland) Act 2011, which allows the court to make a forced marriage protection order in such terms as the court thinks appropriate to provide the necessary protection. Being made a ground for referring a child to the children's hearing for the first time in the Children's Hearings (Scotland) Act 2011, the state itself is now able to take the initiative in providing protection (if only in relation to children). That the child will not be of marriageable age[107] is nothing to the point since the legal validity of the marriage is irrelevant. The ground may be used to protect children who are subject to pressure while they are children in order to enter into marriage when they reach the age of 16, as well as children who are at risk of being taken abroad to a country where the age of marriage is below the age in the United Kingdom. Siblings[108] of children who are subject to pressure to enter a marriage may also be referred under this paragraph, on the ground that they too are likely to face the same pressure when they reach the appropriate age. The ground applies when the child *has been* forced into a marriage as well as when the child is at risk of being so forced at some point in the future. This again emphasises that the validity of the marriage is irrelevant for the forced marriage is itself a nullity.[109]

---

[105] Forced Marriage etc. (Jurisdiction and Procedure) (Scotland) Act 2011 s.1(6).

[106] See for example *Mahmud v Mahmud*, 1994 S.L.T. 599; *Singh v Singh*, 2005 S.L.T. 749.

[107] Though since "child" may in some circumstances include persons above 16 some children, as defined, will in fact be of marriageable age.

[108] Or, more accurately, persons who are members of the same household as the child. "Household" is discussed in relation to ground (d) above.

[109] Marriage (Scotland) Act 1977 s.20A(2), as inserted by Family Law (Scotland) Act 2006 s.2.

CHAPTER FOUR

REPORTERS' DUTIES PRIOR TO THE HEARING

INTRODUCTION

It is the reporter's responsibility to decide whether the circumstances exist that **4–01** would justify referring a child to a children's hearing and, having made that decision, to arrange the hearing and to ensure that proper notifications thereof are given and that appropriate documentation is supplied to those entitled to receive documents. The statute and Rules govern not only procedures at the hearing but also the reporter's duties and role leading up to any children's hearing.

REFERRAL OF CHILD TO REPORTER

There are no means by which a child can be referred to a children's hearing **4–02** otherwise than through the reporter and in the vast majority of cases the reporter is the crucial decision-maker on whether or not that will happen. The reporter must, however, be in possession of sufficient information concerning a child before he or she will be in a position to make the necessary decision. He or she is, therefore, dependent for the proper carrying out of his or her functions on receiving information concerning children from various sources, including local authorities, schools, welfare agencies, the courts and the police. There are different statutory provisions concerning the transmission of information to the reporter, according to whether the information comes from a local authority, from the police, the court or from any other person. Wherever the information comes from, the reporter must keep a record of the name and address of the person who provided it.[1]

Referral from the local authority

Local authorities, through their social services and education departments, **4–03** are uniquely well-placed to acquire information concerning children in their areas, and much of the information that a reporter relies upon comes ultimately from this source. Local authorities are, therefore, duty bound to pass information to the reporter. There are two aspects of their duty, depending upon two similar but essentially distinct judgments that the local authority is required to make. First, the local authority must consider whether it is *likely* that a child is in need of protection, guidance, treatment or control and that it *might* be

---

[1] Children's Hearings (Scotland) Act 2011 (Rules of Procedure in Children's Hearings) Rules 2013 (SSI 2013/194) (hereinafter "2013 Rules") r.12(2)(a).

necessary for a compulsory supervision order to be made in relation to the child: if so, the local authority is obliged by the statute to make all necessary inquiries into the child's circumstances.[2] Inquiries will not be necessary if the authority already has enough information to conclude that the relevant likelihood exists. Secondly, the local authority, having made sufficient inquiries, must consider whether the child is, indeed, in need of protection, guidance, treatment or control and that it *might* be necessary for a compulsory supervision order to be made: if so, the local authority is obliged by the statute to give any information it has about the child to the reporter.[3] The information upon which the local authority bases its judgment in these matters may come from any source and may be of any nature that raises concerns about the health, development or welfare of the child. It must be relevant to the question of whether section 67 grounds of referral exist in relation to the child, for it is only if such grounds exist that the question of whether it is necessary to make a compulsory supervision order arises. Though the local authority may determine that a child is in need of protection, guidance, treatment or control, it is no part of the local authority's judgment to determine that it is actually necessary to make a compulsory supervision order (just as it is not for the police to determine that an alleged offender is guilty) though invariably that question will be uppermost in the minds of the investigators: rather the local authority is entitled to conclude only that the making of a compulsory supervision order *might* be necessary. The importance of making this distinction lies in ensuring that the local authority's duty to involve the reporter arises in cases of doubt as well as cases of (in the authority's view) certainty. It has been said that "to the local authority is given the judgment, in cases in which it receives information, of whether there might be a need for a compulsory supervision order but not of whether there is an actual need. Accordingly, it is obliged to transmit information whenever the view that a compulsory supervision order is necessary could reasonably be entertained even if in its judgment alternative measures, or no action, would be preferable".[4]

4–04   Investigations by the local authority, where necessary, are usually carried out by its social work department, but it must involve other parts of the authority, and indeed other agencies, if necessary to allow it to make the judgments required of it. If the local authority is satisfied that investigations are unnecessary, for example because it is clear that one or more of the section 67 grounds exist, or it is clear that none exists, then the local authority is not obliged to make inquiries. If the local authority's investigations are being frustrated by the unreasonable refusal of parents to allow them access to the child they may seek a child protection order from the sheriff court to allow them to carry out their statutory duty of investigation.[5] Making the threat of seeking such an order might well prove useful in encouraging co-operation with local authority investigations rather more often than it would be appropriate actually to carry out the threat.

4–05   Education authorities (which all local authorities are) are additionally entitled under s.36(3) of the Education (Scotland) Act 1980 to give information

---

[2] Children's Hearings (Scotland) Act 2011 s.60(1).
[3] 2011 Act s.60(2) and (3).
[4] Wilkinson and Norrie, *Parent and Child*, 3rd edn (W. Green, 2013) at para.17.33.
[5] 2011 Act s.38: see further below, para.15–06.

about a child of school age to the reporter where the child has failed to attend a public school regularly, though this entitlement is limited to cases in which there is no requirement on the local authority under s.60 of the Children's Hearings (Scotland) Act 2011 to give information to the reporter. This qualification would seem to have no effect other than to prevent an overlap of provisions and consequent confusion as to the statutory authority under which the local education authority is acting.

If a child has been placed in secure accommodation without a secure accom- **4–06** modation authorisation attached to a compulsory supervision order, an interim compulsory supervision order, a medical examination order or a warrant to secure attendance, or while the child is being provided with accommodation by a local authority under s.25 of the Children (Scotland) Act 1995 or is subject to a permanence order, the chief social work officer of the local authority must immediately, in writing, inform the reporter.[6] Within 72 hours of the placing of the child in secure accommodation the reporter must proceed in accordance with ss.66 to 69 of the Act[7] (i.e. he or she must investigate the case and decide whether or not to arrange a children's hearing, as described below[8]). If a hearing is to be arranged, this must be done within 72 hours of the child's being placed in secure accommodation.[9]

Referral from the police

Another common source of the reporter's information about children is the **4–07** police. If a constable considers that a child is in need of protection, guidance, treatment or control, and that it might be necessary for a compulsory supervision order to be made in relation to the child, then he or she is under a statutory duty to give to the reporter all relevant information which he or she has been able to discover in relation to the child.[10] "Relevant" in this context refers to information that assists in the assessment of whether one or more of the section 67 grounds exist and, if so, whether it is necessary to make a compulsory supervision order in respect of the child: again, the obligation arises whenever the view that a compulsory supervision order might be necessary may rationally be held. In addition, police officers are obliged to report to the appropriate prosecuting authorities the commission of offences that come to their attention,[11] and whenever that duty arises they are also obliged to make such a report to the reporter whenever their report is "in relation to a child".[12] This phrase is not limited to the situation of the child committing an offence, and will include cases in which the child is the victim, for such a report too

---

[6] Secure Accommodation (Scotland) Regulations 2013 (SSI 2013/205) regs.7(4), 8(5) and 9(5).

[7] Secure Accommodation (Scotland) Regulations 2013 reg.10(2). In calculating the 72 hours, Sundays and public holidays are excluded: reg.2(2).

[8] At paras 4–18—4–23.

[9] Secure Accommodation (Scotland) Regulations 2013 regs.7(5), 8(6) and 10(5). Reg.10 covers children accommodated under s.25 of the Children (Scotland) Act 1995 and those subject to a permanence order: in these cases a further 24 hour period is permitted if the reporter considers that it would not be reasonably practicable to arrange a hearing within 72 hours: reg.10(6).

[10] 2011 Act s.61.

[11] Police (Scotland) Act 1967 s.17(1)(b).

[12] 2011 Act s.61(3).

would "relate to a child". If it were intended to limit this duty to cases involving alleged offences by children the statute could easily have said so.[13]

4–08   There is also an obligation on police officers to inform the reporter whenever a child who appears to have committed an offence has been detained in a place of safety[14] but it has been decided that charges are not to be proceeded with against the child.[15] In these circumstances the reporter may either direct that the child be released from the place of safety, or direct that the child continue to be kept in the place of safety until he or she has reached a conclusion as to whether section 67 grounds apply in relation to the child and, if so, whether it is in the reporter's view necessary to make a compulsory supervision order.[16] Having determined that section 67 grounds apply and that a compulsory supervision order is necessary, the reporter must arrange a children's hearing for the purpose of deciding whether a compulsory supervision order should be made in respect of the child[17] and that hearing must take place no later than the third day after the reporter received the information from the police.[18] In the interim, the reporter may either direct that the child be released from the place of safety or continue to be kept there until the children's hearing.[19] The children's hearing that is held on the third day will normally not be in a position to make a final decision and so is likely to defer making a decision (or require the reporter to apply to the sheriff to establish grounds). If the child continues to require to be kept in a place of safety in the meantime this can be effected by the hearing making an interim compulsory supervision order with an appropriate condition of residence.

Referral from other persons

4–09   Any person other than a local authority or a police officer (both of whom have duties), is entitled to give to the reporter all relevant information that he or she has in relation to a child whenever he or she considers that the child is in need of protection, guidance, treatment or control, and that it might be necessary to make a compulsory supervision order in relation to the child.[20] There is no limitation on who has the right to pass information to the reporter, and it may be a medical practitioner, law enforcement officer, school teacher, group leader, neighbour, relative, child protection agency or even the child him or herself. The right to give information exists only if the person genuinely believes that a compulsory supervision order might be necessary, and the information that may be given to the reporter is that which is "relevant" to the question of that necessity. This suggests that there is no right to give information when the belief is not genuinely held, or when the information is not relevant to the question of whether the reporter should arrange a children's hearing. It is clearly not the

---

[13] cf. 2011 Act s.179 (reporter's obligation to share information with prosecuting authorities) which clearly includes cases in which the child is a victim of an alleged offence.
[14] "Place of safety" is defined as in s.202(1) of the Children's Hearings (Scotland) Act 2011, except that for present purposes it does not include a police station: Criminal Procedure (Scotland) Act 1995 s.307.
[15] Criminal Procedure (Scotland) Act 1995 s.43(5).
[16] 2011 Act s.65.
[17] 2011 Act s.69(1) and (2).
[18] 2011 Act s.69(3).
[19] 2011 Act s.72.
[20] 2011 Act s.64.

aim of the Act to discourage the passing of information concerning children to the reporter, even when investigations are likely to show that there is no cause for concern,[21] or that disclosure might be harmful to third parties,[22] but it is important that there be sanctions against persons who waste reporters' time and potentially traumatise children by deliberately passing on false information about them generating perhaps intrusive investigations. A person acting maliciously in giving information concerning a child without a genuine belief that the child might need a compulsory supervision order can be sued for damages. The transmission of information to the reporter is clearly an act which is protected by the defence of qualified privilege in the law of defamation, but it is not protected by absolute privilege and in order to establish civil liability for the wrongful transmission of information the pursuer would have to show both malice on the part of the defender and want of probable cause.[23] In addition, it might in some circumstances amount to a criminal offence knowingly to give false information to the reporter, at least when the information is to the effect that the child has committed an offence,[24] and possibly in any case in which the information suggests that grounds of referral exist.

Referral or remit by the court: general

Another source from which the reporter may receive information is the court, **4–10** for it frequently happens that in the course of other proceedings information comes to light which suggests to the court that section 67 grounds exist in relation to a child. Both civil and criminal courts have the power to refer a child to the reporter but only in certain specified circumstances, and there are different rules depending upon the nature of the court proceedings. Even outwith the specified circumstances a judge or any other person involved in court proceedings can, of course, refer any child to the reporter under the provisions of s.64 discussed immediately above, but there are sometimes procedural advantages (at least for the reporter) if the reference comes formally from the court.

Referral by the court: s.62 of Children's Hearings (Scotland) Act 2011

If, in the course of certain specified proceedings, a court considers that a **4–11** section 67 ground (other than the ground that the child has committed an offence) might apply in relation to a child, the court may refer the matter to the reporter.[25] The proceedings in which the court is able to make a referral under s.62 are as follows: (a) an action for divorce; (b) an action for judicial

---

[21] See further *D v NSPCC* [1978] A.C. 171.

[22] See *Re A (A Child) (Family Proceedings: Disclosure of Information)* [2012] 3 W.L.R. 1484.

[23] See generally Norrie, *Defamation and Related Actions in Scots Law* (Butterworths, 1995), pp.123–124. In *W v Westminster City Council (No.1)* [2005] 1 F.L.R. 816 and *(No.2)* [2005] 4 All E.R. 96 (note) it was held in England that absolute privilege, which applies in all judicial proceedings, does not extend to case conferences in child protection processes and that these are covered only by qualified privilege. These processes tend to be internal to local authorities but the same rule would apply to a meeting between a reporter and a reporter-manager. Proceedings at children's hearings, being quasi-judicial, are on the other hand protected by absolute privilege, with the result that active participants therein cannot be sued at all for any defamatory statement they may utter in the course of the hearing.

[24] See *Stair Memorial Encyclopaedia of the Laws of Scotland* (Butterworths, 1995) Vol.7, paras 524–535.

[25] 2011 Acts.62(1) and (2).

separation; (c) an action for declarator of marriage; (d) an action for declarator of nullity of marriage; (e) an action for dissolution of a civil partnership; (f) an action for separation of civil partners; (g) an action for declarator of nullity of civil partnership; (h) an action for declarator of parentage; (i) an action for declarator of non-parentage; (j) proceedings relating to parental responsibilities or parental rights; (k) an application for an adoption order within the meaning of s.28(1) of the Adoption and Children (Scotland) Act 2007; (l) an application for the making, variation or revocation of a permanence order as defined in s.80(2) of the Adoption and Children (Scotland) Act 2007 (where the child is not already subject to a compulsory supervision order); (m) proceedings relating to an offence under s.35 (failure of parent to secure attendance of child at school) or s.41 (failure to comply with attendance order) or s.42(3) (failure to permit examination of child) of the Education (Scotland) Act 1980; and (n) proceedings under the Forced Marriage etc. (Protection and Jurisdiction) (Scotland) Act 2011.[26]

4–12   Where, in the course of any of these proceedings,[27] the court decides to refer the matter to the reporter, it must give the reporter a "section 62 statement", which is a statement specifying which ground the court considers might apply in relation to the child, setting out the reasons why the court considers that the ground might apply, and setting out any other information about the child which appears to the court to be relevant.[28] On receiving the information from the court, the reporter must then determine whether, in his or her view, a section 67 ground applies in relation to the child and, if so, whether he or she considers it necessary to make a compulsory supervision order in relation to the child.[29] Given that the section 62 statement contains a statement that the court considers that a section 67 ground might apply, it is to be expected that the reporter will, in the generality of cases referred to him or her by a court, come to the view that a section 67 ground does apply, but it is open to the reporter to conclude that the ground specified by the court does not apply, in which case a children's hearing cannot be arranged by the reporter. This emphasises that the court which provides information to the reporter does so on the basis of its judgment that a ground *might* apply, while the reporter, in order to arrange a children's hearing, must make a judgment that a ground *does* apply. And of course even if the reporter considers, with the court, that a section 67 ground does apply, he or she may consider that it is nevertheless not necessary to make a compulsory supervision order (an issue with which the court has no concern), in which case no referral to the hearing will be made. The wording of s.62 would appear to envisage that the court might refer any child to the reporter, and not only a child who is the subject of the relevant proceedings.[30] The "section 62 statement"

---

[26] 2011 Act s.62(5).

[27] "Any proceedings" is not, it is submitted, limited to proceedings at first instance: an appeal court could competently make a referral under s.62.

[28] 2011 Act s.62(3) and (4). If the action is one for divorce, judicial separation, nullity of marriage or dissolution of civil partnership and the court does not consider itself in a position to make such a referral without further consideration, it must postpone its decision on the granting of the decree in the action until it is in such a position, so long as exceptional circumstances make it desirable to do so: Children (Scotland) Act 1995 s.12.

[29] 2011 Act s.66(2).

[30] cf. *McArdle v Orr*, 1994 S.L.T. 463. There may indeed be no child who is directly the subject of proceedings, as in, for example, a divorce action or action for dissolution in which the child's residence is not in dispute.

does not establish that the section 67 grounds apply and they must be proved if denied or not understood.[31]

Referral by the court: s.48 of the Criminal Procedure (Scotland) Act 1995

Where a criminal court has convicted a person of either a Schedule 1 offence[32] **4–13** or the offence of incest with a person aged 17 years or over,[33] or an offence under s.21 of the Children and Young Persons (Scotland) Act 1937,[34] the court may refer either the child victim of the offence, or any child who is or is likely to become a member of the same household as the offender of the Schedule 1 offence or (tautologously) the offence of incest, to the reporter.[35] If the court does so then it will certify that the offence is a ground established for the purposes of the Children's Hearings (Scotland) Act 2011.[36] Certification that a section 67 ground exists does not, however, oblige the reporter to arrange a children's hearing and he or she retains the power to decide not to refer the case to a children's hearing[37]: the reporter is obliged to arrange a hearing only when he or she considers that a section 67 ground applies *and* when he or she considers that it is necessary to make a compulsory supervision order.[38] The reporter is unable to conclude, in light of the court's certification of the ground, that a section 67 ground does not exist,[39] but he or she may well determine that it is nevertheless not necessary to make a compulsory supervision order. If a hearing is arranged by the reporter (having concluded that it is indeed necessary to make a compulsory supervision order) there will be no need for the chairing member of the children's hearing to seek acceptance of the grounds of referral from the child and relevant person (though the grounds referred by the court should nevertheless be explained by the chairing member at the commencement of the hearing[40]), and the hearing can move straight on to the consideration and disposal of the case.

---

[31] This is a change from the position under the Children (Scotland) Act 1995 where, if a court referred a matter under s.54 thereof (the predecessor to s.62 of the 2011 Act) the ground was taken to apply and the reporter, though able to conclude that compulsory supervision was not necessary, could rely on the court's finding if the ground were denied or not understood by the child or relevant person. That this position was highly problematical can be seen in *A v B*, 2011 S.L.T. (Sh Ct) 131.

[32] For scheduled offences, see above, para.3–07.

[33] Which itself is a scheduled offence. Though Schedule 1 to the Criminal Procedure (Scotland) Act 1995 is headed "offences against children under the age of 17", the substantive reference in para.1 is to "Part 1 of the Criminal Law (Consolidation) (Scotland) Act 1995", which contains no age limit.

[34] Vagrants preventing children from receiving education.

[35] Criminal Procedure (Scotland) Act 1995 s.48.

[36] Criminal Procedure (Scotland) Act 1995 s.48(1).

[37] For the conviction and imprisonment of the offender may have removed the source of danger from the child's life.

[38] 2011 Act s.69(2).

[39] 2011 Act s.66(2A), as inserted by the Children's Hearings (Scotland) Act 2011 (Modification of Primary Legislation) Order 2013 (SSI 2013/211) Sch.1 para.20(7). cf. references to the reporter by a civil court under s.62 of the 2011 Act, as discussed above, para.4–11.

[40] 2013 Rules r.60(2)(a) imposes a general duty on the chairing member to inform those present at the hearing of the substance of any report or document: this will include the referral from the court under s.48 of the Criminal Procedure (Scotland) Act 1995.

Referral by the court: s.12 of the Antisocial Behaviour etc (Scotland) Act 2004

4–14   If, on making an antisocial behaviour order (ASBO) or an interim ASBO, the sheriff considers that a section 67 ground (other than that the child has committed an offence) applies in relation to the child, he may require the reporter to arrange a children's hearing.[41] This is not a referral to the reporter in the way that the provisions discussed in the paragraphs immediately above are, entitling the reporter to decide whether or not to arrange a children's hearing, but is rather a requirement on the reporter to arrange a hearing, whether or not he or she is of the view that it is necessary to make a compulsory supervision order in relation to the child. Indeed it is noticeable that the sheriff's focus is on the existence of the section 67 ground, which is the basis of his decision to require a children's hearing to be arranged, rather than the need for a compulsory supervision order. The result is that a child may be referred to a hearing without either the court or the reporter giving formal consideration to the issue of whether a children's hearing has anything to offer the child by way of protection, guidance, treatment or control. However, though the statute does not require sheriffs to give consideration to the question of whether it is necessary to make a compulsory supervision order, it does lie within the sheriff's judgment whether to require the reporter to arrange a hearing and an important, even crucial, factor in making that judgment will be the issue of whether the children's hearing is the appropriate forum to deal with whatever concerns are raised by the existence of the section 67 ground. Nevertheless, the provision leaves reporters in an unfortunate position for in this case alone the reporter may be required to arrange a hearing even when he or she does not believe the child is in need of a compulsory supervision order.[42] This provision may be compared with that relating to parenting orders under the 2004 Act, where the court may merely require the reporter to consider whether to apply for such an order.[43] Section 12 of the 2004 Act does not oblige the sheriff who makes an ASBO to require the reporter to arrange a children's hearing, but merely permits him to do so, and it would be appropriate, it is submitted, for sheriffs to be reticent about exercising this power. It is to be remembered that the reporter is free to arrange a children's hearing in the absence of a direction that he or she does so, based upon the same circumstances as those that led to the making of an ASBO.[44]

---

[41] Antisocial Behaviour etc. (Scotland) Act 2004 s.12, as substituted by Sch.5 para.3 to the Children's Hearings (Scotland) Act 2011.

[42] It was an unfortunate policy choice on the part of the Scottish Parliament not to include proceedings under the Antisocial Behaviour etc. (Scotland) Act 2004 in s.62, as proceedings in which the court could refer the matter to the reporter who would then have to determine whether or not to arrange a children's hearing.

[43] Antisocial Behaviour etc. (Scotland) Act 2004 s.114. The only other two circumstances in which the reporter has no discretion is in relation to a remit by the court under s.49 of the Criminal Procedure (Scotland) Act 1995, discussed at para.4–16 below and when, on a review of a grounds determination, the sheriff has found grounds to be established other than those found at the original grounds determination—on which matter see below, para.8–49.

[44] No question of res judicata will arise since the two processes are designed to achieve quite separate aims.

If the sheriff does require the reporter to arrange a children's hearing he **4–15** must, if the child is not already subject to a compulsory supervision order,[45] give to the reporter a "section 12 statement" which will specify which of the section 67 ground or grounds the sheriff considers to apply, the reasons why the sheriff considers the ground or grounds to apply, and any other information about the child which appears to the sheriff to be relevant.[46] To address the anomaly identified above it would be good practice for sheriffs to indicate to the reporter why they consider that a compulsory supervision order is neces- sary. The requirement of the sheriff is treated as if it were a determination under s.108 of the 2011 Act that the ground specified in the section 12 state- ment had been established by proof and the sheriff had, on that establishment of the ground, directed the reporter to arrange a children's hearing.[47] So the hearing that is arranged will move directly to the question of whether it is necessary, for the protection, guidance, treatment or control of the child, to make a compulsory supervision order, and the section 67 ground is not put to the child and relevant person for acceptance or denial. Again, however, the chairing member has a general duty to ensure that everyone present at the hearing understands why they are there, and the obligation to inform those present of the substance of relevant reports and documents[48] means that he or she must explain the sheriff's section 12 statement.

Remit by the court: s.49 of the Criminal Procecure (Scotland) Act 1995

If the child him or herself has pled guilty to or been found guilty of an **4–16** offence by a criminal court that court may remit the child's case to a children's hearing for consideration and disposal.[49] If it does so, a certificate signed by the clerk of the court stating that the child or person has pled guilty to or been found guilty of the offence to which the remit relates shall be conclusive evidence for the purposes of the children's hearing that the offence has been committed by the child or person.[50] The result again is: (i) that the reporter is not involved in the decision that a children's hearing should be arranged; (ii) that neither the court nor the reporter need formally focus on whether it is necessary to make a compulsory supervision order; and (iii) that the ground (that the child has committed an offence) does not need to be put to the child and relevant person for acceptance. Remits under this provision are, however, appropriate only when the court is of the view that the hearing system is more likely to offer something to the child than the criminal process.

---

[45] If the child is already subject to a compulsory supervision order and the court requires the reporter to arrange a children's hearing, the purpose of that hearing will be to review the existing order. It is odd, however, that in these circumstances a section 12 statement from the sheriff is not required, since the establishment of new grounds may significantly influence the outcome of any review or an existing order. The reporter is, of course, free to draw up new grounds at his or her own initiative, to be put to the child and relevant person at a review: see below, paras 13–03—13–05.

[46] Antisocial Behaviour etc. (Scotland) Act 2004 s.12(1B) and (1C), as inserted by Children's Hearings (Scotland) Act 2011 Sch.5 para.3.

[47] 2011 Act s.70.

[48] 2013 Rules r.60(2)(a).

[49] Criminal Procedure (Scotland) Act 1995 s.49. See below, paras 12–02—12–08.

[50] 2011 Act s.71(2).

INVESTIGATING THE CHILD'S CIRCUMSTANCES

4–17 Having received information concerning a child from any of the sources mentioned above, and some others,[51] the first thing the reporter must decide (except where obliged by the court to arrange a children's hearing) is whether or not to make an initial investigation.[52] The local authority may already have conducted investigations and shared information with the reporter,[53] and further investigations by the reporter will be required only when he or she is not yet in possession of sufficient information to determine whether a children's hearing requires to be arranged (that is to say whether in his or her view section 67 grounds exist and it is necessary, in light of that, to make a compulsory supervision order); no investigation need be undertaken when the reporter is of the view that he or she already has sufficient information to make these two separate, but connected, judgments. If the reporter decides that an initial investigation is required, the form of that investigation can be as the reporter thinks fit. It will normally include requesting the local authority to draw up a social background report, detailing any circumstances that he or she considers necessary, and in particular the reporter may require the local authority to give a report on the child generally and on any particular matter relating to the child that the reporter specifies.[54] The local authority is obliged to supply this report. The report may contain information given to the local authority from any person whomsoever, and it may contain information in addition to that given by the local authority to the reporter when it initially gave the reporter information under s.60.[55] It will often contain recommendations.[56] The reporter may, and often will, also seek reports from others, such as the police or health care providers, though there is no obligation on anyone other than a local authority to supply a report. There is nothing to prevent the reporter from inviting for interview any person who may help the reporter come to the decisions he or she has to make, and this might include, in appropriate cases, the child and his or her parents; there is, however, no power to enforce attendance at any such interview.

DECIDING WHETHER TO ARRANGE A CHILDREN'S HEARING

4–18 Having made such investigation as he or she thinks necessary, the reporter must then decide whether a children's hearing requires to be arranged. This decision depends on the reporter coming to a view on two matters: whether section 67 grounds apply in relation to the child and whether, if so, it is

---

[51] See 2011 Act s.66(1).

[52] 2011 Act s.66(3).

[53] Under 2011 Act s.60(1).

[54] 2011 Act s.66(4).

[55] 2011 Act s.66(5) and (6).

[56] It is open to the local authority to recommend in this report that the child be cared for by their own parents or persons with parental responsibilities and parental rights, by kinship or foster carers, be placed with any other person who is not a relevant person or be placed in a residential establishment: Looked After Children (Scotland) Regulations 2009 (SSI 2009/210) reg.7. The local authority may not, however, recommend that the child be placed in secure accommodation unless it is satisfied (presumably after having investigated the matter) that one or more of the conditions in s.83(6) of the 2011 Act justifying secure accommodation authorisation (see below, paras 11–12—11–15) are satisfied: Secure Accommodation (Scotland) Regulations 2013 (SSI 2013/205) reg.6.

necessary, for the protection, guidance, treatment or control of the child, to make a compulsory supervision order. Neither of these decisions is governed by the general considerations in ss.25 to 29 of the 2011 Act[57] (which refer to decisions made by a court or a children's hearing only and not to decisions made by the reporter), but inevitably in determining the necessity for a compulsory supervision order the reporter will be guided by his or her assessment of the child's welfare. In addition, being a "public authority" for the purposes of the Human Rights Act 1998, the reporter must act at all times, including making decisions, in a manner consistent with the ECHR. This means, in this context, that the reporter must bring to the decision-making process considerations of proportionality: so the reporter must ask him or herself whether it is a proportionate response to the child's difficulties that a hearing be arranged. Whatever determination the reporter makes on this matter he or she must keep a record of it.[58]

Applying for a parenting order

As well as deciding whether to arrange a children's hearing, the reporter **4–19** may, either before or after any hearing, make an application to the sheriff for a parenting order under the Antisocial Behaviour etc (Scotland) Act 2004. The sheriff may make such an order if: (i) the child has been engaged in antisocial behaviour or criminal conduct[59] and making the order is desirable in the interests of preventing the child from engaging in such behaviour or conduct; or (ii) it is desirable in the interests of improving the welfare of the child to make the order.[60] Before applying for a parenting order, the reporter must consult the local authority for the area where the child ordinarily resides.[61] The obligation to "consult" is designed to encourage co-operation but does not inhibit the reporter's discretion in any way. On a request by the reporter for the purpose of determining whether to make an application for a parenting order, the local authority must supply a report on the parent and the child and such circumstances concerning each as appear to the reporter to be relevant.[62] Unlike any power vested in the children's hearing, a parenting order made by a court can require the relevant person to comply with requirements specified in the order,[63] and so this option is suitable when the reporter is of the view that an order over the child is less likely to achieve some good than an order over the relevant person. The 2004 Act is, therefore, a significant additional power in the reporter's armoury.[64] As well as making an application for a parenting

---

[57] For details see below, paras 9–15—9–18.

[58] 2013 Rules r.12(2)(c).

[59] Or conduct that would have been criminal had the child been over the age of eight years: Antisocial Behaviour etc. (Scotland) Act 2004 s.102(7).

[60] Antisocial Behaviour etc. (Scotland) Act 2004 s.102(3).

[61] Antisocial Behaviour etc. (Scotland) Act 2004 s.102(9), The local authority itself may apply for a parenting order, in which case it must consult with the reporter.

[62] Antisocial Behaviour etc. (Scotland) Act 2004 s.113(2).

[63] Antisocial Behaviour etc. (Scotland) Act 2004 s.103.

[64] For a critical view of the likely efficacy of parental orders, see E.E. Sutherland, "Parental Orders: A Culturally Alien Response of Questionable Efficacy", 2004 J.R. 105. They have, in practice, been very little used.

order *ex proprio motu*, the reporter may be required to consider whether to make such an application, either by a court[65] or by a children's hearing.[66]

Decision not to arrange a children's hearing

4–20   The reporter will not, indeed cannot, arrange a children's hearing if he or she considers either that none of the section 67 grounds applies in relation to the child or that, even although such grounds do apply, it is not necessary for a compulsory supervision order to be made.[67] "Necessity" here should be interpreted to include a consideration of "necessity" for interfering with family life in terms of art.8(2) of the ECHR (i.e. would the interference in family life that is an inescapable aspect of a compulsory supervision order pursue a legitimate aim and if so would the means adopted go beyond the minimum necessary to achieve that aim?). The question of whether a compulsory supervision order is necessary can at this stage in the process (though only at this stage) be answered by the reporter him or herself deciding that no such order is necessary. This is an important power, giving to the reporter a vital role in sifting out cases in which section 67 grounds clearly exist but in which, equally clearly, the child is not in need of any compulsory supervision order. The reporter has had this discretion since the children's hearing system was instituted and it has proved to be an essential part of the process, preventing the system from being clogged up with cases in which no reasonable panel member would impose a compulsory supervision order. There are many children who may be involved, for example, in an isolated incident of petty theft or parental defiance, for whom the shock of being investigated is sufficient persuasion not to repeat the incident.[68] Or, the police may have reported that a child has been the victim of a Schedule 1 offence by a stranger in circumstances which no caring parent could have prevented (the crazed gun-man scenario and the like). In such cases, the reporter is able to decide for him or herself that it is not necessary to make a compulsory supervision order and therefore that no children's hearing need be arranged.

4–21   Whenever the reporter has concluded either that no section 67 ground applies or that it is not necessary to make a compulsory supervision order that conclusion—together with the fact that as a consequence a children's hearing will not be arranged—must be intimated to the child, any relevant person, the relevant local authority, any person specified in a child protection order, and the person who gave the reporter information under any statutory provision that led to the reporter's investigation.[69] In addition the reporter may if he or she considers it appropriate, intimate these matters to any other person.[70] The decision not to refer the child to a children's hearing cannot be retracted by the reporter after it has been intimated as required above, unless new information, additional to that held by the reporter when he or she determined either that no section 67 ground applied or that it was not necessary to make a compulsory

---

[65] Antisocial Behaviour etc. (Scotland) Act 2004 s.114.
[66] 2011 Act s.128. When the requirement is that of a children's hearing, see 2013 Rules r.83.
[67] 2011 Act s.68(1).
[68] Some reporters adopt the useful practice of calling a child in and giving a verbal warning of what might happen if the behaviour continues, and some police officers are willing to assist by performing that role too.
[69] 2011 Act s.68(3) and (4).
[70] 2011 Act s.68(3)(b).

supervision order over the child, comes to the attention of the reporter.[71] This new information might indicate a quite different section 67 ground, or it may concern the same—for example, when the evidence was insufficient to persuade the reporter that a section 67 ground applies (or could be established in court) but new and stronger evidence has now come to light.

Having concluded that the conditions allowing him or her to refer the child **4–22** to a children's hearing do not exist, the reporter has three separate powers, to be exercised when he or she considers it appropriate. First, he or she may refer the child to the relevant local authority[72] with a view to the local authority providing (or making arrangements for the provision by another person or body of) advice, guidance and assistance to the child and the child's family under Ch.1 of Pt 2 of the Children (Scotland) Act 1995.[73] Such a reference would be appropriate when the reporter has reason to believe (e.g. having talked to the family and the social work department) that any help offered is likely to be accepted and is likely to prove beneficial to either the child or his or her family, or both. Secondly, the reporter may refer the child to such other person or body as may be specified by the Scottish Ministers with a view to that person or body providing advice, guidance and assistance to the child and the child's family.[74] Thirdly, as described above,[75] the reporter has the power, even when the child is not referred to a children's hearing, to apply to the sheriff for a parenting order under the Antisocial Behaviour etc. (Scotland) Act 2004.

Decision to arrange a children's hearing

The reporter is obliged by s.69(2) to arrange a children's hearing when he or **4–23** she considers: (i) that at least one of the section 67 grounds applies in relation to the child; *and* (ii) that it is necessary for a compulsory supervision order to be made in respect of the child.[76] A ground "applies", it is submitted, only when it can be proved in a court of law: it follows that the reporter can legitimately consider that a section 67 ground applies only when confident that he or she would be able to establish it by evidence before the sheriff if an application under s.93 or s.94 were required to be made. And the reporter can consider that it is necessary for a compulsory supervision order to be made only when confident that an order might be designed by the children's hearing that is likely to do some good and is proportionate to the child's difficulties. If the reporter is required to arrange a children's hearing under this provision, he or she must require a report on the child from the local authority unless he or she has already done so as part of an initial investigation, in which case he or she may request any additional information from the local authority.[77] The local

---

[71] 2011 Act s.68(6).

[72] "The relevant local authority for the child" is defined in s.201 as the local authority in whose area the child predominantly resides or, if the child does not predominantly reside in any such area, the local authority with whose area the child has the closest connection.

[73] 2011 Act s.68(5)(a).

[74] 2011 Act s.68(5)(b).

[75] Above, para.4–19.

[76] 2011 Act ss.69(1) and (2) and 66(2). See also s.7 which imposes a duty on the National Convener to ensure that a children's hearing is held for the purpose of carrying out any of the functions of a children's hearing. The practical obligation lies with the reporter, and the National Convener's obligation here is, therefore, to ensure that it is carried out.

[77] 2011 Act s.69(4) and (5).

authority must provide such reports and information, and any other information concerning the child or his or her circumstances that it considers to be relevant. The reporter is not obliged to wait until the children's hearing is arranged before requesting such a report, and it will normally be sensible for him or her to make the request as soon as the decision to arrange a hearing has been made. Once the decision is made, and some action is taken consequent upon the decision, to refer the child to a children's hearing, the reporter has no power to abandon the case,[78] and its future progress lies in the hands of the children's hearing. If the reference to the reporter was from a local authority or a police officer the reporter must give notice of the decision to arrange a children's hearing to the local authority or, as the case may be, the chief constable of the Police Service of Scotland.[79]

NOTIFICATION OF CHILDREN'S HEARINGS AND SUPPLY OF DOCUMENTS

4–24 Where the reporter arranges any children's hearing (whether after an initial investigation, or to review a current compulsory supervision order, or for any other reason required or permitted under the 2011 Act or any other legislation) or a pre-hearing panel, he or she must notify various individuals and, in order to allow them to prepare properly for the hearing, he or she must also supply various reports, documents and information to them at some time before the hearing takes place.[80] If, when supplying these reports,[81] documents or information, the reporter considers that the disclosure of the whereabouts of the child (to whom the hearing relates[82]) or of any relevant person would be likely to cause significant harm to the child or any relevant person he or she may withhold that information, and the address of the child or relevant person will be given as that of the reporter.[83] The reporter need not notify the child of the date, time and place of the children's hearing or pre-hearing panel, or provide any information, report or other document where, taking account of the child's age and maturity, the child would not be capable of understanding the notification or information.[84] The assessment of the child's capacity to understand lies with the reporter and is likely to be challengeable only when no reasonable reporter would have considered the child incapable. This suggests that, in cases of doubt, notification should be given and information provided. If the reporter

---

[78] Unless, if an application has been made to the sheriff under ss.93 or 94 of the 2011 Act, the reporter abandons the application due to inability to prove the section 67 ground.

[79] 2013 Rules r.12(3).

[80] Prior to the Children (Scotland) Act 1995 neither the child nor the relevant person received background papers: in respect of parents this was held contrary to the ECHR in *McMichael v United Kingdom* (1995) 20 E.H.R.R. 205, and in respect of children was challenged in *S v Miller*, 2001 S.L.T. 531. The 2011 Act now provides for full disclosure, subject to the stated qualifications described in the text above.

[81] And that supply may be done electronically if capable of being reproduced in legible form: s.193.

[82] Notice this important qualification: the reporter is unable to utilise this power for the protection of any other child than the child to whom the hearing relates. cf. *Re A (A Child)* [2012] UKSC 60 where the Supreme Court discussed withholding information for the protection of a person not directly involved in the proceedings.

[83] 2013 Rules r.16.

[84] 2013 Rules r.18.

considers that disclosing to the child any document or part thereof would be likely to cause significant harm to the child, he or she may make a non-disclosure request to the hearing.[85] Information might be withheld for other reasons[86] and if so the reporter must inform the persons to whom information is given under the Rules of the person from whom that information is being withheld, and what the information that is being withheld is.[87]

The 2013 Rules provide for the notification of hearings and supply of docu- **4–25** ments and information and separate (and sometimes different) provision is made for different types of hearing, discussed immediately below. Notification of, and information to be provided for, pre-hearing panels is considered in the following chapter.

Notification of and information to be provided for children's hearings

Where a grounds hearing, a hearing subsequent to a grounds hearing or a **4–26** review hearing is to be held, the reporter must notify the child, each relevant person, any individual who appears to the reporter to have (or recently have had) significant involvement in the upbringing of the child,[88] any appointed safe-guarder, the chief social work officer of the relevant local authority,[89] and the National Convener of the date, time and place of the children's hearing as soon as practicable and no later than seven days before the intended date of the hearing.[90] The three members of the children's panel who will constitute the children's hearing must also, of course, be notified of the date, time and place of the hearing, and this must be done wherever practicable seven days before, and no later than three days before, the intended date of the hearing.[91] The notification to the child and relevant person must include the following:

(a) information on the availability to the child and relevant person of legal advice;

(b) confirmation of the child's duty to attend the children's hearing;

(c) confirmation of the relevant person's duty to attend the hearing;

(d) confirmation of the right of the child and relevant person to request a pre-hearing panel or children's hearing to determine the matters open to a pre-hearing panel to determine;

(e) information on the means by which the child may express views to the children's hearing; and

---

[85] See below, paras 6–49—6–51.

[86] See below, para.6–48.

[87] 2013 Rules r.15.

[88] Notice that this person may not have a right to attend the hearing, and the purpose of the notice is to give such a person the opportunity to seek to be deemed to be a relevant person: the reporter must include in the information he or she supplies to this individual confirmation of the individual's right to require a pre-hearing panel or a children's hearing to determine whether the individual should be deemed to be a relevant person. If the individual does not then request that the reporter arrange a pre-hearing panel for that purpose, but simply shows up at the children's hearing itself, it is open to the chairing member to permit them to attend (2011 Act s.78(2))—in which case the hearing must (if requested to do so) consider whether to deem them a relevant person: 2013 Rules r.55.

[89] The relevant local authority is defined in s.201 of the 2011 Act.

[90] 2013 Rules r.22(1) and (2).

[91] 2013 Rules r.25.

(f) confirmation of the right of the child and relevant person to give any report or other document for the consideration of the children's hearing or pre-hearing panel.[92]

Where the child or any relevant person wishes to give to the children's hearing any report or other document for the consideration by the hearing they must give a copy of such report or document to the reporter, where practicable no later than three days before the intended date of the hearing; and wherever practicable the reporter must circulate this to the child and relevant person (other than where the child or relevant person supplied the report or document), to any appointed safeguarder and to the three panel members no later than three days before the intended date of the hearing.[93] Any information received thereafter by the reporter (including any orally expressed views of the child) must be given to the same people as soon as possible before the beginning of the children's hearing.[94]

Information to be supplied for grounds hearings

4–27   If the children's hearing is a grounds hearing, then in addition to the information specified above, the child, relevant person, safeguarder and the three panel members who will constitute the grounds hearing must also receive the following:

(a) a copy of the statement of grounds drawn up under section 89 of the 2011 Act;

(b) any requirement of a sheriff after an appeal to arrange a children's hearing;

(c) information relating to the retention of the child's DNA and other records kept in connection with the acceptance by the child and relevant person, or the establishment by the sheriff, of an offence specified in an order made by the Scottish Ministers under s.113A(6)(ba) of the Police Act 1997 (though this information is not be sent to the safeguarder or the three panel members);

(d) a copy of any available report or interim report prepared by the safeguarder (not, for obvious reasons, to be sent to the safeguarder);

(e) a copy of any report or information provided by the local authority to the reporter;

(f) a copy of any views of the child given to the reporter whether by the child or any other person; and

(g) a copy of any other report or document material to the children's hearing's consideration.[95]

Wherever practicable this information must be provided seven days before the intended date of the hearing, but the information in paragraphs (d)–(g) must be provided no later than three days before the hearing to the child, relevant person and safeguarder; the information in paragraph (a) must be provided wherever practicable seven days before and no later than three days before the hearing to

---

[92] 2013 Rules r.23.
[93] 2013 Rules r.26(1), (2) and (4).
[94] 2013 Rules r.26(3).
[95] 2013 Rules rr.27 and 28.

the panel members; the information in paragraphs (b) and (d) to (g) must be provided no later than three days before the hearing to the panel members.[96]

If the grounds hearing is in respect of a child who is already subject to a **4–28** compulsory supervision order then in addition to the information above the reporter must no later than three days before the intended date of the hearing give the child, each relevant person, any appointed safeguarder and the three panel members copies of all decisions and reasons for decision of previous pre-hearing panels and children's hearings in relation to the child and a copy of any notice by the local authority seeking a review of the existing compulsory supervision order.[97]

Information to be supplied at hearings after deferral and after grounds established

As soon as practicable and at least three days before the intended date of a **4–29** children's hearing arranged (i) because a previous hearing deferred making a decision, or (ii) after a sheriff has found grounds established, the reporter must give to the child, each relevant person and any appointed safeguarder the following:

> (a) any available report or interim report prepared by the safeguarder (this does not, of course, need to be given by the reporter to the safeguarder);
>
> (b) any report prepared by the local authority;
>
> (c) a copy of any direction by a sheriff at a grounds determination;
>
> (d) a copy of any relevant remit by a court under section 49 of the Criminal Procedure (Scotland) Act 1995;
>
> (e) a copy of any relevant statement by a sheriff referring the case to the hearing under the Antisocial Behaviour etc (Scotland) Act 2004;
>
> (f) a copy of any relevant requirement made by a sheriff at an appeal;
>
> (g) copies of all decisions and their reasons made by all pre-hearing panels and children's hearings arranged in relation to the child;
>
> (h) any other report, document or information relevant to the matter to be considered by the children's hearing.[98]

These must also be given, wherever practicable seven days before and no later than three days before the intended date of the children's hearing, to the three members of the children's hearing, together with a copy of the statement of grounds and a copy of any relevant child protection order.[99]

---

[96] These timescales do not apply where the child is being kept in a place of safety under s.43 of the Criminal Procedure (Scotland) Act 1995 or where the grounds hearing immediately follows the making or implementation of a child protection order: 2013 Rules r.29 provides that notification and information must be given "as soon as practicable before" the beginning of the hearing.

[97] 2013 Rules r.30.

[98] 2013 Rules r.31. It is not stated who determines relevancy for the purpose of paragraph (h) and the decision would seem, therefore, to lie with the reporter. The reporter's decision on relevancy is not unchallengeable and it is a ground of appeal, based on procedural irregularity, that appropriate documentation has not been supplied to the hearing: see for example *D v Sinclair*, 1973 S.L.T. (Sh Ct) 47. It might also interfere with an individual's right to a fair hearing as protected by art.6 ECHR: *McMichael v United Kingdom* (1995) 20 E.H.R.R. 205.

[99] 2013 Rules r.32. There are certain circumstances in which rr.31 and 32 are modified: r.33.

Information to be supplied for review hearings

4–30   As soon as practicable and no later than seven days before the intended date of a children's hearing arranged to review a compulsory supervision order the reporter must give to the child, each relevant person and any appointed safeguuader the following information:

(a) a copy of the compulsory supervision order to be reviewed;
(b) copies of all decisions and their reasons made by pre-hearing panels and children's hearings arranged in relation to the child;
(c) a copy of any remit by the court under section 49 of the Criminal Procedure (Scotland) Act 1995;
(d) a copy of any relevant requirement by a sheriff made under the Antisocial Behaviour etc. (Scotland) Act 2004;
(e) a copy of any relevant requirement made by a sheriff at an appeal;
(f) a copy of any notice by the local authority requiring a review of the compulsory supervision order.[100]

In addition, no later than three days before the intended date of the hearing the reporter must give to the child, relevant person and safeguarder a copy of any available report or interim report from the safeguarder, a copy of any report or other information provided by the local authority for the purpose of the review, a copy of any views of the child given to the reporter (by the child or any other person) and a copy of any other report or document material to the children's hearing's consideration.[101] All of these must also be given to the three panel members no later than three days before the intended date of the children's hearing arranged to review a compulsory supervision order.[102]

Children's hearing held to review contact directions

4–31   If a s.126 hearing[103] is required to be held then as soon as practicable and not later than three days after the children's hearing that makes, varies or continues an order with a contact direction (and so activates s.126), the reporter must inform the following people of the place, date and time of the s.126 hearing to review that contact direction and (other than the last three mentioned) of their right to attend the s.126 hearing:

(a) the child;
(b) each relevant person;
(c) any person (other than a relevant person) who appears to the reporter to have (or recently have had) significant involvement in the upbringing of the child;
(d) any person holding a contact order regulating contact between him and her and the child;

---

[100] 2013 Rules r.34(1)–(3).
[101] 2013 Rules r.34(4)–(6).
[102] 2013 Rules r.35. Where the review is required because the child has been transferred in a case of urgent necessity (under s.143 of the 2011 Act) r.36 provides a modified list of information that has to be given by the reporter.
[103] On which, see below, paras 13–41—13–44.

(e) any person having a right of contact with the child under a permanence order;

(f) any person who requested the s.126 hearing to be held;

(g) any appointed safeguarder;

(h) the three members of the children's hearing;

(i) the chief social work officer of the implementation, or relevant, local authority; and

(j) the National Convener.[104]

The reporter must give to these people, other than the chief social work officer and the National Convener, a copy of the contact direction in the compulsory supervision order, the interim compulsory supervision order or the medical examination order (as the case may be) and the reasons for the contact direction; and any document or part of any document which is relevant to the s.126 hearing's consideration.[105]

Children's hearing held to review child protection order

As soon as practicable before the beginning of a children's hearing held **4–32** under s.45 or s.46 of the 2011 Act (that is to say a hearing arranged on the second working day after a child protection order has been made or implemented), the reporter must give a copy of the child protection order, a copy of the application for the child protection order (or of a child assessment order as the case may be) and a copy of any relevant report or other document which is relevant to the children's hearing's consideration to the following people, together with notification of the date, time and place of the children's hearing:

(a) the child;

(b) each relevant person;

(c) any individual who appears to have (or recently have had) significant involvement in the upbringing of the child[106];

(d) the person who applied for the child protection order (or child assessment order, as the case may be);

(e) the person specified in the child protection order as being authorised to remove the child to a place of safety;

(f) any other person prescribed by rules of court;

(g) the three members of the children's hearing;

(h) any appointed safeguarder; and

(i) the chief social work officer of the relevant local authority.[107]

In addition, the National Convener must be notified of the date, time and place of the children's hearing.[108]

---

[104] 2013 Rules r.42(1) and (2).

[105] 2013 Rules r.42(3) and (4).

[106] This person will not necessarily have any right to attend the children's hearing held under s.45 or s.46 of the 2011 Act but on receiving this notice may seek to be deemed to be a relevant person. The chairing member ought, unless there is good reason otherwise, to permit (under s.78(2)) this person to attend even if he or she cannot satisfy the test to be deemed to be a relevant person.

[107] 2013 Rules r.39.

[108] 2013 Rules r.39(3)(j).

If the hearing has been arranged under s.50 of the 2011 Act (that is to say, in order to provide advice to the sheriff reviewing a child protection order) then the people listed above, and in addition the person who applied for the child protection order to be varied or terminated, must be given by the reporter as soon as practicable copies of the child protection order, the application for the child protection order (or child assessment order, as the case may be), and the application for its variation or termination, together with any other relevant document or information.[109]

Other hearings

4–33 Where a children's hearing is considering making a further interim compulsory supervision order the reporter must, no later than seven days before the intended date of the hearing, give to the child, relevant person, safeguarder and the three panel members: copies of all decisions and reasons for those decisions made by all pre-hearing panels and children's hearings in relation to the child, a copy of any interim compulsory supervision order, and any relevant document or other information.[110]

4–34 Where a children's hearing is arranged because an earlier hearing has deferred determining whether a deemed relevant person should continue to be so deemed, the reporter must, in addition to following the normal notification and provision of information rules in r.22, give any relevant document or other information for the consideration of the children's hearing to the child, relevant person, safeguarder and the three members of the children's hearing.[111]

4–35 Where a children's hearing is required to provide a report under s.49 of the Criminal Procedure (Scotland) Act 1995 the reporter must, as soon as practicable and no later than seven days before the intended date of the hearing notify the child, relevant person, safeguarder, the three members of the children's hearing, the chief social work officer of the relevant local authority and the National Convener of the date, time and place of the hearing, and give the following information to the child, relevant person and safeguarder:

(a) a copy of any relevant remit from the court;
(b) copies of all decisions and their reasons made by pre-hearing panels and children's hearings in relation to the child;
(c) confirmation of the child's duty to attend the hearing;
(d) confirmation of the relevant person's duty to attend the hearing;
(e) information on the means by which the child may express views; and
(f) confirmation of the right of the child and each relevant person to give any report or other document for the consideration of the children's hearing.[112]

---

[109] 2013 Rules r.40.
[110] 2013 Rules r.41.
[111] 2013 Rules r.43.
[112] 2013 Rules r.44.

CHAPTER FIVE

PRE-HEARING PANELS AND
DEEMED RELEVANT PERSONS

INTRODUCTION

Prior to the Children (Scotland) Act 1995, it was not uncommon for members **5–01**
of a children's panel to meet on a non-statutory basis in order to make certain
procedural determinations that would govern the conduct of the children's
hearing when it formally met. When this practice came to the attention of the
Court of Session in *Sloan v B*[1] the validity of such meetings, and the decisions
they made, received judicial sanction as involving no illegality or unfairness.
That sanction was, however, expressly limited to such preliminary meetings
doing no more than giving guidance to the reporter on such matters as who he
or she should invite to the hearing, and the legally efficacious decision on
attendance remained to be made and recorded by a properly constituted children's hearing.[2] Section 64 of the 1995 Act put such advisory meetings on a
statutory basis, and permitted the reporter to arrange what that Act called a
"business meeting" at which certain specified procedural and other matters
could be discussed and determined before the start of the proper children's
hearing.[3] The child and relevant person were able to express views on the
matters discussed, but had no right of attendance. The successor to these business meetings, now called "pre-hearing panels", find their statutory authority
in ss.79–82 of the Children's Hearings (Scotland) Act 2011, but these are very
different from business meetings in at least three respects: (i) pre-hearing
panels may make substantive (and appealable) decisions as well as give advice
to the reporter; (ii) whether a pre-hearing panel will be arranged is no longer
within the sole discretion of the reporter, who may now be obliged to refer
particular questions to a pre-hearing panel; and (iii) the child and relevant
persons are entitled (though not obliged) to attend the pre-hearing panel.

Arranging a pre-hearing panel

A pre-hearing panel is composed of three members of the Children's Panel **5–02**
selected by the National Convener,[4] who must ensure that the pre-hearing panel
consists of members of each sex and, so far as practicable, consists only of
members of the Children's Panel who live or work in the area of the relevant

---

[1] 1991 S.L.T. 530.
[2] per Lord President Hope at 540.
[3] Children (Scotland) Act 1995 s.64(1). For details, see the second edition of this book, at
pp.52–56.
[4] Children's Hearings (Scotland) Act 2011 s.79(2)(a).

local authority.[5] The normal rules of constitution and procedure applicable to hearings will, except in respect of some matters of attendance, apply to pre-hearing panels.[6] The pre-hearing panel must be arranged for a date before the date fixed for the children's hearing,[7] though if it is not practicable to do so the matter will be determined by the children's hearing itself at the start of the hearing and before going on to the matter for which the hearing was arranged.[8] In any case it is competent only "where a children's hearing is to be held in relation to a child".[9] This means, it is submitted, when the reporter has an obligation, however it arises, to arrange a hearing, or a hearing has been arranged. It is competent for pre-hearing panels to be scheduled to take place with three panel members who have previously been scheduled to attend unrelated children's hearings, for there is no requirement that the pre-hearing panel be composed of or even include panel members who will sit on the following children's hearing for the child. The rule is that a member of the children's panel selected for a pre-hearing panel may (but need not) be a member of the children's hearing.[10] The matters that are open for determination by a pre-hearing panel are listed in s.79 of the 2011 Act, though they may be added to by rules made by the Scottish Ministers.[11] In addition, a pre-hearing panel may appoint, if one is not already in place, a safeguarder for the child to whom the children's hearing relates, and if it does so it must record the appointment and give reasons for its decision[12]; any safeguarder appointed by a pre-hearing panel is to be treated for the purposes of the 2011 Act as if he or she were appointed by a children's hearing.[13] The role of the safeguarder appointed by a pre-hearing panel is not to assist it in any of the determinations that it is required to make (for a pre-hearing panel may not defer any determination), but to assist the children's hearing that will follow; if, however, a safeguarder is in post when a pre-hearing panel meets he or she has a right to attend the pre-hearing panel[14] and, as elaborated in the following paragraph, may make representations.

Notification of and information provided for pre-hearing panels

5–03　　Whenever a pre-hearing panel is to be arranged in order to consider whether to deem someone to be a relevant person,[15] the reporter must, wherever practicable at least five days before the intended date of the pre-hearing panel, give notice of the time, date and place of the pre-hearing panel to the child, relevant person, any individual requesting to be deemed to be a relevant person, any individual who appears to the reporter to have (or recently have had) significant involvement in the upbringing of the child, any appointed safeguarder, the

---

[5] Children's Hearings (Scotland) Act 2011 (Rules of Procedure in Children's Hearings) Rules 2013 (SSI 2013/194) (hereinafter "2013 Rules") r.3(2); Children's Hearings (Scotland) Act 2011 s.6 (as extended to pre-hearing panels by Children's Hearings (Scotland) Act 2011 (Modification of Primary Legislation) Order 2013 (SSI 2013/211) Sch.1 para.20(2)).

[6] 2013 Rules, especially rr.3–7.

[7] 2011 Act s.80(2).

[8] 2011 Act s.80(3).

[9] 2011 Act s.79(1).

[10] 2011 Act s.79(6).

[11] 2011 Act ss.79(3) and 177(2)(a).

[12] 2011 Act s.82.

[13] 2011 Act s.82(5).

[14] 2013 Rules r.46(2)(c) and (3)(c)(i).

[15] See below, paras 5–10—5–15.

three members of the pre-hearing panel and the National Convener.[16] These people (except the panel members and the National Convener) must also be informed that they:

(a) have the right to attend the pre-hearing panel;
(b) may make representations relating to whether an individual should be deemed to be a relevant person;
(c) may give any report or other document relevant to whether an individual should be deemed to be a relevant person; and
(d) have the right to request the reporter to take all reasonable steps to enable the child, relevant person or individual in question to attend by way of telephone, video link or by using any other method of communication.[17]

In addition, the individuals who might be deemed to be a relevant person must be informed that if deemed a relevant person they may then request the pre-hearing panel to determine any of the other matters open to a pre-hearing panel.[18] If the pre-hearing panel dealing with a relevant person claim is also to determine any of these other matters the notice from the reporter must state this fact and inform the individual who may be deemed a relevant person that they will not be entitled to take part in any discussion on any of these matters unless they are deemed to be relevant persons; the child, relevant person and safeguarder must be informed that they may make representations orally or in writing or give any report or other document relevant to the matters to be considered by the pre-hearing panel.[19]

Where a pre-hearing panel is arranged to determine matters other than a **5–04** deemed relevant person claim, the reporter must, wherever practicable at least five days before the intended date of the pre-hearing panel, give notice of the date, time and place of the pre-hearing panel to the child, relevant person, safeguuader, the three panel members and the National Convener.[20] Each of these except the National Convener must be informed of the matters to be determined by the pre-hearing panel.[21] The child, relevant person and safeguarder must be informed that they:

(a) have the right to attend the pre-hearing panel;
(b) may make representations (orally or in writing);
(c) may give any report or other document for the consideration of the pre-hearing panel; and
(d) have the right to request that the reporter takes all reasonable steps to enable the child and each relevant person to attend the pre-hearing panel by way of telephone, through video link or using any other method of communication.[22]

---

[16] 2013 Rules r.45(1), (2) and (3)(a).
[17] 2013 Rules r.45(3)(b).
[18] 2013 Rules r.45(3)(c).
[19] 2013 Rules r.45(4).
[20] 2013 Rules r.46(1), (2) and (3)(a).
[21] 2013 Rules r.46(3)(b).
[22] 2013 Rules r.46(3)(c).

Right to attend pre-hearing panels

5–05   The categories of person entitled to attend a pre-hearing panel reflect the categories of person entitled to attend a children's hearing.[23] There are, in addition, supplementary rules of attendance depending on why the pre-hearing panel has been arranged. If the pre-hearing panel has been arranged for reasons other than to deal with a deemed relevant person claim, then the child, relevant person and any appointed safeguarder have the right to attend the pre-hearing panel.[24] If the pre-hearing panel has been arranged to consider a deemed relevant person claim, then these people, as well as the individual wishing to be deemed a relevant person and any one (other than a relevant person) who appears to the reporter to have (or recently have had) significant involvement in the upbringing of the child has a right to attend the pre-hearing panel.[25]

5–06   Whatever the reason for the pre-hearing panel, the attendance of members of area support teams is permitted by s.78.[26] A representative of the child or relevant person is included in s.78, and the 2013 Rules contemplate that an individual seeking to be deemed to be a relevant person may also be accompanied by a representative at a pre-hearing panel.[27] Journalists may likewise attend a children's hearing or a pre-hearing panel by dint of s.78(1)(i) of the Children's Hearings (Scotland) Act 2011, though there will seldom, if ever, be any point of their doing so. The Rule that permits a constable, prison officer or other person who has in their lawful custody "a person who has to attend a pre-hearing panel or a children's hearing" to attend a children's hearing is expressly extended to attendance at a pre-hearing panel[28] notwithstanding that, strictly speaking, no-one "has to" attend a pre-hearing panel:[29] it is suggested that if a prisoner has a right to attend, and is given permission by the prison authorities to attend, a pre-hearing panel then Rule 20 allows a constable or prison officer to insist on accompanying the prisoner.

5–07   Those with a right to attend also have the right to make representations orally or in writing on the matter referred to the pre-hearing panel.[30] They also have the right to give any report or other document relevant to that matter for the consideration of the pre-hearing panel[31]: if they wish to do so they must, as

---

[23] Rights and duties of attendance at children's hearings are dealt with at Ch.6 below. The matter is govered by s.78 of the 2011 Act, the rules in which were extended to pre-hearing panels by the Children's Hearings (Scotland) Act 2011 (Modification of Primary Legislation) Order 2013 Sch.1 para.20(9) by the insertion of s.78(7) under which "children's hearing" includes for the purposes of s.78 a pre-hearing panel.

[24] 2013 Rules r.46(3)(c)(i). Since these people will have a right to attend under s.78, this rule is primarily designed for the avoidance of doubt and should not be taken to prohibit the attendance of individuals listed in s.78 but not in r.46(3) (such as a representative).

[25] 2013 Rules r.45(3)(b)(i).

[26] As amended by the Children's Hearings (Scotland) Act 2011 (Modification of Primary Legislation) Order 2013 (SSI 2013/211) Sch.1 para.20(9).

[27] 2013 Rules r.11(1). The right of the child, relevant person or person seeking to be deemed to be a relevant person to be accompanied by a representative is without prejudice to the right of any of these people to legal representation by a solicitor or counsel: r.11(2).

[28] 2013 Rules r.20.

[29] To argue that this means that there is no such right of attendance is to argue for the meaninglessness of r.20 in respect of pre-hearing panels.

[30] 2013 Rules rr.45(3)(b)(ii) and 46(3)(c)(ii).

[31] 2013 Rules rr.45(3)(b)(iii) and 46(3)(c)(iii).

soon as possible and wherever practicable no later than four days before the intended date of the pre-hearing panel, give those representations, report or other document to the Reporter who must then, wherever practicable no later than three days before the intended date for the pre-hearing panel, give a copy of that information to the other participants at the pre-hearing panel and the panel members.[32] If they are unable to attend in person, they have the right to request that the Reporter takes all reasonable steps to enable the child, relevant person, or the individual in question, as the case may be, to attend the pre-hearing panel by way of telephone, through video link or by using any other method of communication.[33] The rules relating to the prohibition of publication[34] apply to pre-hearing panels as they do to children's hearings.[35]

MATTERS TO BE CONSIDERED AT PRE-HEARING PANEL

Some matters, characterised below as "procedural matters", may be referred to **5–08** a pre-hearing panel at the discretion of the reporter, either acting on his or her own initiative to raise the matter or acting in response to a request from the child, a relevant person or a safeguarder. In addition, the other matter that a pre-hearing panel may consider—whether to deem an individual to be a relevant person—must be referred to a pre-hearing panel whenever the reporter is requested to do so; and even if not requested to refer the matter to a pre-hearing panel the reporter may do so on his or her own initiative. In any case, a determination made by a pre-hearing panel on any matter it is entitled to determine may be made on a majority basis.[36]

Procedural matters to be considered at a pre-hearing panel

Certain matters may be referred to a pre-hearing panel at the discretion of the **5–09** reporter, whether acting on his or her own initiative or following a request from the child, a relevant person or a safeguarder.[37] The reporter cannot be forced to refer any such matter to a pre-hearing panel though, if still live by then, the matter will be open for consideration by a children's hearing. None of these matters is appealable. The matters that fall into this category are as follows:

(a) Whether the child should be excused from attending the children's hearing.[38] The pre-hearing panel may excuse the child from attending the immediately following[39] children's hearing only if (i) the hearing concerns a sch.1 offence and the child's attendance is not necessary

---

[32] 2013 Rules r.47.
[33] 2013 Rules rr.45(3)(b)(iv) and 46(3)(c)(iv).
[34] Considered below, paras 6–42—6–47.
[35] 2011 Act s.182(9), as amended by the Children's Hearings (Scotland) Act 2011 (Modification of Primary Legislation) Order 2013 (SSI 2013/211) Sch.1 para.20(20).
[36] 2011 Act s.202(2A), as inserted by the Children's Hearings (Scotland) Act 2011 (Modification of Primary Legislation) Order 2013 Sch.1 para.20(21).
[37] 2011 Act s.79(2)(c).
[38] 2011 Act s.79(3)(a).
[39] Excusal should be limited only to the immediately following hearing and it would be incompetent, it is submitted, for a pre-hearing panel (or a children's hearing) to excuse a child from all subsequent hearings, or even those to be held within a stated and limited period of time.

for a fair hearing, (ii) the attendance of the child at the hearing would place the child's physical, mental or moral welfare at risk, (iii) taking account of the child's age and maturity, the child would not be capable of understanding what happens at the hearing or (iv) the child is otherwise excused under rules made by the Scottish Ministers.[40] These grounds of excusal are the same as the grounds upon which the children's hearing itself may excuse the child from attendance and are considered more fully below.[41]

(b) Whether a relevant person should be excused from attending the children's hearing.[42] The pre-hearing panel may excuse a relevant person only if (i) it would be unreasonable to require the relevant person's attendance at the hearing, (ii) the attendance of the relevant person at the hearing is unnecessary for the proper consideration of the matter before the hearing or (iii) the relevant person is otherwise excused under rules made by the Scottish Ministers. Again, these grounds of excusal replicate the grounds upon which the children's hearing itself may excuse the relevant person from attendance and are discussed more fully below.[43]

(c) Whether it is likely that the children's hearing will consider making a compulsory supervision order including a secure accommodation authorisation in relation to the child.[44] The question here is not whether the children's hearing is likely to include a secure accommodation authorisation in any compulsory supervision order it makes, but whether it is likely that the hearing will *discuss* the matter. "Likelihood" has the meaning of a real possibility rather than probability, but the possibility must not be fanciful or merely hypothetical. The importance of a pre-hearing panel making this determination is that whenever a hearing is considering such an authorisation legal aid will be automatically available to the child[45] and so once the pre-hearing panel has made its determination on this matter the process of applying for legal aid can be instituted immediately and without waiting for the children's hearing itself to commence its consideration of the child's case. The reporter is obliged, if the pre-hearing panel determines that secure accommodation is likely to be considered, to notify the Scottish Legal Aid Board of that fact, and of the child's name and address.[46]

(d) A matter specified in rules made by the Scottish Ministers.[47] No rules have been made explicitly adding to the list of procedural decisions in s.79(3) but the 2013 Rules do envisage that pre-hearing panels may make at least two other decisions. First, a pre-hearing panel may determine[48] that a child or relevant person is unable to participate

---

[40] 2011 Act s.79(4).
[41] See below, paras 6–03—6–10.
[42] 2011 Act s.79(3)(b). Again, this is limited to the immediately following hearing.
[43] See below, paras 6–17—6–18.
[44] 2011 Act s.79(3)(c).
[45] Legal Aid (Scotland) Act 1986 s.28C(1)(c). And see above, para.1–12.
[46] 2013 Rules r.50(6).
[47] 2011 Act s.79(3)(d).
[48] Under 2013 Rules r.50(7).

effectively in the proceedings before a children's hearing unless represented by a solicitor or counsel, in which case the reporter must, as soon as possible after the pre-hearing panel's determination, notify the Scottish Legal Aid Board of that fact and of the name and address of the child or relevant person. And secondly, a pre-hearing panel may be asked to deal with a non-disclosure request[49]: this matter is examined in detail later.[50]

Before the pre-hearing panel makes its determination on any of these matters, the chairing member must invite the child and relevant person to give any representations, documents or other information that they wish to give for the consideration of the pre-hearing panel, and once the decision is made the chairing member must confirm that determination and its reasons.[51] In coming to its decision the pre-hearing panel is to regard the need to safeguard and promote the welfare of the child throughout his or her childhood as the paramount consideration,[52] and though this is subject to the normal qualification to this principle in s.26,[53] it is difficult to conceive of situations where a determination of a pre-hearing panel would have to be modified in order to protect members of the public from serious harm. The requirement in s.27 to give the child the opportunity to express views applies to pre-hearing panels as it does to children's hearings.[54] It is not required by the Rules but would be good practice for the chairing member to remind the child and relevant person that none of these procedural decisions is appealable.

Deeming an individual to be a relevant person

In addition to these primarily procedural matters that a pre-hearing panel **5–10** may, at the instigation of the reporter, determine there is another, substantive, matter open to a pre-hearing panel's determination which, having been made, is appealable. This is the question of whether an individual who does not meet the definition of "relevant person" as set out in s.200 of the 2011 Act ought nevertheless to be deemed to be a relevant person in relation to the child for the purposes of the children's hearing. This question may be referred to a pre-hearing panel by the reporter at his or her own initiative, and it must be so referred if the reporter has been requested to do so by the individual concerned, the child or a relevant person.[55] The request may only be made "when a children's hearing is to be held in relation to a child"[56] and so an individual who wishes to be deemed to be a relefvant person may not seek this status before a

---

[49] Under 2013 Rules r.84.

[50] Below, paras 6–49—6–51.

[51] 2013 Rules r.49.

[52] 2011 Act s.25.

[53] Allowing a children's hearing, pre-hearing panel or court to make a decision inconsistent with the requirement in s.25 of the 2011 Act if this is necessary to protect members of the public from serious harm.

[54] An amendment was made to both s.26 and s.27 of the 2011 Act as originally passed to achieve this end by the Children's Hearings (Scotland) Act 2011 (Modification of Primary Legislation) Order 2013 Sch.1 para.20(3) and (4). Section 28 of the 2011 Act (the requirement not to make any order unless it would be better for the child for the order to be in force than not) does not apply to pre-hearing panels, because such panels make no orders.

[55] 2011 Act s.79(2)(a) and (b).

[56] 2011 Act s.79(1).

hearing becomes due.[57] If this question is referred to a pre-hearing panel together with any other matter, the deemed relevant person claim must be dealt with before determining the other matter,[58] and if the claim is rejected the individual concerned will not have any right to take part in the discussion on any of the other matters referred to the pre-hearing panel.[59] The question of whether to deem someone a relevant person may also arise even although it is not the matter that the pre-hearing panel has been arranged to determine: if the child, relevant person or safeguarder requests it at a pre-hearing panel arranged to consider one of the procedural matters, that panel must examine the question of whether any person present at the pre-hearing panel satisfies the test for being deemed to be a relevant person.[60] Since no-one other than the child, relevant person and safeguarder has a right to attend a pre-hearing panel arranged only for procedural matters, this provision will apply in respect of individuals allowed to attend the pre-hearing panel at the discretion of the chairing member.[61]

5–11   In order to ensure the preservation of everyone's rights, notification of the pre-hearing panel to determine a relevant person claim must be given not only to the child, relevant person, and safeguarder but also: (i) the individual who has required the reporter to arrange a pre-hearing panel for this purpose and (ii) any individual who appears to the reporter to have (or recently have had) significant contact with the child.[62] So not only the claimant has the right to notification and the right to attend a pre-hearing panel arranged to determine a deemed relevant person claim but so too does anyone who, in the reporter's view, might satisfy the test for being deemed a relevant person. The reporter must, therefore, be pro-active (once a pre-hearing panel is to be arranged to look at the relevant person issue) in identifying individuals who have not themselves asked for a pre-hearing panel to be arranged in order to deem them relevant persons. Indeed, it will be good practice for the reporter to initiate a pre-hearing panel on his or her own initiative whenever, having reviewed the family circumstances, he or she comes to the view that there is an individual who satisfies the test: if not requested to do so, however, it would seem that the reporter is free to decide that even although there is an individual who may satisfy the test there should be no pre-hearing panel to deem them relevant person.[63] At the pre-hearing panel the child, relevant person and individual involved must be invited by the chairing member to give representations, documents or other information

---

[57] An individual may not, for example, seek to be deemed to be a relevant person immediately after a child has been made subject to a compulsory supervision order, but must wait until a review hearing "is to be held": this means when the reporter becomes obliged to start the arrangements for the review, of whatever sort and for whatever reason.

[58] 2011 Act s.81(2).

[59] 2013 Rules r.45(4)(a). In practice, however, if the person is present at the pre-hearing panel and might have something relevant to contribute there is no point in preventing that person from speaking and the chairing member may well exercise his or her general discretion both to permit the individual to remain (2011 Act s.78(2)) and to contribute to the discussion of the other matters (2013 Rules r.7).

[60] 2013 Rules r.48(2). If this happens then the panel proceeds as if the matter had been referred to them in the normal way: r.48(3).

[61] 2011 Act s.78(2), as extended to pre-hearing panels by s.78(7) (inserted by Children's Hearings (Scotland) Act 2011 (Modification of Primary Legislation) 2013 Order Sch.1 para.20(9)), allows the chairing member to permit other persons to attend.

[62] 2013 Rules r.45.

[63] The reporter is not, of course, free to decide not to give notice.

that they have that will assist the determination and may invite such other person as the panel considers appropriate to do so.[64] If the pre-hearing panel determines that the individual does indeed have (or has recently had) significant involvement in the upbringing of the child, then it must deem the individual to be a relevant person.[65] On being deemed to be a relevant person the individual is entitled to receive from the reporter, as soon as practicable after being deemed a relevant person, all the information given to relevant persons,[66] and the deemed relevant person is to be treated as a relevant person for the purposes of the following children's hearing, any subsequent children's hearing, any pre-hearing panel connected with any subsequent children's hearing, any compulsory supervision order, interim compulsory supervision order, medical examination order or warrant to secure attendance made by a hearing or sheriff, any hearing or court proceedings held in connection with such hearings, order or warrant, and the implementation of any such order or warrant.[67]

Meaning of "significant involvement in the upbringing of the child"

The test to be followed by the pre-hearing panel asked to determine a rele- **5–12** vant person claim is whether "the individual has (or has recently had) a significant involvement in the upbringing of the child": if so, then the pre-hearing panel must deem the individual to be a relevant person.[68] The imperative is to be noted: it is not open to the pre-hearing panel (or, if appropriate, the children's hearing) to hold that the test is satisfied but nevertheless the individual should not be deemed to be a relevant person, perhaps on considerations of the welfare of the child.[69] The test is factual rather than judgmental: deeming is not a discretionary power of the pre-hearing panel but an inevitable consequence of the panel having found the factual test to be satisfied. In order to allow the pre-hearing panel to make the determination of whether that test is satisfied, the chairing member must invite the child, relevant person and individual in question, if in attendance, to make representations (orally or in writing) or give any other document or information that he or she wishes to be considered by the pre-hearing panel; the chairing member may also invite any other person that the pre-hearing panel consider appropriate to do so.[70]

"Significant involvement in the upbringing of the child" requires more than **5–13** significant contact with the child and implies that the individual plays an important role in the child's upbringing. It probably does not require that the individual lives with the child, but does require that the individual is involved in upbringing decisions, such as those relating to schooling, medical treatment,

---

[64] 2013 Rules r.48(4) and (5).
[65] 2011 Act s.81(3).
[66] 2013 Rules r.51.
[67] 2011 Act s.81(4).
[68] 2011 Act s.81(3).
[69] Though s.25 of the 2011 Act applies to pre-hearing panels as well as to hearings "coming to a decision about a matter relating to a child", this does not include factual determinations that either a pre-hearing panel or a children's hearing is required to make but is limited, it is submitted, to judgmental decisions made on the basis of facts as found. But see Sheriff McCulloch in *G and T, Appellants* Unreported August 28, 2013 Kirkcaldy Sheriff Court, at [4]. It might also be argued (if rather less persuasively) that a deemed relevant person decision is a matter relating to that person and not a matter relating to the child.
[70] 2013 Rules r.48(4) and (5).

religious observances and the like. Involvement in bringing up a child is quali-
tatively different from being with the child on a regular basis and suggests that
some developmental influence must be exercised. A person may have regular
contact with the child without being involved to a significant extent in the
child's upbringing. The phrase "significant involvement in the upbringing of
the child" should be given a non-technical meaning that is not dependent on
legal rights or legal responsibilities in relation to the child's upbringing. Pre-
hearing panels (and children's hearings) ought not to be too strict in excluding
persons who have a genuine involvement in the child's life. An individual will
be entitled to be deemed to be a relevant person when they recently had, even
although they no longer have, a significant involvement in the child's
upbringing. Again, the concept of "recent" ought not to be too strictly interpreted: the aim is to ensure that those who have had an involvement in the
child's upbringing are not excluded because of recent events. So a person who
loses that involvement through state action should still be able to claim relevant person status, and so protect their right to challenge state action, until such
time as their involvement in the child's upbringing was merely historical and
of no contemporary significance. The timescale of "recent" involvement can
obviously vary from case to case—and with the age of the child—but an
involvement that ended more than a year previously is likely to be considered
"recent" only in unusual circumstances.

5–14   The determination that a person is, or is not, to be deemed to be a relevant
person may be appealed to the sheriff by the individual in question, the child,
a relevant person, or two or more of these persons acting jointly,[71] and these
individuals must be informed of the right to appeal immediately on the decision having been made by the pre-hearing panel.[72] Further appeals may be had
to the sheriff principal or direct to the Court of Session, or to the sheriff principal and then, with leave, to the Court of Session by the individual in question,
the child, a relevant person or two or more of these persons acting jointly.[73]
This further appeal may be on a point or law or in respect of any procedural
irregularity, and a decision of the Court of Session on the matter is final.[74]

5–15   The concept of "significant involvement" in a child's upbringing is not a static
one and, with the passage of time, an individual deemed to be a relevant person
because of significant involvement may reduce, or have reduced, that involvement so that it is no longer significant. While relevant person status, once
conferred by a decision under s.81, will last beyond the instant hearing, it need
not last indefinitely.[75] However, it is not open to a pre-hearing panel to re-examine
the question of an individual's relevant person status: only a children's hearing
at a review of a compulsory supervision order that ends in the order being
continued or varied may do so, and the matter is discussed fully later.[76]

---

[71] 2011 Act s.160(1) and (2). See further below, para.14–37.
[72] 2013 Rules r.48(8) and (9). The reporter must also give notice of that determination, its
reasons, and the right to appeal against it: r.50(1)–(4).
[73] 2011 Act s.164(1)–(3). See further below, paras 14–50—14–51.
[74] 2011 Act s.164(7).
[75] Just as being within the definition of "relevant person" in s.200 is not static and a person, say
by losing all parental responsibilities and parental rights by court order, may fall outwith the definition even although he or she was within the definition when the compulsory supervision order
was first made.
[76] See below, paras 13–37—13–40.

TERMINATION OF DEEMED RELEVANT PERSON STATUS

Other than removal of the status of deemed relevant person by a children's **5–16** hearing, the Act and Rules are silent on how long that status lasts. A person defined as relevant person under s.200 remains a relevant person for the purposes of the children's hearing for so long as he or she remains within the definition. Deemed relevant person status is different, being dependent not only on the satisfaction of a test but also on the child remaining within the children's hearing system. It follows, it is submitted, that if a referral is discharged, or a compulsory supervision order is terminated, anyone who has been deemed to be a relevant person loses that status at that point, with the result that if the child is subsequently referred to another children's hearing the previously deemed relevant person may not rely on that previous deeming, but must persuade a new pre-hearing panel (or children's hearing) that they presently satisfy the test. A relevant person defined as such under s.200 of the Act is able to continue to rely on that definition without having to prove anything new.

CHILDREN'S HEARINGS MAKING DEEMED RELEVANT PERSON DECISIONS

As well as a pre-hearing panel deeming an individual to be a relevant person, the **5–17** children's hearing itself also has the power to do so, in two circumstances. First, if it has not been practicable for the reporter to arrange a pre-hearing panel on a date before the date of the hearing, the children's hearing must determine whatever matter would have been before the pre-hearing panel at the start of the hearing, including of course the relevant person claim.[77] This will only occur when the matter has been referred to a pre-hearing panel on the reporter's own initiative or when the reporter was obliged to refer the matter to a pre-hearing panel on being required to do so by the individual seeking to be deemed a relevant person, by the child, or by an existing relevant person. If the hearing is required to determine other matters open to a pre-hearing panel, the individual will not be entitled to take part in any discussion unless they are first deemed to be a relevant person.[78] The rule applies that the hearing may consider whether to deem any person present to be a relevant person if the appropriate request to do so has been made,[79] as do the other rules applicable to the pre-hearing panel.[80]

Secondly and more broadly, at any grounds hearing, subsequent hearing **5–18** or review hearing, the children's hearing must consider whether to deem an individual who is present at the hearing to be a relevant person.[81] The hearing

---

[77] 2011 Act s.80(3). The reporter must notify those entitled to notification about the pre-hearing panel that the matter will be referred to the children's hearing: 2013 Rules r.52(1) and (2).

[78] 2013 Rules r.52(4). However, it is easy to imagine circumstances in which there is little or no point in excluding the individual from discussions other than the relevant person discussion (such as when that person is likely to have something to contribute to the discussion) and the power remains with the chairing member to permit that individual to remain in the hearing—and to take part in the discussion—even although they are not to be deemed to be a relevant person, for the chairing member may always permit the attendance of others than those with a right to attend: 2011 Act s.78(2).

[79] 2013 Rules r.54, applying r.48(2).

[80] 2013 Rules r.54. And the rules in r.47 applicable to pre-hearing panels concerning the provision of information to the reporter and its transmission to the participants are replicated in r.53.

[81] 2013 Rules r.55.

may not do so at their own initiative, but only when requested to do so by the child, relevant person or the individual in question—though it would be open to the hearing to suggest to those attending that they make such a request. And the hearing may consider the relevant person claim only in respect of a person who is attending the hearing: since this will seldom be a person with a right to attend, the person will be attending at the discretion of the chairing member. The risk exists that permission to attend will be refused in order to prevent the request being made to deem the individual a relevant person. That would, it is suggested, be an illegitimate reason for a chairing member to refuse any individual permission to attend. If the question arises, during a hearing, of whether someone not present would satisfy the test for deemed relevant person status then that matter can only be resolved by a pre-hearing panel. Raising the question might be sufficient justification for the hearing to defer making whatever substantive decision is open to it to allow a pre-hearing panel to consider the matter, and though there is no requirement that the hearing does so this will sometimes be the only way to ensure such a person's right of participation.

5–19   A children's hearing may, at a subsequent review of a compulsory supervision order and as discussed later,[82] remove the deemed relevant person status of any individual who no longer satisfies the test—a pre-hearing panel may not do so.[83]

---

[82] Below, paras 13–37—13–40.
[83] 2011 Act s.142 is limited in its terms to children's hearings.

CHAPTER 6

ATTENDANCE AT THE HEARING, PRIVACY AND CONFIDENTIALITY

INTRODUCTION

It has long been recognised that a child is more likely to feel able to take part **6–01** in a discussion in a private rather than in a public forum, and it has always been the rule, now embodied in s.78(2) of the Children's Hearings (Scotland) Act 2011, that no person other than those who have a right to attend or who have been given permission to attend by the chairing member, may attend a children's hearing or pre-hearing panel. In addition, publication of information in relation to a children's hearings is an offence.[1] There are, however, some individuals who are obliged to be present, some who have a right to choose to be present and some who may, at the discretion of the chairing member of the hearing, be allowed to be present. The presence of those who have an obligation or a right to attend is normally (but not always) necessary for a proper consideration of the case. The discretion to permit the presence of individuals who have no statutory right to attend a children's hearing rests solely with the chairing member, who is constrained in the exercise of that discretion by s.78(4), under which he or she must take all reasonable steps to ensure that the number of persons present at a children's hearing at the same time is kept to a minimum. This does not entitle the chairing member to exclude any person who has a right to attend, except for a reason specified in any statutory provision that permits such exclusion[2]; rather, it does no more than exhort the chairing member to minimise the number of those persons whose presence can be permitted on a discretionary basis. These will be, for the most part, observers rather than active participants, but individuals such as foster carers, family members who are not "relevant persons", or other relatives may well have some role to play in helping the hearing in their determination of whether a compulsory supervision order is necessary. Even when attendance at the hearing is limited to those who have a right to be present, the numbers might easily reach double figures: there may be present three panel members, the reporter, the child, two parents, a lawyer, a safeguarder and a social worker. The chairing member can sanction an arrangement whereby parts only of the hearing take place in the presence of particular individuals. The rules on attendance at pre-hearing panels are broadly similar to those for children's hearings and are considered elsewhere.[3]

---

[1] Children's Hearings (Scotland) Act 2011 s.182: see below, paras 6–42—6–47.
[2] As in s.78(6) in relation to journalists or s.76 in relation to relevant persons.
[3] Above, paras 5–05—5–07.

THE CHILD

6–02 The most important person at any children's hearing is the child. It is the child's hearing, and it is the question of whether the child should be made subject to a compulsory supervision order that the children's hearing is being asked to determine. The child's right to participate in proceedings concerning his or her private and family life is a central element of both art.6 (right to a fair hearing)[4] and art.8 (right to respect for private and family life)[5] of the European Convention on Human Rights. It follows that in most cases the child ought to be present at all stages of the procedure. Under the 2011 Act, whenever a children's hearing is, or is to be, arranged in relation to a child, whether it is a grounds hearing, dispositive hearing, review hearing or an advice hearing, that child is granted the right[6] and placed under an obligation[7] to attend the children's hearing. The current law reflects the position in the Children (Scotland) Act 1995, which itself constituted a significant change from the pre-1995 position, under which the child had a duty but not the right to attend. The practical result of that was that a child could be excluded against his or her wishes from a consideration of his or her own case.[8] The present legislation is more Convention-compliant, for the child has both the duty and the right to attend, and while the children's hearing (or pre-hearing panel) can excuse the child from attending the hearing,[9] it can never remove the child's right to attend if the child wishes to exercise that right. It follows that if the child insists on attending, he or she cannot be excluded from any part of the hearing and that is so even after a pre-hearing panel or children's hearing has excused the child from attending all or part of the hearing. In the absence of any such excusal, the child has a duty to attend his or her own children's hearing, and while breach of that duty is not a criminal offence[10] it may justify the children's hearing in granting a warrant to secure the child's attendance at the children's hearing.[11]

Excusing the child from the duty to attend

6–03   Notwithstanding the child's obligation to attend the children's hearing arranged in relation to him or her, the pre-hearing panel or children's hearing may excuse the child from attending all or part of the hearing. This will permit the children's hearing to consider the child's case in his or her absence if he or she then decides not to exercise the right to attend. The decision to excuse the child can only be made on one or other of three grounds, but the existence of one or more of them does not necessitate excusal. In making the decision to

---

[4] *L v Finland* (2001) 31 E.H.R.R. 30.

[5] *TP & KM v United Kingdom* (2000) 34 E.H.R.R. 2.

[6] 2011 Act s.78(1)(a).

[7] 2011 Act s.73(2). This does not include pre-hearing panels where the child has a right to attend but no obligation to do so: Children's Hearings (Scotland) Act 2011 (Rules of Procedure in Children's Hearings) Rules 2013 (SSI 2013/194) (hereinafter "2013 Rules") rr.45(3)(b)(i) and 46(3)(c)(i). If the child does not attend the pre-hearing panel that panel need not hesitate in making the determination it has been convened to consider in the child's absence.

[8] The competency of excluding a child was one of the major issues in *Sloan v B*, 1991 S.L.T. 530: see Norrie, "Excluding Children from Children's Hearings", 1993 S.L.T. (News) 67.

[9] See below, paras 6–03—6–10.

[10] As it may be for a relevant person: see below, para.6–15.

[11] 2011 Act s.123. See below, paras 6–11—6–14.

excuse the child from attending a children's hearing, the welfare of the child must be the pre-hearing panel's or children's hearing's paramount consideration,[12] but that decision is open to the pre-hearing panel or hearing only once it is established that one or other of the following grounds exists.

(a) In a case concerned with a Schedule 1 offence, the child may be **6–04** excused from attending the hearing if his or her attendance at the hearing or part of the hearing is not necessary for a fair hearing.[13] The aim here is to avoid the possibility of the child being inhibited or influenced in what he or she says by the presence of another person, and also to avoid distress to the child caused by being in the presence of an alleged or actual abuser. However, a "fair hearing" is one that is fair to all parties who may be affected by the outcome and, it is submitted, the children's hearing must consider the interests of more than simply the child (though the child's interests are paramount). A fair hearing will often require that a Schedule 1 offender (whose art.6 and art.8 rights must also be respected) be given the chance to answer any allegation made by the child, and it is only when no such issue is likely to arise that the child's presence can be said to be unnecessary for a fair hearing. This ground of excusal applies only "when the hearing relates to the grounds mentioned in s.67(2)(b), (c), (d) or (g)" but it is unclear what "relates to" means. There is no doubt that a grounds hearing at which any of these grounds are in issue "relate to" these grounds, but review hearings thereafter have a diminishing connection to the original grounds that brought the child to a hearing. It is suggested that at review hearings, unless the relevant section 67 ground remains a live issue, excusal of the child on this basis will not be available because the review hearing will not "relate to" that ground.

(b) In any case, the child may be excused from attending the hearing if **6–05** the children's hearing is satisfied that the attendance of the child at the hearing, or part of the hearing, would place the child's physical, mental or moral welfare at risk.[14] This is a significantly stricter test than applied under the Children (Scotland) Act 1995, where a child could be released from the obligation to attend if the children's hearing was satisfied that it would be detrimental to the interests of the child for him or her to be present at the hearing.[15] Distress at the thought of attending a hearing might have satisfied that test, but it is unlikely, unless shown to have severe and long-lasting consequences, to satisfy the test in the 2011 Act. It would be an unusual circumstance in which the child's physical or moral welfare were at risk by attending a hearing, though extreme cases are not difficult to imagine, such as where the child is too ill to attend. The most common ground for excusing a child from attending a hearing is likely to be that his or her mental welfare is at risk. It is to be noted that the test to be satisfied is

---

[12] 2011 Act s.25 applies to such a decision.
[13] 2011 Act s.73(3)(a). This refers also to offences under the Sexual Offences (Scotland) Act 2009, but these are Sch.1 offences in any case.
[14] 2011 Act s.73(3)(b).
[15] Children (Scotland) Act 1995 s.45(2)(b).

that the child's mental welfare "would be" at risk—not "is likely to be" at risk—and so the risk must be real and inevitable (insofar as risks ever are). A mere preference not to attend is clearly not sufficient nor is, it is submitted, distress at the thought of attending or (far less) of the possible outcomes. A risk to mental welfare requires a threat of some long-lasting damage to the child's emotional state. It also should be noted that if significant distress is caused to the child by the presence of a relevant person, then this provides a ground to exclude the relevant person,[16] making it all the more unnecessary to include such distress within the ambit of mental welfare here.

6–06   (c)   The child may also be excused if, taking account of the age and maturity of the child, he or she would not be capable of understanding what happens at the hearing or part of the hearing.[17] This is designed to allow the hearing to go ahead in the absence of a child who is clearly too young to take any part in the proceedings, such as babies and even toddlers. The ground should not, however, be used as a matter of course in respect of these very young children, because hearings can learn much by observing the interaction between parent and child even in the artificial and stressful environment of the hearing. There is no obligation on hearings to excuse children from attending children's hearings when this, or any other, ground for excusal applies and, making the decision on the basis of the welfare of the child, hearings should always remember that they are likely to be more fully informed about the child by at least seeing the child within his or her family environment. Given that even the youngest child has a right to attend, the presumption should be that an excusal will not be granted unless the ground of excusal is established and, in addition, it is in the interests of the child not to be obliged to attend.

6–07   The decision to excuse a child from attendance is not appealable by a relevant person who is insisting that the child be present.[18] Though the decision is made regarding the welfare of the child as the paramount consideration,[19] it is as well to remember that there are other mechanisms to protect the child from harm which, if practicable, are always to be preferred over excusing a child from attending his or her own children's hearing.

6–08   The language of "excusal" of the child's attendance emphasises that all that s.73 does is to release the child from the obligation to attend and it does not remove the child's right to attend. The pre-hearing panel or children's hearing ought, therefore, to inquire as to the child's wishes in relation to attendance before making its decision one way or the other,[20] and there would be little point in excusing a child who expresses a wish and an intention to attend. If the child wishes to attend a children's hearing but has been excused from attending, r.19 of the 2013 Rules provides that the Scottish Children's Reporter Administration

---

[16] 2011 Act s.76(1)(b). See below, paras 6–21—6–26.

[17] 2011 Act s.73(3)(c).

[18] The question of appeal by the child does not arise since the child may choose to exercise his or her right to attend even after having been excused of the duty to attend.

[19] 2011 Act s.25.

[20] The opportunity to express views by making representations orally or in writing must be afforded the child at pre-hearing panels: see above, paras 5–03—5–07.

must take all reasonable steps to enable the child to attend by way of telephone, through video link or by using any other method of communication, if requested to do so by the child and if the reporter is satisfied that the child has good reason for not attending in person. This is an odd provision in at least two respects. First, it is based on an assumption that an excusal is an exclusion (i.e. that it takes away the right of the child to attend). This is not so.[21] A child who has been excused from attending his or her own hearing is able to choose not to attend and is therefore immune from the granting of a warrant to secure attendance, but if he or she wishes to attend then excusal under s.73(3) does not remove the right to attend under s.78(1)(a) as that latter provision makes explicit.[22] The second oddity in relation to r.19 is that before telephone or video link must be made available the reporter must be satisfied that the child has good reason for not attending—which suggests, surely wrongly, that excusal granted by a hearing on satisfaction of a statutory test (which is, remember, tightly drawn) might not in all cases give the child good reason for not attending in person. It is submitted that if the test for excusal in s.73(3) has been found to be met by a pre-hearing panel or a children's hearing then there is no room for the reporter to consider that there is no good reason for the non-attendance of the child. The real purpose of Rule 19 is to ensure that a child who cannot physically attend a hearing or pre-hearing panel is given the opportunity to participate by video or other link, but it is peculiar that the obligation on SCRA to facilitate this applies only when the child has been excused from attending and not, for example, because it is needed due to physical incapacity (physical incapacity not being, in so many words at least, a ground for excusal).

The main legal effect of exusing a child from attending a hearing is that, on **6–09** excusal, there will be no basis upon which a warrant to secure attendance can be granted. It follows from this that retrospective excusal—excusing a child from attending a hearing that he or she has not, in fact, attended—serves no purpose. If a child has not attended, in breach of the obligation to attend, the hearing may defer making a decision (perhaps granting a warrant to secure attendance if there is no sound reason for the non-attendance) or the hearing may proceed in the absence of the child. The only exception to that is with a grounds hearing where, if the child fails to attend without having previously been excused, the hearing must either require the reporter to arrange another grounds hearing[23] or discharge the referral.[24] And it is to be noted that a child may only be excused from attending that part of a grounds hearing at which the grounds are explained when the hearing is satisfied that, taking account of the child's age and maturity, he or she would not be capable of understanding the explanation.[25] Other than in such circumstances, if a child has attended the explanation of the section 67

---

[21] And the distinction between excusal and exclusion is made explicit in relation to relevant persons, to whom this rule also applies—s.74(3) of the 2011 Act permits the relevant person's excusal, but only on satisfaction of a different test to that in s.76 which allows the relevant person to be excluded.

[22] The right of the child (or relevant person) to attend even when excused from attending is confirmed by r.50(5) of the 2013 Rules, which requires the reporter to inform any child or relevant person who has been excused by a pre-hearing panel from attending that they have a right to attend, as well as a right to request that their attendance be by way of telephone, video link or other method of communication.

[23] 2011 Act s.95(2).

[24] 2013 Rules r.64.

[25] 2011 Act s.73(4).

grounds stated by the reporter, it is difficult to imagine a situation in which the hearing could properly excuse the child before he or she has been given an opportunity to respond to the explanation by accepting or denying the application of the grounds.

6–10 There are some matters that remain unclear from the terms of the statute, in particular the questions: (i) how long does the excusal last; and (ii) can one children's hearing excuse the child from the obligation to attend a future children's hearing? The answer to both these questions turns on the interpretation of the words "all or part of the children's hearing", as they appear in s.73(3). A children's hearing or pre-hearing panel can excuse the child from attending all or part of the children's hearing: this could mean either: (i) all stages conducted on that day by the hearing granting the excusal, or by the hearing immediately following the pre-hearing panel; or (ii) all stages of all hearings, including those held after a hearing defers making a decision, until a dispositive decision is made; or (iii) all hearings until the child leaves the system. The last-mentioned interpretation is clearly wrong, if for no other reason than that circumstances may change from one hearing to the next. The difficulty with adopting the second interpretation is that the disposal of the case will commonly be done by a hearing composed of different members from the hearing at which the child was excused, and they may disagree with the former hearing's excusal of the child's attendance. There is much to be said for the view that all s.73(3) does is to allow a children's hearing to excuse the child from attending that particular hearing and the pre-hearing panel to excuse the child only from the immediately following hearing: this obviates the possibility of, say, a grounds hearing making an important decision which the subsequent hearing might not agree with. However, there is practical awkwardness in adopting this intepretation, since it would require the reporter to arrange for the child's presence in every case until the hearing on the day decides to allow the child to go home again, or arrange a pre-hearing panel before every hearing: in some cases this will serve no purpose at all and might even be harmful to the child's interests. It is submitted, therefore, that an excusal granted by a children's hearing or a pre-hearing panel which is satisfied both that a condition exists for releasing the child of his or her obligation and that it is in the interests of the child to be excused attendance will remain effective until the case has been disposed of by the making of a dispositive decision.[26] A child will not then be obliged to attend at the consideration of his or her case or subsequent hearings where the decision has been deferred but would be obliged to attend at a review of any compulsory supervision order imposed or continued as the disposal (unless a review hearing or pre-hearing panel subsequently decides otherwise). Any children's hearing arranged after the excusal has been granted but before the referral is disposed of may still, of course, come to the view that the child's presence is necessary for it to make a properly informed decision—in which case the hearing can withdraw the excusal previously granted and defer its decision in order to allow the child to attend. In other words, the excusal lasts until the case has been disposed of or, if earlier, until a subsequent children's hearing[27] withdraws the

---

[26] That is to say, to make, vary or terminate a compulsory supervision order, or to discharge the referral.

[27] It is open to argument that a pre-hearing panel (perhaps one arranged before a deferred hearing) may withdraw an earlier excusal: s.79(3)(a) allows it to determine "whether the child should be excused", which may well envisage decisions both ways.

excusal. In practice it will be rare for one hearing to disagree with another on this matter, but the child's circumstances might have changed sufficiently to render the previously granted excusal inappropriate. For example, the grounds hearing might decide that the child's presence is not necessary for a fair hearing due to the risk of the child being intimidated by an alleged abuser; yet when the case comes back to a hearing for disposal after the grounds are found established by a sheriff, the abuser might have indicated that he or she will not attend the hearing and the risk to the child thereby alleviated. In such circumstances if the child has not exercised his or her right to attend, the hearing may well consider it appropriate to defer its decision and withdraw the excusal from attendance.

Ensuring the attendance of the child

The 1995 Act contained a fairly complex range of warrants that could be **6–11** granted by the children's hearings in a number of different situations, including the fact that the child either had not attended a hearing or was unlikely to attend a hearing voluntarily. Most of these warrants disappeared with the passing of the 2011 Act, to be replaced by the interim compulsory supervision order, discussed more fully below.[28] The single warrant that remains available to a children's hearing under the 2011 Act is the warrant to secure the child's attendance at a hearing, which may be granted by a hearing under s.123. The children's hearing may grant such a warrant only on the application of the reporter and not at its own hand, though the hearing (or indeed an individual member thereof) may invite the reporter to make such an application. But if the reporter declines to do so the hands of the hearing are tied and it cannot grant a warrant to secure attendance on its own initiative. Such a warrant is available whenever a children's hearing has been or is to be arranged, or a hearing before the sheriff to establish grounds is to take place. "Any children's hearing" may on cause shown grant such a warrant: this does not include a pre-hearing panel but the word "any" suggests that it does include a hearing arranged to hear a quite separate case involving a quite different child.[29] The cause that needs to be shown is a realistic possibility that the child will not attend the hearing, and though that possibility does not require that the child has already failed to attend a hearing, such failure (at least if no reasonable explanation is offered) will usually be sufficient cause and the hearing at which the child has in fact failed to attend will be the most common hearing that grants a warrant to secure the child's attendance at the subsequent children's hearing. Before granting a warrant the hearing must seek the views of the child, relevant person and safeguarder, if present at the hearing.[30] If granted, the reporter must as soon as practicable give to these people a copy of the warrant and details of the right to appeal against it.[31]

The effect of a warrant to secure attendance is to authorise an officer of the **6–12** law: (i) to search for and apprehend the child; (ii) to take the child to, and detain the child in, a place of safety; (iii) to bring the child before the relevant proceedings (that is, either the children's hearing or the sheriff); and (iv) so far

---

[28] See paras 10–05—10–07.
[29] This is confirmed by the 2013 Rules which contain no provision for notification of a hearing arranged to consider granting a warrant to secure attendance.
[30] 2013 Rules r.78(2).
[31] 2013 Rules r.78(3).

as is necessary for the execution of the warrant, to break open shut and lockfast places.[32] The warrant, once granted, lasts for the period beginning with the granting of the warrant and ending with the earlier of the beginning of the relevant proceedings or the expiry of the period of seven days beginning with the day on which the child is first detained in pursuance of the warrant.[33] This means that a warrant stays effective in terms of the authority that it confers until such time as it is given effect. Once the child is detained in a place of safety under a warrant to secure attendance the reporter must, wherever practicable, arrange a children's hearing to take place on the first working day after the child was first detained in pursuance of the warrant.[34] It is unlikely that that hearing will be in a position to make a dispositive decision and so the outcome will probably be that the hearing defers making its decision: but that allows the hearing to make an interim compulsory supervision order which can last longer than a warrant to secure attendance, though it may contain the same terms.

6–13 A warrant to secure attendance may not be subject to any conditions[35] (for its intent is necessarily short-term and limited), though it may include a secure accommodation authorisation if one or more of the following conditions applies: (a) the child has previously absconded and is likely to abscond again and, if the child were to abscond, it is likely that the child's physical, mental or moral welfare would be at risk; (b) the child is likely to engage in self-harming conduct; or (c) the child is likely to cause injury to another person.[36] In addition, if it is to contain a secure accommodation authorisation, the warrant must authorise the keeping of the child in a residential establishment and, having considered the other options available, the children's hearing must be satisfied that it is necessary to include within the warrant a secure accommodation authorisation.[37]

6–14 The granting of a warrant to secure attendance is appealable to the sheriff at the instance of the child, a relevant person or a safeguarder appointed to the child or two or more of these persons acting jointly.[38] Such an appeal must be made before the expiry of the period of 21 days beginning with the day on which the decision is made,[39] and must be disposed of before the expiry of the period of three days beginning with the day *after the day* on which the appeal is made.[40] Further appeal may be had to the sheriff principal or direct to the Court of Session, or to the sheriff principal and then, with leave, to the Court of Session, by the child, a relevant person, a safeguarder or two or more of

---

[32] 2011 Act s.88(1)(a).

[33] 2011 Act s.88(4)(a). Notice that a warrant granted by a sheriff to ensure the child's attendance at a children's hearing also lasts for seven days (s.88(4)(d)) but that a warrant granted by a sheriff to ensure the child's attendance at the sheriff court hearing lasts for 14 days: s.88(4)(b) and (c).

[34] 2013 Rules r.17.

[35] Other than one prohibiting disclosure (whether directly or indirectly) to any person specified in the warrant of the place of safety to which the child is taken: 2011 Act s.88(1)(b).

[36] 2011 Act s.88(3). These conditions are considered more fully below, para.11–14.

[37] 2011 Act s.88(2).

[38] 2011 Act s.154(2), (3)(g) and (4).

[39] 2011 Act s.154(5). So a warrant granted on 10th July may be appealed against on or before 30th July.

[40] 2011 Act s.157(1)(e) and (2). So an appeal made on 10th August must be disposed of on or before 13th August. The days are *not* working days.

these persons acting jointly[41]: the appeal must be on a point of law or in respect of any procedural irregularity.[42]

THE RELEVANT PERSON

Participation in the decision-making process has long been seen by the **6–15** European Court of Human Rights as a crucial element in the protection of family members' right to a fair hearing and right to respect for their private and family life.[43] The children's hearing system has always encouraged relevant persons to participate fully and indeed the conferral of relevant person status is the primary—though no longer the only—mechanism whereby the participation of those (other than the child) who are directly affected by the process is ensured.[44] Under the 2011 Act, every relevant person has a right to attend the children's hearing[45] and is indeed obliged so to attend.[46] Failure to attend in breach of this obligation is a criminal offence which renders the offender liable on summary conviction to a fine not exceeding level 3 on the standard scale.[47] "Relevant person" for this purpose means all those who come within the definition of that phrase in s.200[48] together with those who are treated as a relevant person having been deemed by a pre-hearing panel or children's hearing to be a relevant person under s.81.[49]

The relevant person's right and duty to attend the children's hearing extends **6–16** to all stages of the hearing, that is to say the explanation of the grounds, the consideration of the case, and the making of the decision by the hearing, as well as any other part of the procedure, whether at a grounds hearing, a dispositive hearing, an advice hearing, or a review hearing. It should, however, be remembered that those who satisfy the definition of relevant person may change through time. A person who holds parental responsibilities and parental rights at one hearing may have had them removed by the time another hearing is held, with the result that he or she is no longer within the definition in s.200 of a relevant person in relation to the child; conversely the conferral by a court of parental responsibilities and parental rights on a person in relation to a child who is subject to a compulsory supervision order (perhaps a grandparent who has been looking after the child in terms of the compulsory supervision order) will bring that person within the definition of relevant person and so require their attendance at subsequent hearings.[50] Likewise, whenever it appears to a

---

[41] 2011 Act s.163(1)(a)(iii). This does not explicitly refer to warrants to secure attendance but rather to "a decision of a children's hearing": it is submitted that this includes all decisions appealable from the hearing to the sheriff, listed in s.154(3).

[42] 2011 Act s.163(9).

[43] *B v United Kingdom* (1987) 10 E.H.R.R. 87; *W v United Kingdom* (1988) 10 E.H.R.R. 29; *Venema v Netherlands* [2003] F.L.R. 552; *TP & KM v United Kingdom* (2002) 32 E.H.R.R. 2.

[44] *Principal Reporter v K*, 2011 S.L.T. 271.

[45] 2011 Act s.78(1)(c).

[46] 2011 Act s.74(2).

[47] 2011 Act s.74(4).

[48] See above, paras 2–14—2–20.

[49] See above, paras 5–10—5–13.

[50] This in fact has long been the case. In *Kennedy v H*, 1988 S.C. 114, 1988 S.L.T. 586 it was held that title to appeal against a decision of a children's hearing inhered only in a person who was a relevant person (then called guardian) at the time of the decision being appealed against. Title to appeal against a decision requires an interest at the time the decision was made.

children's hearing reviewing a compulsory supervision order that an individual who has been deemed to be a relevant person under s.81 may no longer fulfil the criterion for that deeming, the hearing must review whether the individual should, in the future,[51] continue to be deemed to be a relevant person in relation to the child.[52]

Excusing the relevant person from the duty to attend

6–17   The relevant person (defined or deemed) has a duty to attend at all stages of the hearing, unless the children's hearing or pre-hearing panel is satisfied that it would be unreasonable to require his or her attendance at the hearing or that part of the hearing, or that his or her attendance is unnecessary for the proper consideration of the matter before the hearing.[53] It would be unreasonable to require attendance when the cost and inconvenience of attending outweighs the contribution that the person is likely to make to the hearing; this is more likely to be accepted by the hearing when another relevant person is attending than when the only relevant person seeks, or all the relevant persons each seek, not to attend. It will seldom be unreasonable—will usually be reasonable—to require attendance when the child would otherwise be left to attend alone.[54] Attendance would be unnecessary when the relevant person has nothing at all to contribute to the hearing's consideration, for example, when a parent has had no contact with the child for some years and has nothing to offer the child. Attendance of a relevant person at a grounds hearing can never be regarded as "unnecessary for the proper consideration of the matter before the hearing" since the primary matter at a grounds hearing is whether the relevant person and the child accept the grounds; nor would it ever be unreasonable to require a relevant person's attendance at a grounds hearing. It follows that excusal from a grounds hearing will never be appropriate. Failure to attend any hearing without an excusal is a criminal offence,[55] and so the hearing that excuses a relevant person from attending ought to make a positive (and recorded) decision to this effect with reasons and ought not simply to proceed in the absence of the relevant person. A decision to excuse the attendance of the relevant person does no more than take away the legal obligation to attend: it does not take away the right to do so[56] (unless, in addition, a decision to exclude the relevant person under s.76, discussed below, has been made) and a relevant person can still attend if he or she chooses to do so even after the hearing has decided to excuse his or her attendance. The decision to excuse a relevant person's attendance will normally be made prospectively, and often by a pre-hearing panel, permitting a relevant person's non-attendance at a following children's hearing, but it is open to the hearing itself to make the decision in face of the relevant person's failure to attend when he or she had a duty to

---

[51] A decision to remove deemed relevant person status may be made by a children's hearing only after having completed the review for which the hearing was arranged, and only if the outcome of that review is to continue or vary the order.

[52] 2011 Act s.142. See below, paras 13–37—13–40.

[53] 2011 Act s.74(3) in relation to children's hearings, and s.79(5) in relation to pre-hearing panels.

[54] One circumstance in which it might be unreasonable would be when the child is over 16 and no longer living with, and without any continuing relationship in fact with, any relevant person.

[55] 2011 Act s.74(4).

[56] The right of attendance is secured by 2011 Act s.78(1)(c).

attend. This retrospective excusal will prevent a criminal offence having been committed, but in any case of non-authorised non-attendance the children's hearing may, if it considers it appropriate to do so, proceed with the children's hearing in the relevant person's absence.[57]

If the relevant person is excused but wishes to attend then r.19 of the 2013 **6–18** Rules provides for attendance by means of telephone or video link on the same basis as for a child who has been excused attendance.[58]

Ensuring the attendance of the relevant person

A children's hearing has no power to issue a warrant to find and keep and **6–19** bring before the hearing any person other than the referred child. There is no way, therefore, that the hearing can directly ensure that the relevant person fulfils his or her obligation to attend. However, it is open to the hearing to direct the reporter to bring the relevant person's non-attendance to the attention of the procurator fiscal, because a failure to attend in the absence of any excusal granted by the hearing is a criminal offence.[59] Alternatively, if the relevant person is also keeping the child away from a hearing, a warrant to secure attendance might be granted over the child; this will often encourage the unwilling relevant person to attend. However, it is to be remembered that such a warrant can only be granted when it is in the interests of the child to do so (and when requested by the reporter): but it is clearly against the interests of any child for a relevant person to act in such a way as denies the child the effective exercise of the right, granted by s.78(1)(a), to attend his or her own children's hearing.

The reporter does have a means of ensuring the relevant person's attendance **6–20** if this can be shown to be desirable in the interests of improving the welfare of the child. The Antisocial Behaviour etc. (Scotland) Act 2004 permits the reporter to apply for a "parenting order" in these circumstances and this order can require a specified person to comply with any requirement specified in the order[60]: this might include a requirement to attend a children's hearing. However, though the obligation to attend is thereby reinforced, the penalty for failure to comply with the order is the same as that for failure to attend in any case.[61] However, it may well be that a person is more likely to obey a court order specifically directed to him or her than to a statutory provision directed to all relevant persons and the power of reporters to seek this order may well be a persuasive tool to achieve the required end. In practice, parenting orders are very little used.

Exclusion of the relevant person

It sometimes happens that it will be against the interests of the child to be in **6–21** the same room as the relevant person, or one of the relevant persons. This might be because the child is afraid of that person, or is likely to be influenced in what he or she says, or because it would be upsetting and unsettling for the child to have any contact with a parent from whom he or she has been removed in

---

[57] 2011 Act s.75.
[58] See the comments on r.19 above, para.6–08.
[59] 2011 Act s.74(4).
[60] Antisocial Behaviour etc. (Scotland) Act 2004 ss.102(3) and 103(1).
[61] Antisocial Behaviour etc. (Scotland) Act 2004 s.107. The welfare of any child of the relevant person is to be taken into account in determining the penalty.

traumatic circumstances. Under the pre-1995 legislation, the only way to protect the child from such harmful contact was by excluding the child from all or part of the hearing. This did, however, have the serious drawback that the child was thereby denied the chance of participating in the decision-making process; in addition it suggested that the parent had a stronger right to attend the children's hearing than the child had. The rules were changed by the Children (Scotland) Act 1995, and since then the position has been that a child may still be excused from attending the hearing,[62] but alternatively the children's hearing may exclude the relevant person from the hearing for as long as is necessary, where it is satisfied of either of the conditions now laid down in s.76 of the Children's Hearings (Scotland) Act 2011. These conditions are as follows.

6–22   (a) That the presence at the hearing of the relevant person is preventing the hearing from obtaining the views of the child.[63] This deals with a variety of situations such as where there is a risk that the child will be influenced in what he or she says by the presence of the relevant person, or will be inhibited from speaking openly either because he or she is afraid of the relevant person or is embarrassed to talk about the matters being discussed in front of the relevant person. In addition, this ground might also be used if the relevant person is disrupting the hearing or, due to the person insisting on answering for the child, the child is being deprived of the chance to speak for him or herself. In determining whether this condition has been satisfied, the hearing should always bear in mind the fundamental importance of creating an environment in which the child feels able to speak openly and truthfully. Any situation in which the relevant person's attendance risks inhibiting the child from speaking might satisfy this condition. In a provision that allows the chairing member alone to exclude a relevant person, it is additionally provided in the 2013 Rules that at a grounds hearing the chairing member may exclude any relevant person if satisfied that the presence at the grounds hearing of that person is preventing the hearing from obtaining the acceptance or denial of the section 67 grounds from either the child or another relevant person.[64]

6–23   (b) That the presence of the relevant person at the hearing is causing, or is likely to cause, significant distress to the child.[65] This will commonly be because the relevant person has abused the child and the child is afraid of the relevant person, but it might also be, for example, when the child is settled in an environment away from the relevant person and the security of that settlement would be threatened by disturbing contact with the relevant person. In addition, it might also cover the situation in which the relevant person's behaviour at the hearing is so disruptive that the child is distressed as a consequence. The test here is deliberately easier to satisfy than the

---

[62] See above, paras 6–03—6–10.

[63] 2011 Act s.76(1)(a).

[64] 2013 Rules r.59(1). After the exclusion has ended under this provision the chairing member must explain to the relevant person what took place in his or her absence: r.59(2).

[65] 2011 Act s.76(1)(b). On the interplay between "likelihood" and "significant harm" see *Re B (A Child)* [2013] UKSC 33.

test for excusing the child's attendance[66] and so upset to the child will normally be dealt with by excluding the relevant person rather than by excusing the child.

The children's hearing is not obliged to exclude a person even when one or other **6–24** of the grounds for exclusion exists. It is a matter within its discretion. The power to exclude rests with the hearing as a whole and not solely with the chairing member.[67] As usual, decisions are made on a majority basis and the paramount consideration in making the decision is the welfare of the child,[68] but given that the relevant person's as well as the child's family life is being interfered with and, possibly, their civil rights, the relevant person's right to a fair hearing (including in particular their right to participate in the decision-making process[69]) must be taken into account. The children's hearing is required, in other words, to balance the benefit to the hearing process in excluding the relevant person with the fact that exclusion necessarily compromises that person's ECHR rights: the decision to exclude must therefore be proportionate to the legitimate aim of preventing significant harm to the child or ensuring that the child is free to express views. The decision to exclude a relevant person is not in itself appealable,[70] but it will always be good practice to specify in the statement of reasons why a decision to exclude was made. It is a power that should be used sparingly, and with sensitivity. Many parents will not like the thought of leaving their child alone at a hearing and some will refuse to leave, or refuse to leave without the child. The legal power to bring a child before a hearing ought to be explained to such a parent, as well as their right to be informed of what happens in their absence. It will, however, sometimes be better to allow a relevant person to stay if they insist rather than to risk them effectively bringing the hearing to a premature end by removing the child.

The power of exclusion does not extend to pre-hearing panels. Though there **6–25** is no limitation in s.76 to the part or parts of the children's hearing that the relevant person may be excluded from, the power to exclude a relevant person under this provision cannot be used to exclude a relevant person prospectively, that is to say from a subsequent hearing. Nor may the children's hearing exclude a relevant person from that part of a grounds hearing at which the section 67 grounds are put. The need for a relevant person's acceptance of the grounds cannot be avoided by excluding that person before the grounds are put, for "acceptance" of the grounds means acceptance by each relevant person (whether or not they attend) subject only to the relevant person's being excused attendance under s.74 and the hearing's power to proceed in the absence of a relevant person under s.75.[71] It follows that the hearing may never exclude the relevant person from that part of the grounds hearing at which the section 67

---

[66] 2011 Act s.73(3)(b): see above, para.6–05.

[67] Except the power to exclude under r.59(1) of the 2013 Rules: see above, para.6–22.

[68] 2011 Act ss.25 and 202(2).

[69] See fn.43 above.

[70] Though the subsequent dispositive decision might be appealable on the ground that there was a procedural irregularity in excluding the person when no reasonable hearing would have come to the view that one of the grounds for exclusion exists.

[71] 2011 Act ss.91(4) and 93(7). Non-attendance at a grounds hearing where the children's hearing exercises its power to proceed in the absence of the relevant person must be taken as denial of the ground by that relevant person.

grounds are explained and the relevant person's acceptance or denial is sought. There is nothing, however, to prevent section 67 grounds being explained to the child and the relevant person separately.

6–26   If a relevant person is excluded under s.76(2), the chairing member is obliged, at the end of the exclusion, to explain to such a person what took place in his or her absence.[72] The purpose of this requirement is, it is submitted, to protect the relevant person's right to participate in the decision-making process, by giving him or her the chance to respond to anything that happened during his or her exclusion. If this is so then the required explanation must be given *before* the hearing reaches its decision on the matter before it and it would, therefore, be a procedural irregularity for the hearing to make its decision during the exclusion and then explain to the relevant person, after the exclusion has ended, that the decision has been made. What requires to be explained is the generality of the discussion and the procedure during the relevant person's exclusion and not necessarily all the detail. The chairing member's explanation must be such as to allow the relevant person to understand the issues that were discussed in his or her absence, and their relative importance. There will usually be little point in excluding a relevant person solely in order to allow a child to speak freely on matters he or she does not want his or her parents to know about and good practice would require that it be made plain to both relevant person and child that what will take place must be revealed. Section 178 allows the children's hearing not to disclose to any person any information about the child if that disclosure would be likely to cause significant harm to the child.[73] This is a strict test that will not be satisfied merely because of the child's strong preference to keep something confidential. It is not generally possible, therefore, to use the exclusion as a means of protecting the child's confidentiality against a relevant person. The exclusion of the relevant person is likely to be more useful as a means of avoiding distress to the child rather than as a means of encouraging him or her to speak. The difficulty in achieving that aim, however, is that the relevant person must be present at the start of the hearing, at least in order to determine whether an exclusion is justified[74] and towards the end, in order to give the necessary explanation of what took place during the exclusion. In order to avoid the possibility of harmful contact the chairing member of the hearing may therefore sanction an arrangement in which the child is excused while the relevant person is present. There is no requirement that the section 67 grounds be explained, or the decision explained, to the child and the relevant person at the same time.

REPRESENTATIVES

6–27 The 1995 Act did not explicitly give any right to the child or relevant person to be accompanied at the hearing by a representative, though curiously that Act did allow "representatives" to be excluded. The 2011 Act now provides for a right

---

[72] 2011 Act s.76(3).

[73] This explicitly qualifies any obligation to explain what took place at a children's hearing: 2011 Act s.178(2)(a). See below, para.6–48.

[74] It is to be noted that while a pre-hearing panel may determine that a relevant person may be excused from attendance, it has no power to exclude a relevant person from the subsequent children's hearing.

of representatives to attend children's hearings. Section 78(1) provides that various people have a right to attend, including "a person representing the child" and "a person representing a relevant person in relation to the child".[75] This right is without prejudice to any right of the child or relevant person to legal representation at the children's hearing or pre-hearing panel by a solicitor or counsel.[76] There is nothing to prevent the child and the relevant person being represented by the same person. The relevant person's representative, but not (if different)[77] the child's representative, can be excluded from the children's hearing for as long as is necessary[78] on the same terms and conditions as the relevant person can be excluded[79]; if such a representative is excluded then what has taken place in his or absence must be explained to him or her by the chairing member after the exclusion has ended,[80] subject again to the rule in s.178 that nothing need be disclosed if that is likely to cause significant harm to the child. It would seem that a representative may not attend when the person he or she is representing does not (either because of having been excused attendance, exclusion or because of failure to turn up): the 2013 Rules specify the role of the representative as being to assist the accompanied person to discuss the issues arising for discussion before the children's hearing or pre-hearing panel.[81]

There is no limitation on who can act as a representative and it might include, **6–28** for example, a sibling, a cohabitant, a close family friend, a teacher, another member of the child's family who does not qualify as a relevant person, or a solicitor or other legal representative (though solicitor or counsel may accompany the represented person in addition to a representative).[82] The nature of the contribution to the discussion of the representative will depend to a large extent on their relationship with the person they are representing. It is not for the legislation to say how the right to bring a representative is to be exercised, and the role of "assisting the accompanied person to discuss the issues arising for discussion"[83] might include either providing support or advocacy, or where this is needed translation assistance. It is not for the children's hearing to ensure that a child or relevant person has a representative (except in the case where representation by solicitor or counsel is needed to ensure effective participation) but good practice might suggest that in some cases the hearing should defer making its decision with a suggestion to the child or relevant person that they could greatly benefit from the assistance at the next hearing of a representative, legal or otherwise. Indeed, if a children's hearing determines that, for the purpose of enabling the child or relevant person to participate effectively in the proceedings it is necessary that the child or relevant person be represented by a solicitor or counsel, and that it is unlikely that the child or relevant person will arrange to

---

[75] 2011 Act s.78(1)(b) and (d). The 2013 Rules r.11(1), also contemplates a person who wishes to be deemed to be a relevant person being accompanied by a representative at either a pre-hearing panel or a children's hearing.

[76] 2013 Rules r.11(2).

[77] The issue of who the person is representing ought to be clarified at the start of the hearing.

[78] 2011 Act s.77(2).

[79] For which see above, paras 6–21—6–26.

[80] 2011 Act s.77(3).

[81] 2013 Rules r.11(1). The chairing member may, however, permit the individual who would have acted as representative to be present under s.78(2), and ought to do so if he or she considers that the individual will have something relevant to contribute.

[82] 2013 Rules r.11(2).

[83] 2013 Rules r.11(1).

be so represented, the children's hearing or pre-hearing panel may require the reporter to notify the Scottish Legal Aid Board of that determination and of the name and address of the child or relevant person.[84]

SAFEGUARDERS

6–29 If a safeguarder has been appointed to the child by a children's hearing under s.30, or a pre-hearing panel under s.82, he or she has a right and indeed a duty (where reasonably practicable) to attend any children's hearing held while he or she is still in post.[85] A safeguarder appointed by a sheriff under s.31 (e.g. in an application to find established the grounds of referral under ss.93 or 94 or in an appeal under s.154) remains in post until (generally speaking) the time for appeal against a hearing's decision has expired without appeal or an appeal has been finally disposed of and so is likewise entitled to attend hearings subsequent to the sheriff's disposal.

JOURNALISTS

6–30 Though it very seldom happens that journalists attend hearings (for nothing can be published that is either intended to or likely to identify any child concerned in or connected with a hearing, the child's address or the child's school)[86] representatives of a newspaper or news agency do have the right to attend any children's hearing or pre-hearing panel.[87] They probably also have a right to take notes during the proceedings, but they certainly do not have the right to make audio or visual recordings of what is happening. The right to attend is subject to the power vested in the children's hearing to exclude a journalist from part or all of the hearing if either of the following two criteria is satisfied.

6–31   The first ground for exclusion is that it is necessary in order to obtain the views of the child.[88] This deals with the case of the child who is unwilling to speak while the journalist is present, for example because he or she is inhibited due to the large number of people present at the hearing, or is afraid that the journalist will report his or her views, or because the matters being discussed are of a particularly personal or sensitive nature. This provision might, in addition, be used to limit the number of journalists present at any one time. "Necessity" should not, it is submitted, be construed too strictly to mean that the journalist can be excluded only when the child will definitely remain silent if the journalist were to be present. Rather, it will be necessary to exclude a journalist whenever this is likely to make it easier for the child to speak openly, for it is always necessary for the hearing's proper consideration of the case that panel members be able to hear as much as possible from the child.

---

[84] 2013 Rules rr.50(7) and 61(1)(d) and (e).
[85] 2011 Act s.33(1)(b) and s.78(1)(f).
[86] 2011 Act s.182: see further below, paras 6–42—6–46.
[87] 2011 Act s.78(1)(i).
[88] 2011 Act s.78(5)(a).

The second ground for exclusion is that the presence of the journalist is **6–32** causing, or is likely to cause, significant distress to the child.[89] Attention must be paid to the word "significant", though again it should not be construed too strictly.[90] There is probably no requirement that the distress be of a long lasting nature, so long as it is genuine and severe at the moment. A mere preference on the part of the child is not sufficient and the journalist cannot be excluded simply because the child objects to his or her presence.[91]

Since both of the stated grounds for exclusion are directed towards the effect **6–33** on the child, neither would seem to be capable of permitting the exclusion of a journalist when the child is not present. The decision to exclude a journalist lies with the whole hearing and not solely with the chairing member. It is a decision to which both the obligation to regard the child's welfare as paramount and the obligation to take account of the child's views apply but exclusion cannot be justified solely on the basis of the child's welfare or wishes in the absence of one or other of the criteria for exclusion. The decision to exclude a journalist is not appealable.

If a journalist has been excluded from a children's hearing under the terms **6–34** of s.78(5), the chairing member may explain to the journalist, where it is appropriate to do so, the substance of what has taken place in the journalist's absence.[92] "The substance of what has taken place", which may be explained to an excluded journalist, appears on the face of it to be different from "what has taken place", which is what must be explained to an excluded relevant person[93] but it is unlikely that in practice it would ever be considered appropriate to reveal to a journalist more than must be revealed to a relevant person. In both cases it is the generality rather than the detail of what took place that is to be explained. While it is for the chairing member to explain to the journalist the substance of what took place in his absence, it is probably for the children's hearing as a whole to decide whether it is appropriate to give any explanation. The hearing might decide that no explanation should be given if, for example, the matters discussed were particularly personal.[94] If the journalist has been excluded because he or she has deliberately distressed the child, the hearing might quite properly take the view that the journalist has forfeited the right to an explanation. Indeed it is difficult to imagine a situation in which it would be appropriate to reveal to a journalist what occurred during his absence, given that there is so little that can be reported in any case, and given the nature of the criteria for exclusion. If the exclusion is to allow the child to speak freely, that aim could hardly be achieved if matters were subsequently to be revealed; and if the exclusion was because of the child's distress at the journalist's presence, the child's welfare is unlikely to be enhanced by giving information concerning the child. It should be remembered that the decision whether it is appropriate to reveal to a journalist the substance of what took place is to be

---

[89] 2011 Act s.78(5)(b).

[90] cf. in another context *Re B (A Child)* [2013] UKSC 33, per Lord Wilson at [26].

[91] Though there is nothing to stop the hearing requesting that the journalist voluntarily leaves in these circumstances. cf. 2011 Act s.78(3) where the child's or relevant person's objection acts as a veto to the attendance of persons permitted by the chairing member to attend.

[92] 2011 Act s.78(6).

[93] 2011 Act s.76(3) and (in relation to the relevant person's representative) s.77(3).

[94] The rule in 2011 Act s.178 applies here as well: nothing may be disclosed to any person where that disclosure would be likely to cause significant harm to the child.

determined by having regard to the welfare of the child as the paramount consideration[95] and should not be influenced by considerations of "freedom of the press" or "the public's right to know". This is entirely consistent with art.6(1) of the ECHR, which explicitly provides that "the press and public may be excluded ... where the interests of juveniles ... so require". As it is a matter that relates to the child, the child must be given the chance to express views on whether it is appropriate to give the excluded journalist an explanation.[96] It may be that in most cases it is only procedural information that should be revealed, such as "the section 67 grounds were denied and the reporter was directed to make an application to the sheriff for proof of the grounds", or "the hearing has deferred its decision to allow for further investigation". If any information is to be given to a journalist previously excluded, then this must be done in the presence of the child and the relevant person, since they have a right to attend all parts of the hearing.

Persons Attending in an Official Capacity

6–35 Though there is no direct obligation on the reporter to attend the hearing, it is invariable practice that he or she does so and, since the coming into force of the 2011 Act, the reporter has had an explicit right to attend.[97] In practice it will normally be the reporter who has drawn up the statement of grounds who will attend but this is not always possible and, since the Act gives the right to "the Principal Reporter", which includes any person exercising the functions under the Act of that individual,[98] any other reporter may attend in his or her place.

6–36 The reporter will not usually take an active part in the hearing but he or she may well be asked to contribute, for example in explaining why he or she came to the conclusion that it is necessary that a compulsory supervision order be made in respect of the child. Other persons attending in an official capacity will take an entirely passive, observatory, role. So for example members of an area support team,[99] acting in their capacity as such, are entitled to attend a hearing.[100] The statute does not in so many words limit this to members of the area support team serving the instant children's hearing, but the implication that this is so is unavoidable, for attendance at a hearing in their own area will usually have a purpose directed towards the monitoring of the panel members for whom they are responsible (justifying their attendance being a right) while attendance at a hearing in an area for which they have no responsibility can only be for their own educational and observatory purposes. It is suggested, therefore, that members of area support teams wishing to observe hearings in other areas require the chairing member's permission under s.78(2)(b) and their attendance is subject to the veto of the child and relevant person under s.78(3). Also authorised to attend a pre-hearing panel or a children's hearing is

---

[95] 2011 Act s.25.
[96] 2011 Act s.27.
[97] 2011 Act s.78(1)(e).
[98] 2011 Act Sch.3 para.10(1); 2013 Rules r.2(1).
[99] See Children's Hearings (Scotland) Act 2011 Sch.1 para.12.
[100] 2011 Act s.78(1)(h).

a constable, prison officer or other person who has in his or her lawful custody a person who has to[101] attend the pre-hearing panel or children's hearing.[102]

PERSONS ATTENDING WITH THE CHAIRING MEMBER'S PERMISSION

As well as the categories of person discussed above, who all have a right to **6–37** attend a children's hearing, the chairing member may also permit other persons to attend. He or she may give this permission in two separate situations and in deciding whether to do so the chairing member must always bear in mind his or her duty to take all reasonable steps to ensure that the number of people present at the same time is kept to a minimum.[103]

First, a person may attend a children's hearing if that attendance is consid- **6–38** ered by the chairing member to be necessary for the proper consideration of the matter before the children's hearing.[104] The most common category of person to be allowed to attend under this provision is the social worker who is involved in the case (or a stand-in social worker representing the relevant local authority). Though it is not legally mandatory for such a social worker to be present, a children's hearing will seldom be in a position to come to a satisfactory and fully informed decision unless the social worker allocated to the child's case, or a senior social worker with overseeing responsibility for that case, attends. This is because the social worker represents the local authority, whose duty it is to implement any compulsory supervision order. Other persons who can assist in the determination of where the child's interests lie may also be permitted to be present as active participants who are expected to contribute to the discussion, such as school teachers, key workers, groupwork leaders, and relatives and short-term foster carers.

Secondly, the chairing member may, otherwise than because the person's **6–39** attendance is considered necessary for the proper consideration of the matter before the hearing, grant permission to a person to attend the children's hearing.[105] Permission may not be granted by the chairing member under this provision to any person whose attendance is objected to by the child or relevant person.[106] No reason for the objection need be stated by the child or relevant person, and indeed no close inquiry into the child's capacity to object is appropriate. The chairing member ought specifically to ask the child and relevant persons whether they object to the presence of such a person and should not simply assume non-objection until objection is raised—for many children and their families will be unaware of their right to object. The most likely use of this discretion by the chairing member will be to permit observers who wish

---

[101] That is to say is subject to a duty to attend, and is therefore limited to the child or a relevant person.

[102] 2013 Rules r.20. The language used in this rule is that of "authorisation" to attend rather than "right" to attend, but it would appear that such a person cannot be prevented from attending if the person in their custody attends – even if the children's hearing considers it unnecessary or even potentially damaging to the child.

[103] 2011 Act s.78(4).

[104] 2011 Act s.78(2)(a).

[105] 2011 Act s.78(2)(b).

[106] 2011 Act s.78(3). Notice that this qualification does not apply to persons permitted by the chairing member to attend because their attendance is considered necessary for the proper consideration of the matter before the hearing.

to observe a hearing for educational or training purposes. It is considered essential that trainee panel members, as the most obvious example, have the opportunity to witness hearings before they themselves sit and in cases in which there is a small number of active participants it will be appropriate for the chairing member to permit them and their instructors to do so. In addition, trainee reporters, trainee social workers, students and others with a legitimate interest in learning about the children's hearing system may be permitted to attend. Observers take no active part in the hearing, though rules relating to confidentiality apply to them as to the participants. It is a courtesy to introduce any observers to the child and the relevant person before the hearing commences and to explain their role. Some observers, of course, have a right to be present irrespective of the chairing member's permission, such as journalists and members of area support teams, in their capacity as such: objections from the child and relevant persons do not take away these people's right and should not, therefore be invited by the chairing member.

OTHER PERSONS ATTENDING PARTICULAR HEARINGS

6–40 In respect of the limited children's hearing arranged under s.126 of the 2011 Act to review a contact direction,[107] certain additional individuals have the right to attend: any person (other than a relevant person) who appears to the reporter to have (or recently have had) significant involvement in the upbringing of the child, any person who has a contact order regulating contact between the individual and the child, any person who has a right of contact under a permanence order and any person who requested the s.126 hearing in the first place.[108]

6–41 At pre-hearing panels arranged to consider a deemed relevant person claim, the right to attend is extended beyond the child, relevant person and safeguarder to include the person who has requested a pre-hearing panel to determine that he or she be deemed a relevant person, and any individual (other than a relevant person) who appears to the reporter to have (or recently have had) significant involvement in the upbringing of the child.[109]

PROHIBITION ON PUBLICATION OF PROCEEDINGS

6–42 It is a criminal offence for any person to publish "protected information" if that publication is either intended to or likely to identify a child mentioned in the information, or his or her address or school as being that of such a child.[110]

---

[107] See below, paras 13–41—13–44.

[108] 2013 Rules r.42: the only person who may request a s.126 hearing who is not already on the list of attendees is a person who has or has recently had significant involvement in the upbringing of the child (as opposed to appearing to the reporter to have such involvement): Children's Hearings (Review of Contact Directions and Definition of Relevant Person) (Scotland) Order 2013 (SSI 2013/193) art.2(2).

[109] 2013 Rules r.45(2) and (3)(b)(i). See further above, paras 5–05—5–06.

[110] 2011 Act s.182(1). Similar rules apply to proceedings relating to parenting orders made under the Antisocial Behaviour etc. (Scotland) Act 2004 s.111, though no such rules apply to proceedings under that Act relating to ASBOs.

"Protected information" for this purpose means information in relation to a children's hearing,[111] an appeal against a decision of a children's hearing, proceedings before the sheriff either to establish section 67 grounds or to appeal against any decision of the hearing, and any appeal from any decision of the sheriff or sheriff principal made under the Children's Hearings (Scotland) Act 2011; it also includes information given to the reporter in respect of a child in reliance on or satisfaction of any provision in the 2011 Act or any other enactment.[112] The rule protects not only the referred child or child who is the subject of the proceedings but also any other child who becomes concerned in the proceedings, such as a sibling of the referred child or a child witness.[113] Any person who contravenes the prohibition will, subject to the defence mentioned below, be guilty of an offence and will be liable on summary conviction to a fine not exceeding level 4 on the standard scale.[114]

The prohibition is not limited to representatives of the media[115] or publishers **6–43** and distributors of material containing the information but includes individuals who take an active or professional or observational part in the hearing, such as reporters, social workers, panel members, parents, relatives and observers. Indeed it covers all individuals who received, and information contained in, the notice of hearings and pre-hearing panels that reporters are obliged to provide under the 2013 Rules.[116] The extension of the offence to cover such individuals provides an important protection to children's confidentiality.

A limited exception to this prohibition is contained in s.53 of the Criminal **6–44** Justice (Scotland) Act 2003, under which the reporter may inform the victim of an offence of what action he or she has taken in the case, and of any disposal of the case.

Meaning of "publish"

To publish includes: (a) to publish matter in a programme service, as defined **6–45** by s.201 of the Broadcasting Act 1990; and (b) to cause matter to be published.[117] The extent of "publish" is wider than this, and the word has to be interpreted in the light of its clear aim, which is to protect the privacy of children. However, it is likely that for one person to inform another person is not to "publish", which probably requires a more general communication, though it is not necessary that the communication be to a large number of individuals. "Publish" means, it is submitted, to act in any way that makes it likely that the information will fall into the public domain. So it is not a publication for a relevant person to show the documents he or she receives from the reporter to a legal adviser, but it may well be publication to show them to a representative of the press. There is likely to be a large grey area here in which it is unclear whether a sharing of information is or is not a publication, and it is submitted that both the motivation with which the information is passed and the legitimacy of the

---

[111] Or a pre-hearing panel: 2011 Act s.182(9), as amended by the Children's Hearings (Scotland) Act 2011 (Modification of Primary Legislation) Order 2013 (SSI 2013/211) Sch.1 para.20(2).
[112] 2011 Act s.182(9).
[113] *McArdle v Orr*, 1994 S.L.T. 463.
[114] 2011 Act s.182(2).
[115] As was a similar prohibition contained in s.58 of the Social Work (Scotland) Act 1968.
[116] See above, paras 4–24—4–35.
[117] 2011 Act s.182(9).

interest in the child's case that the receiver of the information has are both relevant to the question of whether there is "publication".

Defence

6–46   It is a defence in proceedings relating to this offence for the accused to prove that he did not know, or have reason to suspect, that the publication of the protected information was likely to identify the child mentioned in the protected information, or the address or the school of such a child.[118] The defence will be available, for example, to a distributor of a newspaper which, unknown to him, carries the prohibited material. Those responsible for the contents of the material, such as newspaper editors, will not be able to rely on this defence since they are or should be in a position to know the effect of what they publish. The onus is on the accused to prove his own ignorance.

Permitting publication

6–47   The sheriff,[119] in relation to proceedings before him, the Court of Session in relation to appeal proceedings before them, and the Scottish Ministers in relation to proceedings at a children's hearing or pre-hearing panel are empowered to dispense with the prohibition on publishing protected information, or relax it to such extent as the sheriff, court or Ministers consider appropriate.[120] The children's hearing itself (or pre-hearing panel) has no power to grant such a dispensation. Dispensation can be given only in the interests of justice. In making their decision, however, sheriffs and the Court of Session must regard the child's welfare as their paramount consideration,[121] and this has the result, it is submitted, that the publication ban can be lifted only when this is in the interests of justice *to the child*; circumstances in which this will be so are difficult to visualise but might, for example, cover the case of a child who wishes publicly to clear his or her name from a misrepresentation made in a previous, unauthorised, publication. Beyond that, and in any case, the interests of justice will require that the individual's right to private life be protected and that the decision to dispense with the publication prohibition does not interfere unduly with that important right.[122] The Scottish Ministers are not governed by s.25, but the welfare of the child will in any case be a weighty consideration in their balancing of the interests of justice. If they do decide to lift the publication ban this should be only in the most exceptional circumstances and only to the extent that is absolutely necessary to achieve the particular interests of justice that have been identified. Young people are ill-equipped to deal with media scrutiny which is seldom, if ever, motivated by the interests of the young person.[123] The interests of persons other than the child may well be taken into

---

[118] 2011 Act s.182(3).

[119] Which includes the sheriff principal: Interpretation and Legislative Reform (Scotland) Act 2010 s.25 and Sch.1.

[120] 2011 Act s.182(4)–(6), (9).

[121] 2011 Act s.25 applies here as to any other decision affecting the child.

[122] See *X (Formally Known as Mary Bell) v SO* [2003] E.M.L.R. 37; *Clayton v Clayton* [2006] Fam. 83; *Re B (Children)* [2010] 1 F.L.R. 1708.

[123] The case of *X v BBC*, 2005 S.L.T. 796 provides a salutary warning. There a 17-year-old girl agreed to take part in a documentary about daily business at Glasgow Sheriff Court, including her own court appearances there. She bitterly regretted that involvement and sought to have her agreement reduced either at common law or under the Age of Legal Capacity (Scotland) Act 1991.

account by the Scottish Ministers, but again it is difficult to visualise circumstances in which lifting the publication ban would be appropriate.

CONFIDENTIALITY

The offence of publication, the requirement that the hearing be conducted in **6–48** private, and the limitations on who may attend the hearing are all designed to ensure that the child's circumstances are kept as confidential as possible, privacy being invariably in the interests of the child. That purpose is further strengthened by the rule in s.178(1) that a children's hearing need not disclose to a person any information about the child to whom the hearing relates or about the child's case if disclosure of that information to that person would be likely to cause significant harm to the child. This provision is explicitly given precedence over the rule that a relevant person must be given an explanation of what took place at the hearing while the relevant person was excluded[124] and this allows a hearing, if in limited and tightly drawn circumstances, to offer the child a modicum of confidentiality even against his or her parents. It is, however, to be noted that the grounds upon which a relevant person may be excluded from a part of the hearing are different from the ground upon which information might be withheld.[125] If it wishes to exercise this power, the hearing must perform a balancing exercise between the relevant person's right to a fair hearing and the child's right to be protected from harm. There is always a risk that, if material is not disclosed and the opportunity thereby given for it to be challenged, the wrong decision will be reached as a result and that is *in every case* harmful to the child. So the hearing must be satisfied not only that there is a real (and not a fanciful or over-cautious) possibility of harm that can properly be described as significant being caused by disclosure, but also that, balancing that risk against the interests of the relevant person in having an opportunity to respond to what the child has revealed, and taking into account the harm that wrong decisions inevitably cause, the interests of the child clearly point to non-disclosure.[126] Section 178(1) is also given precedence over the requirement to provide reasons for the decision made by the hearing.[127] That reasons for any judicial or quasi-judicial decision need to be clear, and honest, is an important element of the rule of law as affording those with a right of appeal the basis upon which to do so and for that reason hearings need to be very careful to ensure that information that is, truly, crucial to their decision is withheld from the statement of reasons for that decision only when the likelihood of significant harm to the child from disclosure of the information has unequivocally been made out, and that its withholding is proportionate to the protective aim of the provision. Section 178 does not, in its terms, permit pre-hearing panels to withhold information, though that panel may (as will be seen immediately below) deal with non-disclosure requests.

---

[124] 2011 Act s.178(2)(a).
[125] "Significant distress" in s. 76, and "significant harm" in s.178.
[126] *Re D (Minors) (Adoption Reports: Confidentiality)* [1996] A.C. 593, per Lord Mustill at 615; *Re A (A Child)* [2012] UKSC 60, per Lady Hale at [21].
[127] 2011 Act s.178(2)(b)(ii).

NON-DISCLOSURE REQUESTS

6–49 Section 178 might also be used to justify withholding documents or parts of documents from specified individuals and, though it is the reporter who is obliged to ensure that the relevant information is removed (and who must inform the persons to whom the documents are given the identity of the person from whom the information is being withheld, and what that information is)[128] it is always to be remembered that the decision to withhold information under s.178 rests always and solely with the children's hearing. (The reporter has an independent, but much more limited, right to withhold information concerning the whereabouts of the child or any relevant person if he or she considers that disclosure of that information would be likely to cause significant harm to the child or any relevant person.[129] This might be necessary where, for example, there is a risk of exposing the child or relevant person to domestic abuse).

6–50 A "non-disclosure request" may be made to the children's hearing (or pre-hearing panel)[130] by the reporter or (through the reporter) by any person[131]: this is a request that any document be withheld from the child, relevant person or any other specified person on the ground that disclosure of either the document or any information contained in it would be likely to cause sigificant harm to the child.[132] The request must specify both the part of the document that is sought to be withheld, and why, and also the person to whom the document is not to be disclosed, and why.[133] Other than in the case of a grounds hearing, the children's hearing or pre-hearing panel must consider the non-disclosure request made prior to the hearing or panel at the beginning of the children's hearing or pre-hearing panel; in the case of a grounds hearing it must be considered prior to the making of a decision on whether to make a compulsory supervision order.[134] While considering the matter the person from whom the documents are requested not to be disclosed must be excluded from the children's hearing or pre-hearing panel, but once the decision is made that person must be invited to return and be advised of what the hearing or panel has decided.[135] It is to be remembered that: (i) that person may be the child him or herself; and (ii) disclosure, even when potentially harmful, is a necessary feature of the rule of law not only to ensure a level playing field for the various interests that are involved but also because it is an effective means of avoiding decisions being made on the basis of information that may be inaccurate or incomplete. "Significant harm" to the child must be shown and this is a difficult test to satisfy in other than the clearest of cases: it is the information and not its revelation that must be shown to cause harm, for difficult information, sensitively revealed, may well reduce the harmful effects on the child. If the non-disclosure request is rejected the children's hearing or pre-hearing panel must ensure that the document is given

---

[128] 2013 Rules r.15.

[129] 2013 Rules r.16.

[130] 2013 Rules r.84(4).

[131] The reporter may make a request on his or her own initiative, but must submit a non-disclosure request he or she receives from any other person: 2013 Rules r.85.

[132] 2013 Rules r.84(1).

[133] 2013 Rules r.84(3): there is likely to be substantial overlap in why information should be withheld and who it should be withheld from.

[134] 2013 Rules r.86(1) and (2).

[135] 2013 Rules r.86(3)–(5).

to the excluded person at such time and in such manner as it considers appropriate having regard to the child's best interests.[136] The children's hearing or pre-hearing panel may consider it not in the child's best interests to postpone the hearing to allow the person time to read the document—this will depend on how complex, and how crucial to their decision, the document is. The same process applies where the non-disclosure request is made during the course of the children's hearing or pre-hearing panel by the child, relevant person, safeguarder reporter or author of any document.[137]

A non-disclosure request may not be made in respect of: **6–51**

    (a) the statement of grounds;
    (b) a copy of any remit from a court under s.49 of the Criminal Procedure (Scotland) Act 1995;
    (c) a copy of any requirement of the reporter to arrange a children's hearing made by a sheriff under the Antisocial Behaviour etc. (Scotland) Act 2004 or the sheriff's statement as to which section 67 ground he makes the requirement on; or
    (d) any order or warrant to which the child is subject under the 2011 Act or the 2013 Rules.[138]

---

[136] 2013 Rules r.86(6).
[137] 2013 Rules r.87.
[138] 2013 Rules r.84(2).

CHAPTER 7

THE GROUNDS HEARING

INTRODUCTION

7–01 No compulsory supervision order may be made over a child unless one or more of the section 67 grounds apply in relation to the child (though that is not, as we will see, sufficient on its own to justify the making of an order). Whether or not grounds apply is, therefore, the first substantive determination that a children's hearing must make. Whenever the reporter has drawn up a statement of grounds in respect of a child who is not presently subject to a compulsory supervision order the chairing member must seek acceptance or denial of the grounds set out in the statement of grounds. The hearing at which this is done is called "the grounds hearing".[1] A grounds hearing may also be arranged in respect of a child who is already subject to a compulsory supervision order: this would be appropriate where the reporter wishes the hearing to consider new grounds which he or she considers to have arisen since the compulsory supervision order was made. References to the decision of whether to make a compulsory supervision order are, in these circumstances, to be read as references to the decision to review the existing compulsory supervision order.[2] But here too the hearing will open with the chairing member seeking acceptance or denial of the grounds: if they are accepted then the grounds hearing is to be treated as if it were a hearing to review the compulsory supervision order.[3] Sometimes it is unnecessary to hold a grounds hearing before a children's hearing can consider whether it is necessary to make a compulsory supervision order, because in some limited circumstances a court of law will already have found that section 67 grounds apply.[4]

Introductions and explanations

7–02 The grounds hearing, like all children's hearings and pre-hearing panels, opens with the chairing member introducing him or herself and the other two members of the hearing, by name, to those who are attending and explaining the purpose of the hearing.[5] If it is unclear to the chairing member who any indi-

---

[1] Children's Hearings (Scotland) Act 2011 s.90.

[2] 2011 Act s.97(3).

[3] 2011 Act s.91(2), as substituted in these circumstances by s.97(4).

[4] This happens when a criminal court has established that the child is a victim of a Sch.1 offence (Criminal Procedure (Scotland) Act 1995 s.48) or the child has pled guilty to or been found guilty of a criminal offence (Criminal Procedure (Scotland) Act 1995 s.49) or the reporter has been required to refer the child to a hearing by a court acting under s.12 of the Antisocial Behaviour etc (Scotland) Act 2004. See above, paras 4–13—4–16.

[5] Children's Hearings (Scotland) Act 2011 (Rules of Procedure in Children's Hearings) Rules 2013 (SSI 2013/194) (hereinafter "2013 Rules") r.58(1) and (in relation to pre-hearing panels) r.48(1).

vidual person attending the hearing is, the chairing member ought to require the individual to identify him or herself, for this is the only way that the chairing member can fulfil his or her duty to ensure that only those who have a right or a duty to attend at the hearing do so. Hearing members need to be aware from the start of the status of each attending person. The child, or if too young the relevant person, or if no relevant person is present some other participant who can speak to these matters, should then be asked to give the child's name and address. The chairing member is expressly required to ask the person in respect of whom the hearing has been arranged to declare his or her age (unless the chairing member considers that the person would not be capable of understanding the question).[6] The person may subsequently make another declaration as to his or her age, and the hearing itself may make a determination of the age of the person who is the subject of the hearing.[7] This is to ensure that the person referred is a "child" for the purposes of the hearing[8] and while the hearing will normally take at face-value the age declared by the person asked it is open to the hearing to determine, on the basis of other information it has, that the person's age is other than that declared.[9] Since the purpose is to ensure that the person is a child, and therefore subject to the jurisdiction of the children's hearing, the hearing ought to make a determination of the person's age that is different from the person's declaration only when to do so will make some practical difference in terms of the hearing's right to proceed, or its available options, or to correct an obvious error. The person is taken for the purposes of the Children's Hearings (Scotland) Act 2011 to be of the age worked out on the basis of the person's own declaration or in accordance with the hearing's determination, and nothing done by a children's hearing in relation to a person is invalidated if it is subsequently proved that the age of the person is not that worked out by either of these means.[10] The chairing member must also ask the child whether the documents provided to the child accurately reflect any views expressed by the child,[11] unless the chairing member considers that, taking account of the child's age and maturity, it would not be appropriate to do so.[12] If the child confirms that the documents provided do *not* accurately reflect his or her views, the chairing member must endeavour to clarify the child's views on the relevant matter.[13] Though not required by statute, it is also good practice for the chairing member to allow the relevant persons also to challenge any perceived inaccuracies in the information and documents they have been supplied with.

---

[6] 2011 Act s.124(2) and (4).

[7] 2011 Act s.124(3) and (5).

[8] See above, para.2–10.

[9] See, in the context of an immigration dispute, the challenge to the determination of the petitioner's age in *L v Angus Council*, 2012 S.L.T. 304.

[10] 2011 Act s.124(6) and (7).

[11] And the Rules state that document makers must include the views of the child: 2013 Rules r.8.

[12] 2011 Act s.121. Though this checking might usefully be postponed until the views of the child are being discussed during the substantive part of the hearing, doing so at the opening acts as a useful protection against forgetting to do so later. In any case, the rule in s.121(2) is in absolute terms and applies to all hearings, even those that do not proceed to a substantive discussion such as, typically, a grounds hearing. On balance, therefore, it will be better to make this question part of the opening process, though hearing members should never use any confirmation provided as a reason in itself not to reopen the question of the child's views at the substantive discussion.

[13] 2013 Rules r.58(2).

7–03   Once these preliminary matters have been dealt with the grounds hearing may proceed to its substantive business of determining whether the section 67 grounds specified by the reporter in the statement of grounds prepared under s.89 are accepted or not. What it may do thereafter depends upon whether the grounds are properly accepted or not.

EXPLAINING THE SECTION 67 GROUNDS

7–04   A children's hearing is entitled to consider the question of whether it is necessary to make a compulsory supervision order in respect of a child only when the section 67 grounds upon which the reporter has referred the child to the hearing have been either accepted in whole or in part by the child and each relevant person, or been found established by the sheriff on an application under ss.101–106.[14] It follows that, whenever the reporter has prepared a statement of grounds under s.89, the chairing member of the grounds hearing must, at the opening of the hearing: (i) explain to the child and each relevant person each section 67 ground that is specified in the statement of grounds; and (ii) ask them whether they accept that each ground applies in relation to the child[15]; the "opening of the hearing" means the stage before any discussion on any substantive matter takes place but after the preliminary introductions and determinations discussed immediately above. At this point in the proceedings, the only question for the children's hearing is whether the section 67 grounds are accepted or not.

7–05   Explaining the section 67 grounds to, and seeking their acceptance by, the child and relevant persons serves two purposes. First, the acceptance or denial by the child and relevant persons that the section 67 grounds apply in whole or in part in relation to the child determines which of two different courses of proceeding the hearing must thereafter take. And secondly, it establishes the basis of fact upon which the children's hearing must found its determination, if the grounds do apply, of whether it is necessary to make a compulsory supervision order. The chairing member ought, before explaining the grounds to them, to ensure that the child and relevant person understand that it is not open to the hearing, at this stage of the proceedings, to enter into any discussion of the section 67 grounds, and that all the hearing can do is: (i) explain each section 67 ground that is specified in the statement of grounds drawn up by the reporter; and (ii) determine whether these grounds are accepted or denied by the child and each relevant person. It is sometimes difficult to distinguish an explanation from a discussion, but it must be done. Parents frequently attempt, in response to the chairing member's explanation, to enter into a discussion of how they see the situation, but the hearing are unable, at this point, to give any consideration to what is said. All that should be sought at this point is, effectively, a yes or no answer from the child and relevant person, and it may sometimes be appropriate for the chairing member to inform them that all they are required to do is to give such a one word answer. (It should also be explained, of course, that there will be opportunity for full discussion at a later stage, if the grounds are accepted or found to apply.) If the child or relevant person is unable to give a clear answer

---

[14] On applications to establish grounds, see Ch.8 below.
[15] 2011 Act s.90(1).

then the chairing member should attempt a further explanation, unless it is apparent that no explanation will be sufficient to allow the child or relevant person to give a definite answer. The chairing member must be careful not to appear to put pressure on either the child or the relevant person to secure an acceptance of the grounds of referral: at this stage in the proceedings, the children's hearing is entirely disinterested in whether or not section 67 grounds apply in relation to the child, for it is as much in the interests of a child in respect of whom grounds do not apply to have this established as it is in the interests of a child in respect of whom grounds do apply to have that established. The child and relevant person must be as free from pressure as possible to give one answer rather than another—except pressure to be truthful.[16]

To whom the explanation must be given

The duty to explain the section 67 grounds falls on the chairing member of the **7–06** children's hearing, and the explanation must be given to "the child and each relevant person".[17] The obligation to explain the section 67 grounds does not apply where the grounds hearing is satisfied that the child or relevant person would not be capable of understanding an explanation[18] but other than that the obligation to explain is absolute. It often happens, however, that the child or relevant person does not attend the grounds hearing. If the child fails to attend, the hearing may either require the reporter to arrange another grounds hearing[19] or, alternatively, discharge the referral.[20] Each member of the children's hearing will give their decision on which of these two alternatives to adopt, and the chairing member must confirm the overall decision and its reasons.[21] If the referral is discharged the relevant person and any appointed safeguarder must be informed of their right to appeal that discharge.[22] If the referral is not discharged at this stage (and it would be unusual to do so) then, on the application of the reporter on cause shown, the hearing may grant a warrant to secure attendance of the child at the rearranged grounds hearing.[23] The child's reason for non-attendance, if known, will obviously be central to whether there is any cause to grant such a warrant, which will authorise the detaining of the child in a place of safety and the bringing of the child before the rearranged grounds hearing.[24]

No such warrant is available in respect of a relevant person who has failed to **7–07** attend the grounds hearing, notwithstanding that all relevant persons have a duty, under s.74, to attend at all children's hearings (including, of course, grounds hearings) and failure to do so can be a criminal offence. A relevant person may be absent from a hearing because: (i) he or she has simply failed to show up at the hearing; (ii) he or she has been excused from attending a hearing by a previous

---

[16] The child and relevant person are not, of course, on oath so they have no legal obligation to be truthful. But it should be explained to them that it will *always and without exception* be in the child's interests for truthful answers to be given.

[17] 2011 Act s.90(1)(a).

[18] 2011 Act ss.90(2) and 94(1)(a).

[19] 2011 Act s.95.

[20] 2013 Rules r.64(3).

[21] 2013 Rules r.64(1) and (2).

[22] 2013 Rules r.64(4). In fact, the child who has not attended the grounds hearing has the right to appeal a discharge too.

[23] 2011 Act s.123. See above, paras 6–11—6–14.

[24] 2011 Act s.88(1)(a)(ii) and (iii).

hearing or a pre-hearing panel; or (iii) he or she has been excluded from the hearing. In the first case, the children's hearing is given the power by s.75 to proceed, if it considers it appropriate to do so, in the relevant person's absence. Though the duty to explain the section 67 grounds is not removed when the relevant person fails to attend the hearing,[25] "acceptance" (and non-acceptance) of the grounds is stated to mean acceptance (or non-acceptance) by each relevant person subject to ss.74 and 75.[26] Though it could have been expressed more clearly, this means that a grounds hearing that chooses to proceed in the absence of a relevant person does not need to seek acceptance or non-acceptance of the section 67 grounds from a relevant person who was required to attend the grounds hearing but failed to do so. The second case, that of the relevant person who is excused from attending under s.74, ought never to arise in relation to the grounds hearing (notwithstanding that acceptance or non-acceptance is stated to be subject to s.74)[27], for the basis of excusal will never be made out—a hearing or pre-hearing panel may excuse a relevant person from attending only when it would be unreasonable to require their attendance, or their attendance would be unnecessary for a proper consideration of the matter before the hearing.[28] The only circumstance in which it would be unreasonable to require a relevant person's attendance at a grounds hearing is when that person would not understand the grounds, in which case the duty to explain does not arise[29]: if the relevant person would be able to understand, his or her attendance at the hearing at which acceptance or denial of the section 67 grounds is sought can never, it is submitted, be said to be unnecessary for a proper consideration of the matter before the hearing, since the very matter before the grounds hearing is whether the child and *each* relevant person accepts the grounds. In the third case, that of the relevant person being excluded from the hearing under s.76, it should be noted that acceptance or non-acceptance is not stated to be subject to s.76 and so even if the grounds for exclusion do apply the duty to explain the section 67 grounds and to seek their acceptance still applies. A non-acceptance can never be avoided, therefore, by excluding a relevant person from the grounds hearing even when exclusion is justified.[30]

What must be explained

7–08   The chairing member is obliged to explain "each section 67 ground that is specified in the statement of grounds"[31]: this includes more than a mere recitation of whichever of the section 67 grounds the reporter believes applies in relation to the child, but must also involve an explanation of the facts upon which that belief is based.[32] (It is, however, as explained below, the ground itself rather than the ground and the supporting facts that require to be accepted or denied.)

---

[25] The duty to explain is subject only to 2011 Act s.94 (i.e. the child or relevant person being unable to understand the explanation): s.90(2).
[26] 2011 Act ss.91(4) and 93(7).
[27] 2011 Act ss.91(4) and 93(7).
[28] 2011 Act s.74(3).
[29] 2011 Act s.90(1) is subject to s.94.
[30] If exclusion is necessary (see above, paras 6–21—6–26) the grounds hearing must, it is submitted, give an explanation to and seek acceptance of the grounds from the child and the disruptive relevant person separately.
[31] 2011 Act s.90(1)(a).
[32] 2011 Act s.89(3).

The duty of the chairing member is not simply to read out the statement of grounds prepared by the reporter, but to explain what these grounds mean, in terms that the child and relevant person are likely to understand. Explaining the section 67 grounds is sometimes the most difficult task that faces the chairing member of the children's hearing, for it may involve an explanation of the law, for example the concept of art and part guilt, or the meaning of "reasonable excuse" for not attending school regularly, or the concept of "household" or "close connection", or the nature of a Schedule 1 offence. It is, however, worth spending some time on explaining what the section 67 grounds mean since this will very directly protect the right of the child and the relevant person to deny the stated grounds and so have them tested by evidence in a court. And it is also likely to help the discussion when the children's hearing moves on to a determination of whether it is necessary to make a compulsory supervision order that the child and family understand precisely what it is that has concerned the reporter sufficiently for him or her to decide to arrange a children's hearing. It is to the detriment of a child who may be in need of a compulsory supervision order to have a determination of that question delayed by applying to the sheriff for proof when, with a careful explanation, the child and relevant person could have been brought to an understanding of the section 67 grounds. The chairing member should, therefore, seek advice, whether from the National Convener or elsewhere, before the hearing if the grounds contain references to legal concepts with which he or she is unfamiliar.[33]

ACCEPTANCE OR DENIAL OF GROUNDS

Once the chairing member has explained to the child and each relevant person **7–09** each of the section 67 grounds that are specified in the statement of grounds, and the children's hearing is satisfied that the explanation has been understood,[34] the chairing member must then ask the child and each relevant person to indicate whether or not they accept that the grounds stated by the reporter apply in relation to the child, for it is the very purpose of the explanation to allow the child and the relevant person properly to understand that question, and to respond in an informed manner. There are three possible responses that the child and the relevant person can give, and how the children's hearing can proceed thereafter depends upon which response is given: (1) they may all accept each of the section 67 grounds specified in the statement of grounds: (2) one or more of them may deny completely the grounds specified; or (3) one or more of them may accept the grounds in part and deny them in part.

What must be accepted

The statute requires the acceptance or denial of the grounds specified in "the **7–10** statement of grounds", which is defined in s.89 as a statement setting out "(a) which of the section 67 grounds the Principal Reporter believes applies in relation to the child, and (b) the facts on which that belief is based". The chairing

---

[33] 2011 Act s.8(2)(a). The duty to provide legal advice is not delegable by the National Convener to an Area Support Team: Sch.1 para.14(3). This does not, however, prevent the chairing member accessing other resources such as training manuals and the like.

[34] On lack of understanding, see below, paras 7–20—7–22.

member is obliged to explain to the child and relevant person "each section 67 ground that is specified in the statement of grounds" and to "ask them whether they accept that each ground applies in relation to the child.[35] That explanation will necessarily involve the chairing member explaining the facts contained in the statement of grounds as well as the specified grounds themselves and the distinction between the two may not be readily apparent to the child or relevant person. The chairing member may well ask for acceptance or denial of the supporting facts, but that is only in order to lead to the acceptance or denial of the grounds. A denial of the facts (or some of them) may be accompanied by an acceptance of the grounds and this may be regarded, for statutory purposes, as an acceptance—unless it indicates a lack of understanding.[36] Perhaps more difficult would be if the child and relevant person acknowledge the accuracy of the facts but deny the grounds themselves, perhaps on the assertion that the facts, true in themselves, do not indicate or support the ground specified by the reporter. In that case the chairing member ought to explain again the nature of the grounds and why accepting the facts suggests an acceptance of the grounds: but if, after all, the child or relevant person continues to deny the stated grounds then this is a non-acceptance even when the facts supporting the ground are accepted or not challenged. More frequently there will be an acceptance of some of the facts, or at least an acknowledgement that they are partly true. So long as there are enough of the stated facts accepted to amount to a section 67 ground, together (crucially) with an acceptance of the ground stated by the reporter, the children's hearing may proceed to a consideration of whether it is necessary to make a compulsory supervision order. So for example it is an acceptance of a section 67 ground based on school non-attendance if the child accepts that he or she has not attended school regularly without reasonable excuse, but denies that it is to the extent specified in the statement of facts; likewise it is an acceptance of a ground based on the commission of an offence if the child admits one offence when the reporter has specified another (at least when the two offences can be justified by the same set of facts)[37]. If a fact in the statement of grounds is denied while the ground itself and other facts sufficient to support it are accepted there is nothing to prevent the hearing subsequently discussing the fact that has been denied, but the safer course, if the fact is likely to be central to the outcome, is to treat the denial of the fact as a denial of the essence of the ground, so requiring an application to the sheriff to determine which facts are established by evidence. Indeed in any case of real doubt as to whether there is acceptance or not the only safe course is to treat it as a denial and either discharge the referral or require the reporter to apply to the sheriff for proof.

7–11   The children's hearing may amend the statement of grounds by removing any facts denied,[38] though this is possible only when the hearing is satisfied

---

[35] 2011 Act s.90(1).

[36] For which see below, paras 7–20—7–22.

[37] It would be denial of the ground if, say, the reporter specified a ground of theft and the child admits an assault. cf. Act of Sederunt (Child Care and Maintenance Rules) 1997 (SI 1997/291(S.19)) (as amended by the Act of Sederunt (Children's Hearings (Scotland) Act 2011) (Miscellaneous Amendments) 2013 (SSI 2013/172)) r.3.50, under which the sheriff in an application to establish grounds can determine that an offence has occurred if the evidence establishes it, whether or not it is the offence specified by the reporter. Rule 3.50 does not apply to children's hearings, but only to sheriffs.

[38] 2013 Rules r.59(4).

that the amendment does not call into question the acceptance of the section 67 ground by the child or any relevant person.[39] The ground itself may not be amended.[40]

Acceptance of all of the specified grounds

Where the child and each of the relevant persons who attend the grounds **7–12** hearing have understood the explanation given by the chairing member and they all accept that the section 67 grounds specified in the statement of grounds prepared by the reporter under s.89 apply in relation to the child, the hearing may then move straight on to a discussion of the case in order to determine whether it is necessary to make a compulsory supervision order.[41] The grounds hearing becomes, effectively, a dispositive hearing and it has the same three options available to it as to any other hearing that has been able fully to discuss the child's case: (i) defer making a decision on whether to make a compulsory supervision order until a subsequent hearing; (ii) if satisfied that it is necessary to do so for the protection, guidance, treatment or contol of the child, make a compulsory supervision order; or (iii) if not so satisfied discharge the referral.[42] The latter two options (both of which are governed by the welfare principle)[43] can be adopted by the grounds hearing only after a full discussion of the child's circumstances, in which all attending parties are given an opportunity to express their views as to which of these options would be more appropriate. Deferral, which may be decided upon after the full discussion or at any point before, will be appropriate if the hearing has not had sufficient time to consider the background reports, or the members of the hearing feel that they need more information, or that they need to appoint a safeguarder, or for any other reason they do not feel it appropriate for them to make an immediate decision on whether to make a compulsory supervision order or to discharge the referral. In order to allow the children's hearing to put itself in a position to make a dispositive decision, it has various powers on deferral to seek any report or give such direction as is necessary to enable it to make its decision.[44] In addition, it may appoint a safeguarder, set the date for the subsequent hearing, require the reporter to notify the Scottish Legal Aid Board of the child or relevant person's name and address if it feels the child or relevant person needs to be represented by a solicitor or counsel and require the reporter to arrange for an interpreter.[45] The hearing may also make an interim compulsory supervision order. All these matters are discussed more fully below.[46]

Denial of the grounds

Where either the child and the attending relevant persons or one or more of **7–13** them deny all of the section 67 grounds specified in the statement of grounds drawn up by the reporter under s.89, the grounds hearing has two options: it

---

[39] 2013 Rules r.59(6).
[40] 2013 Rules r.59(5).
[41] See Chs. 9 and 10 below.
[42] 2011 Act s.91(1)(a), (2) and (3).
[43] 2011 Act s.25.
[44] 2013 Rules r.61(1)(b) and (g).
[45] 2013 Rules r.61(1)(a), (c)–(f).
[46] See Ch.10.

may either: (i) discharge the referral in whole; or (ii) direct the reporter to apply to the sheriff for a determination on whether each ground that is not accepted by the child or relevant person is established.[47] The choice of which option to adopt is governed by the welfare principle,[48] but one of the practical difficulties facing the grounds hearing is that this decision has to be made only on the basis of the reports already presented to them. No discussion is permitted with the family or the social worker or anyone else in order to assist the hearing to determine which option is the more appropriate, and the grounds hearing will often not be in a position, without such a discussion, to determine wherein the child's interests lie. The choice, therefore, is usually made by having regard to the seriousness of the allegations made in the statement of grounds. Unless the allegations are considered to be obviously trivial, few children's hearings will be willing to make the dispositive decision of discharging the referral without a full discussion of the child's circumstances in which everyone has a chance to participate. This reluctance is entirely appropriate. Referrals should be discharged after a denial of the grounds only when the grounds hearing is clearly of the view, on the information it has, that even if the section 67 grounds are found established, the decision of the children's hearing would be to not make a compulsory supervision order, or to not vary the terms of any existing order. This will occur most often with referrals of children currently subject to a compulsory supervision order with whom it is felt that the establishment of further grounds would serve no useful purpose, but it could occur (if more rarely) with initial referrals too, for example where the ground was a minor incidence of misbehaviour and the process of being brought before a children's hearing has already persuaded the child that this should not be repeated.

7–14   In deciding whether to discharge the referral or to direct the reporter to make an application to the sheriff, each member of the grounds hearing must state their own decision, and its reasons, and the chairing member must confirm and explain the decision of the hearing[49] (which may, as always, be a majority decision[50]).

7–15   If the grounds hearing decides to direct the reporter to apply to the sheriff for a determination on whether the grounds that are not accepted are established, the chairing member must explain to the child and the relevant person the purpose of the application to the sheriff court, and must inform the child that he or she is obliged to attend the hearing before the sheriff unless excused by the sheriff.[51] If the grounds hearing, having directed the reporter to apply to the sheriff for a determination on whether the non-accepted grounds are established, considers that the nature of the child's circumstances is such that for the protection, guidance, treatment or control of the child it is necessary, as a matter of urgency, that an interim compulsory supervision order be made in relation to the child, the hearing may make such an interim order.[52] That order will last until the sheriff has disposed of the application or until a day specified in the order or on the expiry of a period of 22 days beginning with the day the

---

[47] 2011 Act s.93(1)(b) and (2).
[48] 2011 Act s.25.
[49] 2013 Rules r.63.
[50] 2011 Act s.202(2).
[51] 2011 Act s.93(4).
[52] 2011 Act s.93(5). On interim compulsory supervision orders, see below, paras 10–05—10–07.

interim compulsory supervision order was made or varied (whichever occurs soonest),[53] but a hearing may make further interim compulsory supervision orders until such time as the child has been subject to interim compulsory supervision orders for a continuous period of more than 66 days.[54] Thereafter the reporter may apply to the sheriff for an extension of the order[55] or further extension of the order.[56]

A discussion of the child's present circumstances is permitted at this stage, **7–16** and is probably essential to ensure the child's and relevant person's effective participation in the decision-making process, even although the section 67 grounds have not been accepted, and often the decision of whether to make an interim compulsory supervision order will have to be made on the basis of facts that are vehemently disputed. The hearing members must do their best to judge credibility in assessing disputed allegations and they must, of course, make their decision on whether to make an interim compulsory supervision order by having regard to the child's welfare as their paramount consideration, as well as taking account of the proportionality requirement derived from the European Convention on Human Rights.[57] As well as, or instead of, making an interim compulsory supervision order, the grounds hearing that has directed the reporter to make an application to the sheriff for a determination of whether the denied grounds are established may grant a warrant to secure the child's attendance at the hearing before the sheriff of that application.[58] The chairing member, having confirmed and explained the decisions of the grounds hearing, must also inform the child, each relevant person and any appointed safeguarder of the right to appeal against: (i) the decision to discharge the referral; or (ii) (where the reporter has been directed to make an application to the sheriff) the decision to make an interim compulsory supervision order or grant a warrant to secure attendance (if either has been made or granted).[59] A safeguarder may be appointed by the grounds hearing that directs the reporter to apply to the sheriff. The hearing does not, in this circumstance, have the power to make a medical examination order and, indeed, if it makes an interim compulsory supervision order it may not include within that order a requirement that the local authority arrange a specified medical or other examination of the child.[60]

Acceptance in part

If either the child or the relevant person or both accept only one or more of **7–17** the grounds specified in the statement of grounds but deny other grounds, the grounds hearing may do one of two things. First, if it considers that it is appropriate to make a decision on whether to make a compulsory supervision order on the basis of the ground or grounds that have been accepted, the grounds hearing may proceed to the discussion part of the hearing and may thereafter

---

[53] 2011 Act s.86(3).
[54] 2011 Act s.96(4).
[55] 2011 Act s.98.
[56] 2011 Act s.99.
[57] On proportionality, see above, paras 1–07—1–08.
[58] 2011 Act s.123.
[59] 2013 Rules r.63(3)(iii).
[60] 2011 Act s.93(6). Since this rule refers only to the condition in s.83(2)(f)(i) (which refers to medical examination) it remains competent for the interim compulsory supervision order to contain a condition of medical treatment as in s.83(2)(f)(ii).

either defer the decision, make a compulsory supervision order, or discharge the referral.[61] Secondly, if it does not consider it appropriate to make a decision on whether to make a compulsory supervision order on the basis solely of the grounds that have been accepted, the grounds hearing may either discharge the referral or direct the reporter to make an application to the sheriff for a determination on whether each ground that is not accepted is established.[62] The grounds hearing is not permitted to proceed to consider whether it is necessary to make a compulsory supervision order in respect of the grounds accepted and at the same time refer the denied grounds to the sheriff, for the power to refer the case to the sheriff[63] is expressly stated to exist only when the grounds hearing does not consider it appropriate to make a decision on whether a compulsory supervision order should be made on the basis of the accepted grounds.[64] The decision whether to proceed to a consideration of the accepted grounds, to direct the reporter to make an application to the sheriff for a determination of whether the denied grounds are established, or to discharge the referral is to be made by the grounds hearing regarding the welfare of the child as paramount.[65] Discharge will seldom be appropriate, for the reasons discussed in relation to denial of all the grounds. So the effective choice will normally be between considering the case immediately on the basis of the accepted grounds or sending the matter to the sheriff for proof of the denied grounds.

7–18   That decision will normally turn on whether the hearing considers the denied grounds are likely to affect the eventual outcome of the referral. This is not, however, the only consideration. It may be considered detrimental to the child to delay the consideration of whether it is necessary to make a compulsory supervision order, in which case it would be proper to proceed with the hearing in respect of the grounds that have been accepted, so long as there is enough of a basis of fact in the accepted grounds to allow the children's hearing to conduct a full and proper discussion of the child's needs. Conversely, there are situations in which it would inhibit a proper consideration of the child's circumstances (and therefore be detrimental to the child's welfare) to proceed to a determination of whether it is necessary to make a compulsory supervision order on the basis only of the accepted grounds, such as when there are far more serious grounds which, if established, would fundamentally affect that determination, or the terms contained in any compulsory supervision order. Even if the denied grounds are less serious than those accepted, their existence may colour the case sufficiently that it becomes necessary to establish whether they apply or not. If the grounds hearing decides to proceed in respect of the grounds that are accepted, the hearing members cannot consider in their discussion those grounds or supporting facts that have not been accepted, nor can they allow the denied grounds to influence their dispositive decision, either to make the order or its terms. These problems,

---

[61] 2011 Act s.91(1)(b), (2) and (3). The children's hearing does not "discharge" the denied grounds, but simply proceeds in respect of the accepted grounds. It is the referral as a whole that can be "discharged" (though it is common to talk, inaccurately, of "discharging" denied grounds), or the referral in relation to the grounds denied or not understood. See, however, s.94(2)(b) where "a ground" has not been understood: in that case alone the statute allows the hearing to "discharge the referral in relation to the ground".

[62] 2011 Act s.93(1)(a) and (2).

[63] Contained in 2011 Act s.93(2)(a).

[64] 2011 Act s.93(1)(a). Of course, the application to the sheriff is in respect only of the denied grounds and there is no need to seek establishment of the accepted grounds in addition to these.

[65] 2011 Act s.25.

though they remain real, were lessened to some extent when the 2011 Act introduced the interim compulsory supervision order, for that order may deal with matters when the delay inherent in an application to the sheriff would be detrimental to the child's interests, and, being an interim measure, is well-suited to dealing with the situation when only some grounds but not all of them can be responded to. An interim compulsory supervision order is not, however, available in every case in which some grounds are accepted and some denied or not understood, for a test must be satisfied: that it is necessary as a matter of urgency to make an interim compulsory supervision order.[66]

Difficult questions of emphasis may, therefore, still arise if the grounds **7–19** hearing decides to proceed to a consideration of whether it is necessary to make a compulsory supervision order even in the face of denied grounds, for their consideration of the child's circumstances might well include the fact that allegations have been made but are denied. The proper approach is to treat any ground or supporting fact that is denied as not established fact. For example, a child may be referred to a children's hearing on the ground that he is beyond the control of a relevant person and this may be accepted; in addition, there may be a number of offences specified as grounds which the child denies on the basis that while he was present he did not take part in the offences. If the hearing proceeds on the basis that the child is beyond the control of a relevant person it cannot take into account the allegation that offences have been committed, but it can, it is submitted, take into account the fact that the child is associating with persons who, or indulging in activities which, lead the child to the attention of the police. A discussion of these matters is not a discussion of the denied "grounds", but of circumstances in the child's life which might or might not help the children's hearing to determine the best way forward.

Lack of understanding

It sometimes happens that the grounds hearing is satisfied that the child or a **7–20** relevant person either would not be capable of understanding an explanation of a section 67 ground or has not understood the explanation that has been given. Though the obligation to explain the ground rests with the chairing member of the grounds hearing,[67] the determination that the child or relevant person will not understand or has not understood the explanation is one to be made by the hearing as a whole, and in the unlikely event of disagreement amongst the hearing members a majority decision is, as always, sufficient.[68] The question is one of fact and not, therefore, one to which the welfare test in s.25 applies, and the determination of the hearing on the point is not appealable. To understand a section 67 ground the child and relevant person must be capable of understanding not only the words used by the chairing member but also why the alleged facts are giving cause for concern: it is not sufficient for proper understanding that, for example, a child understands that he or she took goods from

---

[66] 2011 Act s.93(5). See below, paras 10–05—10–07. Notice that while an interim compulsory supervision order may normally include any measure that could have been included in a full compulsory supervision order, it may not, in this circumstance, include a requirement that the local authority arrange a medical or other examination of the child: 2011 Act s.93(6). But see fn.60 above.

[67] 2011 Act s.90(1)(a).

[68] 2011 Act s.202(2).

a shop without paying but does not understand that this is wrongful as the crime of theft. If the decision is that the child or relevant person would not be capable of understanding the explanation, the chairing member need not attempt to give an explanation,[69] though this is likely to be the case only with young children and obviously incapable adults. In cases of doubt, the explanation ought at least to be attempted. It is implicit from the wording of the statute that the child or relevant person may not understand one ground but be capable of understanding other grounds. Whenever an application is made to the sheriff on the basis of lack of understanding it should be made plain which paragraph of s.94(1) the grounds hearing is relying upon to justify the application (that is to say whether the child or relevant person will not understand, or alternatively has not understood, the explanation).[70]

7–21   When the grounds hearing is satisfied that the child or relevant person would not be capable of understanding an explanation of a section 67 ground, or has not understood an explanation given, it must either: (i) discharge the referral in relation to the ground that would not be or has not been understood; or (ii) direct the reporter to apply to the sheriff to determine whether the ground is established.[71] If the first option is chosen, because the referral is discharged only in relation to the ground not understood,[72] the children's hearing may continue to a full discussion and may make a dispositive decision in respect of the grounds that are understood (and accepted). If the second option is chosen, the chairing member must, so far as is reasonably practicable, attempt to explain to the child and relevant person what the purpose of the application to the sheriff is, and must inform the child of the obligation to attend the hearing before the sheriff[73]: there will be many people who do not understand a section 67 ground but are capable of understanding that facts need to be proved. If the reporter is directed to make an application to the sheriff, the grounds hearing may make an interim compulsory supervision order, on the same basis as such an order is made when the grounds are denied.[74] The grounds hearing may also grant a warrant to secure the child's attendance at the hearing before the sheriff.[75] And it may appoint a safeguarder under s.30.

7–22   The reason for the child's or relevant person's lack of understanding is irrelevant, and the hearing should take account of any proferred reason only in so far as it assists the question of whether the child or relevant person has understood or not. In many cases, the age of the child will make it quite obvious that the child would not be capable of understanding any explanation: a baby or toddler, for example, would clearly not understand, however straightforward the statement of grounds is. The chairing member is under no obligation to attempt an explanation in these circumstances.[76] It should be noted that it is one of the justifications for relieving a child of the obligation under s.73(2) to

---

[69] 2011 Act s.94(3).

[70] cf. *Sloan v B*, 1991 S.L.T. 530.

[71] 2011 Act s.94(1) and (2).

[72] 2011 Act s.94(2)(b).

[73] 2011 Act s.94(4), referring to s.93(4).

[74] 2011 Act s.94(5), referring to s.93(5). Section 93(6) also applies (because the interim compulsory supervision order is made under s.93(5)) so that the interim compulsory supervision order may not contain an order requiring a specified medical or other examination of the child (see fn.60 above).

[75] 2011 Act s.123.

[76] 2011 Act s.94(3).

attend a hearing that, taking account of the child's age and maturity, the child would not be capable of understanding the proceedings and this will permit a children's hearing or pre-hearing panel to excuse a young child from attending a grounds hearing.[77] Once the decision is made either to discharge the referral or direct the reporter to apply to the sheriff and, if the latter, to make an interim compulsory supervision order or grant a warrant to secure attendance, the chairing member must confirm and explain the decision and its reasons, and inform the child, each relevant person and any appointed safeguarder of their right to appeal against the decision to discharge the referral, make an interim compulsory supervision order or grant a warrant to secure attendance (as the case may be) within 21 days.[78]

---

[77] See further above, para.6–06.
[78] 2013 Rules r.63(3).

CHAPTER 8

APPLICATION TO THE SHERIFF TO ESTABLISH GROUNDS

INTRODUCTION

8–01 One of the defining characteristics of the children's hearing system is the clear separation of roles between the body that determines whether, and in what terms, a compulsory supervision order should be made, and the body that determines whether, if the matter is disputed, any one or more of the grounds in respect to which the child has been referred to the hearing actually apply in relation to that child. It is only when there is no dispute that a ground applies, or any such dispute has been resolved by a finding that the ground does apply, that the question may be examined by a children's hearing whether or not it is necessary for the protection, guidance, treatment or control of the child to make a compulsory supervision order over the child. The sheriff court has since the inception of the system under the Social Work (Scotland) Act 1968 been the appropriate forum for resolving disputes of fact relating to whether or not (what are now called) section 67 grounds apply in respect of the child, for in that forum evidence can be taken on oath and can be challenged by cross-examination; the children's hearing is the appropriate forum for determining whether to make a compulsory supervision order and its terms, because the hearing is far better placed than a court of law to foster discussion with the child and his or her family of the section 67 grounds, other relevant circumstances, and possible ways forward.

> "It was this separation between the issues of adjudication of the allegations in the grounds for the referral and the consideration of the measures to be applied which lay at the heart of the recommendations of the Kilbrandon *Report on Children and Young Persons, Scotland* (Cmnd. 2306) of April 1964 which were in due course implemented by the Social Work (Scotland) Act 1968. The genius of this reform, which has earned it so much praise which the misfortunes of this case should not be allowed in any way to diminish, was that the responsibility for the consideration of the measures to be applied was to lie with what was essentially a lay body while disputed questions of fact as to the allegations made were to be resolved by the sheriff sitting in chambers as a court of law."[1]

8–02 The reporter may be directed to make an application to the sheriff for a determination on whether grounds are established in any of a number of different

---

[1] *Sloan v B*, 1991 S.L.T. 530, per Lord President Hope at 548D-E.

circumstances: (i) where either the child or any one or more of the relevant persons do not accept any of the grounds as put to them by the chairing member of the children's hearing[2]; (ii) where some but not all of the grounds are accepted and the grounds hearing does not consider it appropriate to make a decision on whether to make a compulsory supervision order on the basis of the ground or grounds that have been accepted[3]; (iii) where the grounds hearing is satisfied that the child or a relevant person would not be capable of understanding an explanation of the grounds[4]; (iv) where the grounds hearing is satisfied that the child or a relevant person has not understood the explanation given by the chairing member of the grounds[5]; or (v) where at a review hearing at which new section 67 grounds have been referred these new grounds are either not accepted or not understood and the hearing does not consider it appropriate to review the existing compulsory supervision order.[6] In any of these circumstances the children's hearing must either discharge the referral or direct the reporter to make an application to the sheriff to determine whether the stated section 67 grounds are established.[7]

The reporter must withdraw the application once it has been made if, before **8–03** the application is determined, due to a change in circumstances or information becoming available to the reporter, he or she no longer considers that any ground to which the application relates applies in relation to the child.[8] If, in that situation, none of the grounds was accepted at the grounds hearing any interim compulsory supervision order or warrant to secure attendance will cease to have effect on the application's withdrawal.[9] If, however, one or more grounds were accepted by the child and relevant persons at the grounds hearing the withdrawal of the application to the sheriff does not bring the process to an end but will require the reporter to arrange a children's hearing to determine, on the basis of the accepted grounds only, whether it is necessary to make a compulsory supervision order.[10] It would appear that an application must be made before it can be withdrawn, and the reporter has no authority to ignore the hearing's direction to make an application to the sheriff. Though it is difficult to fit in to the words of s.107, it is submitted that it is open to the reporter to withdraw an application when the additional information or change of circumstances does not change the reporter's view that a section 67 ground applies, but does persuade the reporter that he or she will no longer be able to establish in court that the section 67 ground applies.[11] This might be due, for example, to the death or disappearance of a vital witness. No ground should be regarded as applying unless it is capable of being proved to apply. If the emergence of new information has put a different light on the circumstances, and persuades the reporter that it is definitely not necessary for a compulsory supervision order to

---

[2] Children's Hearings (Scotland) Act 2011 s.93(1)(b) and (2)(a).
[3] 2011 Act s.93(1)(a) and (2)(a).
[4] 2011 Act s.94(1)(a) and (2)(a).
[5] 2011 Act s.94(1)(b) and (2)(a).
[6] 2011 Act s.97.
[7] 2011 Act s.93(2) and s.94(2).
[8] 2011 Act s.107(1) and (2).
[9] 2011 Act s.107(4).
[10] 2011 Act s.107(3).
[11] *After* the original hearing. It would be extremely bad practice for the reporter to arrange a children's hearing while he or she is of the view that the grounds could not be proved, and in the hope that they will simply be accepted.

be made in respect of the child even although a ground still applies, it would appear that there is no power of withdrawal[12]: this is because once the grounds hearing has been arranged the question of whether it is necessary to make a compulsory supervision order rests solely with the children's hearing and not with the reporter. The reporter must notify withdrawal to the child,[13] any relevant person whose whereabouts are known to the reporter, and any safeguarder and curator *ad litem*.[14] If the application is withdrawn in whole, the sheriff must dismiss the application and discharge the referral.[15]

Time-scale

8–04   The application must be lodged within seven days of the grounds hearing at which the direction to the reporter was made, the day of the hearing counting as the first day.[16] If the application is not made timeously, the referral falls, though there would seem to be nothing to prevent the reporter in that case founding upon the same facts and the same grounds to make a new referral to the children's hearing.[17] As the delay inherent in such a proceeding would clearly be contrary to the interests of a child in respect of whom it may be necessary to make a compulsory supervision order, reporters should make every effort to ensure that applications are made in time. Once the application is lodged, it must be heard by the sheriff no later than 28 days after the day on which it was lodged[18] and if it is not the referral falls though, again, the reporter can found upon the same facts to make a fresh referral.[19] An application is "heard" timeously so long as some substantive step in the process is taken by the sheriff within that period,[20] but the application does not need to be disposed of within that period.[21] Likewise, if the child fails to attend, the granting of a warrant to secure attendance under s.103(5) will amount to a substantive step in the process and the application is not rendered out of time even although the child is not found until after the end of the 28-day period. The decision to continue the hearing is subject to the welfare principle in s.25(2), and it is never in the interests of a child for whom it may be necessary to make a compulsory supervision order for that question to be left unanswered for longer than is practically necessary: this suggests that cases ought not to be continued

---

[12] 2011 Act s.107(2) imposes an obligation to withdraw when the reporter no longer considers any ground applies, *not* when the reporter no longer considers that it is necessary for a compulsory supervision order to be made.

[13] Unless service on the child had previously been dispensed with.

[14] Act of Sederunt (Child Care and Maintenance Rules) 1997 (SI 1997/291 (S.19)), as amended by the Act of Sederunt (Children's Hearings (Scotland) Act 2011 (Miscellaneous Amendments) 2013 (SSI 2013/172), (hereinafter "Child Care and Maintenance Rules 1997") r.3.46(2).

[15] Child Care and Maintenance Rules 1997 r.3.46(3).

[16] Child Care and Maintenance Rules 1997 r.3.45(1). If a safeguarder was appointed by the children's hearing, the reporter must intimate this to the sheriff clerk and lodge along with the application any report made by the safeguarder: r.3.45(2).

[17] See *McGregor v L*, 1983 S.L.T. (Sh Ct) 7.

[18] 2011 Act s.101(2).

[19] *McGregor v L*, 1983 S.L.T. (Sh Ct) 7.

[20] *H v Mearns*, 1974 S.L.T. 184.

[21] *H v McGregor*, 1973 S.L.T. 110, per Lord Wheatley at 115. cf. s.51(3) under which an application for the variation or termination of a child protection order must be "determined", i.e. disposed of, within three working days after the day on which it is made; and s.157(2) under which an appeal against certain decisions of the children's hearing must be disposed of by the sheriff before the expiry of the period of three days beginning the day after the day on which the appeal was made.

for mere administrative convenience but only when it is essential for the proper conduct of the hearing of the application. Concern has been expressed in the higher courts (if in different contexts) about the harm done to children by the uncertainties caused through excessively long proofs and sheriffs have a clear duty to manage proofs in a way that ensures their timeous conclusion without harming the demands for a fair testing of the evidence.[22]

JURISDICTION

The application is to be made by lodging the appropriate forms with the sheriff **8–05** clerk of the sheriff court district in which the child is habitually resident.[23] This is subject to an exception when the ground to be established is that in s.67(2) (j),[24] that is to say the child has committed a criminal offence: in this case the application must be made to the sheriff who would have jurisdiction to try the case if the child were being prosecuted for the offence,[25] and this is so whether or not the application also relates to other section 67 grounds.[26] This creates awkwardness when the allegation is that the child has committed a criminal offence in a sheriff court district other than that in which he or she is habitually resident, but the court rules permit the sheriff with primary jurisdiction to remit the application (once made to him) to another sheriff court on cause shown.[27] It will often be convenient to do so, since the court of the child's habitual residence will be the court that deals, for example, with appeals, or any new (non-criminal) grounds subsequently drawn up. In any case, s.102 does not prevent an application to a sheriff if the ground founded upon is an offence that cannot be tried before a sheriff, like murder or rape. Section 102(2) is to be taken to refer to the sheriff's territorial rather than procedural jurisdiction,[28] for otherwise reporters might be tempted to ensure the sheriff's jurisdiction by presenting serious allegations in a way that diminished their true import (such as, for example, alleging sexual assault under s.3 of the Sexual Offences (Scotland) Act 2009 when the reality was the much more serious offence of rape, dealt with under s.1 of that Act).

Founding jurisdiction on the child's habitual residence within a sheriff court **8–06** district suggests that no application to establish grounds may be made—and therefore the children's hearing has no role—in respect of a child who is not habitually resident somewhere in Scotland. Prior to the 2013 amendments to the Child Care and Maintenance Rules 1997, it was held that the sheriff had no jurisdiction to hear an application for the establishment of grounds of referral in relation to a child who is not present in Scotland at the time the reporter arranged

---

[22] See *B v G*, 2012 UKSC 21; *S v L*, 2012 UKSC 30.

[23] Child Care and Maintenance Rules 1997 r.3.45(1).

[24] Child Care and Maintenance Rules 1997 r.3.45(1A).

[25] 2011 Act s.102(2).

[26] 2011 Act s.102(4).

[27] Child Care and Maintenance Rules 1997 r.3.45(1B), as inserted by Act of Sederunt (Children's Hearings (Scotland) Act 2011) (Miscellaneous Amendments) 2013 art.3 para.32. This was previously a matter that would be dealt with under the *nobile officium*: see for example *Sloan, Petr*, 1991 S.L.T. 527. If the application is remitted to another sheriff court under r.3.45(1B), the hearing may be continued for such reasonable time as the sheriff considers appropriate: r.3.49, as amended.

[28] *Walker v C (No. 2)*, 2003 S.L.T. 293.

a children's hearing,[29] but that the sheriff did have jurisdiction if the child is present in Scotland at that time, regardless of where the child was at the time of the conduct which gave rise to the need for the referral.[30] The state has protective duties over all children who are, for the time being, present in Scotland even if habitually resident elsewhere and r.3.45(1) allows an application to a sheriff other than that of the child's habitual residence "on cause shown". It is submitted that the fact that there is no sheriff court district within which the child is habitually resident is sufficient cause to allow the reporter to lodge an application in the sheriff court district where the child is present, either at the time of the application or the time the reporter arranged the children's hearing. Thereafter neither the children's hearing nor the sheriff loses jurisdiction merely because the child is removed from Scotland.[31] Though it is clear from *Mitchell v S*[32] that there is jurisdiction if the child is present in Scotland at the time the reporter arranges the children's hearing, it was subsequently held by Sheriff Principal Young that the converse (there is never jurisdiction if the child is not present at that time) does not apply.[33] In the case cited a child was already subject to a supervision requirement and it was held that since he was already subject to the jurisdiction of the children's hearing (and therefore the sheriff) a new application to the sheriff was competent even after he had been removed from Scotland. Sheriff Principal Young made the powerful point that to hold presence in Scotland on the date of referral to the hearing essential would mean that a referral in respect of a child being brought up in Scotland would be incompetent if on the date the reporter made the decision so to refer the child happened to be on a family holiday abroad.[34] It would be an odder result still if the reason the child was outwith Scotland was to satisfy the terms of an existing supervision requirement (as in the present case).[35]

ATTENDANCE AT THE SHERIFF COURT HEARING

The child and relevant person

8–07   The child has an explicit obligation to attend the hearing of the application before the sheriff.[36] There is, however, no provision imposing such a duty on the relevant person. Indeed, the statute does not expressly grant the relevant person a right to be present, though the provision entitling both the relevant

---

[29] *Mitchell v S*, 2000 S.L.T. 524.

[30] *Mitchell v S*, 2000 S.L.T. 524, at 527G, founding on *S v Kennedy*, 1996 S.L.T. 1087, where it was held there was jurisdiction even when the offence committed against the child had been committed abroad.

[31] However, removal from Scotland after the reporter has started an investigation but before a children's hearing has been arranged will have exactly that effect: *Mitchell v S*, 2000 S.L.T. 524 at 528D-E.

[32] 2000 S.L.T. 524.

[33] *Walker v C (No 1)*, 2003 S.L.T. (Sh Ct) 31.

[34] *Walker v C (No 1)*, 2003 S.L.T. (Sh Ct) 31, at 33I.

[35] *Walker v C (No 1)*, 2003 S.L.T. (Sh Ct) 31, at 33J. The sheriff principal did go on to interpret *Mitchell v S* as requiring that the child be ordinarily resident outwith Scotland before jurisdiction was lost (at 34C), though that is contrary to an express statement of the Lord Justice Clerk in *Mitchell*.

[36] 2011 Act s.103(2).

person and the child to be legally represented[37] may be taken to imply such a right, as may r.3.47(6) of the Child Care and Maintenance Rules 1997 which permits the relevant person to be excluded while the child is giving evidence. Opportunity to participate is an important element in ensuring that the fact-finding process is compliant with the European Convention on Human Rights and this too suggests the existence of a right to attend.[38] Both the child and the relevant person may be represented by a person other than a solicitor or advocate[39]: this gives them an equal right to the reporter, who has a right of audience even when not legally qualified.[40]

Excusing the child from attending

The sheriff may excuse the child from attending all or part of the hearing of **8–08** the application where any of the following circumstances exist[41]:

(a) The application is to establish one of the grounds involving the commission of a Schedule 1 offence and the attendance of the child at the hearing before the sheriff, or that part of the hearing, is not necessary for a fair hearing. "Fair" in this context means fair both to the child and to the person who is being accused of having committed a schedule 1 offence: often this will require that the accused be faced with his accuser.[42]

(b) The attendance of the child at the hearing, or that part of the hearing, would place the child's physical, mental or moral welfare at risk. Preference, even a strong preference, on the part of the child not to attend does not in itself indicate a risk to mental welfare in requiring attendance.

(c) Taking account of the child's age and maturity, the child would not be capable of understanding what happens at the hearing or that part of the hearing. This will often be decided merely on account of the child's age but the test is one of capacity to understand, not age or maturity.

These are the same grounds upon which a children's hearing or a pre-hearing panel may excuse a child from attending a children's hearing.[43] The decision to excuse the child from attending is one to which the welfare principle in s.25(2) applies; the requirement in s.27 to take account of the child's views will also apply in appropriate cases. In any case in which the sheriff is deciding whether to excuse a child from attending it should be remembered that the child's interests are undoubtedly best served by the sheriff being able to determine the truth

---

[37] 2011 Act s.104.

[38] See *Authority Reporter, Edinburgh v RU,* 2008 Fam.L.R. 70; *Principal Reporter v K,* 2011 S.L.T. 271.

[39] s.104(4) and Child Care and Maintenance Rules 1997 r.3.21.

[40] See Children's Hearings (Scotland) Act 2011 (Rights of Audience of the Principal Reporter) Regulations 2012 (SSI 2012/335) regs 3 and 4. Special training is, however, required: reg.5.

[41] 2011 Act s.103(3).

[42] See *Principal Reporter v K,* 2011 S.L.T. 271 where the Supreme Court considered it a breach of an elementary rule of fairness that a person accused of a sch.1 offence was not given the right to be heard at proceedings designed to determine whether such an offence has occurred.

[43] Reference should be made to the discussion of the grounds in that context above, at paras 6–04—6–06.

of the matter, and very much more will be required to justify the child's absence when his or her presence is likely to assist the sheriff in that quest, for example by acting as a vital witness, than if the child will have little to contribute to the fact-finding process. It is difficult to imagine a situation in which it would be proper to excuse the child from attending when the ground of referral is that he or she has committed an offence. It is perfectly possible that the child might properly be excused from attending the hearing of the evidence before the sheriff but not from the children's hearing that will follow a finding that grounds apply (or vice versa). It is competent to relieve the child from attending part only of the hearing of the application to determine whether grounds have been established. The child may attend the hearing before the sheriff even if excused from doing so,[44] which suggests that the child has a right as well as a duty to attend.

8–09   Where the child has been excused from attending all or part of the hearing of the application any safeguarder, curator ad litem and relevant person is permitted to remain, as is the child's representative.[45]

Ensuring the child's presence

8–10   If the child breaches his or her duty to attend the hearing of the application to the sheriff for a determination on whether the section 67 grounds are established, the sheriff may grant a warrant to secure attendance of the child,[46] as he may do if the hearing of the application is to be continued to another day (for example because the evidence takes more than a day to hear) and the sheriff is satisfied that there is reason to believe that the child will not attend on that other day.[47] This warrant will authorise an officer of law to search for and apprehend the child, to take the child to and detain the child in a place of safety, to bring the child before the sheriff and, so far as is necessary for the execution of the warrant, to break open shut and lockfast places.[48] Such a warrant may include a secure accommodation authorisation, so long as the normal conditions for such an authorisation are met.[49] The warrant will be effective for the period beginning with the granting of the warrant and ending with the earlier of: (i) the beginning of the hearing of the application (or of the continued hearing); or (ii) the expiry of the period of 14 days beginning with the day on which the child is first detained in pursuance of the warrant.[50] Subsequent warrants may, however, be granted. The granting of a warrant to secure attendance may be a proportionate means to ensure the child fulfils his or her obligation to attend only when that attendance is likely to help the sheriff to reach the decision required of him.

The attendance of journalists

8–11   The hearing of the application to determine whether section 67 grounds are established in relation to the child must not be heard in open court,[51] which

---

[44] 2011 Act s.103(4).

[45] Child Care and Maintenance Rules 1997 r.3.47(5).

[46] 2011 Act s.103(5).

[47] 2011 Act s.103(6) and (7).

[48] 2011 Act s.88(1).

[49] 2011 Act s.88(2) and (3). These conditions are discussion below, para.11–14.

[50] 2011 Act s.88(4)(b) and (c). Notice that a warrant granted by a sheriff or a children's hearing to ensure the child's attendance at a children's hearing lasts for seven days only: s.88(4)(a) and (d).

[51] 2011 Act s.101(3).

means that members of the public are not admitted, and journalists have no right to be present.[52] However,

"it is in the discretion of the judge or sheriff to permit anyone including the press to attend the proceedings which are being conducted in his chambers. This is because there is no general rule which prevents this from being done . . . By providing that the proceedings are to be in chambers, Parliament has done what was necessary to allow the sheriff to decide this matter as he thinks fit.[53] It is a matter for his discretion and thus subject entirely to his control as to who, other than those who have a duty or right to be there, may attend and for how long they may remain."[54]

In the case cited, the sheriff had permitted journalists to be present, and Lord President Hope said this:

"We have no criticism to make . . . of the sheriff's decision to allow the journalists to attend . . . The sheriff had to deal with the situation as he found it when he opened the proceedings for which he was responsible in the sheriff court. The press had been present at the proceedings before the children's hearing, and the case had already received a great deal of publicity which was likely to continue. It was suggested that he was wrong to allow the journalists to attend at their request, not on the motion of any party, and to do so when the debate on competency had reached such a stage that they could not get a balanced view of it. But these were matters for the sheriff, and for what it is worth we think that he was right to exercise his discretion as he did in the exceptional circumstances of this case."[55]

It would be wrong to interpret these dicta as indicating that journalists should **8–12** be permitted to be present only in exceptional circumstances. Given the limitations on what may be reported[56] it may be that sheriffs ought usually to permit journalists who wish to be present to be so unless there is good reason why they should not be.[57] Other than journalists and those directly connected to the child or the application, there are few who should ever be permitted to be present at a hearing of an application to determine whether section 67 grounds are established in relation to the child.[58]

---

[52] cf. 2011 Act s.78(1)(i) which permits journalists' presence at children's hearings and pre-hearing panels.

[53] Nothing turns, it is submitted, on the change in statutory expression in the 2011 Act which talks of proceedings "not in open court" as opposed to "proceedings being heard by the sheriff in chambers" (the formulation in s.93(5) of the Children (Scotland) Act 1995 and the sheriff has identical powers of control in both instances.

[54] *Sloan v B*, 1991 S.L.T. 530, per Lord President Hope at 551D-E, G.

[55] 1991 S.L.T. 530 at 551H-I.

[56] See s.182 and discussion thereof above, paras 6–42—6–46.

[57] See, however, the more cautiously expressed view of Sheriff Kearney in *Children's Hearings and the Sheriff Court*, 2nd edn (Butterworths, 2000), para.28.07.

[58] Students, trainees and researchers are an obvious category of person who might appropriately be allowed by the sheriff into a hearing to establish grounds, as observers.

PRELIMINARY MATTERS

Appointing a safeguarder

8–13   Whenever proceedings are being taken before the sheriff in an application to determine whether section 67 grounds are established, and a safeguarder has not already been appointed for these proceedings, the sheriff must consider whether to appoint a safeguarder for the child in the proceedings, and he may make such an appointment, giving reasons for his decision to do so.[59] There is no test laid down in the legislation as to when the appointment might be made other than the welfare principle in s.25(2) and the requirement to take account of the views of the child in s.27. The sheriff may make the appointment on his own initiative or on being requested to do so. It will be appropriate for the sheriff to appoint a safeguarder whenever and however this will protect the child's interests. This might be because, for example, there is a risk that the relevant persons or their representatives will not or cannot look after the child's interests properly, or because the sheriff considers that the appointment is the best way to find out the child's views on the matter at issue (it always being in the child's interests to have his or her views properly expressed). But it should be emphasised that the power to appoint a safeguarder under the 2011 Act is deliberately expressed in wider and vaguer terms than under the previous legislation,[60] with the result, it is submitted, that there is no obligation on the sheriff to identify any positive reason for the appointment of a safeguarder other than that he considers it to be in the interests of the child. It is, however, of great use to the safeguarder to be given some indication beyond that general reason why his or her appointment was considered by the sheriff to be appropriate. The child's interests may be safeguarded by for example the child's receiving advice from a safeguarder as to whether to accept the section 67 grounds that are the subject of the application to the sheriff, and of the implications of doing so. The safeguarder may also be in a position to advise the sheriff whether the sheriff should hear evidence even if the child and relevant person now accept that the section 67 grounds apply,[61] or whether to excuse the child from attending the hearing of the application,[62] or whether to exclude any person while the child is giving evidence.[63] An educative, informative or advisory role will always be appropriate and often sufficient. And since the appointment by a sheriff lasts until the time for appeal has passed (or an appeal has been finally disposed of) against the dispositive decision of the children's hearing,[64] the sheriff may appoint a safeguarder not to assist in the sheriff court proceedings but to safeguard the interests of the child at the children's hearing that will follow a determination that grounds are established.

8–14   Safeguarders appointed by the sheriff in an application to determine whether grounds are established are to be treated for the purposes of the 2011 Act as

---

[59] 2011 Act s.31.

[60] s.34A of the Social Work (Scotland) Act 1968 permitted such an appointment only when there was a risk of a conflict of interests between the child and the parent; s.41 of the Children (Scotland) Act 1995 required that the appointment be "necessary to appoint a person to safeguard the interests of the child in the proceedings."

[61] Under 2011 Act s.105(2).

[62] Under 2011 Act s.103(3).

[63] Under Child Care and Maintenance Rules 1997 r.3.47(6).

[64] See above, para. 2–22.

having been appointed by a children's hearing.[65] They have the powers and duties at common law of a curator ad litem in respect of the child and are entitled to receive from the reporter copies of the application, all productions, and any papers which were before the children's hearing.[66] Safeguarders must determine whether the child wishes to express views in relation to the application and, if the child does so wish, transmit these views to the sheriff; in addition they must make such enquiries so far as relevant to the application as they think appropriate.[67] The safeguarder is entitled to become a party to the proceedings and is obliged to intimate to the sheriff clerk without delay and in any event before the hearing of the application whether or not he or she intends to do so.[68] As a party, the safeguarder may appear personally in the proceedings or instruct an advocate or solicitor to appear on his or her behalf.[69] Whether or not he or she becomes a party the safeguarder is entitled to receive from the sheriff clerk all interlocutors subsequent to his or her appointment.[70] Any report drawn up by the safeguarder and submitted to the sheriff is not evidence as to the existence or otherwise of a section 67 ground, but it may be used by the sheriff as a "check on the view which he had formed on the evidence".[71] A safeguarder appointed by the sheriff in an application to establish grounds also has title to appeal against the sheriff's determination in that matter.[72]

Pleas to the competency of the application

An application to the sheriff for a determination on whether section 67 **8–15** grounds are established cannot be dismissed before the hearing of the evidence on the basis that it is irrelevant,[73] because the proceedings before the sheriff are designed not to establish guilt or innocence but to determine whether the circumstances exist in which the (always relevant) question of whether it is necessary to make a compulsory supervision order in respect of the child may properly be addressed. It follows that technical rules designed to protect accused persons are not appropriate in applications to establish section 67 grounds. The sheriff may, however, disqualify himself from hearing evidence and put the case out for hearing before another sheriff if it is appropriate to do so to avoid, say, perceptions of bias,[74] but other than in that situation the sheriff is normally obliged to hear the evidence tendered by or on behalf of the

---

[65] 2011 Act s.31(4).

[66] Child Care and Maintenance Rules 1997 r.3.8(a) and (b).

[67] Child Care and Maintenance Rules 1997 r.3.8(c) and (d).

[68] Child Care and Maintenance Rules 1997 r.3.8(e).

[69] Child Care and Maintenance Rules 1997 r.3.9(1). If the safeguarder is him or herself an advocate or solicitor, he or she must not also act as advocate or solicitor for the child: r.3.9(2).

[70] Child Care and Maintenance Rules 1997 r.3.8(f), as inserted by Act of Sederunt (Children's Hearings (Scotland) Act 2011) (Miscellaneous Amendments) 2013 art.3 para.11. One welcome curiousity is that in this amendment to r.3.8 a safeguarder is referred to with "his or her", while the rest of that rule refers to the safeguarder in the masculine only.

[71] *Kennedy v M*, 1989 S.L.T. 687, per Lord Brand at 689D.

[72] 2011 Act s.163(3)(c), referring to safeguarders appointed under s.30, which includes appointments under s.31: s.31(4).

[73] *McGregor v D*, 1977 S.L.T. 182, in which the child's solicitor had argued that the statement of fact did not amount to the crime allegedly committed by the child which the reporter sought to establish as a ground of referral.

[74] *F v Constanda*, 1999 S.L.T. 421.

reporter.[75] Sometimes, however, the application can be dismissed on the ground of incompetency, although only when the incompetency is radical. An application which is not heard within 28 days of being lodged[76] must, it is submitted, be dismissed by the sheriff as incompetent (and it is not open to the parties to agree that the proof should go ahead). So must an application that purports to be based on a ground specified in legislation that is no longer extant.[77] Applications which are made timeously and which are otherwise procedurally unchallengeable can be dismissed as incompetent before evidence is led only when the incompetency cannot be put right and the sheriff would be unable, whatever the evidence, to hold the ground of referral established.[78] So in *Merrin v S*[79] a child under the age of eight was referred on the ground of having committed an offence, but no matter what the evidence presented, that particular child could not be guilty of any offence because he was below the age of criminal responsibility[80]: the sheriff was able, therefore, to dismiss the application as incompetent.[81] Similarly, if the sheriff has no jurisdiction, say because the child is habitually resident in a sheriff court district other than the one in which the application is made, then dismissal of the application as incompetent would be appropriate.

LEADING THE EVIDENCE

8–16 The onus lies with the reporter to lead sufficient evidence to persuade the sheriff that the section 67 grounds have been established,[82] and the sheriff must hear the evidence tendered by or on behalf of the reporter.[83] Much of this evidence will already have been obtained by the reporter during the preliminary investigations that he or she is normally obliged to make.[84] In addition, once an application has been made to the sheriff, either to determine whether a section 67 ground is established or to review such a determination,[85] the reporter is entitled to request any prosecutor[86] to give him or her evidence lawfully obtained in the course of, and held by the prosecutor in connection

---

[75] Child Care and Maintenance Rules 1997 r.3.47(1). And see *Kennedy v B*, 1973 S.L.T. 38; *McGregor v D*, 1977 S.L.T. 182; *McGregor v D*, 1981 S.L.T. (Notes) 97; *Kennedy v S*, 1986 S.L.T. 679. The sheriff may dispense with hearing evidence under s.105(2) and s.106(2), discussed below, paras 8–29—8–32.

[76] As required by 2011 Act s.101(2).

[77] cf. *McGregor v A*, 1982 S.L.T. 45.

[78] *Sloan v B*, 1991 S.L.T. 530, per Lord President Hope at 546E-G.

[79] 1987 S.L.T. 193.

[80] Criminal Procedure (Scotland) Act 1995 s.41.

[81] The fact that the child had performed acts which would have amounted to a criminal offence had they been performed by a person over the age of eight did not indicate that it might be necessary to make a compulsory supervision order in relation to the child, because that necessity arises with child offenders due to their possessing *mens rea* which, given the age of this child, was necessarily entirely lacking.

[82] *Ferguson v S*, 1992 S.C.L.R. 866.

[83] Child Care and Maintenance Rules 1997 r.3.47(1).

[84] See further above, para.4–17.

[85] For review, see below, paras 8–37—8–49.

[86] Defined in s.307 of the Criminal Procedure (Scotland) Act 1995 as follows: "(b) for the purposes of summary proceedings, includes procurator fiscal, and any other person prosecuting in the public interest and complainer and any person duly authorised to represent or act for any public prosecutor". This definition applies for the purposes of the 2011 Act: s.202(1).

with, the investigation of a crime or suspected crime, whenever the reporter considers that the evidence might assist the sheriff in determining the application.[87] The evidence may relate to a crime or suspected crime committed by the child or against the child or by or against another member of the child's household or by anyone with whom the child has a close connection. If such a request is made, the prosecutor may refuse to comply with it only when he or she reasonably believes that it is necessary to retain the evidence for the purposes of any proceedings in respect of the crime, whether these proceedings have commenced or not.[88] Even in these circumstances, however, the prosecutor may nevertheless be able to comply with the reporter's request for co-operation, and such a request should be refused only when it is essential to the criminal proceedings that the evidence be retained by the prosecutor.

Once evidence is in the reporter's possession, the leading of that evidence **8–17** before the sheriff is not restricted or excluded on the basis that it would prejudice a fair trial of criminal charges arising from the same facts,[89] for there is no presumption that criminal proceedings take precedence over applications for a determination on whether section 67 grounds are established. The standard of proof required, in all cases except one, is the balance of probabilities, even when to establish the ground would require proof of the commission of a criminal offence (by a person other than the child referred)[90]: the statute imposes a higher standard only for the s.67(2)(j) ground, that is to say that the child has committed an offence, and this has been held to mean that the normal civil standard applies in all other cases.[91] If the ground to be established is that contained in s.67(2)(j), then the standard of proof is that which applies in criminal proceedings, that is to say the sheriff must be satisfied beyond reasonable doubt that the ground applies in relation to the child.[92] The sheriff does not, of course, make a finding of guilt or innocence with any ground, even that in s.67(2)(j): rather he makes a determination that the ground to which the application relates is established or, as the case may be, not established. The only difference in relation to the ground that the child has committed an offence is that the sheriff must be satisfied to a greater degree of certainty than with the other grounds before he can make a determination that the s.67(2)(j) ground is established. With the other grounds, even when the evidence was overwhelming and unchallenged, the findings should not state that the reporter's case has been proved beyond reasonable doubt.[93]

The evidence is to be considered as at the date the sheriff sits and not as at **8–18** the time of the grounds hearing at which the grounds were denied or not

---

[87] 2011 Act s.172(2) and (3).

[88] 2011 Act s.172(4).

[89] *Ferguson v P*, 1989 S.L.T. 681, *P v Kennedy*, 1995 S.L.T. 476.

[90] i.e. a ground under s.67(2)(b), (c), (d), or (g).

[91] *Harris v F*, 1991 S.L.T. 242; *B v Kennedy*, 1987 S.L.T. 765; *B v Authority Reporter*, 2011 S.L.T. (Sh Ct) 55, per Sheriff Principal Taylor at [38]. See also *KA v Finland* [2003] 1 F.L.R. 696 at [119]. The approach in *B v Kennedy* is consistent with that of the House of Lords in English cases: see *Re H & Ors (Minors) (Sexual Abuse: Standard of Proof)* [1996] 1 All E.R. 1 and *Re B (Children) (Sexual Abuse: Standard of Proof)* [2009] 1 A.C. 11. That there are only two standards of proof in Scotland was affirmed in *B v Scottish Ministers*, 2010 S.L.T. 537 and *SA v DA* [2013] CSIH 7.

[92] s.102(3). See *Constanda v M*, 1997 S.L.T. 1396 where it was held that the reporter may not avoid the higher standard by using the same facts to found a different ground.

[93] *P v Kennedy*, 1995 S.L.T. 476 at 482E.

understood. The sheriff is therefore obliged to take account of any changes in the child's circumstances since then.[94]

8–19 In offence cases, once the reporter has led his or her evidence, the sheriff must decide whether that evidence is sufficient to establish the alleged ground, and he must give all the parties an opportunity to be heard on the question of whether the evidence is sufficient for that purpose.[95] If he thinks that the evidence is insufficient he must make a determination to that effect.[96] If he thinks that the evidence tendered by the reporter is sufficient to establish the ground, or any other s.67 ground is in dispute, then the child, the relevant person, and any safeguarder may give evidence and, with the approval of the sheriff, call witnesses with regard to the ground in question.[97]

RULES OF EVIDENCE

8–20 The proceedings, though essentially sui generis and governed by a self-contained code of procedure contained in the Act and the Rules,[98] will follow the normal principles of evidence in summary[99] civil proceedings,[100] except that the interests of the child are not to be thwarted by an over-rigid application of the rules of evidence or procedure.[101] But the interests of the child will always require that the truth be established and rules of evidence and procedure which are designed to achieve that end will be followed. So evidence will be led by the reporter, in the way that a pursuer in a civil suit would lead evidence, and his or her witnesses can be cross-examined by the other parties, and then re-examined. If the sheriff finds that a prima facie case has been established by the reporter, the child and relevant person and, if a party, the safeguarder can then call witnesses who in turn can be cross-examined by the reporter. The relevant person is both competent and compellable as a witness,[102] even when it is alleged that the relevant person has committed an offence against the child. The child, if of an age to be competent to give evidence,[103] will also be compellable, except that in a case in which the ground of referral

---

[94] *Kennedy v B*, 1973 S.L.T. 38. See also *Harris v E*, 1989 S.L.T. 42 in which a change in the law was taken into account. A ground of referral was made out that the child had been the victim of a Sch.1 offence even although the offence was not scheduled at the time of its commission, but had become so by the date of the referral.

[95] Child Care and Maintenance Rules 1997 r.3.47(2). This applies only to offence cases.

[96] Child Care and Maintenance Rules 1997 r.3.47(3).

[97] Child Care and Maintenance Rules 1997 r.3.47(4). The predecessor of this provision, r.8(2) of the Social Work (Sheriff Court Procedure Rules) 1971, imposed a positive obligation on the sheriff to tell the child, etc. that they may give evidence. Though the present provision is not worded in that way it would clearly be good practice for sheriffs to continue so to inform these parties–and it would of course be a procedural irregularity (and thus a ground of appeal) if a failure to do so effectively denied these parties the opportunity to lead evidence.

[98] *McGregor v D*, 1977 S.L.T. 182, per Lord President Emslie at 185.

[99] Child Care and Maintenance Rules 1997 r.3.20.

[100] Even when the ground of referral is that the child has committed an offence: *McGregor v D*, 1977 S.L.T. 182.

[101] *W v Kennedy*, 1988 S.L.T. 583.

[102] *McGregor v T*, 1975 S.L.T. 76.

[103] See below, paras 8–25—8–27.

is that the child has committed an offence the child will be neither compellable nor competent as a witness for the reporter.[104]

Except in cases in which the ground of referral is that the child has committed **8–21** an offence,[105] the presentation of the evidence will be subject to the rules in the Civil Evidence (Scotland) Act 1988.[106] So the sheriff can find a fact proved if satisfied that there is sufficient evidence to do so, even although the evidence is not corroborated.[107] Uncorroborated evidence must, however, be credible and reliable before a sheriff is entitled to hold that it establishes a section 67 ground[108]; the practical result of this is that the reporter should always be in a position to lead corroborating evidence in case the primary witness turns out to be less reliable than expected. Indeed failure to lead corroborating evidence of a fact when that evidence is available might be material to whether the court is satisfied that the fact had been proved by the evidence led.[109] The sheriff is not entitled to hold that a child has committed a criminal offence on the basis of uncorroborated evidence, however credible, for the rule allowing uncorroborated evidence to be sufficient is expressly limited to applications for a determination on whether section 67 grounds other than that contained in s.67(2)(j) are established.[110]

The Civil Evidence (Scotland) Act 1988 also provides that evidence is not to **8–22** be excluded solely on the basis that it is hearsay evidence,[111] and it follows that any party in an application for a determination on whether section 67 grounds are established can lead evidence of statements made which are not repeated or are even denied in court. This is particularly pertinent in relation to statements made by the child to social workers or investigators concerning how he or she has been treated. Evidence can be led that the child made a statement, for example that he or she has been abused, even when the child is unwilling to repeat the statement in court. Indeed, such evidence can be led even when it contradicts the evidence directly given by the child, and if more credible can be preferred by the sheriff.[112] It does not breach the "best evidence" rule[113] for

---

[104] Renton & Brown, *Criminal Procedure* at para.19.73 say that "there seems no reason why" the child should not be compellable and competent, but they give no authority for this and it would appear to be contrary both to natural justice and to the interests of the child to compel the child to give evidence against himself or herself.

[105] For which see below, para.8–24

[106] "Civil proceedings" governed by the 1988 Act are defined in s.9 thereof to include applications for grounds determinations except those based on s.67(2)(j), that the child has committed a criminal offence.

[107] Civil Evidence (Scotland) Act 1988 s.1.

[108] *M v Kennedy*, 1993 S.C.L.R. 69.

[109] *L v L*, 1996 S.L.T. 767; *McGowan v Lord Advocate*, 1972 S.C. 68.

[110] *F v Kennedy (No. 2)*, 1993 S.L.T. 1284, per Lord Justice Clerk Ross at 1287. At the time of writing, the Scottish Government are considering the recommendations of *The Carloway Review* (November 2012), including a recommendation to abolish the requirement for corroboration in all cases. See *Reforming Scots Criminal Law and Practice: Additional Safeguards Following the Removal of the Requirement for Corroboration* (Scottish Government Consultation Paper, December 2012), where the implications for the children's hearing system are not addressed.

[111] Civil Evidence (Scotland) Act 1988 s.2.

[112] *K v Kennedy*, 1993 S.L.T. 1281. Here the sheriff found a ground of referral, that the child had been subjected to a Sch.1 offence, established on the basis of evidence that she had made a statement to that effect, even although she retracted the statement and denied it in her own evidence.

[113] The normal rule in civil proceedings that a party must lead the best evidence available and that any other evidence cannot be led while better evidence is available. See Walker and Walker, *Evidence*, by M. Ross and J. Chalmers, 3rd edn (2008, Tottel), paras 20.1–20.2.

the reporter to lead evidence that the child had earlier made such a statement rather than calling the child to give direct evidence as a witness.[114] There may well be situations in which calling the child is likely to cause him or her harm or distress, for example when the questions relate to domestic abuse within the family, or to deeply personal matters like sexual activity or orientation, and if the reporter feels able to establish the grounds of referral without calling the child, it is neither improper nor incompetent for him or her to attempt to do so. Reporters do, however, have a difficult balance to strike between the short-term protection from distress that not calling the child might ensure and the child's longer term interests which are always served by establishing the section 67 grounds whenever they apply in relation to the child.

8–23   It used to be thought that a qualification to the rule permitting hearsay evidence of what the child has said was that the child (or other person whose hearsay statements are being relied upon[115]) must be admissible as a witness, at the date of the proof hearing.[116] So the statements of a child who was too young to give any evidence could not be led as hearsay evidence.[117] The cases referred to were, however, overruled by the decision of a Court of Five Judges in *T v T*[118] where it was held that hearsay evidence may be led even when the maker of the statement would not have been an admissible witness.[119] Statute has abolished the rule that evidence is inadmissible if the witness is unable to tell the difference between truth and lies.[120]

Evidence to establish the ground in s.67(2)(j)

8–24   If the ground of referral is that the child has committed an offence, the rules in the Civil Evidence (Scotland) Act 1988 do not apply[121] and the normal rules concerning corroboration[122] and hearsay evidence apply instead. How far these rules can be departed from in the interests of the child is open to some doubt. In *W v Kennedy*[123] it was held that the rule against hearsay (which then still applied in all civil proceedings) could not be used to frustrate the search for truth in a case which would now be governed by the Civil Evidence (Scotland) Act 1988; and it might be argued that the same principle should apply in a case today not governed by the 1988 Act (i.e. a case in which the ground of referral is that the child has committed an offence). In support of that it might be argued that one of the important principles underlying the Children's Hearings (Scotland) Act 2011 is that alleged child offenders are to be treated in the same way as other children for whom it may be necessary to make a compulsory supervision order and that in all cases the purpose of an application for a determination on whether a section 67 ground is established is to identify whether that necessity might exist rather than to allocate blame. However, it is submitted that the better view is that the rules on corroboration and hearsay apply in applications to establish

---

[114] *F v Kennedy (No. 2)*, 1993 S.L.T. 1284.
[115] As in *Ferguson v S*, 1993 S.C.L.R. 712.
[116] *L v L*, 1996 S.L.T. 767, per Lord Hamilton at 770H.
[117] *F v Kennedy (No. 1)*, 1993 S.L.T. 1277.
[118] 2000 S.L.T. 1442.
[119] per Lord President Rodger at [37]. See also *SA v DA* [2013] CSIH 7.
[120] Vulnerable Witnesses (Scotland) Act 2004 s.24.
[121] Civil Evidence (Scotland) Act 1988 s.9.
[122] So long as they survive: see fn.110 above.
[123] 1988 S.L.T. 583.

the ground in s.67(2)(j) as they do in criminal trials. To hold otherwise would be inconsistent with the terms of the Civil Evidence (Scotland) Act 1988, which expressly exclude child offender cases from the rules contained therein. Also, the standard of proof being that which applies in criminal proceedings,[124] there is more of a need for corroboration and more of a need to avoid placing reliance on hearsay evidence. The reasoning in *W v Kennedy* should not be applied to applications to establish the ground in s.67(2)(j), for the court there was careful to emphasise that they were not laying down a rule that hearsay evidence is always admissible in applications to establish grounds, and they described the result in the case as only a "marginal relaxation" of the normal rule.[125] In addition, the fact that special rules relating to hearsay in child offender cases are now laid down by statute means that there is no room for arguing that any rules other than these can be applied. The Criminal Procedure (Scotland) Act 1995 sets down circumstances in which, in criminal proceedings, hearsay evidence will be admissible, and the phrase "criminal proceedings" is defined to include applications under s.93 or s.94 of the Children's Hearings (Scotland) Act 2011 to determine whether a ground alleging that the child has committed an offence has been established, or for a review of such a determination.[126] Under s.259(1) of the Criminal Procedure (Scotland) Act 1995, hearsay is admissible if the sheriff is satisfied that the maker of the statement is unavailable for reasons set out in s.259(2),[127] that the evidence would be admissible if the person were available, that the maker of the statement would have been a competent witness, and that there is documentary or oral evidence to the effect that the statement was made. Anyone causing the unavailability of a witness cannot lead hearsay evidence of statements the witness is alleged to have made[128]; evidence of the maker's credibility is competent[129]; notice in writing is normally needed if hearsay evidence is to be led.[130] In addition, s.260 permits the introduction of prior statements by a witness (but not the accused)[131] as evidence of any matter of which direct oral evidence by him would be admissible.

Child witnesses

It frequently happens, and not only in cases involving Schedule 1 offences, **8–25** that the reporter or another party will wish to call the child who has been referred to a children's hearing as a witness in order to establish the ground that is said to apply in relation to that very child. Children, particularly younger children, are often too immature to understand the importance of being truthful while giving evidence. The rule used to be that a child was legally competent

---

[124] 2011 Act s.102(3).

[125] 1988 S.L.T. 583 at 586E.

[126] Criminal Procedure (Scotland) Act 1995 s.262(3), as amended by the Children's Hearings (Scotland) Act 2011 (Modification of Primary Legislation) Order 2013 (SSI 2013/211) Sch.1 para.10(7).

[127] i.e. the person: (a) is dead or unfit; (b) is outwith the UK; (c) cannot be found; (d) refuses to give evidence on the ground that it might incriminate him; or (e) having been called as a witness refuses to take the oath or to affirm or to accept an admonishment to tell the truth, or refuses to give evidence.

[128] Criminal Procedure (Scotland) Act 1995 s.259(3).

[129] Criminal Procedure (Scotland) Act 1995 s.259(4).

[130] Criminal Procedure (Scotland) Act 1995 s.259(5)–(7).

[131] Criminal Procedure (Scotland) Act 1995 s.261: this presumably includes the child referred.

to be a witness only when he or she was adjudged capable of telling the difference between truth and falsehood and if so the child would be admonished to tell the truth.[132] The matter is now one of credibility rather than competency and the evidence of a child (or indeed any other person called as a witness) is not inadmissible solely because he or she does not understand the nature of the duty to give truthful evidence or indeed the difference between truth and lies.[133] The weight to be attached to the evidence of a child is a matter for the sheriff, who will take account of the child's age and maturity and make an assessment of the child's overall credibility.

8–26   The general (but not universal) rule in Scots law is that a witness who is competent is also compellable. One important exception to that rule is that a person may not be called as a witness to give evidence against him- or herself. This would certainly apply in relation to a child for whom the ground that the reporter is seeking to establish is that he or she has committed a criminal offence, notwithstanding the civil nature of the proceedings.[134]

8–27   Special provision is made for evidence given by child witnesses under the Vulnerable Witnesses (Scotland) Act 2004, including in particular the authorisation by the sheriff of the giving of evidence in chief in the form of a prior statement.[135] This permits the evidence to be given in chief without any requirement for the child to adopt or otherwise speak to the statement in giving evidence[136] and is therefore especially useful when the evidence to be given by the child is of a particularly sensitive or personal nature which any child would have difficult sharing in the formal environment of a court. More generally, the sheriff may exclude any person, including a relevant person, while any child is giving evidence if the sheriff is satisfied that this is necessary in the interests of the child and either: (i) the person must be excluded in order to obtain the evidence of the child; or (ii) the presence of the person in question is causing or is likely to cause significant distress to the child.[137]

Evidence of sexual behaviour

8–28   Amendments made to the Children (Scotland) Act 1995 by the Vulnerable Witnesses (Scotland) Act 2004 have been substantially replicated in ss.173–175 of the Children's Hearings (Scotland) Act 2011, which contain restrictions on the types of question that may be asked of a witness in cases in which the ground to be established involves sexual behaviour engaged in by any person (including but not limited to the witness). "Sexual behaviour" for this purpose include references to having undergone or been made subject to any experience of a

---

[132] *Rees v Lowe*, 1990 S.L.T. 507, *Kelly v Docherty*, 1991 S.L.T. 419, *R v Walker*, 1999 S.L.T. 1233.

[133] Vulnerable Witnesses (Scotland) Act 2004 s.24.

[134] Though often said to be "civil proceedings sui generis", the rule against self-incrimination shows that some aspects of criminal procedure might appropriately apply. It is to be noted that the rule against self-incrimination, though not explicitly mentioned in art.6 of the European Convention on Human Rights, has been recognised to lie at the heart of the notion of a fair procedure under art.6: *Murray v United Kingdom* (1996) 22 E.H.R.R. 29; *Saunders v United Kingdom* (1996) 23 E.H.R.R. 313; *Averill v United Kingdom* (2001) 31 E.H.R.R. 36; *Salduz v Turkey* (2009) 49 E.H.R.R. 19. See also *Cadder v HM Advocate*, 2010 S.L.T. 1125.

[135] Vulnerable Witnesses (Scotland) Act 2004 s.22A, as inserted by Children's Hearings (Scotland) Act 2011 s.176(5).

[136] Vulnerable Witnesses (Scotland) Act 2004 s.22A(4).

[137] Child Care and Maintenance Rules 1997 r.3.47(6).

sexual nature.[138] The general rule is that the sheriff may neither admit evidence, nor allow questioning of a witness designed to elicit evidence, which shows or tends to show that either the child or the witness or any other person evidence of whose statements is given for the purposes of the hearing: (a) is not of good character (sexual or otherwise); (b) has engaged in sexual behaviour not forming the subject matter of the ground that is sought to be established; (c) has engaged in non-sexual behaviour that might found an inference that the person is not credible or their evidence is not reliable (other than behaviour shortly before, at the same time as, or shortly after the acts that form part of the subject matter of the ground); and (d) has at any time been subject to any condition or predisposition that might found the inference that the person is not credible or their evidence is not reliable.[139] Such evidence may, however, be taken by order of the sheriff made on application by the child, relevant person, reporter or safeguarder so long as he is satisfied that: (a) the evidence will relate only to a specific occurrence of sexual or other behaviour or specific facts demonstrating the person's character or demonstrating a condition or predisposition to which the person is or has been subject; (b) the occurrence or facts are relevant to establishing the ground; and (c) the probative value of the evidence is significant and likely to outweigh any risk of prejudice to the proper administration of justice arising from its being admitted or elicited.[140]

Dispensing with the evidence

The sheriff has the power, in two distinct circumstances, to determine that **8–29** the section 67 grounds in respect of which the application has been made are established without holding a hearing at which evidence is led. The first circumstance is where the application to the sheriff has been made under s.93 because the section 67 grounds have been denied by either the child or a relevant person, but now both the child and each relevant person *who is present before the sheriff* accept that the section 67 grounds apply in respect of the child.[141] In this case, unless he is satisfied that in all the circumstances evidence in relation to the grounds should be heard, the sheriff is obliged to dispense with hearing evidence and he must determine that the grounds are established.[142] Because this provision is activated by acceptance of the section 67 grounds by the relevant persons who are present before the sheriff, the obligation to dispense with the evidence will arise even when another relevant person, who has not appeared at the sheriff court hearing, denied the grounds at the grounds hearing and there is nothing to suggest that he or she is now accepting

---

[138] 2011 Act s.173(6).

[139] 2011 Act s.173(1)–(4). Identical rules apply with evidence taken by a commissioner appointed under s.19 of the Vulnerable Witnesses (Scotland) Act 2004: s.174.

[140] 2011 Act s.175. The "proper administration of justice" includes: (a) appropriate protection of the person's dignity and privacy; and (b) ensuring the facts and circumstances of which the sheriff is made aware are relevant to the issue to be put before the sheriff and commensurate with the importance of that issue to the sheriff's decision on the question whether the ground is established: s.175(5). The evidence may be in writing or take the form of an audio or audio-visual recording: Child Care and Maintenance Rules 1997 r.3.76A. The lodging of restricted evidence is governed by r.3.81A.

[141] It may be noted that a person who accepted the grounds at the grounds hearing is entitled to withdraw that acceptance at the sheriff court: *Kennedy v R's Curator ad litem*, 1993 S.L.T. 295.

[142] 2011 Act s.105.

the grounds. It follows from this that the only way in which a denying relevant person can insist that the section 67 grounds be proved by evidence is to make sure that he or she attends the sheriff court hearing. So for example if at a grounds hearing the child accepts the grounds (say, of lack of parental care) but his parents deny them, and at the sheriff court hearing the mother now accepts the ground but the father does not attend, the sheriff will be obliged to dispense with hearing the evidence and to determine that the grounds are established. This may, however, be an example of the sort of circumstance in which the sheriff ought to decide that, in all the circumstances, evidence should be heard, for though the sheriff's discretion on the point is deliberately wide, the rule of law itself requires that the interests of all parties be protected, even if a party fails to attend. The sheriff may make his decision to dispense with hearing evidence and to determine that the ground is established at any time, whether before any evidence is led or while evidence is being led. A relevant person who denied grounds before the hearing may, for example, accept the grounds when it is explained by the sheriff what it is that is being accepted or when he or she realises that the evidence is incontrovertible.

8–30   The Child Care and Maintenance Rules 1997[143] provide that if, at the hearing of evidence (or any adjournment or continuation thereof) the section 67 grounds "are no longer in dispute" the sheriff may determine the application without hearing evidence. The grounds will no longer be in dispute, it is submitted, only when those who attended the hearing *and* denied or did not understand them now understandingly accept them. They remain in dispute if a non-accepting relevant person does not attend the sheriff court hearing and has given no indication that he or she now accepts the grounds; likewise they remain in dispute if the grounds were not understood at the children's hearing and there has been no subsequent gaining of understanding.

8–31   The second circumstance in which the sheriff may determine the application without holding a hearing at which evidence is led is when the application has been made under s.94 because the child (but *not* because the relevant person) would not understand or has not understood the explanation of the section 67 grounds, but before the application is determined the ground is accepted by each relevant person who is present at the hearing[144] before the sheriff. The typical example here would be where the relevant persons accept the grounds at the children's hearing but the child was too young to understand and s.106 provides a medium to fast-track the return of the case to the children's hearing when there is no real dispute as to the existence of the section 67 grounds. In this case, the sheriff may, but is not obliged to, determine the application without a hearing[145] (of evidence). This provision does not apply if it is the relevant

---

[143] r.3.47(A1), as inserted by the Act of Sederunt (Children's Hearings (Scotland) Act 2011) (Miscellaneous Amendments) 2013 art.3 para.35.

[144] The wording of this provision is odd: the sheriff may determine the application "without a hearing" (s.106(2)) so long as the grounds are accepted by each relevant person who is "present at the hearing" (s.106(1)). These look like different hearings: that referred to in s.106(1) might be the procedural hearing adverted to in r.3.45 of the Child Care and Maintenance Rules 1997 (as amended by the Act of Sederunt (Children's Hearings (Scotland) Act 2011) (Miscellaneous Amendments) 2013 art.3 para.32) at which the relevant person's acceptance of the grounds obviates the need for the hearing referred to in s.106(2). Alternatively "the hearing" to be attended by relevant persons in s.106(1) is the one at which there might—or might not, if s.106(2) applies—be " a hearing" of evidence. The change from the definite to the indefinite article is suggestive of this alternative.

[145] 2011 Act s.106(1) and (2).

person who has not understood or could not understand the grounds.[146] Even where s.106 does apply, however, the sheriff must not determine the application without a hearing if either: (i) the child, a relevant person, a safeguarder appointed to the child, or the reporter requests that a hearing be held by the sheriff; or (ii) the sheriff considers it would not be appropriate to determine the application without a hearing.[147] It would not be appropriate for the sheriff to determine the application without a hearing if, for example, the sheriff were not convinced that the relevant person really understood what he or she was accepting, or were not convinced that the statement of facts is sufficient to found the grounds of referral, or were of the view that a risk existed that grounds were being accepted for ulterior motives,[148] or if there were an element of fact relating to the ground that might prove contentious and for which a finding by the sheriff may prove useful to a subsequent children's hearing. The decision whether to determine the application without a hearing is governed by the welfare principle in ss.25 and 26, though probably not by the requirement in s.27 to take account of the views of the child since it is the child's incapacity to understand the explanation of the grounds that has activated this provision. If the child would not understand or has not understood the explanation of the grounds given by the chairing member of the grounds hearing it may be reasonable, and in the interests of the child, for the sheriff to determine the application to establish grounds without a hearing when all the parties who can accept are accepting and there is no-one denying or disputing the grounds.

The wording of s.105 (denial of grounds subsequently withdrawn) does not **8–32** permit the sheriff to dispense with the hearing of evidence and then hold the grounds not to be established[149] but there is no such limitation when s.106 (grounds not understood by the child) applies, for the latter provision simply gives the sheriff the power to determine the application without a hearing and the implication is clear that he may, therefore, determine it either by holding the ground to be established or holding it to be not established. It would, however, be a highly unusual case in which a sheriff held, without a hearing, that grounds were not established after they had been accepted by a relevant person. Rule 3.47(A1), however, applies whenever the section 67 grounds are "no longer in dispute" and it is conceivable that this might be because the reporter has come to accept that the grounds do not apply (or cannot be proven to apply) in relation to the child. If the sheriff does determine the application (made on the basis of lack of understanding) without a hearing he must do so before the expiry of the period of seven days beginning with the day on which

---

[146] The wording of s.106(1)(a) makes this plain, but in any case if a relevant person did not understand or could not understand at the children's hearing, it is unlikely that he or she will be able to accept the grounds before the sheriff.

[147] 2011 Act s.106(2) and (3).

[148] It is unfortunately not beyond the realms of imagination that an ill-intentioned mother could allege that her partner had sexually abused the child not to protect the child but to get rid of the partner from her life, or to increase her chances of winning a residence or contact dispute. If such an allegation is made and the child is too young to understand, the sheriff ought, it is submitted, never dispense with the evidence if all there is to suggest sexual or other abuse is the mother's acceptance of the grounds of referral. cf. *A v G*, 1996 S.C.L.R. 787. And see especially *Principal Reporter v K*, 2011 S.L.T. 271 (Sup. Ct.).

[149] 2011 Act s.105(2) requires the sheriff to determine that the ground is established whenever he dispenses with hearing evidence.

the application is made.[150] If the sheriff fails to make the determination in that time scale, then the application does not fall but a hearing at which evidence is led will be required within the normal period of 28 days from the day on which the application is lodged.[151]

THE SHERIFF'S DECISION

8–33　If the sheriff has not dispensed with hearing evidence[152] then, after having heard the evidence presented by all the parties, and having considered the closing submissions made by them, together with any safeguarder's report that has been submitted,[153] the sheriff must determine whether or not one or more of the grounds to which the application relates have been established. The Rules require that the sheriff give his decision orally at the conclusion of the hearing and he may at that time or within seven days thereafter issue a note of the reasons for his decision; a copy of the interlocutor and, if issued, a note of the reasons must be sent to the child, relevant person, safeguarder, curator ad litem, reporter and such other persons as the sheriff may direct.[154] The determination of the sheriff is limited to the question of whether or not the section 67 grounds are established and he is not entitled to go any further and express any view as to whether a compulsory supervision order should be made, for that would be to usurp the function of the children's hearing, in whose remit that question solely lies. Indeed, the sheriff is not entitled to indicate to the children's hearing factors in the case which he considers that the hearing ought to take into account when it is considering whether it is necessary to make a compulsory supervision order.[155] However, he is obliged to make findings on all the grounds that the reporter has attempted to prove established. It is not sufficient for the sheriff to hold one stated ground established and then send the case back to the children's hearing, for the hearing has a statutory obligation to consider all the established grounds.[156]

Grounds found established

8–34　Where the sheriff has determined that one or more of the grounds to which the application relates are established, whether after hearing evidence or on exercising his power to determine that the ground is established without hearing evidence, he is obliged to direct the reporter to arrange a children's hearing to decide whether to make a compulsory supervision order in relation to the child; he must also do so if he determines that none of the grounds to which the application relates is established but one or more other grounds were accepted by the child and each relevant person at the grounds hearing.[157] Having so directed the sheriff may, if one is not already in force, make an

---

[150] 2011 Act s.106(4). There is no equivalent requirement when the sheriff determines the application under s.105.
[151] 2011 Act s.101(2).
[152] Above, paras 8–29—8–32.
[153] See *Kennedy v M*, 1989 S.L.T. 687.
[154] Child Care and Maintenance Rules 1997 r.3.51.
[155] *Kennedy v A*, 1986 S.L.T. 358.
[156] *Harris v F*, 1991 S.L.T. 242 at 246F–G, per Lord Justice Clerk Ross.
[157] 2011 Act s.108(2) and (4).

interim compulsory supervision order in relation to the child,[158] but only when satisfied that the nature of the child's circumstances is such that for the protection, guidance, treatment or control of the child it is necessary as a matter of urgency to make such an order.[159] The interim compulsory supervision order may be in any terms that a compulsory supervision order may be in[160] including, if the usual conditions[161] are satisfied, a secure accommodation authorisation. If the interim compulsory supervision order specifies that the child is to reside at a place of safety, the children's hearing must be arranged to take place no later than the third day after the day on which the child begins to reside at the place of safety.[162] In addition to or instead of making an interim compulsory supervision order, if the sheriff is satisfied that there is reason to believe that the child would not otherwise attend the children's hearing, he may grant a warrant to secure attendance.[163] There is no test of "urgent necessity" for the granting of a warrant to secure attendance and in any case if the aim is simply to ensure the child's attendance it is this warrant rather than an interim compulsory supervision order that the sheriff ought to make. The welfare test in s.25 and the obligation to take account of the child's views in s.27 apply to the sheriff's decision on whether to make an interim compulsory supervision order or grant a warrant to secure attendance, as does the rule in s.29(2) that the sheriff may make the order or grant the warrant only if he considers that it would be better for the child if the order or warrant were in force than not.[164] If the application to the sheriff for a determination on whether section 67 grounds are established was made in relation to a child who is already subject to a compulsory supervision order, the sheriff, instead of making an interim compulsory supervision order, may (on satisfaction of the same test) make an interim variation of the existing compulsory supervision order.[165] On finding new grounds to apply to a child currently subject to a compulsory supervision order, the sheriff must require a review of that compulsory supervision order.[166]

Grounds found not established

If the sheriff determines that none of the grounds to which the application **8–35** relates is established, and none was accepted by the child and each relevant person at the grounds hearing, he must dismiss the application and discharge

---

[158] For the rules on intimation, see Child Care and Maintenance Rules 1997 r.3.64A, as inserted by Act of Sederunt (Children's Hearings (Scotland) Act 2011) (Miscellaneous Amendments) 2013 art.3 para.57.

[159] s.109(2)–(3). If an interim compulsory supervision order is already in force in relation to the child, the sheriff may make a further interim order, on the same test other than that it must be "necessary" to do so rather than necessary "as a matter of urgency": s.109(4)–(5). He may wish to do this either because the existing ICSO is likely to come to an end before a children's hearing can be arranged or because he wishes to include different measures from those included in the existing order.

[160] 2011 Act s.86(1)(a).

[161] Laid down in s.83(5) and (6) and discussed below, paras 11–12—11–14.

[162] 2011 Act s.109(7). So if the child begins to reside at the place of safety in terms of the order on Wednesday 4th November, the children's hearing must take place on or before Saturday 7th November.

[163] 2011 Act s.109(6). This warrant lasts for seven days: s.88(4)(d).

[164] 2011 Act s.29(1)(d).

[165] 2011 Act s.118(3).

[166] 2011 Act s.118(4).

the referral to the children's hearing.[167] It is to be assumed, though oddly the statute does not say this, that the child will be released on that discharge from any interim order or warrant that relates to the grounds. The sheriff has no option in this case and cannot, for example, find that other grounds than those relating to the application have been established.[168] If the evidence suggests the existence of other grounds the reporter may prepare a statement of these new grounds under s.89 and arrange a grounds hearing under s.69(2) in the normal way. If the sheriff finds that some of the grounds are not established and some are established he must direct the reporter to arrange a children's hearing to consider, in light of the grounds that are established, whether it is necessary to make a compulsory supervision order[169] or, if the child is presently subject to a compulsory supervision order, the sheriff must require a review of that compulsory supervision order.[170] In either case the children's hearing must accept as fact that the grounds not established do not apply in relation to the child and it cannot base its decision on them or take them into account in any way.

Amending the statement of grounds

8–36   In an early case, *McGregor v D*,[171] it was held that once the grounds have been put to the child and relevant persons, they could not thereafter be amended either by the reporter or by the sheriff. The rule now is that the sheriff may at any time, on the application of any party or of his own motion, allow amendment of any statement of grounds.[172] The "statement of grounds" is the statement prepared by the reporter setting out both which of the section 67 grounds the reporter believes applies in relation to the child and the facts on which that belief is based.[173] This suggests that the sheriff may allow amendment of either the ground itself or of the supporting facts, which is a change from the previous rule under which amendment was permitted of "any statement supporting" the ground.[174] In addition, it is provided that where in a statement of grounds it is alleged that an offence has been committed by or against any child, the sheriff may find that any other offence established by the facts has been committed.[175] The sheriff should, however, be careful in exercising these powers to ensure that the grounds found established do not depart so substantially from the statement of grounds (including the factual background) that was originally put to the child and relevant persons at the grounds hearing that in effect a case has been found against them that they were not asked to answer.

---

[167] 2011 Act s.108(3).

[168] cf. the power of the sheriff in an application under s.115 to find established different grounds from those previously established and challenged in that application: see below, para.8–49.

[169] 2011 Act s.108(2) and (4)(a). The sheriff may also make an interim compulsory supervision order or grant a warrant to secure attendance under s.109 or, if the child is currently subject to a compulsory supervision order, an interim variation of a compulsory supervision order (s.118(3)).

[170] 2011 Act s.118(4).

[171] 1977 S.L.T. 182. See also *S v Kennedy*, 1996 S.L.T. 1087.

[172] Child Care and Maintenance Rules 1997 r.3.48.

[173] 2011 Act s.89.

[174] Child Care and Maintenance Rules 1997 r.3.48, as originally enacted.

[175] Child Care and Maintenance Rules 1997 r.3.50. See *McGregor v D*, 1977 S.L.T. 182 and *M v Kennedy*, 1996 S.L.T. 434 (on the similar rule contained in the Social Work (Sheriff Court Procedure Rules) 1971 r.10).

SUBSEQUENT REVIEW OF GROUNDS DETERMINATION

Though the Social Work (Scotland) Act 1968 attempted to create a unified and **8–37** comprehensive code for dealing with children who may be in need of compulsory measures of care, the very novelty of the system it set up meant that certain gaps and omissions were inevitable. One omission concerned what was to happen when new evidence came to light some time after the sheriff had found grounds of referral to apply, which raised serious doubts as to the accuracy of that original finding. There were conflicting decisions on whether new evidence could be ordered to be examined by means of a petitition to the *nobile officium*.[176] A whole new procedure was therefore introduced by s.85 of the Children (Scotland) Act 1995, which was designed to put the process for reviewing the grounds of referral onto a statutory basis, to clarify the grounds upon which such reviews can take place, and to specify what was to happen to any order that had been made on the basis of a ground of referral which was subsequently found not to have been made out. The provision was very seldom used.[177] With some changes, which have not served to reduce the complexities of the procedure, s.85 of the 1995 Act has now been replaced by ss.110–117 of the Children's Hearings (Scotland) Act 2011.

When and by whom an application for review of grounds determination may be made

While there are a number of different ways in which the section 67 grounds **8–38** might be shown to apply in relation to a child, a judicial re-examination of the existence of the grounds (other than by means of appeal) is possible only when the grounds have been established by a positive determination of the sheriff on an application made under s.93(2)(a) or s.94(2)(a), that is to say on an application made by the reporter because the child or relevant person has not accepted the grounds or because the child or relevant person would not be capable of understanding, or has not understood, the grounds.[178] No review is permitted under s.110 of a sheriff's determination that grounds do not apply, nor when the grounds are established through the child's and relevant person's acceptance of them under s.91 or s.105 nor, explicitly, when the ground (that the child has committed an offence) is treated as having been established[179] where the child has pled guilty to or been found guilty of an offence in a criminal court which has then remitted the case to the children's hearing for disposal.[180]

There is no limitation on when an application for review of a grounds deter- **8–39** mination can be made, and so it might be made either before a children's hearing has made a compulsory supervision order in respect of the child, or after (even, as in *L, Petitioners*,[181] some years after). The application might be made even if the outcome of the children's hearing was that the referral was

---

[176] *R, Petitioner*, 1993 S.L.T. 910 and *L, Petitioners*, 1993 S.L.T. 1310 and 1342.

[177] The first reported decision which concerned an application under s.85 was that of *D v Children's Reporter*, 2009 Fam. L.R. 88 where the application was rejected on the ground that the applicant was not a "relevant person" as defined in the 1995 Act. Since then, the only other reported decision is that of *G v Authority Reporter*, 2013 S.L.T. (Sh Ct) 15.

[178] 2011 Act s.110, referring to s.108, which itself refers to s.93(2)(a) and s.94(2)(a).

[179] 2011 Act s.71(3).

[180] 2011 Act s.110(1).

[181] 1993 S.L.T. 1310 and 1342.

discharged, and even if a compulsory supervision order had been made but was subsequently terminated. There would seldom be point in making an application under s.110 in such circumstances, but it might well be made as a means of clearing a person's name, unjustly impugned by the sheriff's original determination, or as a means of preventing the establishment of section 67 grounds in respect of other children (e.g. those in the same household as the originally referred child).

8–40   Title to make an application for review of a grounds determination inheres only in: (i) the person who is the subject of the grounds determination, whether or not that person is still a child; and (ii) a person who is, or was at the time the grounds determination was made, a relevant person[182] in relation to the child.[183] No other person may challenge a finding of the sheriff that section 67 grounds apply in relation to the child, even where they feel that they have an interest to do so, for example another member of the child's household who wishes to clear his name from an imputation contained in the original finding, or a sibling of the child seeking to avoid any referral to a children's hearing on the basis of membership of that household: the process is not designed to correct any injustice except that to the child or relevant person or to have consequence for anyone else.

The conditions for making the application

8–41   The sheriff is obliged to review the grounds determination only if the applicant establishes each of the following four conditions[184]; otherwise the sheriff must dismiss the application.[185]

(a)   There is evidence in relation to the ground that was not considered by the sheriff when making the original grounds determination. This new evidence might include evidence which the sheriff did not hear because he dispensed with hearing the evidence under s.105(2) or he determined the application without a hearing under s.106(2). *AND*

(b)   The evidence would have been admissible. *AND*

(c)   There is a reasonable explanation for the failure to lead the evidence on the original application. The onus will be on the applicant to provide an explanation. A reasonable explanation might include the non-availability of the evidence, for whatever reason (so long as that reason is not directly attributable to the applicant), or because of new understandings which have developed since the original finding.[186] If evidence was available at the original proof but for some reason was not led, there will be a heavy onus in providing a reasonable explanation for that failure. *AND*

---

[182] This means a person who falls within the definition of "relevant person" contained in s.200, or a person who enjoyed relevant person status at the relevant time, having been deemed to be a relevant person by a pre-hearing panel or a children's hearing under s.81. It does not therefore include an individual deemed to be a relevant person by the children's hearing that immediately follows the sheriff's determination which might, in some cases at least, be an unfair restriction.

[183] 2011 Act s.110(3). See *D v Children's Reporter*, 2009 Fam. L.R. 88.

[184] 2011 Act s.111(3).

[185] 2011 Act s.111(4).

[186] As in *L, Petitioners*, 1993 S.L.T. 1310 and 1342.

(d) The evidence is significant and relevant to the question of whether the grounds determination should have been made. Evidence is significant and relevant if it is such as to cast genuine doubt on the validity of the original determination that grounds apply. Such evidence might be, for example, a retraction by the child of an allegation of abuse when the child's own previous evidence was the major determinant of the finding,[187] or other evidence that shows that the original evidence founded upon by the sheriff in making the original determination that grounds apply in relation to the child was in some way flawed and is now unreliable, or entirely new evidence which casts a different light on the child's circumstances at the time of the original finding. In exceptional cases the new evidence might be the quashing of a conviction of an alleged Schedule 1 offender but it is always to be remembered that the quashing of a criminal conviction, because proof is not established beyond reasonable doubt, is not in itself conclusive that a finding based on proof on the balance of probabilities ought similarly to be quashed.[188]

The sheriff is entitled to dismiss the application at this stage, exercising a gate- **8–42** keeping role, before considering the evidence[189] though it is suggested that he ought to do so only when in no doubt that the conditions above are not satisfied. Some of the conditions (e.g. that the evidence was not considered) require a factual determination while others (e.g. that the evidence is significant) call for a judgment: with the latter it may well be best to afford any benefit of the doubt to those proferring the evidence.

Procedure for reviewing grounds determination

An application under s.110 must contain the name and address of the appli- **8–43** cant and his or her representative (if any),[190] of the person who was the subject of the grounds determination (even if he or she is no longer a child, and only if the name and address is known), of any safeguarder[191] or curator ad litem, and of any person who is, or was at the time of the grounds determination, a relevant person (if not the applicant); it must include the date and grounds determination made and the place of the sheriff court which made the grounds determination, the grounds for making the application, specification of the nature of the new evidence, the explanation for the failure to lead such evidence

---

[187] cf. *R, Petitioner*, 1993 S.L.T. 910; *H, Petitioners*, 1997 S.L.T. 3. Both these cases held that retraction was not sufficient to justify exercising the *nobile officium*. The test under s.111 is not so strict and the child's evidence that he or she lied before can, it is submitted, be properly regarded as significant and relevant new evidence.

[188] See *R v Cannings* [2004] 1 W.L.R. 2607 and *Re U (A Child) (Serious Injury: Standard of Proof)* [2004] 3 W.L.R. 753, discussed in Norrie, "Identity Crisis" (2004) 49 J.L.S.S. 7/27.

[189] *G v Authority Reporter*, 2013 S.L.T. (Sh Ct) 15.

[190] The applicant may be represented by an advocate or solicitor or any other person who can satisfy the sheriff that he or she is a suitable person to represent the applicant and that he or she is authorised to do so: Child Care and Maintenance Rules 1997 r.3.21.

[191] It will be a rare case indeed in which a safeguarder is still in office when an application under s.110 is made. It might be that this provision refers to any safeguarder who previously acted as such, either at the grounds hearing or when the children's hearing subsequently disposed of the case. But the rule does not say this—though it deals with the point in relation to the relevant person.

in the original application, and any reports, affidavits and productions upon which the applicant intends to rely.[192]

8–44   The sheriff must hear the parties and consider the four conditions listed above, and he may allow such further procedure as he thinks fit to secure the expeditious determination of the application before determining whether the claims have been made out.[193] If the sheriff is satisfied that the four conditions in s.111(3) are satisfied, he must then review the grounds determination.[194] If not so satisfied he must dismiss the application.[195] If the grounds determination is to be reviewed, a safeguarder may be appointed (though presumably only when the subject of the grounds determination remains a child).[196] The child has a duty to attend the review hearing, though only for so long as he or she remains a child,[197] and the sheriff may excuse the child from attendance for the same reasons as he may excuse the child from attending the original hearing of the grounds determination.[198] The child may attend even if excused[199] and it may be supposed that if the person who is subject to the challenged grounds determination is no longer a child that person retains the right to attend. It may also be supposed that the relevant person (or person who was a relevant person when the original grounds determination was made) has a right to attend the review hearing; both the child and relevant person may be represented at the hearing by another person.[200]

8–45   At the conclusion of the hearing of the review, the sheriff will give his decision orally and the sheriff clerk shall forthwith send a copy of the interlocutor containing that decision to the child (unless service on the child has been dispensed with), any relevant person whose whereabouts are known, any safeguarder or curator ad litem, the reporter and such other persons as the sheriff may direct.[201] He may, when giving his decision or within seven days thereafter, issue a note of the reasons for his decision and if he does so the sheriff clerk must forthwith send a copy of such a note to the same people as those to whom the interlocutor must be sent.[202]

Outcome of the review

8–46   Where the sheriff is satisfied on the evidence presented to him that the section 67 ground to which the application relates has been established, he must refuse the application,[203] and any existing order will remain in force without variation, and any current process by which the child is being taken to

---

[192] Child Care and Maintenance Rules 1997 r.3.62(1), as substituted by Act of Sederunt (Children's Hearings (Scotland) Act 2011) (Miscellaneous Amendments) 2013 art.3 para.54. If the applicant does not wish to disclose the address or whereabouts of the child or any other person to anyone who is to receive notice of the application, the applicant must set out the reasons for this: r.3.62(2).

[193] Child Care and Maintenance Rules 1997 r.3.63(3), as substituted by Act of Sederunt (Children's Hearings (Scotland) Act 2011) (Miscellaneous Amendments) 2013 art.3 para.55.

[194] 2011 Act s.111(2).

[195] 2011 Act s.111(4). See *G v Authority Reporter*, 2013 S.L.T. (Sh Ct) 15.

[196] 2011 Act s.31.

[197] 2011 Act s.112(1).

[198] 2011 Act s.112(2), referring to s.103(2).

[199] 2011 Act s.112(3).

[200] 2011 Act s.113. The representative need not be a solicitor or advocate.

[201] Child Care and Maintenance Rules 1997 r.3.63(4) and r.3.51(1) and (2).

[202] Child Care and Maintenance Rules 1997 r.3.51(3).

[203] 2011 Act s.114(2).

a children's hearing will proceed in accordance with the normal rules. If, however, the sheriff determines that the ground to which the application relates is not established he must recall the original grounds determination and make an order discharging the referral of the child to the children's hearing, to the extent that it relates to the ground now found to be not established.[204] There is no provision under the 2011 Act, as there was in the 1995 Act,[205] permitting the sheriff to postpone the termination of the compulsory supervision order until some later specified date.

If the sheriff has discharged the referral in relation to the challenged ground, **8–47** but another section 67 ground specified in the original statement of grounds remains accepted (at the original grounds hearing) or established (at the original grounds determination) and the person to whom the grounds determination relates is still a child the sheriff must direct the reporter to arrange a children's hearing for the purpose of considering whether a compulsory supervision order should be made in relation to the child.[206]

If, on the other hand, the sheriff has discharged the referral in relation to the **8–48** challenged ground, and there are no other grounds in the same statement of grounds which have been accepted or established, any existing compulsory supervision order will be either terminated or reviewed, depending upon when it was made. If the child was already subject to a compulsory supervision order when the original grounds determination was made (and is therefore presently subject to an order that is not dependent on the grounds determination) the sheriff must require a review of that compulsory supervision order.[207] In any other case (that is to say where the child was not subject to a compulsory supervision order when the grounds determination was made, but was made subject to such an order subsequently) the sheriff must terminate any compulsory supervision order that is in force and, if the person is still a child, consider whether the child will require supervision and guidance.[208] If the sheriff considers that the child will require supervision or guidance he must order the relevant local authority[209] to provide it, and the local authority must give such supervision or guidance as the child will accept.[210]

New ground established at review of grounds determination

It may happen that in the course of hearing an application for the review of **8–49** a grounds determination the sheriff is satisfied that there is sufficient evidence

---

[204] 2011 Act s.114(3).

[205] Children (Scotland) Act 1995 s.85(7)(a)(ii). For details, see the second edition of this book, at pp.180–181.

[206] 2011 Act s.115(1) and (2). If the child is already subject to a compulsory supervision order the direction to the reporter will be to arrange a review of the compulsory supervision order: s.118(4). An interim compulsory supervision order may be made by the sheriff (s.115(3)), as may an interim variation of a compulsory supervision order (s.118(3)); the sheriff may grant a warrant to secure attendance at the children's hearing (s.115(4)). If an interim compulsory supervision order is made specifying that the child is to reside in a place of safety, the children's hearing must be arranged to take place no later than the third day after the day on which the child begins to reside in the place of safety: s.115(5), as inserted by the Children's Hearings (Scotland) Act 2011 (Modification of Primary Legislation) Order 2013 Sch.1 para.20(11).

[207] 2011 Act s.116(1) and (2).

[208] 2011 Act s.116(1) and (3).

[209] As defined in 2011 Act s.201.

[210] 2011 Act s.116(4) and (5).

to establish a section 67 ground that had not been specified in the original statement of grounds that led to the grounds determination that is currently being
challenged. If so, the sheriff must determine that this new ground is established
and, if the person to whom the grounds determination relates is still a child,
direct the reporter to arrange a children's hearing for the purposes of considering whether a compulsory supervision order should be made in relation to the
child.[211] It is an important principle of natural justice that those denying the
grounds must be given fair notice of what they are to deny and it follows that
sheriffs who are minded to find established a ground that had never been specified in a statement of grounds must do so only after ensuring that the parties
affected by the finding were given due notice as well as the opportunity to
challenge the allegations upon which the sheriff is making his determination
that a new section 67 ground is established.

---

[211] 2011 Act s.117(1) and (2). If the child is already subject to a compulsory supervision order
the direction to the reporter will be to arrange a review of the compulsory supervision order:
s.118(4). An interim compulsory supervision order may be made by the sheriff (s.117(3)), as may
an interim variation of a compulsory supervision order (s.118(3)); the sheriff may grant a warrant
to secure attendance at the children's hearing (s.117(4)). If an interim compulsory supervision
order is made specifying that the child is to reside in a place of safety, the children's hearing must
be arranged to take place no later than the third day after the day on which the child begins to
reside in the place of safety: s.117(5), as inserted by the Children's Hearings (Scotland) Act 2011
(Modification of Primary Legislation) Order 2013 Sch.1 para.20(12).

CHAPTER 9

DECISION MAKING AT THE HEARING

INTRODUCTION

The establishment of the section 67 grounds, whether by the acceptance by the **9–01** child and the relevant person that they apply in relation to the child[1] or by the sheriff determining that they apply[2] or by a court specifying them to exist,[3] does no more than raise the question of whether it is necessary for the protection, guidance, treatment or control of the child to make a compulsory supervision order in respect of the child,[4] and it neither answers that question nor indicates what form any necessary protection, guidance, treatment or control might take. These matters lie in the hands of the children's hearing who, once the section 67 grounds have been accepted or established, must move on to a consideration of those grounds and any other relevant information that has been made available to them. The two questions that are before the children's hearing at this stage in the proceedings are: (i) whether it is necessary to make a compulsory supervision order; and (ii) if so, what measures that order should contain in order to best serve the child's interests and best meet his or her needs.

At the beginning of any hearing the chairing member must introduce the **9–02** panel members who constitute the children's hearing, and explain the purpose of the hearing; must ask whether the child, each relevant person and any appointed safeguarder has received all the relevant information and documents required under the 2013 Rules to be sent to them; and must confirm whether the child, relevant person and safeguarder has had the opportunity to review that information and these documents and whether they have been understood by the child and relevant person.[5] If the child indicates that the documents do not accurately reflect the child's views the chairing member must endeavour to clarify the child's views on the relevant matter.[6] In addition, the chairing member must in all cases ensure that the child is aware of the availability of children's advocacy services.[7] Once these explanations and confirmations have been given and the hearing is satisfied that, in general terms, they have been understood, and after the other preliminaries such as the introductions

---

[1] Under the Children's Hearings (Scotland) Act 2011 s.91.

[2] On an application under either 2011 Act s.101 or s.110.

[3] Under s.48 or s.49 of the Criminal Procedure (Scotland) Act 1995 or s.12 of the Antisocial Behaviour etc. (Scotland) Act 2004.

[4] 2001 Act ss.91(3) and 119(3).

[5] Children's Hearings (Scotland) Act 2011 (Rules of Procedure in Children's Hearings) Rules 2013 (SSI 2013/194) (hereinafter "2013 Rules") r.58(1).

[6] 2013 Rules r.58(2).

[7] 2011 Act s.122.

and determination of the child's age,[8] the hearing can then move on to consider the two questions mentioned above.

DISCUSSION OF THE CHILD'S CIRCUMSTANCES AND NEEDS

9–03   The central element of any children's hearing that has reached the stage of considering whether it is necessary to make a compulsory supervision order is a discussion, led by the members of the hearing, with the child, the relevant persons who attend the hearing, any representative, safeguarder, the social worker allocated to the case, and anyone else permitted to attend by the chairing member[9] who might be able to make a contribution to the determination of where the child's interests lie. The reporter will not usually take part in the discussion, but it will sometimes be appropriate to ask the reporter questions, such as why he or she considered the child's circumstances serious enough that he or she believes it necessary for a compulsory supervision order to be made,[10] or whether he or she holds any other information that might be relevant. At some point during the hearing, the chairing member must take all reasonable steps to obtain the views of the child, each relevant person and any appointed safeguarder in relation to any relevant report, document or matter being considered by the hearing, and—importantly—what, if any, measures would be in the best interests of the child, and may invite any other person present at the hearing to express their views on, or provide other information relevant to, any matter or action being considered by the hearing.[11] The fact that the Rules require the chairing member to do this should not be taken as a prohibition on either of the other members of the hearing from doing so but is instead a reminder that the chairing member bears ultimate responsibility to ensure that it is done. In practice, individual panel members may engage directly with those attending the hearing and need not direct any invitation to contribute through the chairing member: the Rules are there to ensure that the chairing member involves everyone present if neither of the other panel members do so.

9–04   The aim of this discussion is to allow the members of the hearing properly to determine wherein the child's interests lie, and properly to identify what is the best of the available options for the child's future; in addition, importantly, it is the means by which the child and the relevant persons are afforded the opportunity to participate effectively in the decision-making process. "Effective participation", in this context, means participation that allows an individual a genuine chance to influence the eventual outcome. The assumption underlying this process is that the decision facing the hearing can best be made through an open discussion in which everyone present may take part and put forward their point of view, which the hearing members may weigh and assess and test through questions the answers to which may help them in identifying the best way forward for the child.

---

[8] See above, para.7–02.
[9] See above, paras 6–37—6–39.
[10] The reporter must be of this view before he or she is entitled to arrange a children's hearing: s.66(2).
[11] 2013 Rules r.60(2).

"If there is informality in the procedure at hearings, it is manifested at the discussion stage when panel members must exercise very considerable skills in questioning and listening (and being aware of non-verbal communication signals). In meeting their legal obligations, the hearing must try to open up discussion with what may well be very reluctant family members: there is on-going concern about the 'silent child' phenomenon and the not uncommon problem of ascertaining what the child's view of the situation is."[12]

The child, if old enough, should be the central person in the discussion, though **9–05** hearings must be sensitive to the fact that children attending hearings are likely to be apprehensive and nervous (which can sometimes come across as boorishness and bellicosity). While everyone who can make a contribution must be given the opportunity to do so, this should not be allowed to drown out the child's voice. There is an express statutory obligation on the children's hearing to ensure that, so far as practicable and taking account of the child's age and maturity: (i) the child is given an opportunity to indicate whether he or she wishes to express views; (ii) if he or she does so wish, is given an opportunity to express them; and (iii) regard is had to such views as he or she may express; in addition the chairing member must take all reasonable steps to obtain the child's views on what, if any, measures would be in the best interests of the child.[13] The child should be strongly encouraged to take a full part in the discussion and the role of all the hearing members (and not just the chairing member) is to create an environment during the hearing that encourages the child to feel able to do so. However, the statutory obligation is deliberately worded in terms of giving the child an opportunity to express views *if he or she so wishes* and so, at the end of the day, the child must be permitted to remain silent if he or she so wishes.[14] It is good practice to ask the child at various points throughout the discussion whether he or she is following, and agrees with, what is being said about him or her by the surrounding adults and to give him or her an opportunity to comment.

It is always courteous and usually helpful to allow every other person who **9–06** attends in an active capacity a chance to say what they think, though it should be made plain that the discussion must be directed towards the child's interests, and it falls to the chairing member to ensure that the discussion is not diverted away from that topic. It frequently happens, for example, that members of the child's family attempt to revive old sources of dispute, or attempt to allocate blame for the problems which have arisen. These issues are nearly always irrelevant to the task at hand. Or it may be that the section 67 grounds are again denied: if so it should be made plain that while the grounds must be discussed, they will be treated as established fact at all times. Though consensus may be aimed at—for a way forward that everyone agrees to and buys into is more likely of success than one that continues to be resisted—this is, of course, not always achieved and the child and relevant person, or the social worker or the safeguarder, may radically disagree with some or all of the options that the hearing are considering. The aim of the hearing is not to identify the outcome

---

[12] *Stair Memorial Encyclopaedia of the Laws of Scotland*, Vol.3 (1994), para.1344.

[13] 2011 Act s.27(3); 2013 Rules r.60(2)(b).

[14] There is no obligation, however, on the chairing member to indicate to the child that he or she has a "right to be silent", and it would normally be unhelpful to do so.

that everyone can agree upon but the outcome that best serves the child's interests. It should always be remembered that the sole decision-making power lies in the hands of the children's hearing, and the other participants in the discussion will sometimes need to be reminded that the purpose of the discussion is to assist the three members of the children's hearing in deciding what, in their view, is the best and most appropriate outcome for the child.

Extent of the discussion

9–07   There was previously some dispute as to the extent to which the children's hearing could take account of matters not directly connected to the grounds in respect of which the hearing had been arranged. In *K v Finlayson*[15] the sheriff held that the children's hearing could look no further than the facts established by the acceptance or establishment of the grounds of referral and that it could not, therefore, base its decision on other facts which came to its attention in the course of the hearing. This decision was, however, overruled by the First Division in the important case of *O v Rae*.[16] In this case, it was held that the children's hearing is entitled to take into account all relevant factors and that the test of relevancy of the hearing's consideration is whether the matter is relevant to the question of what course should be taken in the child's best interests.[17] The children's hearing is not, therefore, limited to a narrow consideration of the section 67 grounds alone but is entitled to ask for and consider information across a wide range and from a variety of different people.[18] The grounds in respect of which the children's hearing has been arranged are central to the discussion at the hearing, are always relevant, and must be considered,[19] but there may well be many other additional factors relevant to a determination of whether, and if so in what terms, a compulsory supervision order should be made. While the section 67 grounds are central to the hearing's original consideration of the question of whether it is necessary to make a compulsory supervision order,[20] they are not necessarily determinative of the answer to that question. Indeed the hearing will seldom, if ever, be able to answer the question of whether it is necessary to make a compulsory supervision order by having regard only to the section 67 ground that brought the child before the hearing and the necessity for the order will often be found in other significant concerns around the child's life, lifestyle and family circumstances

---

[15] 1974 S.L.T. (Sh Ct) 51.

[16] 1993 S.L.T. 570.

[17] *O v Rae*, 1993 S.L.T. 570, per Lord President Hope at 574. This case was followed in *M v Kennedy*, 1996 S.L.T. 434, in which the evidence was unclear as to whether the child had been the victim of an offence under s.3 of the Sexual Offences (Scotland) Act 1976 (sexual intercourse with a girl under the age of 13) or under s.4 thereof (sexual intercourse with a girl between the ages of 13 and 16). Because another ground of referral was established, the hearing was held entitled to take account of the undisputed fact that the girl had been subject to unlawful sexual intercourse, even although there was a dispute as to which particular crime of she had been the victim. See also *M v Authority Reporter*, 2011 G.W.D. 2-94 where Sheriff Principal Taylor followed *O v Rae*.

[18] *R, Petitioner*, 1993 S.L.T. 910, per Lord President Hope at 915C.

[19] At least at hearings when the grounds are being considered in order to determine whether or not to make a compulsory supervision order. The grounds are less important and may indeed be irrelevant to hearings at which a compulsory supervision order made some time earlier is being reviewed and the question is whether it should be continued.

[20] They are "the hard core of the material upon which [the hearing's] decision is based", per Lord Justice-Clerk Grant in *Kennedy v B*, 1973 S.L.T. 38 at 40.

of which the grounds are merely indicative. So even the most serious and horrible offences against the child, such as his or her being shot at in a class-room and seriously wounded by a crazed gunman, or being kidnapped and raped by a stranger, might amount to a ground of referral but at the same time say very little about the terms that a compulsory supervision order (if at all necessary) should contain. It is one of the strengths of the system that the existence of a section 67 ground merely raises the question of whether a compulsory supervision order is necessary but does not answer that question: it is for the children's hearing to explore whatever aspect of the child's life needs to be explored in order to allow them to answer the question and to design an order that addresses the child's needs. The policy of the 2011 Act, as with its predecessors, is clearly to leave the children's hearing free from artificial restraint in its exploration of what may be in the interests of the child.

An apparent anomaly resulting from this position is that the children's hearing **9–08** might make its decision on the basis of alleged facts that are disputed by the child or relevant person and that have never been established by proof in a court of law. This raised concerns in *O v Rae*[21] in which a hearing took into account an unproven allegation of sexual abuse against her father made by a sibling of children referred on the basis of lack of parental care. It is, however, a misunderstanding of the system to assume that the children's hearing has no power to resolve disputes of fact.[22] The sheriff is empowered to resolve only disputes as to the existence of the section 67 grounds (and any findings of fact made in the course of resolving such disputes must be accepted by the children's hearing[23]). However, disputes of fact can arise as to very many other circumstances, such as how often the child attends school, whether the parents have co-operated with social workers, or whether a parent's ex-cohabitant continues to have contact with the child. These issues may all significantly affect the outcome of a hearing, yet there is no mechanism to have them resolved by a court of law, and it rests with the children's hearing to resolve these disputes, by the members of the hearing themselves assessing the credibility of statements which are not made on oath.[24] So long as all the parties have the opportunity to influence the decision to be made by the hearing, it does not infringe art.6 of the European Convention on Human Rights for the hearing to take into account allegations and matters that have not been proven by evidence given on oath[25]: the requirement for an adversarial trial "means an opportunity to have knowledge of and comment on the observations filed or evidence adduced by the other party".[26] The theory underpinning this approach is that resolution of a factual dispute is less important than identifying the child's needs, and that if that identification requires dispute resolution, this is best achieved by a non-adversarial discussion in which every participant is able freely to express his or her view and is given an opportunity to

---

[21] 1993 S.L.T. 570. Mitchell described this as "the most fundamental flaw in our children's hearing system", 1997 Scolag 9 at p.11.

[22] See further, Norrie, "In Defence of *O v Rae*", 1995 S.L.T. (News) 353.

[23] *M v Kennedy*, 1993 S.L.T. 431.

[24] A process not dissimilar from a court assessing the worth of hearsay evidence.

[25] *M v Authority Reporter*, 2011 G.W.D. 2-94, per Sheriff Principal Taylor.

[26] *McMichael v United Kingdom* (1995) 20 E.H.R.R. 205 at [80]. In *Engel v Netherlands* (1976) 1 E.H.R.R. 647 the European Court of Human Rights held, at [90], that it is not an infringement of art.6 for a tribunal to take account of factors other than those which brought a party before the tribunal, nor for these factors to determine the outcome.

challenge the views of the others. In that context, many disputes do not, in fact, need to be resolved definitively.[27] Other disputes are easily resolved by accepting the more credible story (e.g. when a teacher says that the child does not attend school at all and the child says that he or she does)[28]; yet other disputes are entirely judgmental and, if relevant to the decision to be made, will clearly require resolution by the hearing (such as, for example, whether the child has benefited from the terms of an existing compulsory supervision order). Disputes of fact which might themselves amount to a section 67 ground will, and should, normally be resolved by the reporter arranging a hearing on the basis of new grounds which, if then denied, can be tested in court. It is only in very rare cases that a disputed fact will clearly and fundamentally affect the outcome. In these cases, the children's hearing must make their judgment of credibility as best they can, and if their judgment is wrong this can be established on appeal to the sheriff, before whom evidence can be led on oath.[29] If the children's hearing is shown to have made a mistaken assessment of fact then its decision may be challenged as being not justified, and this ability for the system itself to be recalibrated protects it (and the case of *O v Rae*) from ECHR challenge. The system would very rapidly break down if every dispute of fact that could influence the hearing's decision required that the hearing be brought to an end so that the matter could be sent off to the sheriff for resolution. A child ought not to be able to postpone a dispositive decision, for example in a case relating to school non-attendance, by denying that there is continued non-attendance since the date the grounds were established, even when that could amount to a new section 67 ground.

Discussing adoption and permanence

9–09   One area of discussion that has for long caused problems is the local authority's plans for the permanent separation of the child from his or her parents. In *R. v Children's Hearing for the Borders Region*[30] a children's hearing purported to exercise their power to specify the child's place of residence by ordering that the child "should reside in a pre-adoptive home chosen by the local authority". The Court of Session held that this was ultra vires of the children's hearing since a condition of residence must specify precisely where the child is to reside. In addition, the opinion was expressed, though obiter, that the challenged condition breached the statutory provision in the adoption legislation[31] prohibiting anyone other than an adoption agency from placing a child for adoption or making arrangements for the adoption of a child. Legislation quickly followed to reverse this opinion[32] and it is now provided[33] that the

---

[27] Such as for example when the child accepts that he or she has not been attending school but suggests that it is less often than the school records indicate.

[28] This is not to suggest that any particular category of person, such as teachers, should always be believed by hearings. The present writer has had experience of a teacher at a special school denying a child's allegation that the teacher continually called him by a highly pejorative name— and finding the child more credible than the teacher.

[29] 2011 Act s.155(5). See further below, para.14–11.

[30] 1984 S.L.T. 65.

[31] Now s.75 of the Adoption and Children (Scotland) Act 2007.

[32] s.27 of the Law Reform (Miscellaneous Provisions) (Scotland) Act 1985.

[33] Adoption and Children (Scotland) Act 2007 s.119(7) and (8), as amended by the Children's Hearings (Scotland) Act 2011 (Modification of Primary Legislation) Order 2013 (SSI 2013/211) Sch.1 para.17(13).

making or varying of a compulsory supervision order or the making of an interim compulsory supervision order which requires the child to reside at a particular place shall not constitute the making of arrangements for the adoption of a child contrary to s.75 of the Adoption and Children (Scotland) Act 2007. This means that a children's hearing can name as a child's residence the home of prospective adopters, knowing and intending that this will facilitate the adoption process in relation to that child.

However, there have been later sheriff court decisions[34] in which it has been **9–10** held that while a children's hearing can require a child to reside with prospective adopters they cannot make any other decision which will facilitate adoption, and in particular they cannot terminate contact between the child and the birth parent for any reason connected with the proposed adoption. The reasoning was that this would amount to "making arrangements" for adoption, which the amended legislation allows children's hearings to do only to the extent of requiring a child to live with prospective adopters. This approach would cause immense difficulties for hearings who, in the full knowledge of the adoption plans, would have to attempt to cast these plans from their minds and make a decision without reference to a factor vitally important to the child's future. It runs the severe risk of misrepresenting the true reasons for a decision if hearings are to skew their stated reasons for decision to avoid all mention of a factor which may have been uppermost in everyone's minds. And it is inconsistent with the proposition of the Inner House in *O v Rae*[35] that "any information which is relevant to the making of a supervision requirement . . . will be relevant information to which the children's hearing may have regard".

The assumption upon which the approach is predicated, that children's hear- **9–11** ings may only take a short-term view of the child's welfare, has never been correct, and there is no Court of Session authority for the proposition that a children's hearing is entitled or obliged to ignore important and influential facts. And indeed it is doubtful whether the sheriff court decisions mentioned above survived (if they were ever good law) the passing of the Children (Scotland) Act 1995. Provision was made in that Act,[36] for the local authority to seek a review of a supervision requirement if the child was to be freed or placed for adoption or an adoption order was pending; and equivalent rules are now found in s.131 of the Children's Hearings (Scotland) Act 2011, which provides that the local authority must require a review of a compulsory supervision order whenever it is satisfied that the best interests of the child would be served by the authority placing the child for adoption and it has the intention to do so,[37] or is aware that an application has been made and is pending, or is about to be made, for an adoption order in respect of the child, or it intends to apply for the making, varying or revocation of a permanence order under the Adoption and Children (Scotland) Act 2007.[38] This places adoption plans at

---

[34] *A v Children's Hearing for Tayside Region*, 1987 S.L.T. (Sh Ct) 126, *M v Children's Hearing for Strathclyde Region*, 1988 S.C.L.R. 592. See also the sheriff's decision appealed against on other grounds in *Kennedy v M*, 1995 S.L.T. 717 (the issue was not discussed in the Inner House).

[35] 1993 S.L.T. 570 at 574.

[36] Children (Scotland) Act 1995 s.73(4).

[37] The same obligation is imposed on other registered adoption services by s.106 of the Adoption and Children (Scotland) Act 2007.

[38] 2011 Act s.131(2)(c).

the forefront of the hearing's consideration. The children's hearing must do two things at this review: it must review the current compulsory supervision order under s.138, and in addition it must prepare a report providing advice as to the circumstances to which the review relates—that is to say advice as to the proposals for an adoption or a permanence order.[39] This report is for both the local authority and the court dealing with the adoption or permanence application and the court must have regard to it in coming to its decision.[40] It would be entirely unrealistic to expect a children's hearing to ignore the adoption or permanence plans for the purposes of the review and at the same time to give advice about these plans for the purposes of the report to be sent to the court. Also, s.25(2) requires the children's hearing to regard the need to safeguard and promote the welfare of the child *throughout his or her childhood* as the paramount consideration, and this requires the hearing to take a long-term view. It is submitted that a children's hearing can and must take account of the local authority's plans for the future of the child, even when these plans involve possible adoption or permanent separation from the parents, in determining what measures should be included in any compulsory supervision order; and if it believes that adoption or permanence is best for the child the hearing can and must make whatever decision will, in its view, further the child's best interests by advancing these plans.

MAKING THE DECISION

9–12   Once the hearing members have given consideration to all the issues that they consider relevant, it is good practice for the chairing member to inquire of all those present whether there are any other issues that ought to be raised and given consideration. Then, after having given consideration, through discussion, to all the circumstances relating to the child which have been put before it, the children's hearing must make a decision of which of the available options open to the hearing most appropriately meets the child's needs. "The hearing should have attempted to ascertain the family's views and discussed the range of options on offer. The decision should not, therefore, come as a surprise to anyone."[41] Depending on the type of hearing, the decision will be to make, vary or terminate a compulsory supervision order, discharge the referral or defer making a decision; if the decision is anything other than to terminate an existing compulsory supervision order or discharge a referral without making one, there are numerous subsidiary decisions that will be required, including whether any interim order is required or whether any terms or conditions are to be attached to or removed from the compulsory supervision order.

9–13   Decisions are, as always, made on a majority basis,[42] and no decision will have been made unless it attracts the support of at least two members of the hearing. It is possible (though highly unlikely) that each member of the hearing will prefer a different one of the various options open to the hearing, in which

---

[39] 2011 Act s.141(2). See below, paras 12–16—12–18.

[40] 2011 Act s.141(4).

[41] *Stair Memorial Encyclopaedia of the Laws of Scotland*, Vol.3 (1994), para.1353.

[42] 2011 Act s.202(2). Curiously, there was no equivalent express provision in the pre-2011 legislation but majority decision-making was always the practice.

case no decision can be said to have been made. There is no provision made for the hearing failing to come to a decision and unless one of the members of the children's hearing then wishes to reconsider his or her decision (which is competent if the chairing member so permits), the only option in these circumstances is deferral: failure to reach a majority decision amounts, it is submitted, to an agreement that the decision must be deferred until a subsequent children's hearing. The deferring hearing will then be faced with the decision of whether or not to make an interim compulsory supervision order[43] but, that question raising only two options, there will always be a majority, one way or the other.

Making the decision is as much a part of the hearing as the explanation of **9–14** the grounds and the discussion of the child's circumstances, and it follows that those persons who have a right and a duty to attend the children's hearing (i.e. the child and the relevant person) must be present when the decision is being made.[44] The members of the children's hearing are not permitted to go into a closed session to discuss matters outwith the hearing or presence of the child and relevant person, though there is nothing to prevent them from discussing amongst themselves, openly before the child and relevant person, what the decision should be. It is not common practice for an individual member of the hearing to attempt to persuade his or her colleagues as to what decision to make and while this would not be contrary to the terms of the statute or the Rules it is unlikely to be particularly helpful. The three members of the hearing have an equal vote and are entitled to make their own decision without reference to the reasoning of their colleagues.[45] Hearings should not be afraid of majority decisions rather than unanimous decisions, for they sometimes serve useful symbolic purposes for the child and the relevant person (as well as informative purposes for future hearings). It is one of the strengths of the system that there are three members of the hearing who may come from a very wide cross-section of the community and who may bring to the decision-making process very different perspectives and, indeed, attitudes and values. While the decision is that of the children's hearing as a whole, that decision is made up of the contributions of all three members.[46]

The overarching principles: general

Children's hearings are given statutory guidance as to how they should come **9–15** to their decisions, in the form of three overarching principles laid down by the 2011 Act, which must be taken into account in determining which of the various options open to it should be adopted. These are discussed in the following paragraphs.

---

[43] 2011 Act s.92 (grounds hearings) and s.120 (subsequent hearings). A review hearing may make an interim variation of a compulsory supervision order under s.140: see below, paras 13–26—13–27.

[44] The 1995 Act provided that the child and the relevant person had a right to be present "at all stages of the hearing" (s.45(1)(a) and s.45(8)(a)). The equivalent provisions in the 2011 Act are to the effect that the child (s.73(2) and (3)) and the relevant person (s.74(2) and (3)) "must attend the children's hearing" unless excused from "all or part of the children's hearing", and both "have a right to attend a children's hearing" (s.78(1)). This amounts, it is submitted, to a right and duty to attend at all stages (including the decision-making stage) unless excused.

[45] So for example in r.61 of the 2013 Rules it is provided that each member of the hearing must state their decision and reasons. This obligation is replicated throughout the Rules.

[46] See (for example) 2013 Rules r.61(2)(a) and (3)(i).

The paramountcy of the child's welfare

9–16   First, the children's hearing must regard the need to safeguard and promote the child's welfare throughout his or her childhood as the paramount consideration.[47] This applies whenever a children's hearing or a pre-hearing panel is coming to a decision about a matter relating to a child[48]: that will include dispositive decisions such as to discharge the referral, to make, continue or vary a compulsory supervision order; interim measures such as the making of an interim compulsory supervision order, a warrant to secure attendance or a medical examination order; and also decisions upon the terms of any of these measures or orders, such as whether to include contact directions, a secure accommodation authorisation, or any other term or condition that will have legal effect. The children's hearing and (since the amendments to the Children's Hearings (Scotland) Act 2011 contained in subsidiary legislation[49]) the pre-hearing panel[50] may make a decision which is inconsistent with that requirement if the hearing considers that, for the purpose of protecting members of the public from serious harm (whether or not physical harm), it is necessary that the decision be made; in doing so, however, the hearing is to regard the need to safeguard and promote the welfare of the child throughout his or her childhood as a primary consideration rather than the paramount consideration.[51] This might be used, for example, when it is not the best option for the child to be kept in secure accommodation but the risk to the public from the child's continued liberty is such as to outweigh the child's own needs. The welfare consideration applies to any decision made by a children's hearing or pre-hearing panel under the Act about a matter relating to a child,[52] though some decisions, such as for example questions of right to attend the hearing, must be excluded by implication as not raising an issue which calls for a welfare judgment. The reference to the whole of the child's childhood, which first appeared in the 1995 Act,[53] requires that children's hearings take a long-term view. Often it is difficult to predict what is in the child's interests beyond the immediate future, and the provision probably requires little more than that the hearing at least give consideration to the child's long-term future. Short-term gains are not, of course, to be dismissed as unimportant, especially since a child's perception of time-scale is very different from an adult's, but nor are long-term gains to be sacrificed for some immediate benefit. The balance is very difficult to strike correctly is every case, and children's hearings are not to be criticised (nor their decisions overruled) if, with hindsight, it becomes obvious that a decision other than the one they have reached would have served the child's interests better.

---

[47] 2011 Act s.25(2).

[48] 2011 Act s.25(1).

[49] Children's Hearings (Scotland) Act 2011 (Modification of Primary Legislation) Order 2013 (SSI 2013/211) Sch.1 para.20(3).

[50] Though given the limited range of decisions open to a pre-hearing panel the issue of protecting the public can hardly arise. See further above, para.5–09.

[51] 2011 Act s.26.

[52] As such, the consideration is of more general application than the equivalent principle in the Children (Scotland) Act 1995: see *S v Proudfoot*, 2002 S.L.T. 743 where the welfare principle was held not to apply to matters of law or procedural decisions.

[53] Children (Scotland) Act 1995 s.16(1).

The child's views and effective participation

The second overarching principle that a children's hearing needs to take **9–17**
account of in coming to a decision about a matter relating to a child concerns
the views of the child. The hearing must, so far as practicable and taking
account of the age and maturity of the child: (a) give the child an opportunity
to indicate whether or not he or she wishes to express views; (b) if he or she
does so wish, give him or her an opportunity to express these views; and (c)
have regard to any views expressed by the child.[54] This principle is (at least) as
important as the welfare principle for the child—the central person at the
hearing and the person most affected by its outcome—must be allowed and
indeed encouraged to participate as fully as possible in the decision-making
process. This is ensured in a number of different statutory provisions, as well
as the 2011 Act itself. The chairing member is obliged by the 2013 Rules to
take all reasonable steps to obtain the views of the child (and relevant person
and safeguarder) in relation to any matter being considered by the hearing and
what, if any, measures would be in the best interests of the child.[55] Even where
the child is not present at the hearing, having been excused attendance, the
Scottish Children's Reporter Administration must take all reasonable steps to
enable the child to attend by way of telephone, video link or any other method
of communication.[56] It is presumed that a child who is aged 12 or over is of
sufficient age and maturity to form a view.[57] These rules apply whenever the
children's hearing is coming to a decision about a matter relating to a child and
this includes procedural questions (such as whether to exclude a relevant
person) as well as when the hearing is considering whether to make, or is
reviewing, a compulsory supervision order; in addition it applies to the hearing's decision whether to make or grant any other order open to it under the
2011 Act and to the measures that may be included in any order. The requirement relating to the child's views expressly applies when hearings are providing
advice to a sheriff considering whether to continue a child protection order and
when they are drawing up a report for a court considering making an adoption
or permanence order in respect of the child.[58] The general right of participation, in any case, requires that the child be given the opportunity to express
views, so far as practicable and taking account of the child's age and maturity.
As well as giving the child the opportunity to express views, the chairing
member of the hearing is obliged (unless, taking account of the child's age and
maturity, he or she considers it inappropriate to do so) to ask the child, at some
point during the hearing, whether the documents provided to the child in which
the child's views are recorded accurately reflect these views.[59] This provision,
which had no counterpart in the 1995 Act, reinforces the importance of the

---

[54] 2011 Act s.27(1)–(3).
[55] 2013 Rules r.60(2)(b).
[56] 2013 Rules r.19. See further above, para.6–08.
[57] 2011 Act s.27(4). This is stated to be without prejudice to the generality of the requirement to
have regard to any views expressed and so it cannot be taken from the presumption of maturity that
a child under the age of 12 years is presumed insufficiently mature. Such presumptions, which may
have some place in court proceedings, are inappropriate within the context of the children's
hearing where each child is dealt with as an individual and with the part they are to play in the
discussion depending upon the hearing's own assessment of the child's capabilities.
[58] 2011 Act s.27(5).
[59] 2011 Act s.121.

hearing taking into account such views as the child is willing to express, and the obligation must not, therefore, be carried out in a merely mechanical manner. That importance is further reinforced by the 2013 Rules which provide that if, in response to the request to confirm the accuracy of any recorded views, the child indicates they are not accurate, the chairing member must endeavour to clarify the child's views on the relevant matter.[60] A further provision designed to ensure the child's effective participation is found in the 2013 Rules, which allow a hearing that defers making a decision to determine that, for the purpose of enabling the child to participate effectively, he or she should be represented by a solicitor or counsel and to require the reporter to notify the Scottish Legal Aid Board of that determination and of the child's name and address.[61] The deferring hearing might also require the reporter to make arrangements for an interpreter for the child or to take any other steps with a view to securing the child's participation in the hearing.[62] The obligations to have regard to the child's views and to facilitate the child's effective participation apply to pre-hearing panels,[63] and the 2013 Rules require that the child (and relevant person) who attends any pre-hearing panel must be invited to make representations (orally or in writing).[64]

Minimum (proportionate) intervention

9–18   The third overarching principle that the children's hearing must always give effect to is that it may make, vary or continue an order, interim variation or warrant only if the hearing considers that it would be better for the child if the order, interim variation or warrant were in force than not.[65] This applies whenever a children's hearing is considering whether to: (a) make, vary or continue a compulsory supervision order; (b) make an interim compulsory supervision order or an interim variation of a compulsory supervision order; (c) make a medical examination order; or (d) grant a warrant to secure attendance.[66] This consideration is based on the premise that the state should get involved in the upbringing of children only when intervention is necessary and can be shown to be likely to be better for the child than if the state did not get involved. As such, the consideration reflects the test for making a compulsory supervision order, which is that it is necessary to do so for the protection, guidance, treatment or control of the child. The children's hearing must be persuaded, in other words, not only that the order it is proposing to make is objectively "necessary" but that it is likely to improve the child's situation. Aligned with this principle in the 2011 Act, and as important, is the "proportionality" principle of ECHR law,[67] which requires that such measures of state intervention as are necessary should be designed in a way that involves the minimum interference in family life that is necessary to achieve the aim of the interference: the terms

---

[60] 2013 Rules r.58(2).
[61] 2013 Rules r.61(1)(d) and (e).
[62] 2013 Rules r.61(2)(f).
[63] 2011 Act s.27, as amended by the Children's Hearings (Scotland) Act 2011 (Modification of Primary Legislation) Order 2013 Sch.1 para.20(4); 2013 Rules r.50(7).
[64] 2013 Rules r.48(4)(a) in relation to pre-hearing panels arranged to consider a relevant person claim; r.49(1)(a) in relation to pre-hearing panels arranged for any other reason.
[65] 2011 Act s.28(2).
[66] 2011 Act s.28(1).
[67] See above, para.1–07.

of the order will be disproportionate to the legitimate aim of the order if they go any further than is necessary for the achievement of that aim. The legitimate aim of any decision that a children's hearing makes is easy to identify: making the child's life better. More difficult is ensuring that the means adopted to achieve that aim do not interfere any further than is necessary with the child's—and the relevant persons'—right to family life as protected by art.8 of the ECHR. Clearly the more serious the child's circumstances are the more intrusive the interference might need to be, but it is to be remembered that, the section 67 grounds themselves giving at best an incomplete indication of the seriousness of the child's circumstances, proportionality must exist between the child's needs (the legitimate aim) and the outcome, rather than between the section 67 grounds and the outcome. So even very minor grounds may justify a serious outcome if that is the only way—and the minimal way—to achieve the identified goal. The requirement in s.28 of the 2011 Act that it be better for the child that the order or warrant is in force than not and the proportionality principle from ECHR jurisprudence coalesce within the idea that the action of the state must be "necessary", which thus takes on a double meaning: a compulsory supervision order, or a warrant, or any other decision made in respect of a child that interferes with his or her private or family life must be necessary in the domestic sense of being better for the child than not making the order, and it must be necessary in the ECHR sense of being a proportionate response to the child's needs: this is, however, a single rather than a double hurdle and in many respects is simply two different ways of saying the same thing.

STATING THE DECISION

Whatever the type of children's hearing, and whatever decision the hearing makes, the final substantive part of any hearing is the announcement of what that decision is and, where appropriate, of the right to appeal against it. Different types of hearing are governed by different Rules,[68] but the overall picture is the same: after the discussion at which everyone has been able to make their contribution each member of the children's hearing must state his or her decision and its reasons; the chairing member must them summarise this by confirming the overall decision of the hearing (that is to say the decision that is supported by at least two of the three members of the children's hearing) and explain its reasons and effect; and the chairing member must also inform those who are present of their right to appeal and the timescale for doing so[69]

9–19

---

[68] 2013 Rules r.61(2) and (3) for grounds hearings held after deferral and review hearings (where the decision is to defer (or further defer) making a decision); r.62(2) and (3) for grounds hearings held after deferral and review hearings (where a substantive decision is made); r.63(2) and (3) (at grounds hearing where the reporter is directed to make an application to the sheriff to establish the s.67 grounds); r.66(4) (where a review hearing is considering whether an individual previously deemed to be a relevant person should continue to be so deemed); r.70(3) and (4) (hearings held on the second working day after a child protection order is made or implemented); r.73(3) and (4) (where the hearing is considering a further interim compulsory supervision order); r.74(6) and (7) (where the hearing is reviewing a contact direction under s.126); and r.95(3) and (4) (where the hearing is reviewing a secure accommodation authorisation). There is no rule explicitly applying this process to pre-hearing panels, but it is a sensible model to follow there too.
[69] If the child, relevant person or safeguarder is not present then the Reporter must in any case give information about the right of appeal and its timescale: 2013 Rules r.88(3)(d).

and, where appropriate, the right to seek suspension of the decision.[70] Once this has been done, it is good practice to inquire whether the child and relevant person understand the decision and whether they want to ask anything about it. As part of the explanation of the decision to make, vary or continue a compulsory supervision order, the chairing member should explain to the child and the relevant person the nature and effect of the order—that is to say who is bound by it and what is expected of the child under its terms and the support that the family can expect to receive—and also how long it will last and when it might be reviewed. These explanations bring the hearing to an end.

9–20 At the conclusion of the children's hearing the chairing member will write or cause to be written a statement of the reasons for the decision to which the hearing has come and this must be given by the reporter to the child, each relevant person, and any appointed safeguarder within five days of the children's hearing.[71] This is so for every hearing, whether it makes a substantive or procedural decision; there is in addition an explicit statutory obligation for the children's hearing to record the appointment of a safeguarder and to give reasons for that decision.[72] These statements are necessary for the purpose of maintaining an accurate record of what has been decided, and also of explaining why. Those affected by the decision are entitled to an explanation of the basis on which it has been reached.[73] The reasons should therefore be a clear statement of the material considerations to which the children's hearing had regard in their decision and it must be intelligible to the persons to whom it is addressed—including those who were not present at the hearing—and it must deal with all the substantial questions which were the subject of the decision.[74] The decision is that of the hearing as a whole, even when made on the basis of a majority. There is no requirement that it be noted that the decision was a majority decision, but nor is there any prohibition on the chairing member doing so and if the decision of the majority is to make, vary or continue a compulsory supervision order it is often helpful to the subsequent review hearing to know that there was a dissent, and why.

---

[70] On suspension, see below, paras 10–20—10–21 and 14–30—14–35.

[71] 2013 Rules r.88(1), (2) and (3)(a) and (b). Though the Rules do not explicitly require the chairing member to draw up a written statement of the decision and its reasons (as was required by the predecessor Children's Hearings (Scotland) Rules 1996 r.10(5)) this will always be the best way of ensuring that the information that requires to be sent to the child, relevant person and safeguarder is an accurate reflection of what the hearing decided and why.

[72] 2011 Act s.30(3) and (4). The decision to appoint a safeguarder and the reasons for doing so must be given by the reporter to the appointed safeguarder: 2013 Rules r.56(3)(c).

[73] per Lord President Hope in *DH & JH v Kennedy* Unreported December 20, 1991. In *Wordie Property v Secretary of State for Scotland*, 1984 S.L.T. 345 at 348 it was stated, in a different context, that an administrative decision, appealable to a court, had to be such as to "leave the informed reader, and the court, in no real and substantial doubt as to what the reasons for it were and what were the material considerations which were taken into account in reaching it".

[74] per Lord President Hope in *Kennedy v M*, 1995 S.L.T. 717 at 723H, citing his own comments in *DH & JH v Kennedy* Unreported December 20, 1991. A failure to make the reasons intelligible is a ground of appeal to the sheriff: see for example *D v Strathclyde Regional Council*, 1991 S.C.L.R. 185. And see also *H v Kennedy*, 1999 S.C.L.R. 961.

NOTIFICATION OF THE DECISION

Within five days of the children's hearing making its decision the reporter must **9–21** give to the child, each relevant person and any appointed safeguarder the following information:

(a) the decision of the children's hearing;

(b) the reasons for that decision;

(c) a copy of any compulsory supervision order,[75] interim compulsory supervision order, medical examination order made or warrant to secure attendance granted;

(d) a notice of any right to appeal the children's hearing's decision under s.154 (general appeals) or s.160 (appeals against relevant person decisions);

(e) where the child or any relevant person is subject to an order relating to frivolous or vexatious appeals, confirmation of the need for that person to seek leave from the sheriff to appeal the decision;

(f) details of any right to seek a suspension of the children's hearing's decision; and

(g) details of the child's and each relevant person's right to seek a review of a compulsory supervision order.[76]

The reporter must also give to the chief social work officer of the relevant local **9–22** authority and any person who under an order or warrant made under the 2011 Act is responsible for providing any service, support or accommodation in respect of the child the following information within five days of the children's hearing:

(a) the decision of the children's hearing;

(b) the reasons for that decision; and

(c) a copy of any compulsory supervision order, interim compulsory supervision order, medical examination order made or warrant to secure attendance granted.[77]

Specified information must also be given by the reporter to the chief constable **9–23** of the Police Service of Scotland, though the purposes for which that information may be used are limited.[78] The notification rules for second working day hearings, s.126 hearings and decisions on requests to suspend decisions are dealt with in their appropriate places elsewhere in this book.[79]

---

[75] This will include a continued compulsory supervision order, with or without variation, and an interim variation of a compulsory supervision order.

[76] 2013 Rules r.88. This rule does not apply to decisions with their own notification rules: r.88(4).

[77] 2013 Rules r.89.

[78] 2013 Rules r.90.

[79] See below, para.15–20 for 2nd working day hearings, para.13–42 for s.126 hearings and para.14–31 for suspension decisions.

CHAPTER 10

DISPOSAL OF THE REFERRAL

INTRODUCTION

10–01 Having fully discussed all relevant matters with those attending the hearing, and having given consideration to the question of whether it is necessary for the protection, guidance, treatment or control of the child to make a compulsory supervision order, the children's hearing has three primary options open to it: it may (i) defer making a decision on whether to make a compulsory supervision order until a subsequent children's hearing; (ii) discharge the referral; or (iii) make a compulsory supervision order. Choosing either of the first or the third of these primary options will require the hearing to consider additional measures. In deciding which of the primary options to adopt, and whether to include any of the additional measures, the children's hearing must regard the need to safeguard and promote the welfare of the child throughout the child's childhood as the paramount consideration,[1] must give the child the opportunity to express views and have regard to such views as are expressed by the child,[2] and may make, vary or continue a compulsory supervision order only if it considers that it would be better for the child if the order were in force than not.[3] These three general considerations were examined in detail above.[4]

DEFERRING MAKING A DECISION

10–02 Of the three options available to the children's hearing after the discussion of the child's circumstances, two are dispositive (i.e. they dispose of the referral one way or the other) and are appealable, and one, deferral, is procedural and is not appealable. The Children's Hearings (Scotland) Act 2011 gives little guidance as to when the hearing should defer making a decision on whether to make or continue a compulsory supervision order and simply empowers the hearing to do so whenever the hearing considers that it is appropriate.[5] However, the hearing's consideration of the child's circumstances is completed only when the hearing members are in a position to make a decision as to what course of action is in the best interests of the child. It follows that deferring making a decision is the appropriate course whenever (and for whatever reason) the

---

[1] Children's Hearings (Scotland) Act 2011 s.25. This is subject to s.26 under which the hearing may make a decision inconsistent with s.25 in order to protect members of the public from serious harm, but even then the child's welfare is to be regarded as a primary consideration.
[2] 2011 Act s.27.
[3] 2011 Act s.28.
[4] Above, paras 9–15—9–18.
[5] 2011 Act ss.91(2) (grounds hearings), 119(2) (other hearings) and 138(2) (review hearings).

children's hearing is not in possession of sufficient information, and cannot obtain that information in the course of the current hearing, to make a definitive decision on the matter and it is therefore necessary to have further investigation of the child's circumstances. If it is likely that the missing information can be obtained within the working hours of that same day, the hearing may, instead of deferring its decision, adjourn the hearing-though this is possible only when the hearing can re-convene on the same day.[6] It is not laid down how long the deferral is to be for but the children's hearing has the power to set the date on which the subsequent hearing is to be held.[7] If the hearing does not do so, it rests with the reporter to arrange the subsequent hearing at a date sufficiently distant in time to allow the further investigations which have been identified as necessary to be carried out, but sufficiently close to the original hearing that the child is not left in limbo longer than is necessary. It should, in addition, be remembered that any warrant to secure attendance, interim compulsory supervision order or (on review) interim variation of a compulsory supervision order will have strict time-limits attached to them. A subsequent hearing can, again, defer making a decision on whether to make or vary a compulsory supervision order[8] and indeed there is no limit on the number of times this can be done (though the longer the delay in making a decision disposing of the referral, the more likely it is that the child's interests will be prejudiced).

A hearing that defers making a decision ought to be clear, and ought to **10–03** specify in its statement of reasons, why it considers that further investigations are necessary, the nature of these investigations, and what it is that is hoped to be learned in the course of these investigations. Deferral might be considered appropriate, for example:

- because a particular report has not been completed in time; or
- because the hearing has been convened on an emergency basis and the members of the hearing are not in possession of, or have not had time to digest, the various reports; or
- because an in-depth residential or community-based assessment is considered essential in order to identify the child's needs or the source of his or her difficulties; or
- because the accuracy of a report is being challenged and the hearing feels that further investigation is necessary to help it resolve a consequent dispute of fact; or
- because a particular resource which the members of the hearing consider might be appropriate has not been investigated and considered by the local authority, or
- in order to appoint a safeguarder,[9] it being felt that a safeguarder might be able to identify significant features of the child's case that the social background report from the local authority has been unable to investigate, or will be able to comment on (say) the desirability of increasing or decreasing contact between the child and another person or the

---

[6] Children's Hearings (Scotland) Act 2011 (Rules of Procedure in Children's Hearings) Rules 2013 (SSI 2013/194) (hereinafter "2013 Rules") r.7(2) and (3).

[7] 2013 Rules r.61(1)(c).

[8] 2011 Act s.119(1) and (2).

[9] Power to do so is contained in s.30 of the Act and confirmed on deferral by the 2013 Rules r.61(1)(a).

efficacy of some other measure that the hearing are minded to include in the compulsory supervision order; or

- because the safeguarder has produced for the hearing only an interim report and statement, in which case the hearing must consider that interim report and statement and may set a further date up to a maximum of 35 days for the provision of a full report for consideration at the deferred hearing[10]; or

- because the hearing needs to take legal (or other) advice from the National Convener under s.8 of the Act, in which case the chairing member must prepare a request for advice specifying the nature of the advice sought and such other details as the children's hearing considers appropriate[11]; or

- because it is felt that the child who is appearing without legal representation needs time to appoint a lawyer and to apply for legal aid, the lawyer being necessary because the child is unable to participate in the discussion effectively, or because secure accommodation is, for the first time, under active consideration.

10–04 Deferring making a decision is not appropriate when the hearing is of the view that, whatever the further investigation shows, the dispositive decision is likely to be the same (except where, for due process reasons, the child is entitled to but does not have legal representation), nor when the members of the hearing simply cannot make up their minds. The decision to defer should be made only when the members of the hearing feel either that they do not have enough information to make a proper decision in the child's interests, or that some other piece of information might change the decision they would otherwise be inclined to make. Nor is deferral appropriate simply in order to see whether things will improve in the child's life in the meantime (e.g. to see whether he or she can keep out of trouble with the police or can attend school on a regular basis, or to give the child's parents the chance to show that they can look after the child properly). A referral, once made, should not be used as a sword of Damocles hanging over the child: children appreciate, above all else, certainty and security and such continuing uncertainty is invariably against any child's welfare. If there is a fear that short-term improvements in the child's position might not be long-lasting, the correct approach, it is submitted, is to make a supervision requirement but to set an early review date under s.125(3).[12] Deferral in order to seek legal or other advice from the National Convener will be rare, and appropriate only when the answer to the question that has arisen cannot be obtained through a short adjournment and reference to guidance materials and the like. In any case it is to be noted that neither the National Convener nor the Principal Reporter is permitted to direct or guide a children's hearing in carrying out the functions conferred on it by the 2011 Act or any other legislation[13]: it follows from this that it would be

---

[10] 2013 Rules r.60(3) and (4).

[11] 2013 Rules r.79(2). The reporter must then forward this request for advice to the National Convener as soon as practicable and within five days; the National Convener must respond within 14 days; on receipt of the advice the reconvened children's hearing must share that advice with everyone present (and not just those who are entitled to receive notification and background papers): r.79(3)–(5).

[12] For which, see below, para.10–22.

[13] 2011 Act s.9.

incompetent for a hearing to seek (and unlawful for the National Convener to give) advice on whether the hearing *should* follow a particular course of action, as opposed to whether any proposed course of action would be lawful.

Making an interim compulsory supervision order

Whenever a children's hearing decides to defer making a decision on whether **10–05** to make a compulsory supervision order, it may make an interim compulsory supervision order if it considers that the nature of the child's circumstances is such that for the protection, guidance, treatment or control of the child it is necessary as a matter of urgency to do so.[14] This is the same test as that for the making of a compulsory supervision order,[15] except for the addition of the requirement that the necessity be urgent. This is designed to ensure that it is only when some imminent threat to the child's wellbeing exists that a hearing will be able to make an interim compulsory supervision order in circumstances in which it is not yet able to determine whether to make a compulsory supervision order. Interim orders are not to be used to "tide things over" or to see how the child (and family) respond to being under a legal order but are only to be used when the child's immediate circumstances require that he or she be subject to an order. If the child is already subject to a compulsory supervision order and the hearing is reviewing that order then, on deferral, instead of making an interim compulsory supervision order the hearing may make an interim variation of a compulsory supervision order.[16]

An interim compulsory supervision order (or, on review, an interim varia- **10–06** tion of a compulsory supervision order) may include any of the measures that may be included in a compulsory supervision order, and it must specify the local authority which is to be responsible for giving effect to the measures in the order ("the implementation authority").[17] The interim order may, instead of specifying the place where the child is to reside, specify that the child is to reside at any place of safety away from the place where the child predominantly resides[18]: this allows the interim order to authorise the child being kept in a place of safety without specifying the actual address of that place, which may be useful in circumstances in which a decision that the child needs to be kept safe can be made but a place has not yet been identified. When making an interim compulsory supervision order the children's hearing should consider whether to include a contact direction, and the order may include a movement restriction condition or a secure accommodation authorisation[19] so long as the conditions for such condition or authorisation are satisfied.[20]

---

[14] 2011 Act ss.92(2) and 120(3).

[15] 2011 Act ss.91(3)(a) and 119(3)(a).

[16] 2011 Act s.97(5). See below, paras 13–26—13–27.

[17] 2011 Act s.86(1)(a) and (b). For the measures that a compulsory supervision order may include see below, Ch.11.

[18] 2011 Act s.86(2). "Place of safety" is defined in s.202(1).

[19] Though with ICSOs the requirement in 2011 Act s.83(5)(a) to name both secure and non-secure accommodation does not apply.

[20] 2011 Act s.86(4), applying s.83(3)–(6) (other than s.83(5)(a)). The reference to s.83(3) is no longer apt since that subsection was repealed before the 2011 Act came into force by the Children's Hearings (Scotland) Act 2011 (Modification of Primary Legislation) Order 2013 (SSI 2013/211) Sch.2. The result (surely unintentional) is that the obligation to consider contact does not apply to a hearing considering making an ICSO: it remains good practice to do so nevertheless.

10–07   An interim compulsory supervision order has effect during the period beginning with its making and ending with the earliest of: (i) the holding of the next
children's hearing in relation to the child; (ii) a day specified in the order; (iii) the
expiry of the period of 22 days beginning with the day on which the order was
made or extended.[21] Though an interim order lasts, therefore, a maximum of 22
days, once it has been made a children's hearing, convened either specifically for
the purpose or to continue consideration of the question whether to make a full
compulsory supervision order, may make a further interim compulsory supervision order, so long as it is satisfied that the nature of the child's circumstances is
such that for the protection, guidance, treatment or control of the child it is necessary that a further interim order be made.[22] This is the same test as for the original
making of the interim compulsory supervision order, other than that at this stage
there is no need to show the order to be necessary "as a matter of urgency": it is
therefore the same test as to be applied when making a full compulsory supervision order. Once interim measures are in place their withdrawal before a final
order can be determined will often be harmful even when the urgency of the situation has receded. There would seem to be no limit to the number of consecutive
interim compulsory supervision orders that a children's hearing (other than a
grounds hearing) having deferred a decision may make.[23]

Making a medical examination order

10–08   An interim compulsory supervision order may contain, as one of the measures included within it, a requirement (subject to the capable child's right to
refuse) that the implementing local authority arrange a specified medical or
other examination of the child, or specified medical or other treatment for the
child.[24] In addition, a children's hearing that defers making a decision may, if
it considers that it is necessary to do so for the purpose of obtaining any further
information, or carrying out any further investigation that is needed before the
subsequent children's hearing, make a medical examination order.[25] This is an
order authorising any of the following measures:

---

[21] 2011 Act s.86(3). If made while the sheriff determines whether section 67 grounds apply or
not, the ICSO lasts until the earliest of these events or, if earlier than any, the disposal by the sheriff
of the application.

[22] 2011 Act s.120(4) and (5): this applies to both interim compulsory supervision orders and
interim variations of compulsory supervision orders and it applies both when interim orders are
made at a grounds hearing or review hearing, or a hearing after the sheriff has found grounds to be
established: (s.97(5) and 119(1)), or a further grounds hearing after deferral (2013 Rules r.68). The
normal duties of the chairing member and of each member of the children's hearing (to inform of
the substance of reports, take views, state decisions and reasons, and confirm rights of appeal) are
governed by the 2013 Rules r.73.

[23] It is, however, different where the ICSO was made at a grounds hearing where the reporter is
directed to make an application to the sheriff for a determination on whether section 67 grounds
apply: in that situation consecutive ICSOs may not be made if the effect would be that the child
would be subject to an ICSO for a continuous period of more than 66 days: s.96(4). On reaching
that maximum, however, the reporter may apply to the sheriff for an extension of the order (s.98)
or further extension of the order (s.99): so all ICSOs may be extended at 22 day intervals beyond
66 days and the difference lies only in the tribunal with the power to grant the extension.

[24] 2011 Act s.86(1)(a) and s.83(2)(f). Note that an ICSO made under s.93 (when grounds are
denied or not understood and the reporter is directed to apply to the sheriff to establish these
grounds) may not contain a requirement that the local authority arrange a specified medical or
other examination of the child: s.93(6).

[25] 2011 Act ss.92(3) and 120(6).

   (a) a requirement that the child attend or reside at a clinic, hospital or other establishment[26];

   (b) subject to the child's right to refuse medical[27] treatment or examination, a requirement that a specified local authority arrange a specified medical examination of the child;

   (c) a prohibition on the disclosure (whether directly or indirectly) of a place specified in paragraph (a);

   (d) a secure accommodation authorisation[28];

   (e) a direction regulating contact between the child and a specified person or class of person; and

   (f) any other specified condition appearing to the children's hearing to be appropriate for the purpose of ensuring that the child complies with the order.[29]

Whenever, in terms of such an order, a person other than the relevant local authority or a relevant person is to have control over the child and the local authority holds a report which would assist that person in the care and supervision of the child, the local authority must as soon as practicable and, in any case, no later than two working days after receiving notice of the making or varying of the medical examination order, give a copy of the report to that person.[30]

There is an unfortunate degree of overlap between a requirement in an interim **10–09** compulsory supervision order that the implementation authority arrange a specified medical or other examination of the child[31] and a requirement in a medical examination order that a specified local authority arrange a specified medical examination of the child[32] and the statute gives no indication of the circumstances in which one order rather than the other ought to be made (except where the orders do not overlap).[33] The terms of a medical examination order overlap more generally with the terms of an interim compulsory supervision order—so for example both may include a secure accommodation authorisation.[34] Though the statute states that an interim compulsory supervision order and a medical

---

[26] If the child cannot immediately be received in the named clinic, hospital or other establishment, the relevant local authority must arrange for the child to be temporarily accommodated in another suitable place, for a period not exceeding 22 days from the date of the order: Children's Hearings (Scotland) Act 2011 (Compulsory Supervision Orders etc.: Further Provision) Regulations 2013 (SSI 2013/149) reg.8.

[27] "Medical" for this purpose includes psychological: 2011 Act s.87(5).

[28] This is permitted only if the order authorises the keeping of the child in a residential establishment and it is considered by the hearing necessary to grant the authorisation; in addition *either*: (a) the child has previously absconded and is likely to abscond again and, if the child were to abscond, it is likely that his or her physical, mental or moral welfare would be at risk; (b) the child is likely to engage in self-harming conduct; or (c) the child is likely to cause injury to another person:2011 Act s.87(3) and (4).

[29] 2011 Act s.87(1) and (2).

[30] Children's Hearings (Scotland) Act 2011 (Compulsory Supervision Orders etc.: Further Provision) Regulations 2013 reg.5.

[31] 2011 Act s.83(2)(f)(i).

[32] 2011 Act s.87(2)(b). Notice that the local authority in this provision is not limited to the implementation authority and so this provision must be used if the obligation is to be imposed on a local authority other than the implementation authority.

[33] For example, medical "treatment" may be arranged only by means of an ICSO, for a medical examination order involves only "examination".

[34] 2011 Act s.83(2)(e) for ICSOs and s.87(2)(d) for MEOs.

examination order means an order authorising "any" of the stated measures,[35] it is submitted that this must be read in light of the purpose for which the particular order is made. So a medical examination order is designed to allow the obtaining of further information about the state of the child's physical or mental health and the measures attached to that order must, it is submitted, be directed towards that aim. If this is so, then a medical examination order cannot be made with, say, a direction regulating contact between the child and a specified person if this contact does not in some way facilitate the obtaining of health-related information. Even more obviously, a medical examination order whose only term is a secure accommodation authorisation may not be made for the sole purpose of keeping the child in secure accommodation: that would be disproportionate to the only legitimate aim of the medical examination, which is set out clearly in s.92(3) as the obtaining of further information or the carrying out of further investigation. If the aim is to keep the child in secure accommodation this can be achieved by means of an interim compulsory supervision order.[36]

10–10　　A medical examination order may authorise whatever is necessary to achieve its purpose, such as for example requiring the child to reside in an assessment centre, or to attend an educational psychologist, or otherwise to undergo medical or psychological examination during the specified period, in order to give the subsequent hearing a fuller picture of his or her circumstances and needs. But it does *not* authorise the medical treatment of the child and if that is required as a matter of urgency then such examination may be included as a measure in an interim compulsory supervision requirement.[37] However, neither a requirement in an interim compulsory supervision order that the local authority arrange a medical examination or medical or other treatment for the child nor the making of a medical examination order takes away the child's right to consent or refuse consent to any medical, surgical or dental procedure or treatment granted by s.2(4) of the Age of Legal Capacity (Scotland) Act 1991 to persons under the age of 16 who understand the nature and consequences of the procedure or treatment.[38]

10–11　　A medical examination order is effective from the time of its making to whichever of the following first occurs: (a) the beginning of the next child's hearing arranged in relation to the child; (b) a day specified in the order; or (c) the expiry of the period of 22 days beginning on the day on which the order is made.[39] So when the child is required to reside at a specified clinic, hospital or other establishment, he or she cannot be kept there beyond the period of 22 days from the day on which the order is made (which might, of course, be some days before the child commences residing at the clinic or hospital). The order automatically ceases to have effect at the end of the period of 22 days, whether or not any medical investigation has been undertaken. This means that if an appointment (say, with an educational psychologist) cannot be had until after 22 days after the hearing that made the medical examination order, the child cannot be required to attend that appointment. It is unclear from the statute whether, at the subsequent hearing, a further medical examination order can then be made. On the one hand,

---

[35] 2011 Act s.83(1)(a) for ICSOs and s.87(1) for MEOs.
[36] That would be permitted under 2011 Act s.92(2) and s.120(3) with reference to s.86(1)(a) and s.83(2)(e).
[37] 2011 Act ss.83(2)(f)(ii) and 86(1)(a).
[38] 2011 Act s.186.
[39] 2011 Act s.87(5).

this is not explicitly prohibited; on the other hand, the making of a further interim compulsory supervision order is explicitly provided for under s.120(5), beyond that granted under s.120(3), and it might be assumed that if the intention had been to permit the making of a further medical examination order this would have similarly been expressly provided for. An interim compulsory supervision order is, however, usually more intrusive and therefore requires more in the way of statutory authority for it to be renewed. The lack of prohibition of subsequent medical examination orders probably means that they are permitted, though the hearing is likely to require an explanation as to why the original order was not given effect to or did not achieve its aim.

Though a sheriff may make, on the same terms as a children's hearing, an **10–12** interim compulsory supervision order[40] there is no provision permitting him to make a medical examination order. Nor, however, is there any prohibition on the sheriff including a requirement on the local authority to arrange a medical examination of the child as a measure included within an interim compulsory supervision order.[41]

Other decisions on deferral

Deferral is commonly thought necessary in order to allow a safeguarder to **10–13** provide a report. A children's hearing that defers making a decision whether to make a compulsory supervision order must, if one is not already in post, consider whether to appoint a person to safeguard the interests of the child, and may make the appointment.[42] Reasons must be given by the hearing for the appointment but there is no limitation in the Act or Rules as to what these reasons might be. As well, a hearing may—but only on the application of the reporter, and for cause shown—grant a warrant to secure the child's attendance at the subsequent children's hearing.[43] "Cause" is any indication that suggests that the child might breach his or her obligation to attend at the subsequent hearing. Appointment of a safeguarder is not an appealable decision, though the grant of a warrant to secure attendance is appealable.

On deferral the children's hearing may require the reporter to obtain any **10–14** report from any person which the hearing considers would be relevant to the matter being determined.[44] The hearing may also come to the view that, for the purposes of enabling the child or any relevant person to participate effectuively in the proceedings it is necessary that he or she be represented by a solicitor or counsel but that it is unlikely that he or she will arrange to be so represented. If so, the hearing may require the reporter to notify the Scottish Legal Aid Board of this.[45] The hearing may give any other direction on any other matter that is necessary to enable the hearing to make its decision, including requiring the reporter to arrange for an interpreter or take any other steps necessary to secure the participation of the child or relevant person in the hearing.[46]

---

[40] 2011 Act s.109(3) and s.117(3).
[41] The prohibition on children's hearings doing so in 2011 Act s.93(6) is not replicated in s.109 or s.117.
[42] 2011 Act s.30.
[43] 2011 Act s.123.
[44] 2013 Rules r.61(1)(b).
[45] 2013 Rules r.61(1)(d) and (e). SLAB will thereafter have the onus of contacting the child or relevant person.
[46] 2013 Rules r.61(1)(f) and (g).

DISCHARGING THE REFERRAL

10–15 A children's hearing may make a compulsory supervision order only when satisfied that it is necessary to do so for the protection, guidance, treatment or control of the child.[47] If, after a full consideration of the child's circumstances, the grounds and the reports, and being guided in that consideration by the overarching principles in ss.25–28,[48] and taking account of the views expressed by the child, relevant person and anyone else who has contributed to the discussion, the children's hearing is not so satisfied its decision must be to discharge the referral.[49]

10–16 The power to discharge the referral, even when section 67 grounds apply, is important in emphasising that it is the children's hearing alone that decides, once the matter has been referred to it, whether it is necessary to make a compulsory supervision order, and that such need is not conclusively proved by the mere acceptance or establishment of the section 67 grounds. There are many circumstances in which it might be considered appropriate to discharge a referral even in the face of the existence of section 67 grounds. The discussion might indicate to the members of the hearing that the event which led to the referral (e.g. an incident of petty theft) is unlikely to be repeated. Or the problem that led to the referral may have resolved itself (e.g. school attendance may no longer be a problem due to the removal from the school of a bully or because the child has lawfully left school). Or the threat to the child's well-being may have been removed from the child's environment (e.g. by the imprisonment of an abuser or the departure of an anti-educationalist). Or the hearing may consider that the section 67 grounds contained in the reporter's statement of grounds are simply not serious enough to raise any real concerns for the welfare of the child, or that a compulsory supervision order simply has nothing to offer the particular child. In a case in which the members of the hearing are thinking of discharging the referral without making a compulsory supervision order, it will usually be good practice to inquire of the reporter why he or she referred the case to the hearing, for the reporter will previously have investigated the case and come to a positive conclusion that the circumstances merited the making of a compulsory supervision order.[50] The reporter's original concerns are always to be taken into account.

Effect of discharge

10–17 A reporter cannot found upon the same facts as the sole or primary basis of a new section 67 ground after an earlier referral has been discharged since this would, in effect, be the reporter seeking a review of a children's hearing's decision, which he or she has no legitimate interest to do. However, the facts of a previous referral can be used as part of the statement of facts with which the

---

[47] 2011 Act ss.91(3)(a) and 119(3)(a).

[48] Paramountcy of the child's welfare, taking account of the child's views, and determining whether it would be better that the order were in force than not.

[49] 2011 Act ss.91(3)(b) and s.119(3)(b).

[50] The reporter must arrange a children's hearing under 2011 Act s.69(1) whenever he or she is of the view that it is necessary for a compulsory supervision order to be made in respect of the child, and a decision of the children's hearing to discharge the referral without making such an order is, therefore, a decision to disagree with the reporter.

reporter seeks to establish new grounds, so long as there is sufficient new material to suggest that there is, in essence, a new case for the subsequent children's hearing to consider.

MAKING A COMPULSORY SUPERVISION ORDER

Where a children's hearing does not consider it necessary to defer making a **10–18** decision until a subsequent hearing and, after considering the child's circumstances and taking into consideration the need to safeguard and promote the child's welfare throughout his or her childhood as the paramount consideration, as well as the views of the child, relevant person and anyone else who has contributed to the discussion, the children's hearing is satisfied that it is necessary, for the child's protection, guidance, treatment or control, to make a compulsory supervision order, and that it would be better for the child that the order be in force than not, it must make such an order.[51] There would seem to be no discretion, as there was under the pre-2011 law,[52] for the hearing to decide not to make a compulsory supervision order in circumstances in which, even although such an order is considered "necessary" it is of the opinion that the order will not, in fact, succeed in achieving any good (for example in the case of a child nearing 16 who refuses to co-operate with any help offered). The mandatory nature of the present statutory wording must, however, be read with the injunction in s.28(2) against making any order except where the children's hearing considers that it would be better for the child if the order were in force than not: an order may well be objectively "necessary" (imposing the obligation to make it) while at the same time likely to make no difference to the child (in which case its making could not be said to be "better" than not making it), for example if the child absolutely refuses to co-operate with any order and compulsion is considered inappropriate. So the change from discretion to obligation to make an order may be more apparent than real, though discretion is now to be exercised within the context of the judgment whether or not the order is "necessary" or "better" rather than whether it should be made. A compulsory supervision order is necessary whenever the children's hearing is of the view that the child either would not receive or would not accept protection, guidance, treatment or control without the making of the order. If the local authority offers appropriate help and the child is willing to receive it, the provision of that help will seldom need to be compulsory; if the child indicates an absolute unwillingness to co-operate and the hearing sees no benefit in seeking to enforce co-operation then it cannot be said that the making of a compulsory supervision order is necessary. An order will only be "necessary" if its making—and enforcement—would be "better" for the child than not making it.

The Social Work (Scotland) Act 1968 contained a provision permitting the **10–19** children's hearing to postpone the operation of a supervision requirement,[53] though the power was very seldom used. Neither the 1995 Act nor the 2011 Act contains such a provision, and though the hearing's power to attach conditions

---

[51] 2011 Act ss.91(3)(a) and 119(3)(a).

[52] See the second edition of this work at p.132.

[53] Social Work (Scotland) Act 1968 s.44(3).

to a compulsory supervision order is wide,[54] the wording of the relevant section[55] is inept to include a condition as to when the order is to come into effect. It is submitted, therefore, that a compulsory supervision order in all cases comes into effect as soon as the order has been signed by the chairing member of the hearing.

OTHER DECISIONS

Suspension of decision

10–20 A children's hearing is able to suspend a decision to make, vary, continue or terminate a compulsory supervision order pending an appeal against that decision.[56] Though the matter could have been expressed more clearly it would seem competent for the hearing to suspend one or more of the measures it includes in the compulsory supervision order. For what is suspended is not the order itself but the hearing's decision, and if the decision is to vary an existing order by attaching an additional measure to it the suspension of the decision will involve only a suspension of the additional measure: it would be anomalous not to permit suspension of a measure (but not otherwise the order itself) when it is first made.[57] There is no power to suspend a decision to make an interim compulsory supervision order or an interim variation of a compulsory supervision order, or to grant a warrant to secure attendance or any other decision that is not dispositive of the question in relation to the compulsory supervision order.

10–21 The application to suspend a decision of a children's hearing must be made by the person who is appealing the decision[58] and if that person is required to attend the hearing that will consider the request but he or she fails to do so then the children's hearing may, if it considers it appropriate, take no further action in relation to the application.[59] The fact that this rule is not worded as an imperative suggests that the hearing may, instead, rearrange another hearing to allow the person's attendance; the choice will normally turn on the reason for the person's failure to attend. The children's hearing must, before making its decision, invite the child, relevant person and any appointed safeguarder who is present at the hearing to make such representations as they wish to make[60] though these should be limited to the sole question before the hearing—whether to suspend the decision now being appealed against and the discussion must not be allowed to reopen matters the previous hearing made its decision upon.

---

[54] See below, para.11–28.

[55] 2011 Act s.83(2)(h) (previously, s.70(3)(b) of the Children (Scotland) Act 1995).

[56] 2011 Act s.158. See further below, paras 14–30—14–35.

[57] *S v Proudfoot*, 2002 S.L.T. 743, which held that only the whole order could be suspended and not an individual element thereto, was decided under the previous statutory wording, in terms of which (Children (Scotland) Act 1995, s.51(9)) it was the order itself and not the hearing's decision that was suspended.

[58] 2011 Act s.158(1)(b).

[59] 2013 Rules r.76(3). This applies to the child and relevant person only. If it is the safeguarder who has appealed and sought suspension then the option of taking no further action would appear not to be open to the hearing.

[60] 2013 Rules r.76(4).

Specifying when a review is to take place

A children's hearing that makes, varies or continues a compulsory supervi- **10–22** sion order may at the same time require the order to be reviewed by a subsequent children's hearing on a day or within a period specified in the order.[61] If the order contains a movement restriction condition[62] the hearing must exercise its power under this provision,[63] but otherwise it has a discretion of whether or not to do so.[64]

Educational referrals

Whenever a child has been referred to a children's hearing (and not only, it **10–23** would seem, when grounds of referral are accepted or established) and the children's hearing considers that an education authority has a duty under s.14(3) of the Education (Scotland) Act 1980 to provide education to that child who has been excluded from school but that the authority is failing to comply with the duty, the hearing may require the National Convener to refer the matter to the Scottish Ministers.[65] If such a requirement is made, the chairing member must include in the record of the hearing's decision details of the ways in which the education authority is in breach of its duty and make or cause to be made a report for the National Convener providing such additional information on the matter as the hearing considers appropriate.[66] The reporter must as soon as practicable give to the National Convener a copy of the hearing's decision and its reasons and any such report.[67] The National Convener must make the referral and give a copy of it to the education authority to which it relates and to the Principal Reporter.[68] It is not stated what action the Scottish Ministers may take against a local authority that they consider to be in breach of its duties under the 1980 Act.

Parenting orders

The Antisocial Behaviour etc. (Scotland) Act 2004 is designed to control the **10–24** behaviour of unruly persons, and to provide protection from such behaviour to others.[69] Children over the age of 12 years as well as adults may be made subject to antisocial behaviour orders,[70] but the processes created by the 2004 Act sit uneasily with the existing children's hearing system. The 2004 Act does, however, attempt to help the hearing system achieve its overall aims more effectively, by permitting the hearing to require the reporter to refer certain matters on for further action in other fora.

---

[61] 2011 Act s.125.
[62] See below, paras 11–08—11–09.
[63] 2011 Act s.125(2).
[64] This matter is discussed more fully below, paras 13–15—13–17.
[65] 2011 Act s.127(1) and (2).
[66] 2013 Rules r.82(1).
[67] 2013 Rules r.82(2).
[68] 2011 Act s.127(3).
[69] See generally, T. Guthrie, *Antisocial Behaviour Legislation* (W. Green, 2005).
[70] Antisocial Behaviour etc. (Scotland) Act 2004 s.4(2)(a).

10–25   Whenever a children's hearing has been constituted for any purpose[71] in respect of a child[72] and the hearing is satisfied that it might be appropriate for a parenting order to be made in respect of a parent of the child under s.102 of the Antisocial Behaviour etc. (Scotland) Act 2004, the hearing may require the reporter to consider whether to apply for a parenting order under that provision.[73] This power is available whenever it appears to the hearing "that it might be appropriate for a parenting order to be made", but the Act gives no indication of when it might be considered so appropriate, or the basis upon which a hearing can make that judgment. But a parenting order is an order that requires something of the parent (unlike a compulsory supervision order, which can require something only of the child and the local authority) and when it is perceived that, for example, a change in behaviour of the parent is needed more than a change in behaviour of the child then it might well be considered that the child's welfare would be better served by the reporter obtaining a parenting order than the hearing making a compulsory supervision order. Indeed, a package of measures in the child's interests might suggest that both a compulsory supervision order and a parenting order is appropriate. If the hearing does require the reporter to consider applying for a parenting order, it must include in the record of its decision details of the reason why it considers that a parenting order might be appropriate and provide in a report such additional information on the matter as the hearing considers appropriate.[74] The reporter must take these into account in determining whether to make the application.

10–26   The children's hearing may require the reporter to consider making an application to the sheriff for a parenting order, but it cannot require him or her actually to make the application. The child's welfare is paramount in the hearing's decision whether to require the reporter to consider applying for a parenting order,[75] and the requirement to take account of the child's views applies also.[76] The decision of the hearing on the matter is not appealable.

10–27   Section 102 of the 2004 Act allows a parenting order to be made in respect of a "parent" of the child, and it is to be noted that this word is defined differently from the definition in the Children's Hearings (Scotland) Act 2011 of "relevant person". The definition in the 2004 Act[77] originally referred to the definition of "relevant person" as it then appeared in s.93(2)(b) of the Children (Scotland) Act 1995, and the definition of "parent" in the 2004 Act was amended by the Children's Hearings (Scotland) Act 2011 (Modification of Primary Legislation) Order 2013 to ensure that the definition remains for the purposes of that Act unchanged—notwithstanding that "relevant person" is now defined in the 2011

---

[71] So a grounds hearing may utilise this provision even though grounds are not accepted or not understood, as may a review hearing that is terminating a compulsory supervision order. A pre-hearing panel has no equivalent power.

[72] And not just a child in respect of whom an ASBO may be made—children, that is to say, below as well as above the age of 12 years.

[73] s.128. For a critical analysis of parenting orders, see A. Cleland and K. Tisdall "The Challenge of Antisocial Behaviour: New Relationships Between the State, Children and Parents" (2005) 19 Int. J. Law Pol. & Fam. 395.

[74] 2013 Rules r.83.

[75] 2011 Act s.25. It is difficult to envisage a situation in which the qualification to this in s.26 would apply in relation to a decision in respect of a parenting order.

[76] 2011 Act s.27.

[77] Antisocial Behaviour etc. (Scotland) Act 2004 s.117.

Act differently. It follows that the jurisprudence interpreting s.93(2)(b) of the 1995 Act[78] continues to inform how "parent" under the 2004 Act is to be defined. "Parent" for the purposes of s.128 of the 2011 Act is defined in s.117 of the 2004 Act to mean:

(a) any person enjoying parental responsibilities or parental rights under Pt 1 of the Children (Scotland) Act 1995;

(b) any individual in whom parental responsibilities or parental rights are vested by, under or by virtue of the 1995 Act;

(c) any individual in whom parental responsibilities or parental rights are vested by, under or by virtue of a permanence order made under the Adoption and Children (Scotland) Act 2007; and

(d) any individual who appears to be an individual who ordinarily (and other than by reason only of the individual's employment) has charge of, or control over, the child.

The difficulties caused by the disjunction between the definitions of "parent" for this purpose and "relevant person" for all other purposes are likely in practice to be minimal since children's hearings very seldom consider it appropriate to require the reporter to consider whether to apply for a parenting order.

---

[78] Including in particular *S v N*, 2002 S.L.T. 589, *Authority Reporter v S*, 2010 S.L.T. 765 and *Principal Reporter v K*, 2011 S.L.T. 271.

CHAPTER ELEVEN

COMPULSORY SUPERVISION ORDERS

11–01 A compulsory supervision order may be made by a children's hearing under s.91(3)(a) or s.119(3)(a) of the Children's Hearings (Scotland) Act 2011. It may contain one or more of a number of measures specified in s.83(2) and, like the making of the order itself, the decision to include these measures is governed by the welfare principle in s.25, its qualification in s.26, and the requirement in s.27 to take account of the child's views.[1] The terms, as opposed to the making, of the compulsory supervision order are not explicitly governed by the injunction in s.28 against making the order unless the hearing considers that it would be better for the child if the order were in force than not, but the minimum intervention principle, traced to the proportionality principle of ECHR law,[2] does apply and so hearings ought to include in the order it makes only those measures that the hearing members believe are likely to make a positive difference to the child's life or circumstances and constitute no more interference in private and family life than is necessary to achieve that purpose. The measures that might be included in a compulsory supervision order are listed in s.83(2) of the 2011 Act, and form the subject matter of this chapter. They may also be included in an interim compulsory supervision order.[3]

REQUIRING THE CHILD TO RESIDE IN A SPECIFIED PLACE

11–02 A compulsory supervision order or interim compulsory supervision order may contain a requirement that the child reside at a specified place.[4] So the hearing might require the child to reside in a residential establishment, or with foster carers,[5] or with relatives, or with one parent, or in any other place deemed to

---

[1] The terms of the order are "matters relating to a child" and therefore governed by ss.25–27.

[2] In *In Re O (Care or Supervision Order)* [1996] 2 F.L.R. 755 at 760 Hale J said this: "the court should begin with a preference for the less interventionist rather than the more interventionist approach. This should be considered to be in the better interests of the children . . . unless there are cogent reasons to the contrary". Thorpe L.J. was to similar effect in *In Re B (Care: Interference with Family Life)* [2003] 2 F.L.R. 813 when he said at [34] that a judge "must not sanction an interference with family life unless he is satisfied that that is both necessary and proportionate and that no other less radical form of order would achieve the essential end of promoting the welfare of the children". Both passages were cited with approval by Lord President Hamilton in *S v L*, 2011 S.L.T. 1204 and similar comments were made by Lord Reed when the case reached the Supreme Court: 2012 UKSC 30. Though that case concerned adoption, the principle as stated by Hale J. is of wide application.

[3] Children's Hearings (Scotland) Act 2011 s.86(1)(a).

[4] s.83(2)(a).

[5] As in, for example, *Kennedy v H*, 1988 S.L.T. 586, *Catto v Pearson*, 1990 S.L.T. (Sh Ct) 77, *M v Kennedy*, 1993 S.L.T. 431, and *Kennedy v M*, 1995 S.L.T. 717.

be in the best interests of the child. Any such requirement supersedes, during its currency, any other court order regulating the child's residence (such as an order under s.11 of the Children (Scotland) Act 1995) to the extent that the residence requirement is inconsistent with the court order[6]; likewise it necessarily supersedes any general right of a parent to determine the child's residence under s.2 of the 1995 Act, or it temporarily prevents the exercise of such rights.[7] It is an important principle of human rights law that any requirement on the child to reside outwith the family home ought normally to be regarded as a temporary measure, to be discontinued as soon as circumstances permit, and any measures implementing such a requirement should be consistent with the ultimate aim of reuniting the relevant person and the child.[8] In practice, this means ensuring that contact arrangements between the child and those with whom he or she shares family life are maintained until such time as contact is shown to be harmful.

If a children's hearing makes a compulsory supervision order with a require-   **11–03** ment that the child reside somewhere, that place must be "specified", that is to say expressly named in the order.[9] The requirement cannot be to the effect that the child is to reside, say, "otherwise than with the parents", or "in an establishment chosen by the local authority", or "with foster carers selected by the local authority".[10] If the specified place requires that the child will be under the charge and control of someone who is not a relevant person, the children's hearing must first receive and consider a report or information provided by the local authority with recommendations on the needs of the child and the suitability to meet those needs of the place to be named and the person to be in charge or control of the child; in addition, the local authority must confirm that they have carried out the procedures and gathered the information required by regs 3 and 4 of the Looked After Children (Scotland) Regulations 2009.[11] These regulations also provide for the local authority to review any such placement and visit the child there.[12] Other than this, however, the power of the children's hearing to specify a place for the child's residence is unlimited. It is, however, almost certainly incompetent to require a child to reside outwith the United Kingdom as a condition in a compulsory supervision order, for that would be a decision to remove the child from the jurisdiction of the hearing.[13] If the child is required to reside with a named individual who does not have parental responsibilities and parental rights

---

[6] *Aitken v Aitken*, 1978 S.L.T. 183; *P v P*, 2000 S.L.T. 781.

[7] *Aitken v Aitken*, per Lord President Emslie at 185. The compulsory supervision order does not, however, make it incompetent for a court to make a residence order whose effect will be suspended until the residence requirement in the compulsory supervision order is terminated: *W v Glasgow Corporation*, 1974 S.L.T. (Notes) 5. See also s.3(4) of the 1995 Act.

[8] *Johansen v Norway* (1997) 23 E.H.R.R. 33 at [78]; *Kutzner v. Germany* (2002) 35 E.H.R.R. 25 at [76]; *Levin v Sweden* [2012] 1 F.C.R. 569 at [57]–[60].

[9] If it is an interim compulsory supervision order that is being made, the order may, instead of specifying a place or places where the child is to reside, specify that the child is to reside at any place of safety away from the place where the child predominantly resides: 2011 Act s.86(2).

[10] *R v Children's Hearing for Borders Region*, 1984 S.L.T. 65.

[11] Children's Hearings (Scotland) Act 2011 (Rules of Procedure in Children's Hearings) Rules 2013 (SSI 2013/194) (hereinafter "2013 Rules") r.80.

[12] Looked After Children (Scotland) Regulations 2009 regs 45 and 46.

[13] Though a compulsory supervision order which does not specify a place of residence does not in itself prohibit the removal of the child from Scotland or the UK. cf. s.134 which envisages that a child can be taken to live outwith Scotland without infringing the terms of a compulsory supervision order.

in relation to the child, that individual will be obliged to do what is reasonable in all the circumstances to safeguard the child's health, development and welfare and in fulfilling that obligation will be entitled to consent to any surgical, medical or dental treatment or procedure.[14] A compulsory supervision order that specifies the place of residence of the child may also contain a direction authorising the person who is in charge of the place specified to restrict the child's liberty to the extent that the person considers appropriate having regard to the measures included in the order.[15] If the compulsory supervision order authorises the keeping of a child in a particular place then an officer of law may enforce the order by searching for and apprehending the child, by taking the child to that place and, where it is not reasonably practicable to take the child there immediately, by taking the child to and detaining the child in a place of safety for as short a period of time as possible.[16]

11–04 A requirement to reside in a residential establishment will normally be made only when the hearing is assured that there is a place for the child in such an establishment, but there is no prohibition on the hearing naming an establishment even in the absence of such a place. The hearing must make its decision in the child's best interests, and while that in practice will normally mean the best that is actually available to the child there is sometimes merit in making a decision knowing that the residential condition cannot be satisfied. This may indicate to the local authority that greater efforts should be made to find a suitable place. If the implementation authority is unable to make immediate arrangements for the child's reception in the named residential establishment, the authority must arrange for the child to be temporarily accommodated in another suitable place for a period not exceeding 22 days from the date of the order containing the residential requirement.[17] Where a child is required to reside at a particular place but it is in the interests of either the child him or herself or of another child in the place that the child be moved out of that place as a matter of urgent necessity, the chief social work officer may transfer the child to another place.[18] If this occurs, the reporter must arrange a review of the compulsory supervision order which contains the requirement to reside at the original place.[19] The children's hearing is not obliged to vary the compulsory supervision order if the members of the hearing remain of the view that the place originally named is still the best for the child, but if there is no realistic possibility of that place being available the hearing may in practice be forced to confirm the change that has already been made.

Non-disclosure of child's place of residence

11–05 If the compulsory supervision order or interim compulsory supervision order requires the child to reside in a specified place, the children's hearing may in addition prohibit the disclosure (whether directly or indirectly) of the

---

[14] Children (Scotland) Act 1995 s.5(1).

[15] 2011 Act s.83(2)(b).

[16] 2011 Act s.168. The officer of law may also, so far as necessary to achieve this, break open shut and lockfast places: s.168(2)(d).

[17] Children's Hearings (Scotland) Act 2011 (Compulsory Supervision Orders etc: Further Provision) Regulations 2013 (SSI 2013/149) reg.6: for interim compulsory supervision orders, see reg.7.

[18] 2011 Act s.143.

[19] 2011 Act s.136. Notification provisions are contained in the 2013 Rules r.36.

place specified.[20] The statute gives no indication as to when it would be appropriate for the children's hearing to exercise the power to prohibit disclosure of the child's place of residence, and there is nothing to prevent them from doing so for the benefit of someone other than the child, such as foster carers, kinship carers or prospective adopters with whom the child has been placed. The prohibition will, however, normally be considered appropriate when contact between the child and another person is likely to be harmful to the child, and when it is believed that there is a risk that the other person will attempt to make contact.

The previous legislation permitting the hearing to prohibit disclosure[21] **11–06** required that the prohibition be directed towards a named individual but the present provision is substantially wider: it authorises a "prohibition on the disclosure . . . of a place specified" without indicating to whom the prohibition is directed. This suggests that the child's place of residence may be disclosed to no-one if such a prohibition is made, but that must necessarily be qualified to allow disclosure to at least those responsible for giving effect to the order. To avoid dispute, it will remain good practice under the 2011 Act for hearings which include a non-disclosure element to the compulsory supervision order to specify the person to whom the child's residence is not to be disclosed: this will normally be a relevant person or other family member (but might include, for example, a source of danger to the child who has no family connection with the child). A requirement of non-disclosure is likely to be effective in achieving that end only when the child is being moved to a new address[22]: there would be no point in making such a requirement when the individual from whom the child (or the child's carer) is to be protected knows the child's current address and the child is remaining there. And it is incompetent to make a non-disclosure requirement when the compulsory supervision order does not include within its terms a requirement that the child reside at a named place (which can, of course, be the place where the child is already residing). So if a child is to remain at home (or be returned home) and the children's hearing wishes to keep this fact from a particular person, it must first name the child's residence as a requirement in the compulsory supervision order.

Though the children's hearing may include a prohibition on the disclosure **11–07** of the child's residence (if that residence is specified in the compulsory supervision order or interim compulsory supervision order) on its own initiative, it may also be asked to do so by someone else. The procedure for dealing with the rather wider "non-disclosure request" was considered above[23] and, though the link is not made by the statute or the Rules, much of that procedure will be appropriately followed when the hearing is considering including this measure in the order itself.[24]

---

[20] 2011 Act s.83(2)(c). The power to include a non-disclosure measure in the terms of the compulsory supervision order is independent of non-disclosure requests to withhold information or documents from specified persons made in terms of rr.84–87 of the 2013 Rules. See further below, para.11–07. The reporter also has an independent power to withhold information about the whereabouts of the child when fulfilling his or her duty to notify people of a children's hearing or pre-hearing panel: 2013 Rules r.16.

[21] Children (Scotland) Act 1995 s.70(6).

[22] It is competent and not uncommon for a compulsory supervision order to require the child to reside where he or she is presently residing (for example when there is dispute as to with whom the child is better off living).

[23] Above, paras 6–49—6–51.

[24] Remembering that, except where otherwise specified, the chairing member determines procedure: 2013 Rules r.7(1).

MOVEMENT RESTRICTION CONDITIONS

11–08 The compulsory supervision order or interim compulsory supervision order may contain a movement restriction condition,[25] which is a restriction on the child's movements in a way specified in the condition and a requirement that the child comply with arrangements specified in the condition for monitoring compliance with the restriction.[26] Any monitoring arrangements must include the preparation by the implantation authority of a child's plan[27] and the hearing must designate a responsible local authority officer who is to monitor the child's compliance.[28] It is for the children's hearing to determine the nature of the restrictions to be imposed but in any case, what must be specified are: (a) the place where the child is to reside; (b) the days of the week during which the child is to remain there and the periods he or she is to remain there (which is not to exceed 12 hours in any one day); and (c) the period for which the movement restriction condition is to have effect, which is not to exceed six months.[29] In addition, conditions may be imposed: (a) specifying places where the child is required not to enter; (b) any requirements relative to allowing the monitoring official to discharge his or her functions; (c) any requirements relating to the child's participation in or co-operation with the child's plan; (d) contingent arrangements; and (e) respite care arrangements.[30] Arrangements for monitoring compliance might include requiring the child to report his or her movements regularly, or to wear some form of electronic tracking device.[31]

11–09 A movement restriction condition may be included in a compulsory supervision order or interim compulsory supervision order only if the children's hearing is satisfied that it is necessary to include such a condition in the order.[32] In addition, one or more of the following conditions must apply: (a) the child has previously absconded and is likely to abscond again and, if he or she were to abscond, it is likely that the child's physical, mental or moral welfare would be at risk; (b) the child is likely to engage in self-harming conduct; (c) the child is likely to cause injury to another person.[33] These conditions are considered more fully in relation to secure accommodation authorisations, discussed immediately below.

AUTHORISING SECURE ACCOMMODATION

11–10 The compulsory supervision order or interim compulsory supervision order may include a secure accommodation authorisation,[34] which is an authorisation

---

[25] 2011 Act s.83(2)(d).

[26] 2011 Act s.84. If a movement restriction condition is included in a compulsory supervision order the children's hearing that makes, varies or continues that order must specify the day on or the period within which the order is to be reviewed: s.125(2).

[27] Children's Hearings (Scotland) Act 2011 (Movement Restriction Conditions) Regulations 2013 (SSI 2013/210) (hereinafter "Movement Restriction Conditions Regulations 2013") reg.3.

[28] Movement Restriction Conditions Regulations 2013 reg.4: this designation may be varied by a hearing under reg.5.

[29] Movement Restriction Conditions Regulations 2013 reg.6(1).

[30] Movement Restriction Conditions Regulations 2013 reg.6(2).

[31] Movement Restriction Conditions Regulations 2013 regs 7 and 8. Tracking devices are those authorised under the Restriction of Liberty Order etc (Scotland) Regulations 2013 (SSI 2013/6).

[32] 2011 Act s.83(4)(b).

[33] 2011 Act s.83(4)(a) and (6).

[34] 2011 Act s.83(2)(e).

enabling the child to be placed and kept in secure accommodation within a residential establishment.[35] It is appropriate to grant such an authorisation when it is in a child's welfare to have his or her movements physically restrained, by being required to reside in an establishment that has the ability to lock the child in. Other measures contained in a compulsory supervision order may well require the child to live at one place rather than another, but these do not in themselves carry the right of physical enforcement and they do not, therefore, engage Art.5 of the European Convention on Human Rights (the right to liberty and security of person).[36] But keeping a child in secure accommodation, which necessarily involves physical enforcement of any requirement to reside there, does engage art.5[37] and it follows that the procedures which lead to a child's detention in secure accommodation must not only satisfy art.6 (due process) and art.8 (private and family life) but must also be justified in terms of art.5.[38] The most important requirement in art.5 is that everyone deprived of their liberty shall be entitled to take proceedings by which the lawfulness of the detention shall be decided speedily by a court and his or her release ordered if the detention is not lawful.[39] Possibly the single most common complaint taken to the European Court is the claim that detention has been too long before a case has been heard in a court, and for that reason alone it is important that our law lays down—and practice adheres to—strict time-limits when secure accommodation is authorised. It was held by the First Division before the passing of the 2011 Act that since the child has the right to challenge the hearing's decision to authorise secure accommodation within 21 days, the requirements for speedy determination in art.5(4) are satisfied.[40]

The children's hearing has no power to require that the child be kept in secure **11–11** accommodation; rather they simply authorise the placing of the child there. The actual decision that the child is to be placed in secure accommodation rests with the chief social work officer of the implementation authority, but that officer may implement the authorisation only with the consent of the person in charge of the residential establishment containing the secure accommodation in which the child is to be placed.[41] Though the decision to implement the authorisation is not made by a tribunal, implementation of a secure accommodation authorisation is lawful only when that authorisation has been given by an independent tribunal established by law, that is to say the children's hearing, and for that reason the process by which the child is subjected to the limitation in his or her liberty through the implementation of the authorisation is consistent with the European Convention and in particular art.5 thereof.[42] The 2011 Act added to

---

[35] 2011 Act s.85. "Residential establishment" is defined in s.202 to mean an establishment in Scotland (whether managed by a local authority, by a voluntary organisation or by any other person) which provides residential accommodation for children for the purposes of the 2011 Act, the Children (Scotland) Act 1995 or the Social Work (Scotland) Act 1968 (or equivalent homes in England, Wales or Northern Ireland).

[36] *S v Miller*, 2001 S.L.T. 531.

[37] *Martin v N*, 2004 S.L.T. 249.

[38] See *Bouamer v Belgium* (1989) 11 E.H.R.R. 1, *Neilsen v Denmark* (1988) 11 E.H.R.R. 175; *Re K (A Child) (Secure Accommodation Order: Right to Liberty)* [2001] 2 W.L.R. 1141.

[39] European Convention on Human Rights art.5(4).

[40] *Martin v N*, 2004 S.L.T. 249.

[41] 2011 Act s.151(3).

[42] *J v Children's Reporter for Stirling*, 2010 Fam.L.R. 140. Cf. *Re K (A Child) (Secure Accommodation: Right to Liberty)* [2001] Fam. 377.

the existing provision by conferring the right to appeal against not only the authorisation but its implementation (or non-implementation)[43] and the fact that such an appeal (which must be made before the expiry of 21 days beginning with the day on which the decision to implement the order was made) has to be heard and disposed of before the expiry of the period of three days beginning with the day on which the appeal is made[44] satisfies the requirement in art.5 of the ECHR for speedy review of the determination.

Conditions to be satisfied

11–12   There are a number of conditions that require to be satisfied before a children's hearing may include a secure accommodation authorisation in a compulsory supervision order or interim compulsory supervision order. First, emphasising that keeping a child locked up is a measure of last resort, it is provided that before giving the authorisation the hearing must consider the other options available (including a movement restriction condition) and must thereafter come to the conclusion that it is necessary to include a secure accommodation authorisation in the order.[45] The implication of this requirement is that if the desired effect can be achieved by a movement restriction condition, or any lesser infringement of liberty, then this should be the option chosen by the hearing instead of secure accommodation, as being the more proportionate and less intrusive response to the child's circumstances. In giving their reasons for making a secure accommodation authorisation, it would be sensible for hearings always to set out why a movement restriction condition, or any less intrusive measure, is not sufficient to achieve the aim sought by the order.

11–13   Secondly, a secure accommodation authorisation may be included in a compulsory supervision order only when the order includes a requirement that the child reside at a specified place, and that place must be either a residential establishment which contains both secure accommodation and non-secure accommodation, or two or more residential establishments one of which contains accommodation which is not secure accommodation.[46] This is designed to ensure that if the secure accommodation authorisation is not given effect to, either because the chief social work officer chooses not to implement the authorisation or because the head of the unit that contains the secure accommodation authorisation does not consent to its implementation, the terms of the compulsory supervision order laid down by the children's hearing can still be given effect to. In other words, the children's hearing is obliged, in all cases in which it may include a secure accommodation authorisation, also to decide where the child is to reside in the event that secure accommodation is not made available to the child. In this way the children's hearing retains control of where the child is to be, even when its first choice has not proved possible. This requirement does not apply to a secure accommodation authorisation in an interim compulsory supervision order or in a warrant to secure attendance.[47]

---

[43] 2011 Act s.162. See further below, paras 14–39—14–41.

[44] Children's Hearings (Scotland) Act 2011 (Implementation of Secure Accommodation Authorisation) (Scotland) Regulations 2013 (SSI 2013/212) reg.11.

[45] 2011 Act s.83(5)(c).

[46] 2011 Act s.83(5)(a).

[47] 2011 Act s.86(4) and s.88(2), disapplying s.83(5)(a).

Thirdly, before a secure accommodation authorisation can be included as a **11–14** measure in a compulsory supervision order or an interim compulsory supervision order, one or more of the following conditions must be satisfied:

(a) the child has previously absconded and is likely[48] to abscond again and, if he or she were to abscond, it is likely that the child's physical, mental or moral welfare would be at risk;
(b) the child is likely to engage in self-harming conduct;
(c) the child is likely to cause injury to another person.[49]

Risk to physical welfare is a risk that the child will be bodily injured; risk to mental welfare is a risk that the child's mind or emotional state will be damaged; risk to moral welfare is a risk that the child will be deprived of appropriate moral guidance and support, or will be subject to immoral or otherwise harmful influences. It would seem at first sight that this paragraph is not sufficiently broad to allow the children's hearing to authorise secure accommodation in order to prevent the child making his or her position worse by continued offending.[50] However, allowing a child freedom to continue with habits of criminality can, it is submitted, be said to put the child at mental or moral risk since it is likely to deny the child appropriate moral guidance and may well threaten to turn a child who offends into an habitual offender. It is in any child's interests to be protected from that risk. "Injury to another person" is limited, it is submitted, to physical or mental or, perhaps, moral injury and does not include economic injuries such as damage to property.[51]

In English law, a decision to place a child in secure accommodation is not **11–15** one in which the child's welfare is the paramount consideration. In *Re M (A Minor) (Secure Accommodation)*[52] it was held that welfare, though always relevant, was not paramount since s.1 of the (English) Children Act 1989 makes welfare paramount only in relation to questions with respect to "the upbringing of the child", which the decision to place the child in secure accommodation was held not to be. Section 25(2) of the Children's Hearings (Scotland) Act 2011, however, is significantly wider and provides that the requirement to regard the need to safeguard and promote the welfare of the child throughout his or her childhood as the paramount consideration applies whenever the hearing "is coming to a decision about a matter relating to the child". Whether to authorise the placing of a child in secure accommodation is clearly a matter relating to that child. Section 26 should, however, also be noted, for it is provided there that the children's hearing may make a decision

---

[48] The word "likely" in this context means a real possibility, which can be established by a past history of absconding: *S v Knowsley Borough Council* [2004] 2 F.L.R. 716.

[49] 2011 Act s.83(5)(b) and (6). The local authority may submit a report to the children's hearing recommending secure accommodation for the child only when it is satisfied that one or more of these conditions is satisfied: Secure Accommodation (Scotland) Regulations 2013 (SSI 2013/205) reg.6.

[50] In *Humphries v S*, 1986 S.L.T. 683, it was held that detention in a place of safety "in the child's own interests" (the wording in the 1968 Act) could be authorised for this reason and that it would be too narrow an interpretation of "the child's own interests" to limit that phrase to the child's mental, physical or moral well-being.

[51] The paragraph does not refer to "some other person's interests", which would include economic injuries. Cf. 2011 Act s.26 which expressly includes harm "whether physical or not".

[52] [1995] 2 W.L.R. 302.

inconsistent with the requirement to give paramountcy to the child's welfare if the hearing considers it necessary to do so for the purpose of protecting members of the public from serious harm (whether physical or not). In that situation the hearing must regard the need to safeguard and promote the child's welfare throughout his or her childhood as a primary consideration rather than as the paramount consideration. This means that the child's welfare is always relevant and one of the first factors to be taken into account but if, at the end of the day, it is contrary to the child's welfare to be kept in secure accommodation that fact may be outweighed by the serious harm to the public that might be caused by failing to keep the child secure. The interplay between s.26 and s.83(6)(c) is not clear, particularly since the reference to harm to others is wider (being physical or not) in s.26 than in s.86(3)(c) (which refers simply to "injury to another person"). The problem is perhaps best illustrated by the question of whether secure accommodation can be authorised to prevent the child causing serious economic injuries to others (such as destoying their property). It is suggested that the answer to that question is no. To grant a secure accommodation authorisation one or more of the conditions in s.83(6) must be satisfied, and these conditions (which, as suggested above, do not permit authorisation to protect economic interests) are not enlarged by s.26. Section 26 merely downplays the place of welfare from paramount to primary in the specified circumstances, but does not in itself authorise the making of any decision that is not authorised by another express provision in the statute. Sections 25 and 26 contain the criteria according to which particular decisions must be made, not the conditions which have to be satisfied before these decisions may be addressed. So a children's hearing may include in the compulsory supervision order a secure accommodation authorisation only if the conditions in s.83(6) are satisfied and if such a decision is contrary to the child's welfare it can be made only if, *in addition,* the criterion for decision in s.26 is also satisfied. It is unlikely, however, that reliance will often have to be placed on s.26 for there are many situations, as shown above, where it is entirely consistent with giving paramountcy to the interests of a child who is a danger to the public to authorise the placing of that child in secure accommodation. This decision, perhaps more than any other, must crucially take account of the proportionality test: is secure accommodation truly the least invasive method of achieving the legitimate aim of improving the child's life?

Removal of child from secure accommodation

11–16   A child may be removed from secure accommodation by the chief social work officer who implemented the authorisation if he or she considers it unnecessary for the child to be kept there or is required to do so by the regulations[53]: if he or she does so the secure accommodation authorisation ceases to have effect and may no longer be relied upon if thereafter it appears that the child needs to be kept in secure accommodation.[54] It is noticeable, and to be regretted, that there is no provision requiring the chief social work officer to

---

[53] For example after a review under reg.10 of the Children's Hearings (Scotland) Act 2011 (Implementation of Secure Accommodation Authorisation) (Scotland) Regulations 2013 where the chief social work officer considers placement in secure accommodation to be no longer in the child's best interests.

[54] 2011 Act s.151(4) and (5).

take account of the views of the child when making a decision to remove the child from secure accommodation. It would be error to assume that all children, in all circumstances, would prefer to be accommodated elsewhere than in secure accommodation and so good practice will usually demand what the law does not in terms of taking account of the child's views.

Placement in secure accommodation without authority of a children's hearing

The chief social work officer and the person in charge of the residential **11–17** establishment providing secure accommodation can place and keep a child who is subject to a compulsory supervision order that does not contain a secure accommodation authorisation in secure accommodation provided the criteria in s.83(6)[55] are satisfied and in addition (i) they are both satisfied that it is in the child's best interests to be so placed and (ii) the chief social work officer is satisfied that the placement in that establishment is appropriate to the child's needs, having regard to the residential establishment's statement of functions and objectives.[56] When the child is placed in secure accommodation, the chief social work officer must immediately inform the reporter and each relevant person in relation to the child, and immediately and in any event not later than 24 hours after the placement require a review of the compulsory supervision order; the reporter must arrange a children's hearing within 72 hours of the placement to review the compulsory supervision order.[57] Similar rules apply if the child placed in secure accommodation is subject to an interim compulsory supervision order, or a medical examination order[58] or is a looked after child[59] or is detained by an order under s.44 or s.51 of the Criminal Procedure (Scotland) Act 1995.[60] The maximum period during which a child may be kept in secure accommodation without the authority of a children's hearing or sheriff is an aggregate of 72 hours (whether or not consecutive) in any period of 28 consecutive days.[61]

Duties towards children in secure accommodation

If a child has been placed and kept in secure accommodation, it is the duty **11–18** of the managers and person in charge of the residential establishment to ensure that the child's welfare is safeguarded and promoted.[62] The child's placement in secure accommodation must be reviewed by the chief social work officer within seven days of the placement, then one month thereafter and then within one month of each previous review, or when the child or relevant person

---

[55] Either: (i) that the child has absconded, is likely to abscond again, and by doing so will put him or herself at risk; (ii) that the child is likely to engage in self-harming conduct, or (iii) that the child is likely to cause injury to another person.

[56] 2011 Act s.152; Secure Accommodation (Scotland) Regulations 2013 (SSI 2013/205) reg.7(2) and (3).

[57] Secure Accommodation (Scotland) Regulations 2013 reg.7(4) and (5).

[58] Secure Accommodation (Scotland) Regulations 2013 reg.8.

[59] Secure Accommodation (Scotland) Regulations 2013 regs 9 and 10.

[60] Secure Accommodation (Scotland) Regulations 2013 regs 11 and 12.

[61] Secure Accommodation (Scotland) Regulations 2013 reg.5. An extra 24 hours is granted in cases of looked after children where the reporter considers it would not be reasonably practicable to arrange a children's hearing within 72 hours: Secure Accommodation Regulations reg.10(6).

[62] Secure Accommodation Regulations 2013 reg.4.

requests a review.[63] In conducting the review, regard must be had to whether the criteria for authorising secure accommodation[64] continue to apply, whether the placement is still in the best interests of the child and how the child's needs are being met.[65] If the criteria for authorising secure accommodation do not continue to apply the authorisation does not immediately fall, though this will be a strong indicator to the chief social work officer that he should remove the child from secure accommodation.

REQUIRING MEDICAL EXAMINATION OR TREATMENT

11–19 Another measure that the children's hearing may include in a compulsory supervision order or an interim compulsory supervision order is a requirement that the implementation authority arrange: (i) a specified medical or other examination of the child; or (ii) specified medical or other treatment of the child.[66] Such a requirement aims to ensure that there is carried out any medical examination of the child that is necessary to determine what medical treatment the child might need, and to ensure that such treatment as is necessary is made available. That the children's hearing must "specify" what examination or treatment the local authority is to arrange ensures that this provision may be used only when the hearing has a clear idea of what is, or might be, needed and it cannot authorise a general examination in the absence of good reason to suspect that some form of medical intervention is advisable. Though this requirement may also be attached to an interim compulsory supervision order when the hearing defers making its decision its purpose when a full compulsory supervision order is made is to provide the improvement in the child's circumstances that has been identified as necessary in the interests of the child.[67] This measure, though primarily designed to deal with the child's medical needs, is worded deliberately widely and refers to "medical or other examination" and "medical or other treatment": this would cover things like drug rehabilitation treatment or psychiatric or psychological assessment and treatment or an educational assessment.

11–20 It is unclear from the terms of the statute what the strict legal effect of the requirement is, for in its terms it simply requires the local authority to make arrangements. Enforcing these arrangements is another matter, and while normally the measure will be used in the light of parental failure, due to inadequacy, to provide appropriate medical facilities for the child it might also be used in the face of parental refusal, for example for religious reasons, to ensure that the child receives appropriate medical treatment.[68] It is to be noted that a requirement that the local authority arranges specified medical or other

---

[63] Children's Hearings (Scotland) Act 2011 (Implementation of Secure Accommodation Authorisation) (Scotland) Regulations 2013 reg.10(2).

[64] That is to say: (a) the child has absconded and is likely to abscond again and it is likely that the child's physical, mental or moral welfare would be at risk; (b) that the child is likely to engage in self-harming conduct; or (c) that the child is likely to cause injury to another person.

[65] Children's Hearings (Scotland) Act 2011 (Implementation of Secure Accommodation Authorisation) (Scotland) Regulations 2013 reg.10(4).

[66] 2011 Act s.83(2)(f).

[67] The question for the hearing is always whether a compulsory supervision order is necessary for the "protection, guidance, *treatment* or control of the child": ss.91(3)(a) and 119(3)(a).

[68] cf. *Finlayson, Applicant*, 1989 S.C.L.R. 601.

examination or treatment does not replace the consent to medical examination or treatment that is generally required, either from the child (if capable) or the child's parent exercising the responsibility and right to act as the child's legal representative. Under the 1995 Act the requirement was worded as a condition on the child who could be "required to submit to any medical or other examination or treatment"[69] but this language is noticeably absent from the 2011 Act. It follows that the doctor whom the local authority has arranged to carry out the examination or treatment would not be able to rely on the requirement in the compulsory supervision order in the face of parental refusal to grant consent to the child's medical examination or treatment. This is expressly so in the case of a refusing child, at least if capable of consenting or withholding consent to his or her own medical treatment. If the child is mature enough to understand the nature and consequences of the proposed medical examination or treatment then that child has capacity to consent or refuse consent, under the terms of s.2(4) of the Age of Legal Capacity (Scotland) Act 1991.[70] That provision is expressly preserved by s.186 of the Children's Hearings (Scotland) Act 2011, to which s.83(2)(f) is made subject, and which is in these terms:

> "(1) Nothing in this Act prejudices any capacity of a child enjoyed by virtue of section 2(4) of the Age of Legal Capacity (Scotland) Act 1991
> . . .
> (2) in particular, where (a) [under an order made under the 2011 Act] any examination or treatment is arranged for the child and (b) the child has the capacity mentioned in section 2(4) [of the 1991 Act] the examination or treatment may be carried out only if the child consents to it".

In other words, any requirement on the local authority to arrange medical treatment does no more than impose a duty on the local authority and it does not provide the doctor with the necessary authority for carrying out the treatment: the child's consent is that authority, and a doctor who carries out the treatment without the patient's consent may be guilty of assault.

The children's hearing may in addition impose a condition on the child that **11–21** he or she submits to medical treatment under s.83(2)(h)[71] but neither is such a condition any legal authority for carrying it out,[72] because the terms of s.186 are general even although not explicitly referred to in s.83(2)(h). Rather, a child who refuses to submit in the face of such a condition will be regarded as having breached that condition, and treated in the same way as any child who breaches a condition in a compulsory supervision order, that is to say will be brought back to a children's hearing for a review under s.131(2)(b). A children's hearing, however, ought to give especially careful consideration to the appropriateness of imposing such a condition when they know that the child is

---

[69] Children (Scotland) Act 1995 s.70(5)(a).

[70] Though the 1991 Act is worded in terms of capacity to consent and not capacity to refuse, it is submitted that the one includes the other since the whole point of a doctor asking a patient for consent is to allow the patient the opportunity to refuse. A more difficult question is whether something like psychiatric or psychological assessment, which is clearly covered by s.83(2)(f) of the 2011 Act, is within the phrase "medical, dental or surgical treatment or procedure" as used in s.2(4) of the 1991 Act. It is submitted that the 1991 Act is to be read broadly to include all legitimate health care provision.

[71] Considered in more detail below, para.11–28.

[72] Just as a requirement on a child to reside at a specified address is not authority to lock the child in.

refusing. A failure on the part of a parent to consent to necessary medical treatment will, in itself, amount to a section 67 ground[73] but a term in a compulsory supervision order does not provide a health-care provider with the legal authority to act in the face of a refusing parent. It may well be that the only way to grant legal authority to provide necessary medical treatment in these circumstances would be through the mechanism of a child protection order, with a special authorisation under s.37(3).[74] Even that, however, is an impotent provision in the face of a capable child's refusal to consent.[75]

11–22   A children's hearing that makes a compulsory supervision order may not, at the same time, grant a medical examination order, for the latter order may competently be made only when the hearing defers making a decision on whether to make a compulsory supervision order.[76]

DIRECTION REGULATING CONTACT

11–23   In every case in which a children's hearing decides to make, vary or continue a compulsory supervision order it is expressly obliged[77] to consider whether to include in the order one particular measure, that is to say a direction regulating contact between the child and a specified person or class of person.[78] This obligation was originally contained in s.83(3) and s.138(5) and was extended to interim compulsory supervision orders by s.86(4). But both s.83(3) and s.138(5) were repealed before the 2011 Act came into force,[79] and replaced with a new s.29A. That new section does not extend the rule to interim compulsory supervision orders, in what was almost certainly a mistake on the part of the legislature. But there is really no point in a hearing which is considering making an interim compulsory supervision order (or an interim variation of a compulsory supervision order) *not* considering the issue of contact[80] and so good practice probably demands what the legislation does not. There is no obligation to impose such a direction, but merely to consider whether it would be in the interests of the child to include one.[81] If a contact direction is not included in the compulsory supervision order or interim compulsory supervision order, the local authority will have the right to regulate contact whenever the child is being looked after by them in accommodation provided by the local authority and it is to be remembered that the local authority will have the duty to take such steps to promote, on a regular basis, personal relations and direct contact between the child and any person with parental responsibilities

---

[73] cf. *Finlayson, Applicant*, 1989 S.C.L.R. 601.

[74] "A child protection order may also include any other authorisation or requirement necessary to safeguard or promote the welfare of the child".

[75] 2011 Act s.186(2) and (3)(b).

[76] See above, paras 10–08—10–12.

[77] 2011 Act s.29A(1) (as inserted by the Children's Hearings (Scotland) Act 2011 (Modification of Primary Legislation) Order 2013 (SSI 2013/211) Sch.1 para.20(5).

[78] 2011 Act s.29A and s.83(2)(g). A sheriff varying or continuing a compulsory supervision order must do so too: s.29A(2): a sheriff has no power to *make* a compulsory supervision order, and "varying" includes, it is submitted, interim variation.

[79] Children's Hearings (Scotland) Act 2011 (Modification of Primary Legislation) Order 2013 Sch.2.

[80] 2011 Act s.126 provides consequences for contact directions made as part of an ICSO.

[81] *Kennedy v M*, 1995 S.L.T. 717.

in relation to the child as appear to the local authority to be both practicable and reasonable, having regard to their duty to safeguard and promote the child's welfare.[82] If, however, the children's hearing considers it best to leave the matter in the hands of the local authority this is not properly a matter to be included as a direction in the compulsory supervision order and it should not appear as such.[83] That decision would not be appropriate in circumstances in which the local authority is likely to respond by applying a policy rather than making individual decisions, such as when the child is being placed for adoption and the local authority policy is to reduce contact: in these and similar circumstances the hearing should make its own decision in relation to the particular child appearing before it.[84] In many cases, for example when contact is not an issue, the consideration that must be given to the question of contact can be dealt with speedily, though, in order to show that the statutory obligation has been satisfied, it would be good practice to record as a positive decision the hearing's determination that it is not necessary to include such a requirement in the compulsory supervision order or interim compulsory supervision order.

The obligation to consider the issue of contact applies generally and is not **11–24** limited to situations in which the child is required to reside somewhere.[85] If it is to be made, the direction should be in clear and unambiguous terms. A direction regulating contact will normally be appropriate when the child is required to live away from home and it is in his or her interests to maintain contact with his or her parents or guardians, or other family members, but the condition may also be imposed when the child remains at home and the child's interests would be served by some other person, such as an absent parent, or a previous foster carer to whom the child has become attached, having contact. Or, since the direction is to "regulate" contact, it can be used to require that no contact be permitted between the child and a stated person. This whole provision is, however, slightly peculiar since the measures in a compulsory supervision order are enforceable against only the child and the local authority. The direction included in the compulsory supervision order may purport to "regulate" contact between the child and another person, but steps can be taken to enforce that part of the order only when it is the child (or local authority) who breaches it. The real aim of the provision is to ensure that the local authority permits and facilitates contact and to emphasise that the power to regulate contact with a child subject to a compulsory supervision order rests with the children's hearing and not the local authority. A parent's failure to maintain contact with the child when the children's hearing has considered such contact to be in the interests of the child will not automatically activate a review under s.131(2)(b), but it may well oblige the local authority to require a review under s.131(2)(a).[86]

The regulation of contact by means of a direction included in a compulsory **11–25** supervision order or interim compulsory supervision order can be as prescriptive or as non-prescriptive as the children's hearing considers appropriate, so long as the person or class of person with whom contact is to be regulated

---

[82] Children (Scotland) Act 1995 s.17(1)(c) and (6)(b).
[83] *Kennedy v M*, 1995 S.L.T. 717.
[84] *H v Petrie*, 2000 S.L.T. (Sh Ct) 145.
[85] cf. the power under s.83(2)(c) to prohibit disclosure of where the child resides.
[86] See below, para.13–08.

is specified. So the hearing might set out where contact is to take place, how often, and whether it is to be supervised or not.[87] The hearing may allow contact to be at the discretion of the implementation local authority, or of the relevant person who is the primary carer of the child, or even of the child him or herself.[88] The hearing may specify particular days and particular hours during which contact is to take place, if this is considered necessary. In general, however, it is likely that a child's interests will best be served by laying down only the general parameters of contact without too much prescription of detail. Children's lives tend to change more rapidly than adults and prescribed times have a habit of interfering with new interests or new friendships that the child subsequently develops. It is competent for a condition to prohibit contact between a child and a specified person, but if any form of family life exists between them the European Court will impose a stricter scrutiny on such limitations to the parties' art.8 rights and the justification for prohibiting contact will require to be particularly cogent and persuasive.[89]

11–26   A direction included in a compulsory supervision order or interim compulsory supervision order that regulates contact between the child and any specified person or class of person supersedes any other legal right of contact, to the extent that such a right is inconsistent with the condition. So, for example, a person with the parental right to maintain personal relations and direct contact with the child under s.2 of the Children (Scotland) Act 1995 cannot exercise that right during the currency of the compulsory supervision order if a contact direction is included to the effect that the child is to have no contact with the person with the s.2 right.[90] And any court order under s.11(2)(d) of the 1995 Act regulating the arrangements for maintaining personal relations and direct contact between the child and another person is put in suspension during the currency of the compulsory supervision order, in so far as the court order is inconsistent with any term or direction included in the compulsory supervision order.[91] If no direction regulating contact is included in the compulsory supervision order, pre-existing rights of contact (in so far as it is apt to refer to them as "rights") are unaffected. So a court decree[92] allowing or requiring contact at stated times should still be given effect to if the children's hearing does not consider it appropriate to attach any direction regulating contact and it is not otherwise inconsistent with the terms of the compulsory supervision order or interim compulsory supervision order. In the absence of a court decree, however, contact between the child and any other person is within the practical control of the person who has care and control of the child, which might well be the local authority. A relevant person who is dissatisfied with the level of contact with the child that he or she is being permitted by the local authority cannot ask the court to make an order under s.11 which has immediate effect

---

[87] So, for example, in *O v Rae*, 1993 S.L.T. 570 the father was allowed supervised access for one hour per fortnight with each of his children.

[88] See for example *C v Principal Reporter*, 2010 Fam. L.R. 14.

[89] *Olsson v Sweden (No. 2)* (1994) 17 E.H.R.R. 134; *Johansen v Norway* (1997) 23 E.H.R.R. 33 at [64]; *K & T v Finland* [2000] 2 F.L.R. 79 at [139]; *Levin v Sweden* [2012] 1 F.C.R. 569 at [57]–[59]. And see *Principal Reporter v K*, 2011 S.L.T. 271.

[90] Children (Scotland) Act 1995 s.3(4).

[91] *Dewar v Strathclyde Regional Council*, 1985 S.L.T. 114.

[92] Granted under Children (Scotland) Act 1995 ss.11(2)(d).

different from the terms of the compulsory supervision order,[93] but must seek a review of the compulsory supervision order and ask the children's hearing to attach a condition regulating contact in more favourable terms.

The inclusion of a direction regulating contact may affect the civil rights of **11–27** persons other than a relevant person—and other than those who may require a review of the compulsory supervision order. Persons other than a relevant person do, however, have protection of their civil rights, and in particular their right to participate in a process that might affect their rights, by the procedure created by s.126 of the Children's Hearings (Scotland) Act 2011. This provides that if a children's hearing makes, continues or varies a compulsory supervision order or makes an interim compulsory supervision order, an interim variation of a compulsory supervision order or a medical examination order which is to have effect for more than five working days, and the order contains (or is varied to contain) a contact direction then in certain circumstances that contact direction must be reviewed by a children's hearing no later than five working days[94] after the hearing that made (or continued or varied) the order to which the contact direction is attached.[95] This is not necessary in all cases in which a contact direction is made but only when there is in force a contact order made under s.11(2)(d) of the Children (Scotland) Act 1995 or a permanence order within the meaning of s.80(2) of the Adoption and Children (Scotland) Act 2007, and either order regulates contact between the child and an individual who is not a relevant person in relation to the child.[96] In addition, an individual who has or has recently had significant involvement in the upbringing of the child[97] may require the reporter to arrange a children's hearing within the same timescale to review the contact direction.[98] The hearing may confirm the compulsory supervision order, or vary it but only by varying or removing the contact direction.[99] This limited review is examined more fully below.[100]

ANY OTHER SPECIFIED CONDITION

The compulsory supervision order may include a requirement that the child **11–28** comply with any other specified condition.[101] The discretion of the children's hearing is very wide here and it may impose any condition that it considers likely to do some good for the child. A condition on the child might be that he

---

[93] In *P v P*, 2000 S.L.T. 781 (at 788L) the Inner House accepted that it would be competent to seek a contact order, but inappropriate other than in exceptional circumstances for a court to make an order that at the time of its making would be inconsistent with a condition attached to a supervision requirement. This was approved in *Principal Reporter v K*, 2010 S.L.T. 308 at [63] (and the point was not commented upon when that decision was overruled by the Supreme Court: 2011 S.L.T. 271).

[94] "Working day": every day except Saturdays and Sundays, 25th and 26th December, and 1st and 2nd January: s.202(1).

[95] 2011 Act s.126(1) and (4).

[96] 2011 Act s.126(2)(a) and (3).

[97] 2011 Act s.126(2)(b); Children's Hearings (Scotland) Act 2011 (Review of Contact Directions and Definition of Relevant Person) Order 2013 (SSI 2013/193) art.2(2).

[98] 2011 Act s.126(2)(b).

[99] 2011 Act s.126(6).

[100] Below, paras 13–41—13–44.

[101] 2011 Act s.83(2)(h).

or she attends school regularly, or attends some group-work or training project, or meets with a social worker on a stated basis, or co-operates with the plans drawn up by the social work department, or attends at a drug or alcohol rehabilitation unit or anger-management programme, or does any other thing (or ceases doing anything) specified by the hearing. The only limitation is that the condition must require something of the child, and that its purpose is to protect, guide, treat or control the child.[102] A children's hearing has no power to impose conditions on any other person[103] (other than a local authority, for which see immediately below), such as a relevant person (though the relevant person's responsibilities and rights are affected in that they cannot be exercised during the currency of the compulsory supervision order or interim compulsory supervision order in any way that would be incompatible with that order[104]). If the children's hearing decides to impose a condition on the child it must do so expressly and the condition must be specified in the relevant form: a passage in the statement of reasons issued by the hearing is not a condition attached to the compulsory supervision order.[105] And the condition must be expressed in clear and unambiguous terms.[106] The same will apply to duties imposed on local authorities.

REQUIREMENTS ON LOCAL AUTHORITIES

11–29 The children's hearing may also include as a measure in the compulsory supervision order or interim compulsory supervision order a requirement that the relevant local authority carry out specified duties in relation to the child.[107] In giving effect to a compulsory supervision order or interim compulsory supervision order, the implementation authority is obliged to comply with any requirements imposed on it in relation to the child by the order, and the duties that may be imposed on it include the duty to secure or facilitate the provision for the child of services of a kind which the implementation authority does not itself provide.[108] The only implicit qualification is that the duty be directed to the achievement of the overall aim of the compulsory supervision order. This means that it is probably incompetent for the children's hearing to impose a requirement on a local authority to carry out a duty in relation to the child that has no connection with the current difficulties the child has nor the hearing's attempts to resolve them. However, if a large view is taken of the scope of intervention available to the hearing which has jurisdiction over the child, there will be few functions of the local authority that may not be included in a

---

[102] Kearney points out (*Children's Hearings and the Sheriff Court*, 2nd edn (Butterworths, 2000), para.25.41) that theoretically this is so wide that the condition could be to the effect that an offending child make reparation to his or her victim, or undertake some form of community service but that such conditions would not be "in the spirit of the Act". This is undoubtedly so. There is a huge difference between teaching the child how to fit properly into society and teaching the child a lesson. The former is a right and proper, the latter an illegitimate, basis for a children's hearing's decision.

[103] *P v P,* 2000 S.L.T. 781 at 786D.

[104] Children (Scotland) Act 1995 s.3(4), as amended by the Children's Hearings (Scotland) Act 2011 (Modification of Primary Legislation) Order 2013 Sch.1 para.9(2).

[105] *Kennedy v M,* 1995 S.L.T. 717.

[106] *D v Strathclyde Regional Council,* 1991 S.C.L.R. 185 at 186F.

[107] 2011 Act s.83(2)(i).

[108] 2011 Act s.144.

requirement under this provision. Extreme cases are not beyond the imagination (such as a hearing requiring the local authority to provide the child with a place at a particular school when there is no indication that schooling is a problematical issue for the child) and such a requirement in these circumstances may well be held to be not justified. The local authority will, in any case, have a range of duties to any child over whom a compulsory supervision order has been made, beyond those explicitly specified in the order, for all such children are "looked after" in terms of s.17 of the Children (Scotland) Act 1995.[109]

Another duty that the local authority is subject to without this being imposed **11–30** on it by the terms of the compulsory supervision order is that whenever the local authority holds a report concerning the child and the terms of a compulsory supervision order require that someone other than a local authority is to have control over the child (whether as foster carer or manager of a residential establishment) the local authority must give the person a copy of that report if it appears to the local authority that the report would assist the person in the care and supervision of the child.[110] It is also the local authority's duty to take the child to any place in which he or she is required to reside or be taken under a compulsory supervision order, an interim compulsory supervision order, a medical examination order or under another provision in the 2011 Act.[111]

---

[109] As amended by the Children's Hearings (Scotland) Act 2011 Sch.5 para.2(4).

[110] Children's Hearings (Scotland) Act 2011 (Compulsory Supervision Orders etc: Further Provision) Regulations 2013 (SSI 2013/149) reg.3. The same applies with interim compulsory supervision orders, though in that case the report must be given no later than two working days after receiving notice of the making or variation of the interim compulsory supervision order: reg.4.

[111] Children's Hearings (Scotland) Act 2011 (Compulsory Supervision Orders etc: Further Provision) Regulations 2013 reg.9.

CHAPTER TWELVE

ADVICE AND REMIT HEARINGS

INTRODUCTION

12–01 Sometimes a children's hearing is convened not in order to consider whether to make or review a compulsory supervision order, but instead to give advice about the referred child to a court that is required to make a decision over the child. Proceedings at such hearings follow that at any other hearing, with the chairing member commencing the hearing by introducing the panel members, checking the status of all those who are attending, and explaining the purpose of the hearing.[1] The discussion and the consideration of the options that will follow, and be the heart of the hearing, are governed by the type of court that has sought advice, and what the court is asking the hearing to do.

CRIMINAL CASES

12–02 Though in the generality of cases a child who commits an offence will be dealt with by having his or her case referred to a children's hearing[2] instead of being prosecuted in a criminal court, there will be some situations in which the Crown or the procurator fiscal takes the decision that the appropriate course is to prosecute the child for the offence in the normal criminal courts.[3] This might be, for example, because of the seriousness of the alleged offence,[4] or because the child has committed a large number of offences, or because the children's hearing system has exhausted the good it can realistically do for the particular child. If the child, on prosecution, pleads guilty to or after trial is found guilty of an offence, the criminal court (whether the High Court, the sheriff court or the Justice of the Peace Court) has the power and sometimes the duty, under the Criminal Procedure (Scotland) Act 1995, to seek advice from a children's

---

[1] See further above, para.7–02.

[2] The ground upon which the child is referred being that contained in the Children's Hearings (Scotland) Act 2011 s.67(2)(j).

[3] There is nothing in the statute that says that if a child is prosecuted he or she cannot later be referred to a children's hearing in respect of the same offence, but it is likely that the principle of res judicata would render any such referral incompetent. It could be argued that the children's hearing system, being sui generis and designed to protect the child's welfare, remains open in appropriate cases. A criminal court, on conviction, might determine that the child does or does not require punishment; this is irrelevant to the question of whether the child's welfare requires a compulsory supervision order to be made. However, it is submitted that this line of reasoning is not good. The court's power to remit the child's case to a children's hearing should be taken to exclude the reporter's power to refer the child when the court decides not to do so.

[4] As in, for example, *Codona v HM Advocate*, 1996 S.L.T. 1100, where a 14-year-old girl had been charged and convicted of murder.

hearing as to how it should dispose of the case (i.e. what sentence, if any, is appropriate); in addition the court may remit the case of the child to the children's hearing for disposal by the hearing itself. The court may neither seek advice from, nor remit a case to, a children's hearing when the offence is one the sentence for which is fixed by law.[5]

The rules governing when a criminal court can seek advice from a children's **12–03** hearing or remit the case for disposal to a children's hearing differ according to whether or not the child is currently subject to a compulsory supervision order, and for that reason any court in which a child is being prosecuted should take care to ascertain whether this is so or not. There are also differences in some circumstances depending upon the age of the child or young person.

Child not currently subject to compulsory supervision order

Where a child, that is to say a person under 16, is not subject to a compulsory **12–04** supervision order, has been prosecuted in a criminal court and has pled guilty to or been found guilty of an offence, the court has three options: (i) it may dispose of the case itself according to its normal criminal jurisdiction; (ii) it may remit the case for disposal by a children's hearing[6]; or (iii) it may request the reporter to arrange a children's hearing for the purpose of obtaining the hearing's advice as to the treatment of the child.[7] If the third option is chosen it is open to the hearing to advise the court to dispose of the case itself, and to suggest which of the sentences that are available to the court is the most likely to serve the interests of the child; alternatively the hearing may advise the court to remit the case back to the children's hearing for disposal. In either case the terms of the advice ought to explain to the court why the hearing favours one disposal over another. Advice to the court to remit the case back to a children's hearing would be appropriate when the hearing considers that the welfare-based system still has something to offer the child in the way of protection, guidance, treatment or control; advice to the court to dispose of the case itself would be appropriate whenever the hearing considers that realistically it has nothing beneficial to offer the child. The court must consider the advice obtained and having done so may either dispose of the case itself or remit it back to the children's hearing for its disposal,[8] whether this is what the children's hearing advised or not (though it would be unusual for a court to remit the case back to a children's hearing at this stage against the advice of the hearing). If the case is remitted back to the children's hearing, a certificate signed by the clerk of court stating that the child whose case is remitted has pled guilty to or has been found guilty of the offence to which the remit relates is conclusive evidence for the purposes of the remit that the offence was committed by the child,[9] and the hearing will thereafter proceed as if an offence ground under s.67(2)(j) had been established by the sheriff[10] (that is to say will move on to a consideration of whether it is necessary to make a compulsory supervision order in light of the establishment of the ground).

---

[5] Criminal Procedure (Scotland) Act 1995 s.49(5).

[6] Criminal Procedure (Scotland) Act 1995 s.49(1)(a).

[7] Criminal Procedure (Scotland) Act 1995 s.49(1)(b). The reporter must, of course, comply with this "request".

[8] Criminal Procedure (Scotland) Act 1995 s.49(2).

[9] Children's Hearings (Scotland) Act 2011 s.71(2).

[10] 2011 Act s.71(3).

Person aged 16 or over not currently subject to compulsory supervision order

12–05   When a person aged 16 years or over, but who is more than six months short of his or her 18th birthday, is not currently subject to a compulsory supervision order, has been prosecuted in a criminal court in summary proceedings[11] and has pled guilty to or been found guilty of an offence, the court has two options—it may either: (i) dispose of the case itself according to its normal criminal jurisdiction; or (ii) request the reporter to arrange a children's hearing for the purpose of obtaining its advice as to the treatment of the person.[12] If it does the latter, then, having considered the advice that the children's hearing gives, the court may either dispose of the case itself (whether in accordance with the advice it receives or not) or (but in this case only if this is what the children's hearing recommended in its advice) remit the case back to the hearing for it to dispose of the case.[13] The court may not both dispose of part of the case itself and at the same time remit the case back to the hearing.[14] If the case is remitted back to the children's hearing for disposal (following the hearing's advice to do so) a certificate signed by the clerk of court stating that the person concerned has pled guilty to or has been found guilty of the offence to which the remit relates shall be conclusive evidence for the purposes of the remit that the offence was committed by the person,[15] and the hearing will proceed as if an offence ground under s.67(2)(j) had been established by the sheriff.[16] This is the main circumstance in which a person who is not subject to a compulsory supervision order on his or her 16th birthday can be made subject to such an order thereafter.[17] If the person is less than six months short of his or her 18th birthday (or is over the age of 18), the court cannot refer the case for advice and must therefore deal with the case itself.

Child currently subject to compulsory supervision order

12–06   Where a child who is currently subject to a compulsory supervision order or an interim compulsory supervision order has been prosecuted in the High Court and has pled guilty to or been found guilty of an offence, the court may as it thinks fit either: (i) dispose of the case itself according to its normal criminal jurisdiction; or (ii) request the reporter to arrange a children's hearing for the purpose of obtaining its advice as to the treatment of the child[18]; the High Court may not, at this stage, remit the case for disposal by a children's hearing. If the child has been prosecuted in the sheriff court or the Justice of the Peace

---

[11] This will not include the High Court, which does not conduct summary trials.

[12] Criminal Procedure (Scotland) Act 1995 s.49(6). The reporter must, of course, comply with this "request".

[13] Criminal Procedure (Scotland) Act 1995 s.49(7).

[14] *McCulloch v Murray*, 2005 S.C.C.R. 775.

[15] Children's Hearings (Scotland) Act 2011 s.71(2).

[16] 2011 Act s.71(3).

[17] Such a person is not a "child" for the purposes of the Children's Hearings (Scotland) Act 2011, but the terms of that Act will apply as if the person were a child whenever a court has remitted a case to the children's hearing for disposal under this provision: s.199(8) and (9). The other circumstance is when a referral to a children's hearing is made before a child's 16th birthday but the reference is not disposed of until after that date: s.199(3)–(5). See above, para.2–10.

[18] Criminal Procedure (Scotland) Act 1995 s.49(3)(a). The reporter must, of course, comply with this "request".

court and had pled guilty to or been found guilty of an offence, the sheriff (whether the procedure is solemn or summary) or the JP *must* refer the case to a children's hearing for such advice[19] and the court may, at this stage, neither dispose of the case itself nor remit the case to a children's hearing for disposal.[20] On receiving advice, the court (whether High Court, sheriff court or Justice of the Peace Court) must consider that advice and, as it thinks proper, may now either dispose of the case itself or remit it back to the children's hearing for its disposal, whether this is what the children's hearing advised or not. If, however, the offence to which the child has pled guilty or been found guilty of is one of various crimes under the Firearms Act 1968 or the Violent Crime Reduction Act 2006, to which minimum sentences apply, then the court must dispose of the case itself[21]: but even in such cases the advice of the hearing, if it has been given, must be considered.

Procedure at advice hearings

When the reporter is required to arrange a children's hearing at the behest **12–07** of a criminal court seeking advice as to how it should dispose of the child's case, he or she must, as soon as practicable and no later than seven days before the intended date of the hearing, notify the child, each relevant person, any safeguarder, the three members of the children's hearing, the chief social work officer of the relevant local authority and the National Convener of the date, time and place of the hearing.[22] As soon as possible and no later than three days before the intended date of the hearing the reporter must give to the child, relevant person and safeguarder:

(a) a copy of the remit from the court;
(b) copies of all decisions and reasons made by all pre-hearing panels and children's hearings in respect of the child;
(c) confirmation of the child's duty to attend the advice hearing;
(d) confirmation of the relevant person's duty to attend;
(e) information on the means by which the child may express views to the hearing; and
(f) confirmation of the right of the child and relevant person to give any report or other document for the consideration of the children's hearing.[23]

Copies of the remits and decisions must, on the same timescale, be given to the three panel members who will make up the children's hearing.[24]

The procedure to be followed at a children's hearing convened in order to **12–08** give advice to a criminal court is similar to that at any other hearing held after grounds have been established, except that there is no dispositive (nor appealable) decision for the hearing to make. The provisions concerning attendance

---

[19] Criminal Procedure (Scotland) Act 1995 s.49(3)(b).
[20] *Anderson v McGlennan*, 1998 S.C.C.R. 552.
[21] Criminal Procedure (Scotland) Act 1995 s.49(3).
[22] Children's Hearings (Scotland) Act 2011 (Rules of Procedure in Children's Hearings) Rules 2013 (SSI 2013/194) (hereinafter "2013 Rules") r.44(1) and (2).
[23] 2013 Rules r.44(3) and (4).
[24] 2013 Rules r.44(5).

at children's hearings, and warrants to secure attendance, apply with equal force. The children's hearing does not, however, review any current compulsory supervision order the child may be subject to (unless a review hearing, competently arranged, is being held at the same time) and the sole purpose of the advice hearing is to examine the child's circumstances through a discussion with the persons present, and to draw up a report for the court containing such advice as the hearing thinks appropriate. The chairing member of the hearing must, before the children's hearing proceeds to consider what advice to give, inform those present at the hearing of the substance of any relevant report or other document.[25] Procedure will follow the normal pattern of a discussion of the issue—being in this case what advice to give to the court—and as always the chairing member must take all reasonable steps to obtain the views of the child, relevant person, and any appointed safeguarder in relation to the reporters and documents and what, if any, advice or measures would be in the interests of the child,[26] and may invite any other person present at the hearing, as the children's hearing considers appropriate, to express views on that issue.[27] Once the hearing has decided what advice to give the chairing member must confirm to the child, relevant person and safeguarder what that advice will be and then make, or cause to be made,[28] a report of the advice.[29] Though there is no express statutory obligation to do so, it is good practice for the chairing member, at the end of the hearing, to remind the child that the court is not legally bound to follow the advice. Thereafter the report containing the advice must then be signed and dated by the chairing member and given to the reporter at the conclusion of the hearing. The reporter must, as soon as possible following receipt of the report, give a copy of the report to the child, each relevant person, the safeguarder, the chief social work officer of the relevant local authority and, of course, the court that made the request for the advice.[30]

Powers of advice hearings; appointing a safeguarder

12–09   The criminal court may accept or reject the hearing's advice and dispose of the case on grounds other than the child's welfare but members of the children's hearing have neither training nor competence to give advice about any matter other than the child's welfare, such as the need for exemplary punishment or the need to deter others. The role of the children's hearing, in advice hearings, is therefore to advise the court as to what would be in the interests of the child.

12–10   An advice hearing has no explicit statutory power to defer making a decision as to the advice it wishes to give (except that the general power to adjourn[31]— and reconvene the same day—applies to all hearings). However, the rule in r.7(1) that procedure is as the chairing member determines explicitly applies to "any children's hearing . . . required to be held by virtue of [the 2011 Act] or any other enactment" and this gives, it is submitted, the chairing member the

---

[25] 2013 Rules r.75(2)(a).

[26] 2013 Rules r.75(2)(b).

[27] 2013 Rules r.75(2)(c).

[28] In practice the chairing member should never delegate this task to anyone other than one of the other members of the hearing: the advice is the hearing's advice and it is best to be drawn up in the hearing's own words.

[29] 2013 Rules r.75(2)(d) and (3).

[30] 2013 Rules r.75(4).

[31] 2013 Rules r.7(2).

power to defer the decision at an advice hearing until a subsequent hearing. This might be useful if, for example, an up-to-date social background report is not yet available. However, an advice hearing may not make any medical examination order, interim compulsory supervision order, or other order that might be made when a dispositive hearing defers making its decision. Power to make these orders is specifically granted at various stages, such as when grounds of referral have been accepted[32] or established,[33] but no such power is granted to a children's hearing convened for the purposes of giving advice,[34] and there is no basis upon which the power may be implied. The chairing member's power under r.7 of the 2013 Rules is to determine procedure, which includes deferral, but not to make orders not explicitly provided for.

Under the Children (Scotland) Act 1995 an advice hearing arranged under **12–11** s.49 of the Criminal Procedure (Scotland) Act 1995 had no power to appoint a safeguarder, because that power applied only to hearings arranged under the Children (Scotland) Act 1995.[35] The power to appoint a safeguarder under the 2011 Act, on the other hand, applies "at any time when the children's hearing is still deciding matters in relation to the child"[36] and it is initially unclear whether determining what advice to give amounts to "deciding a matter" for this purpose. On a strict reading of the statute, giving advice is different from making a decision (which carries an implication of disposition). However, the same limitation is imposed on the requirements to regard the need to safeguard and promote the child's welfare as the paramount consideration and to take account of the child's views,[37] and if "coming to a decision about a matter relating to a child" did not include giving advice then these requirements would not apply to the determination of what advice to give. It is an implausible interpretation that the advice may be determined upon without regarding the child's welfare as the paramount, or at least a primary,[38] consideration and at least in relation to the child's views the phrase "coming to a decision" includes advice in one particular context.[39] There would be little point in the requirement in the 2013 Rules for the chairing member to seek the child's, relevant person's and safeguarder's views on what advice "would be in the best interests of the child"[40] unless that were the paramount consideration (i.e. unless s.25 of the 2011 Act applied here as elsewhere). This all suggests that a broader meaning should be given to "coming to a decision" than making a dispositive decision, and that it might include deciding what advice to give. If that is so then advice hearings may, since the coming into force of the 2011 Act, appoint a safeguarder, though it would be appropriate to do so only if the hearing considered that some element beyond advice it is able to give might be discovered by a safeguarder.[41] The criminal court has no statutory

---

[32] 2011 Act s.92(2) and (3).

[33] 2011 Act s.120(5) and (6).

[34] 2011 Act s.71(3), which will carry all these powers, applies only when the case has been remitted to the hearing for disposal (s.71(1)(a)) and not for advice.

[35] Children (Scotland) Act 1995 s.41.

[36] 2011 Act s.30(2).

[37] 2011 Act ss.25 and 27.

[38] 2011 Act s.26.

[39] That of advising whether a child protection order should be continued: see 2011 Act s.27(5).

[40] 2013 Rules r.75(2)(b)(ii).

[41] And the power to appoint a safeguarder confirms the advice hearing's power to defer making its decision on what advice to give.

obligation to receive any report of a safeguarder appointed by an advice hearing but in the generality of cases there will be no reason for it not to. A more solid role for a safeguarder appointed in these circumstances would be if the children's hearing were confident that the child's case will be referred back to it for disposal.

Remit hearings

12–12   The procedure in advice hearings is quite different from the procedure to be followed in cases remitted from a criminal court to the children's hearing for disposal, for in the latter the role of the children's hearing is not to give advice but to make a dispositive decision of whether to make, vary or continue a compulsory supervision order. If a case is remitted to the children's hearing from the court for disposal, the jurisdiction of the court in respect of the child ceases and the child's case stands referred to the children's hearing.[42] The powers and duties of the children's hearing are the same as if the reporter had arranged a hearing after a sheriff had found section 67 grounds established,[43] and the procedure to be adopted is also the same. So the children's hearing must consider the case, taking account of the section 67 ground (that the child has committed the offence that he or she pled guilt to or was found guilty of in the criminal proceedings that led to the remit), any reports and any other information that it has, and it can discharge the referral, defer making a decision, or make, vary or continue a compulsory supervision order in such terms as it thinks fit. Rules of attendance, including excusal and exclusion, apply as in other hearings, warrants to secure attendance may be granted, medical examination orders, interim compulsory supervision orders or interim variations of compulsory supervision orders may be made, secure accommodation authorisations may be given, and if the child is already subject to a compulsory supervision order that order must be reviewed at the same time.[44]

NON-CRIMINAL ADVICE HEARINGS

Advice relating to antisocial behaviour orders

12–13   The Antisocial Behaviour etc. (Scotland) Act 2004 allows the court, on the application of a local authority, to make an antisocial behaviour order (ASBO) in respect of a child[45] if the following three conditions are satisfied:

---

[42] Criminal Procedure (Scotland) Act 1995 s.49(4).

[43] 2011 Act s.71(3)(b). Sheriff Kearney, *Children's Hearings and the Sheriff Court*, 2nd edn (Bloomsbury, 2000) at para.24.19 suggests a constraint on the powers of a hearing when a previous hearing has advised a remit back to the hearing, to follow the advice. But it is difficult to see how this can be so. There is no express rule to this effect and two differently constituted hearings may well come to opposing conclusions, both reasonable and both justified in all the circumstances of the case. Most fact scenarios faced by hearings allow judgment to be exercised in determining welfare (the paradigm "judgment case") and judgment, by definition, contains a margin of appreciation. Just as one hearing is not to be criticised because another hearing (or a sheriff) would have decided differently, so too one hearing giving advice cannot be taken to bind another hearing called upon to make the dispositive decision.

[44] 2011 Act s.130(2).

[45] Defined as a person under the age of 16 years: Antisocial Behaviour etc. (Scotland) Act 2004 s.18.

(a) the child is at least 12 years of age;
(b) the child has engaged in antisocial behaviour[46] towards a person within the local authority area, unhelpfully entitled in the 2004 Act a "relevant person"[47]; and
(c) an ASBO is considered by the sheriff to be necessary for the purpose of protecting "relevant persons" from further antisocial behaviour by the child.[48]

Before determining whether to make an ASBO, and whether or not the child is **12–14** presently subject to a compulsory supervision order, the court is obliged to take advice from a children's hearing, and then to have regard to that advice.[49] However, very oddly, this is not advice as to whether it is in the child's welfare to make an ASBO, but rather advice as to whether the third of the conditions mentioned above is satisfied, that is to say whether making the ASBO is necessary for the purpose of protecting "relevant persons" (as defined) from further antisocial behaviour by the child. Not being advice relating to the child's interests, but more akin to advice to a sheriff as to whether a section 67 ground applies or not, this form of advice from a children's hearing is unique and poses some difficulties for hearings since their major expertise, identifying what is in the welfare of the child, is not called upon at all[50]: this is especially anomalous when the child is not otherwise subject to the jurisdiction of the children's hearing. The condition upon which the hearing must give advice is a matter of judgment upon the likely efficacy—from a third party's point of view—of the proposed order. Children's hearings are unlikely to be able to make that judgment any better than a sheriff and their advice, for the most part, will serve no real (as opposed to procedural) purpose in the ASBO process. This is even more so in those cases in which the "relevant person" to be protected is not a relevant person as understood by the 2011 Act and so without any explicit right to attend the hearing to explain why an ASBO might be necessary to protect them. It is open to a children's hearing, and would be by no means bad practice, to advise the court that it cannot make the judgment, just as it is open to the sheriff to ignore any more substantive advice the hearing does feel able to give.

No specific procedure is laid down for this eminently repealable type of **12–15** hearing (which in practice is vanishingly rare), though the general power of the chairing member to determine procedure in r.7(1) of the 2013 Rules clearly applies. There is nothing in the Rules that indicate to the Reporter who to notify of such a hearing, and no rules about attendance at the hearing.

Advice relating to adoption and permanence orders

As will be seen in the next chapter, a review of an existing compulsory **12–16** supervision order must be required by the implementation authority whenever:

---

[46] Defined in s.143 of the 2004 Act as acting in a manner or pursuing a course of conduct that causes or is likely to cause alarm or distress to at least one person who is not in the same household as the child.
[47] Antisocial Behaviour etc. (Scotland) Act 2004 s.4(13).
[48] Antisocial Behaviour etc. (Scotland) Act 2004 s.4(2).
[49] Antisocial Behaviour etc. (Scotland) Act 2004 s.4(4).
[50] This may be compared with the advice a hearing may be called upon to give to a court in relation to adoption or permanence order plans (discussed immediately below) for there the advice will invariable be on whether the proposed order is in the child's interests.

(i) it is satisfied that the best interests of the child would be served by the authority making (and it intends to make) an application for a permanence order or its variation or amendment or revocation; or (ii) it is satisfied that the best interests of the child would be served by the authority placing (and it intends to place) the child for adoption; or (iii) it is aware that an application has been made or is about to be made for an adoption order in respect of the child.[51] When a children's hearing is arranged to review a compulsory supervision order for any of these reasons it must, in addition to carrying out the review, prepare a report providing advice about the circumstances to which the review relates for both the implementation authority (in the case of (i) and (ii) above) and any court that requires to come to a decision about the application (referred to in (i) and (iii) above).[52] The hearing must do so irrespective of the outcome of the review of the existing compulsory supervision order, that is to say whether it is continued, varied or terminated. Before deciding upon the advice to be contained in the report, the chairing member must explain to the child and relevant person the purpose of the report to be prepared, and must inform them of the substance of any document or information material to the advice to be contained in the report.[53] Before preparing the report, the children's hearing must discuss the case with the child, relevant person and any safeguarder and seek their views as to what they think would be in the best interests of the child.[54] Taking these views into account, the hearing must then determine what advice to include in their report and it must inform the child, relevant person and safeguarder of what that advice is.[55] The chairing member must then make or cause to be made the report, sign and date it, and give it to the reporter at the conclusion of the hearing; the reporter then has five days to give a copy of the report to the child, relevant person, safeguarder, the court that requires to come to a decision on the subject matter of the report, the chief social work officer of the implementation authority, and (where it is adoption that is being proposed) the prospective adopters.[56]

12–17   This report should be wider than the statement of reasons for a decision that the hearing normally makes, which is limited to justifying the decision made in respect of the compulsory supervision order. Rather, the report should take the form of the hearing's opinion as to the appropriateness of the order that the court will be asked to make or of the proposed placing for adoption. Since the court making an adoption order or a permanence order must terminate an existing compulsory supervision order if satisfied that on the making of an adoption order or a permanence order the compulsory supervision order is no longer necessary,[57] it will usually be appropriate for the advice to include a recommendation as to whether or not the court should indeed, if it does make an adoption order or a permanence order, terminate the existing compulsory supervision order. The court is obliged to have regard to this report when coming to its decision about the application for an adoption order or a

---

[51] 2011 Act s.131(2)(c), (d) and (e).
[52] 2011 Act s.141(2).
[53] 2013 Rules r.65(1).
[54] 2013 Rules r.65(2).
[55] 2013 Rules r.65(2)(c).
[56] 2013 Rules r.65(3) and (4).
[57] Adoption and Children (Scotland) Act 2007 s.36 (adoption order) and s.89 (permanence order).

permanence order.[58] The court will of course already have before it many different reports which it must consider in an application for an adoption order or a permanence order and there will seldom be any issue of fact that might come out of a children's hearing's report which the court will not otherwise be aware of. Nevertheless, the report may have some use if the members of the children's hearing are convinced that the adoption or permanence plans are quite wrong for the particular child, since it provides them with a direct line to the court through which they can communicate their doubts.

In what might be regarded as an example of legislative overkill, reviews of **12–18** compulsory supervision orders are required, and reports have to be drawn up, at each of the stages of the adoption and permanence processes. So a report will be required when the child is placed for adoption and another when an adoption application is made; a report will be required when a permanence order is sought and another when an application for its variation is made. If these events are relatively close in time, the children's hearing may feel that it has little to add to its previous reports. The obligation to prepare a report under s.141 is absolute, but its contents are left to the hearing and, if the child's circumstances have not substantially changed since a previous report was prepared, it would be competent and sometimes appropriate for the children's hearing's report simply to repeat advice previously given or even to do no more than refer to advice given in a previously prepared report.

Advice to permanence courts—section 95 reports

A quite different sort of advice hearing might be held once an application **12–19** has been made to a sheriff to make a permanence order (or its variation or amendment). While it is normally in the child's interests not to be subject to more than one legal process at any one time, this is sometimes unavoidable. A review of an existing compulsory supervision order might fall due during the permanence process (that is to say after the date the application is made to the court but before the date of the granting of the order, or of the application's withdrawal or abandonment), or the reporter might consider it appropriate to arrange a children's hearing due to the occurrence of circumstances that amount to one or more of the section 67 grounds, even while permanence proceedings are underway, perhaps as a response to the same circumstances.[59] If a children's hearing is held during the permanence process, either to put new grounds or to review an existing order, the children's hearing is prohibited from making or varying any compulsory supervision order, other than by interim variation.[60] The thrust of the legislation is that the permanence court

---

[58] 2011 Act s.141(4).

[59] It is to be remembered that local authorities, which apply for permanence orders, have an obligation to share information with reporters whenever it might be necessary to make a compulsory supervision order: s.60. It would not be legitimate for a local authority to conclude that, since it was itself applying for a permanence order, it is not necessary to make a compulsory supervision order and therefore the reporter should not be informed of the child's circumstances. A reporter, however, on receipt of information from a local authority and knowing that a permanence order is being applied for may not consider it necessary, in these circumstances, to arrange a children's hearing: s.66(2) and s.68(1)(b). The point is, the decision is the reporter's and not the local authority's.

[60] Adoption and Children (Scotland) Act 2007 s.96(1) and (2), as amended by the Children's Hearings (Scotland) Act 2011 (Modification of Primary Legislation) Order 2013 Sch.1 para.17(9).

should deal with all issues confronting the child, both once the order is made and during the process in which it is applied for. However, the children's hearing that is subject to this prohibition must nevertheless hold a full hearing, at the end of which it may come to the view that a compulsory supervision order should be made or varied. If the matter is one of urgent necessity, it may make an interim compulsory supervision order[61] or an interim variation of an existing compulsory supervision order[62] but if the test for an interim order is not satisfied the children's hearing that proposes to make or vary a compulsory supervision order must, instead of doing so, prepare a report under s.95 of the Adoption and Children (Scotland) Act 2007, setting out the terms of the proposed compulsory supervision order or the terms of its proposed variation, together with the reason the children's hearing has for making or varying the compulsory supervision order; in addition (if the child is already subject to a compulsory supervision order—which will normally be the case) the report drawn up under s.141 of the Children's Hearings (Scotland) Act 2011 (that is to say the report drawn up at any review giving advice to the court as to permanence proposals)[63] must also be included in the s.95 report.[64]

12–20   The s.95 report explains what the hearing thinks the hearing should do; the s.141 report explains what the hearing thinks the court should do. It would be sensible to include within these reports the children's hearing's reasons why the hearing system should retain some control over the case even when the permanence process is underway (if that is what the hearing believes). The two processes are designed with different aims and operate to different timeframes: it follows that continued involvement of the children's hearing in a child's life even when a permanence order has been applied for or has been granted would be appropriate when there is still volatility in the child's circumstances. The permanence order (which is named well) is designed to regularise a permanent situation and the permanence court is likely to be far less dexterous in responding to short-term difficulties or rapidly evolving circumstances. Whenever these exist the children's hearing system is usually the better forum and this point should be made in any s.95 report in which a children's hearing is trying to persuade a permanence court to allow it to make or vary a compulsory supervision order even while the permanence process is underway.

12–21   Whenever a report is to be drawn up under s.95, the chairing member must explain to the child, relevant person and safeguarder the purpose of the report and must consider the child's case as it would at any other hearing arranged to decide whether it is necessary that a compulsory supervision order be made or ought to be varied, taking account of the views of those present at the hearing.[65] The chairing member must, if the hearing then wishes to make or vary a compulsory supervision order, explain to the child, relevant person and safeguarder that it wishes to do so (and why) but that it cannot do so while the permanence application is undecided, or until the court remits the case back to

---

[61] For the rule in s.96(2) of the 2007 Act does not prohibit the making or varying of an interim compulsory supervision order, or the granting of a warrant to secure attendance, or of any other order available to the hearing other than a compulsory supervision order itself.

[62] Under 2011 Act s.139(3).

[63] Above, paras 12–16—12–18.

[64] Adoption and Children (Scotland) Act 2007 (Supervision Reports in Applications for Permanence Orders) Regulations 2009 (SSI 2009/169).

[65] 2013 Rules r.77(2) and (3).

the hearing after considering the report.[66] The chairing member then makes (or causes to be made) the report and gives it to the reporter, who then has five days to give it to the permanence court, the child, relevant person, safeguarder and chief social work officer of the relevant local authority.[67]

The court to which the application for a permanence order has been made **12–22** must consider the s.95 report and may then, in light of this report, decide to refer the child's case to the reporter. This referral has the effect of removing the prohibition on the hearing making or modifying a compulsory supervision order while permanence proceedings are underway.[68] The reconvened children's hearing may now, therefore, make or modify the compulsory supervision order.

It has been suggested that a hearing, reconvened after referral from a court in **12–23** these circumstances, may do only that which the previous hearing that drew up the s.95 report wanted to do and which, therefore, has been authorised by the sheriff making the referral,[69] but there is no statutory authority for this suggestion nor is it a necessary implication from the process. The reconvened hearing is as bound as any other hearing by s.25, which requires it to regard the need to safeguard and promote the welfare of the child throughout childhood as the paramount consideration, and this requires the reconvened hearing, it is submitted, to come to its own judgment as to what is best for the child. In no other circumstance must a hearing defer to the welfare assessment made by either an earlier hearing or a sheriff and had the statute intended to impose an obligation on the subsequent hearing to follow the review hearing it could easily have done so expressly—or even more easily allowed the sheriff to endorse the earlier hearing's proposals. In any case, if the court that subsequently makes, varies or amends a permanence order disagrees with the decision of the reconvened children's hearing, the court may terminate the compulsory supervision order if it considers that that order is no longer necessary.[70] And if the permanence court is not yet in a position to make its final decision, it may make an interim order[71] which prevails over any inconsistent terms of a compulsory supervision order.[72] (In any case other than an interim (permanence) order, if a child is concurrently subject to both a compulsory supervision order and a permanence order, any inconsistency between the two is resolved by giving precedence to the terms of the compulsory supervision order.)[73] These are the ways in which the permanence court retains ultimate say over the future of the child.

Advice in relation to child protection orders

If a sheriff has made a child protection order over a child under either s.38 **12–24** or s.39 of the Children's Hearings (Scotland) Act 2011 an application to vary or terminate that order may be made to the sheriff.[74] If so, the reporter may (but

---

[66] 2013 Rules r.77(4).
[67] 2013 Rules r.77(5) and (6).
[68] Adoption and Children (Scotland) Act 2007 s.96(3).
[69] *City of Edinburgh, Petitioners*, 2011 Fam. L.R. 83, per Sheriff Holligan at [8].
[70] Adoption and Children (Scotland) Act 2007 s.89.
[71] Adoption and Children (Scotland) Act 2007 s. 97(2).
[72] Adoption and Children (Scotland) Act 2007 s. 97(5).
[73] Adoption and Children (Scotland) Act 2007 s. 90.
[74] 2011 Act s.48. See further below, paras 15–26—15–33.

is not obliged to) arrange a children's hearing for the purpose of providing any advice the children's hearing may consider appropriate to assist the sheriff in the determination of the application to vary or terminate the child protection order.[75] The application for the sheriff to review the order may be made either before or after a children's hearing has already reviewed the child protection order and if the hearing has already done so there will usually be little that a hearing convened to provide advice can add. Nevertheless, the chairing member must inform all those present at the hearing of the substance of any relevant report or other relevant document, and take all reasonable steps to obtain the views of the child, relevant person and any appointed safeguarder in relation to these reports and documents and what, if any, advice to be given to the sheriff would be in the child's best interests; the chairing member may invite any other person present to express their views; and the chairing member must confirm the advice that the hearing determines to give, to the child, relevant person, any appointed safeguarder, and the person who applied for the child protection order or its variation or termination.[76] The nature of the advice given is entirely for the members of the children's hearing themselves to decide, but it should, of course, be directed towards the question before the sheriff, which is whether the conditions for the making of the child protection order are satisfied and, if so, what terms the order should include. The child's welfare is not directly relevant to the first of these questions, but is central to the second—notwithstanding that providing advice under s.50 is explicitly included in the words "coming to a decision about a matter relating to a child" for the purposes of the obligation in s.27 to have regard to the views of the child[77] but it is not so explicitly included in the identical phrase for the purposes of the application of the welfare test in s.25. The advice will invariably, in other words, include the hearing's opinion on whether it is in the child's interests that the child protection order be continued, varied or terminated. The sheriff is not, of course, obliged to accept any advice the hearing offers, but it is implicit that he must take the advice into account in reaching his decision. The statute gives no guidance to the reporter as to how and when to exercise his or her discretion to arrange this advice hearing, and often the matter will be determined by the availability of time: the arranging of this hearing does not interrupt the running of the three working days within which the sheriff must determine the application and on that time-scale it will seldom be possible for a children's hearing to give sufficiently deep consideration to the child's circumstances to be able to say anything very useful.

---

[75] 2011 Act s.50. The reporter's notification and provision of information obligations are governed by the 2013 Rules r.40.

[76] 2013 Rules r.72(1) and (2). The reporter must then give a copy of the report of the advice to various people, listed in r.72(4).

[77] 2011 Act s.27(5)(a).

CHAPTER 13

REVIEW HEARINGS

INTRODUCTION

One of the underlying principles of the whole children's hearing system—and **13–01** a requirement of ECHR jurisprudence—is that a child in respect of whom a compulsory supervision order has been made is to remain subject to that order only for so long as his or her interests require it. The main way in which this is done is to provide for regular reviews of the compulsory supervision order to which the child is subject. Regular reviews are necessary not only because the child's circumstances may change fairly rapidly, and his or her needs may develop (often very much more quickly than adults'), but also to ensure that the child does not remain subject to state intervention in his or her life longer than is necessary to achieve the purposes of that intervention. If not timeously reviewed, a compulsory supervision order will cease to have effect and to bring the child back into the system would require new section 67 grounds to be accepted or established. There are various circumstances in which the reporter will be obliged to initiate a review of a compulsory supervision order and to arrange a children's hearing to do so. A review must be initiated by the reporter when he or she has been requested to do so by certain people and also, in the absence of any such request, in certain specified circumstances and at stated periods. On arranging a review hearing, the reporter must require the implementation authority to give him or her any reports that the authority has prepared in relation to the child and any other information which the authority may wish to give to assist the children's hearing; in addition the reporter may require the implementation authority to give him or her a report on the child generally or on any particular matter relating to the child specified by the reporter.[1] The powers and duties of a children's hearing reviewing a compulsory supervision order are, by and large, conterminous (though not quite identical) with the powers and duties of a children's hearing arranged to consider the original section 67 grounds that brought the child into the system in the first place, as are the opening preliminaries.[2] The possible disposals at a review hearing are rather different from, though there is some overlap with, the disposals available to a hearing that first imposes a compulsory supervision order on a child.

---

[1] Children's Hearings (Scotland) Act 2011 s.137(4) and (5). The implementation authority may include information it has received from another person: 2011 Act s.137(6).

[2] For which see above, para.7–02.

CIRCUMSTANCES IN WHICH A REVIEW HEARING
MUST BE ARRANGED

Reviews at instigation of reporter

13–02   There are two circumstances in which the reporter, without being required to do so by any other person or body, must arrange a review hearing, and a third circumstance in which he or she may do so. First, a compulsory supervision order, if it has not otherwise been reviewed within that time, will remain effective for one year and it cannot remain in force for a period longer than one year unless it has been continued, with or without variation, within a year of its imposition or last continuation.[3] If the reporter has not been required to initiate a review before then, he or she must do so if it will expire within three months and would not otherwise be reviewed before it expires.[4] This review is commonly, though not wholly accurately, referred to as the annual review. Secondly, a person cannot remain subject to a compulsory supervision order after reaching the age of 18 years, and any subsisting order automatically ceases to have effect on the person's 18th birthday, even without the meeting of a hearing to terminate it. The reporter's obligation to arrange a review within three months of the expiry of the compulsory supervision order applies in this situation also, though any continuation of the order in these circumstances would last only until that date.[5] In either of these cases, if the reporter fails to arrange a review hearing the compulsory supervision order will cease to have effect on the person's 18th birthday or on the anniversary of its being imposed or continued; but reporters who are of the view that it is no longer necessary that the child be subject to a compulsory supervision order should not simply fail to arrange a hearing, for not only would that breach their statutory obligation but it would also usurp the function of the children's hearing, in whose sole remit the question of whether the order remains necessary lies.

13–03   Thirdly, the reporter, at his or her discretion, may also instigate a review of a compulsory supervision order by arranging a children's hearing to consider new or additional section 67 grounds that have come to his or her attention. The reporter might do so, rather than waiting for a review to be required or to fall due in the normal way because, for example, the new grounds are pointing to a deteriorating situation or are indicating that the existing measures contained in the order are not, or are no longer, appropriate. In any situation in which the child is already subject to a compulsory supervision order, Part Nine of the Act (general rules relating to children's hearings, and grounds hearings) applies with references to "making a compulsory supervision order" being read as references to "reviewing the order",[6] and with references to interim compulsory supervision orders being read as references to interim variations of compulsory supervision orders.[7] So the reporter is required to

---

[3] 2011 Act s.83(7)(a) and (b).
[4] 2011 Act s.133.
[5] Though it will only be in very rare circumstances indeed that a compulsory supervision order will be continued so close to its subject's 18th birthday.
[6] 2011 Act s.97(3), subject to the non-application of s.96(4) which imposes timelimits for interim compulsory supervision orders.
[7] 2011 Act s.97(5).

prepare a statement of grounds[8] when he or she considers that a new[9] section 67 ground applies and must arrange a children's hearing for the purpose of reviewing the existing order.[10] A grounds hearing will follow,[11] with the grounds being put to the child and relevant person and, as with a normal grounds hearing, procedure thereafter will depend upon whether the new grounds are accepted, or not understood or denied.

If the new grounds are accepted by the child and relevant person the provisions relating to review hearings apply,[12] and the children's hearing may exercise any of the powers laid down in ss.138 and 139 for review hearings (discussed later in this chapter).[13] The outcome of the review of the existing compulsory supervision order will inevitably be influenced by the existence of the new section 67 grounds (though it does not always follow that the order will be altered in any way). **13–04**

If, on the other hand, the new grounds are denied, or are denied in part, or are not understood, the hearing may, in relation to the new grounds, either direct the reporter to make an application to the sheriff to determine whether the new grounds are established[14] or discharge the referral of these new grounds.[15] If the reporter is directed to apply to the sheriff for establishment of the new grounds the hearing may continue the compulsory supervision order until the subsequent children's hearing.[16] The fact that this is not expressed as an imperative means that the hearing may, if it wishes, immediately review the existing compulsory supervision order, but given that the existence—or otherwise—of the new grounds is likely to be a strong influence on the outcome of the review[17] it will usually be more appropriate not to proceed to a review of the existing order while at the same time directing the reporter to apply to the sheriff for a determination of whether the new grounds apply or not. The hearing would normally, in these circumstances, be better deferring making its decision until the sheriff has made his determination,[18] and if any change in the terms of the order is considered necessary in the meantime, as a matter of urgency, then it may make an interim variation of the existing compulsory supervision order.[19] The matter is somewhat different if the referral of the new grounds is discharged for in that case the hearing may proceed, where appropriate, to a review of the existing order.[20] Again, this is not an imperative and so the hearing may consider it more appropriate to terminate the hearing there **13–05**

---

[8] 2011 Act s.89.

[9] That is to say, additional to the grounds upon which the child was originally made subject to a compulsory supervision order, and nearly always since the date the order was made.

[10] 2011 Act s.69(2), though not in Part 9 of the Act, is referred to in s.89 (which is) and so is similarly modified by s.97(3). The reporter must satisfy the notification and provision of information rules that apply in relation to both grounds hearings and review hearings: Children's Hearings (Scotland) Act 2011 (Rules of Procedure in Children's Hearings) Rules 2013 (SSI 2013/194), hereinafter "2013 Rules", r.38.

[11] See Ch.7 above.

[12] 2011 Act s.97(4).

[13] Below, paras 13–25—13–32.

[14] 2011 Act s.93(2)(a) and s.94(2)(a).

[15] 2011 Act s.93(2)(b) and s.94(2)(b).

[16] 2013 Rules r.69(2).

[17] If they are not, then it will often be better to discharge the referral of those grounds.

[18] 2011 Act s.138(2).

[19] 2011 Act s.139(3).

[20] 2013 Rules r.69(3).

and then, allowing the existing order to be reviewed in the normal course of events. It should, however, be borne in mind that too many hearings inevitably stress the child, and it may be that in most cases it will be good practice to review an existing order at the hearing that has already been convened even when new grounds are discharged.

Local authority requiring review

13–06   The most common circumstance (apart from the annual review) in which a review of a compulsory supervision order will be held is when a local authority has required it. The implementation authority, that is to say the local authority that is responsible for giving effect to the order, must require (by way of notice to the reporter) a review of the compulsory supervision order in a number of different circumstances,[21] and when it does so the reporter then has an obligation to arrange a review hearing.[22] The matter is one of obligation on the part of the local authority (and, indeed, of the reporter) and if one of the stated circumstances exists the local authority cannot decide simply to let the matter lie until the annual review (unless, probably, the annual review is imminent in any case). The different circumstances in which the local authority must require a review are described in the following paragraphs.

13–07   First, a review must be required whenever the local authority is satisfied that the current compulsory supervision order ought to be terminated or varied.[23] The local authority may come to this view because some change (good or bad) has taken place in the child's circumstances since the compulsory supervision order was made or last reviewed which indicates to the authority that the terms and conditions of the order are no longer appropriate. It might be, for example, that the plans for the child have worked successfully, or the threat to the child's well-being has been lifted, and that a compulsory supervision order is therefore thought by the local authority to be no longer necessary, or to have served its purpose. Or it might be that the plans are not working and some change in the terms of the order is considered necessary to give effect to new plans which the local authority has drawn up and which it believes would better serve the child's needs. Or the child's circumstances may now be such that different measures are now needed to be included in the compulsory supervision order, for example in relation to contact or where the child is to live, or indeed whether a secure accommodation authorisation is needed.

13–08   Secondly, a review must be required by the local authority whenever it is satisfied that the compulsory supervision order is not being complied with.[24] It does not matter why the order is not being complied with, whether it is because of a radical change in the child's circumstances, or non-co-operation by the child, or lack of resources by the local authority, or for any other reason. Conditions are frequently imposed upon the child as part of the terms of the order,[25] and any breach of such conditions of which the local authority is aware will oblige it to require a review. The local authority is therefore required to keep a watchful eye on the situation in order to monitor whether or not each of

---

[21] 2011 Act s.131.
[22] 2011 Act s.137(2).
[23] 2011 Act s.131(2)(a).
[24] 2011 Act s.131(2)(b).
[25] See above, Ch.11.

the terms and conditions of the order are being fulfilled. However, there is no sanction in the Act for the failure on the part of a local authority to bring the case back to a hearing when conditions are not fulfilled,[26] but it is no excuse for such a breach of a statutory obligation that those charged with giving effect to the order do not consider the terms of the order appropriate (for that does not lie within their judgment). If that is considered to be the case, the local authority must require a review[27] and explain to the children's hearing why it would be better for the child that the order be varied.

Thirdly, a review must be required whenever the local authority is satisfied **13–09** that the best interests of the child would be served by the authority making an application for a permanence order under s.80 of the Adoption and Children (Scotland) Act 2007, or an application for its variation under s.92 or its amendment under s.93 or its revocaction under s.98 of the 2007 Act, and in addition the authority intends to make such an application.[28] A children's hearing arranged as a result of a referral for any of these reasons must not only review the existing compulsory supervision order, but must also prepare a report providing advice about the circumstances to which the review relates for both the local authority and the court to which the application will go.[29] Indeed, this will usually be the main purpose of the review hearing since it has been arranged as a result of an intended, as opposed to actual, change in the child's circumstances,[30] and in any case a court that makes a permanence order is obliged to terminate any compulsory supervision order (unless satisfied that it remains necessary)[31] so that any remaining issues in the child's life are dealt with by means of the provisions in the long-term permanence order rather than the shorter-term provisions in the compulsory supervision order. All the more important, therefore, that the report to the court drawn up under s.141 is directed to the child's welfare under the permanence regime rather than the children's hearing system.

Fourthly, a review must be required whenever the local authority is satisfied **13–10** that the best interests of the child would be served by the authority placing the child for adoption and it intends to do so.[32] Again, the children's hearing will be required both to review the existing compulsory supervision order and to

---

[26] It is arguable that an action for breach of statutory duty might be possible at the instance of a child who suffers loss by being subject to a compulsory supervision order longer than his or her welfare requires, but such an argument is unlikely to be sustained in the light of *M (A Minor) v Newham London Borough Council* [1995] 2 A.C. 633. But it is not entirely impossible: see *Barrett v Enfield London Borough Council* [2001] 2 A.C. 550. A failure by a local authority to ensure appropriate monitoring of vulnerable children, as a result of which the children are subjected to inhuman or degrading treatment, may amount to a breach of art.3 of the ECHR: see *E v United Kingdom* (2003) 36 E.H.R.R. 31 and *DP & JC v United Kingdom* (2003) 36 E.H.R.R. 14.

[27] Under 2011 Act s.131(2)(a).

[28] 2011 Act s.131(2)(c).

[29] 2011 Act s.141(2). See above, paras 12–16—12–18.

[30] Note that the review must be arranged when an order is applied for rather than when it is granted. And recall that a compulsory supervision order may not be varied (other than by interim variation) while an application for a permanence order or its variation or amendment is pending: Adoption and Children (Scotland) Act 2007 s.96(2), discussed above, para.12–19.

[31] Adoption and Children (Scotland) Act 2007 s.89.

[32] 2011 Act s.131(2)(d). See also Adoption and Children (Scotland) Act 2007 s.106 which imposes a similar duty on registered adoption services (but does not follow the duty through by requiring a review on receipt of reports). This does not supersede the local authority's duties under s.131(2).

prepare a report providing advice to the local authority about the circumstances to which the review relates.[33] The local authority must then take that advice into account in determining whether to go ahead with the placement.

13–11　　Fifthly, a review must be required by the local authority whenever it becomes aware that an adoption application has been made and is pending, or is about to be made, in respect of the child under s.29 or s.30 of the Adoption and Children (Scotland) Act 2007.[34] At a review required for this reason, the children's hearing must both review the existing compulsory supervision order and (again the main purpose of the hearing) prepare advice about the circumstances to which the review relates to both the implementation authority and the court to which the adoption application has been made or will be made.[35] The making of an adoption order obliges the court to terminate any compulsory supervision order (unless satisfied that the compulsory supervision order remains necessary[36]).

Review required by child or relevant person

13–12　　The child or relevant person is able to require a review at any time after three months beginning with the day on which the order is made, continued or varied,[37] and if either or both do so the reporter is obliged to arrange a children's hearing.[38] The months are calendar months and the review may take place on any date after three months have expired since the compulsory supervision order was made, continued or varied.[39] The notice requiring the review that the child or relevant person gives to the reporter may be given at a time before the expiry of the three months, but the children's hearing cannot consider the case until after that expiry.

13–13　　The age at which a child has capacity to call for a review is not specified, nor has it been discussed in any reported case. There would be acute awkwardness in attempting to apply the rules contained in the Age of Legal Capacity (Scotland) Act 1991 to this question.[40] Requiring a review may be seen as a"transaction having legal effect", that effect being to impose on the reporter an obligation to arrange the review; but if s.2(1) of the Age of Legal Capacity (Scotland) Act 1991 applies, this would mean that a review could be called for by a child only when the child is of an age at which it is"common" for persons of the child's age and circumstances to do so and on terms that are not unreasonable. It is, in fact, highly unusual for children to call for reviews[41] and the requirement that the terms of the transaction be not unreasonable is redundant in this context. It is submitted that the 1991 Act is not designed to cover this situation and that the better view is that the terms of s.132(2), permitting "a

---

[33] 2011 Act s.141(2).

[34] 2011 Act s.131(2)(e).

[35] 2011 Act s.141. See above, paras.12–16—12–18.

[36] Adoption and Children (Scotland) Act 2007 s.36.

[37] 2011 Act s.132(2), (3) and (4).

[38] 2011 Act s.137(1) and (2).

[39] For example, a compulsory supervision order made, varied or continued on March 23 may be reviewed at the instance of the child or relevant person on or after June 24.

[40] The child's capacity to appeal is a different issue and is expressly dealt with in s.2(4A) and (4B) of the 1991 Act.

[41] Though "common", as used in the 1991 Act, refers not to numerical frequency but to the unexceptionality of the act. It would be unexceptional for a child of 14 to call for a review, and exceptional for a five-year-old to do so.

child" to call for a review, implicitly confers capacity on all children who are subject to compulsory supervision orders, however young, or alternatively that the right to call for a review is not a right the exercise of which requires any formal legal capacity at all.[42] In practice, reporters are likely to arrange a review called for by a child unless the child clearly has no understanding of what it means to do so.

The relevant person who may call for a review under this provision will **13–14** normally be the same person as is obliged under s.74(2) to attend the children's hearing. However, it is by no means inconceivable that a person may have acquired parental responsiblities and parental rights by court action since the previous hearing, in which case he or she will immediately come within the definition of relevant person in s.200 and so acquire a right to call for a review, even of an order made or continued before he or she became a relevant person. On the other hand, a person who has become, since the last hearing, significantly involved in the child's upbringing and so able to seek to be deemed to be a relevant person under s.81 will not be entitled to call for a review until such time as a pre-hearing panel (or children's hearing) has deemed him or her, on that basis, to be a relevant person: such a person may require a pre-hearing panel to determine that issue "where a chidlren's hearing is to be held", which probably means when a review is due, but he or she may not require the review itself. Conversely, a person who was earlier deemed to be a relevant person retains the right to call for a review even after ceasing to have significant involvement in the child's upbringing, though the children's hearing may well remove his or her relevant person status at that review.[43]

Review required by children's hearing

A children's hearing that makes, varies or continues a compulsory supervi- **13–15** sion order may require the order to be reviewed on a day or within a period specified in the order, and sometimes must do so.[44] This allows the hearing to ensure that the compulsory supervision order will be reviewed at some point before it otherwise would be, that is to say within a year (though it may not postpone a review required by other provisions). This might be appropriate when, for example, the child is over 16 and is thought to need only a few months to settle down, or a child has been returned to a parent's care in an attempt at rehabilitation but it remains unclear whether rehabilitation will succeed. This useful provision allows the children's hearing to make long-term plans for the child's future, by taking account of, and making provision to respond to, any foreseeable changes in the child's short-term circumstances. It would, however, be a misuse for children's hearings to require a review under this provision for no reason other than to "keep their eye on the situation".[45] It would be a proper use of this provision to utilise it to further definite plans, such as changes in the child's residence which will foreseeably become

---

[42] Just as the right to attend one's own children's hearing is not a right the exercise of which requires formal legal capacity.

[43] See below, paras 13–37—13–40.

[44] 2011 Act s.125. The circumstances in which the power to set a review date becomes an obligation to do so are discussed below, para.13–17.

[45] It should never be forgotten how stressful hearings are for many children, and it cannot be doubted that too many unnecessary hearings are not conducive to the child's welfare.

appropriate within a few months, or to give an older child a shorter period to prove that he or she can live satisfactorily without local authority involvement, or to provide a short-term safety net during a difficult transitional period in the child's life. A circumstance in which this power can most usefully be employed is when the child is nearing school leaving age and the children's hearing is minded to terminate the compulsory supervision order. If the order is continued until shortly after the child attains school leaving age, the local authority will be obliged to provide guidance and assistance (in cash or in kind) until the child is 19, under the after-care provisions contained in s.29 of the Children (Scotland) Act 1995, and may do so until the child is 21.[46] Maintaining the order for a few months in order to obtain this very real benefit that would otherwise be denied the child would be justified even when there is nothing else to indicate that a compulsory supervision order is necessary: and requiring an early review will ensure that the order is not continued after its purpose has been achieved.

13–16 The hearing may either specify the date on which the order is to be reviewed, or the period within which the review is to be held. In the vast majority of cases it will be sensible to specify the period within which the review is to be held rather than being too precise as to the actual date upon which the review is to be held, for practical considerations, including scheduling of panel members and availability of relevant persons, may constrain the setting of the date. It would be good practice for hearings intending to use this power to take advice from the reporter as to the practicality of arranging a review on the date, or within the period, specified. The requirement to specify "a period" indicates that the hearing cannot require a review on the happening of an event as opposed to the passing of a certain period. If the future event is one that is likely to change the child's circumstances to such an extent that a review will be indicated, the hearing can do no more than require a review within the period that it predicts the event will occur, or rely on the local authority to call for a review, as it must when satisfied that the compulsory supervision order ought to be terminated or varied.[47]

13–17 There are two circumstances in which the children's hearing must exercise its power to require a review. First, it must specify a date on, or period within which, the compulsory supervision order is to be reviewed whenever the order being made is to contain a movement restriction order, or is being varied to include such a condition.[48] This ensures that this restriction on personal liberty is re-examined at regular intervals to ensure that it remains appropriate. No period is specified in the statute to guide a children's hearing setting a review date,[49] but it is to be remembered that a movement restriction condition cannot have effect for more than six months[50] so a review of the order containing such a condition ought normally to be set at least within that timeframe. The second situation in which a children's hearing must set a review date is whenever, at a

---

[46] At the time of writing the Children and Young People (Scotland) Bill 2013 proposes raising the age of 21 to 26.

[47] 2011 Act s.131(2)(a): see above, para.13–07.

[48] 2011 Act s.125(2).

[49] The implementation authority, on the other hand, as part of the child's plan that it must prepare for children subject to movement restriction conditions, must review that plan within three months: Children's Hearings (Scotland) Act 2011 (Movement Restriction Conditions) Regulations 2013 (SSI 2013/210) reg.3(7).

[50] Children's Hearings (Scotland) Act 2011 (Movement Restriction Conditions) Regulations 2013 reg.6(1).

review hearing, the children's hearing directs the National Convener to give the local authority notice of an intended application to the sheriff principal to enforce the local authority's duties under the compulsory supervision order:[51] when it does so the hearing must also require a further review of the order on or as soon as reasonably practicable after the expiry of a period of 28 days beginning on the day the notice is given.[52] This latter provision requires a review on or after a particular date while a review of a compulsory supervision order with a movement restriction order (or otherwise) may be required on or before a particular date.

Review required by court

There are a number of circumstances in which a court may require the reporter to arrange a review hearing in respect of child who is presently subject to a compulsory supervision order. First, if an ASBO or an interim ASBO has been made under the Antisocial Behaviour etc. (Scotland) Act 2004, in respect of a child who is currently subject to a compulsory supervision order, and the sheriff considers that a section 67 ground (except that the child has committed an offence) applies in relation to the child, the sheriff may require the reporter to arrange a children's hearing.[53] It is left to implication that the new ground that the sheriff considers to apply will be put to the child and relevant person[54] to be accepted or denied. In such circumstances the hearing may proceed in the same way, already discussed,[55] as when the reporter him or herself draws up new grounds in relation to a child already subject to a compulsory supervision order by arranging a review.[56] Secondly, if a criminal court, having found a child guilty of an offence or having accepted the child's guilty plea, has remitted a case to the reporter for disposal of the case under s.49 of the Criminal Procedure (Scotland) Act 1995[57] then, if the child is presently subject to a compulsory supervision order, the reporter must initiate a review of that existing order.[58] In this case, the new ground will be treated as having been established under s.108[59] and so will not need to be put to the child and relevant person for acceptance or denial: the review of the existing order will take into account that the new offence has occurred. Thirdly, if a sheriff, reviewing a grounds determination on an application under s.110[60] in relation to a child already subject to a compulsory supervision order recalls the grounds determination that is the subject of the application but other grounds remain accepted or established, the sheriff must direct the reporter to arrange a review of that compulsory supervision order.[61] This allows the hearing to revisit the child's

13–18

---

[51] See further below, paras 13–34—13–36.

[52] 2011 Act s.146(5).

[53] Antisocial Behaviour etc. (Scotland) Act 2004 s.12(1) and (1A).

[54] cf. the situation when the child is not currently subject to a compulsory supervision order, for in that situation the sheriff must make a "section 12 statement" specifying the ground he considers to apply (2004 Act, s.12(1B)) and this statement will act as if it were a determination under s.108 that the ground applies: s.70.

[55] Above, paras 4–14—4–15.

[56] 2011 Act s.129.

[57] See above, para.4–16.

[58] 2011 Act s.130(1) and (2). Procedure at such hearings is governed by the 2013 Rules r.75.

[59] 2011 Act s.130(4).

[60] See above, paras 8–37—8–49.

[61] 2011 Act s.115(2) (as modified by s.116(2) and s.118(4)).

circumstances in the light of the newly established fact that not all of the original grounds apply in relation to the child. Fourthly, if on determining an appeal under s.154 the sheriff continues or varies a compulsory supervision order he must, if the order contains (or is varied to contain) a movement restriction condition and he may, in any other case, require that the order be reviewed on a day or within a specified period.[62] This is to be interpreted in the same way as the similar rule for children's hearings setting a review date.[63]

Review conducted by the court

13–19   Any court that makes an adoption order or a permanence order over a child who is subject to a compulsory supervision order must make an order providing that, on the making of the adoption order or permanence order, the compulsory supervision order ceases to have effect.[64] The court may, however, do so only when it is satisfied that, were it to make the adoption order or the permanence order, the compulsory supervision order would no longer be necessary for the protection, guidance, treatment or control of the child.[65] Though technically this is not a review, the court must, in order to come to its decision on this point, consider the same matters as a children's hearing would in reviewing a compulsory supervision order and, it is submitted, sheriffs and judges ought to conduct the proceedings in a manner as like a review by a children's hearing as possible. Since a decision by an adoption court on the compulsory supervision order is "a decision relating to the adoption of a child", s.14 of the Adoption and Children (Scotland) Act 2007 governs the decision. That section provides that the court must regard the need to safeguard and promote the welfare of the child concerned throughout his or her life as the paramount consideration and must have regard, so far reasonably practicable, to: (a) the value of a stable family unit in the child's development; (b) the child's ascertainable views taking account of his or her age and maturity; (c) the child's religious persuasion, racial origin, and cultural and linguistic background; and (d) the likely effect on the child, throughout his or her life, of the making of an adoption order. It may be expected that similar matters, mutatis mutandis, will be taken into account by a permanence court determining whether a compulsory supervision order ought to be terminated.[66]

Proposal to remove child from Scotland

13–20   The jurisdiction of the children's hearing extends only to Scotland, and the removal of the child from Scotland will render it practically impossible for the implementation authority, whose duty it is to give effect to the compulsory

---

[62] 2011 Act s.156(3A), as inserted by the Children's Hearings (Scotland) Act 2011 (Modification of Primary Legislation) Order 2013 Sch.1 para.20(15).

[63] Above, para.13–16.

[64] Adoption and Children (Scotland) Act 2007 ss.36 (adoption orders) and 89 (permanence orders).

[65] Adoption and Children (Scotland) Act 2007 ss.36(1)(b) and 89(1)(b).

[66] The welfare principle, the minimum intervention principle, and the requirement to take account of the child's views are expressed to apply only in relation to the making of a permanence order, its variation, amendment to include authority to adopt, and revocation: Adoption and Children (Scotland) Act 2007 ss.84(3), (4) and (5), 92(6), 93(5) and 98(3) respectively. The principles do not apply generally or, as with adoption, to any decision "relating to" permanence orders.

supervision order,[67] to fulfil that duty. In order that the efficacy of the compulsory supervision order is not frustrated by such removal, an obligation is imposed on any relevant person who intends to take the child to live outwith Scotland to notify the reporter at least 28 days before the day on which he or she intends to remove the child from Scotland.[68] On receiving notice under this subsection, the reporter must then initiate a review of the compulsory supervision order.[69] There are two limitations to the circumstances in which the obligation to inform the reporter of a proposal to remove the child from Scotland arises. First, such notice is required only when the proposal is that the child be removed long-term from Scotland and not merely for a holiday: the wording of the statute is that the child is to be taken "*to live* outwith Scotland". Extended holidays may well cause problems here, and the test is probably whether the intention is that the child should have a new life abroad (or elsewhere in the UK). Permanence, or at least a long-term plan, is necessary. Secondly, notice is required only when the proposal to take the child to live outwith Scotland is not in accordance with the compulsory supervision order or an order made by a court under s.11 of the Children (Scotland) Act 1995. It will be rare (but not incompetent) for a hearing to attach as one of the terms of the compulsory supervision order an explicit requirement that the child remains in Scotland but, by specifying a place of residence for the child within Scotland, the hearing will more commonly achieve that effect, at least to the extent that any proposal to remove the child from Scotland will oblige the relevant person to notify the reporter, who will then be obliged to initiate a review of the compulsory supervision order. Few terms or conditions other than a requirement to reside at a specified place will carry the implication that the child is to remain in Scotland, but the statutory test is that the proposal be "not in accordance with the order." This does not require, it is submitted, an absolute conflict between the proposal and the terms of the order. It must be remembered that the implementation authority may well have positive duties imposed upon it by the order[70] which it is obliged to comply with[71] and any proposal to take the child to live outwith Scotland that prevents the authority from fulfilling these duties should be regarded as being "not in accordance with the order" even if there is no explicit requirement on the child to live in a particular place in Scotland. Difficult questions may arise if the proposal simply makes it more difficult for the implementation authority to carry out its duties, without making it impossible. It is suggested that if the terms of a compulsory supervision order are designed on an understanding that the local authority will be able to fulfil responsibilities imposed upon it by the order in its normal course of business, a proposal that significantly increases the burden on the local authority should not be regarded as being "in accordance with the order", with the result that the relevant person is obliged to notify the reporter of the proposal.

As with other review provisions, this provision is designed to ensure that a **13–21** review takes place whenever there is, or is likely soon to be, a significant change in the child's circumstances. However, it is noticeable that the statute

---

[67] 2011 Act s.144.
[68] 2011 Act s.134(1) and (2).
[69] 2011 Act s.134(3).
[70] Under 2011 Act s.83(2)(i).
[71] 2011 Act s.144(2).

lays down no sanction on a relevant person who fails to give the reporter the appropriate notification—or indeed any other person who breaches the condition by removing the child.[72]

Child subject to secure accommodation authorisation

13–22   If the existing compulsory supervision order includes a secure accommodation authorisation and that authorisation has not ceased to have effect by the child's removal from such accommodation, the reporter must initiate a review of the order before the end of the period of three months beginning with the day on which the order was made, varied or continued.[73] It should be noted that the review is required within three months of the making, continuing or varying of the order that contains the secure accommodation authorisation, and *not* within three months of the authorisation being implemented. In other words, a review is still required even although the child never was placed in secure accommodation, or has been so placed a short time before the three month period expires. If no such review is held it may be supposed that the authorisation ceases to have effect and the child, if then being held in secure accommodation, must either be released forthwith or kept there under the provisions of the Secure Accommodation (Scotland) Regulations 2013,[74] which themselves require a review within 72 hours.[75] In addition, there are special rules if the child is not placed in secure accommodation because the head of unit decided to withhold consent to that placement.[76] In that case, the reporter must arrange a children's hearing for the purpose of reviewing the compulsory supervision order, interim compulsory supervision order or medical examination order in which the secure accommodation authorisation is contained; this review hearing must take place no later than the third working day after the reporter received notice from the chief social work officer of the head of unit's withholding of consent, and the hearing may vary the order only to the extent of varying or removing the secure accommodation authorisation.[77] At this review the children's hearing must provide the opportunity to make representations to the child, relevant person, safeguarder, chief social work officer and the

---

[72] Removal of a child outwith the United Kingdom who is subject to a compulsory supervision order may well constitute a "wrongful removal" within the terms of the Hague Convention on International Child Abduction, with the result that the child's immediate return to the United Kingdom may be sought: see for example *W v B* [2010] IEHC 160 where the Irish High Court ordered the return of a child who had been removed to Ireland contrary to the terms of a compulsory supervision order. The local authority itself may even be held to have "rights of custody" for Hague Convention purposes: *Nottinghamshire County Council v B* [2010] IEHC 9.

[73] 2011 Act s.135.

[74] SSI 2013/205. See above, para.11–17.

[75] Secure Accommodation (Scotland) Regulations 2013 reg.7(4) and (5).

[76] Children's Hearings (Scotland) Act 2011 (Implementation of Secure Accommodation Authorisation) (Scotland) Regulations 2013 (SSI 2013/212) reg.8.

[77] Children's Hearings (Scotland) Act 2011 (Implementation of Secure Accommodation Authorisation) (Scotland) Regulations 2013 reg.9. For the reporter's notification and provision of information obligations, see 2013 Rules r.94; procedure at the hearing itself is governed by r.95; and notification of the hearing's decision and rights of appeal by r.96. The chief social work officer must also review the placement under reg.10 of the Implementation of Secure Accommodation (Scotland) Regulations 2013 but whatever the outcome of that review a children's hearing's review is not activated, unless the review suggests that the order itself (as opposed to the placement) requires variation or termination in which case the local authority's duty to require a review is activated.

head of the unit that provides secure accommodation, if they are present at the hearing.[78]

Transfer of child in case of urgent necessity

Where a child is residing at a particular place by virtue of a compulsory **13–23** supervision order which contains a residence requirement, but the chief social work officer of the relevant local authority has transferred the child to another place because it is in the interests of the child or in the interests of another child in the place,[79] the reporter must initiate a review of the compulsory supervision order, and the review hearing must be arranged to take place before the expiry of the period of three working days beginning with the day on which the child is transferred.[80] This covers the situation of the child's placement breaking down for some reason to such an extent that the child will not or cannot remain where he or she is required to reside, and removal to another place was done as a matter of urgent necessity. The children's hearing will normally be requested to remove the existing requirement that the child resides in the place from which he or she has just been removed and to replace it by naming another place of residence (if a suitable place has been identified). It would seem that if a review is not timeously held the obligation on the child to reside at any particular place falls. Usually the children's hearing that is held within three working days is arranged on an emergency basis which does not allow panel members sufficient time to digest the reports and usually, therefore, the hearing will need to exercise its power to defer making a long-term decision. It follows that the main purpose of the hearing held within three working days is primarily to ensure the child's safety in the meantime, by making an interim variation of the existing compulsory supervision order (on which see below).[81]

Return of fugitive child

A child who is kept in a particular place by virtue of a compulsory supervi- **13–24** sion order and who absconds from that place or, at the end of a period of leave, fails to return to that place, may be arrested without warrant and taken back to that place.[82] If, however, the occupier of the place is unwilling or unable to receive the child back, that circumstance must be intimated to the reporter and the child must be kept in a place of safety until a children's hearing sits, the local authority having required the reporter to arrange a review because the compulsory supervision order is not being complied with.[83] No time limit is laid down for how long the child can be kept in a place of safety under this provision, though the reporter ought probably to arrange a review as soon as is practicable: it is to be noted that the child must be kept in a place of safety until the review has been held and there is no authority to release the child before

---

[78] 2013 Rules r.95(2).
[79] 2011 Act s.143.
[80] 2011 Act ss.136 and 137(3). The reporter's notification and provision of information obligations are set out in the 2013 Rules r.36.
[81] Below, para.13–26. An interim variation of a compulsory supervision order need not specify the child's place of residence but may simply specify that the child is to reside in a place of safety other than where he or she predominantly resides: s.140(2).
[82] 2011 Act s.169(1) and (2).
[83] 2011 Act s.169(5) and (6)(f), with reference to s.131(2)(b).

then. There are identical provisions in relation to a child who absconds from a person who has control of the child by virtue of the terms of a compulsory supervision order.[84]

POWERS AND DUTIES OF THE CHILDREN'S HEARING ON REVIEW

13–25 At a review hearing there is no need to have accepted or established the existence of any section 67 ground and the hearing can, once the introductions and other preliminaries[85] (including an explanation of the purpose of the hearing) have been carried out, move straight on to a consideration of whether the compulsory supervision order should be continued, varied or terminated. The original section 67 grounds may retain some relevance and will sometimes require reconsideration, but the further back in time they occurred the less likely they are to be relevant to the child's present situation and future needs and there is, indeed, no statutory obligation on a review hearing to give any fresh consideration to the grounds that originally brought the child into the hearing system. There is usually little point in going over old grounds, though occasionally this must be done. For example, if the original ground was that the child had a close connection with a Schedule 1 offender, the ground may well require examination in order to determine whether that connection still exists or has been re-established and whether it still poses a risk to the child. On the other hand, the fact that the child committed a single criminal offence well over a year previously will seldom be relevant to a consideration of what is best for the child now. A review hearing should conduct a wide-ranging discussion into the child's present circumstances in order to determine whether the child still requires to be subject to a compulsory supervision order. A consideration of how successful the current order has been in tackling the problems facing the child is inevitable. If a review has been specifically required (i.e. it is not an annual review initiated by the reporter) it will be sensible for the person or body who required the review to be asked why he or she did so. With these specialties, the actual discussion will follow much the same lines as a discussion at the hearing that originally made the compulsory supervision order,[86] with the same requirements to ensure participation and seek views from all those attending the hearing in an active capacity. The options available to a review hearing are, however, in the nature of the case, somewhat different. The four primary options (within which there may be several subsidiary decisions to be made) that are available to the review hearing are: (i) to defer making a decision; (ii) to terminate the compulsory supervision order; (iii) to vary the order; or (iv) to continue the order without variation.

Deferring the decision

13–26   Where the children's hearing that is carrying out a review of a compulsory supervision order considers it appropriate to do so, it may defer making a decision about the compulsory supervision order until a subsequent children's

---

[84] 2011 Act s.170(1)(a)(vi), (2), (5) and (6)(f), with reference to s.131(2)(b).

[85] See above, para 7–02.

[86] Part 15 of the 2013 Rules applies to review hearings as it does to hearings that first made a compulsory supervision order.

hearing.[87] As at the original hearing, this is the proper decision to come to when the members of the hearing feel that they need more information before they will be in a position to determine what to do about the compulsory supervision order. If the review hearing defers its decision it may continue the compulsory supervision order until the subsequent children's hearing[88] and this would be appropriate if the order would otherwise run out of time. That the children's hearing "may" continue the order indicates that it does not have to, but that does not mean that the compulsory supervision order will immediately come to an end if it is not.[89] Rather, the compulsory supervision order, if not formally continued under s.139(2), will continue in effect until its time limit has been reached—so there is no need to continue the order under s.139 only when the subsequent hearing will certainly be held before the order's time-limit has expired. In any case, the hearing that defers its decision on the review may make an interim variation of the compulsory supervision order.[90] An interim variation is a variation of the existing order that has effect until the earliest occurring of: (i) the next children's hearing; (ii) the disposal by the sheriff of an application to establish grounds[91]; (iii) a day specified in the variation; or (iv) the expiry of the period of 22 days beginning with the day on which the order is varied.[92] An interim variation may be made only where the hearing defers making its decision but considers that the nature of the child's circumstances is such that for the protection, guidance, treatment or control of the child it is necessary as a matter of urgency to make an interim variation of the existing compulsory supervision order[93]: the test is therefore the same as for making an interim compulsory supervision order in respect of a child who is not yet subject to a compulsory supervision order.[94] Likewise, the test for making a further interim variation is the same as for making a further interim compulsory supervision order[95]—that is to say a test of necessity but not urgency. There is no limit to the number of times an interim variation may be made to a compulsory supervision order,[96] though the inherent uncertainty of interim orders suggests that they should not be used repeatedly unless a final decision remains, for some good reason, impossible to make. Since an interim varaiation is not in itself a new order, but merely a variation of an existing order, a limitation of time does apply: that which is implicit in the compulsory supervision order itself. If, after a number of interim variations the compulsory supervision order itself is about to terminate a hearing that is not (yet) in a position to conclude a review will be obliged to continue the compulsory

---

[87] 2011 Act s.138(2).

[88] 2011 Act s.139(1) and (2).

[89] If the order is not continued it continues in effect until the end of the period for which it was last continued (or, if earlier, until the day the child attains the age of 18): 2011 Act s.83(7).

[90] 2011 Act s.139(3).

[91] In cases in which, at the review hearing, a new statement of grounds has been drawn up by the reporter: see above, paras 13–03—13–05.

[92] 2011 Act s.140(1) and (4).

[93] 2011 Act s.139(3).

[94] See above, paras 10–05—10–07.

[95] 2011 Act s.96, applied to interim variations by s.97(5).

[96] If it remains appropriate to include, for example, a residence condition as an interim variation then once the time limit for that has been reached the next hearing will again make an interim variation of the existing compulsory supervision order: this is not technically a continuation of the interim variation, though it will have the same effect.

supervision order under s.139(2). In deciding whether to defer and to use these interim powers, children's hearings should bear in mind the harm that continuing uncertainty does to any child.

13–27   It is explicitly provided in s.140(2) that an interim variation may vary the order so that, instead of specifying a place or places at which the child is to reside under s.83(2)(a) (the measure in the existing order), the order specifies that the child is to reside at any place of safety away from the place where the child predominantly resides. This provision carries no implication that this is the only variation permissible, for the definition of "interim variation" is contained in s.140(1) and not s.140(2)—and there is no such limitation to an original hearing making an interim compulsory supervision order to which an interim variation is, in the context of reviews, analogous). The importance of this provision is that while a compulsory supervision order itself must specify the place of the child's residence (if the hearing wishes to require the child to reside at any particular place), any interim protection to be afforded the child need not. So likewise in making an interim compulsory supervision order, the children's hearing is not obliged to specify a place of residence but may similarly specify that the child is to reside at any place of safety.[97] It may not be possible to identify where a child should reside for an interim period, even while a children's hearing determines that the child needs to be kept in a place of safety until a long-term decision can be made. It is open to the hearing to make an interim variation of the compulsory supervision order to include (or remove) any measure that may competently be included in a compulsory supervision order, and this includes granting a secure accommodation authorisation: if the hearing does grant such an authorisation in an interim variation it need not specify two or more residential establishments or a residential establishment with both secure accommodation and non-secure accommodation.[98] Again, this reflects the position in relation to interim compulsory supervision orders.[99]

13–28   Other interim measures, such as warrants to secure attendance, may be made by a review hearing that defers making a decision.[100] A medical examination order may not, however, be made by a hearing reviewing an existing order.[101] At some point during the review hearing the children's hearing must consider whether to appoint a person to safeguard the interests of the child to whom the hearing relates[102] and, if the outcome of the review is to defer a decision about the compulsory supervision order, a safeguarder may be appointed.

13–29   If the child or relevant person had been excused from attending the review hearing,[103] and that hearing defers making its decision until a subsequent

---

[97] 2011 Act s.86(2).
[98] 2011 Act s.140(3).
[99] 2011 Act s.86(4).
[100] 2011 Act s.123.
[101] The power to make a medical examination order exists only in situations in which the child is not presently subject to a compulsory supervision order, under 2011 Act s.92 (where deferral follows the acceptance of grounds) or s.120 (where deferral follows consideration of grounds established by the sheriff). If medical examination is necessary then this can be a measure included in the compulsory supervision order—though not its interim variation since s.97(5) applies the rules for interim compulsory supervision orders to interim variations, and an interim compulsory supervision order may not include a requirement for medical examination (s.93(6)).
[102] 2011 Act s.30(2).
[103] Under 2011 Act ss.73, 74 or 79, for which see above, paras 6–03—6.10, 6–17—6–18.

children's hearing, it is not obliged to excuse the child or relevant person from attending that subsequent hearing.[104] This power to remove the excusal is a useful provision for the avoidance of doubt, for it may be that the children's hearing has deferred making a decision because it felt unable to do so without hearing directly from the child or relevant person: subsequent hearings are not bound in this matter[105] by the decision of earlier hearings.

Termination of the compulsory supervision order

The second option available to a children's hearing at a review of a compulsory supervision order is to terminate that order.[106] If the order itself is terminated then all measures attached to it similarly come to an end. Termination will normally be appropriate if the order has been found at the review to have achieved its aim, or if the child's problems have otherwise been resolved.[107] In any situation in which the children's hearing terminates a compulsory supervision order, it must consider whether supervision or guidance is needed by the child and, if so, make a statement to that effect:[108] it is then the duty of the relevant local authority to give such supervision or guidance as the child will accept.[109] This is a slightly odd provision, because if the children's hearing considers that the child still needs supervision or guidance, then a continuation of the compulsory supervision order will normally be the correct decision. The key lies in the difference between what order is "necessary" and what the child "needs". An order is "necessary" when some enforcement is required and in that case the hearing should continue the order under s.138(5). But a child may "need" supervision or guidance even when it is not necessary to enforce that upon the child. It is therefore when the child is willing voluntarily to accept the supervision or guidance that he or she needs that the hearing should make a statement under s.138(6) instead of continuing the compulsory supervision order.

13–30

Variation of the existing order

The third option available to a children's hearing reviewing a compulsory supervision order is to vary its terms[110]: this necessarily involves that the order is continued, though in varied form. Variation would be appropriate where the hearing is satisfied that, for the protection, guidance, treatment or control of the child, it is necessary that one or more of the measures included in the existing compulsory supervision order ought to be removed, or new measures added, or existing measures altered in some way. It is open to the children's hearing to include in the varied order any of the measures that the original order might have contained,[111] subject to the usual conditions upon which these measures may be included in a compulsory supervision order. A decision to vary the

13–31

---

[104] 2011 s.138(8) and (9).

[105] Or indeed in any matter.

[106] 2011 Act s.138(3)(a).

[107] If, for example, the child's problem was nothing other than school attendance and he or she has now reached the school-leaving age it may be appropriate to terminate the compulsory supervision order even when it failed to achieve its purpose of returning the child to school.

[108] 2011 Act s.138(6).

[109] 2011 Act s.138(7).

[110] 2011 Act s.138(3)(b).

[111] Listed in 2011 Act s.83(2): see above, Ch.11.

compulsory supervision order might be appropriate if the child's circumstances have changed, for the better or for the worse, and a different form of supervision is now required to address the difficulties that the child continues to face. It might also be appropriate when the child's circumstances have not changed at all, but the existing measures have not been effectual in achieving the aim of the order and different measures are considered more likely to do so.

Continuation of the compulsory supervision order

13–32   The fourth option open to a children's hearing reviewing a compulsory supervision order is to continue it for a period not exceeding one year.[112] Continuation without variation would be the appropriate decision where the hearing is satisfied that it remains necessary for the protection, guidance, treatment or control of the child to maintain the compulsory supervision order in its existing terms.[113] This might be because the order needs more time to achieve its aim, or because the child's circumstances have not changed but the existing measures remain the best way of addressing the issues that brought the child to the hearing in the first place.

OTHER OUTCOMES AT REVIEW HEARINGS

13–33 As well as reviewing the compulsory supervision order, there are a number of other outcomes available to the review hearing that were also available to the hearing that originally made the compulsory supervision order, such as suspending the decision pending an appeal under s.158, making an educational referral under s.127 and requiring the reporter under s.128 to consider whether to apply for a parenting order under the Antisocial Behaviour etc. (Scotland) Act 2004.[114] There are, however, two other decisions open to a review hearing that are not available to hearings deciding whether to make a compulsory supervision order in the first place.

Enforcing the local authority's duties

13–34   Where it appears to a children's hearing that has completed a review of a compulsory supervision order that the local authority responsible for its implementation is in breach of a duty under the order in relation to the child, the hearing may direct the National Convener to give the local authority notice of an intended application to the sheriff principal for an order to enforce the implementation authority's duty.[115] This notice must set out the respects in which the authority is in breach of its duty in relation to the child and contain a statement that if the authority does not perform that duty before the expiry of the period of 21 days beginning with the day the notice is given, the National Convener, on the direction of the children's hearing, will make an application to enforce the authority's duty.[116] The children's hearing giving such a direction

---

[112] 2011 Act s.138(3)(c).
[113] 2011 Act s.138(4).
[114] See above, paras 10–24—10–25.
[115] 2011 Act s.146(1) and (2).
[116] 2011 Act s.146(3). A copy of this notice must be sent to the child and each relevant person: s.146(4).

to the National Convener must also require that a further review of the compulsory supervision order take place on or as soon as is reasonably practicable after the expiry of a period of 28 days beginning on the day the notice is given (*i.e.* a week after the expiry of the 21 days the local authority has to fulfil its duties).[117] If on that further review, it appears to the children's hearing that the local authority continues to be in breach, the hearing may direct the National Convener to make an application to the sheriff principal.[118] It is to be noted that the matter rests entirely with the children's hearing as to whether to direct the National Convener to give the warning notice, and also whether to direct the National Convener to make an application to the sheriff principal.[119] The hearing's decision at both points is governed by the welfare principle in s.25 and the need to take account of the child's views in s.27 and these matters must be addressed during the review. The statute explicitly provides that in determining whether to direct the National Convener to make an application to the sheriff principal to enforce the authority's duty, the children's hearing must not take into account any factor relating to the adequacy of the means available to the authority to enable it to comply with its duty.[120]

Unlike the children's hearing, the National Convener has no discretion in **13–35** this matter and, if directed to do so by the hearing, must apply to the sheriff principal[121] for an order to enforce the implementation authority's duty in relation to the child.[122] The National Convener may not, however, make the application, despite being directed to do so, unless proper notice has been given, and unless the authority has failed to carry out the duty within the period specified in the notice.[123] So while the direction may only be given by the children's hearing if it is of the view that the authority continues to be in breach,[124] the National Convener must come to an independent view on whether that is so or not, and may decline to make the application if it appears to him or her that the duty has now been carried out or (even when the children's hearing thought otherwise) it was indeed carried out within the time specified.

On an application by the National Convener, the sheriff principal may (but **13–36** is not obliged to) make an order, which is final, requiring the implementation authority to carry out the duty that it is in breach of.[125] The sheriff principal may decline to make an order for enforcement if, for example, the implementation authority is no longer in breach of its duty, or if circumstances have moved on sufficiently that enforcing the duty is no longer appropriate, or if enforcing

---

[117] 2011 Act s.146(5).

[118] 2011 Act s.146(6).

[119] It is submitted, however, that it would be incompetent to make either direction to the National Convener if the conclusion of the review is that the compulsory supervision order ought to be terminated, for the only point of these provisions is to enforce a duty which, on termination, will necessarily become no longer extant.

[120] 2011 Act s.146(7). It is noticeable that this rule does not apply to the hearing's earlier decision whether or not to direct the National Convener to give notice of the intended application. This suggests that at the further review, held after 28 days after the original review, the focus of enquiry should be on the local authority rather than (directly) on the child.

[121] That is to say, the sheriff principal of the sheriffdom in which the principal office of the implementation authority is situated: 2011 Act s.147(2).

[122] 2011 Act s.147(1).

[123] 2011 Act s.147(3).

[124] 2011 Act s.146(6).

[125] 2011 Act s.148.

the order would be unduly burdensome on the local authority—for there is no injunction against the sheriff principal taking account of the means available to the authority, as there is in relation to the children's hearing's decision whether to direct the National Convener to make the application to the sheriff principal. This is an important power, though the Act is silent as to the consequences of the local authority's failure to follow the order. Presumably the normal remedies for contempt of court will be available.

Review of Relevant Person Status

13–37   Whenever: (i) the outcome of a review is that the compulsory supervision order is to be continued, with or without variation; (ii) there is an individual who at that time is a deemed relevant person; and (iii) it appears that the individual no longer has (nor recently has had) a significant involvement in the upbringing of the child, the children's hearing must review whether that individual should continue to be deemed to be a relevant person.[126] The hearing should do this on its own initiative, though of course it might be requested to do so by any person present at the hearing. (A children's hearing reviewing a compulsory supervision order must also, irrespective of the outcome of the review, consider whether any individual who is present at the hearing should be deemed to be a relevant person, but only if requested to do so by the child, the relevant person or the individual in question.)[127] Relevant person status previously recognised can only be removed at a review hearing whose outcome is that the compulsory supervision order is to be continued or varied: in other words, after the review of the compulsory supervision order has been concluded and the decision made. A hearing that defers making a decision about the compulsory supervision order until a subsequent hearing may not do so, with the result that the person whose deemed relevant person status is in question retains full participation rights during the whole review process: if the relevant person status is removed, that occurs at the end of the hearing at which, of course, the individual has had the opportunity to argue that he or she should continued to be deemed to be a relevant person. A decision to remove relevant person status will mean that the individual has no right to participate at any subsequent hearing, nor will he or she have the right to call for a review of the continued or varied compulsory supervision order, but he or she will retain the right of appeal against both the decision to remove relevant person status and (irrespective of that appeal) the decision of the review hearing in respect of the compulsory supervision order.[128] If the outcome of the review is that the compulsory supervision order is to be terminated, the deemed relevant person status falls in any case, or (more accurately) will fall when the time for appeal has passed or any appeal has been finally disposed of.

13–38   Though the hearing is directed by the statute to review "whether the individual *should* continue to be deemed to be a relevant person",[129] this is not a welfare judgment and the hearing must not determine the issue on the basis of whether or not they consider it would be better for the child that the individual continue to be deemed to be a relevant person. Rather, the question is

---

[126] 2011 Act s.142.
[127] 2013 Rules r.55. See above, para.5–18.
[128] 2011 Act s.142(4)(b).
[129] 2011 Act s.142(2).

determined on the same basis and by the same test as that which governed the pre-hearing panel's (or children's hearing's) decision to confer relevant person status in the first place, though it is the present circumstances that are relevant rather than those that applied when the pre-hearing panel (or children's hearing) made its original decision. This test is factual rather than judgmental: it is whether the individual continues to have, or has recently had, a significant involvement in the upbringing of the child.[130] The decision may be different on review from that of a pre-hearing panel or children's hearing that conferred relevant person status if there has been a change of circumstances, though sometimes the mere passage of time may be enough—an individual may have "recently" had significant involvement in the child's upbringing at the time of the pre-hearing panel but not a year or more later at the time of a review hearing.

If the review hearing determines that the deemed relevant person no longer **13–39** has nor recently has had significant involvement in the upbringing of the child, the hearing must direct that he or she is no longer to be deemed to be a relevant person and that individual will no longer be treated as a relevant person for the specified statutory purposes. Before coming to this decision the chairing member of the hearing must have explained the purpose of the review of relevant person status to those present,[131] and this needs to be done *after* the review of the compulsory supervision order has been completed. The review of relevant person status cannot be carried in the minds of the hearing members while reviewing the compulsory supervision order, to be announced at the end of that review. The child, relevant person (including, of course, the deemed relevant person whose status is in question) must be invited to express views on the relevant person matter, and the chairing member may, in addition, invite anyone else present at the hearing to do so.[132] After discussion of the relevant person matter the members of the hearing must then give their decision and the chairing member must sum up, confirm the hearing's decision and its reasons, and inform the child, relevant person, and individual whose relevant person status was in issue of the right to appeal the determination, one way or the other, within seven days.[133] The reporter must then give the child, relevant person and individual whose relevant person status was in issue a copy of the hearing's determination and details of the right of appeal no later than two working days from the date of the children's hearing.[134]

The hearing may defer making its decision on relevant person status until "a **13–40** subsequent hearing"[135] but (remembering that the compulsory supervision order has been continued) that subsequent hearing will not be one convened solely to look at the relevant person status of the individual in question: rather it will be the hearing convened in the normal way to review the compulsory supervision order.[136] And again, at that review of the order, the relevant person question can be dealt with only after the review of the order is completed, and

---

[130] This test is examined in detail above, paras 5–12—5–15.
[131] 2013 Rules r.66(1).
[132] 2013 Rules r.66(2).
[133] 2013 Rules r.66(3) and (4).
[134] 2013 Rules r.66(5)–(7).
[135] 2011 Act s.142(3).
[136] Deferral of the relevant person question is "until a subsequent children's hearing under this section" (s.142(3)) and a children's hearing under s.142 is one that "determines a review of a compulsory supervision order by varying or continuing the order" (s.142(1)).

only if the outcome at that review is that the compulsory supervision order is to be continued or varied. Effectively, therefore, a decision of a children's hearing to defer making its decision on relevant person status is a decision that that status should continue.[137] Yet there is this difference between deferring the decision and deciding that the individual still meets the test: the latter is appealable under s.160(1)(b) while the former is not. For this reason alone deferral of the relevant person question should be avoided for other than very good reason. In any case, the child or another relevant person who is dissatisfied with the review hearing's relevant person decision may call for a subsequent review of the compulsory supervision order three months after its continuation,[138] even if their own motivation for doing so is to reopen the relevant person matter.

REVIEW OF CONTACT DIRECTIONS: SECTION 126 HEARINGS

13–41 Though not a review of the compulsory supervision order itself (and therefore not subject to the outcomes discussed in the previous section of this chapter), it is convenient here to deal with hearings arranged under s.126 to review contact directions that have been included in certain types of order. Whenever a children's hearing makes, varies or continues a compulsory supervision order, or makes an interim compulsory supervision order, or makes an interim variation of a compulsory supervision order, or makes a medical examination order and that order (having effect for more than five working days) contains a direction regulating contact between the child and a specified person or class of person, the reporter must, in one or other of two stated circumstances, arrange a children's hearing for the purpose of reviewing the contact direction. The stated circumstances are as follows:

(i) that there is in force either a contact order made by a court under section 11(2)(d) of the Children (Scotland) Act 1995 regulating contact between the child and an individual other than a relevant person, or a permanence order made under s.80 of the Adoption and Children (Scotland) Act 2007 which specifies arrangements for contact between the child and such an individual; or

(ii) the reporter has been requested to arrange such a review hearing by an individual who is not a relevant person but who has or recently has had a significant involvement in the upbringing of the child.[139]

If neither of these circumstances exists then a s.126 review will not be required. The purpose of this review is to protect the interests of individuals who, not being relevant persons, are not entitled to attend the children's hearing but whose civil rights (of contact, whether traced to a s.11 contact order or a

---

[137] And the chairing member must confirm that this is so: 2013 Rules r.66(3)(c).

[138] 2011 Act s.132.

[139] 2011 Act s.126(1)–(3) and Children's Hearings (Review of Contact Directions and Definition of Relevant Person) (Scotland) Order 2013 (SSI 2013/193) art.2. Whenever a s.126 hearing is being arranged, the reporter must inform, and provide documents to, not only the person who requested the hearing but also any other person (other than a relevant person) who appears to the reporter to have (or recently have had) significant involvement in the upbringing of the child: 2013 Rules r.42(2)(c) and (f).

permanence order) or traced to the fact that they have been involved in the child's upbringing might be affected by the children's hearing making an order that contains a contact direction. To ensure the efficacy of that protection, the reporter must notify those people before any children's hearing that may make a contact direction of that hearing and inform them that, in the event of the hearing making a contact direction, they have the right to request a s.126 hearing to review that direction.[140] Before this procedure was introduced by the 2011 Act, the only means by which persons with a right of contact (a civil right protected by art.6 of the European Convention on Human Rights) or family life (protected by art.8 thereof) with the child could be guaranteed the right to participate in the decision-making process was to recognise them as relevant persons, and for this reason the courts utilised the interpretative power of s.3 of the Human Rights Act 1998 to expand the definition of "relevant person" then contained in s.93(2) of the Children (Scotland) Act 1995 so that it included such individuals.[141] This however was perceived as giving such individuals more rights to participate than they actually needed to protect their own interests, especially (perhaps) in giving them access to all the background papers that the child's parents would receive. It is this issue that s.126 of the Children's Hearings (Scotland) Act 2011 seeks to address, by providing a means of access to the hearing for individuals who are unable either to bring themselves within the definition of relevant person in s.200 of the 2011 Act, and have not yet been deemed to be relevant persons under s.81. Such individuals are able to argue their point of view at this new type of hearing, where the discussion is limited to the matter that directly affects them: that is to say the contact direction in the order. But the s.126 procedure is only partial protection for individuals who may be affected by the terms of a compulsory supervision order. A person who may claim to enjoy family life, as protected by art.8 of the European Convention on Human Rights, with the child but who cannot show significant involvement in the child's upbringing[142] will not be able to seek a review of any contact direction, even if it is to the effect that contact is to be prohibited with that person, unless he or she already holds a contact order or has contact rights under a permanence order.[143]

---

[140] 2013 Rules r.81. Providing this information is confirmation of the right of these people to attend the s.126 hearing: r.81(5)—*not* the hearing that imposes the contact direction.

[141] See *Authority Reporter v S*, 2010 S.L.T. 765; *M, Appellant*, 2010 Fam. L.R. 152; *Principal Reporter v K*, 2011 S.L.T. 271; *CW, Appellant* Unreported July 29, 2013 Sheriff Court at Glasgow.

[142] The concept of "family life" in art.8 ECHR is substantially wider than the concept of significant involvement in the child's upbringing: family life has been found to exist by the European Court of Human Rights between a child and an adult with only minimal involvement in the child's life: see for example *Keegan v Ireland* (1994) 18 E.H.R.R. 342, *Brauer v Germany* (2012) 51 E.H.R.R. 23; *Anayo v Germany* (2012) 55 E.H.R.R. 5.

[143] Before the coming into force of the 2011 Act, the sheriff utilised his power under s.3 of the Human Rights Act 1998 to read words into s.51 of the Children (Scotland) Act 1995 so that an appeal against a warrant (the predecessor of the 2011 Act's ICSO) could be made by a grandparent, limited to the issue of contact: *J, Appellant*, 2013 S.L.T. (Sh Ct) 18. Under the 2011 Act, the sheriff may vary any order, including an ICSO and so it is no longer necessary to rely on the Human Rights Act to read in words to the statute, but that does not deal with the title point. The grandfather in *CW, Appellant* (Unreported July 29, 2013 Sheriff Court at Glasgow), who saw his grandchildren around four times a year and who attended hearings as their mother's representative, was held to be a relevant person under the 1995 Act because he enjoyed family life with the children. But he would not be able to protect the contact he had by the s.126 procedure.

13–42   A s.126 hearing must take place no later than five working days after the hearing that made, varied or continued the order that contains the contact direction.[144] If the hearing has been required by an individual who claims to have or recently have had significant involvement in the upbringing of the child but the hearing considers that the individual does not have such involvement, nor recently has had it then the hearing must take no further action[145]: in other words, it must terminate the hearing forthwith. This means that the hearing must commence its consideration by determining the nature of the involvement of the individual who sought the review in the child's life before reviewing the contact direction,[146] and the individual must be given an opportunity to argue his or her case. The test is the same as for deeming an individual to be a relevant person.[147] Whatever decision the hearing makes at this stage is not, however, appealable—which is an inherently suspicious position since the individual who claims to have significant involvement in the upbringing of the child will, if that claim is rejected, have no means of influencing the terms of an order that might (if the rejection is wrong) impinge upon his or her civil rights. As at a pre-hearing panel[148] the question of whether or not the individual has or has recently had significant involvement in the upbringing of the child is to be decided *without* considerations of the welfare of the child: entitlement to attend hearings (like being a relevant person) is a matter of adults' rights rather than children's welfare. Though the test is the same, it should be noted that it is not open to a s.126 hearing to consider whether a person should be deemed to be a relevant person.[149]

13–43   Once the hearing has accepted that the individual who called for a review of the contact direction has or recently has had significant involvement in the upbringing of the child, or the review has been required because of the existence of a contact order or a permanence order, the children's hearing must then review the contact direction in the compulsory supervision order, interim compulsory supervision order, interim variation of a compulsory supervision order or medical examination order, with the aim of determining whether to confirm the previous hearing's decision to include that contact direction or to vary it.[150] Before making its decision the children's hearing must seek the views on the matter from the

---

[144] 2011 Act s.126(4). The reporter must, as soon as practicable and no later than three days after that children's hearing, inform the following people of the place, date and time of the children's hearing, and of their right to attend the s.126 hearing: the child, each relevant person, any person (other than a relevant person) who appears to the reporter to have (or recently have had) significant involvement in the upbringing of the child, any person with a contact order, any person with a right of contact under a permanence order, the person who requested the s.126 hearing, any appointed safeguarder, the three members of the children's hearing, the chief social work officer of the implementation or relevant local authority, and the National Convener (2013 Rules r.42(2)). As well, and in all cases no later than three working days prior to the date of the s.126 hearing, the reporter must give to those people a copy of the contact direction, the reasons why the direction was made, and any other document or part of document which is relevant to the s.126 hearing: 2013 Rules r.42(3). The days here are calendar days (cf. s.126(4) which requires the s.126 hearing to be held no later than five working days of the hearing that made the contact direction).

[145] 2011 Act s.126(5).

[146] 2013 Rules r.74(2).

[147] See above, paras 5–12—5–15.

[148] See above, para.5–12.

[149] 2013 Rules r.55 specifies the types of hearings at which this might be done, and it does *not* include hearings in Pt 12 of the Act. And s.142 of the 2011 Act, which allows hearings to review relevant person status applies only when a compulsory supervision order is being reviewed, which does not happen in a s.126 hearing.

[150] 2011 Act s.126(6).

child, relevant person, any appointed safeguarder, any person who has or recently has had significant involvement in the upbringing of the child, any person with a contact order and any person who has a permanence order regulating contact between him and her and the child.[151] The hearing's decision on the contact direction is, of course, governed by the welfare test in s.25, its public safety qualification in s.26, and the requirement to take account of any views the child wishes to express in s.27.[152] Hearings arranged under s.126 have no locus to discuss any other issue than whether to confirm or vary or remove the contact direction in the compulsory supervision order (except insofar as another issue cannot realistically be separated from the issue of the contact direction) nor can they make any other decision than confirmation, variation or removal of the contact direction:[153] it is not the whole compulsory supervision order or its efficacy that is open to discussion and alteration, but only the contact direction.

The children's hearing arranged under s.126 must make its decision on the **13–44** day and there is no provision for deferring making the decision.[154] There is nothing, however, to prevent a s.126 hearing (which is still a children's hearing, though with limited decision-making powers) from exercising the power to adjourn, so long as it is able to reconvene on the same day.[155] A decision under s.126(6) to confirm, vary or remove the contact direction is appealable[156] but as we have seen the decision of the hearing that an individual who called for the review does not or did not recently have significant involvement in the upbringing of the child is not appealable.[157]

---

[151] 2013 Rules r.74(5).

[152] The child, however, has no obligation to attend the hearing:2011 Act s.126(7), disapplying s.73. It may be that any views expressed at the full hearing will be sufficient to satisfy the requirements of s.27, or that a decision by the child not to attend the s.126 hearing can be taken to be an implicit declaration of the child that he or she has no views to express on the matter of contact. Both approaches have some dangers and the hearing ought to make a positive effort to satisfy its obligation under s.27.

[153] 2011 Act s.126(6).

[154] The power to defer a review hearing, contained in 2011 Act s.138(2), is limited to reviews of compulsory supervision orders under s.138(1).

[155] 2013 Rules r.7(2) and (3).

[156] 2011 Act s.161: see below, para.14–38.

[157] That decision is made under 2011 Act s.126(5) while s.161 allows appeals to be taken in respect of decisions made under 2011 Act s.126(6) only. This is to be compared with the identical decision being made by a pre-hearing panel, which is appealable: see below, para.14–37.

Chapter Fourteen

APPEALS

14-01 All decisions of the children's hearing have legal effect, and are frequently far-reaching for the child and his or her family. It is an essential aspect of fairness, therefore, that these decisions be open to appeal and it is no exaggeration to say that the integrity of the whole system, as well as its consistency with the due process requirements of (in particular) art.6 of the European Convention on Human Rights, is dependent to a large extent on the appeal mechanisms that are laid down in Part 15 of the Children's Hearings (Scotland) Act 2011 and the associated rules and regulations. The Act allows various decisions of the children's hearing to be appealed against to the sheriff. In addition, decisions of the sheriff, whether on appeal from the children's hearing or on an application for a grounds determination, may be appealed against either to the sheriff principal or direct to the Court of Session; and decisions of the sheriff principal may be appealed against, with leave of the sheriff principal, to the Court of Session. No appeal from the Court of Session to the Supreme Court can be taken, for decisions of the Court of Session made under the Children's Hearings (Scotland) Act 2011 are final.[1] The rules applicable to any individual appeal depend upon the nature of the decision being appealed against: most substantive decisions made by a children's hearing are appealable under the general rules laid down in ss.154–159 of the 2011 Act but a number of specified appeals, considered later in this chapter, are subject to their own special rules.

General Appeals from the Hearing to the Sheriff

14-02 Though the previous legislation talked of appeals to the sheriff from "any decision of the children's hearing",[2] case law had already established that appeals could be taken only against: (i) substantive decisions of the children's hearing (that is to say decisions discharging referrals or imposing, varying, continuing or terminating supervision requirements); and (ii) decisions granting, varying, or renewing warrants; there was, however, sometimes doubt as to whether a decision amounted to a dispositive decision.[3] In order to avoid any such doubt,

---

[1] Children's Hearings (Scotland) Act 2011 s.163(11). The rules governing children's hearings may be examined by the Supreme Court only if the issue reaches that body by some other route: as for example in *Principal Reporter v K*, 2011 S.L.T. 271.

[2] Children (Scotland) Act 1995 s.51(1)(a) and, prior to that, Social Work (Scotland) Act 1968 s.49(1).

[3] For details, see the second edition of this book at pp.211–213. The most recent discussion is to be found in *G v Authority Reporter*, 2013 S.L.T. 538 where a decision to continue a hearing to

the present legislation explicitly lists the decisions open to a children's hearing against which an appeal may be had to the sheriff under the general rules about to be discussed[4]:

(a)   a decision to make, vary or continue a compulsory supervision order;
(b)   a decision to discharge a referral by the reporter;
(c)   a decision to terminate a compulsory supervision order[5];
(d)   a decision to make an interim compulsory supervision order;
(e)   a decision to make an interim variation of a compulsory supervision order;
(f)   a decision to make a medical examination order; or
(g)   a decision to grant a warrant to secure attendance.

Any other decision that a hearing might make but which is not listed either here or elsewhere in Part 15 of the 2011 Act,[6] such as a decision to appoint a safe-guarder, or to defer making a decision, or to direct the reporter to make an application to the sheriff for a determination of whether or not section 67 grounds are established, is not in itself directly appealable, but it should be remembered that irregularities in making any such decision can amount to a ground of appeal against the dispositive decision that follows.[7]

Title to appeal

In keeping with the essentially private nature of the children's hearing **14–03** system, title to appeal against a decision of the children's hearing inheres only in certain specified individuals, or jointly by two or more of these individuals.[8] The appeal must be dismissed if made by a person with no title.[9] The reporter, of course, has no title or interest in appealing a decision of the hearing, whether in relation to the disposal of the case or the making of an interim order, but is the contradictor in any appeal made to the sheriff. The individuals with title to appeal against a hearing's decision are as follows[10]:

(a) The child   **14–04**

The child has title to appeal and may do so on his or her own behalf if possessed of legal capacity to do so. A person under the age of 16 years has legal capacity to instruct a solicitor and to sue in or to defend any civil proceedings (including, it is submitted, appeals from decisions of children's hearings) where

---

a future date was held not to be appealable, following *H v McGregor*, 1973 S.L.T. 110, on the ground that it was essentially academic and had no practical consequences since a hearing would have to be held in any case.

[4] 2011 Act s.154(3).

[5] It would be rare in the extreme for the child or relevant person to appeal against such a decision, but it has always been competent: see for example *Thomson, Petr*, 1998 S.L.T. 1066.

[6] For appeals against decisions other than those in 2011 Act s.154(3), see below, paras 14–36—14–41.

[7] *H v McGregor*, 1973 S.L.T. 110, per Lord Avonside at 116; *M v Kennedy*, 1995 S.L.T. 123, per Lord President Hope at 126F–1.

[8] 2011 Act s.154(1), (2) and (4).

[9] *Kennedy v H*, 1988 S.L.T. 586; *Catto v Pearson*, 1990 S.L.T. (Sh Ct) 77. See also *B v Kennedy*, 1992 S.L.T. 870.

[10] 2011 Act s.154(2).

that person has a general understanding of what it means to do so; and without prejudice to that generality a person 12 years of age or more will be presumed to be of sufficient age and maturity.[11] When the child lacks capacity in this sense the child's legal representative (that is to say a person who has the parental responsibility and parental right of legal representation under s.1(1)(d) and s.2(1)(d) of the Children (Scotland) Act 1995) may appeal on behalf of the child, and he or she may do so too if acting as the capable child's agent. The child's legal representative or agent will usually be a relevant person in any case.

14–05 *(b) The relevant person*

Each relevant person has the right and obligation to attend the children's hearing and to dispute the grounds of referral, and to appeal against decisions made by that hearing. The right of appeal inheres in the relevant person even when he or she did not attend the hearing against whose decision the appeal is being taken. It was held under previous legislation that the appellant would have title to appeal only if he or she were a relevant person at the time of the hearing from whose decision the appeal is being taken, and that a person does not subsequently acquire title to appeal on becoming a relevant person at some later date,[12] but it is unlikely that this rule survives the passing of the 2011 Act, under which it is easier than before for a person to move in and out of the category of "relevant person".[13] It is submitted that the natural reading of s.154(2)(b) is that a person has title to appeal as a "relevant person" if he or she meets the definition in s.200, or has been deemed to be a relevant person under s.81 and retains that status, at the time the appeal is made irrespective of whether the person was a relevant person at the time the decision being appealed against was made.[14] Conversely, an individual who loses his or her status as a relevant person does not lose the right of appeal against decisions made when he or she was a relevant person[15]; and a decision of the hearing to remove relevant person status conferred by a pre-hearing panel does not remove such a person's right to appeal against the hearing's substantive decision.[16]

14–06 *(c) The safeguarder*

In a significant change from the position under the 1995 Act[17] the safe-guarder is given a right of appeal that is independent of the child's right of

---

[11] Age of Legal Capacity (Scotland) Act 1991 s.2(4A) and (4B).

[12] *Kennedy v H*, 1988 S.L.T. 586. This case was decided under the Social Work (Scotland) Act 1968, which referred to "guardian" as opposed to "relevant person".

[13] A person deemed to be a relevant person by a pre-hearing panel is treated as a relevant person for the purposes of appeals: 2011 Act s.81(4).

[14] cf. 2011 Act s.163(7)(b) where, in relation to appeals to the sheriff principal or the Court of Session, the "relevant person" is stated to "include" a person who was a relevant person at the time the ground was established, which clearly suggests that the concept of "relevant person" includes others, i.e. those who are relevant persons at the time of the appeal. If this is so, there is no reason why the rule should be any different in relation to appeals to the sheriff and an absence of any express equivalent to s.163(7)(b) should not be taken to indicate a parliamentary intent that "relevant person" should include fewer individuals for the purposes of s.154 than for the purposes of s.163.

[15] This is explicitly so in relation to appeals from the sheriff against determinations as to whether a s.67 ground is established: s.163(6) and (7).

[16] 2011 Act s.142(4)(b).

[17] See the second edition of this book at pp.206–207.

appeal, with the result that the safeguarder may appeal against a decision even when the child (and relevant person) do not wish to do so and actively oppose an appeal. There is no incompetency in the safeguarder appearing as a respondent in an appeal.[18] Though s.154(2)(c) confers title to appeal on safeguarders appointed under s.30 (i.e. appointed by a children's hearing) it is to be recalled that s.31(4) provides that a safeguarder appointed by a sheriff under s.31 is to be treated for the purposes of the Act as if appointed under s.30 and so a safeguarder appointed by a sheriff has as much title to appeal as a safeguarder appointed by a hearing so long as he or she is still in office.

Time-scale

An appeal under s.154 to the sheriff must be made before the expiry of the **14–07** period of 21 days beginning with the day on which the decision of the children's hearing being appealed is made.[19] There is no general provision in the statute requiring the sheriff to dispose of the appeal within a specified time-scale, except in relation to appeals against certain specified decisions[20] where it is provided that the appeal must be heard and disposed of before the expiry of the period of three days beginning the day after the day on which the appeal is made.[21] The days here are calendar days.[22] There had under the 1995 Act been some dispute over the day from which the periods specified in the time-scales would run,[23] but the present legislation is worded much more unambiguously and there seems to be little room for dispute. When s.154(5) of the 2011 Act says that an appeal must be made "before the expiry of the period of 21 days beginning with the day on which the decision is made", this means that if a decision is made on, say, Monday 1st February, the 21 day period begins to run on that day and any appeal must therefore be made before the expiry of that period, that is to say on or before Sunday 21st February. On the other hand the rule for the disposal of appeals against certain decisions is specified differently: the appeal must be heard and disposed of before the expiry of the period of 3 days beginning the day *after the day* on which the appeal is made."[24] So if an appeal is made on, say, Friday 1st September, the three day period begins to run on the day after that (i.e. on Saturday 2nd September), and the appeal must be disposed of before the expiry of that period, that is to say on or before Monday 4th September. The absence from these provisions of a general power to allow an appeal out of time does not breach art.6 of the European Convention on Human Rights.[25]

---

[18] *R v Grant*, 2000 S.L.T. 372 at 374C.

[19] 2011 Act s.154(5).

[20] That is to say, decisions to: (i) make a compulsory supervision order including a secure accommodation authorisation or movement restriction condition (which presumably includes decisions to vary an order to include such an authorisation or condition); (ii) make an interim compulsory supervision order; (iii) make an interim variation of a compulsory supervision order; (iv) make a medical examination order; or (v) grant a warrant to secure attendance.

[21] 2011 Act s.157(2).

[22] *B v Kennedy*, 1992 S.L.T. 870.

[23] See *S, Appeallants*, 1979 S.L.T. (Sh Ct) 37; *B v Kennedy*, 1992 S.L.T. 870; *J v Caldwell*, 2001 S.L.T. (Sh Ct) 164; *M, Appellant*, 2003 S.L.T. (Sh Ct) 112.

[24] 2011 Act s.157(2).

[25] *AB v Children's Reporter*, 2009 G.W.D. 16–260. See also *BM v Reporter to the Children's Panel*, 2006 S.C.L.R. 246.

14–08   After the appeal is lodged, the date assigned for the hearing must be within the prescribed time limits and in any event no later than 28 days after the lodging of the appeal.[26]

Procedure

14–09   The appeal, in appropriate form and accompanied by a copy of the decision complained of and any document relevant to it that was before the children's hearing, must be lodged with the sheriff clerk of the sheriff court district in which the child is habitually resident (or on cause shown such other court), having been signed by the appellant or his or her representative; an appeal by the child may be signed on his or her behalf by any safeguarder.[27] Thereafter, the sheriff clerk will assign a date for the hearing and intimate it, together with a copy of the appeal to: (a) the reporter; (b) if not the appellant, the child (unless the sheriff dispenses with intimation where he considers this appropriate); (c) if not the appellant, any relevant person; (d) any safeguarder; and (e) any other person the sheriff considers necessary including the author or compiler of a report or statement and (in appropriate circumstances) the person in charge of the secure accommodation specified in a secure accommodation authorisation and the chief social work officer of the relevant local authority.[28] Any person on whom service of the appeal has been made may lodge answers to the appeal not later than seven days before the diet fixed for the hearing of the appeal.[29] It is the responsibility of the reporter to lodge with the sheriff clerk all the appropriate documentation relevant to the appeal, which includes the decisions and reasons for decision of the children's hearing, all information provided under the rules, and the report of the children's hearing.[30]

14–10   As soon as reasonably practicable after an appeal has been lodged, the sheriff must, where a safeguarder has not been appointed for the child, consider whether to appoint a safeguarder for the child and he may make such an appointment at any later stage of the appeal.[31] The safeguarder, on appointment, will have all the powers and duties at common law of a curator ad litem in respect of the child and will be entitled to receive from the sheriff clerk all interlocutors subsequent to his or her appointment.[32] The safeguarder must

---

[26] Act of Sederunt (Child Care and Maintenance Rules) 1997 (SI 1997/291 (S.19)), as amended by the Act of Sederunt (Children's Hearings (Scotland) Act 2011) (Miscellaneous Amendments) 2013 (SSI 2013/172) (hereinafter "Child Care and Maintenance Rules 1997"), r.3.54(5): to be consistent with the 2011 Act (see for example ss.154(5) and 165(4)) this period will commence on the day the appeal is lodged. So if the appeal is lodged on August 1, the date assigned may be up to August 28, but not thereafter.

[27] Child Care and Maintenance Rules 1997 r.3.53(1)–(3), as substituted by Act of Sederunt (Children's Hearings (Scotland) Act 2011) (Miscellaneous Amendments) 2013. Where leave to appeal is required due to a previous appeal having been deemed to be frivolous or vexatious (see below, paras 14–28—14–29), application for leave must be made by letter to the sheriff clerk setting out the grounds on which the application is made, accompanied by a copy of the decision that the previous appeal was frivolous or vexatious, and lodged with the sheriff clerk with the relevant form of appeal: r.3.53(4).

[28] Child Care and Maintenance Rules 1997 r.3.54, as so amended.

[29] Child Care and Maintenance Rules 1997 r.3.55(1): this does not apply to all appeals: r.3.55(1A). A copy of these answers must be intimated to any person on whom service of the appeal has been made: r.3.55(2).

[30] 2011 Act s.155(2).

[31] 2011 Act s.31 and Child Care and Maintenance Rules 1997 r.3.7(1).

[32] Child Care and Maintenance Rules 1997 r.3.8.

without delay intimate in writing to the sheriff clerk whether or not he or she intends to become a party to the proceedings, and if he or she does become a party may appear personally or instruct an advocate or solicitor to appear on his or her behalf.[33] Where an appeal has been heard in part and a safeguarder thereafter becomes a party to the appeal, the sheriff may order the hearing of the appeal to commence of new.[34]

The appeal must not be heard in open court.[35] The sheriff may (but need not) **14–11** hear evidence from: (i) the child; (ii) a relevant person in relation to the child; (iii) an author or compiler of a report or statement provided to the children's hearing that made the decision now being appealed against; (iv) the reporter; (v) where the appeal is against a decision to make, grant, vary or continue an order or warrant including a secure accommodation authorisation in respect of the child, any person in charge of the specified secure accommodation and the chief social work officer; and (vi) any other person who the sheriff considers may give material additional evidence.[36] The sheriff may require any person to give a report to the sheriff for the purpose of assisting him in determining the appeal.[37] In hearing an appeal from a decision of the children's hearing the sheriff must first hear the appellant or his or her representative and any party to the appeal (that is the child, the relevant person, the reporter and, if appropriate, any safeguarder).[38] It is in the discretion of the sheriff whom he wants to examine and he may call for any further report which he considers may assist him in deciding the appeal, such as an updated social background report, educational report, medical report, safeguarder's report, or any other report that was not available to the children's hearing.[39] It has been suggested[40] that these powers indicate that the sheriff should take a more inquisitorial role in appeals from children's hearings than would normally be appropriate in the sheriff court. The sheriff may hear evidence as to any alleged irregularity if that is the ground of appeal, and in any other case he may hear evidence when he considers it appropriate to do so.[41] The evidence must be kept strictly within the bounds of the appeal, that is to say directed towards the question of whether the hearing's decision was justified. It would be incompetent to lead evidence directed to other questions, for example whether accepted section 67 grounds apply in relation to the child.[42] The sheriff may, on the motion of any party or on his own motion, adjourn or continue the hearing of the appeal for such

---

[33] Child Care and Maintenance Rules 1997 r.3.8 and r.3.9.

[34] Child Care and Maintenance Rules 1997 r.3.56(7).

[35] 2011 Act s.155(3).

[36] 2011 Act s.155(5). Other than in relation to the factual occurrences at the hearing, additional evidence should not be sought from panel members: judicial decision-makers do not give evidence to justify their decisions on appeal. See, further, fn.37 below.

[37] 2011 Act s.155(6). This includes safeguarders: Children's Hearings (Scotland) Act 2011 (Safeguarders: Further Provision) Regulations 2012 (SSI 2012/336) reg.6. It is conceivable that a sheriff might require a report from the chairing member of the hearing to give further explanation of the decision that the hearing made.

[38] Child Care and Maintenance Rules 1997 r.3.56(1). Procedure for obtaining the views of the child is specified in r.3.5.

[39] On receipt of such further reports, the sheriff must direct the reporter to send a copy thereof to every party to the appeal: Child Care and Maintenance Rules 1997 r.3.56(2).

[40] Kearney, *Children's Hearings and the Sheriff Court*, 2nd edn (Butterworths, 2000), Ch.35.

[41] Child Care and Maintenance Rules 1997 r.3.56(3).

[42] See *G v Authority Reporter*, 2013 S.L.T. 538 where it was attempted to use the appeal process to challenge matters not open to appeal.

reasonable time and for such purposes as may in the circumstances be appropriate, and if he does so he may make such order as he deems necessary to secure the expeditious determination of the appeal.[43]

14–12　　The child may be excluded from the hearing by the sheriff where he is satisfied that the nature of the appeal or of any evidence is such that it is in the child's interests not to be present, though in that event any safeguarder and any relevant person or[44] representative of the child shall be permitted to remain during the absence of the child.[45] Likewise, any relevant person and/or his or her representative can be excluded from the hearing where the sheriff considers it is necessary in the interests of any child[46] where he is satisfied that: (a) he must do so in order to obtain the views of the child in relation to the hearing; or (b) the presence of the person in question is causing or is likely to cause significant distress to the child; where any relevant person has been excluded the sheriff shall, after that exclusion has ended, explain the substance of what took place in his or her absence and shall give him or her an opportunity to respond to any evidence given by the child by leading evidence or otherwise.[47]

Grounds of appeal

14–13　　The grounds of appeal to the sheriff are not laid down in the 2011 Act except for the requirement in s.156(1) that the sheriff must confirm the decision if satisfied that the decision to which the appeal relates is justified: the sole ground of appeal, therefore, is that the decision was not justified. It has long been accepted that the sheriff may not allow an appeal merely because he takes a different view from the hearing as to the correct disposal of the case. It is perfectly conceivable that two different, even opposing, decisions are each justifiable in the circumstances of a single case. It follows from this, Sheriff Principal Nicholson held,[48] "that the task facing a sheriff to whom an appeal has been taken is not to reconsider the evidence which was before the hearing with a view to making his own decision on that evidence. Instead, the sheriff's task is to see if there has been some procedural irregularity in the conduct of the case; to see whether the hearing has failed to give proper, or any, consideration to a relevant factor in the case; and in general to consider whether the decision reached by the hearing can be characterised as one which could not, upon any reasonable view, be regarded as being justified in all the circumstances of the case". These words were spoken in the context of the 1995 Act, where appeals were allowed if the sheriff was satisfied "that the decision of the children's hearing is not justified in all the circumstances of the case", but the restructuring of the rules for appeal in the 2011 Act and in particular the removal of the words "in all the circumstances of the case" do not, it is thought, change the underlying principle expressed by Sheriff Principal

---

[43] Child Care and Maintenance Rules 1997 r.3.57, as amended by Act of Sederunt (Children's Hearings (Scotland) Act 2011) (Miscellaneous Amendments) 2013 art.3 para.46.

[44] The use of the word "or" suggests that the child's representative cannot remain if the relevant person insists on remaining. Since appeals are heard in chambers, however, the sheriff will have a discretion and unless there is good reason why the representative should not remain, in most cases it will be appropriate for the sheriff to allow him or her to do so.

[45] Child Care and Maintenance Rules 1997 r.3.56(4).

[46] Not just the referred child.

[47] Child Care and Maintenance Rules 1997 r.3.56(5) and (6).

[48] *W v Schaffer*, 2001 S.L.T. (Sh Ct) 86 at 87K–88A.

Nicholson. This leaves unaffected (if unspoken) the basis upon which a sheriff might today hold a decision of a children's hearing to be not justified, and it is submitted that the case law on the pre–2011 legislation continues to hold good on the matter.

Procedural irregularity is explicitly a ground of appeal from the sheriff to the **14–14** sheriff principal or to the Court of Session under s.163(9)(b), from which it may be inferred that procedural irregularity is also among the grounds on which a decision of the children's hearing may be appealed to the sheriff under s.154.[49] The irregularity alleged in the case cited was that the children's hearing had proceeded on the assumption that the grounds of referral had been accepted when, in fact, they had not been. Other irregularities might be failing to consider contact (as required by s.83(3)), requiring the child to live with foster or kinship carers although the procedures in the Looked After Children (Scotland) Regulations 2009 had not been carried out, excluding a relevant person from the children's hearing for no good reason, failing to convene time-ously, purporting to make a decision without giving appropriate opportunity to the child, relevant person, safeguarder or representative to express views,[50] taking into account allegations which have been expressly found by the sheriff not to be proved,[51] or failing to give consideration to the appointment of a safeguarder. However, before the appeal can be upheld, the irregularity must be such that it had a material effect on the conduct of or outcome of the proceedings, or such that it materially prejudices the child or relevant person. A decision might well remain justified even when there was a failure, for example, on the part of the chairing member to check a toddler's age. In *McGregor v A*[52] the irregularity was constituted by the statement of grounds referring to the wrong statute: that was held to create no prejudice and there-fore the decision of the children's hearing was upheld. The Court of Session, in the context of an appeal against a decision of a sheriff, has held that for an irregularity to found a successful appeal, it is necessary that the occurrence was damaging to the justice of the proceedings,[53] and this is likely to be true also in relation to appeals from a children's hearing to the sheriff.

It is clear that procedural irregularity is not the only ground of appeal.[54] **14–15** Error of law, if different from procedural irregularity, will also be a ground of appeal because a decision of a children's hearing is unlikely to be justified if it is based upon a misunderstanding of the law. This might be constituted, for example, by a misinterpretation of a statutory provision, such as the circum-stances in which secure accommodation can be authorised or in which an interim compulsory supervision order can be made, or in which a person is to be deemed to be a relevant person.[55] Likewise, unfairness in the determination

---

[49] *M v Kennedy*, 1995 S.L.T. 123, per Lord President Hope at 126E. That this is a ground of appeal from the hearing to the sheriff is assumed in the rules: see Child Care and Maintenance Rules 1997 r.3.56(3)(a).

[50] cf. *Kennedy, Petitioner*, 1988 S.C.L.R. 149 in which the sheriff held that there was a proce-dural irregularity when one member of the children's hearing stated his decision before the conclu-sion of the consideration of the case–some two and a half hours into the hearing!

[51] *M v Kennedy*, 1993 S.L.T. 431.

[52] 1982 S.L.T. 45.

[53] *C v Miller*, 2003 S.L.T. 1379.

[54] In *M v Kennedy*, 1995 S.L.T. 123 Lord President Hope described irregularity as being "among the grounds on which that decision may be appealed against".

[55] *S v Authority Reporter, Edinburgh*, 2008 Fam. L.R. 84; *M, Appellant*, 2010 Fam. L.R. 152.

of the parties' civil rights (if, again, different from procedural irregularity) is a ground of appeal,[56] as is any other breach of the ECHR rights of anyone affected by the hearing process.[57] In addition, a lack of clarity in the decision, such as to the effect of any of the measures included in a compulsory supervision order, has been a successful ground of appeal.[58] Lack of clarity in the stated reasons for decision may be a ground of appeal for if the reasons are stated ambiguously it may be impossible for the sheriff to determine whether or not the decision is justified: if the sheriff cannot so determine, the decision, it is submitted, cannot stand.[59] The European Court of Human Rights has frequently found an infringement of art.6 (right to a fair trial) when reasons for decision are insufficient to allow a party the know-how to structure an appeal.[60]

14–16   More generally, it is open to the sheriff to uphold an appeal on the basis that the decision made by the children's hearing was entirely inappropriate, though this will be so only where the decision is one that no reasonable children's hearing would have reached on the information that was properly before them.[61] This might be because the hearing has founded its decision on irrelevant considerations, or has failed to take into account relevant considerations,[62] or has not been made aware of relevant considerations.[63] A decision might not be justified if it proceeds upon the basis of information which, in the event, turns out to be factually inaccurate. This is unlikely to eventuate in relation to the children's hearing that initially makes a compulsory supervision order (for such a hearing is entitled to act upon the section 67 grounds accepted or established and an appeal cannot be used to reopen these grounds[64]) but it might arise at a review hearing if inaccurate reports, written or verbal, are given to the hearing.[65] This is an important check against a children's hearing relying too heavily on unsubstantiated allegations which have not been included in the statement of grounds. In *O v Rae*,[66] had the decision to remove the children

---

[56] Per Sheriff Ross in *M v Caldwell*, 2001 S.L.T. (Sh Ct) 106 at [15].

[57] Though not an appeal under the children's hearing legislation, in *Principal Reporter v K*, 2011 S.L.T. 271 the Supreme Court held that it was contrary to natural justice for a hearing to seek to remove a father's contact with a child without affording him the right to participate.

[58] *D v Strathclyde Regional Council*, 1991 S.C.L.R. 185. In this case, access was stated "to be at the discretion of the local authority" and the evidence showed that the intention had been to terminate access completely.

[59] *K v Finlayson*, 1974 S.L.T. (Sh Ct) 51 (overruled on another point in *O v Rae*, 1993 S.L.T. 570). See also *Kennedy v M*, 1995 S.L.T. 717 in which Lord President Hope held that the sheriff's criticism of the children's hearing's statement of reasons was unjustified and that the reasons were not so ambiguous as to be open to challenge.

[60] *Hadjianastassiou v Greece* (1992) 16 E.H.R.R. 219; *H v Belgium* (1987) 10 E.H.R.R. 339; *Sanchez Cardenas v Norway* (2009) 49 E.H.R.R. 6. The domestic law on the matter was discussed in some detail in *Megrahi v HM Advocate*, 2002 J.C. 99. See also (in a different context) the discussion of adequacy of reasons in *Uprichard v The Scottish Ministers* [2013] UKSC 21, per Lord Reed at [47].

[61] *O v Rae*, 1993 S.L.T. 570, per Lord President Hope at 575I.

[62] As in *D v Sinclair*, 1973 S.L.T. (Sh Ct) 47 where the hearing had failed to consider an up-to-date social background report.

[63] Which the sheriff can discover by exercising his power under 2011 Act s.155(6) to call for further reports.

[64] The procedure to do that is contained in ss.110–117: see above, paras 8–37—8–49.

[65] Such inaccuracy can be established before the sheriff on appeal since evidence can be led and the sheriff is entitled to examine the authors or compilers of reports or statements: 2011 Act s.155(5)(c).

[66] 1993 S.L.T. 570.

from their mother's care been made primarily or exclusively on the basis that the father had sexually abused another sibling, and that allegation been shown by evidence led on appeal to be false, the decision would not have been justified and the appeal would have been sustained.[67]

There is some authority under the pre–2011 legislation to suggest that the **14–17** assessment of whether a decision is justified or not was to be made on the basis of the circumstances pertaining at the date of the appeal rather than at the date of the decision being appealed against.[68] Section 51(5) of the 1995 Act provided that appeals should be allowed if the hearing's decision was "not justified in all the circumstances of the case" and the argument was that changes since the hearing made its decision were part of the circumstances of the case. There was, however, a conceptual illogicality in this since to uphold an appeal on the basis of a change of circumstances would be to allow an appeal against a decision that was *ex hypothesi* justified at the time it was made, in order to ensure that the decision be looked at again in the light of subsequent developments. The issue will not arise under the 2011 Act, for not only have the words "in all the circumstances of the case" not been re-enacted, but the sheriff is given the express power (discussed below) to vary the children's hearing's decision because there has been a change of circumstances even when he is upholding that decision. It follows that if the hearing's decision was justified at the time it was made then, notwithstanding any subsequent change, the sheriff is obliged to confirm the decision under s.156(1)(a) but, if there has been a change of circumstances, he may vary the terms of the compulsory supervision order under s.156(1)(b), as discussed more fully below.[69]

Disposal of the Appeal

Having heard the parties and considered any evidence tendered and reports **14–18** submitted, the sheriff must then decide whether to reject or to allow the appeal. He must give his decision orally either at the conclusion of the appeal or on such day (subject to the provisions of the 2011 Act) as he shall appoint.[70] He may issue a note of the reasons for his decision, and must do so if, on allowing the appeal, he decides to take any of the steps available to him under s.156(2) or (3)[71]; any such note must be issued at the time the sheriff gives his decision or within seven days thereafter.[72] The sheriff's decision in this regard is determined

---

[67] In the event, the appeal in that case was unsuccessful since the allegation was not the primary basis of the decision and there were various other grounds upon which the decision could be justified. But care needs to be taken with unsubstantiated allegations of sexual abuse to ensure that they do not influence the decision unduly, for that might amount to an infringement of art.6 of the ECHR: see *Sanchez Cardenas v Norway* (2009) 49 E.H.R.R. 6.

[68] In *D v Sinclair*, 1973 S.L.T. (Sh Ct) 47 the sheriff allowed an appeal on the ground that the child's circumstances had changed sufficiently since the last hearing (five weeks previously) to justify the hearing looking at the matter again. See also *Kennedy v B*, 1973 S.L.T. 38.

[69] See para.14–20.

[70] Child Care and Maintenance Rules 1997 r.3.58(1).

[71] These steps are to recall a warrant, terminate an ICSO or medical examination order, require the reporter to arrange a hearing, continue, vary or terminate any order, interim variation or warrant, discharge the child from any further proceedings, make an ICSO or interim variation of a compulsory supervision order, or grant a warrant to secure attendance.

[72] Child Care and Maintenance Rules 1997 r.3.58(2) and (3).

only by whether he is satisfied that the decision being appealed against was justified or not, and is not dependent on the application of the principles in ss.25, 26, 27 and 29.[73] And as we have already seen, the decision is not to be made according to whether the sheriff agrees with the hearing's decision or not. Under the Social Work (Scotland) Act 1968, this important principle (based on the proposition that it is the hearing and not the sheriff that is the most appropriate forum for making the decision as to which, from a range of justifiable options, is in the best interests of the child) was underpinned by the fact that the only option available to a sheriff who allowed an appeal was to remit the case back to the hearing for reconsideration. The Children (Scotland) Act 1995 qualified that position to some extent by permitting sheriffs, on a successful appeal, to substitute for the disposal of the children's hearing any requirement which could be imposed by the hearing on the child.[74] Sheriffs proved themselves reticent in using this new power, accepting that in most cases the children's hearing remains the better forum for determining what form of supervision will best meet the child's needs. The power was nevertheless valuable in circumstances in which it was clear, on appeal, that there was only one possible option that would serve the child's interests and when, therefore, it would be a procedural waste of time to send the matter back to the children's hearing for disposal. The Children's Hearings (Scotland) Act 2011 further extends the sheriff's power, by allowing the sheriff to vary or terminate an order even when the appeal is unsuccessful (though only if there has been a change of circumstances since the decision appealed against was made).[75] It is expected, and to be hoped, that sheriffs will continue to show reticence and use this enhanced power only when it achieves the only possible good outcome, or an order has to be changed as a matter of urgency. A useful by-product of this change is, however, that an appeal by a person who wishes to challenge not the whole order but only one of its terms[76] can achieve that end (so long as a change in circumstances can be shown). Nevertheless, in the generality of cases, if a range of justifiable measures is available it is all the more important that the child and relevant persons are able fully to participate in the choice of which measure to include in the order, and in most cases this will be best assured by returning the case to the children's hearing for disposal. In one respect at least, as we will see, the power of the sheriff under the 2011 Act is actually narrower than it was under the 1995 Act.[77]

Appeal rejected

14–19   If the sheriff is satisfied that the decision of the children's hearing to which the appeal relates is justified, the appeal fails and the sheriff must confirm the decision of the hearing.[78] Any previously granted suspension of a compulsory supervision order[79] will be lifted on the rejection of the appeal.[80]

---

[73] Paramountcy or primacy of welfare, children's views and minimum intervention.

[74] Children (Scotland) Act 1995 s.51(5)(c)(iii).

[75] 2011 Act s.156(1)(b).

[76] As did the appellant in *J, Appellant*, 2013 S.L.T. (Sh Ct) 18.

[77] See below, para.14–23, fn.91.

[78] 2011 Act s.156(1)(a).

[79] Granted under 2011 Act s.158: see above, paras 10–20—10–21 and below, paras.14–30—14–35.

[80] The wording of 2011 Act s.158(2) suggests that suspension lasts only while the determination of an appeal is "pending".

In a change to the previous law, the 2011 Act provides that even where a **14–20** decision is confirmed as being justified and the appeal, therefore, rejected the sheriff may nevertheless take one or more of the steps[81] that he is able to take when he upholds the appeal, and this will invariably involve altering the child's position vis-a-vis a compulsory supervision order. The sheriff may take such steps, however, only if satisfied that the circumstances of the child have changed since the decision was made.[82] The change in circumstances must, one assumes, be such as to justify a change in the terms of the order and it would be an abuse of process for a sheriff to found on an inconsequential change in order to make a decision different from the justifiable decision of a children's hearing which he happens to disagree with but has no reason to overturn. Whether there has been a change in circumstances is a question of fact and not one to which the principles in ss.25–29 apply, but, having determined that there has been a change of circumstances, the sheriff's decision whether to exercise the power to vary the child's position is governed by: (i) the principle in s.25 that he is to regard the need to safeguard and promote the welfare of the child throughout his or her childhood as the paramount consideration (or, if s.26 applies, a primary consideration); and (ii) the principle in s.29(2) that the sheriff may make, vary, continue or extend an order, interim variation or warrant only if he considers that it would be better for the child if the order etc were in force than not. Section 27 also applies when the sheriff is deciding whether to do more than simply confirm a decision of the hearing and so he is obliged to: (i) give the child an opportunity to indicate whether he or she wishes to express views; (ii) if the child wishes to do so, give him or her an opportunity to express these views; and (iii) have regard to any views expressed by the child. There is no provision requiring a sheriff to take account of the views of the relevant person, but human rights considerations require that a relevant person be given the opportunity for effective participation in all the decision-making processes that might affect their interests[83] and it follows that any sheriff minded to exercise this power will need to offer such an opportunity to a relevant person, at least if its exercise will have a real effect on the position of the relevant person. If varying or continuing a compulsory supervision order the sheriff must give consideration to whether to include a contact direction in the order.[84]

Appeal allowed

If the sheriff is not satisfied that the decision being appealed against is **14–21** justified, he will allow the appeal. He must recall the warrant (if the decision being appealed against is to grant a warrant to secure attendance) and he must terminate the order (if the decision being appealed against is to make either an interim compulsory supervision order or a medical examination order).[85] In

---

[81] Discussed below, paras 14–22—14–16.

[82] 2011 Act s.156(1)(b).

[83] *W v United Kingdom* (1988) 10 E.H.FR.R. 29; *McMichael v United Kingdom* (1995) 20 E.H.R.R. 205; *Venema v The Netherlands* [2003] 1 F.LR. 552; *S v Miller*, 2001 S.L.T. 531. See also (in different contexts) *Principal Reporter v K*, 2011 S.L.T. 271 (Sup. Ct.) and *A v B*, 2011 S.L.T. (Sh Ct) 131.

[84] 2011 Act s.29A(2), as inserted by the Children's Hearings (Scotland) Act 2011 (Modification of Primary Legislation) Order 2013 Sch.1 para.20(5).

[85] 2011 Act s.156(2)(a).

any case, including appeals against the making, varying, continuing or terminating of a compulsory supervision order, or against a decision to include in that order any particular measure, he may take one or more of the steps listed in s.156(3)[86] (and discussed immediately below). His decision of which of the specified steps to take must, of course, be made taking account of the welfare principle in ss.25 and 26, the views of the child as required by s.27, and the no-order principle in s.29. Again, an opportunity to participate must be afforded to the relevant person, if this has not already been done in the course of hearing the appeal. The steps open to the sheriff when satisfied that the decision of the hearing is not justified are as follows:

14–22　*(a)　He may require the reporter to arrange a children's hearing for any purpose for which a hearing can be arranged under the 2011 Act*

What that purpose is will depend upon the nature of the decision that has been found to be not justified. The usual case will involve the hearing being arranged to review a compulsory supervision order that was made, continued or varied by the decision appealed against, this in light of the sheriff's finding that that decision was not justified. The compulsory supervision order itself is not, by the sheriff taking this step, terminated or varied or suspended. When the sheriff takes this step, he must give reasons for his decision, but he is not entitled to give any directions as to how the hearing should proceed with the case or dispose of it: such matters lie solely in the hands of the children's hearing.[87] His statement of reasons must, therefore, be limited to a statement of why he has found the decision appealed against to be not justified. The subsequent hearing is under no obligation to change its previous decision.[88] It is to be expected that in the generality of cases this will be the step taken by sheriffs who allow appeals against decisions of children's hearings.

14–23　*(b)　The sheriff may continue, vary or terminate any order, interim variation or warrant which is in effect*

This is the provision that allows the sheriff, on determining an appeal, to replace the hearing's decision with his own. It will be noticed that it is expressly within the power of a sheriff allowing an appeal to decide to continue the order appealed against without variation. Continuation of a compulsory supervision order without variation will have no effect on its terms but will have effect on its length, for the terms of s.83(7)(b) suggest that the one year that orders are effective for will run from the sheriff's decision to continue the order rather than from the date of the hearing's decision to impose it. Continuation without

---

[86] 2011 Act s.156(2)(b).

[87] *Kennedy v A*, 1986 S.L.T. 358. Nor may the sheriff give procedural directions as to, for example, the makeup of the children's hearing. That function lies with the area support team and there is no statutory authority for a sheriff giving directions to that team. It follows that the sheriff's decision which led to the case *Kennedy, Petitioner*, 1988 S.C.L.R. 149, that the hearing to which a case was remitted after appeal be composed of panel members other than those who made the decision appealed against, was incompetent (or, at any rate, would be incompetent under the current regime).

[88] It might be, for example, that the hearing should simply specify better or clearer reasons for their original decision: see, for example, *D v Strathclyde Regional Council*, 1991 S.C.L.R. 185 in which the appeal was allowed in order that the children's hearing make clear what their decision actually was.

variation of an order found on appeal to be not justified might be appropriate if there has been a change in the child's circumstances that now justifies its terms. Variation of an order is appropriate when the sheriff considers that while it remains justified for the child to be subject to a compulsory supervision order, that order nevertheless needs to be altered in order to include a measure that will better ensure the welfare of the child than the existing terms, or to remove a measure that is inhibiting the achievement of that aim.[89] Termination of a compulsory supervision order will be an unusual decision for a sheriff to make, and both an interim compulsory supervision order and a warrant to secure attendance must be terminated in any case if the decision to make or grant such an order or warrant was unjustified.[90] It should be noted that the sheriff does not have the power to *make* a compulsory supervision requirement.[91] An appeal may be had (perhaps by a safeguarder, or a relevant person wanting to access support that he or she considers the child needs) against a decision to discharge a referral to the hearing,[92] and if the sheriff finds that decision to be not justified and he considers that a compulsory supervision order needs to be made, then his only option is to return the case to the hearing under para.(a) above, perhaps making also an interim compulsory supervision order, as permitted under para.(d) below. Even then, however, the hearing might again decide to discharge the referral.[93] If the sheriff continues or varies a compulsory supervision order he must (if it contains a movement restriction condition) and may (in any other case) require that the order be reviewed by a children's hearing on a day or within a period specified in the order.[94] And when varying or continuing a compulsory supervision order he must consider whether to include a contact direction.[95] "Vary" includes, it is submitted, an interim variation.

(c)   The sheriff may discharge the child from any further hearing or other   **14–24**
proceedings in relation to the grounds that gave rise to the decision, and if he
does so he must also terminate any order or warrant which is in effect in
relation to the child[96]

It would be appropriate to choose this option if the sheriff is in no doubt that, the decision being appealed against not being justified, the only option that properly serves the child's interests is to release the child from the jurisdiction of the children's hearing system. If discharge is merely one of a range of options that might serve the child's interests, it will normally be better for the sheriff to require the reporter to arrange a children's hearing under paragraph (a) above in order for the hearing to review the order found to be not justified.

---

[89] This could be achieved only with some awkwardness under the pre–2011 law: see *J, Appellant*, 2013 S.L.T. (Sh Ct) 18.

[90] 2011 Act s.156(2)(a).

[91] This may be compared with the more extensive power under s.51(5)(c)(iii) of the Children (Scotland) Act 1995 which allowed the sheriff to make any disposal that was open to the children's hearing.

[92] 2011 Act s.154(3)(b).

[93] cf. 2011 Act s.156(5) where the matter is made explicit in relation to most other decisions available to a hearing.

[94] 2011 Act s.156(3A), as inserted by the Children's Hearings (Scotland) Act 2011 (Modification of Primary Legislation) Order 2013 Sch.1 para.20(15).

[95] 2011 Act s.29A(2), as so inserted, Sch.1 para.20(5).

[96] 2011 Act s.156(3)(c) and (4).

The option of discharge should be chosen by the sheriff only when he is satisfied that the child should no longer be subject to a compulsory supervision order or the jurisdiction of the children's hearing; a procedural irregularity that founds the appeal will seldom in itself lead to this conclusion, which is more likely to follow a finding that the hearing's decision to make or retain a compulsory supervision order over a child was one that no reasonable hearing would have made. After discharge, the child cannot then be brought back to a children's hearing by the reporter founding upon the section 67 grounds previously established, for that would amount to seeking a review by the children's hearing of the sheriff's decision.[97] The sheriff's discharge of the child has the same effect as a children's hearing's discharge of the referral under s.91(3)(b), except that it will not take effect until the time for appealing against it has passed.[98]

14–25 *(d) The sheriff may make an interim compulsory supervision order, or an interim variation of a compulsory supervision order*

The only circumstance in which this would be appropriate would be when the matter is being returned to the hearing for reconsideration of the decision being appealed against. It is thought, though not explicitly provided, that a sheriff may take either of these interim steps only when it is necessary as a matter of urgency to do so, for this is the test that needs to be satisfied for the making of interim orders in other circumstances.[99]

14–26 *(e) The sheriff may grant a warrant to secure attendance*

As with para.(d) above it is not explicitly provided but probably implied that the normal conditions[100] for the granting of a warrant to secure attendance will need to be satisfied before it is appropriate for the sheriff to utilise this power—in other words, the sheriff must be satisfied that there is reason to believe that the child would not otherwise attend the subsequent children's hearing. In any case, the power is limited to situations in which there are further proceedings for the child to attend, and so it would be incompetent (fairly obviously) to grant a warrant under s.156(3)(e) while at the same time discharging the child from any further hearing or other proceedings under s.156(3)(c).

14–27 However the sheriff decides, any subsequent hearing is not bound to endorse his decision, and so it may continue, vary or terminate any order or warrant made, continued or varied by the sheriff.[101]

Frivolous and vexatious appeals

14–28 Where a sheriff has determined an appeal against any of the decisions of a children's hearing listed in s.154(3) by confirming the decision of the hearing to vary or continue a compulsory supervision order, and he is satisfied that the

---

[97] The reporter is able to appeal from the sheriff's decision under 2011 Act s.163: see below, paras 14–42—14–48.

[98] *Stirling v D*, 1995 S.L.T. 1089: see below, para.14–47.

[99] As for example in 2011 Act s.109(3) where the sheriff has made a grounds determination finding grounds established, required the reporter to arrange a children's hearing and in the interim made an ICSO.

[100] Found, for sheriffs after a grounds determination, in 2011 Act s.109(6).

[101] 2011 Act s.156(5).

appeal was "frivolous or vexatious", he may order that, during the period of 12 months beginning on the day of the order, the appellant must obtain leave from the sheriff before making another appeal under s.154 against a decision of a children's hearing in relation to the compulsory supervision order.[102] There are a number of limitations to the application of this provision which need to be noted. First, it applies only to appeals under s.154 or s.161[103] and so is inapplicable in relation to the special appeals under other sections of the 2011 Act (discussed below) such as an appeal under s.160 against a relevant person determination or an appeal under s.162 against a decision to implement a secure accommodation authorisation. Secondly, it applies only after unsuccessful appeals against decisions to vary or continue a compulsory supervision order but not against decisions to make or to terminate such an order. Thirdly, the sheriff may make an order under this provision only when he confirms the hearing's decision, though he may of course confirm the decision while at the same time varying the compulsory supervision order found to be justified, because of some change in the child's circumstances: in that case too he may make an order requiring leave for further appeal.[104] Fourthly, and in a limitation that did not apply under the Children (Scotland) Act 1995, an order under this provision inhibits appeals only by the unsuccessful applicant and does not impose a requirement to seek leave to appeal on anyone else.[105] If the sheriff makes an order under s.159 that leave to appeal must be obtained, this requirement is limited to subsequent appeals against decisions "in relation to the compulsory supervision order", but it is not immediately apparent that a hearing's decision to grant a warrant to secure attendance[106] would be regarded as a decision "in relation to *the* compulsory supervision order". It is suggested, if tentatively, that granting a warrant to secure attendance is indeed an order in relation to an existing compulsory supervision order since it is made in the process in which the hearing is determining whether or not to vary or continue the compulsory supervision order. The same is true, and more obviously so, for a decision to make an interim variation of a compulsory supervision order. If this is so, then leave will be required before an appeal against either of these decisions can be made whenever an order under s.159 is extant.

The Act does not define what a frivolous or vexatious appeal is, though the **14–29** concept is commonly used in statutory appeal processes.[107] The words need to be interpreted in light of the aims of the provision, which are clear: (i) to ensure that the courts are not cluttered by appeals that have no chance of success; (ii) to protect the child from the needless uncertainties caused by appeals when no change whatsoever has occurred in the child's circumstances since the last hearing; and (iii) to avoid the possibility of the appeal process being used for

---

[102] 2011 Act s.159. This also applies to appeals under s.161 against contact decisions made by hearings under s.126, for which see below, para.14–38.

[103] The reference to 2011 Act s.161 was added by the Children's Hearings (Scotland) Act 2011 (Modification of Primary Legislation) Order 2013 Sch.1 para.20(16).

[104] There will be few cases in which an appeal could be described as frivolous when, as a result of the appeal, the sheriff alters the terms of the order. Even a sound appeal might, however, be made vexatiously.

[105] For this reason if no other, it may sometimes be tactically sensible for appellants to avoid appealing jointly.

[106] Appealable under 2011 Act s.154(3)(f) and (g).

[107] For a discussion of the concept in another context, see *Council of the Law Society of Scotland v Scottish Legal Complaints Commission*, 2011 S.C. 94.

illegitimate motives, such as to prolong the procedure or to create trouble and unnecessary effort on the part of others.

Suspension of compulsory supervision order pending appeal

14–30   It is a general rule in appeals that any order appealed against does not need to be executed until the appeal has been determined.[108] This rule, however, applies only when there is no statutory provision to the contrary. Compulsory supervision orders are to be enforced immediately they are made, even when an appeal is lodged, because there is a procedure in the Children's Hearings (Scotland) Act 2011 allowing a person who appeals against a decision of the children's hearing under s.154 to make, vary, continue or terminate a compulsory supervision order to request the reporter to arrange a children's hearing to consider whether the decision should be suspended until the appeal has been heard and determined.[109] It is implicit in this provision that the compulsory supervision order remains effective unless and until such an application has been successfully made.[110] The local authority's duties to give effect to the compulsory supervision order[111] therefore come into effect immediately and are not suspended by the lodging of an appeal: they will be suspended only if an application to suspend the order has been granted.

14–31   An application to suspend the effect of a compulsory supervision order can be made when an appeal is made, but not before, so the hearing against whose decision the appeal is being taken cannot itself deal with an application to suspend the compulsory supervision order it has just made, varied, continued or terminated. It is the responsibility of the reporter to arrange, as soon as practicable after the request is made, a children's hearing to consider whether the decision should be suspended pending the determination of the appeal[112] and he or she must give notice to the child, relevant person, any appointed safeguarder, the three members of the children's hearing, the chief social work officer of the relevant local authority and the National Convener of the date, time and place of the children's hearing at which the application will be considered.[113] If the applicant fails to attend at that hearing, the hearing may, if it considers it appropriate, take no further action in relation to the application[114] or, if the children's hearing feels able to make a decision one way or the other, the application may be determined even in the absence of the person who made it.[115]

14–32   The right to seek a suspension of the decision being appealed against is limited to those decisions listed in s.154(3)(a) and (c) and so there is no power

---

[108] *Macleay v Macdonald*, 1928 S.C. 776.

[109] 2011 Act s.158(1). See further above, paras 10–20—10–21.

[110] It is different with appeals from the sheriff to the sheriff principal or to the Court of Session for, in the absence of any statutory provision analogous to 2011 Act s.158, the general rule applies: *Kennedy v M*, 1995 S.L.T. 717, per Lord President Hope at 720K–721B.

[111] See above, paras 2–35—2–37.

[112] 2011 Act s.158(2).

[113] Children's Hearings (Scotland) Act (Rules of Procedure in Children's Hearings) Rules 2013 (SSI 2013/194) (hereinafter "2013 Rules") r.76(1) and (2).

[114] 2013 Rules r.76(3). It is presumably open to the reporter to rearrange a children's hearing if, on receipt of the notice, the applicant indicates that he or she cannot attend on the date specified.

[115] The applicant may participate by other means of communication, but a failure to do so is likely to encourage the children's hearing not to suspend the decision.

to suspend a decision pending an appeal under s.160 relating to a relevant person determination, under s.161 relating to a contact direction varied or removed by a hearing under s.126, or under s.162 against a decision to implement a secure accommodation authorisation. Nor is suspension of an interim compulsory supervision order, an interim variation of a compulsory supervision order, a warrant to secure attendance or a medical examination order possible. It was held under the 1995 Act that it was not competent to suspend a condition in a supervision requirement without also suspending the requirement itself,[116] for the suspension of a condition would amount to a variation of the supervision requirement which was not possible under s.55(9) of the 1995 Act. This is unlikely to remain the case under the 2011 Act, for while the 1995 Act talked about "suspension of the requirement appealed against", the 2011 Act talks of the children's hearing considering whether its "decision should be suspended pending the determination of the appeal". Given that it is the hearing's decision that is appealed against (and the decision that may now be suspended) rather than the order that is imposed, the effect of a decision to vary a compulsory supervision order may be suspended leaving the original terms of the order in force. If this is so then there is no reason why a term of an order made (as opposed to varied) by a hearing might not also be suspended without suspending the order itself. "Decision" includes parts thereof, such as which measures to attach to a compulsory supervision order that the hearing decides to make.

There is no indication as to what criteria the children's hearing should use to **14–33** determine requests to suspend a decision (which are very uncommon in practice), but the question is clearly one governed by the welfare of the child as the paramount consideration,[117] or at least a primary consideration.[118] The child, relevant person and any appointed safeguarder present at the hearing must be invited to make such representations as they wish to make.[119] The hearing must also, so far as practicable and taking account of the age and maturity of the child, give the child the opportunity to indicate whether he or she wishes to express views, if the child does wish to express views give him or her the opportunity to do so, and have regard to these views.[120] Suspension will not be appropriate when the children's hearing is of the view that the child is in need of immediate protection, guidance, treatment or control because, for example, he or she is likely to continue to face the risks that founded the section 67 ground; it might, on the other hand, be in the interests of the child to suspend the operation of the compulsory supervision order pending an appeal when little or no work can in fact be done with the child in the interim (e.g. when there is no place yet available at a day care unit, or group work, or other resource which has been identified as appropriate for the child) or when, in the light of further information, the hearing believes that an appeal is likely to be successful.[121] It is difficult to imagine a situation in which suspension of a decision to continue a

---

[116] *S v Proudfoot*, 2002 S.L.T. 743.

[117] 2011 Act s.25.

[118] 2011 Act s.26. It is very difficult to envisage circumstances in which suspension of a compulsory supervision order would be necessary to protect members of the public, though suspension of a provision freeing the child from an earlier restriction might be so.

[119] 2013 Rules r.76(4).

[120] 2011 Act s.27.

[121] The hearing arranged under s.158 to consider suspension has no power to review the compulsory supervision order itself.

compulsory supervision order without variation will be appropriate, especially if it involves a continuing plan of work with the child. Suspension is rather more likely to be appropriate when the child was not subject to a compulsory supervision order before the hearing or when the measures included in the existing order are being radically changed, or the order itself is being terminated while the person seeking suspension believes it is continuing to do some good.

14–34　At the conclusion of the discussion, each member of the children's hearing must state his or her decision and its reasons, and the chairing member must confirm the overall decision of the children's hearing and the reasons for that decision.[122] The decision on suspension is itself not appealable, nor it would seem is it open to judicial review.[123]

14–35　Suspension lasts until the appeal has been determined by the sheriff. The compulsory supervision order itself cannot last longer than until "the day one year after the day on which the order is made,"[124] which is a different formulation of the same rule in the 1995 Act (under which "no supervision requirement shall remain in force for a period of longer than one year").[125] The 1995 Act formulation suggested that suspension of the supervision requirement interrupted the running of the period of one year (since during suspension it was not "in force") but that implication is entirely absent from the 2011 Act. It may therefore be that suspension no longer interrupts the running of the period of one year before which a review must be held. Likewise, suspension of the decision does not interrupt the running of the three-month period after which the child or relevant person can require a review.[126]

OTHER APPEALS TO THE SHERIFF

14–36　Other than the decisions listed in s.154(3) which are appealable under the rules contained in ss.154–159, there are three other determinations or decisions against which an appeal may be had to the sheriff, each subject to its own special rules.

Appeals against relevant person determination

14–37　An appeal may be made to the sheriff against a determination of a pre-hearing panel or a children's hearing that an individual either is or is not to be deemed under s.81 to be a relevant person in relation to a child[127]; likewise an appeal may be made against a determination (either way) of a children's hearing at a review under s.142 of the relevant person status of a person deemed to be a relevant person.[128] Title to appeal is limited to the individual in question (that is to say the

---

[122] 2013 Rules r.76(5) and (6). As always, the decision may be made by a majority of the hearing: 2011 Act s.202(2).

[123] See *S v Proudfoot*, 2002 S.L.T. 743.

[124] 2011 Act s.83(7)(a)(i).

[125] Children (Scotland) Act 1995 s.73(2).

[126] 2011 Act s.132(4) provides that the order must not be reviewed during the period of three months beginning with the day on which it was made, continued or varied. There is no suggestion here that the requirement be in force for three months before a review can be called for.

[127] On such determinations see above, paras 5–10—5–19. An early example of an appeal against a pre-hearing panel's determination is *G & T, Appellants* Unreported August 28, 2013 Sheriff Court at Kirkcaldy.

[128] 2011 Act s.160(1).

person being deemed or not being deemed to be a relevant person), the child, a relevant person (defined or deemed), or two or more of these persons acting jointly.[129] A safeguarder has no title to appeal against a relevant person determination. If satisfied that the determination being appealed against is justified the sheriff must confirm the determination[130]: as always the question is not whether the sheriff agrees with the assessment made by the children's hearing but whether that assessment (of whether or not the individual has a significant involvement in the upbringing of the child)[131] can be justified or not. If the sheriff is not satisfied that the determination of the children's hearing or pre-hearing panel is justified he must, if the determination was that the relevant person test was satisfied, quash that determination[132]: this will have the effect of removing any relevant person status that the determination had granted. If the determination being appealed against was to the effect that the individual should not be deemed to be a relevant person because the test is not satisfied, but the sheriff is not satisfied that that determination is justified, he must quash the determination and make an order deeming that individual to be a relevant person.[133] Thereafter the individual will be treated as a relevant person for all the purposes listed in s.81(4).[134] An appeal against a relevant person determination must be made before the expiry of the period of seven days beginning with the day on which the determination is made, and it must be heard and disposed of by the sheriff before the expiry of the period of three days beginning with the day on which the appeal is made.[135] There is no express requirement that the appeal not be heard in open court[136] but it is to be expected that the same procedure in chambers will be followed.

Appeals against decisions affecting contact or permanence orders

A children's hearing that makes, continues or varies a compulsory supervision order, or makes an interim compulsory supervision order, an interim variation of a compulsory supervision order or a medical examination order which is to have effect for more than five working days,[137] may include in that order a contact direction.[138] If so, and there is in force at the same time a contact order made under s.11(2)(d) of the Children (Scotland) Act 1995 or a permanence order made under the Adoption and Children (Scotland) Act 2007 specifying

14–38

---

[129] 2011 Act s.160(2).

[130] 2011 Act s.160(3). See *G & T, Appellants* Unreported August 28, 2013 Sheriff Court at Kirkcaldy.

[131] 2011 Act s.81(3).

[132] 2011 Act s.160(4)(a).

[133] 2011 Act s.160(4)(a) and (b).

[134] 2011 Act s.160(5).

[135] 2011 Act s.160(6). It is to be noted that the three day period within which the appeal must be dealt with commences on the day on which the appeal is made: this may be compared with s.157(2) where the three day period within which appeals against certain decisions must be dealt with commences on the day *after* the day on which the appeal is made. So sheriffs have one day less to dispose of appeals under s.160 than they have in relation to (some) appeals under s.154. An appeal lodged on a Friday under s.160 needs to be disposed on by the Sunday immediately following, while an appeal governed by s.157 (say, against the making of an interim compulsory supervision order) needs to be disposed of by the Monday immediately following. Sheriff McCulloch in *G & T, Appellants* Unreported August 28, 2013 Sheriff Court at Kirkcaldy, at [10] talked of "the almost impossible timescale allowed to me in this case".

[136] cf. s.155(3) in relation to ordinary appeals and s.162(6) in relation to appeals in relation to the implementation of secure accommodation authorisations.

[137] "Working days" being defined in 2011 Act s.202.

[138] 2011 Act ss.83(2)(g) and 87(2)(e). See above, paras 11–23—11–27.

arrangements between an individual (other than a relevant person) and the child, then the reporter must arrange for the hearing's order to be reviewed no later than five working days after the order was made, continued or varied.[139] That review hearing may either confirm the original hearing's decision, or vary it (though only to the extent of varying or removing the contact direction).[140] The child, relevant person or safeguarder may appeal against either the original decision or its variation at the s.126 review,[141] but the s.11 order or permanence order may regulate contact between the child and some person other than a relevant person. Since that person's civil rights, as embodied in the court order, may be affected by the decision of the children's hearing[142] it is necessary that that person is also able to appeal against such a decision and the right to do so is provided for in s.161. This appeal is not against the original decision but against the limited decision on contact made by the hearing reviewing that single issue under s.126. Title to appeal under s.161 against a decision made under s.126(6) rests solely with any person (other than a relevant person) in relation to whom a contact or permanence order is in force or who has significant involvement in the upbringing of the child.[143] If the sheriff is satisfied that the hearing's decision on review of the contact direction is justified then he must confirm that decision.[144] If not so satisfied he must vary the compulsory supervision order, though only by varying or removing the contact direction[145]: the sheriff has no power, in an appeal under s.161, to take any of the steps listed in s.156(3) available to him in appeals under s.154. This emphasises that this whole process is restricted to the issue of contact and does not open up the general issue of whether the compulsory supervision order was necessary and, if so, on what terms. An appeal under s.161 must be made before the expiry of the period of 21 days beginning with the day on which the decision was made, and it must be heard and disposed of before the expiry of the period of three days beginning with the day on which[146] the appeal is made.[147] Again, there is no express requirement that the appeal not be heard in open court[148] but it is to be expected that the same

---

[139] 2011 Act s.126.

[140] 2011 Act s.126(6). For full details see above, paras 13–41—13–44.

[141] 2011 Act s.154(2) and (3)(a). Though s.161 allows no-one other than the individual to appeal a decision of a s.126 hearing, this should be interpreted as being in addition to, as opposed to instead of, those who have a right to appeal under s.154 against a decision to continue or vary the order. Otherwise a child, happy with the original hearing's decision (say) to prohibit contact and unhappy with the s.126 hearing's removal of that prohibition would—for no sound reason—be unable to challenge the latter decision.

[142] It being remembered that in case of a clash of terms between a court order and a compulsory supervision order it is the latter that prevails: Children (Scotland) Act 1995 s.3(4); *Aitken v Aitken*, 1978 S.C. 297; *P v P*, 2000 S.L.T. 781.

[143] 2011 Act s.161(2); Children's Hearings (Scotland) Act 2011 (Review of Contact Directions and Definition of Relevant Person) Order 2013 (SSI 2013/193) art.2(2).

[144] 2011 Act s.161(4).

[145] 2011 Act s.161(5).

[146] Again, cf. 2011 Act s.157(2) which talks of the period commencing the day *after* the day on which the appeal is made. An appeal under s.161 lodged on a Friday needs to be disposed on by the Sunday immediately following, while an appeal governed by s.157 needs to be disposed of by the Monday immediately following.

[147] 2011 Act s.161(6). Oddly, an appeal (say, by a relevant person) against a decision of a s.126 hearing taken under s.154 is *not* subject to the requirement to be disposed of within three days.

[148] cf. s.155(3) in relation to ordinary appeals and s.162(6) in relation to appeals in relation to the implementation of secure accommodation authorisations.

procedure in chambers will be followed. The rules relating to frivolous and vexatious appeals[149] apply to appeals under s.161 as well as those under s.154.[150]

Appeals against decision to implement or not to implement secure accommodation authorisation

A compulsory supervision order, an interim compulsory supervision order, a **14–39** medical examination order and a warrant to secure attendance may all contain a secure accommodation authorisation, that is to say an authorisation made by the children's hearing or by a sheriff enabling the child to be placed and kept in secure accommodation within a residential establishment.[151] The making of any of these orders with a secure accommodation authorisation is itself open to appeal by the normal process under s.154,[152] considered above. However, the authorisation itself does not amount to a requirement that the child be placed in secure accommodation[153]: rather, it simply allows the chief social work officer of the relevant local authority to give effect to it, though he or she requires the consent of the person in charge of the residential establishment containing the secure accommodation.[154] The decision of the chief social work officer to implement the secure accommodation authorisation, or not to implement the authorisation, or to remove the child from secure accommodation after the child has been placed there, is, since the coming into force of the 2011 Act, open to appeal by the child or relevant person (acting alone or jointly) under s.162.[155] Such an appeal must be made before the expiry of 21 days beginning with the day on which the decision appealed against is made and then heard and disposed of before the expiry of the period of three days beginning with the day on which the appeal is made.[156] The appeal must not be heard in open court.[157] The sheriff may hear evidence from the child, relevant person, the chief social work officer, the person in charge of the named residential establishment containing the secure accommodation, the reporter and any other person whom the sheriff considers may give material evidence.[158] In addition, the sheriff may require any person to give a report to the sheriff for the purpose of assisting him in determining the appeal.[159]

Where the decision being appealed against was to implement the secure **14–40** accommodation authorisation and the sheriff is satisfied that the decision is justified, the sheriff must confirm the decision; if not so satisfied the sheriff may[160]

---

[149] Above, paras 14–28—14–29.

[150] 2011 Act s.159, as amended by the Children's Hearings (Scotland) Act 2011 (Modification of Primary Legislation) Order 2013 (SSI 2013/211) Sch.1 para.20(16).

[151] 2011 Act s.85.

[152] Other than that the decision to make a compulsory supervision order with a secure accommodation authorisation must be appealed within the very much shorter time-frame specified in 2011 Act s.157.

[153] See further, above paras 11–10—11–11.

[154] 2011 Act s.151(3).

[155] 2011 Act s.162(3).

[156] Children's Hearings (Scotland) Act 2011 (Implementation of Secure Accommodation Authorisation) (Scotland) Regulations 2013 (SSI 2013/212) reg.11(2).

[157] 2011 Act s.162(6).

[158] Children's Hearings (Scotland) Act 2011 (Implementation of Secure Accommodation Authorisation) (Scotland) Regulations 2013 reg.11(4) and (6).

[159] Children's Hearings (Scotland) Act 2011 (Implementation of Secure Accommodation Authorisation) (Scotland) Regulations 2013 reg.11(5).

[160] The sheriff must do one or other, or both, but not neither.

direct the chief social work officer to remove the child from secure accommodation and/or require the reporter to arrange a children's hearing.[161] Where the decision being appealed against was not to implement the secure accommodation authorisation and the sheriff is satisfied that the decision is justified, the sheriff must confirm the decision and may require the reporter to arrange a children's hearing; if not so satisfied the sheriff may[162] direct the chief social work officer to place the child in secure accommodation and/or require the reporter to arrange a children's hearing.[163] If the decision being appealed against is to remove the child from secure accommodation and the sheriff is satisfied that the decision is justified, the sheriff must confirm the decision and may require the reporter to arrange a children's hearing; if not so satisfied the sheriff may[164] direct the chief social work officer to place the child in secure accommodation and vary the order or warrant that is in effect to include a secure accommodation authorisation and/ or require the reporter to arrange a children's hearing.[165]

14–41   No appeal to the sheriff principal or Court of Session is provided for under either the Children's Hearings (Scotland) Act 2011 or the associated regulations from the sheriff's decision in an appeal under s.162.[166]

APPEALS FROM THE SHERIFF

Appealable decisions

14–42   Appeals can be taken from the following decisions of the sheriff:

(i) a determination of an application to determine whether a section 67 ground is established;[167]

(ii) a determination of an application for a review of a grounds determination;

(iii) a determination of an appeal against a decision of a children's hearing;

(iv) a determination of an application to the sheriff for an extension, or a further extension, of an interim compulsory supervision order;

(v) a decision of the sheriff to make an interim compulsory supervision order or an interim variation of a compulsory supervision order.[168]

No appeal lies under the 2011 Act from any decision that the sheriff makes under the Act, other than those listed either here or elsewhere in Part 15. So

---

[161] Children's Hearings (Scotland) Act 2011 (Implementation of Secure Accommodation Authorisation) (Scotland) Regulations 2013 reg.12.

[162] The sheriff must do one or other, or both, but not neither.

[163] Children's Hearings (Scotland) Act 2011 (Implementation of Secure Accommodation Authorisation) (Scotland) Regulations 2013 reg.13.

[164] The sheriff must do one or other, or both, but not neither.

[165] Children's Hearings (Scotland) Act 2011 (Implementation of Secure Accommodation Authorisation) (Scotland) Regulations 2013 reg.14.

[166] This involves no incompatibility with the European Convention, for the right to appeal against the implementation of a secure accommodation authorisation is a new procedure added into the system by the 2011 Act, additional to the pre-existing appeal mechanisms which were in themselves held to be Convention-compliant in *BJ v Proudfoot*, 2011 S.C. 201.

[167] Other than when, acting as a criminal court, a sheriff has determined that the 2011 Act s.67(2)(j) ground that the child has committed an offence applies and he has remitted the case to the hearing for disposal: s.163(1)(a)(i).

[168] 2011 Act s.163(1).

there is no appeal under the Act, for example, against the sheriff's order made under s.159 that no further appeal may be made without leave by a frivolous or vexatious appellant for the following 12 months. Nor is there an appeal under the Act against the decision of a sheriff under s.109(6) to grant a warrant to secure attendance, or indeed a decision of the sheriff in an appeal under s.154(3)(g) against the granting of such a warrant by a children's hearing. It may, however, be that some of these decisions are open to judicial review.[169] Decisions of the sheriff on the special appeals relating to deemed relevant person status and to contact and permanence orders[170] are themselves appealable under separate provisions,[171] but a decision of the sheriff on appeal against the implementation by the chief social work officer of the relevant local authority of a secure accommodation authorisation is not further appealable to the sheriff principal or the Court of Session.

Title

Title to appeal under s.163 from any of the decisions of the sheriff listed in **14–43** s.163(1) inheres in the child, the relevant person or two or more of them acting jointly.[172] The reporter may appeal against these decisions, except that he or she may not appeal against a determination of the sheriff confirming a decision of a children's hearing.[173] A safeguarder, whether appointed by the children's hearing or by the sheriff,[174] and acting alone or jointly with the child or a relevant person, has title to appeal from a decision of the sheriff in an appeal against a decision of a children's hearing, or a sheriff's determination of an application for an extension or further extension of an interim compulsory supervision order: explicitly, a safeguarder may not appeal against the sheriff's decision in a grounds determination (or review of grounds determination) or the sheriff's decision to make an interim compulsory supervision order or an interim variation of a compulsory supervision order.[175]

The court appealed to

The appeal can be taken either to the sheriff principal of the sheriffdom in **14–44** which the sheriff, from whose determination the appeal is being taken, sits or direct to the Court of Session[176]; and if the appeal is taken to the sheriff principal there is a further appeal, with leave, from his decision to the Court of Session.[177] It is a matter for the appellant to decide which court to appeal to. It is to be expected that appeals will be taken direct to the Court of Session when the point of law is

---

[169] cf. *S v Proudfoot*, 2002 S.L.T. 743 (where, in the event, judicial review was not available to the decision at issue). If judicial review is possible, this would bring the case to the Outer House, and thereafter provide one of the very few routes for a children's hearing case to go ultimately to the Supreme Court.

[170] Which are governed by their own rules, discussed above, paras 14–37—14–38.

[171] ss.164 and 165, discussed below, paras 14–49—14–51.

[172] 2011 Act s.163(3).

[173] 2011 Act s.163(3) and (5).

[174] 2011 Act s.163(3)(c) lists only safeguarders appointed under s.30, which refers to appointments by children's hearings, but s.31(4) provides that safeguarders appointed by a sheriff are to be treated for the purposes of the Act as having been appointed under s.30.

[175] 2011 Act s.163(4).

[176] 2011 Act s.163(1).

[177] 2011 Act s.163(2). Leave to appeal ought to be sought at the same time as the application to state a case, in order to avoid delays and risk running out of time: *M v Irvine*, 2006 Fam.L.R. 36.

particularly difficult or contentious, or raises an important matter of principle or statutory interpretation. Leave is not required to appeal from the sheriff to the sheriff principal nor direct from the sheriff to the Court of Session, but if an appeal has already been taken from the sheriff to the sheriff principal a further appeal to the Court of Session will require the leave of the sheriff principal. No statutory guidance is given to the sheriff principal as to the circumstances in which it would be appropriate to grant or to withhold leave to appeal, but the aim of the requirement for leave is to ensure that appeal to the sheriff principal is not used simply as a delaying tactic. Leave ought to be refused, it is submitted, when an appeal to the sheriff principal has failed and it is his view that the ground of appeal put forward was not arguable. Leave ought to be granted without hesitation if appeal to the Court of Session is necessary to resolve a difference which has arisen between sheriffs principal[178]; and, it is submitted, in the generality of cases unless there is good reason to deny leave it should be granted. The system has benefited immensely over the years by the clarifications provided by the Court of Session in appeal cases. The decision of the Court of Session on any appeal under this provision is final[179] and so there is no further appeal to the Supreme Court.[180]

Grounds of appeal

14–45 The appeal from the sheriff may be taken either on a point of law or in respect of any procedural irregularity.[181] A point of law might, for example, concern the sheriff's interpretation of one of the section 67 grounds,[182] or his failure to take account of the whole facts of the case,[183] or his interpretation of when he could grant or recall a warrant,[184] or his adopting the wrong standard of proof,[185] or his misapplying the rules of evidence,[186] or his paying insufficient regard to, or misapplying, ECHR jurisprudence,[187] for example in interpreting the definition of "relevant person".[188] Irregularity in the conduct of the children's hearing is a ground of appeal to the sheriff, and the sheriff's decision on whether or not there was any irregularity is appealable; likewise irregularity in the proceedings before the sheriff will give a ground of appeal.[189] Kearney,[190]

---

[178] As in, for example, *K & F, Applicants*, 2002 S.L.T. (Sh Ct) 38.

[179] 2011 Act s.163(11).

[180] Issues relevant to children's hearings may come before the Supreme Court in other proceedings, as in an appeal relating to whether an order under s.11 of the Children (Scotland) Act 1995 can confer "relevant person" status on an individual: *Principal Reporter v K*, 2011 S.L.T. 271 (Sup. Ct.).

[181] 2011 Act s.163(9).

[182] See, for example, *McGregor v L*, 1981 S.L.T. 194; *McGregor v H*, 1983 S.L.T. 626; *B v Harris*, 1990 S.L.T. 208; *D v Kelly*, 1995 S.L.T. 1220; *S v Kennedy*, 1996 S.C.L.R. 34; *M v McClafferty*, 2008 Fam. L.R. 22.

[183] As in *M v McGregor*, 1982 S.L.T. 41 and *Authority Reporter, Edinburgh v RU*, 2008 Fam. L.R. 70.

[184] As in *McGregor v K*, 1982 S.L.T. 293 and *Humphries v S*, 1986 S.L.T. 683.

[185] As in *Harris v F*, 1991 S.L.T. 242.

[186] As in *F v Kennedy (No.1)*, 1993 S.L.T. 1277; *Ferguson v S*, 1993 S.C.L.R. 712; *T v Watson*, 1995 S.L.T. 1062.

[187] *W v Schaffer*, 2001 S.L.T. (Sh Ct) 86.

[188] As in *Knox v S*, 2010 S.C. 531. See also *M v Irvine*, 2005 Fam. L.R. 113, where the sheriff was overruled without reliance on the ECHR for misinterpreting the definition in the 1995 Act of "relevant person".

[189] As in *H v Mearns*, 1974 S.L.T. 184 when the statutory timetable for applications for (what is now called) a grounds determination was not followed.

[190] *Children's Hearings and the Sheriff Court*, 2nd edn (Butterworths, 2000), para.49.07.

in a passage approved by the Inner House,[191] said this: "for an appeal based on such grounds to succeed, however, it would seem that the defect must be 'material' in the sense of causing real prejudice to the person affected by the irregularity or, presumably, to the interests of the child". Such an irregularity may, for example, be when the sheriff refuses to hear one or other of the parties to an appeal,[192] or wrongly excludes a relevant person from the hearing of a s.68 application,[193] or has purported to make a disposal which is not open to him or has given directions he is not permitted to give,[194] or has heard an appeal from parties with no title to appeal,[195] or has given inadequate reasons for his decision.[196] The irregularity may lie in the actions of the reporter rather than the sheriff.[197] It is not for the appeal court to conduct a rehearing or reconsideration of the decision taken by the sheriff.[198]

Procedure

An appeal from a decision of the sheriff or the sheriff principal is by way of **14–46** stated case[199] and the application to state a case must be made before the expiry of the period of 28 days beginning with the day on which the determination or decision appealed against was made,[200] otherwise the right of appeal is lost.[201] Within 21 days of the lodging of a note of appeal against a decision of the sheriff, the sheriff must issue a draft stated case.[202] Within seven days of issuing the draft stated case the appellant or any party to whom intimation has been made[203] may lodge with the sheriff clerk a note of any adjustments which he or she seeks to make and may state any point of law or procedural irregularity which he or she wishes to raise in the appeal; a note of such adjustment or point of law or procedural irregularity must be intimated to the appellant and the other parties.[204] The sheriff may allow a hearing on adjustments of the stated case, and must do so where he proposes to reject any proposed adjustments.[205] Within 14 days after the latest date on which a note of adjustments has been or may be lodged, or after the hearing on adjustments, the sheriff must, after considering such note and any representations made to him at the hearing, state and sign the case.[206] The stated

---

[191] *C v Miller*, 2003 S.L.T. 1379 at [71].

[192] As in *Authority Reporter, Edinburgh v RU*, 2008 Fam. L.R. 70, where Sheriff Principal Bowen pointed out that the right to be heard, protected by art.6 of the ECHR, was absolute and its breach would always give ground to appeal, even when no real prejudice followed.

[193] As in *C v Kennedy*, 1991 S.L.T. 755 and *S v N*, 2002 S.L.T. 589.

[194] As in *Kennedy v A*, 1986 S.L.T. 358.

[195] As in *Kennedy v H*, 1988 S.L.T. 586.

[196] *C v Miller*, 2003 S.L.T. 1379 at [71].

[197] *C v Miller*, 2003 S.L.T. 1379.

[198] *W v Schaffer*, 2001 S.L.T. (Sh Ct) 86.

[199] 2011 Act s.163(1) and Child Care and Maintenance Rules 1997 r.3.59(A1).

[200] 2011 Act s.163(8). So a decision made on Thursday 1st July may be appealed on or before Wednesday 28th July.

[201] As in *M v Irvine*, 2006 Fam. L.R. 36.

[202] Child Care and Maintenance Rules 1997 r.3.59(3).

[203] In terms of Child Care and Maintenance Rules 1997 r.3.59(2) (as amended by Act of Sederunt (Children's Hearings (Scotland) Act 2011) (Miscellaneous Amendments) 2013, art.3 para.50(c)).

[204] Child Care and Maintenance Rules 1997 r.3.59(4), the parties being the reporter, the child (if not the appellant), any relevant person (if not the appellant), any safeguarder and any other party to the proceedings: r.3.59(2).

[205] Child Care and Maintenance Rules 1997 r.3.59(5).

[206] Child Care and Maintenance Rules 1997 r.3.59(6).

case must include, as the case may be, (a) questions of law, framed by the sheriff, arising from the points of law stated by the parties and such other questions of law as he may consider appropriate, (b) any proposed adjustments which were rejected by him, and (c) a note of the procedural irregularity averred by the parties and any questions of law or other issues which he considers arise therefrom.[207] The procedure on appeals must be followed strictly in accordance with these rules.[208]

14–47   No new evidence can be placed before the appeal court, since that would not bear upon any irregularity in the conduct of the case or assist the court in determining a point of law.[209] An appeal under s.163 cannot involve a general review of the decisions of fact made by the sheriff: the only matters of fact that can properly be raised are those associated with the alleged error of law or procedural irregularity.[210] There is no provision similar to that contained in s.158 under which the appellant can apply to have the decision that is the subject of the appeal suspended pending the outcome of the appeal.[211] However, if an appeal from an order made by the sheriff is lodged, the order itself does not need to be complied with: so if the sheriff remits the case back to a children's hearing for a review of the compulsory supervision order under s.156(3) (a) the reporter is not obliged to arrange a children's hearing if the sheriff's decision is being appealed against[212]; likewise if the sheriff discharges the child from any further hearing or other proceedings under s.156(3)(c) the child remains subject to an extant compulsory supervision order while the appeal from the sheriff is pending[213] (and that order must be reviewed and continued at the appropriate point before the appeal has been heard if it is not to lapse a year after its making or last continuation).[214] It would also follow from these authorities that if the sheriff varies the order under s.156(3)(b) and that disposal is appealed against, it is the original terms of the compulsory supervision order made or continued by the children's hearing rather than the terms substituted by the sheriff that should be complied with until the appeal from the sheriff has been disposed of.

14–48   Once the appeal has been decided, the sheriff principal or the Court of Session must remit the case back to the sheriff for disposal in accordance with such directions as the court may give.[215] The breadth of this provision allows the court on appeal from the sheriff to go further than the sheriff on appeal from the hearing could go, for a sheriff cannot give the hearing directions as to

---

[207] Child Care and Maintenance Rules 1997 r.3.59(7).

[208] *Kennedy v A*, 1986 S.L.T. 358 at 361A and *Sloan v B*, 1991 S.L.T. 530 at 544J–L.

[209] *Stirling v R*, 1996 S.C.L.R. 191 (Notes).

[210] *C v Miller*, 2003 S.L.T. 1379 at [79].

[211] See above, paras 14–30—14–35. A suspension lapses on the sheriff's decision and cannot continue even after an appeal from the sheriff's decision has been lodged.

[212] *Kennedy v M*, 1995 S.L.T. 717.

[213] *Stirling v D*, 1995 S.L.T. 1089. It was also stated in this case that a consequence of this rule is that such a discharge is inoperative in all cases until the time for appeals has passed, otherwise the right to appeal would be negated.

[214] *Stirling v D*, 1995 S.L.T. 1089. As the commentator to this case points out, the delays in hearing appeals may mean that a child remains subject to a compulsory supervision order for many months after the sheriff has discharged the referral. See, in another context, *Lessani v Lessani*, 2007 Fam. L.R. 81.

[215] 2011 Act s.163(10). This applies only to appeals made under s.163(1), that is to say from the sheriff to the sheriff principal or Court of Session and it does not apply to appeals made under s.163(2), that is to say from the sheriff principal to the Court of Session.

how to dispose of the case: the sheriff principal or the Court of Session may, however, so direct the sheriff.

Appeals with special rules

Just as certain appeals to the sheriff are governed by their own special rules, **14–49** separate from the generality of appeals, so too are certain appeals from the sheriff to the sheriff principal or Court of Session.

First, an appeal from a decision of a sheriff in an appeal against the determi- **14–50** nation of a pre-hearing panel or a children's hearing that an individual is or is not to be deemed to be a relevant person in relation to the child is governed by s.164 instead of the general rules in s.163. An appeal may be taken by the individual in question, the child, a relevant person in relation to the child, or two or more of these persons acting jointly, to either the sheriff principal or the Court of Session and, if appeal is taken to the sheriff principal, a further appeal is permitted, with leave of the sheriff principal, to the Court of Session.[216] Secondly, appeals to the sheriff principal and Court of Session against the decision of a sheriff in an appeal under s.161 relating to contact and permanence orders are governed by s.165 instead of the general rules in s.163. An appeal to the sheriff principal or the Court of Session and, with leave of the sheriff principal, an appeal from the sheriff principal to the Court of Session may be taken by the individual who had title to appeal to the sheriff in the first place[217] (that is to say a person other than a relevant person whose civil rights may be affected by the decision).[218] The child, relevant person, or safeguarder has no right to appeal under this provision but may do so under s.163(1)(a)(iii): the rule in s.165 under consideration here is expansive of the categories of those with title to appeal and is not restrictive.

In both types of appeal, the appeal must be made before the expiry of the **14–51** period of 28 days beginning with the day on which the decision appealed against is made[219] and it may be made on a point of law or in respect of any procedural irregularity.[220] On deciding the appeal the sheriff principal or the Court of Session must remit the case to the sheriff for disposal in accordance with such directions as the court may give.[221] The decision of the Court of Session in either type of appeal is final and there is no further appeal to the Supreme Court.[222]

---

[216] 2011 Act s.164(1)–(3).

[217] See above, para.14–38.

[218] 2011 Act s.165(1)–(3).

[219] 2011 Act s.164(4) and s.165(4). So a decision made on Wednesday 1st May must be made on or before Tuesday 28th May.

[220] 2011 Act s.164(5) and s.165(5).

[221] 2011 Act s.164(6) and s.165(6). This rule applies only to the initial appeal from the decision of the sheriff and does not apply when a decision of the sheriff principal is appealed to the Court of Session.

[222] 2011 Act s.164(7) and s.165(7).

CHAPTER FIFTEEN

EMERGENCY PROTECTION OF CHILDREN

INTRODUCTION

15–01 It sometimes happens that a child's circumstances give rise to the belief that protective measures need to be taken immediately, without the delay necessarily inherent in a referral to the reporter and the arranging of a children's hearing.[1] This might arise, for example, if social workers or teachers or health care workers notice apparently non-accidental physical injuries on a child, or if the child's home is discovered to be in a grossly unhygienic state, or if the child discloses continuing sexual abuse. Prior to the coming into force of the Children (Scotland) Act 1995, emergency protective measures which could not wait until a children's hearing was convened took the form of a place of safety order, granted by a court or justice of the peace under s.37 of the Social Work (Scotland) Act 1968, which authorised the removal of a child to a place of safety. Though the rules in that section were straightforward, there were a number of criticisms that could be, and were, made of the operation of the provision, in particular that there was no means by which the granting of the order could be challenged before the matter came into the hands of the children's hearing: the system made no provision for the family who were willing to attend a children's hearing (perhaps confident that they would be able to rebut any allegations made) but who wanted their child back home in the meantime. The system of emergency protection came under the spotlight during the public inquiry that followed the Orkney case, and the publication of the Clyde Report.[2] The whole system of emergency protection of children was redesigned as a result of that Report and the place of safety order under the 1968 Act was replaced by the child protection order under the Children (Scotland) Act 1995. The rules in the 1995 Act were in turn replaced, with some significant changes, by ss.37–56 of the Children's Hearings (Scotland) Act 2011, which contain the current law on the granting and the effect of a child protection order (hereinafter CPO). The provisions are fairly complicated and the time-scale short in which the CPO is granted, reviewed and terminated. The procedure relating to child protection orders is separate from the children's hearing system, though it will usually lead into that system. The order itself can last only for a maximum of eight working days, and there will always

---

[1] The reporter has various investigative and preparatory functions to carry out before arranging a children's hearing and, generally speaking, once arranged, the hearing members require at least three days' notice. See Children's Hearings (Scotland) Act 2011 (Rules of Procedure in Children's Hearings) Rules 2013 (SSI 2013/194) (hereinafter "2013 Rules") Pts 7–12.

[2] *Report of the Inquiry into the Removal of Children From Orkney in February 1991* (HC Papers 1992–1993, No.195).

be one, and sometimes two, reviews to determine whether it is or was necessary to remove the child and whether it remains necessary to keep the child
away from home.

THE GROUNDS FOR GRANTING A CPO

A CPO can be applied for under one of two separate sections, and the application **15–02**
must, of course, specify which of these sections is being founded upon.

Section 39: reasonable grounds for believing harm

An application for a CPO may be made under s.39 by a local authority or **15–03**
any other person, such as a reporter, a parent, a constable, or even the child him
or herself, and the sheriff may make the order if satisfied:

    (a) that there are reasonable grounds to believe that the child[3]—
        (i)   has been or is being so treated in such a way that he or she is
            suffering or is likely to suffer significant harm; or
        (ii) has been or is being neglected and as a result of the neglect the
            child is suffering or is likely to suffer significant harm, or
        (iii) is likely to suffer significant harm if the child is not removed to
            and kept in a place of safety, or
        (iv) is likely to suffer signficant harm if the child does not remain in
            the place at which the child is staying (whether or not the child
            is resident there), and
    (b) the order is necessary to protect the child from that harm or from
        further harm.

Both paragraphs must be fulfilled. Under paragraph (a)(i) and (ii) the sheriff
must be satisfied that there is evidence sufficient to ground a reasonable belief
that the child has been, is being or is likely to be treated in the specified manner
or neglected with the specified result. These subparagraphs primarily concern
the way that some other person is presently acting or failing to act towards the
child and it covers, for example, the child who is being assaulted or who is not
being fed or washed. "Has been or is being treated" suggests a state of affairs
brought about by someone other than the child and it does not cover significant
harm caused by the child's own acts or omissions. "Is suffering or is likely to
suffer" looks to the child's suffering in the present and in the future, and so a
child who was beaten some time in the past will not be covered by this provision unless the injuries he or she sustained are still being suffered from (or the
past injury suggests a likelihood of future injury). Likelihood of harm in both
subparagraphs is to be tested on the balance of probabilities,[4] and the greater

---

   [3] "Child" does not include an unborn child. There is conflicting authority as to whether the
parents of an unborn child can lodge a caveat for notice of any application by the local authority
which intends to apply for a CPO as soon as the child is born: compare *C, Petitioner*, 2002 Fam.
L.R. 42 with *K & F, Applicants*, 2002 S.L.T. (Sh Ct) 38. See further, *J & H v Lord Advocate* [2013]
CSOH 27. The application may well be made before delivery of the child, but it may not be dealt
with until after the child is born alive.
   [4] *Re B (Children) (Care Proceedings: Standard of Proof)* [2009] 1 A.C. 11; *Wilson, Petr*, 2008
S.L.T. 753.

the likelihood of harm the less it needs to be to be considered significant (and vice versa).[5] Paragraph (a)(iii) and (iv) are capable of covering both significant harm that another person will cause to the child in the future and harm that is being or will be caused by the child him or herself. Harm inflicted upon the child in the past (whether by the child or some other person) may well provide reasonable grounds for believing that harm will be suffered in the future. So a parent who has previously beaten a child will give reasonable grounds for believing that the child"will suffer" harm, if it is reasonable to believe that the beating is likely to be repeated. A parent who has inflicted harm on one child in the past may well give reasonable grounds to believe that he or she will inflict harm on another child in the future, as will (the Supreme Court held on very different statutory wording) a parent who is "likely" to have been the perpetrator of proven harm on the other child.[6] A child may be presently harming him or herself, say, by abusing alcohol or drugs, or by associating with thieves or prostitutes: such actions may well give reasonable ground to believe that the child will suffer significant harm if not removed to a place of safety and kept there, so long as it can be shown that those presently looking after the child are not protecting the child from harm.

15–04   Whichever subparagraph is founded upon, the harm that the child must be suffering or threatened with is "significant" harm, that is to say harm of a not minor, transient or superficial nature. It may be physical or emotional and will include developmental harm.[7] "The categories of harm are never closed."[8] The subjecting of the child to any sexual activity is likely always to be considered significant (though in itself it may not always amount to harm),[9] as is any physical assault consisting of a blow to the head, shaking or the use of an implement.[10] There is, however, no necessary connection between "significant harm" and harm that would lead to a criminal charge against the perpetrator: the latter does not have to be "significant" and the test is not that the child is a victim of an offence. Emotional harm will be significant when it can properly be described as trauma; distress and upset will not usually be sufficient. Harm will always be significant when it is clearly more detrimental than the potential trauma that removal from home will cause almost every child.

15–05   Reasonable grounds to believe harm in these terms is not on its own sufficient, for the applicant must also satisfy the sheriff that the making of a CPO is "necessary" to protect the child from the actual or threatened significant harm.[11] If the harm is not such as to require, in the eyes of the reasonable person, immediate action to protect the child from any continuation of the harm, then the making of the order cannot be said to be necessary. This does

---

[5] *Re B (A Child)* [2013] UKSC 33.

[6] *Re J (Care Proceedings: Past Possible Perpetrators in a New Family Unit)* [2013] UKSC 9; [2013] 1 F.L.R. 1373.

[7] The English Children Act 1989 defines "harm" to mean "ill-treatment or the impairment of health or development": s.31(9). There is no definition of"harm" in the Children's Hearings (Scotland) Act 2011 but interpreting the words "significant harm" in light of the aim of s.39 thereof suggests that developmental impairment is included.

[8] M. Freeman, *Children, their Families and the Law* (Macmillan, 1992), p.93.

[9] For example in the case of a 15-year-old who has been experiencing consensual and non-exploitative sexual activity with another person of around the same age.

[10] These sorts of assault are never "justifiable" as the parental right of chastisement: Criminal Justice (Scotland) Act 2003 s.51(3).

[11] 2011 Act s.39(2)(b).

not mean that the CPO must be shown to be the only possible way in which the child can be protected. Rather the word "necessary" has, it is submitted, a somewhat looser meaning, and this condition is fulfilled when the CPO is shown to be either the only, or the most efficacious, or in the circumstances the most appropriate, means of protecting the child. Necessity must be interpreted in the light of a continuing risk to the child, for the whole point of the order is to give immediate protection to the child from risk. So even when significant harm has been unquestionably caused, a CPO will not be necessary unless there is a likelihood, that is to say a real chance, of the harm continuing or being repeated. A parent may admittedly injure his or her child but suffer genuine remorse and contrition: the question of whether the making of a compulsory supervision order is necessary always arises but if the event is unique and the contrition genuine the making of a CPO before a children's hearing can be arranged to consider that question may well not be "necessary". It will certainly not be necessary if the source of the harm has been removed from the child's home and taken, say, into police custody."Necessity", in this context as in others, also imports the ECHR proportionality test. In *KA v Finland*[12] the European Court of Human Rights held that with emergency orders the proportionality test is satisfied if: (i) there are relevant and sufficient reasons for making the order; and (ii) the parent had the opportunity to participate adequately in the decision making. In *Langley v Liverpool City Council*[13] it was held that there was an infringement of art.8 of the European Convention when emergency provisions had been used to remove children from their home though the circumstances did not show an immediate risk.[14] The more draconian the measure, the greater must be the risk facing the child before the proportionality test is satisfied and this is especially so with new-born babies. In *P, C & S v United Kingdom*[15] the European Court of Human Rights said this: "the taking of a new-born baby into public care at the moment of its birth is an extraordinarily harsh measure. There must be extraordinarily compelling reasons before a baby can be physically removed from its mother, against her will, immediately after birth".

Section 38: frustration of enquiries

A CPO might be sought under s.38 by a local authority but by no-one else, **15–06** and the sheriff may make the order if satisfied:

(a) that the local authority has reasonable grounds to suspect[16] that the child—
    (i) has been or is being treated in such a way that the child is suffering or is likely to suffer significant harm,

---

[12] [2003] 1 F.L.R. 696 at [103]–[104].

[13] [2006] 1 W.L.R. 375.

[14] The children had been removed from their home on the ground that their father, who was registered blind, had continued to insist on driving them to school, but there was no imminent risk to the children from the father's driving at the time the order was implemented.

[15] (2002) 35 E.H.R.R. 31 at [116]; *Haase v Germany* (2005) 40 E.H.R.R. 19 at [91].

[16] On the difference between "grounds to suspect" and "grounds to believe" (as required in 2011 Act s.39) see *Eastenders Cash and Carry Plc v South Western Magistrates' Court* [2011] EWHC 937 (Admin), per Sullivan L.J. at [13].

      (ii) has been or is being neglected and as a result of the neglect the child is suffering or is likely to suffer significant harm, or

      (iii) will be treated or neglected in such a way that is likely to cause significant harm to the child,

  (b) that the local authority is making enquiries to allow it to decide whether to take action to safeguard the welfare of the child, or is causing those enquires to be made,

  (c) those enquiries are being frustrated by access to the child being unreasonably denied, and

  (d) the local authority has reasonable cause to believe that such access is required as a matter of urgency.

The enquiries must be rendered wholly ineffectual in allowing the local authority to determine whether or not its suspicions are justified, because of the denial of access for no good cause, by the person with control over who has contact with the child. Merely hampering or making more difficult these enquiries will not be sufficient. The requirement that the local authority believes access be required "urgently" indicates the purpose for the making of the order under this section, which is to protect evidence that might be used to test the local authority's suspicion.

The sheriff's decision

15–07   Whichever section the application for a CPO is made under, it must identify the applicant, so far as practicable identify the child in respect of whom the order is sought, state the grounds on which the application is made, and be accompanied by supporting evidence, whether documentary or otherwise, sufficient to enable the sheriff to determine the application.[17] On receipt of an application for a CPO, the sheriff, having considered the grounds for the application, the supporting evidence and, within reason,[18] any interested party, must forthwith grant or refuse it.[19] He cannot adjourn and give his decision at a later date. The sheriff is not entitled to appoint a safeguarder at this stage in the proceedings in order to assist him or to safeguard the interests of the child, for that would inevitably require an adjournment until a safeguarder could be contacted. Sheriff Kearney[20] describes the process as follows:

> "The hearing before the sheriff is not a 'proof'. The strict rules of evidence do not apply. The sheriff is entitled to have regard to hearsay evidence and will consider the whole *information* which has been presented and draw such inferences as common sense may suggest. The sheriff has to be 'satisfied'."

15–08   Even when the sheriff is satisfied as to the existence of the circumstances set out in either s.38 or s.39, the sheriff retains a discretion and he is not obliged to make the order sought. He is guided in the exercise of that discretion by

---

[17] 2011 Act s.37(5).

[18] See *C, Petitioner*, 2002 Fam. L.R. 42.

[19] Act of Sederunt (Child Care and Maintenance Rules) 1997, as amended by Act of Sederunt (Children's Hearings (Scotland) Act 2011) (Miscellaneous Amendments) 2013 (SSI 2013/172) (hereinafter "Child Care and Maintenance Rules 1997") r.3.31.

[20] *Children's Hearings and the Sheriff Court*, 2nd edn (Butterworths, 2000), para.6.06.

s.25, under which the welfare of the child throughout childhood must be his paramount consideration.[21] This may well indicate that no order should be made if, for example, it appears that the making of an order is likely to do more harm (perhaps psychological) to the child than good. Welfare, as always, is to be given broad scope and is not limited to the immediate circumstances which would otherwise justify the making of a CPO. A CPO can quite conceivably be both necessary to protect a child from significant harm and at the same time be against the welfare of the child. The removal of a child from familiar surroundings might sometimes be so traumatic and cause such distress to the child as to be a greater, psychological, injury than the physical harm it is designed to bring a stop to. Though the requirement to have regard to the views of the child is explicitly excluded when the sheriff is deciding whether to make a child protection order in relation to a child,[22] sheriffs should not ignore the fact that it is common experience for children to express a preference to remain in a highly unsatisfactory home than to be summarily removed to the alien environment most children would regard a residential establishment (or even a foster home) to be, and their opinions, if known, are not to be dismissed lightly on that matter. This is not, of course, to deny that in many cases the child's welfare will indeed require immediate removal of the child from a source of risk even at the cost of serious emotional distress to the child. The sheriff may make, vary, continue or extend a child protection order only if he considers that it would be better for the child if the order were in force than not.[23]

Making a CPO on application for a child assessment order

Instead of applying for a CPO, the local authority may apply for a child **15–09** assessment order, on satisfaction of very similar conditions to those applicable to CPOs. The local authority must have "reasonable cause to suspect" that the conditions apply to justify an application for a child assessment order under s.36, and must have "reasonable grounds to suspect" that the conditions apply to justify an application for a child protection order under s.38. "Cause to suspect" is, if only marginally, a lesser test than "grounds to suspect" but the distinction is subtle and in most cases the establishing of the conditions under s.36 will also establish the conditions under s.38. So the sheriff is given the discretion[24] to make a child protection order where, on an application for a child assessment order in which the local authority seeks to show that it has reasonable cause to suspect significant harm, he is satisfied that the local authority has reasonable grounds to suspect that harm. There is no equivalent power to make a child assessment order when, on an application for a child protection order, the sheriff considers that the conditions for the making of the former order are satisfied (which, invariably, they will be). It is likely that the discretion to make a child protection order on an application for a child assessment order will be

---

[21] He is also guided by s.26, in terms of which he may make a decision that is inconsistent with s.25 if it is necessary to do so for the purpose of protecting members of the public from serious harm: in this case the child's welfare must be regarded as a primary consideration rather than the paramount consideration. It is, however, difficult to envisage circumstances in which, in an application for a CPO, harm to the public would be in issue.

[22] 2011 Act s.27(2).

[23] 2011 Act s.29(1)(b) and (2).

[24] 2011 Act s.36(3).

exercised only very rarely. The assessment order is a lesser interference in family life than a protection order is and, not involving the procedural complexities that a child protection order involves, it better achieves the aim of minimum, or proportionate, intervention. Also, local authorities are the bodies entrusted with the power to decide which process they should activate in order to obtain the information that they need to make child protection decisions, and their decisions ought not to be interfered with by a court unless it is very clear that the more complex order is, in the circumstances and though it has not been sought by the local authority, the more appropriate for the sheriff to grant.

MATTERS AUTHORISED

15–10   Whichever section the application is made under, the effect of the order, if granted, is the same, as are the matters it may authorise and the procedures that its implementation activates. A child protection order may require or authorise one or more of the actions listed in s.37(2), as follows.

The CPO may:

  (a) require any person in a position to do so to produce the child to a specified person,
  (b) authorise the removal of the child by the specified person to a place of safety, and the keeping of the child in that place,
  (c) authorise the prevention of the removal of the child from any place where he or she is staying (whether or not the child is resident there),
  (d) authorise the carrying out[25] of an assessment either of the child's health or development or of the way in which he or she has been or is being treated or neglected.

The CPO may also include any other authorisation or requirement necessary to safeguard or promote the welfare of the child.[26] This significantly widens out the powers that the sheriff has in making a CPO from those he previously had under the Children (Scotland) Act 1995.

15–11   It is likely that most CPOs will authorise the action in either paragraphs (b) or (c) of s.37(2). An order under paragraph (b) authorises the taking of the child by the specified person to a place of safety[27] and the keeping of the child there.[28] The wording of this paragraph, with its reference to removal, suggests that it cannot be used when the child is already in a place of safety, but is to be used only to take a child to a place of safety and keep him or her there. An authorisation of the carrying out of an assessment of the child's health or development (paragraph (d)) may be included only if the order includes an authorisation under paragraph (b) or (c).[29] There is nothing to prevent a requirement

---

[25] Subject to 2011 Act s.186, which preserves the child's capacity to refuse to give consent to any medical or dental procedure or treatment.
[26] 2011 Act s.37(3).
[27] Defined in 2011 Act s.202(1).
[28] If the place of safety is provided by a local authority, that authority will have the same duties towards the child as if the child were looked after by the local authority: s.44. These duties are specified in s.17 of the Children (Scotland) Act 1995.
[29] 2011 Act s.37(4).

under paragraph (a) being made without any other authorisation, and this might be approproiate where the mere production of the child would be sufficient to lay the suspicions of the local authority to rest. But when the local authority is the applicant it will usually be appropriate to include a requirement for a person to produce the child in conjunction with the authorisation under paragraph (b). And if the applicant is some other person than the local authority, such as the parent, the requirement under paragraph (a) may well, in some circumstances, properly stand alone.[30] The order under paragraph (c), preventing the removal of the child from the place where he or she is staying, will cover (but is not limited to) the situation of the child already in a place of safety,[31] but its wording initially suggests that it cannot be used to detain the child there against his or her will: the word "removal" indicates that the order is designed to prevent someone else from taking the child away but does not authorise the prevention of the child leaving a place on his or her own volition. However, paragraph (b) deals only with a child taken to a place of safety and not a child already there and a strict interpretation would mean that a child already in a place of safety could not be protected under that paragraph. The Act must be interpreted in such a way as does not frustrate the intention to protect all children in need of protection and the word "removal" in paragraph (c) should therefore be read to include removal of the child by the child him or herself from the place of safety. Alternatively, this might be achieved by utilising the power in s.37(3) to make any authorisation or requirement that the sheriff considers necessary to safeguard or promote the welfare of the child. In any case the applicant for (or any other person specified in) a CPO may only take such steps to implement the order as the applicant (or other person) reasonably believes are necessary to safeguard or promote the welfare of the child.[32]

Once made, the applicant must, as soon as practicable, give notice of the **15–12** making of the CPO to: (i) the person specified in the order as obliged to produce the child; (ii) the child in respect of whom the order is made; (iii) any relevant person; (iv) the relevant local authority (unless the local authority is the applicant); (v) the Principal Reporter; and (vi) any other person to whom the applicant is required to give notice under rules of court (being such other persons as the sheriff may direct), and serve a copy of the order that has been made on the person specified in the order, the relevant persons, the relevant local authority and the Principal Reporter, as well as such other persons as the sheriff may direct.[33] On receiving this notice, the reporter must give notice of the making of the order to any person (other than a relevant person) who the reporter considers to have (or to recently have had) a significant involvement in the upbringing of the child.[34] This will allow such a person to exercise his or her right, for example, to apply for a variation or termination of the CPO.[35]

---

[30] The CPO procedure might be used by a parent, say, seeking to recover a child from grandparents who are refusing to return the child and who pose some threat to the child. While this might be quicker than a common law action of recovery, it would have the invariable consequence that a children's hearing will require to be held.

[31] Perhaps having been taken there under the provisions of ss.55 and 56 (justice of the peace authorisations and police officer removals: see below, paras 15–41—15–52).

[32] 2011 Act s.58.

[33] 2011 Act s.43(1) and Child Care and Maintenance Rules 1997 r.3.32.

[34] 2011 Act s.43(2).

[35] 2011 Act s.48(1)(c).

ANCILLARY MEASURES ATTACHED TO CPO

15–13 As well as the authorisations and requirements that make up the primary effect of a CPO, the sheriff must also, where he makes a CPO, consider whether to include an information non-disclosure direction,[36] and a contact direction;[37] as well, he may make, but only if sought by the applicant at the same time as the application for a CPO is made, a parental responsibilities and parental rights direction.[38] The decision to include any such ancillary direction is a "decision about a matter relating to a child" and so subject to the welfare principle in s.25.[39] Since the inclusion of an ancillary direction is an essential part of the decision to make a CPO, the requirement to have regard to the views of the child does not apply,[40] but the injunction not to make the order (in this context, not to include the direction) unless the sheriff considers that it would be better for the child than if the direction were not in force does apply.[41] Each of these ancillary provisions will cease to have effect when it is terminated by a children's hearing or a sheriff reviewing the CPO or when the CPO in which it is included itself ceases to have effect.[42]

Information non-disclosure directions

15–14 An information non-dislosure direction, the inclusion of which must be considered whenever the sheriff makes a CPO, is a direction that: (a) the location of any place of safety at which the child is being kept; and (b) any other information specified in the direction relating to the child, must not be disclosed (directly or indirectly) to any person or class of person specified in the direction.[43] The purpose of such a direction is protective and, because it involves withholding information from persons who might otherwise be entitled to receive such information, it should be made by the sheriff only when this is necessary for the protection of the child. Withholding the location of the child will seldom, if ever, interfere with the participation rights of others, but withholding other information may do so and requires, therefore, greater justification in terms of its necessity for the child's protection. The sheriff may include an information non-disclosure direction in a CPO even when not asked to include such a direction.

Contact directions

15–15 A contact direction, the inclusion of which must be considered whenever a sheriff makes a CPO, is a direction: (a) prohibiting contact between the child and a person mentioned below; (b) making contact between the child and such a person subject to any condition which the sheriff considers appropriate to

---

[36] 2011 Act s.40(2).
[37] 2011 Act s.41(2).
[38] 2011 Act s.42.
[39] And its qualification in 2011 Act s.26, though it is difficult to imagine a situation in which either making or not making an information non-disclosure direction will be necessary for the purpose of protecting members of the public from serious harm.
[40] 2011 Act s.27(2).
[41] 2011 Act s.29(1)(b).
[42] 2011 Act ss.40(4), 41(5) and 42(3).
[43] 2011 Act s.40(3).

safeguard and promote the welfare of the child; (c) making such other provision as the sheriff considers appropriate about contact between the child and such a person.[44] The persons whose contact with the child may be prohibited or regulated by a contact direction included in a CPO are: (a) a parent of the child[45]; person with parental responsibilities for the child or other person specified in the direction; or (b) a person falling within a class of person specified in the direction.[46] A contact direction is the means by which the sheriff ensures that appropriate contact is maintained while the child is kept in a place of safety, and the terms of the direction may be as directive as the sheriff considers appropriate taking into account, as always, the welfare of the child. In contradistinction to the previous wording under s.58(1) of the Children (Scotland) Act 1995, there is no test laid down for the sheriff nor requirement that the contact direction be included only when "necessary". The matter lies wholly in the discretion of the sheriff, subject to the provisions, already noted, in ss.25–29 of the 2011 Act. The sheriff may include a contact direction in a CPO even when not asked to include such a direction, but the direction ought not to be given simply because the sheriff wants everything to remain within judicial control. The philosophy here, as in other parts of the Act, is that the court should get involved in directing children's lives only when not to do so would be against the child's interests. It might be appropriate to include a contact direction when, for example, the applicant is minded not to allow contact and the sheriff thinks that contact would be in the child's interests, or when the applicant cannot come to an agreement with a person who is seeking to have contact with the child. When the applicant is the person who will be looking after the child it is good practice for the sheriff to inquire of the applicant what arrangements for contact they would be minded to make in the absence of any direction. It is to be remembered that various people will have a right of contact with the child, which should be prohibited or otherwise regulated by a direction in a CPO only when the proposed arrangements are not, in the sheriff's opinion, satisfactory and the child's interest requires that better arrangements be made.

The direction given by the sheriff may require that contact be permitted **15–16** between the child and another person (or class of person), or may prohibit it, or may subject it to such conditions as the sheriff considers appropriate. So the sheriff may direct that contact always be supervised, or he may direct where it is to take place or how often, or he may direct that any specified person or class of person is not to have any contact at all. Different arrangements can be made for different people so that, for example, it may be required that the mother's contact with the child be supervised at all times and that the father have no contact at all. The sheriff's discretion is wide, and the statute does not require that, having decided that a direction is necessary, the sheriff must prescribe all the terms and conditions under which contact will take place, relating to time,

---

[44] 2011 Act s.41(3).

[45] It may be noted that this is one of the very rare occasions in which the "parent" of a child appears in the Children's Hearings (Scotland) Act 2011. There is no limitation on the term other than that the person must be recognised by the law as the child's "parent", by whatever means, including the presumptions in the Law Reform (Parent and Child) (Scotland) Act 1986 and the rules in the Human Fertilisation and Embryology Act 2008.

[46] 2011 Act s.41(4).

place, frequency, duration and supervision. Such prescription might in some cases be appropriate, and in others not.

Parental responsibilities and parental rights directions

15–17   It is important to note that a CPO does not transfer parental responsibilities and parental rights to the applicant, even for the short period of its operation, and these remain with whomsoever had them before the making of the order.[47] Nevertheless, the applicant can, at the same time as applying for the CPO itself, apply to the sheriff for a parental responsibilities and parental rights direction, which is a direction about how parental responsibilities are to be fulfilled or how parental rights are to be exercised in relation to: (a) the treatment of the child arising out of any assessment authorised by the CPO; or (b) any other matter that the sheriff considers appropriate.[48] The sheriff cannot give any such direction *ex proprio motu*, as he can with a contact direction or an information non-disclosure direction, but must be asked to give it by the applicant "at the same time" as the CPO itself is applied for.[49] (This suggests that an applicant cannot amend the application during its consideration by the sheriff to seek the addition of such a direction.) Usually the applicant will not be a person with parental responsibilities or parental rights and so any direction given will not be directed towards the applicant (as would be the case with a contact direction), but towards the person whose fulfilment or exercise of parental responsibilities or parental rights is to be regulated. The purpose is to provide directions as to how parental responsibilities and parental rights should be carried out. The statute lays down no sanction for failure to follow the directions given, though such a failure could be regarded as contempt of court.

15–18   The applicant may request the sheriff to give any direction in relation to the fulfilment or exercise of any parental responsibilities or parental rights, such as, for example, prohibiting the parent from removing the child to another part of Scotland or furth of the jurisdiction, or directing the parent as to the education that is to be provided to the child. It will not normally be appropriate to deal with matters of long-term significance by means of a parental responsibilities and parental rights direction, unless there is some urgency, such as the need to provide the child with medical treatment. It is explicitly provided that the direction may in particular be in relation to the treatment of the child arising out of any assessment authorised by the CPO[50] and, given the very short-term nature of a CPO, this is likely to prove the most useful form of direction under this section.

---

[47] But see Kearney, *Children's Hearings and the Sheriff Court*, 2nd edn (Butterworths, 2000), para.5.07, who suggests that the order, if combined with directions as to parental responsibilities and parental rights, does indeed effect such a transfer. It is difficult to see how this can be so. A local authority has the same duties towards the child subject to a CPO as if he or she were a"looked after" child under s.17 of the Children (Scotland) Act 1995, whenever the child is removed to a place of safety provided by the local authority (Children's Hearings (Scotland) Act 2011 s.44(2)) and many of the responsibilities this imposes on a local authority will be similar to those held by parents. But even being "looked after" does not in itself transfer the whole gamut of parental responsibilities and parental rights and it would be reading too much into s.42(2) of the 2011 Act to say that a direction applied for by an applicant about how parental responsibilities or parental rights are to be fulfilled or exercised amounts to a transfer, to the applicant, of all parental responsibilities and parental rights.

[48] 2011 Act s.42(1) and(2).

[49] 2011 Act s.42(1).

[50] 2011 Act s.42(2)(a).

"Treatment" is not limited in any way but medical treatment is what is primarily envisaged. It should be noted that the power to include a parental responsibilities and parental rights direction in a CPO does not allow the sheriff to authorise examination, assessment or treatment, nor can he authorise the applicant to carry it out.[51] Rather, the sheriff can simply direct the parent or guardian to exercise their parental responsibilities and parental rights in a particular manner. This may include a direction that the parent, say, provides consent to the child's medical examination, assessment or treatment, but that would be competent only when the parent or guardian retains the right to provide such consent. Such a direction will not, therefore, be competent in relation to many older children, for s.186 of the Children's Hearings (Scotland) Act 2011 preserves the child's capacity to consent or refuse consent under s.2(4) of the Age of Legal Capacity (Scotland) Act 1991, and s.15(5)(b) of the Children (Scotland) Act 1995 ensures that a person with parental responsibilities and parental rights can consent only when the child cannot consent or refuse on his or her own behalf.[52] It follows that a direction as to medical examination, assessment or treatment would be competent only when the child is too young to consent to that examination or treatment him- or herself, for only then does the question of the fulfilment of parental responsibilities or the exercise of parental rights arise.[53]

Review of CPO

A CPO can be made by a sheriff even before the child and his or her parents **15–19** have been given a chance to oppose it, or to attempt to state reasons why the order ought not to be made. Indeed, the first that the parents may know about the making of a CPO could be when an attempt is made to implement it by removing the child from their care. Even when they are given notice of the application being made, the time-scale may not give them sufficient time to prepare any proper arguments against its making.[54] For these reasons the statute requires that, once the CPO is in force, matters must be looked at again very shortly after its making, either by a children's hearing reviewing the order under ss.45 or 46, or by a sheriff determining an application for the variation or termination of the CPO under s.48. A review by a children's hearing must be held on the second working day after the day on which the child was taken to a place of safety or, if the CPO prevents the child's removal from a place of safety, the second working day after the day on which the CPO was made.[55] The application to the sheriff for variation or termination may be made at any time before the commencement of the children's hearing, and if it is made at that point the children's hearing will not be required.[56] In addition, if a chil-

---

[51] For child assessment orders, see 2011 Act ss.35–36.

[52] That the rule in 2011 Act s.15(5) applies to consent to medical treatment is explained in Norrie, *Children (Scotland) Act 1995*, 2nd edn (W. Green, 2004), pp.48–49.

[53] The CPO itself, of course, may authorise the carrying out of an assessment of the child's health or development: 2011 Act s.37(2)(d)(i).

[54] Though if they are in a position to argue their case there is no reason to refuse them the opportunity to do so: *J & H v Lord Advocate* [2013] CSOH 27. Non-participation of parents in the initial application for a CPO is not necessarily a breach of the ECHR: see *KA v Finland* (2003) 1 F.L.R. 696.

[55] 2011 Act ss.45(3) and 46(3).

[56] 2011 Act s.45(1)(c).

dren's hearing has reviewed the CPO and it is continued (with or without variation), an application to the sheriff can be made within two working days of that continuation.[57]

Review by children's hearing: second working day hearing

15–20   Where a CPO is in force in respect of a child, the child has been taken to a place of safety by virtue of the order, and the reporter has not received notice of an application to the sheriff to terminate or vary the order, the reporter must arrange a children's hearing to take place on the second working day[58] after the day on which the child is taken to the place of safety.[59] Likewise, where a CPO is in force in respect of a child authorising the prevention of the removal of the child from a place, and the reporter has not received notice of an application to the sheriff to terminate or vary the order, the reporter must arrange a children's hearing to take place on the second working day after the day on which the CPO was made.[60] In either case the reporter must as soon as practicable before the beginning of the hearing supply a copy of the CPO, a copy of the application for the CPO (or child assessment order), and a copy of any report or other document which is relevant to the children's hearing's consideration, to the child, relevant person, person who appears to the reporter to have (or recently have had) significant involvement in the upbringing of the child, the applicant for the order, the person specified in the order, any appointed safeguarder,[61] the members of the hearing and the chief social work officer of the relevant local authority.[62]

15–21   It would be incompetent to hold the hearing on any other day than the second working day, such as the day before, even when that is practicable. It was explicit under the 1995 Act that failure to hold a hearing on the second working day will bring the CPO to an end, for the order could survive beyond that day only if the hearing continued it.[63] That provision has not been replicated in the 2011 Act, but the result is, it is submitted, the same: the continued operation of a CPO after the second working day depends upon its having been continued (with or without variation) by a children's hearing. It is not open to the children's hearing to defer making its decision beyond the second working day in order to obtain further information: the only options specified by the Act are to continue the order, to continue and vary the order, or to terminate the order[64] and there is no equivalent to the provisions elsewhere in the Act allowing a children's hearing, arranged for other reasons, to defer making its decision.[65]

---

[57] 2011 Act s.48(3)(b).

[58] "Working day" is defined in s.202(1) to be every day except Saturdays and Sundays, December 25 and 26, and January 1 and 2. All other public holidays count as working days. It follows that if a CPO is made or implemented on a Monday, the children's hearing must sit on the immediately following Wednesday; if the CPO is made or implemented on a Friday, the children's hearing must sit on the following Tuesday; if made or implemented on Friday 22nd December, the second working day after that will be Thursday 28th December.

[59] 2011 Act s.45.

[60] 2011 Act s.46.

[61] It might happen that a child over whom a CPO is made has previously been referred to a children's hearing and a safeguarder is presently in post.

[62] 2013 Rules r.39.

[63] Children (Scotland) Act 1995 s.60(6)(a).

[64] 2011 Act s.47(1).

[65] See, for example, 2011 Act ss.91(2), 119(2) and 138(2).

Adjournment of the hearing under the 2013 Rules is, however, permitted so long as the hearing can reconvene on the same day.[66]

The children's hearing arranged under either ss.45 or 46 is subject to the **15–22** same rules of constitution and procedure[67] as any other children's hearing, except that its role is more limited and, since it is unable to defer making a decision, it may not exercise any of the usual powers on deferral. It can make no dispositive decision, nor review any compulsory supervision order that the child is already under. Rather, the children's hearing held on the second working day is limited to considering whether it is satisfied that the conditions for the making of the CPO, set out in s.38(2) or s.39(2), are met or not.[68] This is a matter of fact, which leaves no room for discretion, though there is sometimes room for the exercise of judgment as to whether the fact exists or not (and that judgment may well be different from the sheriff's). It is not made clear whether the hearing has to determine that the conditions are met as at the time of the granting of the order, or as at the time the hearing is looking at the matter, though the latter interpretation is probably to be preferred both in principle[69] and as a more natural reading of the statute.[70] Given the shortness of time between the making of the order and the children's hearing it will be unusual for there to have been any significant change in circumstances, but extreme cases (such as death or imprisonment of the source of danger) are not beyond the realms of possibility. If the hearing is not satisfied that the conditions are met then the only option for the children's hearing is to terminate the order.[71] There is no appeal from a children's hearing's decision to terminate the CPO.

If the conditions for the granting of a CPO are found by the children's **15–23** hearing to be met, then the options open to the hearing are: (i) to continue the order; or (ii) to continue and vary the order, including by terminating, varying or including an information non-disclosure direction, a contact direction or a parental responsibilities and parental rights direction.[72] In determining which option to adopt, the hearing must regard the need to safeguard and promote the welfare of the child as the paramount consideration and must take account of any views the child has expressed after being given the opportunity to do so.[73]

A children's hearing reviewing a CPO is subject to the normal rules for **15–24** attendance and participation.[74] It is unclear whether a children's hearing reviewing a CPO has the power to appoint a safeguarder: the doubt arises from the wording of s.30(2) under which "*a* children's hearing may appoint a safeguarder at any time when *the* children's hearing is still deciding matters in rela-

---

[66] 2013 Rules r.7(2) and (3).

[67] The role of the chairing member and each member of the children's hearing is set out in the 2013 Rules r.70.

[68] 2011 Act s.47(1).

[69] cf. *Kennedy v B*, 1973 S.L.T. 38 in which it was held that a sheriff in determining whether grounds of referral are established must look at the facts that exist on the day he sits and not at the time of the original hearing.

[70] 2011 Act s.47(1)(a): a children's hearing may continue or vary the order "if satisfied that the conditions for making the order *are* met . . .". This suggests that the conditions need to be met at present rather than in the past when the sheriff decided that they were met.

[71] 2011 Act s.47(1)(b).

[72] 2011 Act s.47(1)(a). For these directions, see above, paras 15–13—15–18. The powers of the chilren's hearing at this point are the same as those of the sheriff in relation to directions.

[73] 2011 Act ss.25 and 27.

[74] 2011 Act s.78.

tion to the child". If "the children's hearing", second mentioned, is a reference back to "a children's hearing", first mentioned, then a hearing held under s.45 or s.46 will not have the power to appoint a safeguarder since it must make the decision it has been arranged to make at that hearing and will therefore not be "still deciding matters".[75] This may, however, be too narrow a reading of s.30(2) and "*the* children's hearing" may refer to the children's hearing system: if that is so then it is at least arguable that, since most children over whom a CPO has been made will be brought within the children's hearing system on or before the eighth working day, the power in s.30(2) extends to hearings on the second working day. It will seldom be appropriate for a children's hearing that continues a CPO to appoint a safeguarder in any case. The grounds hearing that will usually follow on or before the eighth working day after the day the child was removed to a place or safety or, if not so removed, after the day on which the CPO was made will be in possession of much more information upon which to judge the necessity of appointing a safeguarder and, since that hearing will nearly always defer making a substantive decision in any case, no time is lost by postponing appointment until then. However, a safeguarder is entitled to adopt an advisory role in relation to the child and appointment by a children's hearing reviewing a CPO might be appropriate in order to ensure that the child receives independent advice at the grounds hearing that will almost invariably follow on or before the eighth working day.

15–25   As soon as practicable after the decision has been made the reporter must give the decision of the hearing and its reasons and, where the decision was to continue the CPO, confirmation of the right to apply to the sheriff for a further review of the CPO, to the child, each relevant person, any individual (not being a relevant person) who appears to the reporter to have (or recently have had) significant involvement in the upbringing of the child, the person who applied for the CPO (or child assessment order), the person specified in the CPO, any other person prescribed by rules of court, and any appointed safeguarder.[76]

Review by sheriff

15–26   If an application to the sheriff to vary or terminate the CPO has been made before the sitting of the children's hearing (which must otherwise sit on the second working day after either the order was made or the child was removed to a place of safety) then no such children's hearing may take place,[77] and the re-examination of the issue will be conducted by the sheriff. There is nothing to prevent the sheriff who made the original order hearing the application for variation or termination: this is unlikely to be incompatible with Art.6 ECHR since the process is not an appeal but a review. The application to the sheriff to vary the CPO may be made by any one or more of the following persons, that is to say:

---

[75] It may also be noted that sheriffs do not have the power to appoint a safeguarder while either making or reviewing a child protection order: the sheriff may do so only in proceedings under Pts 10 or 15 of the 2011 Act.

[76] 2013 Rules r.91(1) and (2). In addition, the reporter must give to the chief social work officer of the relevant local authority and any person responsible under the order for providing a service, support or accommodation to the child, both the decision of the children's hearing and its reasons: r.91(3)–(5).

[77] 2011 Act ss.45(1)(c) and 46(1)(c).

(a) the child in respect of whom the CPO is made;
(b) a relevant person in relation to the child;
(c) a person (other than a relevant person) who has (or recently had) a significant involvement in the upbringing of the child[78];
(d) the person who applied for the CPO;
(e) the person specified in the CPO as being required to produce the child;
(f) the reporter; or
(e) any other person prescribed by rules of court.[79]

The same persons, other than the reporter, may apply to the sheriff for the termination of the CPO.[80]

No-one else can make an application to the sheriff, even when they appear **15–27** to have an interest in doing so, such as a stranger seeking to clear his or her name of an allegation of abuse against the child. The application to vary or terminate the order may be made by the child, so long as he or she has capacity (determined by the Age of Legal Capacity (Scotland) Act 1991 s.2(4A) and (4B)) to conduct civil proceedings.[81] If the child lacks capacity then the application may be made on his or her behalf by his or her legal representative (that is to say person with the parental responsibility and parental right of legal representation); and even when the child does have capacity the application may be made on his or her behalf if he or she consents to be represented in proceedings by someone who used to be his or her legal representative.[82]

If the application to the sheriff is not made within the strict time-limits laid **15–28** down in s.48(3) then it cannot be made thereafter. The application must be made *either* before the commencement of a children's hearing arranged to review the CPO under ss.45 or 46 *or,* if that hearing continues the CPO (with or without variation), within two working days after the day on which the CPO is continued.[83] In either situation, the sheriff must determine the application within three working days after the day on which it is made.[84] If he has not determined the application by then, the CPO ceases to have effect[85]: generally, however, the sheriff ought to be able to make his decision on the day the application is made.[86]

The person applying to the sheriff for variation or termination of a CPO **15–29** must, as soon as practicable after making the application, give notice of it to the following people:

---

[78] That is to say a person who may claim relevant person status under 2011 Act s.81. The change there from "or recently had" to "or has recently had" is too subtle to indicate any difference in substantive meaning. See also the reference in 2011 Act s.51(2)(d) to a person the sheriff considers "to recently have had" significant involvement.

[79] 2011 Act s.48(1).

[80] 2011 Act s.48(2).

[81] Capacity is dependent upon the child having a general understanding of what it means to conduct civil proceedings.

[82] Children (Scotland) Act 1995 s.15(6).

[83] 2011 Act s.48(3).

[84] 2011 Act s.51(3). So for example, if the application is made on a Friday the sheriff must determine it by the following Wednesday.

[85] 2011 Act s.51(4).

[86] cf. the original making of the CPO: Child Care and Maintenance Rules 1997 r.3.31 requires the sheriff to decide whether to grant or refuse the application "forthwith".

(a) the person who applied for the CPO (unless that person is the applicant for the variation or termination);

(b) the person specified in the CPO as being required to produce the child (unless that person is the applicant for the variation or termination);

(c) the child (unless the child is the applicant);

(d) each relevant person in relation to the child (unless the relevant person is the applicant for the variation or termination);

(e) the relevant local authority for the child (unless it is the applicant for the variation or termination);

(f) the reporter (unless he or she is the applicant for variation or termination); and

(g) any other person to whom the applicant is required to give notice under rules of court.[87]

15–30 The sheriff must, before determining the application, give the following persons an opportunity to make representations:

(a) the applicant;

(b) the child in respect of whom the CPO is made;

(c) each relevant person in relation to the child;

(d) any person who is not a relevant person but who the sheriff considers to have (or to recently have had) a significant involvement in the upbringing of the child;

(e) the applicant for the CPO;

(f) the relevant local authority (if not the applicant); and

(g) the reporter.[88]

15–31 The sheriff is not entitled to appoint a safeguarder in order to safeguard the interests of the child in the proceedings at such a review.[89]

15–32 After hearing the parties to the action and having allowed such further procedure as he thinks fit, the sheriff must make his decision[90] and, where the sheriff so directs, intimation of that decision must be given by the applicant to such persons as the sheriff directs.[91] The first decision for the sheriff is whether or not the conditions for the making of the CPO were met, and only if he is not satisfied that they are met may he terminate the CPO.[92] If he does so the CPO ceases to have effect at the end of the hearing before the sheriff.[93] If, on the other hand, the sheriff is satisfied that the conditions for the making of the order (whether under s.38 or s.39) are met the sheriff may not terminate the CPO but must decide whether: (i) to vary it, including by terminating, varying or including an information non-disclosure direction, a contact direction or a

---

[87] 2011 Act s.49.

[88] 2011 Act s.51(2).

[89] s.31 limits the power of the sheriff to appoint a safeguarder to proceedings under Pts 10 or 15 of the 2011 Act. CPOs are reviewed under Pt 5.

[90] Child Care and Maintenance Rules 1997 r.3.33(4).

[91] Child Care and Maintenance Rules 1997 r.3.33(6).

[92] 2011 Act s.51(5)(a). Though the terminology of "may" is used, termination is the only available option when the sheriff is not satisfied that the conditions for making the order are met.

[93] 2011 Act s.51(6).

parental responsibilities and rights direction[94]; or (ii) to confirm the CPO without variation.[95] In determining whether to vary or confirm the CPO (being satisfied that the conditions for its making continue to be met) the sheriff must take account of the welfare principle in ss.25 and 26, the obligation to have regard to the child's views in s.27 and the obligation in s.29 to vary or continue the CPO only if he considers that it would be better for the child if the order (as varied or continued) were in force than not. The issue for the sheriff is not, however, whether the continuation in force of the CPO is in the best interests of the child, for the focus of inquiry is on the existence of the conditions for its making: if he is satisfied that these conditions are met the sheriff may not terminate the order, and if he is not satisfied that these conditions are met he must terminate the order. The principles in ss.25–29 do not assist in determining whether the CPO is to continue in force, but do apply to its design.

Review by sheriff after children's hearing's review

An application to the sheriff to vary or terminate the CPO may also be made **15–33** within two working days after the day on which the children's hearing continued the CPO under s.47(1)(a), effectively giving a second review.[96] If this is done, then the same rules and procedure apply as when the application to the sheriff is made before the children's hearing's review, except that the sheriff will have at his disposal the reasons why the children's hearing considered it appropriate to continue (or continue and vary) the order, and for that reason it will seldom, if ever, be appropriate for the reporter to arrange an advice hearing under s.50.

Advice hearings

Whether the application to the sheriff to vary or terminate the CPO has been **15–34** made before or after the children's hearing's review, the reporter may arrange a children's hearing for the purpose of providing any advice it considers appropriate to assist the sheriff in the determination of the application.[97] This matter was considered more fully elsewhere in this book.[98]

TERMINATION OF CPO

Termination on the eighth working day

The CPO is designed to be used as an emergency short-term procedure, **15–35** providing immediate protection to the child when this is necessary as a matter of urgency to prevent significant harm. It will usually be followed by a children's hearing, which will have to examine the question of whether more long-term measures are required to achieve that aim, but that process is effectively quite separate. In no circumstance can a CPO ever remain effective at the end of the period of eight working days beginning on the day the child was removed to a

---

[94] 2011 Act s.51(5)(b).
[95] 2011 Act s.51(5)(c).
[96] 2011 Act s.48(3)(b).
[97] 2011 Act s.50.
[98] See above, para.12–24.

place of safety (if the order contained an authorisation so to remove the child),[99] or on the day the order was made (in any other case).[100] The Children (Scotland) Act 1995 required that a children's hearing be held on the eighth working day[101] at which grounds of referral would be put to the child and relevant person for acceptance or denial. The current legislation is less precise and the children's hearing may be held on or before the eighth working day. It may, indeed, be held after then by the reporter arranging a grounds hearing, but the CPO will in any case have ended by the end of the eighth working day. So the reporter will normally arrange a grounds hearing under s.69 of the 2011 Act before the expiry of the eight working days to ensure that there is no hiatus in the protection given to the child. Given the short period of time between the making of a CPO and the holding of a grounds heading before the CPO loses its force, it is unlikely that the hearing will be in a position to determine whether or not it is necessary in the child's interests for the child to be made subject to a compulsory supervision order. The most common outcome is that the grounds hearing defers making its decision on that matter and, if it is felt that the child should remain in the place of safety in which he or she was detained under the CPO, the hearing may make an interim compulsory supervision order under s.92(2), or an interim variation of an existing compulsory supervision order with residence in the place of safety as one of its measures, and with other terms effectively the same (if they remain appropriate) as those the now-defunct CPO contained. It follows that as soon as the CPO has been made, the reporter must commence those investigative duties that he or she has under s.66,[102] decide whether it is necessary for a compulsory supervision order to be made (or reviewed) in respect of the child and, if so,[103] must prepare a statement of grounds under s.89. Procedure then follows that of any other grounds hearing.[104]

Non-implementation of the order

15–36   In order to obtain a CPO, the applicant must have been able to persuade the sheriff that the order is necessary for the protection of the child from harm. If, however, the applicant delays in attempting to implement it after it has been made, it can be assumed that such necessity to act no longer exists and the order, for that reason, ought to fall. The rule is, therefore, that a CPO that contains an authorisation to remove a child to a place of safety will cease to have effect at the end of the period of 24 hours beginning with the making of the order if there has been no attempt to implement it within that period; if attempts have been made within that period but these have not been successful, and therefore the order remains extant but the child has not been removed to a place of safety, then the order ceases to have effect at the end of the period of 6 days[105] beginning with the making of the order.[106] The applicant can be said to make an attempt to implement the order when he takes necessary steps

---

[99] 2011 Act s.54(c).

[100] 2011 Act s.54(d).

[101] Children (Scotland) Act 1995 s.65(2).

[102] 2011 Act s.66(1)(a)(i).

[103] In the vast majority of cases in which a CPO has been made the reporter will determine that a compulsory supervision order is necessary, but it does not always follow.

[104] 2011 Act ss.90–97.

[105] Note: *not* working days.

[106] 2011 Act s.52.

directed to that end. The attempt might not be successful until after the 24 hours have passed, but the order does not come to an end so long as the attempt commences before then. So, for example, if the CPO authorises the removal of a child to a place of safety the order ceases if the applicant does nothing for more than 24 hours, but it does not cease if the applicant attempts within that time to obtain the child but the attempt is frustrated by the parents of the child spiriting him or her away or the child running away. If the CPO remains unimplemented at the end of the period of 6 days, for whatever reason, but protection of the child remains necessary, this must be sought by means of either a further CPO or the holding of a children's hearing that may grant a warrant to secure attendance[107] which itself will authorise the detaining of the child in a place of safety.[108]

Termination or non-determination at review

The CPO will also come to an end if, after it has been reviewed, it is termi- **15–37** nated by the children's hearing,[109] or, implicitly, if the hearing that ought to have been held to review the order has not been held on the second working day. The order comes to an end in the former case at the conclusion of the children's hearing and in the latter case at the end of the second working day. If an application has been made to the sheriff to terminate or vary the CPO, either before or after a review by a children's hearing, the order comes to an end if the sheriff either terminates the order[110] or he fails to determine the application within three working days after the day on which it is made.[111] The order comes to an end in the former case at the end of the hearing before the sheriff[112] and in the latter case at the end of the period of three working days.[113]

Termination of order by reporter

If the reporter is satisfied that the conditions for the making of a CPO in **15–38** respect of a child are no longer satisfied, he or she may terminate the order by giving notice to the person specified in the order as required to produce the child or, where there is no such person specified, the applicant for the order.[114] It follows that the child must be returned home or freed, unless some other statutory authority[115] to keep the child can be invoked; and conditions attached

---

[107] Under 2011 Act s.123: in this case the reporter must, whenever practicable, arrange the children's hearing to take place on the first working day after the child was first detained in pursuance of the warrant: 2013 Rules r.17.

[108] 2011 Act s.88(1)(a)(ii).

[109] 2011 Act s.47(1)(b).

[110] Under 2011 Act s.51(5)(a).

[111] 2011 Act s.51(3).

[112] 2011 Act s.51(6).

[113] 2011 Act s.51(4).

[114] 2011 Act s.53(1). Whenever such notice is given, the reporter must also notify the sheriff who granted the order: s.53(5).

[115] Such as a warrant to secure attendance granted by a children's hearing under s.123. It might sometimes be appropriate for a reporter to seek such a warrant even when of the view that the conditions for the making of a CPO are no longer satisfied, for the purpose of the warrant under s.123 will be to secure the child's attendance rather than to protect him or her from harm. Any hearing may grant a warrant whenever "a children's hearing . . . is to be arranged" and so the reporter may both terminate a CPO and seek a warrant to secure attendance, so long as he or she has made the decision to arrange a children's hearing (and so long as there is a real risk of the child's non-attendance).

to the CPO similarly cease to have effect. The reporter can reach the view that the conditions for the making of the CPO are no longer satisfied either because he or she has received further information relating to the case or because of a change in the circumstances of the case; the reporter cannot release a child simply because he or she disagrees with the sheriff who made the order, though the further information that comes to the attention of the reporter might suggest that the conditions never were, in fact, satisfied. Evidence that the child's welfare is suffering due to the implementation of the CPO will be a persuasive (and usually sufficient) change in circumstances that might well suggest that the CPO is not "necessary to protect the child from ... further harm".[116] Similarly the removal of the source of danger[117] will be a material change in circumstances. It is the notification to the appropriate person of the reporter's view that takes away that person's authority to keep the child. It remains open to the reporter to arrange a children's hearing under s.69 after having terminated the CPO to which the child was subject.

15–39   The reporter may also by the same means terminate one or more of the ancillary directions in a CPO, that is to say an information non-disclosure direction, a contact direction or a parental responsibilities and rights direction, if satisfied that the conditions for including the direction in a CPO are no longer satisfied.[118] Again, the words "no longer satisfied" imply that a change of circumstances has occurred since the CPO was made with the relevant direction. The reporter may not vary the CPO by adding in a direction that was not included by the sheriff, but may vary the order by removing one or more of these directions. The ancillary direction is terminated by the giving of notice to the person who is required to produce the child under the CPO or, where there is no such person, to the applicant for the order.[119]

15–40   The aim of s.53 is to allow the reporter to react speedily to sudden changes in circumstances. The effect of that provision is, however, limited by s.53(4), which provides that the reporter cannot terminate or even vary the order after the commencement of a children's hearing that is held under ss.45 or 46 or the commencement of any application to the sheriff to terminate or vary the order under s.48. This means that the reporter's power under s.53 to terminate or vary the CPO lasts only until the end of the second working day after the implementation or making of the CPO and he or she is powerless to bring the order to an end thereafter, however much the circumstances change or whatever the nature of the new evidence he or she acquires. If a children's hearing has been held on the second working day, it will be open to the reporter, up to two working days thereafter, to apply to the sheriff to vary the CPO, but not to terminate it.[120] If, however, there was no children's hearing because the application had been made immediately to the sheriff, the reporter's hands will be

---

[116] Which is the test in 2011 Act s.39(2)(b).

[117] For example by the implementation of an exclusion order under s.76 of the Children (Scotland) Act 1995.

[118] 2011 Act s.53(2) and (3).

[119] 2011 Act s.53(2). Notice must also be given to the sheriff who granted the order: s.53(5). There is an odd error in s.53(5), because it refers to the reporter terminating or varying a CPO under s.53(1). In fact the reporter may only terminate the order under s.53(1) and the power to vary is traced to s.53(2). The provision only makes sense if it is interpreted to impose a requirement to notify the sheriff when the reporter has either terminated the order under s.53(1) or varied it under s.53(2).

[120] 2011 Act s.48(1) and (2).

tied for up to six working days. The CPO may, however, be terminated at the instigation of the reporter by his or her giving notice under s.68(3) to either the person required to produce the child or, if there is no such person, the applicant for the order that the question of whether a compulsory supervision order should be made in respect of the child will not be referred to a children's hearing.[121] In other words, if the reporter, having investigated the case, decides under s.68 either that none of the grounds of referral applies or that it is not necessary for a compulsory supervision order to be made, he or she may bring the CPO to an end by intimating that decision. This does not, however, cover the situation where the reporter believes that a compulsory supervision order is indeed necessary but that there is no need for the child to be kept away from home before the children's hearing can assess the situation: in that case the CPO must remain in effect until it comes to an end by some other means.

EMERGENCY PROTECTION IN THE ABSENCE OF A SHERIFF

It will sometimes happen that either a sheriff is not available to grant a CPO or **15–41** it appears that a child's safety can be secured only by his or her immediate and summary removal from a source of danger. In these circumstances a CPO, though designed to be granted quickly, might not be available quite quickly enough. Sections 55 and 56 attempt to address that difficulty by permitting, respectively, a justice of the peace to make an order that authorises certain of the acts that could be achieved through a CPO, and by authorising police officers to remove a child from an immediate source of danger. These provisions are simpler than those relating to CPOs and have no reviews or appeals, but they are designed to be holding measures only, until a CPO can be sought. The expectation is that an application for a CPO will be made during the period in which the order or authorisation granted under ss.55 or 56 lasts.

Justice of the peace orders

When the conditions specified in either s.38(2)[122] or s.39(2)[123] for **15–42** the granting of a CPO are satisfied, but a justice of the peace is satisfied that it is not practicable in the circumstances for an application for a CPO to be made to or considered by a sheriff, then the justice of the peace may make an order:

---

[121] 2011 Act s.54(b).

[122] i.e. (a) the local authority has reasonable grounds to suspect that the child has been, is being or will be treated or neglected in such a way that the child is suffering or is likely to suffer significant harm, (b) the local authority is making or causing to be made enquiries to allow it to decide whether to take action to safeguard the welfare of the child, (c) those enquiries are being frustrated by access to the child being unreasonably denied, and (d) the authority has reasonable cause to believe that access is required as a matter of urgency.

[123] i.e. (a) there are reasonable grounds to believe that (i) the child has been or is being treated in such a way that he or she is suffering or is likely to suffer significant harm, (ii) the child has been or is being neglected and as a result of the neglect he or she is suffering or is likely to suffer significant harm, (iii) the child is likely to suffer significant harm if he or she is not removed to and kept in a place of safety, or (iv) the child is likely to suffer significant harm if he or she does not remain in the place at which he or she is staying; and (b) the order is necessary to protect the child from that harm or from further harm.

(a) requiring any person in a position to do so to produce the child to a specified person;

(b) authorising the removal of the child by the specified person to a place of safety and the keeping of the child in that place;

(c) authorising the prevention of the removal of the child from any place where he or she is staying.[124]

These acts are the same as those authorised by a CPO itself,[125] except for the authorisation in s.37(2)(d), to carry out an assessment of the child's health or development or the way in which the child has been or is being treated or neglected. The justice of the peace order may not include ancillary measures such as an information non-disclosure direction,[126] a contact direction or a parental responsibilities and rights direction. In any case the applicant for the order may only take such steps to implement the order as the applicant (or other person) reasonably believes are necessary to safeguard or promote the welfare of the child.[127] As with CPOs sought under s.39, there is no limitation on who may apply for an authorisation under s.55: the applicant can be "a person", though normally it will be a local authority. The only situation in which it would be not practicable to obtain a CPO from a sheriff is when no sheriff is, for whatever reason, available in sufficient time to deal with the particular emergency that has arisen. This eventuality is unlikely to occur in large urban areas such as Glasgow or Edinburgh in which there are many sheriffs, but it may occur more frequently in rural areas such as the Western or the Northern Isles. It will often remain practicable to approach a sheriff even when it is easier and quicker to approach a justice of the peace: the test, it is to be remembered, is impracticality rather than inconvenience.

15–43   In deciding whether to make the order the justice of the peace will be governed by the obligation to regard the welfare of the child as paramount[128] but, not being a sheriff, his decision is not governed by the requirement in s.27 to have regard to the views of the child or by the rule in s.29 that an order may be made "only if the sheriff considers that it would be better for the child if the order . . . were in force than not". A justice of the peace is, however, a public authority for the purposes of the Human Rights Act 1998[129] with the result that the proportionality principle applies, as does his obligation to allow the child and family to participate in the decision-making process if that is possible without compromising the child's safety. The very emergency that gives a justice of the peace authority to make an order in this context is likely, in many cases, to make such participation impossible and lack of opportunity to

---

[124] 2011 Act s.55(1) and (2).

[125] See 2011 Act s.37(2).

[126] Though some information may be withheld: Children's Hearings (Scotland) Act 2011 (Child Protection Emergency Measures) Regulations 2012 (SSI 2012/334) (hereinafter "Emergency Measures Regulations 2012") reg.6.

[127] 2011 Act s.58.

[128] 2011 Act s.25, which applies when a "court is coming to a decision about a matter relating to a child". Sheriff Kearney points out in *Children's Hearings and the Sheriff Court*, 2nd edn (Butterworths, 2000), para.11.07, that a justice of the peace is not a"court" and so not directly governed by s.25. However, he suggests that given that the justice of the peace must be satisfied that a sheriff would grant a CPO, the welfare test is equally applicable.

[129] Human Rights Act 1998 s.6.

participate is not in such a context necessarily contrary to the European Convention on Human Rights.[130]

The order made by a justice of the peace must be implemented within **15–44** 12 hours of the authorisation having been granted, otherwise the order ceases to have effect,[131] and in any case the authorisation must be implemented as soon as reasonably practicable.[132] If it has not ceased to have effect before then, the order will cease to have effect on the earlier of: (i) the end of the period of 24 hours beginning with the making of the order (note, not after having been given effect to); or (ii) the determination by the sheriff of an application for a CPO.[133] The reporter may terminate the order before then if satisfied that the conditions for the making of the order are no longer satisfied *or* it is no longer in the best interests of the child for the order to continue to have effect.[134]

There is no requirement to seek a CPO after the obtaining of an order under **15–45** this section, but doing so will allow the child can be kept in a place of safety for longer than the periods provided here, and it is expected that this is what will normally happen. The reporter may also seek a warrant to secure the child's attendance,[135] with a condition that the child be detained in a place of safety,[136] so long as the conditions for its granting are met, including the requirement that a children's hearing is being arranged.

As soon as practicable after implementing a s.55 order, the specified person **15–46** (or, if there is no person specified in the order as being the person to whom the child must be produced, the applicant) must inform the relevant persons, any person with whom the child was residing immediately before the making of the order, the relevant local authority (where neither the specified person nor the applicant is the local authority), the local authority for the area in which the place of safety or other place in which the child is kept is situated, the local authority for the area in which the child was residing immediately before the making of the order, and the Principal Reporter, of:

(a) the steps taken to implement the order;
(b) the location of the place of safety where the child is being kept or other place where the child is staying;
(c) the reasons for the making of the order; and
(d) any other steps which the specified person or the applicant has taken or is likely to take to safeguard the welfare of the child.[137]

---

[130] In *KA v Finland* (2003) 1 F.L.R. 696 the European Court of Human Rights said this at [95]: "When an emergency care order has to be made, it may not always be possible, because of the urgency of the situation, to associate fully in the decision-making process those having custody of the child. Nor may it even be desirable, even if possible, to do so if those having custody of the child are seen as the source of an immediate threat to the child".

[131] 2011 Act s.55(4). The JP and persons notified of the making of the order must be informed of its ceasing to have effect: Emergency Measures Regulations 2012 reg.7.

[132] Emergency Measures Regulations 2012 reg.3.

[133] 2011 Act s.55(5).

[134] 2011 Act s.55(6). If the reporter does so, he or she must inform the person specified in the order as being the person to whom the child must be produced, if different from the applicant: Emergency Measures Regulations 2012 reg.8.

[135] 2011 Act s.123.

[136] 2011 Act s.88(1)(a)(ii).

[137] Emergency Measures Regulations 2012 regs.4 and 5.

15-47   After making the order the specified person or applicant must regard the need to safeguard the welfare of the child as the paramount consideration.[138] As soon as practicable on or after implementing the order the specified person or applicant must so far as practicable and taking account of the age and maturity of the child inform the child of the reasons for making the order and of any other steps taken or to be taken to safeguard his or her welfare, and give the child the opportunity to express views and have regard to any views expressed.[139] The specified person or applicant may permit contact between the child and any person, subject to such conditions as are thought appropriate to safeguard the welfare of the child.[140] The address of the place of safety and details of other steps taken can be withheld from the relevant person and persons with whom the child was residing if to do so is necessary to safeguard the welfare of the child.[141]

Emergency protection by a constable

15-48   A child can be removed from, or kept away from, a source of immediate danger without any involvement of a sheriff or justice of the peace by a police officer if the conditions in s.56 of the Children's Hearings (Scotland) Act 2011 are satisfied. These are that it is not practicable in the circumstances for an application for a CPO to be made to or considered by a sheriff, but the constable is satisfied that:

(i)   the child has been or is being treated in such a way that he or she is suffering or is likely to suffer significant harm; or

(ii)   the child has been or is being neglected and as a result of the neglect he or she is suffering or is likely to suffer significant harm; or

(iii) the child is likely to suffer significant harm if not removed to and kept in a place of safety; or

(iv)   the child is likely to suffer significant harm if he or she does not remain in the place at which he or she is staying (whether or not the child is resident there); *and*

(v)   the removal of the child is necessary to protect the child from that harm or from further harm.[142]

15-49   The necessity for the removal must be immediate, otherwise an order may be sought from a justice of the peace, or a CPO itself can be sought, and removal must be a proportionate response. A police officer can, for example, step in and remove a child to a place of safety if he or she witnesses the child being beaten up by his or her parents, or if a child is brought to a female and child unit at a police station in a distressed state, or if the police officer comes across a child who has been expelled from the family home in conditions that create a risk of significant harm. Once taken to a place of safety by a constable, the constable may continue to keep the child there only for so long as he remains satisfied that the original conditions allowing him to remove

---

[138] Emergency Measures Regulations 2012 reg.9(1).
[139] Emergency Measures Regulations 2012 reg.9(2).
[140] Emergency Measures Regulations 2012 reg.9(3).
[141] Emergency Measures Regulations 2012 reg.6.
[142] 2011 Act s.56(1), referring to the conditions in s.39(2)(a).

the child still apply and that it is necessary to keep the child in a place of safety to protect the child from the harm or further harm referred to in the grounds.[143] After removal to a place of safety, the constable must regard the need to safeguard the welfare of the child as the paramount consideration, and must, as soon as practicable after removal and taking account of the age and maturity of the child inform the child of the reasons for the removal to a place of safety and of any other steps taken or to be taken to safeguard his or her welfare, and give the child the opportunity to express views and to have regard to these views.[144]

If a child is removed to and kept in a place of safety by a police officer under **15–50** the terms of s.56, the constable must as soon as practicable inform any relevant person, any person with whom the child was residing immediately before being removed to a place of safety, the revelant local authority, the local authority for the area in which the place of safety is situated, the local authority for the area in which the child was residing immediately before being removed to a place of safety, and the Principal Reporter, of:

(a) the removal of the child to a place of safety;
(b) the location of that place of safety;
(c) the reasons for the removal; and
(d) any other step taken or to be taken by the constable to safeguard the welfare of the child in the place of safety.[145]

Information concerning the location of the place of safety and the other steps being taken to safeguard the welfare of the child may be withheld from a relevant person or person with whom the child was residing where the constable considers it necessary to do so in order to safeguard and promote the welfare of the child.[146]

The child may be kept in the place of safety only for a maximum period of **15–51** 24 hours after first being removed or kept from the source of danger.[147] If the child is to be kept for any longer period than that, a CPO must be sought and obtained: if obtained the authority to keep the child comes from that order rather than from s.56,[148] and if an application has been made to a sheriff for a CPO or to a justice of the peace for an order under s.55 on the basis of the facts before the constable, but that application has been refused, the authorisation under s.56 comes to an end.[149]

The reporter may, by giving notice to the constable, require the constable **15–52** to release the child if the reporter is satisfied that the conditions for placing the child in a place of safety under s.56 are no longer satisfied, *or* that it is no longer in the best interests of the child to be kept in a place of safety.[150]

---

[143] Emergency Measures Regulations 2012 reg.13.
[144] Emergency Measures Regulations 2012 reg.14.
[145] Emergency Measures Regulations 2012 regs.10 and 11.
[146] Emergency Measures Regulations 2012 reg.12.
[147] 2011 Act s.56(3).
[148] 2011 Act s.56(4)(a).
[149] 2011 Act s.56(4)(b).
[150] 2011 Act s.56(5).

OFFENCES IN CONNECTION WITH EMERGENCY PROTECTION MEASURES

It is an offence, making the offender liable on summary conviction to a fine not exceeding level three on the standard scale, for any person intentionally to obstruct a person who is acting either under a CPO or under an order made by a justice of the peace under s.55 or to obstruct a constable removing a child to a place of safety under s.56.[151] It is also an offence for any person knowingly to assist or induce a child to abscond from a place of safety, to harbour or conceal a child who has so absconded, or to prevent a child from returning to a place of safety.[152] However, a local authority is not "harbouring" a child where the child appears to it to be at risk of harm and at the child's request it provides him or her with a refuge in a residential establishment or arranges for refuge to be provided in an approved household.[153]

---

[151] 2011 Act s.59.
[152] 2011 Act s.171.
[153] Children (Scotland) Act 1995 s.38.

APPENDIX ONE

CHILDREN'S HEARINGS (SCOTLAND) ACT 2011

(asp 1)

CONTENTS

Section

PART 2

THE PRINCIPAL REPORTER AND THE SCOTTISH CHILDREN'S REPORTER ADMINISTRATION

The Principal Reporter and SCRA

The Principal Reporter

Functions of SCRA

Transfer of staff, property etc.

PART 3

GENERAL CONSIDERATIONS

PART 4

SAFEGUARDERS

PART 5

CHILD ASSESSMENT AND CHILD PROTECTION ORDERS

Child assessment orders

Child protection orders

Consideration of application by sheriff

Ancillary measures

Notice of order

Obligations of local authority

Review by children's hearing of certain orders

Decision of children's hearing

Variation or termination of order by sheriff

Termination of order

PART 6

INVESTIGATION AND REFERRAL TO CHILDREN'S HEARING

Provision of information to Principal Reporter

Investigation and determination by Principal Reporter

PART 7

ATTENDANCE AT CHILDREN'S HEARING

PART 11

SUBSEQUENT CHILDREN'S HEARINGS

PART 12

CHILDREN'S HEARINGS: GENERAL

PART 13

REVIEW OF COMPULSORY SUPERVISION ORDER

PART 16

ENFORCEMENT OF ORDERS

PART 17

PROCEEDINGS UNDER PART 10: EVIDENCE

PART 18

MISCELLANEOUS

PART 19

LEGAL AID AND ADVICE

PART 20

GENERAL

Formal communications

Forms

Subordinate legislation

Interpretation

General

PART 1

THE NATIONAL CONVENER AND CHILDREN'S HEARINGS SCOTLAND

The National Convener and CHS

The National Convener

1.—(1) There is to be an officer to be known as the National Convener of Children's Hearings Scotland (referred to in this Act as "the National Convener").

(2) The Scottish Ministers are to appoint a person as the first National Convener.

(3) The Scottish Ministers must take reasonable steps to involve persons who are under 21 years of age in the process for selection of a person for appointment under subsection (2).

(4) The period for which the person is appointed is 5 years.

(5) The terms and conditions on which the person holds and vacates office are to be determined by the Scottish Ministers.

Children's Hearings Scotland

2. There is established a body corporate to be known as Children's Hearings Scotland (referred to in this Act as "CHS").

Further provision about National Convener and CHS

3. Schedule 1 makes further provision about the National Convener and CHS.

The Children's Panel

The Children's Panel

4.—(1) The National Convener must appoint persons to be members of a panel to be known as the Children's Panel.

(2) The National Convener must endeavour to ensure that—
(a) the number of persons that the National Convener considers appropriate is appointed, and
(b) the panel includes persons from all local authority areas.

(3) Schedule 2 makes further provision about the Children's Panel.

Children's hearings

Children's hearing

5. A children's hearing consists of three members of the Children's Panel selected in accordance with section 6 for the purpose of carrying out functions conferred on a children's hearing by virtue of this Act or any other enactment.

Selection of members of children's hearing

6.—(1) This section applies where a children's hearing requires to be arranged by virtue of, or for the purposes of, this Act or any other enactment.

(2) The members of the children's hearing are to be selected by the National Convener.

(3) The National Convener must ensure that the children's hearing—

(a) includes both male and female members of the Children's Panel, and

(b) so far as practicable, consists only of members of the Children's Panel who live or work in the area of the local authority which is the relevant local authority for the child to whom the hearing relates.

(4) The National Convener may select one of the members of the children's hearing to chair the hearing.

[1](5) In this section "children's hearing" includes a pre-hearing panel.

NOTE

1. As inserted by the Children's Hearings (Scotland) Act 2011 (Modification of Primary Legislation) Order 2013 (SSI 2013/211) Sch.1 para.20(2) (effective June 24, 2013—this being the date on which the 2011 (asp 1) came into force).

Holding of children's hearing

7. The National Convener must ensure that a children's hearing is held for the purpose of carrying out any function conferred on a children's hearing by virtue of this Act or any other enactment.

Provision of advice to children's hearing

8.—(1) The National Convener may provide advice to children's hearings about any matter arising in connection with the functions conferred on children's hearings by virtue of this Act or any other enactment.

(2) The National Convener may in particular provide—

(a) legal advice,

(b) advice about procedural matters,

(c) advice about the consequences of decisions of the children's hearing,

(d) advice about how decisions of children's hearings are implemented.

(3) In this section, "children's hearing" includes pre-hearing panel.

Independence of children's hearings

9. Nothing in this Act authorises the National Convener or the Principal Reporter to direct or guide a children's hearing in carrying out the functions conferred on children's hearings by virtue of this Act or any other enactment.

Power to change National Convener's functions

Power to change National Convener's functions

10.—(1) The Scottish Ministers may by order—

(a) confer additional functions on the National Convener,

(b) remove functions from the National Convener,

(c) transfer functions from another person to the National Convener,

(d) transfer functions from the National Convener to another person,

(e) specify the manner in which, or period within which, any function conferred on the National Convener by virtue of this Act is to be carried out.

(2) An order under this section is subject to the super-affirmative procedure (other than an order under subsection (1)(e), which is subject to the affirmative procedure).

Functions of CHS

Provision of assistance to National Convener

11. CHS must—

(a) assist the National Convener in carrying out the functions conferred on the National Convener by virtue of this Act or any other enactment,

(b) facilitate the carrying out of those functions.

Independence of National Convener

12.—(1) Nothing in this Act authorises CHS or any other person to direct or guide the National Convener in carrying out the functions conferred on the National Convener by virtue of this Act or any other enactment.

(2) This section is subject to section 10(1)(e).

Directions

13.—(1) The Scottish Ministers may give CHS general or specific directions about the carrying out of its functions.

(2) CHS must comply with a direction under subsection (1).

(3) The Scottish Ministers may vary or revoke a direction under subsection (1) by giving a subsequent direction under that subsection.

PART 2

THE PRINCIPAL REPORTER AND THE SCOTTISH CHILDREN'S REPORTER ADMINISTRATION

The Principal Reporter and SCRA

The Principal Reporter

14. There continues to be an officer known as the Principal Reporter.

The Scottish Children's Reporter Administration

15. There continues to be a body corporate known as the Scottish Children's Reporter Administration (in this Act referred to as "SCRA").

Further provision about Principal Reporter and SCRA

16. Schedule 3 makes further provision about the Principal Reporter and SCRA.

The Principal Reporter

Duty as respects location of children's hearing

17. The Principal Reporter must ensure that, so far as practicable, a children's hearing takes place in the area of the relevant local authority for the child to whom the hearing relates.

Power to change Principal Reporter's functions

18.—(1) The Scottish Ministers may by order—

(a) confer additional functions on the Principal Reporter,

(b) remove functions from the Principal Reporter,

(c) transfer functions from another person to the Principal Reporter,

(d) transfer functions from the Principal Reporter to another person,

(e) specify the manner in which, or period within which, any function conferred on the Principal Reporter by virtue of this Act or the Criminal Procedure (Scotland) Act 1995 (c.46) is to be carried out.

(2) An order under this section is subject to the super-affirmative procedure (other than an order under subsection (1)(e), which is subject to the affirmative procedure).

Rights of audience

19.—(1) The Scottish Ministers may by regulations—

(a) empower the Principal Reporter to conduct proceedings which by virtue of this Act require to be conducted before the sheriff or the sheriff principal,

(b) prescribe qualifications or experience that must be acquired or training that must be undertaken by the Principal Reporter before conducting such proceedings.

(2) References in subsection (1) to the Principal Reporter include references to a person carrying out a function on behalf of the Principal Reporter by virtue of paragraph 10(1) of schedule 3.

Functions of SCRA

Assisting Principal Reporter

20. SCRA must—

(a) assist the Principal Reporter in carrying out the functions conferred on the Principal Reporter by virtue of this Act or any other enactment, and

(b) facilitate the carrying out of those functions.

Provision of accommodation for children's hearings

21.—(1) SCRA must provide suitable accommodation and facilities for children's hearings.

(2) Accommodation and facilities must, so far as practicable, be provided in the area of each local authority.

(3) Accommodation and facilities must be dissociated from courts exercising criminal jurisdiction and police stations.

Independence of Principal Reporter

22.—(1) Nothing in this Act authorises SCRA or any other person to direct or guide the Principal Reporter in carrying out the functions conferred on the Principal Reporter by virtue of this Act or any other enactment.

(2) This section is subject to section 18(1)(e).

Directions

23.—(1) The Scottish Ministers may give SCRA general or specific directions about the carrying out of its functions.

(2) SCRA must comply with a direction under subsection (1).

(3) The Scottish Ministers may vary or revoke a direction under subsection (1) by giving a subsequent direction under that subsection.

Transfer of staff, property etc.

Transfer of staff, property etc.

24. Schedule 4 makes provision about the transfer of staff, property, rights, liabilities and obligations to CHS.

PART 3

GENERAL CONSIDERATIONS

Welfare of the child

25.—(1) This section applies where by virtue of this Act a children's hearing, pre-hearing panel or court is coming to a decision about a matter relating to a child.

(2) The children's hearing, pre-hearing panel or court is to regard the need to safeguard and promote the welfare of the child throughout the child's childhood as the paramount consideration.

Decisions inconsistent with section 25

[1]**26.**—(1) A children's hearing or a court may make a decision that is inconsistent with the requirement imposed by section 25(2) if—

(a) the children's hearing, pre-hearing panel or court considers that, for the purpose of protecting members of the public from serious harm (whether physical or not), it is necessary that the decision be made, and

(b) in coming to the decision, the children's hearing, pre-hearing panel or court complies with subsection (2).

(2) The children's hearing, pre-hearing panel or court is to regard the need to safeguard and promote the welfare of the child throughout the child's childhood as a primary consideration rather than the paramount consideration.

1. As amended by the Children's Hearings (Scotland) Act 2011 (Modification of Primary Legislation) Order 2013 (SSI 2013/211) Sch.1 para.20(3) (effective June 24, 2013—this being the date on which the 2011 (asp 1) came into force).

Views of the child

[1]**27.**—(1) This section applies where by virtue of this Act a children's hearing, pre-hearing panel or the sheriff is coming to a decision about a matter relating to a child.

(2) This section does not apply where the sheriff is deciding whether to make a child protection order in relation to a child.

(3) The children's hearing, pre-hearing panel or the sheriff must, so far as practicable and taking account of the age and maturity of the child—

(a) give the child an opportunity to indicate whether the child wishes to express the child's views,

(b) if the child wishes to do so, give the child an opportunity to express them, and

(c) have regard to any views expressed by the child.

(4) Without prejudice to the generality of subsection (3), a child who is aged 12 or over is presumed to be of sufficient age and maturity to form a view for the purposes of that subsection.

(5) In this section "coming to a decision about a matter relating to a child", in relation to a children's hearing, pre-hearing panel, includes—

(a) providing advice by virtue of section 50,

(b) preparing a report under section 141(2).

NOTE

1. As amended by the Children's Hearings (Scotland) Act 2011 (Modification of Primary Legislation) Order 2013 (SSI 2013/211) Sch.1 para.20(4) (effective June 24, 2013—this being the date on which the 2011 (asp 1) came into force).

Children's hearing: pre-condition for making certain orders and warrants

28.—(1) Subsection (2) applies where a children's hearing is—

(a) considering whether to make a compulsory supervision order,

(b) considering whether to vary or continue a compulsory supervision order,

(c) considering whether to make an interim compulsory supervision order,

(d) considering whether to make an interim variation of a compulsory supervision order,

(e) considering whether to make a medical examination order, or

(f) considering whether to grant a warrant to secure attendance.

(2) The children's hearing may make, vary or continue the order or interim variation or grant the warrant, only if the children's hearing considers that it would be better for the child if the order, interim variation or warrant were in force than not.

Sheriff: pre-condition for making certain orders and warrants

29.—(1) Subsection (2) applies where—

(a) the sheriff is considering making a child assessment order,

(b) the sheriff is considering making or varying a child protection order,

(c) by virtue of section 156(1)(b) or (2)(b), the sheriff is considering—

    (i) varying or continuing a compulsory supervision order,

    (ii) making or varying an interim compulsory supervision order or an interim variation of a compulsory supervision order,

    (iii) varying a medical examination order, or

    (iv) granting a warrant to secure attendance,

(d) the sheriff is otherwise considering—

    (i) making an interim compulsory supervision order or an interim variation of a compulsory supervision order, or

    (ii) granting a warrant to secure attendance, or

(e) the sheriff is considering extending or varying an interim compulsory supervision order under section 98 or 99.

(2) The sheriff may make, vary, continue or extend the order or interim variation or grant the warrant, only if the sheriff considers that it would be better for the child if the order, interim variation or warrant were in force than not.

Duty to consider including contact direction

[1]**29A.**—(1) A children's hearing must, when making, varying or continuing a compulsory supervision order in relation to a child, consider whether to include in the order a measure of the type mentioned in section 83(2)(g).

(2) A sheriff must, when varying or continuing a compulsory supervision order in relation to a child, consider whether to include in the order a measure of the type mentioned in section 83(2)(g).

NOTE
1. As inserted by the Children's Hearings (Scotland) Act 2011 (Modification of Primary Legislation) Order 2013 (SSI 2013/211) Sch.1 para.20(5) (effective June 24, 2013—this being the date on which the 2011 (asp 1) came into force).

Children's hearing: duty to consider appointing safeguarder

30.—(1) A children's hearing must consider whether to appoint a person to safeguard the interests of the child to whom the children's hearing relates (a "safeguarder").

(2) A children's hearing may appoint a safeguarder at any time when the children's hearing is still deciding matters in relation to the child.

(3) A children's hearing must record an appointment made under subsection (2).

(4) If a children's hearing appoints a safeguarder, it must give reasons for its decision.

(5) Subsection (1) does not apply where a safeguarder has already been appointed.

Sheriff: duty to consider appointing safeguarder

31.—(1) This section applies where—
(a) proceedings are being taken before the sheriff under Part 10 or 15 in relation to a child, and
(b) a safeguarder has not been appointed for the child in relation to proceedings under those Parts.

(2) The sheriff must consider whether to appoint a safeguarder for the child.

(3) The sheriff may appoint a safeguarder for the child.

[1](4) A safeguarder appointed under this section is to be treated for the purposes of this Act (other than this section and section 33) as having been appointed by a children's hearing by virtue of section 30.

(5) An appointment under subsection (3) must be recorded.

(6) If the sheriff appoints a safeguarder, the sheriff must give reasons for the decision.

NOTE
1. As amended by the Children's Hearings (Scotland) Act 2011 (Modification of Primary Legislation) Order 2013 (SSI 2013/211) Sch.1 para.20(6) (effective June 24, 2013—this being the date on which the 2011 (asp 1) came into force).

PART 4

SAFEGUARDERS

The Safeguarders Panel

32.—(1) The Scottish Ministers must establish and maintain a panel of persons (to be known as the Safeguarders Panel) from which any appointment under this Act of a safeguarder is to be made.

(2) The Scottish Ministers may by regulations make provision for or in connection with—

(a) the recruitment and selection of persons who may be appointed as members of the Safeguarders Panel,

(b) the appointment and removal of members of the Safeguarders Panel,

(c) qualifications to be held by members of the Safeguarders Panel,

(d) the training of members and potential members of the Safeguarders Panel,

(e) the payment of expenses, fees and allowances by the Scottish Ministers to members and potential members of the Safeguarders Panel,

(f) the operation and management of the Safeguarders Panel.

(3) For the purpose of complying with the requirements imposed by subsection (1) and regulations under subsection (2), the Scottish Ministers may enter into arrangements (contractual or otherwise) with any person other than CHS or SCRA.

Functions of safeguarder

33.—(1) A safeguarder appointed in relation to a child by virtue of section 30 must—

(a) except where subsection (2) applies, on being so appointed, prepare a report setting out anything that, in the opinion of the safeguarder, is relevant to the consideration of the matter before the children's hearing,

(b) so far as reasonably practicable, attend the children's hearing, and

(c) prepare any report that the safeguarder is required to prepare by a children's hearing.

(2) This subsection applies where the children's hearing directs the Principal Reporter under section 93(2)(a) or 94(2)(a) to make an application to the sheriff.

Safeguarders: regulations

34.—(1) The Scottish Ministers may by regulations make further provision about safeguarders.

(2) Regulations under this section may in particular make provision for or in connection with—

(a) imposing additional requirements on safeguarders,

(b) conferring additional powers (including rights of appeal) on safeguarders,

(c) the termination of safeguarders' appointments.

Child assessment orders

Child assessment orders

35.—(1) A local authority may apply to the sheriff for a child assessment order in respect of a child.

(2) A child assessment order is an order authorising an officer of a local authority or a person authorised by that officer to carry out (subject to section 186) an assessment of—

(a) the child's health or development, or

(b) the way in which the child has been or is being treated or neglected.

(3) An order may—

(a) require any person in a position to do so to produce the child to the officer,

(b) for the purpose of carrying out the assessment, authorise the taking of the child to any place and the keeping of the child at that place or any other place for a period specified in the order,

(c) where it contains an authorisation of the type mentioned in paragraph (b), include directions about contact between the child and any other person.

(4) A child assessment order must specify the period during which it has effect.

(5) That period must—

(a) begin no later than 24 hours after the order is granted, and

(b) not exceed 3 days.

Consideration by sheriff

36.—(1) This section applies where an application for a child assessment order in respect of a child is made by a local authority.

(2) The sheriff may make the order if the sheriff is satisfied that—

(a) the local authority has reasonable cause to suspect—

(i)   that the child has been or is being treated in such a way that the child is suffering or is likely to suffer significant harm, or

(ii) that the child has been or is being neglected and as a result of the neglect the child is suffering or is likely to suffer significant harm,

(b) an assessment of the kind mentioned in section 35(2) is necessary in order to establish whether there is reasonable cause to believe that the child has been or is being so treated or neglected, and

(c) it is unlikely that the assessment could be carried out, or carried out satisfactorily, unless the order was made.

(3) The sheriff may, instead of making a child assessment order, make a child protection order if the sheriff considers the conditions in section 38(2) are satisfied.

Child protection orders

Child protection orders

37.—(1) A person may apply to the sheriff for a child protection order in respect of a child.

(2) A child protection order is an order doing one or more of the following—

(a) requiring any person in a position to do so to produce the child to a specified person,

(b) authorising the removal of the child by the specified person to a place of safety and the keeping of the child in that place,

(c) authorising the prevention of the removal of the child from any place where the child is staying (whether or not the child is resident there),

(d) authorising the carrying out (subject to section 186) of an assessment of—

(i) the child's health or development, or

(ii) the way in which the child has been or is being treated or neglected.

(3) A child protection order may also include any other authorisation or requirement necessary to safeguard or promote the welfare of the child.

(4) A child protection order may include an authorisation of the type mentioned in paragraph (d) of subsection (2) only if it also includes an authorisation of a type mentioned in paragraph (b) or (c) of that subsection.

(5) An application for a child protection order must—

(a) identify the applicant,

(b) in so far as is practicable, identify the child in respect of whom the order is sought,

(c) state the grounds on which the application is made, and

(d) be accompanied by supporting evidence, whether documentary or otherwise, sufficient to enable the sheriff to determine the application.

(6) In subsection (2), "specified" means specified in the order.

Consideration of application by sheriff

Consideration by sheriff: application by local authority only

38.—(1) This section applies where an application for a child protection order in respect of a child is made by a local authority.

(2) The sheriff may make the order if the sheriff is satisfied that—

(a) the local authority has reasonable grounds to suspect that—

(i) the child has been or is being treated in such a way that the child is suffering or is likely to suffer significant harm,

(ii) the child has been or is being neglected and as a result of the neglect the child is suffering or is likely to suffer significant harm, or

(iii) the child will be treated or neglected in such a way that is likely to cause significant harm to the child,

(b) the local authority is making enquiries to allow it to decide whether to take action to safeguard the welfare of the child, or is causing those enquiries to be made,

(c) those enquiries are being frustrated by access to the child being unreasonably denied, and

(d) the local authority has reasonable cause to believe that access is required as a matter of urgency.

Consideration by sheriff: application by local authority or other person

39.—(1) This section applies where an application for a child protection order in respect of a child is made by a local authority or other person.

(2) The sheriff may make the order if the sheriff is satisfied that—

(a) there are reasonable grounds to believe that—

(i) the child has been or is being treated in such a way that the child is suffering or is likely to suffer significant harm,

(ii) the child has been or is being neglected and as a result of the neglect the child is suffering or is likely to suffer significant harm,

(iii) the child is likely to suffer significant harm if the child is not removed to and kept in a place of safety, or

(iv) the child is likely to suffer significant harm if the child does not remain in the place at which the child is staying (whether or not the child is resident there), and

(b) the order is necessary to protect the child from that harm or from further harm.

Ancillary measures

Information non-disclosure directions

40.—(1) This section applies where the sheriff makes a child protection order in respect of a child.

(2) The sheriff must consider whether to include an information non-disclosure direction in the order.

(3) An information non-disclosure direction is a direction that—

(a) the location of any place of safety at which the child is being kept, and

(b) any other information specified in the direction relating to the child, must not be disclosed (directly or indirectly) to any person or class of person specified in the direction.

(4) An information non-disclosure direction ceases to have effect when—

(a) it is terminated by a children's hearing under section 47(1)(a)(ii) or the sheriff under section 51(5)(b), or

(b) the child protection order in which it is included ceases to have effect.

Contact directions

41.—(1) This section applies where the sheriff makes a child protection order in respect of a child.

(2) The sheriff must consider whether to include a contact direction in the order.

(3) A contact direction is a direction—

(a) prohibiting contact between the child and a person mentioned in subsection (4),

(b) making contact between the child and such a person subject to any conditions which the sheriff considers appropriate to safeguard and promote the welfare of the child,

(c) making such other provision as the sheriff considers appropriate about contact between the child and such a person.

(4) The persons are—

(a) a parent of the child, person with parental responsibilities for the child or other person specified in the direction,

(b) a person falling within a class of person specified in the direction.

(5) A contact direction ceases to have effect when—

(a) it is terminated by a children's hearing under section 47(1)(a)(ii) or the sheriff under section 51(5)(b), or

(b) the child protection order in which it is included ceases to have effect.

Parental responsibilities and rights directions

42.—(1) A person applying to the sheriff for a child protection order in respect of a child may, at the same time, apply to the sheriff for a parental responsibilities and rights direction.

(2) A parental responsibilities and rights direction is a direction about the fulfilment of parental responsibilities or exercise of parental rights in relation to—
- (a) the treatment of the child arising out of any assessment authorised by the child protection order, or
- (b) any other matter that the sheriff considers appropriate.

(3) A parental responsibilities and rights direction ceases to have effect when—
- (a) it is terminated by a children's hearing under section 47(1)(a)(ii) or the sheriff under section 51(5)(b), or
- (b) the child protection order in which it is included ceases to have effect.

Notice of order

Notice of child protection order

43.—(1) As soon as practicable after the making of a child protection order, the applicant must give notice to—
- (a) the person specified in the order under section 37(2)(a) (unless the person is the applicant),
- (b) the child in respect of whom it is made,
- (c) each relevant person in relation to the child,
- (d) the relevant local authority for the child (unless the local authority is the applicant),
- (e) the Principal Reporter,
- (f) any other person to whom the applicant is required to give notice under rules of court.

(2) Where the Principal Reporter receives notice under subsection (1)(e), the Principal Reporter must give notice of the making of the order to any person (other than a relevant person in relation to the child) who the Principal Reporter considers to have (or to recently have had) a significant involvement in the upbringing of the child.

Obligations of local authority

Obligations of local authority

44.—(1) This section applies where, by virtue of a child protection order, a child is removed to a place of safety provided by a local authority.

(2) Subject to the child protection order, the local authority has the same duties towards the child as the local authority would have by virtue of section 17 of the 1995 Act if the child were looked after by the local authority.

Review by children's hearing of certain orders

Review by children's hearing where child in place of safety

45.—(1) This section applies where—
- (a) a child protection order is in force in respect of a child,
- (b) the child has been taken to a place of safety by virtue of the order, and

(c) the Principal Reporter has not received notice under section 49 of an application to the sheriff to terminate or vary the order.

(2) The Principal Reporter must arrange a children's hearing.

(3) The Principal Reporter must arrange for the children's hearing to take place on the second working day after the day on which the child is taken to the place of safety.

Review by children's hearing where order prevents removal of child

46.—(1) This section applies where—

(a) a child protection order is in force in respect of a child,

(b) the order authorises the prevention of the removal of the child from a place, and

(c) the Principal Reporter has not received notice under section 49 of an application to the sheriff to terminate or vary the order.

(2) The Principal Reporter must arrange a children's hearing.

(3) The Principal Reporter must arrange for the children's hearing to take place on the second working day after the day on which the child protection order is made.

Decision of children's hearing

Decision of children's hearing

47.—(1) A children's hearing arranged under section 45 or 46 may—

(a) if it is satisfied that the conditions for making the order are met—

   (i) continue the order, or

   (ii) continue and vary the order (including by terminating, varying or including an information non-disclosure direction, a contact direction or a parental responsibilities and rights direction), or

(b) if it is not satisfied that those conditions are met, terminate the order.

(2) In subsection (1), the "conditions for making the order" are—

(a) where the order was made under section 38, the matters mentioned in subsection (2)(a) to (d) of that section,

(b) where the order was made under section 39, the matters mentioned in subsection (2)(a) and (b) of that section.

Variation or termination of order by sheriff

Application for variation or termination

48.—(1) An application may be made by any of the following persons to the sheriff to vary a child protection order—

(a) the child in respect of whom the order is made,

(b) a relevant person in relation to the child,

(c) a person not falling within paragraph (b) who has (or recently had) a significant involvement in the upbringing of the child,

(d) the person who applied for the child protection order,

(e) the person specified in the child protection order under section 37(2)(a),

(f) the Principal Reporter,

(g) any other person prescribed by rules of court.

(2) An application may be made by any of the persons mentioned in subsection (1)(a) to (g) (other than the Principal Reporter) to the sheriff to terminate a child protection order.

(3) An application under this section may be made only—

(a) before the commencement of a children's hearing arranged under section 45 or 46, or

(b) if the children's hearing arranged under section 45 or 46 continues the child protection order (with or without variation), within 2 working days after the day on which the child protection order is continued.

Notice of application for variation or termination

49. A person applying under section 48 for variation or termination must, as soon as practicable after making the application, give notice of it to—

(a) the person who applied for the child protection order (unless the person is the applicant),

(b) the person specified in the child protection order under section 37(2)(a) (unless the person is the applicant),

(c) the child (unless the child is the applicant),

(d) each relevant person in relation to the child (unless the relevant person is the applicant),

(e) the relevant local authority for the child (unless the local authority is the applicant),

(f) the Principal Reporter (unless the Principal Reporter is the applicant), and

(g) any other person to whom the applicant is required to give notice under rules of court.

Children's hearing to provide advice to sheriff in relation to application

50. The Principal Reporter may arrange a children's hearing for the purpose of providing any advice the children's hearing may consider appropriate to assist the sheriff in the determination of an application under section 48.

Determination by sheriff

51.—(1) This section applies where an application is made under section 48 in relation to a child protection order.

(2) The sheriff must, before determining the application, give the following persons an opportunity to make representations—

(a) the applicant,

(b) the child in respect of whom the child protection order is made,

(c) each relevant person in relation to the child,

(d) any person not falling within paragraph (c) who the sheriff considers to have (or to recently have had) a significant involvement in the upbringing of the child,

(e) the applicant for the child protection order,

(f) the relevant local authority for the child (if the authority did not apply for the child protection order),

(g) the Principal Reporter.

(3) The application must be determined within 3 working days after the day on which it is made.

(4) The child protection order ceases to have effect at the end of that period if the application is not determined within that period.

(5) The sheriff may—

(a) terminate the child protection order if the sheriff is not satisfied of—

  (i) where the order was made under section 38, the matters mentioned in subsection (2)(a) to (d) of that section, or

  (ii) where the order was made under section 39, the matters mentioned in subsection (2)(a) and (b) of that section,

(b) vary the child protection order (including by terminating, varying or including an information non-disclosure direction, a contact direction or a parental responsibilities and rights direction), or

(c) confirm the child protection order.

(6) If the sheriff orders that the child protection order is to be terminated, the order ceases to have effect at the end of the hearing before the sheriff.

Termination of order

Automatic termination of order

52.—(1) This section applies where a child protection order contains an authorisation of the type mentioned in section 37(2)(b).

(2) The order ceases to have effect at the end of the period of 24 hours beginning with the making of the order if the person specified in the order under section 37(2)(a) has not attempted to implement it within that period.

(3) The order ceases to have effect at the end of the period of 6 days beginning with the making of the order if the child to whom the order relates has not been removed to a place of safety within that period.

Power of Principal Reporter to terminate order

53.—(1) If the Principal Reporter is satisfied that the conditions for the making of a child protection order in respect of a child are no longer satisfied, the Principal Reporter may terminate the order by giving notice to—

(a) the person specified in the order under section 37(2)(a), or

(b) where there is no such person specified, the applicant for the order.

(2) If the Principal Reporter is satisfied that the conditions for including a relevant direction in a child protection order in respect of a child are no longer satisfied, the Principal Reporter may vary the child protection order so as to terminate the direction by giving notice to—

(a) the person specified in the order under section 37(2)(a), or

(b) where there is no such person specified, the applicant for the order.

(3) A relevant direction is—

(a) an information non-disclosure direction,

(b) a contact direction,

(c) a parental responsibilities and rights direction.

(4) The Principal Reporter may not terminate or vary the order if—

(a) a children's hearing arranged under section 45 or 46 has commenced, or

(b) proceedings before the sheriff in relation to an application under section 48 have commenced.

(5) Where the Principal Reporter terminates or varies a child protection order under subsection (1), the Principal Reporter must notify the sheriff who granted the order.

Termination of order after maximum of 8 working days

54. A child protection order in respect of a child ceases to have effect on the earliest of—
  (a) the beginning of a children's hearing arranged under section 69 in relation to the child,
  (b) the person specified in the order under section 37(2)(a) or, where there is no such person specified, the applicant for the order receiving notice under section 68(3) that the question of whether a compulsory supervision order should be made in respect of the child will not be referred to a children's hearing,
  (c) where the order contains an authorisation of the type mentioned in section 37(2)(b), the end of the period of 8 working days beginning on the day the child was removed to a place of safety, or
  (d) where the order does not contain such an authorisation, the end of the period of 8 working days beginning on the day the order was made.

Other emergency measures

Application to justice of the peace

55.—(1) A person may apply to a justice of the peace for an order in respect of a child—
  (a) requiring any person in a position to do so to produce the child to a specified person,
  (b) authorising the removal of the child by the specified person to a place of safety and the keeping of the child in that place,
  (c) authorising the prevention of the removal of the child from any place where the child is staying.
  (2) A justice of the peace may make an order under this section if—
  (a) the justice of the peace is satisfied of—
    (i) in a case where the applicant for the order is a local authority, the matters mentioned in section 38(2)(a) to (d), or
    (ii) in a case where the applicant for the order is a local authority or any other person, the matters mentioned in section 39(2)(a) and (b), and
  (b) the justice of the peace is satisfied that it is not practicable in the circumstances for an application for a child protection order to be made to or considered by the sheriff.
  (3) As soon as practicable after the making of the order, the applicant must inform—
  (a) the Principal Reporter,
  (b) the person specified in the order under subsection (1)(a) (unless the person is the applicant).
  (4) The order ceases to have effect at the end of the period of 12 hours beginning with the making of the order if—
  (a) where the order authorises the removal of the child to a place of safety, the child has not been taken, or is not being taken, to that place within that period,

(b) where the order authorises the prevention of the removal of the child from a place where the child is staying, arrangements have not been made within that period to prevent that removal.

(5) Otherwise, the order ceases to have effect on the earlier of—

(a) the end of the period of 24 hours beginning with the making of the order, or

(b) the determination by the sheriff of an application to the sheriff for a child protection order in respect of the child.

(6) The Principal Reporter may, by giving notice to the applicant, terminate the order if—

(a) the Principal Reporter is satisfied that the conditions for the making of an order under this section are no longer satisfied, or

(b) the Principal Reporter is satisfied that it is no longer in the best interests of the child for the order to continue to have effect.

(7) In subsection (1), "specified" means specified in the order.

Constable's power to remove child to place of safety

56.—(1) A constable may remove a child to a place of safety and keep the child there if—

(a) the constable is satisfied—

　(i) of the matters mentioned in section 39(2)(a), and

　(ii) that the removal of the child is necessary to protect the child from the harm mentioned there or from further harm, and

(b) it is not practicable in the circumstances for an application for a child protection order to be made to or considered by the sheriff.

(2) As soon as practicable after a constable removes a child under this section, the constable must inform the Principal Reporter.

(3) The child may not be kept in a place of safety under this section for a period of more than 24 hours.

(4) The child may not be kept in a place of safety under this section if—

(a) a child protection order is in force in respect of the child, or

(b) an application has been made to the sheriff for a child protection order or to a justice of the peace for an order under section 55 on the basis of the facts before the constable and that application has been refused.

(5) The Principal Reporter may, by giving notice to the constable, require the constable to release the child if—

(a) the Principal Reporter is satisfied that the conditions for placing the child in a place of safety under this section are no longer satisfied, or

(b) the Principal Reporter is satisfied that it is no longer in the best interests of the child to be kept in a place of safety.

Sections 55 and 56: regulations

57.—(1) The Scottish Ministers may by regulations make further provision in respect of a child removed to or kept in a place of safety—

(a) under an order under section 55,

(b) under section 56.

(2) In particular, the regulations may require notice to be given to a person specified in the regulations of—

(a) the removal of the child to the place of safety,

(b) the location of the place of safety,

(c) an order under section 55 ceasing to have effect by virtue of subsection (4) or (5) of that section.

Implementation of orders: welfare of child

Implementation of orders: welfare of child

58.—(1) An applicant for (and any other person specified in) an order mentioned in subsection (2) may only take such steps to implement the order as the applicant (or other person) reasonably believes are necessary to safeguard or promote the welfare of the child.

(2) The orders are—

(a) a child assessment order,

(b) a child protection order,

(c) an order under section 55.

Offences

Offences

59.—(1) A person who intentionally obstructs—

(a) a person acting under a child assessment order,

(b) a person acting under a child protection order,

(c) a person acting under an order under section 55, or

(d) a constable acting under section 56(1),

commits an offence.

(2) A person guilty of an offence under subsection (1) is liable on summary conviction to a fine not exceeding level 3 on the standard scale.

PART 6

INVESTIGATION AND REFERRAL TO CHILDREN'S HEARING

Provision of information to Principal Reporter

Local authority's duty to provide information to Principal Reporter

60.—(1) If a local authority considers that it is likely that subsection (2) applies in relation to a child in its area, it must make all necessary inquiries into the child's circumstances.

(2) This subsection applies where the local authority considers—

(a) that the child is in need of protection, guidance, treatment or control, and

(b) that it might be necessary for a compulsory supervision order to be made in relation to the child.

(3) Where subsection (2) applies in relation to a child the local authority must give any information that it has about the child to the Principal Reporter.

Constable's duty to provide information to Principal Reporter

61.—(1) This section applies where a constable considers—

(a) that a child is in need of protection, guidance, treatment or control, and

(b) that it might be necessary for a compulsory supervision order to be made in relation to the child.

(2) The constable must give the Principal Reporter all relevant information which the constable has been able to discover in relation to the child.

[1](3) If the constable makes a report under section 20(1)(d) of the Police and Fire Reform (Scotland) Act 2012 (asp 8) in relation to the child, the constable must also make the report to the Principal Reporter.

NOTE
1. As amended by the Police and Fire Reform (Scotland) Act 2012 (asp 8) Sch.7(1) para.44 (effective June 24, 2013: substitution came into force on April 1, 2013 but could not take effect until the commencement of 2011 (asp 1) s.61(3) on June 24, 2013).

Provision of information by court

62.—(1) This section applies where, in the course of relevant proceedings, a court considers that a section 67 ground (other than the ground mentioned in section 67(2)(j)) might apply in relation to a child.

(2) The court may refer the matter to the Principal Reporter.

(3) If the court refers the matter under subsection (2) it must give the Principal Reporter a section 62 statement.

(4) A section 62 statement is a statement—
(a) specifying which of the section 67 grounds the court considers might apply in relation to the child,
(b) setting out the reasons why the court considers that the ground might apply, and
(c) setting out any other information about the child which appears to the court to be relevant.

[1](5) In this section "relevant proceedings" means—
(a) an action for divorce,
(b) an action for separation,
(c) an action for declarator of marriage,
(d) an action for declarator of nullity of marriage,
(e) an action for dissolution of a civil partnership,
(f) an action for separation of civil partners,
(g) an action for declarator of nullity of a civil partnership,
(h) an action for declarator of parentage,
(i) an action for declarator of non-parentage,
(j) proceedings relating to parental responsibilities or parental rights,
(k) an application for an adoption order (as defined in section 28(1) of the Adoption and Children (Scotland) Act 2007 (asp 4)),
(l) an application for the making, variation or revocation of a permanence order (as defined in section 80(2) of the Adoption and Children (Scotland) Act 2007) in respect of a child who is not subject to a compulsory supervision order,
(m) proceedings relating to an offence under any of the following sections of the Education (Scotland) Act 1980 (c.44)—
   (i) section 35 (failure by parent to secure regular attendance by child at a public school),
   (ii) section 41 (failure to comply with attendance order),
   (iii) section 42(3) (failure to permit examination of child),
(n) an application for the making, variation, recall or extension of—

(i) a forced marriage protection order (as defined in section 1(6) of the Forced Marriage etc. (Protection and Jurisdiction) (Scotland) Act 2011 (asp 15)), or

(ii) an interim forced marriage protection order (as defined in section 5(2) of that Act),

(o) civil proceedings in which a court makes an order such as is mentioned in sub-paragraph (i) or (ii) of paragraph (n) by virtue of section 4(1) of that Act (power to make order without application), or

(p) proceedings relating to an offence under section 9(1) of that Act (offence of breaching order).

NOTE

1. As amended by the Forced Marriage etc. (Protection and Jurisdiction) (Scotland) Act 2011 (asp 15) Pt 1 s.13(2) (effective November 28, 2011).

Provision of evidence from certain criminal cases

63.—(1) The Lord Advocate may direct that in any specified case or class of case evidence lawfully obtained in the investigation of a crime or suspected crime must be given to the Principal Reporter.

(2) The evidence must in that case, or in a case of that class, be given to the Principal Reporter even if the Principal Reporter has not made a request under section 172.

Provision of information by other persons

64.—(1) This section applies where a person considers—

(a) that a child is in need of protection, guidance, treatment or control, and

(b) that it might be necessary for a compulsory supervision order to be made in relation to the child.

(2) The person may give the Principal Reporter all relevant information which the person has in relation to the child.

Provision of information by constable: child in place of safety

65.—(1) Subsection (2) applies where a constable informs the Principal Reporter under subsection (5) of section 43 of the Criminal Procedure (Scotland) Act 1995 (c.46) that—

(a) a child is being kept in a place of safety under subsection (4) of that section, and

(b) it has been decided not to proceed with the charge against the child.

(2) The Principal Reporter may direct—

(a) that the child be released from the place of safety, or

(b) that the child continue to be kept in the place of safety until the Principal Reporter makes a determination under section 66(2).

Investigation and determination by Principal Reporter

Investigation and determination by Principal Reporter

¹**66.**—(1) This section applies where—

(a) the Principal Reporter receives in relation to a child—

(i) notice under section 43 of the making of a child protection order,

(ii) information from a local authority under section 60,

(iii)   information or a report from a constable under section 61,

(iv)   a section 62 statement,

(v)   evidence under section 63,

(vi)   information from a person under section 64,

(vii)   information from a constable under section 43(5) of the Criminal Procedure (Scotland) Act 1995 (c.46),

(viii)   a reference from a court under section 48(1) of the Criminal Procedure (Scotland) Act 1995 (c.46), or

(b)   it appears to the Principal Reporter that a child might be in need of protection, guidance, treatment or control.

(2) The Principal Reporter must determine—

(a)   whether the Principal Reporter considers that a section 67 ground applies in relation to the child, and

(b)   if so, whether the Principal Reporter considers that it is necessary for a compulsory supervision order to be made in respect of the child.

(2A)   In a case where a certificate is supplied under section 48(1) of the Criminal Procedure (Scotland) Act 1995, the Principal Reporter is deemed to have determined under subsection (2)(a) that the Principal Reporter considers that a section 67 ground applies in relation to the child.

(3) The Principal Reporter may make any further investigations relating to the child that the Principal Reporter considers necessary.

(4) The Principal Reporter may require a local authority to give the Principal Reporter a report on—

(a)   the child generally,

(b)   any particular matter relating to the child specified by the Principal Reporter.

(5) A local authority may include in a report given to the Principal Reporter under subsection (4) information given to the local authority by another person.

(6) The report may contain information in addition to any information given to the Principal Reporter under section 60.

NOTE

1. As amended by the Children's Hearings (Scotland) Act 2011 (Modification of Primary Legislation) Order 2013 (SSI 2013/211) Sch.1 para.20(7) (effective June 24, 2013—this being the date on which the 2011 (asp 1) came into force).

Meaning of "section 67 ground"

67.—(1) In this Act "section 67 ground", in relation to a child, means any of the grounds mentioned in subsection (2).

(2) The grounds are that—

(a)   the child is likely to suffer unnecessarily, or the health or development of the child is likely to be seriously impaired, due to a lack of parental care,

(b)   a schedule 1 offence has been committed in respect of the child,

(c)   the child has, or is likely to have, a close connection with a person who has committed a schedule 1 offence,

(d)   the child is, or is likely to become, a member of the same household as a child in respect of whom a schedule 1 offence has been committed,

(e)   the child is being, or is likely to be, exposed to persons whose conduct is (or has been) such that it is likely that—

(i)   the child will be abused or harmed, or

(ii) the child's health, safety or development will be seriously adversely affected,

(f) the child has, or is likely to have, a close connection with a person who has carried out domestic abuse,

(g) the child has, or is likely to have, a close connection with a person who has committed an offence under Part 1, 4 or 5 of the Sexual Offences (Scotland) Act 2009 (asp 9),

(h) the child is being provided with accommodation by a local authority under section 25 of the 1995 Act and special measures are needed to support the child,

(i) a permanence order is in force in respect of the child and special measures are needed to support the child,

(j) the child has committed an offence,

(k) the child has misused alcohol,

(l) the child has misused a drug (whether or not a controlled drug),

(m) the child's conduct has had, or is likely to have, a serious adverse effect on the health, safety or development of the child or another person,

(n) the child is beyond the control of a relevant person,

(o) the child has failed without reasonable excuse to attend regularly at school,

(p) the child—

[1](i) has been, is being, or is likely to be, subjected to physical, emotional or other pressure to enter into a civil partnership, or

(ii) is, or is likely to become, a member of the same household as such a child.

[2](q) the child—

(i) has been, is being or is likely to be forced into a marriage (that expression being construed in accordance with section 1 of the Forced Marriage etc. (Protection and Jurisdiction) (Scotland) Act 2011 (asp 15)) or,

(ii) is, or is likely to become, a member of the same household as such a child.

(3) For the purposes of paragraphs (c), (f) and (g) of subsection (2), a child is to be taken to have a close connection with a person if—

(a) the child is a member of the same household as the person, or

(b) the child is not a member of the same household as the person but the child has significant contact with the person.

(4) The Scottish Ministers may by order—

(a) amend subsection (2) by—

(i) adding a ground,

(ii) removing a ground for the time being mentioned in it, or

(iii) amending a ground for the time being mentioned in it, and

(b) make such other amendments of this section as appear to the Scottish Ministers to be necessary or expedient in consequence of provision made under paragraph (a).

(5) An order under subsection (4) is subject to the affirmative procedure.

(6) In this section—

"controlled drug" means a controlled drug as defined in section 2(1)(a) of the Misuse of Drugs Act 1971 (c.38),

"permanence order" has the meaning given by section 80(2) of the Adoption and Children (Scotland) Act 2007 (asp 4), "schedule 1 offence" means an offence mentioned in Schedule 1 to the Criminal Procedure (Scotland) Act 1995 (c.46) (offences against children under 17 years of age to which special provisions apply).

NOTE
1. As amended by the Forced Marriage etc. (Protection and Jurisdiction) (Scotland) Act 2011 (asp 15) Pt 1 s.13(3) (effective November 28, 2011) and further by the Children's Hearings (Scotland) Act 2011 (Modification of Primary Legislation) Order 2013 (SSI 2013/211) Sch.1 para.20(8) (effective June 24, 2013—this being the date on which the 2011 (asp 1) came into force).
2. As inserted by the Forced Marriage etc. (Protection and Jurisdiction) (Scotland) Act 2011 (asp 15) Pt 1 s.13(3) (effective November 28, 2011).

Determination under section 66: no referral to children's hearing

68.—(1) This section applies where, having made a determination under section 66(2) in relation to a child, the Principal Reporter considers that—
 (a) none of the section 67 grounds applies in relation to the child, or
 (b) it is not necessary for a compulsory supervision order to be made in respect of the child.

(2) If the child is being kept in a place of safety under section 65(2)(b) the Principal Reporter must direct that the child be released from the place of safety.

(3) The Principal Reporter—
 (a) must inform the persons mentioned in subsection (4) of the determination and the fact that the question of whether a compulsory supervision order should be made in respect of the child will not be referred to a children's hearing, and
 (b) may, if the Principal Reporter considers it appropriate, inform any other person of the determination and that fact.

(4) Those persons are—
 (a) the child,
 (b) each relevant person in relation to the child,
 (c) the relevant local authority for the child,
 (d) any person specified in a child protection order in force in relation to the child under section 37(2)(a),
 (e) any person who has given the Principal Reporter—
   (i) notice under section 43 of a child protection order,
   (ii) information under section 60, 61, 64 or 66,
   (iii) a report under section 61 or 66,
   (iv) a section 62 statement,
   (v) evidence under section 63, or
   (vi) information under section 43(5) of the Criminal Procedure (Scotland) Act 1995 (c.46).

(5) The Principal Reporter may refer the child to—
 (a) the relevant local authority for the child with a view to the authority providing (or making arrangements for the provision by another person or body of) advice,
   guidance and assistance to the child and the child's family in accordance with Chapter 1 of Part 2 of the 1995 Act (support for children and their families),
 (b) such other person or body as may be specified by the Scottish Ministers by order for the purposes of this subsection, with a view to that person or body providing advice, guidance and assistance to the child and the child's family.

(6) After complying with the requirements imposed by subsection (3)(a), the Principal Reporter must not refer the question of whether a compulsory supervision order should be made in respect of the child to a children's hearing unless the Principal Reporter receives new information about the child.

Determination under section 66: referral to children's hearing

69.—(1) This section applies where, having made a determination under section 66(2) in relation to a child, the Principal Reporter considers that it is necessary for a compulsory supervision order to be made in respect of the child.

(2) The Principal Reporter must arrange a children's hearing for the purpose of deciding whether a compulsory supervision order should be made in respect of the child.

(3) If the child is being kept in a place of safety under subsection (4) of section 43 of the Criminal Procedure (Scotland) Act 1995 (c.46) at the time the determination is made, the children's hearing must be arranged to take place no later than the third day after the Principal Reporter receives the information under subsection (5) of that section.

(4) If the Principal Reporter has required a local authority to give the Principal Reporter a report under section 66(4), the Principal Reporter may request additional information from the local authority.

(5) If the Principal Reporter has not required a local authority to give the Principal Reporter a report under section 66(4), the Principal Reporter must require a local authority to give the Principal Reporter a report under that section.

Requirement under Antisocial Behaviour etc. (Scotland) Act 2004

70.—(1) This section applies where—
(a) under section 12(1A) of the Antisocial Behaviour etc. (Scotland) Act 2004 (asp 8) the sheriff requires the Principal Reporter to arrange a children's hearing in respect of a child, and
(b) a compulsory supervision order is not in force in relation to the child.

(2) This Act applies as if—
(a) the requirement of the sheriff were a determination of the sheriff under section 108 that the section 67 ground specified in the statement given to the Principal Reporter under section 12 of the Antisocial Behaviour etc. (Scotland) Act 2004 was established in relation to the child, and
(b) the sheriff had directed the Principal Reporter under section 108(2) to arrange a children's hearing.

Case remitted under section 49 of Criminal Procedure (Scotland) Act 1995

71.—(1) This section applies where under section 49 of the Criminal Procedure (Scotland) Act 1995 (c.46)—
(a) a court remits a case to the Principal Reporter to arrange for the disposal of the case by a children's hearing, and
(b) a compulsory supervision order is not in force in relation to the child or person whose case is remitted.

(2) A certificate signed by the clerk of the court stating that the child or person whose case is remitted has pled guilty to, or been found guilty of, the

offence to which the case relates is conclusive evidence for the purposes of the children's hearing that the offence was committed by the child or person.

(3) This Act applies as if—

(a) the plea of guilty, or the finding of guilt, were a determination of the sheriff under section 108 that the ground in section 67(2)(j) was established in relation to the child, and

(b) the sheriff had directed the Principal Reporter under section 108(2) to arrange a children's hearing.

Child in place of safety: Principal Reporter's powers

72.—(1) Subsection (2) applies where—

(a) the Principal Reporter is required by section 69(2) to arrange a children's hearing in relation to a child, and

(b) the child is being kept in a place of safety under section 65(2)(b).

(2) The Principal Reporter may direct—

(a) that the child be released from the place of safety, or

(b) that the child continue to be kept in the place of safety until the children's hearing.

PART 7

ATTENDANCE AT CHILDREN'S HEARING

Child's duty to attend children's hearing

73.—(1) This section applies where by virtue of this Act a children's hearing is, or is to be, arranged in relation to a child.

(2) The child must attend the children's hearing unless the child is excused under subsection (3) or rules under section 177.

(3) A children's hearing may excuse the child from attending all or part of the children's hearing if the children's hearing is satisfied that—

(a) the hearing relates to the ground mentioned in section 67(2)(b), (c), (d) or (g) and the attendance of the child at the hearing, or that part of the hearing, is not necessary for a fair hearing,

(b) the attendance of the child at the hearing, or that part of the hearing, would place the child's physical, mental or moral welfare at risk, or

(c) taking account of the child's age and maturity, the child would not be capable of understanding what happens at the hearing or that part of the hearing.

(4)   Where the children's hearing is a grounds hearing, the children's hearing may excuse the child from attending during an explanation given in compliance with section 90(1) only if it is satisfied that, taking account of the child's age and maturity, the child would not be capable of understanding the explanation.

Relevant person's duty to attend children's hearing

74.—(1) This section applies where by virtue of this Act a children's hearing is, or is to be, arranged in relation to a child.

(2) Each relevant person in relation to the child who is notified of the children's hearing by virtue of rules under section 177 must attend the children's hearing unless the relevant person is—

(a) excused under subsection (3) or rules under section 177, or

(b) excluded from the children's hearing under section 76(2).

(3) A children's hearing may excuse a relevant person from attending all or part of the children's hearing if the children's hearing is satisfied that—

(a) it would be unreasonable to require the relevant person's attendance at the hearing or that part of the hearing, or

(b) the attendance of the relevant person at the hearing, or that part of the hearing, is unnecessary for the proper consideration of the matter before the hearing.

(4) A relevant person who is required to attend a children's hearing under subsection (2) and fails to do so commits an offence and is liable on summary conviction to a fine not exceeding level 3 on the standard scale.

Power to proceed in absence of relevant person

75.—(1) This section applies where a relevant person in relation to a child is required by section 74(2) to attend a children's hearing and fails to do so.

(2)   The children's hearing may, if it considers it appropriate to do so, proceed with the children's hearing in the relevant person's absence.

Power to exclude relevant person from children's hearing

76.—(1) This section applies where a children's hearing is satisfied that the presence at the hearing of a relevant person in relation to the child—

(a) is preventing the hearing from obtaining the views of the child, or

(b) is causing, or is likely to cause, significant distress to the child.

(2) The children's hearing may exclude the relevant person from the children's hearing for as long as is necessary.

(3) After the exclusion has ended, the chairing member of the children's hearing must explain to the relevant person what has taken place in the relevant person's absence.

Power to exclude relevant person's representative from children's hearing

77.—(1) This section applies where a children's hearing is satisfied that the presence at the hearing of a representative of a relevant person in relation to the child—

(a) is preventing the hearing from obtaining the views of the child, or

(b) is causing, or is likely to cause, significant distress to the child.

(2) The children's hearing may exclude the representative from the children's hearing for as long as is necessary.

(3)   After the exclusion has ended, the chairing member of the children's hearing must explain to the representative what has taken place in the representative's absence.

Rights of certain persons to attend children's hearing

78.—(1) The following persons have a right to attend a children's hearing—

(a) the child (whether or not the child has been excused from attending),

(b) a person representing the child,

(c) a relevant person in relation to the child (unless that person is excluded under section 76(2)),

(d) a person representing a relevant person in relation to the child (unless that person is excluded under section 77(2)),

(e) the Principal Reporter,

(f) if a safeguarder is appointed under this Act in relation to the child, the safeguarder,

[2](g) [. . .]

(h) a member of an area support team (acting in that person's capacity as such),

(i) subject to subsection (5), a representative of a newspaper or news agency.

(2) No other person may attend a children's hearing unless—

(a) the person's attendance at the hearing is considered by the chairing member of the children's hearing to be necessary for the proper consideration of the matter before the children's hearing,

(b) the person is otherwise granted permission to attend by the chairing member of the children's hearing, or

(c) the person is authorised or required to attend by virtue of rules under section 177.

(3) The chairing member may not grant permission to a person under subsection (2)(b) if the child or a relevant person in relation to the child objects to the person attending the children's hearing.

(4) The chairing member must take all reasonable steps to ensure that the number of persons present at a children's hearing at the same time is kept to a minimum.

(5) The children's hearing may exclude a representative of a newspaper or news agency from any part of the hearing where it is satisfied that—

(a) it is necessary to do so to obtain the views of the child, or

(b) the presence of that person is causing, or is likely to cause, significant distress to the child.

(6) Where a person is excluded under subsection (5), after the exclusion has ended, the chairing member may explain to the person, where appropriate to do so, the substance of what has taken place in the person's absence.

[1](7) In this section "children's hearing" includes a pre-hearing panel.

NOTE
1. As amended by the Children's Hearings (Scotland) Act 2011 (Modification of Primary Legislation) Order 2013 (SSI 2013/211) Sch.1 para.20(9) (effective June 24, 2013—this being the date on which the 2011 (asp 1) came into force).
2. Repealed by the Public Bodies (Abolition of Administrative Justice and Tribunals Council) Order 2013 (SI 2013/2042) Sch.1 para.42 (effective August 19, 2013).

PART 8

PRE-HEARING PANEL

Referral of certain matters for pre-hearing determination

79.—(1) This section applies where a children's hearing is to be held in relation to a child by virtue of section 69(2) or Part 9 to 11 or 13.

(2) The Principal Reporter—

(a) must refer the matter of whether a particular individual should be deemed to be a relevant person in relation to the child for determination

by three members of the Children's Panel selected by the National Convener (a "pre-hearing panel") if requested to do so by—
  (i)   the individual in question,
  (ii) the child, or
  (iii) a relevant person in relation to the child,
(b) may refer that matter for determination by a pre-hearing panel on the Principal Reporter's own initiative,
(c) may refer a matter of a type mentioned in subsection (3) for determination by a pre-hearing panel—
  (i)   on the Principal Reporter's own initiative, or
  (ii) following a request to the Principal Reporter from the child, a relevant person in relation to the child, or if a safeguarder has been appointed for the child, the safeguarder.
(3) Those matters are—
(a) whether the child should be excused from attending the children's hearing,
(b) whether a relevant person in relation to the child should be excused from attending the children's hearing,
(c) whether it is likely that the children's hearing will consider making a compulsory supervision order including a secure accommodation authorisation in relation to the child,
(d) a matter specified in rules under section 177(2)(a).
(4) For the purposes of subsection (3)(a), the pre-hearing panel may excuse the child from attending the children's hearing only if—
(a) the pre-hearing panel is satisfied that any of paragraphs (a) to (c) of section 73(3) applies, or
(b) the child may be excused under rules under section 177.
(5) For the purposes of subsection (3)(b), the pre-hearing panel may excuse a relevant person in relation to the child from attending the children's hearing only if—
(a) the pre-hearing panel is satisfied that section 74(3)(a) or (b) applies, or
(b) the relevant person may be excused under rules under section 177.
(6) A member of the Children's Panel selected for a pre-hearing panel may (but need not) be a member of the children's hearing.

Determination of matter referred under section 79

80.—(1) This section applies where the Principal Reporter refers a matter to a pre-hearing panel under section 79(2).

(2) The Principal Reporter must arrange a meeting of the pre-hearing panel for a date before the date fixed for the children's hearing.

(3) If it is not practicable for the Principal Reporter to comply with subsection (2), the children's hearing must determine the matter referred at the beginning of the children's hearing.

Determination of claim that person be deemed a relevant person

81.—(1) This section applies where a matter mentioned in section 79(2)(a) (a "relevant person claim") is referred to a meeting of a pre-hearing panel.

(2) Where the relevant person claim is referred along with any other matter, the pre-hearing panel must determine the relevant person claim before determining the other matter.

(3) The pre-hearing panel must deem the individual to be a relevant person if it considers that the individual has (or has recently had) a significant involvement in the upbringing of the child.

(4) Where the pre-hearing panel deems the individual to be a relevant person, the individual is to be treated as a relevant person for the purposes of Parts 7 to 15, 17 and 18 in so far as they relate to—

(a) the children's hearing,

(b) any subsequent children's hearing under Part 11,

(c) any pre-hearing panel held in connection with a children's hearing mentioned in paragraph (a), (b) or (e),

(d) any compulsory supervision order, interim compulsory supervision order, medical examination order, or warrant to secure attendance made by—

    (i) a hearing mentioned in paragraph (a) or (b),

    (ii) the sheriff in any court proceedings falling within paragraph (f),

(e) any children's hearing held for the purposes of reviewing a compulsory supervision order falling within paragraph (d),

(f) any court proceedings held in connection with a hearing mentioned in paragraph (a), (b) or (e),

(g) any court proceedings held in connection with an order or warrant falling within paragraph (d),

(h) the implementation of an order or warrant falling within paragraph (d).

(5) The Scottish Ministers may by order—

(a) amend subsection (3),

(b) in consequence of provision made under paragraph (a), make such other amendments as appear to the Scottish Ministers to be necessary or expedient to—

    (i) section 43,

    (ii) section 48,

    (iii) section 51,

    (iv) this section,

    (v) section 142.

(6) An order under subsection (5) is subject to the affirmative procedure.

(7) Where, by virtue of section 80(3), the children's hearing is to determine the relevant person claim, references in subsections (2) to (4) (other than paragraph (c) of subsection (4)) to the pre-hearing panel are to be read as references to the children's hearing.

Appointment of safeguarder

82.—(1) A pre-hearing panel may appoint a safeguarder for the child to whom the children's hearing relates.

(2) A pre-hearing panel must record an appointment made under subsection (1).

(3) If a pre-hearing panel appoints a safeguarder, it must give reasons for the decision.

(4) Subsection (1) does not apply where a safeguarder has already been appointed.

(5) A safeguarder appointed under this section is to be treated for the purposes of this Act (other than this section) as being appointed by a children's hearing by virtue of section 30.

PART 9

CHILDREN'S HEARING

Key definitions

Meaning of "compulsory supervision order"

83.—(1) In this Act, "compulsory supervision order", in relation to a child, means an order—

(a) including any of the measures mentioned in subsection (2),

(b) specifying a local authority which is to be responsible for giving effect to the measures included in the order (the "implementation authority"), and

(c) having effect for the relevant period.

(2) The measures are—

(a) a requirement that the child reside at a specified place,

(b) a direction authorising the person who is in charge of a place specified under paragraph (a) to restrict the child's liberty to the extent that the person considers appropriate having regard to the measures included in the order,

(c) a prohibition on the disclosure (whether directly or indirectly) of a place specified under paragraph (a),

(d) a movement restriction condition,

(e) a secure accommodation authorisation,

(f) subjecttosection186,arequirementthattheimplementationauthorityarrange—

  (i) a specified medical or other examination of the child, or

  (ii) specified medical or other treatment for the child,

(g) a direction regulating contact between the child and a specified person or class of person,

(h) a requirement that the child comply with any other specified condition,

(i) a requirement that the implementation authority carry out specified duties in relation to the child.

[1](3) [. . .]

(4) A compulsory supervision order may include a movement restriction condition only if—

(a) one or more of the conditions mentioned in subsection (6) applies, and

(b) the children's hearing or, as the case may be, the sheriff is satisfied that it is necessary to include a movement restriction condition in the order.

(5) A compulsory supervision order may include a secure accommodation authorisation only if—

(a) the order contains a requirement of the type mentioned in subsection (2)(a) which requires the child to reside at—

  (i) a residential establishment which contains both secure accommodation and accommodation which is not secure accommodation, or

  (ii) two or more residential establishments, one of which contains accommodation which is not secure accommodation,

(b) one or more of the conditions mentioned in subsection (6) applies, and

(c) having considered the other options available (including a movement restriction condition) the children's hearing or, as the case may be, the sheriff is satisfied that it is necessary to include a secure accommodation authorisation in the order.

(6) The conditions are—
(a) that the child has previously absconded and is likely to abscond again and, if the child were to abscond, it is likely that the child's physical, mental or moral welfare would be at risk,
(b) that the child is likely to engage in self-harming conduct,
(c) that the child is likely to cause injury to another person.

(7) In subsection (1), "relevant period" means the period beginning with the making of the order and ending with—
(a) where the order has not been continued, whichever of the following first occurs—
 (i) the day one year after the day on which the order is made,
 (ii) the day on which the child attains the age of 18 years,
(b) where the order has been continued, whichever of the following first occurs—
 (i) the end of the period for which the order was last continued,
 (ii) the day on which the child attains the age of 18 years.

(8) In subsection (2)—
 "medical" includes psychological,
  "specified" means specified in the order.

NOTE
1. Repealed by the Children's Hearings (Scotland) Act 2011 (Modification of Primary Legislation) Order 2013 (SSI 2013/211) Sch.2 (effective June 24, 2013—this being the date on which the 2011 (asp 1) came into force). *Rule now contained in section 29A.*

Meaning of "movement restriction condition"

84.—In this Act, "movement restriction condition", in relation to a child, means—
(a) a restriction on the child's movements in a way specified in the movement restriction condition, and
(b) a requirement that the child comply with arrangements specified in the movement restriction condition for monitoring compliance with the restriction.

Meaning of "secure accommodation authorisation"

85.—In this Act, "secure accommodation authorisation", in relation to a child, means an authorisation enabling the child to be placed and kept in secure accommodation within a residential establishment.

Meaning of "interim compulsory supervision order"

86.—(1) In this Act "interim compulsory supervision order", in relation to a child, means an order—
(a) including any of the measures mentioned in section 83(2),
(b) specifying a local authority which is to be responsible for giving effect to the measures included in the order ("the implementation authority"), and
(c) having effect for the relevant period.

(2) An interim compulsory supervision order may, instead of specifying a place or places at which the child is to reside under section 83(2)(a), specify that the child is to reside at any place of safety away from the place where the child predominantly resides.

(3) In subsection (1), "relevant period" means the period beginning with the making of the order and ending with whichever of the following first occurs—

(a) the next children's hearing arranged in relation to the child,

(b) the disposal by the sheriff of an application made by virtue of section 93(2)(a) or 94(2)(a) in relation to the child,

(c) a day specified in the order,

(d) where the order has not been extended under section 98 or 99, the expiry of the period of 22 days beginning on the day on which the order is made,

(e) where the order has been extended (or extended and varied) under section 98 or 99, the expiry of the period of 22 days beginning on the day on which the order is extended.

(4)   Subsections (3) to (6) (except subsection (5)(a)) of section 83 apply to an interim compulsory supervision order as they apply to a compulsory supervision order.

Meaning of "medical examination order"

87.—(1) In this Act "medical examination order", in relation to a child, means an order authorising for the relevant period any of the measures mentioned in subsection (2).

(2) The measures are—

(a) a requirement that the child attend or reside at a specified clinic, hospital or other establishment,

(b) subject to section 186, a requirement that a specified local authority arrange a specified medical examination of the child,

(c) a prohibition on the disclosure (whether directly or indirectly) of a place specified under paragraph (a),

(d) a secure accommodation authorisation,

(e) a direction regulating contact between the child and a specified person or class of person,

(f) any other specified condition appearing to the children's hearing to be appropriate for the purposes of ensuring that the child complies with the order.

(3) A medical examination order may include a secure accommodation authorisation only if—

(a) the order authorises the keeping of the child in a residential establishment,

(b) one of the conditions mentioned in subsection (4) applies, and

(c) having considered the other options available the children's hearing is satisfied that it is necessary to do so.

(4) The conditions are—

(a) that the child has previously absconded and is likely to abscond again and, if the child were to abscond, it is likely that the child's physical, mental or moral welfare would be at risk,

(b) that the child is likely to engage in self-harming conduct,

(c) that the child is likely to cause injury to another person.

(5) In this section—

"medical" includes psychological,

"relevant period", in relation to a medical examination order, means the period beginning with the making of the order and ending with whichever of the following first occurs—

(a) the beginning of the next children's hearing arranged in relation to the child,

(b) a day specified in the order,

(c) the expiry of the period of 22 days beginning on the day on which the order is made,

"specified" means specified in the order.

Meaning of "warrant to secure attendance"

88.—(1) In this Act, "warrant to secure attendance", in relation to a child, means a warrant effective for the relevant period—

(a) authorising an officer of law—
    (i) to search for and apprehend the child,
    (ii) to take the child to, and detain the child in, a place of safety,
    (iii) to bring the child before the relevant proceedings, and
    (iv) so far as is necessary for the execution of the warrant, to break open shut and lockfast places,

(b) prohibiting disclosure (whether directly or indirectly) to any person specified in the warrant of the place of safety.

(2) A warrant to secure attendance may include a secure accommodation authorisation but only if—

(a) the warrant authorises the keeping of the child in a residential establishment,

(b) one or more of the conditions mentioned in subsection (3) applies, and

(c) having considered the other options available the children's hearing or sheriff is satisfied that it is necessary to do so.

(3) The conditions are—

(a) that the child has previously absconded and is likely to abscond again and, if the child were to abscond, it is likely that the child's physical, mental or moral welfare would be at risk,

(b) that the child is likely to engage in self-harming conduct,

(c) that the child is likely to cause injury to another person.

(4) In this section—

"relevant period", in relation to a warrant to secure attendance, means—

    (a) where the warrant is granted by a children's hearing, the period beginning with the granting of the warrant and ending with the earlier of—
        (i) the beginning of the relevant proceedings, or
        (ii) the expiry of the period of 7 days beginning with the day on which the child is first detained in pursuance of the warrant,

    (b) where the warrant is granted by the sheriff under section 103(7), the period beginning with the granting of the warrant and ending with the earlier of—
        (i) the beginning of the continued hearing, or
        (ii) the expiry of the period of 14 days beginning with the day on which the child is first detained in pursuance of the warrant,

    (c) where the warrant is granted by the sheriff under any other provision in respect of attendance at proceedings under Part 10, the period beginning with the granting of the warrant and ending with the earlier of—
        (i) the beginning of the relevant proceedings, or
        (ii) the expiry of the period of 14 days beginning with the day on which the child is first detained in pursuance of the warrant,

    (d) where the warrant is granted by the sheriff in respect of attendance at a children's hearing arranged by virtue of section 108, 115,

117(2)(b) or 156(3)(a), the period beginning with the granting of the warrant and ending with the earlier of—

(i) the beginning of the relevant proceedings, or

(ii) the expiry of the period of 7 days beginning with the day on which the child is first detained in pursuance of the warrant,

"relevant proceedings", in relation to a warrant to secure attendance, means the children's hearing or, as the case may be, proceedings before the sheriff in respect of which it is granted.

Statement of grounds

Principal Reporter's duty to prepare statement of grounds

89.—(1) This section applies where the Principal Reporter is required by virtue of section 69(2) to arrange a children's hearing in relation to a child.

(2) The Principal Reporter must prepare the statement of grounds.

(3) In this Act "statement of grounds", in relation to a child, means a statement setting out—

(a) which of the section 67 grounds the Principal Reporter believes applies in relation to the child, and

(b) the facts on which that belief is based.

Grounds hearing

Grounds to be put to child and relevant person

90.—(1) At the opening of a children's hearing arranged by virtue of section 69(2) or 95(2) (the "grounds hearing") the chairing member must—

(a) explain to the child and each relevant person in relation to the child each section 67 ground that is specified in the statement of grounds, and

(b) ask them whether they accept that each ground applies in relation to the child.

(2)   This section is subject to section 94.

Grounds accepted: powers of grounds hearing

91.—(1) This section applies where—

(a) each ground specified in the statement of grounds is accepted, or

(b) at least one of the grounds specified in the statement of grounds is accepted and the grounds hearing considers that it is appropriate to make a decision on whether to make a compulsory supervision order on the basis of the ground or grounds that have been accepted.

(2) If the grounds hearing considers that it is appropriate to do so, the grounds hearing may defer making a decision on whether to make a compulsory supervision order until a subsequent children's hearing.

(3) If the grounds hearing does not exercise the power conferred by subsection (2) the grounds hearing must—

(a) if satisfied that it is necessary to do so for the protection, guidance, treatment or control of the child, make a compulsory supervision order, or

(b) if not so satisfied, discharge the referral.

(4) In subsection (1), "accepted" means accepted by the child and (subject to sections 74 and 75) each relevant person in relation to the child.

Powers of grounds hearing on deferral

92.—(1) This section applies where under section 91(2) the grounds hearing defers making a decision in relation to a child until a subsequent children's hearing.

(2) If the grounds hearing considers that the nature of the child's circumstances is such that for the protection, guidance, treatment or control of the child it is necessary as a matter of urgency that an interim compulsory supervision order be made, the grounds hearing may make an interim compulsory supervision order in relation to the child.

(3)   If the grounds hearing considers that it is necessary to do so for the purpose of obtaining any further information, or carrying out any further investigation, that is needed before the subsequent children's hearing, the hearing may make a medical examination order.

Grounds not accepted: application to sheriff or discharge

93.—(1) This section applies where—
(a) at least one of the grounds specified in the statement of grounds is accepted but the grounds hearing does not consider that it is appropriate to make a decision on whether to make a compulsory supervision order on the basis of the ground or grounds that have been accepted, or
(b) none of the grounds specified in the statement of grounds is accepted.

(2) The grounds hearing must—
(a) direct the Principal Reporter to make an application to the sheriff for a determination on whether each ground that is not accepted by the child and (subject to sections 74 and 75) each relevant person in relation to the child is established, or
(b) discharge the referral.

(3) Subsections (4) and (5) apply if the grounds hearing gives a direction under subsection (2)(a).

(4) The chairing member must—
(a) explain the purpose of the application to the child and (subject to sections 74 and 75) each relevant person in relation to the child, and
(b) inform the child that the child is obliged to attend the hearing before the sheriff unless excused by the sheriff.

(5) If the grounds hearing considers that the nature of the child's circumstances is such that for the protection, guidance, treatment or control of the child it is necessary as a matter of urgency that an interim compulsory supervision order be made, the grounds hearing may make an interim compulsory supervision order in relation to the child.

(6) An interim compulsory supervision order made under subsection (5) may not include a measure of the kind mentioned in section 83(2)(f)(i).

(7) In subsection (1), "accepted" means accepted by the child and (subject to sections 74 and 75) each relevant person in relation to the child.

Child or relevant person unable to understand grounds

94.—(1) Subsection (2) applies where the grounds hearing is satisfied that the child or a relevant person in relation to the child—

(a) would not be capable of understanding an explanation given in compliance with section 90(1) in relation to a ground, or

(b) has not understood the explanation given in compliance with section 90(1) in relation to a ground.

(2) The grounds hearing must—

(a) direct the Principal Reporter to make an application to the sheriff to determine whether the ground is established, or

(b) discharge the referral in relation to the ground.

(3) In the case mentioned in subsection (1)(a), the chairing member need not comply with section 90(1) in relation to that ground as respects the person who would not be capable of understanding an explanation of the ground.

(4) If the grounds hearing gives a direction under subsection (2)(a), the chairing member must—

(a) in so far as is reasonably practicable comply with the requirement in paragraph (a) of section 93(4), and

(b) comply with the requirement in paragraph (b) of that section.

(5) If the grounds hearing gives a direction under subsection (2)(a), section 93(5) applies.

Child fails to attend grounds hearing

95.—(1) This section applies where—

(a) a child fails to attend a grounds hearing arranged by virtue of section 69(2) or subsection (2), and

(b) the child was not excused from attending the grounds hearing.

(2) The grounds hearing may require the Principal Reporter to arrange another grounds hearing.

Children's hearing to consider need for further interim order

Children's hearing to consider need for further interim compulsory supervision order

96.—(1) This section applies where—

(a) under section 93(5) a grounds hearing makes an interim compulsory supervision order in relation to a child, and

(b) the order will cease to have effect before the disposal of the application to the sheriff to which it relates.

(2) The Principal Reporter may arrange a children's hearing for the purpose of considering whether a further interim compulsory supervision order should be made in relation to the child.

(3) If the children's hearing is satisfied that the nature of the child's circumstances is such that for the protection, guidance, treatment or control of the child it is necessary that a further interim compulsory supervision order be made, the children's hearing may make a further interim compulsory supervision order in relation to the child.

(4) The children's hearing may not make a further interim compulsory supervision order in relation to the child if the effect of the order would be that the child would be subject to an interim compulsory supervision order for a continuous period of more than 66 days.

Application of Part where compulsory supervision order in force

Application of Part where compulsory supervision order in force

97.—(1) This Part has effect in relation to a child mentioned in subsection (2) with the modifications set out in subsections (3) to (6).

(2) The child is a child in relation to whom a compulsory supervision order is in force.

(3) References to a decision on whether to make a compulsory supervision order are to be read as references to a decision on whether to review the compulsory supervision order.

(4) Section 91 applies as if for subsections (2) and (3) there were substituted—

"(2) The grounds hearing is to be treated as if it were a hearing to review the compulsory supervision order (and sections 138, 139 and 142 apply accordingly).".

(5) References to an interim compulsory supervision order are to be read as references to an interim variation of the compulsory supervision order.

(6)   Section 96(4) does not apply.

PART 10

PROCEEDINGS BEFORE SHERIFF

Application for extension or variation of interim compulsory supervision order

Application for extension or variation of interim compulsory supervision order

98.—(1) This section applies where—

(a) a child is subject to an interim compulsory supervision order ("the current order"), and

[1](b) either—

(i) the current order is made under section 93(5) and by virtue of section 96(4) a children's hearing would be unable to make a further interim compulsory supervision order, or

(ii) the current order is made under section 100(2).

(2) The Principal Reporter may, before the expiry of the current order, apply to the sheriff for an extension of the order.

(3) The Principal Reporter may, at the same time as applying for an extension of the current order, apply to the sheriff for the order to be varied.

(4)   The current order may be extended, or extended and varied, only if the sheriff is satisfied that the nature of the child's circumstances is such that for the protection, guidance, treatment or control of the child it is necessary that the current order be extended or extended and varied.

NOTE
1. As amended by the Children's Hearings (Scotland) Act 2011 (Modification of Primary Legislation) Order 2013 (SSI 2013/211) Sch.1 para.20(10) (effective June 24, 2013—this being the date on which the 2011 (asp 1) came into force).

Further extension or variation of interim compulsory supervision order

99.—(1) This section applies where an interim compulsory supervision order is—

(a) extended, or extended and varied, under section 98(4), or

(b) further extended, or further extended and varied, under subsection (4).

(2) The Principal Reporter may, before the expiry of the order, apply to the sheriff for a further extension of the order.

(3) The Principal Reporter may, at the same time as applying for a further extension of the order, apply to the sheriff for the order to be varied.

(4) The sheriff may further extend, or further extend and vary, the order if the sheriff is satisfied that the nature of the child's circumstances is such that for the protection, guidance, treatment or control of the child it is necessary that the order be further extended or, as the case may be, further extended and varied.

Power to make interim compulsory supervision order

Sheriff's power to make interim compulsory supervision order

100.—(1) This section applies where—

(a) a child is not subject to an interim compulsory supervision order, and

(b) an application to the sheriff by virtue of section 93(2)(a) or 94(2)(a) in relation to the child has been made but not determined.

(2) If the sheriff is satisfied that the nature of the child's circumstances is such that for the protection, guidance, treatment or control of the child it is necessary as a matter of urgency that an interim compulsory supervision order be made, the sheriff may make an interim compulsory supervision order in relation to the child.

Application to establish grounds

Hearing of application

101.—(1) This section applies where an application is made to the sheriff by virtue of section 93(2)(a) or 94(2)(a).

(2) The application must be heard not later than 28 days after the day on which the application is lodged.

(3) The application must not be heard in open court.

Jurisdiction and standard of proof: offence ground

102.—(1) This section applies where an application is to be made to the sheriff to determine whether the ground mentioned in section 67(2)(j) is established in relation to a child.

(2) The application must be made to the sheriff who would have jurisdiction if the child were being prosecuted for the offence or offences.

(3) The standard of proof in relation to the ground is that which applies in criminal proceedings.

(4) It is immaterial whether the application also relates to other section 67 grounds.

Child's duty to attend hearing unless excused

103.—(1) This section applies where an application is made to the sheriff by virtue of section 93(2)(a) or 94(2)(a).

(2) The child to whom the application relates must attend the hearing of the application unless the child is excused from doing so under subsection (3).

(3) The sheriff may excuse the child from attending all or part of the hearing of the application where—

    (a) the hearing relates to the ground mentioned in section 67(2)(b), (c), (d) or (g) and the attendance of the child at the hearing, or that part of the hearing, is not necessary for a fair hearing,

    (b) the attendance of the child at the hearing, or that part of the hearing, would place the child's physical, mental or moral welfare at risk, or

    (c) taking account of the child's age and maturity, the child would not be capable of understanding what happens at the hearing or that part of the hearing.

(4) The child may attend the hearing of the application even if the child is excused from doing so under subsection (3).

(5) If the child is not excused from attending the hearing but the child does not attend the sheriff may grant a warrant to secure attendance in relation to the child.

(6) Subsection (7) applies if—

    (a) the hearing of the application is to be continued to another day, and

    (b) the sheriff is satisfied that there is reason to believe that the child will not attend on that day.

(7) The sheriff may grant a warrant to secure attendance in relation to the child.

Child and relevant person: representation at hearing

104.—(1) This section applies where an application is made to the sheriff by virtue of section 93(2)(a) or 94(2)(a).

(2) The child may be represented at the hearing of the application by another person.

(3) A relevant person in relation to the child may be represented at the hearing of the application by another person.

(4) A person representing the child or relevant person at the hearing need not be a solicitor or advocate.

Ground accepted before application determined

Application by virtue of section 93: ground accepted before determination

105.—(1) This section applies where—

    (a) an application is made to the sheriff by virtue of section 93(2)(a) in relation to a ground, and

    (b) before the application is determined, the ground is accepted by the child and each relevant person in relation to the child who is present at the hearing before the sheriff.

(2) Unless the sheriff is satisfied in all the circumstances that evidence in relation to the ground should be heard, the sheriff must—

    (a) dispense with hearing such evidence, and

    (b) determine that the ground is established.

Application by virtue of section 94: ground accepted by relevant person before determination

106.—(1) This section applies where—

(a) an application to the sheriff is made by virtue of section 94(2)(a) in relation to a ground on the basis that the child would not understand, or has not understood, an explanation given in compliance with section 90(1)(a), and

(b) before the application is determined the ground is accepted by each relevant person in relation to the child who is present at the hearing before the sheriff.

(2) The sheriff may determine the application without a hearing unless—

(a) a person mentioned in subsection (3) requests that a hearing be held, or

(b) the sheriff considers that it would not be appropriate to determine the application without a hearing.

(3) The persons are—

(a) the child,

(b) a relevant person in relation to the child,

(c) if a safeguarder has been appointed, the safeguarder,

(d) the Principal Reporter.

(4) If the sheriff determines the application without a hearing, the sheriff must do so before the expiry of the period of 7 days beginning with the day on which the application is made.

Withdrawal of application: termination of orders etc.

Withdrawal of application: termination of orders etc. by Principal Reporter

107.—(1) This section applies where—

(a) an application is made to the sheriff by virtue of section 93(2)(a) or 94(2)(a), and

(b) before the application is determined, due to a change of circumstances or information becoming available to the Principal Reporter, the Principal Reporter no longer considers that any ground to which the application relates applies in relation to the child.

(2) The Principal Reporter must withdraw the application.

(3) If one or more grounds were accepted at the grounds hearing which directed the Principal Reporter to make the application, the Principal Reporter must arrange a children's hearing to decide whether to make a compulsory supervision order in relation to the child.

(4) If none of the grounds was accepted at the grounds hearing, any interim compulsory supervision order or warrant to secure attendance which is in force in relation to the child ceases to have effect on the withdrawal of the application.

Determination of application

Determination: ground established

108.—(1) This section applies where the sheriff determines an application made by virtue of section 93(2)(a) or 94(2)(a).

(2) If subsection (4) applies, the sheriff must direct the Principal Reporter to arrange a children's hearing to decide whether to make a compulsory supervision order in relation to the child.

(3) In any other case, the sheriff must—

(a) dismiss the application, and

(b) discharge the referral to the children's hearing.

(4) This subsection applies if—

(a) the sheriff determines that one or more grounds to which the application relates are established, or

(b) one or more other grounds were accepted at the grounds hearing which directed the Principal Reporter to make the application.

(5) In subsection (4)(b), "accepted" means accepted by the child and (subject to sections 74 and 75) each relevant person in relation to the child.

Determination: power to make interim compulsory supervision order etc.

109.—(1) This section applies where the sheriff directs the Principal Reporter to arrange a children's hearing to decide whether to make a compulsory supervision order in relation to the child.

(2) Subsection (3) applies if immediately before the hearing at which the sheriff determined the application made by virtue of section 93(2)(a) or 94(2)(a) an interim compulsory supervision order was not in force in relation to the child.

(3) If the sheriff is satisfied that the nature of the child's circumstances is such that for the protection, guidance, treatment or control of the child it is necessary as a matter of urgency that an interim compulsory supervision order be made, the sheriff may make an interim compulsory supervision order in relation to the child.

(4) Subsection (5) applies if immediately before the hearing at which the sheriff determined the application made by virtue of section 93(2)(a) or 94(2) (a) an interim compulsory supervision order was in force in relation to the child.

(5) If the sheriff is satisfied that the nature of the child's circumstances is such that for the protection, guidance, treatment or control of the child it is necessary that a further interim compulsory supervision order be made, the sheriff may make a further interim compulsory supervision order in relation to the child.

(6) If the sheriff is satisfied that there is reason to believe that the child would not otherwise attend the children's hearing, the sheriff may grant a warrant to secure attendance.

(7) If the sheriff makes an interim compulsory supervision order under subsection (3) or (5) specifying that the child is to reside at a place of safety, the children's hearing must be arranged to take place no later than the third day after the day on which the child begins to reside at the place of safety.

Review of sheriff's determination

Application for review of grounds determination

110.—(1) This section applies where the sheriff makes a determination under section 108 that a section 67 ground (other than the ground mentioned in section 67(2)(j) if the case was remitted to the Principal Reporter under section 49 of the Criminal Procedure (Scotland) Act 1995) is established in relation to a child (a "grounds determination").

(2) A person mentioned in subsection (3) may apply to the sheriff for a review of the grounds determination.

(3) The persons are—

(a) the person who is the subject of the grounds determination (even if that person is no longer a child),
(b) a person who is, or was at the time the grounds determination was made, a relevant person in relation to the child.

Sheriff: review or dismissal of application

111.—(1) This section applies where an application is made under section 110.

(2) If subsection (3) applies the sheriff must review the grounds determination.

(3) This subsection applies if—
(a) there is evidence in relation to the ground that was not considered by the sheriff when making the grounds determination,
(b) the evidence would have been admissible,
(c) there is a reasonable explanation for the failure to lead that evidence before the grounds determination was made, and
(d) the evidence is significant and relevant to the question of whether the grounds determination should have been made.

(4) If subsection (3) does not apply, the sheriff must dismiss the application.

Child's duty to attend review hearing unless excused

112.—(1) This section applies where—
(a) a hearing is to be held by virtue of section 111(2) for the purpose of reviewing a grounds determination, and
(b) the person who is the subject of the grounds determination is still a child.

(2) The child must attend the hearing unless the child is excused by the sheriff on a ground mentioned in section 103(3).

(3) The child may attend the hearing even if the child is excused under subsection (2).

(4) If the sheriff is satisfied that there is reason to believe that the child would not otherwise attend the hearing, the sheriff may grant a warrant to secure attendance.

Child and relevant person: representation at review hearing

113.—(1) This section applies where a hearing is to be held by virtue of section 111(2) for the purpose of reviewing a grounds determination.

(2) The person who is the subject of the grounds determination ("P") may be represented at the hearing by another person.

(3) A relevant person in relation to P (or, where P is no longer a child, a person who was a relevant person in relation to P at the time the grounds determination was made) may be represented at the hearing by another person.

(4)   A person representing P or the relevant person (or person who was a relevant person) at the hearing need not be a solicitor or advocate.

Sheriff's powers on review of grounds determination

114.—(1) This section applies where the sheriff reviews a grounds determination by virtue of section 111(2).

(2) If the sheriff is satisfied that the section 67 ground to which the application relates is established, the sheriff must refuse the application.

(3) If the sheriff determines that the ground to which the application relates is not established, the sheriff must—

(a) recall the grounds determination, and

(b) make an order discharging (wholly or to the extent that it relates to the ground) the referral of the child to the children's hearing.

Recall: power to refer other grounds

115.—(1) This section applies where—

(a) the sheriff makes an order under section 114(3), but

(b) another section 67 ground specified in the same statement of grounds that gave rise to the grounds determination is accepted or established.

(2) If the person to whom the grounds determination relates is still a child, the sheriff must direct the Principal Reporter to arrange a children's hearing for the purpose of considering whether a compulsory supervision order should be made in relation to the child.

(3) If the sheriff is satisfied that the nature of the child's circumstances is such that for the protection, guidance, treatment or control of the child it is necessary as a matter of urgency that an interim compulsory supervision order be made, the sheriff may make an interim compulsory supervision order in relation to the child.

(4) If the sheriff is satisfied that there is reason to believe that the child would not otherwise attend the children's hearing, the sheriff may grant a warrant to secure attendance.

[1](5) If the sheriff makes an interim compulsory supervision order under subsection (3) specifying that the child is to reside at a place of safety, the children's hearing must be arranged to take place no later than the third day after the day on which the child begins to reside at the place of safety.

NOTE

1. As amended by the Children's Hearings (Scotland) Act 2011 (Modification of Primary Legislation) Order 2013 (SSI 2013/211) Sch.1 para.20(11) (effective June 24, 2013—this being the date on which the 2011 (asp 1) came into force).

Recall: powers where no grounds accepted or established

116.—(1) This section applies where—

(a) the sheriff makes an order under section 114(3), and

(b) none of the other section 67 grounds specified in the statement of grounds that gave rise to the grounds determination is accepted or established.

(2) If a compulsory supervision order that is in force in relation to the person who is the subject of the grounds determination was in force at the time of the grounds determination, the sheriff must require a review of the compulsory supervision order.

(3) In any other case, the sheriff must—

(a) terminate any compulsory supervision order that is in force in relation to the person who is the subject of the grounds determination, and

(b) if that person is still a child, consider whether the child will require supervision or guidance.

(4) Where that person is still a child and the sheriff considers that the child will require supervision or guidance, the sheriff must order the relevant local authority for the child to provide it.

(5) Where the sheriff makes such an order, the relevant local authority for the child must give such supervision or guidance as the child will accept.

New section 67 ground established: sheriff to refer to children's hearing

117.—(1) This section applies where—
- (a) by virtue of section 110 the sheriff is reviewing a grounds determination, and
- (b) the sheriff is satisfied that there is sufficient evidence to establish a section 67 ground that is not specified in the statement of grounds that gave rise to the grounds determination.

(2) The sheriff must—
- (a) determine that the ground is established, and
- (b) if the person to whom the grounds determination relates is still a child, direct the Principal Reporter to arrange a children's hearing for the purpose of considering whether a compulsory supervision order should be made in relation to the child.

(3) If the sheriff is satisfied that the nature of the child's circumstances is such that for the protection, guidance, treatment or control of the child it is necessary as a matter of urgency that an interim compulsory supervision order be made, the sheriff may make an interim compulsory supervision order in relation to the child.

(4) If the sheriff is satisfied that there is reason to believe that the child would not otherwise attend the children's hearing, the sheriff may grant a warrant to secure attendance.

[1](5) If the sheriff makes an interim compulsory supervision order under subsection (3) specifying that the child is to reside at a place of safety, the children's hearing must be arranged to take place no later than the third day after the day on which the child begins to reside at the place of safety.

NOTE
1. As amended by the Children's Hearings (Scotland) Act 2011 (Modification of Primary Legislation) Order 2013 (SSI 2013/211) Sch.1 para.20(12) (effective June 24, 2013—this being the date on which the 2011 (asp 1) came into force).

Application of Part where compulsory supervision order in force

Application of Part where compulsory supervision order in force

118.—(1) This Part has effect in relation to a child mentioned in subsection (2) with the modifications set out in subsections (3) to (5).

(2) The child is a child in relation to whom a compulsory supervision order is in force.

(3) References to an interim compulsory supervision order are to be read as references to an interim variation of the compulsory supervision order.

(4) References to the sheriff directing the Principal Reporter to arrange a children's hearing to decide whether to make a compulsory supervision order in relation to the child are to be read as references to the sheriff requiring a review of the compulsory supervision order.

(5) Sections 98 and 99 do not apply.

Children's hearing following deferral or proceedings under Part 10

119.—(1) This section applies where a children's hearing is arranged by the Principal Reporter by virtue of section 91(2), 107(3), 108, 115(2) or 117(2)(b) or subsection (2).

(2) If the children's hearing considers that it is appropriate to do so, the children's hearing may defer making a decision on whether to make a compulsory supervision order until a subsequent children's hearing.

(3) If the children's hearing does not exercise the power conferred by subsection (2) the children's hearing must—

(a) if satisfied that it is necessary to do so for the protection, guidance, treatment or control of the child, make a compulsory supervision order, or

(b) if not so satisfied, discharge the referral.

(4) Subsection (5) applies where—

(a) the child is excused by virtue of section 73(3) or 79(3)(a) or rules under section 177, or

(b) a relevant person in relation to the child is excused by virtue of section 74(3) or 79(3)(b) or rules under section 177.

(5) The children's hearing may, despite the excusal, defer its decision to a subsequent children's hearing under this section without further excusing the person.

Powers of children's hearing on deferral under section 119

120.—(1) This section applies where under subsection (2) of section 119 a children's hearing defers making a decision in relation to a child until a subsequent children's hearing under that section.

(2) Subsection (3) applies if immediately before the children's hearing which takes place under section 119 an interim compulsory supervision order was not in force in relation to the child.

(3) If the children's hearing considers that the nature of the child's circumstances is such that for the protection, guidance, treatment or control of the child it is necessary as a matter of urgency to make an interim compulsory supervision order, the children's hearing may make an interim compulsory supervision order in relation to the child.

(4) Subsection (5) applies if immediately before the children's hearing which takes place under section 119 an interim compulsory supervision order was in force in relation to the child.

(5) If the children's hearing is satisfied that the nature of the child's circumstances is such that for the protection, guidance, treatment or control of the child it is necessary that a further interim compulsory supervision order be made, the children's hearing may make a further interim compulsory supervision order in relation to the child.

(6) If the children's hearing considers that it is necessary to do so for the purpose of obtaining any further information, or carrying out any further investigation, that is needed before the subsequent children's hearing, the hearing may make a medical examination order.

PART 12

CHILDREN'S HEARINGS: GENERAL

Views of child

Confirmation that child given opportunity to express views before hearing

121.—(1) This section applies where a children's hearing is held in relation to a child by virtue of this Act.

(2) The chairing member of the children's hearing must ask the child whether the documents provided to the child by virtue of rules made under section 177 accurately reflect any views expressed by the child.

(3) The chairing member need not comply with subsection (2) if, taking account of the age and maturity of the child, the chairing member considers that it would not be appropriate to do so.

Children's advocacy services

Children's advocacy services

122.—(1) This section applies where a children's hearing is held in relation to a child by virtue of this Act.

(2) The chairing member of the children's hearing must inform the child of the availability of children's advocacy services.

(3) The chairing member need not comply with subsection (2) if, taking account of the age and maturity of the child, the chairing member considers that it would not be appropriate to do so.

(4) The Scottish Ministers may by regulations make provision for or in connection with—

(a) the provision of children's advocacy services,

(b) qualifications to be held by persons providing children's advocacy services,

(c) the training of persons providing children's advocacy services,

(d) the payment of expenses, fees and allowances by the Scottish Ministers to persons providing children's advocacy services.

(5) The Scottish Ministers may enter into arrangements (contractual or otherwise) with any person other than a local authority, CHS or SCRA for the provision of children's advocacy services.

(6) Regulations under this section are subject to the affirmative procedure.

(7) In this section, "children's advocacy services" means services of support and representation provided for the purposes of assisting a child in relation to the child's involvement in a children's hearing.

Warrants to secure attendance

General power to grant warrant to secure attendance

123.—(1) This section applies where in relation to a child—

(a) a children's hearing has been or is to be arranged, or

(b) a hearing is to take place under Part 10.

(2) On the application of the Principal Reporter, any children's hearing may on cause shown grant a warrant to secure the attendance of the child at the children's hearing or, as the case may be, the hearing under Part 10.

Child's age

Requirement to establish child's age

124.—(1) This section applies where a children's hearing is held by virtue of this Act.

(2) The chairing member of the children's hearing must ask the person in respect of whom the hearing has been arranged to declare the person's age.

(3) The person may make another declaration as to the person's age at any time.

(4) The chairing member need not comply with the requirement in subsection (2) if the chairing member considers that the person would not be capable of understanding the question.

(5) Any children's hearing may make a determination of the age of a person who is the subject of the hearing.

(6) A person is taken for the purposes of this Act to be of the age—

(a)   worked out on the basis of the person's most recent declaration, or

(b)   if a determination of age by a children's hearing is in effect, worked out in accordance with that determination.

(7) Nothing done by a children's hearing in relation to a person is invalidated if it is subsequently proved that the age of the person is not that worked out under subsection (6).

Compulsory supervision orders: review

Compulsory supervision order: requirement to review

125.—(1) This section applies where a children's hearing is making, varying or continuing a compulsory supervision order.

(2) Where the order being made contains a movement restriction condition (or the order is being varied so as to include such a condition), the children's hearing must require the order to be reviewed by a children's hearing on a day or within a period specified in the order.

(3) In any other case, the children's hearing may require the order to be so reviewed.

Contact orders and permanence orders

Review of contact direction

126.—(1) This section applies where, in relation to a child—

(a)   a children's hearing—

(i)   makes a compulsory supervision order,

(ii) makes an interim compulsory supervision order, an interim variation of a compulsory supervision order or a medical examination order which is to have effect for more than 5 working days, or

(iii) continues or varies a compulsory supervision order under section 138, and

(b) the order contains (or is varied so as to contain) a measure of the type mentioned in section 83(2)(g) or 87(2)(e) ("a contact direction").

(2) The Principal Reporter must arrange a children's hearing for the purposes of reviewing the contact direction—

(a) if an order mentioned in subsection (3) is in force, or

(b) if requested to do so by an individual who claims that the conditions specified for the purposes of this paragraph in an order made by the Scottish Ministers are satisfied in relation to the individual.

(3) The orders are—

(a) a contact order regulating contact between an individual (other than a relevant person in relation to the child) and the child, or

(b) a permanence order which specifies arrangements for contact between such an individual and the child.

(4) The children's hearing is to take place no later than 5 working days after the children's hearing mentioned in subsection (1)(a).

(5) If a children's hearing arranged by virtue of paragraph (b) of subsection (2) considers that the conditions specified for the purposes of that paragraph are not satisfied in relation to the individual, the children's hearing must take no further action.

(6) In any other case, the children's hearing may—

(a) confirm the decision of the children's hearing mentioned in subsection (1)(a), or

(b) vary the compulsory supervision order, interim compulsory supervision order or medical examination order (but only by varying or removing the contact direction).

(7) Sections 73 and 74 do not apply in relation to a children's hearing arranged by virtue of subsection (2).

Referral where failure to provide education for excluded pupil

Referral where failure to provide education for excluded pupil

127.—(1) This section applies where it appears to a children's hearing that—

(a) an education authority has a duty under section 14(3) of the Education (Scotland) Act 1980 (c.44) (education authority's duty to provide education for child excluded from school) in relation to the child to whom the children's hearing relates, and

(b) the authority is failing to comply with the duty.

(2) The children's hearing may require the National Convener to refer the matter to the Scottish Ministers.

(3) If a requirement is made under subsection (2), the National Convener must—

(a) make a referral to the Scottish Ministers, and

(b) give a copy of it to the education authority to which it relates and the Principal Reporter.

Parenting order

Duty to consider applying for parenting order

128.—(1) This section applies where a children's hearing constituted for any purpose in respect of a child is satisfied that it might be appropriate for a parenting order to be made in respect of a parent of the child under section 102 of the Antisocial Behaviour etc. (Scotland) Act 2004 (asp 8) (the "2004 Act").

(2) The children's hearing may require the Principal Reporter to consider whether to apply under section 102(3) of the 2004 Act for such an order.

(3) The children's hearing must specify in the requirement—

(a) the parent in respect of whom it might be appropriate for the order to be made, and

(b) by reference to section 102(4) to (6) of the 2004 Act, the condition in respect of which the application might be made.

(4) In this section, "parent" and "child" have the meanings given by section 117 of the 2004 Act.

PART 13

REVIEW OF COMPULSORY SUPERVISION ORDER

Requirement for review

Requirement under Antisocial Behaviour etc. (Scotland) Act 2004

129.—(1) Subsection (2) applies where—

(a) under section 12(1A) of the Antisocial Behaviour etc. (Scotland) Act 2004 (asp 8) the sheriff requires the Principal Reporter to arrange a children's hearing in respect of a child, and

(b) a compulsory supervision order is in force in relation to the child.

(2) The Principal Reporter must initiate a review of the compulsory supervision order.

Case remitted under section 49 of Criminal Procedure (Scotland) Act 1995

130.—(1) This section applies where, in relation to a child—

(a) a court remits a case under section 49 of the Criminal Procedure (Scotland) Act 1995 to the Principal Reporter to arrange for the disposal of the case by a children's hearing, and

(b) a compulsory supervision order is in force in relation to the child.

(2) The Principal Reporter must initiate a review of the compulsory supervision order.

(3) A certificate signed by the clerk of the court stating that the child has pled guilty to, or been found guilty of, the offence to which the case relates is conclusive evidence for the purposes of the children's hearing held for the purposes of reviewing the order that the offence was committed by the child.

(4) This Act applies as if the plea of guilty, or the finding of guilt, were a determination of the sheriff under section 108 that the ground in section 67(2)(j) was established in relation to the child.

Duty of implementation authority to require review

131.—(1) The implementation authority must, by notice to the Principal Reporter, require a review of a compulsory supervision order in relation to a child where the authority is satisfied that one or more of the circumstances set out in subsection (2) exist.

(2) Those circumstances are—

(a) the compulsory supervision order ought to be terminated or varied,

(b) the compulsory supervision order is not being complied with,

(c) the best interests of the child would be served by the authority making one of the following applications, and the authority intends to make such an application—

    (i) an application under section 80 of the Adoption and Children (Scotland) Act 2007 (asp 4) (the "2007 Act") for a permanence order,

    (ii) an application under section 92 of the 2007 Act for variation of such an order,

    (iii) an application under section 93 of the 2007 Act for amendment of such an order,

    (iv) an application under section 98 of the 2007 Act for revocation of such an order,

(d) the best interests of the child would be served by the authority placing the child for adoption and the authority intends to place the child for adoption,

(e) the authority is aware that an application has been made and is pending, or is about to be made, under section 29 or 30 of the 2007 Act for an adoption order in respect of the child.

(3) The Scottish Ministers may by regulations specify the period within which a requirement under subsection (1) must be made where the implementation authority is satisfied as to the existence of the circumstances mentioned in subsection (2)(a) to (d).

(4) Different periods may be specified for different circumstances, or classes of circumstances.

(5) Where an implementation authority is under a duty to require a review under subsection (1) by virtue of being satisfied as to the existence of the circumstances mentioned in subsection (2)(e), the authority must do so as soon as practicable after the authority becomes aware of the application.

Right of child or relevant person to require review

132.—(1) This section applies where a compulsory supervision order is in force in relation to a child.

(2) The child may by giving notice to the Principal Reporter require a review of the order.

(3) A relevant person in relation to the child may by giving notice to the Principal Reporter require a review of the order.

(4) The order may not be reviewed—

(a) during the period of 3 months beginning with the day on which the order is made,

(b) if the order is continued or varied, during the period of 3 months beginning with the day on which it is continued or varied.

(5) The Scottish Ministers may by regulations provide that, despite subsection (4), where the order includes a secure accommodation authorisation, the order may be reviewed during a period specified in the regulations.

Principal Reporter's duty to initiate review

133. The Principal Reporter must initiate a review of a compulsory supervision order in relation to a child if—

(a) the order will expire within 3 months, and

(b) the order would not otherwise be reviewed before it expires.

Duty to initiate review if child to be taken out of Scotland

134.—(1) This section applies where—

(a) a child is subject to a compulsory supervision order,

(b) a relevant person in relation to the child proposes to take the child to live outwith Scotland, and

(c) the proposal is not in accordance with the order or an order under section 11 of the 1995 Act.

(2) The relevant person must give notice of the proposal to the Principal Reporter and the implementation authority at least 28 days before the day on which the relevant person proposes to take the child to live outwith Scotland.

(3) If the Principal Reporter receives notice under subsection (2), the Principal Reporter must initiate a review of the compulsory supervision order.

Duty to initiate review: secure accommodation authorisation

135.—(1) Subsection (2) applies where a compulsory supervision order includes a secure accommodation authorisation (which has not ceased to have effect by virtue of section 151(5)).

(2) The Principal Reporter must initiate a review of the order—

(a) before the end of the period of 3 months beginning with the day on which the order is made, and

(b) if the order is varied or continued, before the end of the period of 3 months beginning with the day on which it is varied or continued.

Duty to initiate review where child transferred

136. The Principal Reporter must initiate a review of a compulsory supervision order in relation to a child where the child is transferred under section 143(2).

Functions of Principal Reporter and children's hearing

Duty to arrange children's hearing

137.—(1) This section applies where a compulsory supervision order is in force in relation to a child and—

(a) a review of the order is required or initiated by virtue of any of—

(i)   sections 107, 108, 115 and 117 (all as modified by section 118),

(ii) sections 116, 125, 129 to 136 and 146, or

(b) the child's case is referred to the Principal Reporter under section 96(3) or 106 of the Adoption and Children (Scotland) Act 2007 (asp 4).

(2) The Principal Reporter must arrange a children's hearing to review the compulsory supervision order.

(3) If the review is initiated under section 136, the children's hearing must be arranged to take place before the expiry of the period of 3 working days beginning with the day on which the child is transferred.

(4) The Principal Reporter must require the implementation authority to give the Principal Reporter any reports that the authority has prepared in relation to the child and any other information which the authority may wish to give to assist the children's hearing.

(5) The Principal Reporter may require the implementation authority to give the Principal Reporter a report on—

(a) the child generally,

(b) any particular matter relating to the child specified by the Principal Reporter.

(6) The implementation authority may include in a report given to the Principal Reporter under subsection (4) or (5) information given to the authority by another person.

Powers of children's hearing on review

138.—(1) This section applies where a children's hearing is carrying out a review of a compulsory supervision order in relation to a child.

(2) If the children's hearing considers that it is appropriate to do so, the children's hearing may defer making a decision about the compulsory supervision order until a subsequent children's hearing under this section.

(3) Otherwise, the children's hearing may—

(a) terminate the compulsory supervision order,

(b) vary the compulsory supervision order,

(c) continue the compulsory supervision order for a period not exceeding one year.

(4) The children's hearing may vary or continue a compulsory supervision order only if the children's hearing is satisfied that it is necessary to do so for the protection, guidance, treatment or control of the child.

[1](5) [. . .]

(6) If the children's hearing terminates the compulsory supervision order, the children's hearing must—

(a) consider whether supervision or guidance is needed by the child, and

(b) if so, make a statement to that effect.

(7) If the children's hearing states that supervision or guidance is needed by the child, it is the duty of the relevant local authority for the child to give such supervision or guidance as the child will accept.

(8) Subsection (9) applies where—

(a) a child or relevant person in relation to the child is excused under section 73(2), 74(2) or 79 from attending the children's hearing, and

(b) the hearing defers its decision until a subsequent children's hearing.

(9) The children's hearing need not excuse the child or relevant person in relation to the child from attending the subsequent children's hearing.

NOTE
1. Repealed by the Children's Hearings (Scotland) Act 2011 (Modification of Primary Legislation) Order 2013 (SSI 2013/211) Sch.2 (effective June 24, 2013—this being the date on which the 2011 (asp 1) came into force). *Rule now contained in section 29A.*

Powers of children's hearing on deferral under section 138

139.—(1) This section applies where under subsection (2) of section 138 a children's hearing defers making a decision about the compulsory supervision order in relation to a child until a subsequent children's hearing under that section.

(2) The children's hearing may continue the compulsory supervision order until the subsequent children's hearing.

(3) If the children's hearing considers that the nature of the child's circumstances is such that for the protection, guidance, treatment or control of the child it is necessary as a matter of urgency that the compulsory supervision order be varied, the children's hearing may make an interim variation of the compulsory supervision order.

Interim variation of compulsory supervision order

140.—(1) In this Act, "interim variation", in relation to a compulsory supervision order made in relation to a child, means a variation of the order having effect for the relevant period.

(2) An interim variation may vary the order so that, instead of specifying a place or places at which the child is to reside under section 83(2)(a), the order specifies that the child is to reside at any place of safety away from the place where the child predominantly resides.

(3) Section 83(5)(a) does not apply to the varied order.

(4) In subsection (1), the "relevant period" means the period beginning with the variation of the order and ending with whichever of the following first occurs—

  (a) the next children's hearing arranged in relation to the child,
  [1](b) the disposal by the sheriff of an application made by virtue of section 93(2)(a) or 94(2)(a) relating to the child,
  (c) a day specified in the variation,
  (d) the expiry of the period of 22 days beginning with the day on which the order is varied.

NOTE
1. As amended by the Children's Hearings (Scotland) Act 2011 (Modification of Primary Legislation) Order 2013 (SSI 2013/211) Sch.1 para.20(13) (effective June 24, 2013—this being the date on which the 2011 (asp 1) came into force).

Preparation of report in circumstances relating to permanence order or adoption

141.—(1) This section applies where a review of a compulsory supervision order in relation to a child is required under subsection (1) of section 131 in the circumstances mentioned in subsection (2)(c), (d) or (e) of that section.

(2) On determining the review under section 138(3), the children's hearing must prepare a report providing advice about the circumstances to which the review relates for—

  (a) the implementation authority, and
  (b) any court that requires (or may subsequently require) to come to a decision about an application of the type mentioned in section 131(2)(c) or (e).

(3) The report must be in such form as the Scottish Ministers may determine.

(4) If an application of the type mentioned in section 131(2)(c) or (e) is (or has been) made, the court must have regard to the report when coming to its decision about the application.

Review of relevant person determination

Review of determination that person be deemed a relevant person

142.—(1) This section applies where, in relation to a child—

(a) a children's hearing determines a review of a compulsory supervision order by varying or continuing the order,

(b) an individual is deemed to be a relevant person by virtue of section 81, and

(c) it appears to the children's hearing that the individual may no longer have (nor recently have had) a significant involvement in the upbringing of the child.

(2) The children's hearing must review whether the individual should continue to be deemed to be a relevant person in relation to the child.

(3) If the children's hearing considers that it is appropriate to do so, the children's hearing may defer determining the review under subsection (2) until a subsequent children's hearing under this section.

(4) Otherwise, if the children's hearing determines that the individual does not have (and has not recently had) a significant involvement in the upbringing of the child then—

(a) the children's hearing must direct that the individual is no longer to be deemed to be a relevant person, and

(b) section 81(4) ceases to apply in relation to the individual (except in relation to any appeal arising from the determination mentioned in subsection (1)(a)).

PART 14

IMPLEMENTATION OF ORDERS

Power to transfer child in cases of urgent necessity

Transfers in cases of urgent necessity

143.—(1) Subsection (2) applies where a child is residing at a particular place by virtue of a compulsory supervision order or interim compulsory supervision order containing a measure of the type mentioned in section 83(2)(a).

(2) If it is in the interests of the child or another child in the place that the child be moved out of the place as a matter of urgent necessity then, despite the order, the chief social work officer may transfer the child to another place.

Implementation of compulsory supervision order

Implementation of compulsory supervision order: general duties of implementation authority

144.—(1) The implementation authority must give effect to a compulsory supervision order.

(2) The implementation authority must in particular comply with any requirements imposed on it in relation to the child by the compulsory supervision order.

(3) The duties which an implementation authority may be required to carry out under a compulsory supervision order include securing or facilitating the provision for the child of services of a kind which the implementation authority does not provide.

Duty where order requires child to reside in certain place

145.—(1) Subsection (2) applies where, under a compulsory supervision order, a child is required to reside—

(a) in accommodation provided by the parents or relatives of the child, or by any person associated with them or the child, or

(b) in any other accommodation not provided by a local authority.

(2) The implementation authority must from time to time—

(a) investigate whether, while the child is resident in that accommodation, any conditions imposed under the compulsory supervision order are being complied with, and

(b) if the authority considers that conditions are not being complied with, take such steps as the authority considers reasonable.

Breach of duties imposed by sections 144 and 145

146.—(1) This section applies where, on determining the review of a compulsory supervision order under section 138(3), it appears to the children's hearing that the implementation authority is in breach of a duty in relation to the child imposed on the authority under section 144 or 145.

(2) The children's hearing may direct the National Convener to give the authority notice in accordance with subsection (3) of an intended application by the National Convener to enforce the authority's duty.

(3) The notice must—

(a) set out the respects in which the authority is in breach of its duty in relation to the child, and

(b) state that if the authority does not perform that duty before the expiry of the period of 21 days beginning with the day on which the notice is given, the National Convener, on the direction of the children's hearing, is to make an application to enforce the authority's duty.

(4) The National Convener must, at the same time as giving the notice, send a copy of the notice to—

(a) the child,

(b) each relevant person in relation to the child.

(5) If a children's hearing gives a direction under subsection (2), the children's hearing must require that a further review of the compulsory supervision order take place on or as soon as is reasonably practicable after the expiry of the period of 28 days beginning on the day on which the notice is given.

(6) If, on that further review, it appears to the children's hearing carrying out the further review that the authority continues to be in breach of its duty, the children's hearing may direct the National Convener to make an application under section 147.

(7) In determining whether to direct the National Convener to make an application under section 147 to enforce the authority's duty, the children's hearing must not take into account any factor relating to the adequacy of the means available to the authority to enable it to comply with the duty.

Application for order

147.—(1) The National Convener must, if directed to do so under section 146(6), apply to the relevant sheriff principal for an order to enforce an implementation authority's duty in relation to a child.

(2) The relevant sheriff principal is the sheriff principal of the sheriffdom in which the principal office of the implementation authority is situated.

(3) The National Convener may not make such an application, despite the direction given under section 146(6), unless—

(a) the National Convener has given the authority notice in relation to the duty in compliance with a direction given under section 146(2), and

(b) the authority has failed to carry out the duty within the period specified in the notice.

(4) The application is to be made by summary application.

Order for enforcement

148.—(1) The sheriff principal may, on an application by the National Convener under section 147, make an order requiring the implementation authority that is in breach of a duty imposed by virtue of a compulsory supervision order to carry out that duty.

(2) Such an order is final.

Compulsory supervision orders etc.: further provision

Compulsory supervision orders etc.: further provision

149.—(1) The Scottish Ministers may by regulations make provision about—

(a) the transmission of information relating to a child who is the subject of an order or warrant mentioned in subsection (2) to any person who, by virtue of the order or warrant, has or is to have control over the child,

(b) the provision of temporary accommodation for the child,

(c) the taking of the child to any place in which the child is required to reside under the order or warrant,

(d) the taking of the child to—

  (i) a place of safety under section 169 or 170,

  (ii) a place to which the child falls to be taken to under section 169(2), or

  (iii) a person to whom the child falls to be taken to under section 170(2).

(2) The orders and warrants are—

(a) a compulsory supervision order,

(b) an interim compulsory supervision order,

(c) a medical examination order,

(d) a warrant to secure attendance.

Movement restriction conditions: regulations etc.

Movement restriction conditions: regulations etc.

150.—(1) The Scottish Ministers may by regulations prescribe—

(a) restrictions, or

(b) monitoring arrangements,

that may be imposed as part of a movement restriction condition.

(2) Regulations under subsection (1) may in particular—

(a) prescribe the maximum period for which a restriction may have effect,

(b) prescribe methods of monitoring compliance with a movement restriction condition,

(c) specify devices that may be used for the purpose of that monitoring,

(d) prescribe the person or class of person who may be designated to carry out the monitoring, and

(e) require that the condition be varied to designate another person if the person designated ceases to be prescribed, or fall within a class of person, prescribed under paragraph (d).

(3) Regulations under subsection (1) are subject to the affirmative procedure.

(4) The Scottish Ministers may—

(a) make arrangements (contractual or otherwise) to secure the services of such persons as they think fit to carry out monitoring, and

(b) make those arrangements in a way that provides differently for different areas or different forms of monitoring.

(5) Nothing in any enactment or rule of law prevents the disclosure to a person providing a service under an arrangement made under subsection (4) of information relating to a child where the disclosure is made for the purposes only of the full and proper provision of monitoring.

Secure accommodation

Implementation of secure accommodation authorisation

151.—(1) Subsections (3) and (4) apply where a relevant order or warrant made in relation to a child includes a secure accommodation authorisation.

(2) A relevant order or warrant is—

(a) a compulsory supervision order,

(b) an interim compulsory supervision order,

(c) a medical examination order,

(d) a warrant to secure attendance.

(3) The chief social work officer may implement the authorisation only with the consent of the person in charge of the residential establishment containing the secure accommodation in which the child is to be placed (the "head of unit").

(4) The chief social work officer must remove the child from secure accommodation if—

(a) the chief social work officer considers it unnecessary for the child to be kept there, or

(b) the chief social work officer is required to do so by virtue of regulations made under subsection (6).

(5) A secure accommodation authorisation ceases to have effect once the child is removed from secure accommodation under subsection (4).

(6) The Scottish Ministers may by regulations make provision in relation to decisions—

(a) by the chief social work officer—

(i) whether to implement a secure accommodation authorisation,

(ii) whether to remove a child from secure accommodation,

(b) by the head of unit whether to consent under subsection (3).

(7) Regulations under subsection (6) may in particular—

(a) specify—

(i) the time within which a decision must be made,

(ii) the procedure to be followed,

(iii) the criteria to be applied,

(iv) matters to be taken into account or disregarded,

(v) persons who must be consulted,

(vi) persons who must consent before a decision has effect,

(b) make provision about—

(i) notification of decisions,

(ii) the giving of reasons for decisions,

(iii) reviews of decisions,

(iv) the review of the order or warrant containing the secure accommodation authorisation where the head of unit does not consent.

(8) Regulations under subsection (6) are subject to the affirmative procedure.

Secure accommodation: placement in other circumstances

152.—(1) The Scottish Ministers may by regulations make provision specifying circumstances in which a child falling within subsection (3) may be placed in secure accommodation.

(2) Regulations under subsection (1) may in particular include provision for and in connection with—

(a) the procedure to be followed in deciding whether to place a child in secure accommodation,

(b) the notification of decisions,

(c) the giving of reasons for decisions,

(d) the review of decisions,

(e) the review of placements by a children's hearing.

(3) A child falls within this subsection if—

(a) a relevant order or warrant is in force in relation to the child, and

(b) the relevant order or warrant does not include a secure accommodation authorisation.

(4) A relevant order or warrant is—

(a) a compulsory supervision order,

(b) an interim compulsory supervision order,

(c) a medical examination order,

(d) a warrant to secure attendance.

(5) Regulations under subsection (1) are subject to the affirmative procedure.

Secure accommodation: regulations

153.—(1) The Scottish Ministers may by regulations make provision about children placed in secure accommodation by virtue of this Act.

(2) Regulations under subsection (1) may in particular include provision—

(a) imposing requirements on the Principal Reporter,

(b) imposing requirements on the implementation authority in relation to a compulsory supervision order or an interim compulsory supervision order,

(c) imposing requirements on the relevant local authority for a child in relation to a medical examination order or a warrant to secure attendance,

(d) in connection with the protection of the welfare of the children.

(3) Regulations under subsection (1) are subject to the affirmative procedure.

PART 15

APPEALS

Appeal against decision of children's hearing

Appeal to sheriff against decision of children's hearing

154.—(1) A person mentioned in subsection (2) may appeal to the sheriff against a relevant decision of a children's hearing in relation to a child.

(2) The persons are—

(a) the child,

(b) a relevant person in relation to the child,

(c) a safeguarder appointed in relation to the child by virtue of section 30.

(3) A relevant decision is—

(a) a decision to make, vary or continue a compulsory supervision order,

(b) a decision to discharge a referral by the Principal Reporter,

(c) a decision to terminate a compulsory supervision order,

(d) a decision to make an interim compulsory supervision order,

(e) a decision to make an interim variation of a compulsory supervision order,

(f) a decision to make a medical examination order, or

(g) a decision to grant a warrant to secure attendance.

(4) An appeal under subsection (1) may be made jointly by two or more persons mentioned in subsection (2).

(5) An appeal under subsection (1) must be made before the expiry of the period of 21 days beginning with the day on which the decision is made.

Procedure

155.—(1) This section applies where an appeal under section 154 is made.

(2) The Principal Reporter must lodge with the sheriff clerk a copy of—

(a) the decision, and the reasons for the decision, of the children's hearing,

(b) all information provided by virtue of rules under section 177 to the children's hearing, and

(c) the report of the children's hearing.

(3) The appeal must not be heard in open court.

(4) The sheriff may (but need not) hear evidence before determining the appeal.

(5) The sheriff may hear evidence from—

(a) the child,

(b) a relevant person in relation to the child,

(c) an author or compiler of a report or statement provided to the children's hearing that made the decision,

(d) the Principal Reporter,

(e) where the appeal is against a decision to make, grant, vary or continue an order or warrant including a secure accommodation authorisation in respect of the child—

(i) the person in charge of the secure accommodation specified in the secure accommodation authorisation, and

(ii) the chief social work officer, and

(f) any other person who the sheriff considers may give material additional evidence.

(6) The sheriff may require any person to give a report to the sheriff for the purpose of assisting the sheriff in determining the appeal.

[1](7) Subsection (6) applies in relation to a safeguarder only if regulations under section 34 so provide.

NOTE

1. As amended by the Children's Hearings (Scotland) Act 2011 (Modification of Primary Legislation) Order 2013 (SSI 2013/211) Sch.1 para.20(14) (effective June 24, 2013—this being the date on which the 2011 (asp 1) came into force).

Determination of appeal

156.—(1) If satisfied that the decision to which an appeal under section 154 relates is justified, the sheriff—

(a) must confirm the decision, and

(b) may take one or more of the steps mentioned in subsection (3) if satisfied that the circumstances of the child in relation to whom the decision was made have changed since the decision was made.

(2) In any other case, the sheriff—

(a) must—

   (i) where the decision is a decision to grant a warrant to secure attendance, recall the warrant,

   (ii) where the decision is a decision to make an interim compulsory supervision order or a medical examination order, terminate the order,

(b) may take one or more of the steps mentioned in subsection (3).

(3) Those steps are—

(a) require the Principal Reporter to arrange a children's hearing for any purpose for which a hearing can be arranged under this Act,

(b) continue, vary or terminate any order, interim variation or warrant which is in effect,

(c) discharge the child from any further hearing or other proceedings in relation to the grounds that gave rise to the decision,

(d) make an interim compulsory supervision order or interim variation of a compulsory supervision order, or

(e) grant a warrant to secure attendance.

[1](3A) If the sheriff continues or varies a compulsory supervision order under subsection (3)(b), the sheriff—

(a) must, if the order contains a movement restriction condition (or is being varied so as to include such a condition), require the order to be reviewed by a children's hearing on a day or within a period specified in the order,

(b) may, in any other case, require the order to be so reviewed.

(4) If the sheriff discharges a child under subsection (3)(c), the sheriff must also terminate any order or warrant which is in effect in relation to the child.

(5) The fact that a sheriff makes, continues or varies an order, or grants a warrant, under subsection (1)(b) or (2)(b) does not prevent a children's hearing from continuing, varying or terminating the order or warrant.

NOTE

1. As inserted by the Children's Hearings (Scotland) Act 2011 (Modification of Primary Legislation) Order 2013 (SSI 2013/211) Sch.1 para.20(15) (effective June 24, 2013—this being the date on which the 2011 (asp 1) came into force).

Time limit for disposal of appeal against certain decisions

157.—(1) This section applies where an appeal under section 154 relates to a decision of a children's hearing to—

(a) make a compulsory supervision order including a secure accommodation authorisation or movement restriction condition,

(b) make an interim compulsory supervision order,

(c) make an interim variation of a compulsory supervision order,

(d) make a medical examination order, or

(e) grant a warrant to secure attendance.

(2) The appeal must be heard and disposed of before the expiry of the period of 3 days beginning the day after the day on which the appeal is made.

(3) If the appeal is not disposed of within that period, the authorisation, condition, order, variation or, as the case may be, warrant ceases to have effect.

Compulsory supervision order: suspension pending appeal

Compulsory supervision order: suspension pending appeal

158.—(1) This section applies where—

(a) an appeal is made under section 154 against a decision to make, vary, continue or terminate a compulsory supervision order, and

(b) the person making the appeal requests the Principal Reporter to arrange a children's hearing to consider whether the decision should be suspended pending the determination of the appeal.

(2) As soon as practicable after the request is made, the Principal Reporter must arrange a children's hearing to consider whether the decision should be suspended pending the determination of the appeal.

Frivolous and vexatious appeals

Frivolous and vexatious appeals

[1]**159.**—(1) This section applies where the sheriff—

(a) determines an appeal under section 154 or 161 by confirming a decision of a children's hearing to vary or continue a compulsory supervision order, and

(b) is satisfied that the appeal was frivolous or vexatious.

(2) The sheriff may order that, during the period of 12 months beginning on the day of the order, the person who appealed must obtain leave from the sheriff before making another appeal under section 154 or 161 against a decision of a children's hearing in relation to the compulsory supervision order.

NOTE

1. As amended by the Children's Hearings (Scotland) Act 2011 (Modification of Primary Legislation) Order 2013 (SSI 2013/211) Sch.1 para.20(16) (effective June 24, 2013—this being the date on which the 2011 (asp 1) came into force).

Other appeals

Appeal to sheriff against relevant person determination

160.—(1) A person mentioned in subsection (2) may appeal to the sheriff against—

(a) a determination of a pre-hearing panel or children's hearing that an individual is or is not to be deemed a relevant person in relation to a child,

(b) a determination of a review under section 142(2) that an individual is to continue to be deemed, or no longer to be deemed, a relevant person in relation to a child.

(2) The persons are—

(a) the individual in question,

(b) the child,

(c) a relevant person in relation to the child,

(d) two or more persons mentioned in paragraphs (a) to (c) acting jointly.

(3) If satisfied that the determination to which the appeal relates is justified, the sheriff must confirm the determination.

(4) If not satisfied, the sheriff must—

(a) quash the determination, and

(b) where the determination is a determination of a pre-hearing panel or children's hearing under section 81 that the individual should not be deemed a relevant person in relation to the child, make an order deeming the individual to be a relevant person in relation to the child.

(5) Where the sheriff makes an order under subsection (4)(b), section 81(4) applies to the individual as if a pre-hearing panel had deemed the individual to be a relevant person.

(6) An appeal under this section must be—

(a) made before the expiry of the period of 7 days beginning with the day on which the determination is made,

(b) heard and disposed of before the expiry of the period of 3 days beginning with the day on which the appeal is made.

Appeal to sheriff against decision affecting contact or permanence order

161.—(1) A person mentioned in subsection (2) may appeal to the sheriff against a relevant decision of a children's hearing in relation to a child.

(2) The person is an individual (other than a relevant person in relation to the child) in relation to whom—

(a) a contact order is in force regulating contact between the individual and the child,

(b) a permanence order is in force which specifies arrangements for contact between the individual and the child, or

(c) the conditions specified for the purposes of section 126(2)(b) are satisfied.

(3) A relevant decision is a decision under section 126(6) relating to a compulsory supervision order.

(4) If the sheriff is satisfied that the relevant decision is justified, the sheriff must confirm the decision.

(5) If not satisfied, the sheriff must vary the compulsory supervision order by varying or removing the measure contained in the order under section 83(2)(g).

(6) An appeal under this section must be—

(a) made before the expiry of the period of 21 days beginning with the day on which the relevant decision is made,

(b) heard and disposed of before the expiry of the period of 3 days beginning with the day on which the appeal is made.

Appeal to sheriff against decision to implement secure accommodation authorisation

162.—(1) This section applies where a relevant order or warrant made in relation to a child includes a secure accommodation authorisation.

(2) A relevant order or warrant is—

(a) a compulsory supervision order,

(b) an interim compulsory supervision order,

(c) a medical examination order,

(d) a warrant to secure attendance.

(3) The child or a relevant person in relation to the child may appeal to the sheriff against a relevant decision in relation to the authorisation.

(4) A relevant decision is a decision by the chief social work officer—

(a) to implement the authorisation,

(b) not to implement the authorisation,

(c) to remove the child from secure accommodation.

(5) An appeal under subsection (3) may be made jointly by—

(a) the child and one or more relevant persons in relation to the child, or

(b) two or more relevant persons in relation to the child.

(6) An appeal must not be held in open court.

(7) The Scottish Ministers may by regulations make further provision about appeals under subsection (3).

(8) Regulations under subsection (7) may in particular—

(a) specify the period within which an appeal may be made,

(b) make provision about the hearing of evidence during an appeal,

(c) make provision about the powers of the sheriff on determining an appeal,

(d) provide for appeals to the sheriff principal and Court of Session against the determination of an appeal.

(9) Regulations under subsection (7) are subject to the affirmative procedure.

Appeals to sheriff principal and Court of Session

Appeals to sheriff principal and Court of Session: children's hearings etc.

163.—(1) A person mentioned in subsection (3) may appeal by stated case to the sheriff principal or the Court of Session against—

(a) a determination by the sheriff of—

   (i) an application to determine whether a section 67 ground (other than the ground mentioned in section 67(2)(j) if the case was remitted to the Principal Reporter under section 49 of the Criminal Procedure (Scotland) Act 1995) is established,

   (ii) an application under section 110(2) for review of a finding that a section 67 ground is established,

   (iii) an appeal against a decision of a children's hearing,

   (iv) an application under section 98 for an extension of an interim compulsory supervision order,

   (v) an application under section 99 for a further extension of an interim compulsory supervision order,

(b) a decision of the sheriff under section 100 to—

   (i) make an interim compulsory supervision order,

   (ii) make an interim variation of a compulsory supervision order.

(2) A person mentioned in subsection (3) may, with leave of the sheriff principal, appeal by stated case to the Court of Session against the sheriff principal's decision in an appeal under subsection (1).

(3) The persons are—

(a) the child,

(b) a relevant person in relation to the child,

(c) a safeguarder appointed in relation to the child by virtue of section 30,

(d) two or more persons mentioned in paragraphs (a) to (c) acting jointly, and

(e) the Principal Reporter.

(4) Despite subsections (1) and (2), a safeguarder may not—

(a) appeal against a determination by the sheriff of a type mentioned in subsection (1)(a)(i) or (ii), or a decision of the sheriff of a type mentioned in subsection (1)(b),

(b) appeal to the Court of Session against the sheriff principal's decision in such an appeal.

(5) Despite subsection (1), the Principal Reporter may not appeal against a determination by the sheriff confirming a decision of a children's hearing.

(6) Subsection (7) applies in relation to—

(a) an appeal against a determination by the sheriff of an application under section 110(2) for review of a finding that a section 67 ground is established,

(b) an appeal to the Court of Session against the sheriff principal's decision in such an appeal.

(7) In subsection (3)(a) and (b)—

(a) the references to the child are to the person in relation to whom the section 67 ground was established (even if that person is no longer a child),

(b) the reference to a relevant person in relation to the child includes a person who was, at the time the section 67 ground was established, a relevant person in relation to the child.

(8) An appeal under this section must be made before the expiry of the period of 28 days beginning with the day on which the determination or decision appealed against was made.

(9) An appeal under this section may be made—

(a) on a point of law, or

(b) in respect of any procedural irregularity.

(10) On deciding an appeal under subsection (1), the sheriff principal or the Court of Session must remit the case to the sheriff for disposal in accordance with such directions as the court may give.

(11) A decision in an appeal under subsection (1) or (2) by the Court of Session is final.

(12) In subsection (1)(a)(ii), the reference to a determination by the sheriff of an application under section 110(2) for review of a finding that a section 67 ground is established includes a reference to a determination under section 117(2)(a) that a ground is established.

Appeals to sheriff principal and Court of Session: relevant persons

164.—(1) A person mentioned in subsection (3) may appeal by stated case to the sheriff principal or the Court of Session against a decision of the sheriff in an appeal against a determination of a pre-hearing panel or children's hearing that an individual is or is not to be deemed a relevant person in relation to the child.

(2) A person mentioned in subsection (3) may, with leave of the sheriff principal, appeal by stated case to the Court of Session against the sheriff principal's decision in an appeal under subsection (1).

(3) The persons are—

(a) the individual in question,

(b) the child,

(c) a relevant person in relation to the child,

(d) two or more persons mentioned in paragraphs (a) to (c) acting jointly.

(4) An appeal under this section must be made before the expiry of the period of 28 days beginning with the day on which the decision appealed against is made.

(5) An appeal under this section may be made—

(a) on a point of law, or

(b) in respect of any procedural irregularity.

(6) On deciding an appeal under subsection (1), the sheriff principal or the Court of Session must remit the case to the sheriff for disposal in accordance with such directions as the court may give.

(7) A decision in an appeal under subsection (1) or (2) by the Court of Session is final.

Appeals to sheriff principal and Court of Session: contact and permanence orders

165.—(1) A person mentioned in subsection (3) may appeal by stated case to the sheriff principal or the Court of Session against a decision of the sheriff in an appeal under section 161.

(2) A person mentioned in subsection (3) may, with leave of the sheriff principal, appeal by stated case to the Court of Session against the sheriff principal's decision in an appeal under subsection (1).

(3) The person is an individual (other than a relevant person in relation to the child) in relation to whom—

(a) a contact order is in force regulating contact between the individual and the child,

(b) a permanence order is in force which specifies arrangements for contact between the individual and the child, or

(c) the conditions specified for the purposes of section 126(2)(b) are satisfied.

(4) An appeal under this section must be made before the expiry of the period of 28 days beginning with the day on which the decision appealed against was made.

(5) An appeal under this section may be made—

(a) on a point of law,

(b) in respect of any procedural irregularity.

(6) On deciding an appeal under subsection (1), the sheriff principal or the Court of Session must remit the case to the sheriff for disposal in accordance with such directions as the court may give.

(7) A decision in an appeal under subsection (1) or (2) by the Court of Session is final.

Requirement imposed on local authority: review and appeal

Review of requirement imposed on local authority

166.—(1) This section applies where a duty is imposed on a local authority by virtue of—

(a) a compulsory supervision order,

(b) an interim compulsory supervision order, or

(c) a medical examination order.

(2) If the local authority is satisfied that it is not the relevant local authority for the child in respect of whom the duty is imposed, the local authority may apply to the sheriff for a review of the decision or determination to impose the duty on it.

(3) The sheriff may review the decision or determination to impose the duty with or without hearing evidence.

(4) The sheriff may hear evidence from—

(a) any local authority,

(b) the National Convener,

(c) the child in respect of whom the duty is imposed,

(d) a person representing that child,

(e) a relevant person in relation to that child,

(f) a person representing that person.

(5) Where the duty is imposed on the local authority by a children's hearing, the sheriff may require the Principal Reporter to lodge with the sheriff clerk a copy of the decision (and reasons) of the children's hearing.

(6) The sheriff must determine which local authority is the relevant local authority for the child.

(7) Where the local authority that made the application under subsection (2) is the relevant local authority for the child, the sheriff must confirm the decision of the children's hearing or the determination of the sheriff.

(8) Where another local authority is the relevant local authority for the child, the sheriff—

(a) must vary the order which imposed the duty so that the duty falls on that local authority, and

(b) may make an order for that local authority to reimburse such sums as the sheriff may determine to the local authority which made the application under subsection (2) for any costs incurred in relation to the duty.

Appeals to sheriff principal: section 166

167.—(1) A local authority may appeal by stated case to the sheriff principal against—

(a) the determination by the sheriff under section 166(6) of which local authority is the relevant local authority for a child,

(b) the making of an order by the sheriff under section 166(8)(b).

(2) A person mentioned in subsection (3) may appeal by stated case to the sheriff principal against the determination by the sheriff under section 166(6) of which local authority is the relevant local authority for a child.

(3) The persons are—

(a) the child to whom the determination relates,

(b) a person representing that child,

(c) a relevant person in relation to that child,

(d) a person representing that person.

(4) An appeal under this section must be made before the expiry of the period of 28 days beginning with the day on which the determination or, as the case may be, order was made.

(5) An appeal under this section may be made—

(a)　on a point of law, or

(b)　in respect of any procedural irregularity.

(6) On determining an appeal under this section, the sheriff principal must remit the case to the sheriff for disposal in accordance with such directions as the court may give.

(7) A determination of an appeal under this section is final.

PART 16

ENFORCEMENT OF ORDERS

Enforcement of orders

168.—(1) Subsection (2) applies where a relevant order authorising the keeping of a child in a particular place (an "authorised place") is in force in relation to a child.

(2) An officer of law may enforce the order—

(a)　by searching for and apprehending the child,

(b)　by taking the child to the authorised place,

[1](c)　where—

(i)　it is not reasonably practicable to take the child immediately to the authorised place,

(ii)　[. . .]

by taking the child to and detaining the child in a place of safety for as short a period of time as is practicable, and

(d)　so far as is necessary, by breaking open shut and lockfast places.

(3) In this section, "relevant order" means—

(a)　a child assessment order,

(b)　a child protection order,

(c)　an order under section 55,

(d)　a compulsory supervision order,

(e)　an interim compulsory supervision order,

(f)　a medical examination order.

NOTE

1. As amended by the Children's Hearings (Scotland) Act 2011 (Modification of Primary Legislation) Order 2013 (SSI 2013/211) Sch.1 para.20(17) (effective June 24, 2013—this being the date on which the 2011 (asp 1) came into force).

Child absconding from place

169.—(1) This section applies where—

(a)　a child requires to be kept in a particular place by virtue of—

(i)　a child assessment order,

(ii)　a child protection order,

(iii)　an order under section 55,

(iv)　section 56,

(v)　section 65,

(vi)　a compulsory supervision order,

(vii)　an interim compulsory supervision order,

(viii)　a medical examination order,

(ix)　a warrant to secure attendance, or

(x)　section 143, and

(b) the child absconds from that place or, at the end of a period of leave, fails to return to that place.

(2) The child may be arrested without warrant and taken to that place.

(3) If a court is satisfied that there are reasonable grounds for believing that the child is within premises, the court may grant a warrant authorising an officer of law to—

(a) enter premises, and

(b) search for the child.

(4) The court may authorise the officer of law to use reasonable force for those purposes.

(5) Where the child is returned to the place mentioned in subsection (1), but the occupier of that place is unwilling or unable to receive the child—

(a) the officer of law returning the child must immediately notify the Principal Reporter of that fact, and

(b) the child must be kept in a place of safety until the occurrence of the relevant event.

(6) In subsection (5), the relevant event is—

(a) in the case mentioned in sub-paragraph (i) of subsection (1)(a), the end of the period specified in the child assessment order,

(b) in the case mentioned in sub-paragraph (ii) of that subsection, whichever of the following first occurs—

  (i) the children's hearing arranged under section 45 or 69,

  (ii) the termination of the child protection order,

(c) in the case mentioned in sub-paragraph (iii) of that subsection, whichever of the following first occurs—

  (i) the order ceasing to have effect under section 55(4) or (5),

  (ii) the determination by the sheriff of an application for a child protection order in respect of the child,

(d) in the case mentioned in sub-paragraph (iv) of that subsection, whichever of the following first occurs—

  (i) the giving of notice under subsection (5) of section 56, or

  (ii) the end of the period mentioned in subsection (3) of that section,

(e) in the case mentioned in sub-paragraph (v) of that subsection, whichever of the following first occurs—

  (i) the giving of a direction by the Principal Reporter under section 68(2) or 72(2)(a), or

  (ii) the children's hearing arranged by virtue of section 69(2),

(f) in the case mentioned in sub-paragraph (vi) of that subsection, the children's hearing arranged by virtue of section 131(2)(b),

(g) in the cases mentioned in sub-paragraphs (vii) and (ix) of that subsection whichever of the following first occurs—

  (i) the next children's hearing that has been arranged in relation to the child,

  (ii) the next hearing before the sheriff relating to the child that is to take place by virtue of this Act,

(h) in the cases mentioned in sub-paragraphs (viii) and (x) of that subsection, the next children's hearing that has been arranged in relation to the child.

Child absconding from person

170.—(1) This section applies where—

    (a) a person has (or is authorised to have) control of a child by virtue of—
        (i)   a child assessment order,
        (ii)   a child protection order,
        (iii)   an order under section 55,
        (iv)   section 56,
        (v)   section 65,
        (vi)   a compulsory supervision order,
        (vii) an interim compulsory supervision order,
        (viii) a medical examination order,
        (ix)   a warrant to secure attendance, or
        (x)   section 143, and
    (b) the child absconds from that person.

(2) The child may be arrested without warrant and taken to that person.

(3) If a court is satisfied that there are reasonable grounds for believing that the child is within premises, the court may grant a warrant authorising an officer of law to—

    (a) enter premises, and
    (b) search for the child.

(4) The court may authorise the officer of law to use reasonable force for those purposes.

(5) Where the child is returned to the person mentioned in subsection (1), but the person is unwilling or unable to receive the child—

    (a) the officer of law returning the child must immediately notify the Principal Reporter of that fact, and
    (b) the child must be kept in a place of safety until the occurrence of the relevant event.

(6) In subsection (5), the relevant event is—

    (a) in the case mentioned in sub-paragraph (i) of subsection (1)(a), the end of the period specified in the child assessment order,
    (b) in the case mentioned in sub-paragraph (ii) of that subsection, whichever of the following first occurs—
        (i)   the children's hearing arranged under section 45 or 69,
        (ii) the termination of the child protection order,
    (c) in the case mentioned in sub-paragraph (iii) of that subsection, whichever of the following first occurs—
        (i)   the order ceasing to have effect under section 55(4) or (5),
        (ii) the determination by the sheriff of an application for a child protection order in respect of the child,
    (d) in the case mentioned in sub-paragraph (iv) of that subsection, whichever of the following first occurs—
        (i)   the giving of notice under subsection (5) of section 56, or
        (ii) the end of the period mentioned in subsection (3) of that section,
    (e) in the case mentioned in sub-paragraph (v) of that subsection, whichever of the following first occurs—
        (i)   the giving of a direction by the Principal Reporter under section 68(2) or 72(2)(a), or
        (ii) the children's hearing arranged by virtue of section 69(2),
    (f) in the case mentioned in sub-paragraph (vi) of that subsection, the children's hearing arranged by virtue of section 131(2)(b),
    (g) in the cases mentioned in sub-paragraphs (vii) and (ix) of that subsection whichever of the following first occurs—

    (i)   the next children's hearing that has been arranged in relation to the child,

    (ii) the next hearing before the sheriff relating to the child that is to take place by virtue of this Act,

  (h) in the cases mentioned in sub-paragraphs (viii) and (x) of that subsection, the next children's hearing that has been arranged in relation to the child.

Offences related to absconding

171.—(1) This section applies where—

  (a) a child requires to be kept in a particular place by virtue of—

    (i)   a child assessment order,

    (ii) a child protection order,

    (iii) a compulsory supervision order,

    (iv) an interim compulsory supervision order,

    (v) a medical examination order, or

    (vi) a warrant to secure attendance, or

  (b) a person has (or is authorised to have) control of a child by virtue of such an order or warrant.

(2) A person commits an offence if the person—

  (a) knowingly assists or induces the child to abscond from the place or person,

  (b) knowingly harbours or conceals a child who has absconded from the place or person, or

  (c) knowingly prevents a child from returning to the place or person.

(3) The person is liable on summary conviction to a fine not exceeding level 5 on the standard scale, to imprisonment for a term not exceeding 6 months or to both.

(4) This section is subject to—

  (a) section 38(3) and (4) of the 1995 Act,

  (b) section 51(5) and (6) of the Children Act 1989 (c.41), and

  (c) Article 70(5) and (6) of the Children (Northern Ireland) Order 1995 (S.I. 1995/755 (N.I. 2)).

PART 17

PROCEEDINGS UNDER PART 10: EVIDENCE

Use of evidence obtained from prosecutor

172.—(1) This section applies where an application is made to the sheriff—

  (a) to determine whether a section 67 ground is established, or

  (b) to review a grounds determination.

(2) The Principal Reporter may request a prosecutor to give the Principal Reporter evidence held by the prosecutor in connection with the investigation of a crime or suspected crime if the Principal Reporter considers that the evidence might assist the sheriff in determining the application.

(3) The request may relate only to evidence lawfully obtained in the course of the investigation.

(4) The prosecutor may refuse to comply with the request if the prosecutor reasonably believes that it is necessary to retain the evidence for the purposes

of any proceedings in respect of a crime (whether or not the proceedings have already commenced).

Cases involving sexual behaviour: evidence

173.—(1) This section applies where—
  (a) an application is made to the sheriff—
      (i) to determine whether a section 67 ground is established, or
      (ii) to review a grounds determination, and
  (b) the ground involves sexual behaviour engaged in by any person.

(2) In hearing the application the sheriff must not, unless the sheriff makes an order under section 175, admit evidence, or allow questioning of a witness designed to elicit evidence, which shows or tends to show one or more of the circumstances mentioned in subsection (3) in relation to a person mentioned in subsection (4).

(3) The circumstances are that the person—
  (a) is not of good character (whether in relation to sexual matters or otherwise),
  (b) has, at any time, engaged in sexual behaviour not forming part of the subjectmatter of the ground,
  (c) has, at any time (other than shortly before, at the same time as or shortly after the acts which form part of the subject-matter of the ground), engaged in behaviour (not being sexual behaviour) that might found an inference that the person is not credible or the person's evidence is not reliable,
  (d) has, at any time, been subject to any condition or predisposition that might found the inference that the person is not credible or the person's evidence is not reliable.

(4) The persons are—
  (a) the child,
  (b) a person giving evidence for the purposes of the hearing,
  (c) any other person evidence of whose statements is given for the purposes of the hearing.

(5) In subsection (4)(c), "statements" includes any representations, however made or expressed, of fact or opinion.

(6) In this section and section 174, references to sexual behaviour engaged in include references to having undergone or been made subject to any experience of a sexual nature.

Cases involving sexual behaviour: taking of evidence by commissioner

174.—(1) Subsection (2) applies where—
  (a) a commissioner is appointed under section 19 of the Vulnerable Witnesses (Scotland) Act 2004 (asp 3) to take evidence for the purposes of a hearing before the sheriff—
      (i) to determine whether a section 67 ground is established, or
      (ii) to review a grounds determination, and
  (b) the ground involves sexual behaviour engaged in by any person.

(2) The commissioner must not, unless the sheriff makes an order under section 175, take evidence which shows or tends to show one or more of the circumstances mentioned in section 173(3) in relation to a person mentioned in section 173(4).

Sections 173 and 174: application to sheriff for order as to evidence

175.—(1) On the application of a person mentioned in subsection (2), the sheriff may, if satisfied as to the matters mentioned in subsection (3) make an order—

(a) admitting evidence of the kind mentioned in section 173(2),

(b) allowing questioning of the kind mentioned in that section,

(c) enabling evidence of the kind mentioned in section 174(2) to be taken.

(2) Those persons are—

(a) the child,

(b) a relevant person in relation to the child,

(c) the Principal Reporter,

[1](d) a safeguarder appointed in relation to the child by virtue of section 30.

(3) Those matters are—

(a) the evidence or questioning will relate only to—

    (i) a specific occurrence or specific occurrences of sexual behaviour or other behaviour demonstrating the character of the person,

    (ii) specific facts demonstrating the character of the person,

    (iii) a specific occurrence or specific occurrences of sexual behaviour or other behaviour demonstrating a condition or predisposition to which the person is or has been subject, or

    (iv) specific facts demonstrating a condition or predisposition to which the person is or has been subject,

(b) the occurrence, occurrences or facts are relevant to establishing the ground, and

(c) the probative value of the evidence is significant and is likely to outweigh any risk of prejudice to the proper administration of justice arising from its being admitted or elicited.

(4) References in this section to an occurrence or occurrences of sexual behaviour include references to undergoing or being made subject to any experience of a sexual nature.

(5) In this section "proper administration of justice" includes—

(a) appropriate protection of the person's dignity and privacy, and

(b) ensuring the facts and circumstances of which the sheriff is made aware are relevant to an issue to be put before the sheriff and commensurate with the importance of that issue to the sheriff's decision on the question whether the ground is established.

NOTE

1. As amended by the Children's Hearings (Scotland) Act 2011 (Modification of Primary Legislation) Order 2013 (SSI 2013/211) Sch.1 para.20(18) (effective June 24, 2013—this being the date on which the 2011 (asp 1) came into force).

Amendment of Vulnerable Witnesses (Scotland) Act 2004

176.—(1) The Vulnerable Witnesses (Scotland) Act 2004 (asp 3) is amended as follows.

(2) In section 11 (interpretation of Part 2 of Act), in subsection (5)—

(a) after "Part—" insert—

" "the 2011 Act" means the Children's Hearings (Scotland) Act 2011 (asp 1),",

(b) in the definition of "civil proceedings", for the words from "any proceedings" to the end substitute "relevant proceedings", and

[1](c) after the definition of "court" insert—
" "relevant proceedings" means proceedings under Part 10 of the 2011 Act (other than section 98 or 99),".

(3) In section 12 (order authorising the use of special measures for vulnerable witnesses), after subsection (7) add—

"(8) In the case of relevant proceedings, the child witness notice or vulnerable witness application—

(a) must be lodged or made before the commencement of the hearing at which the child or, as the case may be, vulnerable witness is to give evidence,

(b) on cause shown, may be lodged or made after the commencement of that hearing.".

(4) After section 16 insert—

"16A Relevant proceedings: Principal Reporter's power to act for party to proceedings

(1) Subsection (2) applies where a child witness or other person who is giving or is to give evidence in or for the purposes of relevant proceedings (referred to in this section as "the party") is a party to the proceedings.

(2) The Principal Reporter may, on the party's behalf—

(a) lodge a child witness notice under section 12(2),

(b) make a vulnerable witness application for an order under section 12(6),

(c) make an application under section 13(1)(a) for review of the current arrangements for taking a witness's evidence.".

(5) After section 22 insert—

"22A Giving evidence in chief in the form of a prior statement

(1) This section applies to proceedings in relation to—

(a) an application made by virtue of section 93 or 94 of the 2011 Act to determine whether the ground mentioned in section 67(2)(j) of that Act is established, or

(b) an application under section 110 of that Act for review of a finding that the ground mentioned in section 67(2)(j) of that Act is established.

(2) The special measures which may be authorised by virtue of section 12 or 13 for the purpose of taking the evidence of a vulnerable witness at a hearing to consider such an application include (in addition to those listed in section 18(1)) the giving of evidence in chief in the form of a prior statement in accordance with subsections (3) to (10).

(3) Where that special measure is to be used, a statement made by the vulnerable witness (a "prior statement") may be lodged in evidence for the purposes of this section by or on behalf of the party citing the vulnerable witness.

(4) A prior statement is admissible as the witness's evidence in chief, or as part of the witness's evidence in chief, without the witness being required to adopt or otherwise speak to the statement in giving evidence.

(5) A prior statement is admissible as evidence of any matter stated in it of which direct oral evidence by the vulnerable witness would be admissible if given at the hearing.

(6) A prior statement is admissible under this section only if—

(a) it is contained in a document, and

(b) at the time the statement was made, the vulnerable witness would have been a competent witness for the purposes of the hearing.

(7) Subsection (6) does not apply to a prior statement—

(a) contained in a precognition on oath, or

(b) made in other proceedings (whether criminal or civil and whether taking place in the United Kingdom or elsewhere).

(8) A prior statement of a type mentioned in subsection (7) is not admissible for the purposes of this section unless it is authenticated in such manner as may be prescribed by regulations made by statutory instrument by the Scottish Ministers.

(9) This section does not affect the admissibility of any statement made by any person which is admissible otherwise than by virtue of this section.

(10) In this section—

"document" has the meaning given by section 262(3) of the Criminal Procedure (Scotland) Act 1995 (c.46),

"statement"—

(a) includes—

(i) any representation, however made or expressed, of fact or opinion, and

(ii) any part of a statement, but

(b) does not include a statement in a precognition other than a precognition on oath.

(11) For the purposes of this section, a statement is contained in a document where the person who makes it—

(a) makes the statement in the document personally,

(b) makes a statement which is, with or without the person's knowledge, embodied in a document by whatever means or by any person who has direct personal knowledge of the making of the statement, or

(c) approves a document as embodying the statement.

(12) A statutory instrument containing regulations under subsection (8) is subject to annulment in pursuance of a resolution of the Scottish Parliament.".

NOTE
1. As amended by the Children's Hearings (Scotland) Act 2011 (Modification of Primary Legislation) Order 2013 (SSI 2013/211) Sch.1 para.20(19) (effective June 24, 2013—this being the date on which the 2011 (asp 1) came into force).

PART 18

MISCELLANEOUS

Children's hearings: procedural rules

Children's hearings: procedural rules

177.—(1) The Scottish Ministers may make rules about the procedure relating to children's hearings.

(2) Rules may in particular make provision for or in connection with—

(a) specifying matters that may be determined by pre-hearing panels,

(b) constituting children's hearings,

(c) arranging children's hearings,

(d) notifying persons about children's hearings,

(e) attendance of persons at children's hearings,

(f) specifying circumstances in which persons may be excused from attending children's hearings,

(g) specifying circumstances in which persons may be excluded from children's hearings,

(h) obtaining the views of the child to whom a children's hearing relates,
    (i)   provision of specified documents to—
    (i)   members of children's hearings,
    (ii) the child to whom a children's hearing relates,
    (iii) relevant persons in relation to the child to whom a children's hearing relates,
    (iv) any other specified persons,

(j) withholding of specified documents from persons mentioned in paragraph (i),

(k) prescribing the form of the statement of grounds,

(l) the recording and transmission of information,

(m) representation of persons at children's hearings,

(n) payment of expenses,

(o) appeals.

(3) In making rules in pursuance of subsection (2)(i)(i), the Scottish Ministers must ensure that any views expressed by the child to whom a children's hearing relates are reflected in a specified document.

(4) Rules containing provision of the type mentioned in subsection (2)(a), (e), (f), (g), (j) or (m) are subject to the affirmative procedure.

(5) In this section—
    "children's hearing" includes pre-hearing panel,
    "specified" means specified in the rules.

Disclosure of information

Children's hearing: disclosure of information

178.—(1) A children's hearing need not disclose to a person any information about the child to whom the hearing relates or about the child's case if disclosure of that information to that person would be likely to cause significant harm to the child.

(2) Subsection (1) applies despite any requirement under an enactment (including this Act and subordinate legislation made under it) or rule of law for the children's hearing—

(a) to give the person an explanation of what has taken place at proceedings before the hearing, or

(b) to provide the person with—
    (i)   information about the child or the child's case, or
    (ii) reasons for a decision made by the hearing.

Sharing of information: prosecution

179.—(1) This section applies where—

(a) by virtue of this Act, the Principal Reporter, a children's hearing or the sheriff has determined, is determining or is to determine any matter relating to a child,

(b) criminal proceedings have been commenced against an accused,

(c) the proceedings have not yet been concluded, and

(d) the child is connected in any way with the circumstances that gave rise to the proceedings, the accused or any other person connected in any way with those circumstances.

(2) The Principal Reporter must make available to the Crown Office and Procurator Fiscal Service any information held by the Principal Reporter relating to the prosecution which the Service requests for the purpose of—

    (a) the prevention or detection of crime, or

    (b) the apprehension or prosecution of offenders.

Sharing of information: panel members

180.—(1) A local authority must comply with a request from the National Convener to provide to the National Convener information about the implementation of compulsory supervision orders by the authority.

(2) The National Convener may disclose information provided by a local authority under subsection (1) to members of the Children's Panel.

Implementation of compulsory supervision orders: annual report

Implementation of compulsory supervision orders: annual report

181.—(1) The National Convener must, as soon as is reasonably practicable after the end of each financial year, prepare and submit to the Scottish Ministers a report about implementation of compulsory supervision orders during the year—

    (a) in Scotland as a whole, and

    (b) in each local authority area.

(2) The National Convener must give a copy of the report to each member of the Children's Panel.

(3) The Scottish Ministers must lay the report before the Scottish Parliament.

(4) For the purposes of preparing the report, the National Convener may require each local authority to provide to the National Convener for each financial year—

    (a) information about—

        (i) the number of compulsory supervision orders for which the authority is the implementation authority,

        (ii) changes in the circumstances that led to the making of the orders,

        (iii) the ways in which the overall wellbeing of children who are subject to the orders has been affected by them, and

    (b) such other information relating to the implementation of the orders as the National Convener may require.

(5) Information provided under subsection (4) must not identify (or enable the identification of) a particular child.

(6) In this section, "financial year" has the meaning given by paragraph 24(3) of schedule 1.

Publishing restrictions

Publishing restrictions

182.—(1) A person must not publish protected information if the publication of the information is intended, or is likely, to identify—

    (a) a child mentioned in the protected information, or

    (b) an address or school as being that of such a child.

(2) A person who contravenes subsection (1) commits an offence and is liable on summary conviction to a fine not exceeding level 4 on the standard scale.

(3) It is a defence for a person ("P") charged with a contravention of subsection (1) to show that P did not know or have reason to suspect that the publication of the protected information was likely to identify a child mentioned in the protected information, or, as the case may be, an address or school of such a child.

(4) In relation to proceedings before a children's hearing, the Scottish Ministers may in the interests of justice—

(a) dispense with the prohibition in subsection (1), or

(b) relax it to such extent as they consider appropriate.

(5) In relation to proceedings before the sheriff under Part 10 or 15, the sheriff may in the interests of justice—

(a) dispense with the prohibition in subsection (1), or

(b) relax it to such extent as the sheriff considers appropriate.

(6) In relation to proceedings in an appeal to the Court of Session under this Act, the Court may in the interests of justice—

(a) dispense with the prohibition in subsection (1), or

(b) relax it to such extent as the Court considers appropriate.

(7) The prohibition in subsection (1) does not apply in relation to the publication by or on behalf of a local authority or an adoption agency of information about a child for the purposes of making arrangements in relation to the child under this Act or the Adoption and Children (Scotland) Act 2007 (asp 4).

(8) In subsection (7), "adoption agency" has the meaning given by the Adoption and Children (Scotland) Act 2007.

[1](9) In this section—

"children's hearing" includes a pre-hearing panel,
"protected information" means—
(a) information in relation to—
(i) a children's hearing,
(ii) an appeal against a decision of a children's hearing,
(iii) proceedings before the sheriff under Part 10 or 15, or
(iv) an appeal from any decision of the sheriff or sheriff principal made under this Act, or
(b) information given to the Principal Reporter in respect of a child in reliance on, or satisfaction of, a provision of this Act or any other enactment,
"publish" includes in particular—
(a) to publish matter in a programme service, as defined by section 201 of the Broadcasting Act 1990 (c.42), and
(b) to cause matter to be published.

NOTE

1. As amended by the Children's Hearings (Scotland) Act 2011 (Modification of Primary Legislation) Order 2013 (SSI 2013/211) Sch.1 para.20(20) (effective June 24, 2013—this being the date on which the 2011 (asp 1) came into force).

Mutual assistance

Mutual assistance

183.—(1) A person mentioned in subsection (2) must comply with a request by another such person for assistance in the carrying out of functions conferred by virtue of this Act.

(2) The persons are—

(a) CHS,

(b) the National Convener,

(c) SCRA,

(d) the Principal Reporter.

(3) A person mentioned in subsection (4) must comply with a request by a local authority for assistance in the carrying out of the local authority's functions under this Act.

(4) The persons are—

(a) another local authority,

(b) a health board constituted under section 2 of the National Health Service (Scotland) Act 1978 (c.29).

(5) A request under this section must specify the assistance that is required.

(6) Nothing in this section requires a person to comply with a request if—

(a) it would be incompatible with any function (whether conferred by statute or otherwise) of the person to whom it is directed, or

(b) it would unduly prejudice the carrying out by the person to whom the request is directed of the person's functions.

Enforcement of obligations on health board under section 183

184.—(1) This section applies where—

(a) the implementation authority in relation to a compulsory supervision order has made a request for assistance from a health board under section 183(3),

(b) the request is in connection with the implementation of the compulsory supervision order, and

(c) the implementation authority is satisfied that the health board has unreasonably failed to comply with the request.

(2) The implementation authority may refer the matter to the Scottish Ministers.

(3) On receiving a reference under subsection (2), the Scottish Ministers may, if they are satisfied that the health board has unreasonably failed to comply with the request, direct the health board to comply with the request.

(4) The health board must comply with a direction under subsection (3).

Proceedings before sheriff under Act

Amendment of section 32 of Sheriff Courts (Scotland) Act 1971

185.—(1) Section 32 of the Sheriff Courts (Scotland) Act 1971 (c.58) (power of Court of Session to regulate civil procedure in sheriff court) is amended as follows.

(2) In subsection (1)—

(a) after paragraph (eb) insert—

"(ec) enabling a witness (including a witness who is outwith Scotland) in proceedings under Part 10 or 15 of the Children's Hearings (Scotland) Act 2011 to give evidence by a means specified in the act of sederunt that does not require the witness to be physically present in court in such circumstances, and subject to such conditions, as may be specified in the act of sederunt,

(ed) prescribing circumstances in which a party to proceedings under Part 10 or 15 of the Children's Hearings (Scotland) Act 2011 may be prohibited from personally conducting the examination of witnesses,",

(b) after paragraph (i) insert—

"(ia) permitting a party to proceedings under the Children's Hearings (Scotland) Act 2011 to be represented (including through the making of oral submissions to the sheriff on the party's behalf), in such circumstances as may be specified in the act of sederunt, by a person who is neither an advocate nor a solicitor,", and

(c) after paragraph (k) insert—

"(ka) prescribing functions of safeguarders appointed by the sheriff in relation to proceedings under Part 10 or 15 of the Children's Hearings (Scotland) Act 2011,

(kb) prescribing rights of safeguarders appointed by the sheriff in relation to proceedings under Part 10 or 15 of the Children's Hearings (Scotland) Act 2011 to information relating to the proceedings,".

(3) After subsection (4) add—

"(5) In subsection (1), "civil proceedings" includes proceedings under the Children's Hearings (Scotland) Act 2011.".

Consent of child to medical examination or treatment

Consent of child to medical examination or treatment

186.—(1) Nothing in this Act prejudices any capacity of a child enjoyed by virtue of section 2(4) of the Age of Legal Capacity (Scotland) Act 1991 (c.50) (capacity of child with sufficient understanding to consent to surgical, medical or dental procedure or treatment).

(2) In particular, where—

(a) under an order mentioned in subsection (3) any examination or treatment is arranged for the child, and

(b) the child has the capacity mentioned in section 2(4) of the Age of Legal Capacity (Scotland) Act 1991, the examination or treatment may be carried out only if the child consents to it.

(3) Those orders are—

(a) a child assessment order,

(b) a child protection order,

(c) a compulsory supervision order,

(d) an interim compulsory supervision order,

(e) a medical examination order.

Rehabilitation of offenders

Rehabilitation of Offenders Act 1974: treatment of certain disposals by children's hearings

187.—(1) The Rehabilitation of Offenders Act 1974 (c.53) is amended as follows.

(2) In section 8B (protection afforded to spent alternatives to prosecution: Scotland)—

(a) after subsection (1) insert—

"(1A) For the purposes of this Act, a person has also been given an alternative to prosecution in respect of an offence if (whether before or after the commencement of this section) in proceedings before a children's hearing to which subsection (1B) applies—

(a) a compulsory supervision order (as defined in section 83 of the 2011 Act) has been made or, as the case may be, varied or continued in relation to the person, or

(b) the referral to the children's hearing has been discharged (whether wholly or in relation to the ground that the person committed the offence).

(1B) This subsection applies to proceedings if the proceedings were taken in relation to the person on the ground (whether alone or with other grounds) that the person had committed the offence and—

(a) the ground was accepted for the purposes of the 2011 Act by—
   (i) the person, and
   (ii) any person who was a relevant person as respects those proceedings, or

(b) the ground was established or treated as established for the purposes of the 2011 Act.

(1C) In subsections (1A) and (1B)—
"the 2011 Act" means the Children's Hearings (Scotland) Act 2011,
"relevant person"—

(a) has the meaning given by section 200 of the 2011 Act, and

(b) includes a person who was deemed to be a relevant person by virtue of section 81(3), 160(4)(b) or 164(6) of that Act.

(1D) For the purposes of this Act, a person has also been given an alternative to prosecution in respect of an offence if (whether before or after the commencement of this section) in proceedings before a children's hearing to which subsection (1E) applies—

(a) a supervision requirement has been made or, as the case may be, varied or continued under the Children (Scotland) Act 1995 ("the 1995 Act") in relation to the person, or

(b) the referral to the children's hearing has been discharged (whether wholly or in relation to the ground that the person committed the offence).

(1E) This subsection applies to proceedings if the proceedings were taken in relation to the person on the ground (whether alone or with other grounds) that the person had committed the offence and—

(a) the ground was accepted for the purposes of the 1995 Act by the person and, where necessary, the relevant person (as defined in section 93(2) of that Act), or

(b) the ground was established, or deemed to have been established, for the purposes of that Act.", and

(b) in subsection (2), for "subsection (1)" substitute "subsections (1), (1A) and (1D)".

(3) In Schedule 3 (protection for spent alternatives to prosecution: Scotland), after subparagraph (1)(a) of paragraph 1 insert—

"(aa) in the case of—

(i) a compulsory supervision order referred to in paragraph (a) of subsection (1A) of that section, the period of 3 months beginning on the day the compulsory supervision order is made or, as the case may be, varied or continued, or

(ii) a discharge referred to in paragraph (b) of subsection (1A) of that section, the period of 3 months beginning on the day of the discharge,

(ab) in the case of—

(i) a supervision requirement referred to in paragraph (a) of subsection (1D) of that section, the period of 3 months beginning on the day the supervision requirement is made or, as the case may be, varied or continued, or

(ii) a discharge referred to in paragraph (b) of subsection (1D) of that section, the period of 3 months beginning on the day of the discharge,".

Criminal record certificates

Criminal record certificates

188.—In section 113A of the Police Act 1997 (c.50) (criminal record certificates)—

(a) in subsection (6), in the definition of "relevant matter", after paragraph (b) insert—

"(ba) an alternative to prosecution of the type mentioned in section 8B(1A) or (1D) of that Act which relates to an offence specified in an order made by the Scottish Ministers by statutory instrument, including any such alternative to prosecution which so relates and which is spent under Schedule 3 to that Act,

(bb) a supervision requirement made in relation to a person by a children's hearing under section 44 of the Social Work (Scotland) Act 1968 in the circumstances mentioned in subsection (6A) if the supervision requirement relates to an offence specified in an order under paragraph (ba),

(bc) the discharge under section 43 of the Social Work (Scotland) Act 1968 of the referral of a person to a children's hearing in the circumstances mentioned in subsection (6A) if the discharge relates to an offence specified in an order under paragraph (ba),",

and

(b) after that subsection, insert—

"(6A) The circumstances are—

(a) the person was referred to the children's hearing on the ground (whether alone or among other grounds) mentioned in section 32(2)(g) of the Social Work (Scotland) Act 1968 (commission of offence), and

(b) the ground was accepted by the person and, where necessary, by the person's parent or established to the satisfaction of the sheriff under section 42 of that Act.

(6B) An order under paragraph (ba) of the definition of "relevant matter" in subsection (6) may specify an offence by reference to a particular degree of seriousness.

(6C) A statutory instrument containing an order under paragraph (ba) of the definition of "relevant matter" in subsection (6) may not be made unless a draft of the instrument containing the order has been laid before, and approved by resolution of, the Scottish Parliament.".

Places of safety

Places of safety: restrictions on use of police stations

189.—(1) This section applies where a person is authorised or required under this Act to keep or detain a child in a place of safety.

(2) A child may be kept or detained in a police station only if it is not reasonably practicable to keep or detain the child in a place of safety which is not a police station.

(3) Where a child is being kept or detained in a police station, the person must take steps to identify a place of safety which is not a police station and transfer the child to that place as soon as is reasonably practicable.

Orders made outwith Scotland

Effect of orders made outwith Scotland

190.—(1) The Scottish Ministers may by regulations make provision for a specified non-Scottish order which appears to them to correspond to a compulsory supervision order to have effect as if it were such an order.

(2) Regulations under subsection (1)—

(a) may provide that a non-Scottish order is to have such effect only—
  (i) in specified circumstances,
  (ii) for specified purposes,
(b) may modify the following enactments in their application by virtue of the regulations to a non-Scottish order—
  (i) the Social Work (Scotland) Act 1968,
  (ii) this Act,
(c) are subject to affirmative procedure.

(3) In this section—

"non-Scottish order" means an order made by a court in England and Wales or in Northern Ireland,
"specified" means specified in the regulations.

PART 19

LEGAL AID AND ADVICE

Legal aid and advice

191.—After section 28A of the Legal Aid (Scotland) Act 1986 (c.47) insert—

"PART 5A

CHILDREN'S LEGAL AID

28B Children's legal aid

(1) This Part applies to children's legal aid.

(2) In this Act, "children's legal aid" means representation by a solicitor and, where appropriate, by counsel in proceedings mentioned in subsection (3), on the terms provided for in this Act, and includes all such assistance as is usually given by a solicitor or counsel in the steps preliminary to or incidental to those proceedings.

(3) The proceedings are—

(a) proceedings before the sheriff in relation to an application under section 48 of the 2011 Act (application for variation or termination of child protection order),

(b) proceedings before a children's hearing arranged by virtue of section 45 or 46 of the 2011 Act (children's hearing following making of child protection order),

(c) proceedings before a children's hearing or a pre-hearing panel if the children's hearing or the panel considers that it might be necessary to make a compulsory supervision order including a secure accommodation authorisation in relation to the child to whom the proceedings relate,

(d) proceedings before a children's hearing to which section 69(3) of the 2011 Act applies (children's hearing following arrest of child and detention in place of safety),

(e) proceedings under Part 10 or 15 of the 2011 Act.

(4) In this Part—

"compulsory supervision order" has the meaning given by section 83 of that Act,

"pre-hearing panel" has the meaning given by section 79 of that Act,

"secure accommodation authorisation" has the meaning given by section 85 of that Act.

28C Circumstances where children's legal aid automatically available

(1) Subsection (2) applies where—

(a) an application is made under section 48 of the 2011 Act for variation or termination of a child protection order,

(b) a children's hearing is arranged in relation to a child by virtue of section 45 or 46 of the 2011 Act,

(c) a children's hearing or a pre-hearing panel considers that it might be necessary to make a compulsory supervision order including a secure accommodation authorisation in relation to a child, or

(d) a children's hearing to which section 69(3) of the 2011 Act applies is arranged in relation to a child.

(2) If assistance by way of representation has not been made available to the child, children's legal aid is available to the child for the purposes of—

(a) proceedings before the sheriff in relation to the application mentioned in paragraph (a) of subsection (1),

(b) the children's hearing mentioned in paragraph (b) or, as the case may be, (c) or (d) of that subsection, and

(c) if that children's hearing is deferred, any subsequent children's hearing held under Part 11 of the 2011 Act.

(3) The Scottish Ministers may by regulations—

(a) modify subsection (1),

(b) modify subsection (2) and section 28B(3) and (4) in consequence of modifications made under paragraph (a).

28D Availability of children's legal aid: child

(1) Subsection (2) applies in relation to proceedings under Part 10 or 15 of the 2011 Act (other than an appeal to the sheriff principal or the Court of Session).

(2) Children's legal aid is available to the child to whom the proceedings relate if, on an application made to the Board, the Board is satisfied that the conditions in subsection (3) are met.

(3) The conditions are—

(a) that it is in the best interests of the child that children's legal aid be made available,

(b) that it is reasonable in the particular circumstances of the case that the child should receive children's legal aid, and

(c) that, after consideration of the disposable income and disposable capital of the child, the expenses of the case cannot be met without undue hardship to the child.

(4) Subsection (5) applies in relation to an appeal to the sheriff principal or the Court of Session under Part 15 of the 2011 Act.

(5) Children's legal aid is available to the child to whom the proceedings relate if, on an application made to the Board, the Board is satisfied that—

(a) the conditions in subsection (3) are met, and

(b) the child has substantial grounds for making or responding to the appeal.

28E Availability of children's legal aid: relevant person

(1) Subsection (2) applies in relation to—

(a) proceedings before the sheriff in relation to an application under section 48 of the 2011 Act (application for variation or termination of child protection order), and

(b) proceedings under Part 10 or 15 of the 2011 Act (other than an appeal to the sheriff principal or the Court of Session).

(2) Children's legal aid is available to a relevant person in relation to the child to whom the proceedings relate if, on an application made to the Board, the Board is satisfied that the conditions in subsection (3) are met.

(3) The conditions are—

(a) that it is reasonable in the particular circumstances of the case that the relevant person should receive children's legal aid, and

(b) that, after consideration of the disposable income and disposable capital of the relevant person, the expenses of the case cannot be met without undue hardship to the relevant person.

(4) Subsection (5) applies in relation to an appeal to the sheriff principal or the Court of Session under Part 15 of the 2011 Act.

(5) Children's legal aid is available to a relevant person in relation to the child to whom the appeal relates if, on an application made to the Board, the Board is satisfied that—

(a) the conditions in subsection (3) are met, and

(b) the relevant person has substantial grounds for making or responding to the appeal.

(6) In this Part, "relevant person"—

(a) has the meaning given by section 200 of the 2011 Act, and

(b) includes a person deemed to be a relevant person by virtue of section 81(3), 160(4)(b) or 164(6) of that Act.

28F Availability of children's legal aid: appeals relating to deemed relevant person

(1) Subsection (2) applies in relation to—

(a) an appeal under section 154 or 163(1)(a)(iii) or (2) of the 2011 Act arising from a determination of a children's hearing mentioned in section 142(1)(a) if by virtue of section 142(4) (b) an individual is no longer to be deemed to be a relevant person,

(b) an appeal to the sheriff under section 160(1)(a) of that Act against a determination of a pre-hearing panel or children's hearing that an individual is not to be deemed a relevant person in relation to a child,

(c) an appeal to the sheriff under section 160(1)(b) of that Act against a direction under section 142(4)(a) that an individual is no longer to be deemed a relevant person in relation to a child,

(d) an appeal to the sheriff principal or the Court of Session under section 164(1) of that Act against a decision of the sheriff in an appeal under section 160(1)—

    (i) confirming a determination that an individual is not to be deemed a relevant person in relation to a child, or

    (ii) quashing a determination that an individual is to be deemed a relevant person in relation to a child, and

(e) an appeal to the Court of Session under section 164(2) of that Act against a determination of the sheriff principal where the effect of the sheriff principal's determination is that an individual is not to be deemed a relevant person in relation to a child.

(2) Children's legal aid is available to the individual if, on an application made to the Board, the Board is satisfied—

(a) that it is reasonable in the particular circumstances of the case that the individual should receive children's legal aid,

(b) that, after consideration of the disposable income and disposable capital of the individual, the expenses of the case cannot be met without undue hardship to the individual, and

(c) that—

    (i) in relation to an appeal mentioned in paragraph (a) of subsection (1), the individual has substantial grounds for making or, as the case may be, responding to the appeal,

    (ii) in relation to an appeal mentioned in any other paragraph of that subsection, the individual has substantial grounds for making the appeal.

28G Conditions

The Board may make the grant of children's legal aid subject to such conditions as the Board considers expedient; and such conditions may be imposed at any time.

28H Board to establish review procedures

(1) The Board must establish a procedure under which a person whose application for children's legal aid has been refused may apply to the Board for a review of the application.

(2) The Board must establish a procedure under which any person receiving children's legal aid which is subject to conditions by virtue of section 28G may apply to the Board for a review of any such condition.

28J Board's power to require compliance with conditions

The Board may require a person receiving children's legal aid to comply with such conditions as it considers expedient to enable it to satisfy itself from time to time that it is reasonable for the person to continue to receive children's legal aid.

28K Contributions to the Fund

(1) A person in receipt of children's legal aid (the "assisted person") may be required by the Board to contribute to the Fund in respect of any proceedings in connection with which the assisted person is granted children's legal aid.

(2) A contribution under subsection (1) is to be determined by the Board and may include—

   (a) if the assisted person's disposable income exceeds £3,355 a year, a contribution in respect of income which is not to be more than one-third of the excess (or such other proportion of the excess, or such amount, as may be prescribed by regulations made under this section), and

   (b) if the assisted person's disposable capital exceeds £7,504, a contribution in respect of capital which is not to be more than the excess (or such proportion of the excess or such lesser amount as may be prescribed by regulations made under this section).

(3) Regulations under this section may prescribe different proportions or amounts for different amounts of disposable income and for different cases or classes of case.

28L Power of Scottish Ministers to modify circumstances in which children's legal aid to be available

(1) The Scottish Ministers may by regulations modify this Part so as to—

   (a) extend or restrict the types of proceedings before a children's hearing in connection with which children's legal aid is to be available, and

   (b) specify the persons to whom children's legal aid is to be available.

(2) If regulations are made making children's legal aid available to a child, the regulations must include provision—

   (a) requiring the Board to be satisfied that—

      (i) one of the conditions in subsection (3) is met, and

      (ii) the conditions in section 28D(3) are met before children's legal aid is made available, and

(b) requiring the Board, in determining for the purposes of subsection (3)(b)(ii) whether the child would be able to participate effectively in the proceedings, to take into account in particular the matters mentioned in subsection (4).

(3) The conditions are—

(a) that it might be necessary for the children's hearing to decide whether a compulsory supervision order or, as the case may be, an interim compulsory supervision order should include or (where a compulsory supervision order is being reviewed) continue to include a secure accommodation authorisation, and

(b) that—

  (i) the condition in paragraph (a) is not met, and

  (ii) for the purpose of enabling the child to participate effectively in the proceedings before the children's hearing, it is necessary that the child be represented by a solicitor or counsel.

(4) The matters are—

(a) the nature and complexity of the case (including any points of law),

(b) the ability of the appropriate person, with the assistance of any accompanying person, to consider and challenge any document or information before the children's hearing,

(c) the ability of the appropriate person, with the assistance of any accompanying person, to give the appropriate person's views at the children's hearing in an effective manner.

(5) If regulations are made making children's legal aid available to a person other than the child to whom the proceedings relate, the regulations must include provision—

(a) requiring the Board to be satisfied that the conditions in subsection (6) are met before children's legal aid is made available, and

(b) requiring the Board, in determining for the purposes of the condition in subsection (6)(a) whether the person would be able to participate effectively in the proceedings, to take into account in particular the matters mentioned in subsection (4).

(6) The conditions are—

(a) that, for the purpose of enabling the person to participate effectively in the proceedings before the children's hearing, it is necessary that the person be represented by a solicitor or counsel,

(b) that it is reasonable in the particular circumstances of the case that the person should receive children's legal aid, and

(c) that, after consideration of the disposable income and disposable capital of the person, the expenses of the case cannot be met without undue hardship to the person or the dependants of the person.

(7) In subsection (4)—

"accompanying person" means a person entitled to accompany the child or other person to the children's hearing by virtue of rules under section 177 of the 2011 Act, "appropriate person" means—

(a) for the purposes of subsection (2)(b), the child,

(b) for the purposes of subsection (5)(b), the other person.

(8) The Scottish Ministers may by regulations modify—

(a) the matters for the time being set out in subsection (4),

(b) the definition of "accompanying person" for the time being set out in subsection (7).

PART 5B

CHILDREN'S LEGAL ASSISTANCE

28M Register of solicitors and firms eligible to provide children's legal assistance

(1) The Board must establish and maintain a register of—

(a) solicitors who are eligible to provide children's legal assistance, and

(b) the firms with which such solicitors are connected.

(2) A sole solicitor who wishes to provide children's legal assistance must be included in the register maintained under this section both as a solicitor and as a firm.

(3) Only those solicitors who are included in the register maintained under this section may provide children's legal assistance.

(4) Subject to subsection (5), a solicitor may provide children's legal assistance only when working in the course of a connection with a firm included in the register maintained under this section.

(5) Where the Board employs a solicitor under sections 26 and 27 to provide children's legal assistance—

(a) the Board may only employ a solicitor who is included in the register maintained under this section,

(b) the entry in the register relating to the solicitor's name must include a note that the solicitor is so employed,

(c) the Board is not to be regarded as a firm for the purposes of this section and is not required to be included in the register.

(6) The Scottish Ministers may by regulations make provision about qualifications to be held by persons who may be included in the register maintained under this section.

(7) Subsections (5) to (15) of section 25A apply in relation to the register maintained under this section as they apply in relation to the Register subject to the modifications mentioned in subsection (8).

(8) Those modifications are—

(a) subsections (8) and (9) are to be read as if references to the code were references to the code of practice under section 28N for the time being in force, and

(b) subsection (9) is to be read as if the reference to criminal legal assistance were a reference to children's legal assistance.

28N Code of practice

(1) The Board must prepare a draft code of practice in relation to the carrying out by solicitors of their functions with regard to the provision of children's legal assistance.

(2) Different provision may be made for different cases or classes of case.

(3) Subsections (3) to (8) of section 25B apply in relation to a draft code prepared under subsection (1) above as they apply in relation to a draft code prepared under subsection (1) of that section.

28P Duty to comply with code of practice

(1) Solicitors and firms included in the register maintained under section 28M(1) must comply with the requirements of the code of practice under section 28N for the time being in force.

(2) The Board must monitor the carrying out by those solicitors and firms of their duty under subsection (1).

(3) For the purpose of carrying out its duty under subsection (2) the Board may use the powers conferred on it by sections 35A and 35B.

28Q Non-compliance with code of practice

(1) Section 25D applies in relation to a solicitor or firm included in the register maintained under section 28M(1) and the code of practice under section 28N for the time being in force as it applies in relation to a registered solicitor or registered firm and the code subject to the modifications mentioned in subsection (2).

(2) Those modifications are—

(a) references to the Register are to be read as if they were references to the register maintained under section 28M(1),

(b) subsection (6) is to be read as if the references to criminal legal assistance were references to children's legal assistance.

28R Further provision as to removal of name from register

(1) Subsection (2) applies where the Board is satisfied (whether on being informed by the solicitor concerned or otherwise) that a solicitor who is included in the register maintained under section 28M(1)—

(a) has become connected with a firm whose name is not included in that register, and

(b) is no longer connected with a firm whose name is included in that register.

(2) The Board must remove the solicitor's name from the register.

(3) Subsections (6) to (9) of section 25D (as applied by section 28Q) apply in relation to a solicitor whose name is removed from the register under subsection (2) above as they apply in relation to a solicitor whose name is removed from the register under subsection (4) of that section (as applied by section 28Q).

28S Publication of register etc.

Section 25F applies in relation to the register maintained under section 28M(1) as it applies in relation to the Register.".

Power to make regulations about contracts for provision of children's legal aid

192.—After section 33A of the Legal Aid (Scotland) Act 1986 insert—

"Contracts for the provision of children's legal assistance

33B Contracts for the provision of children's legal assistance

(1) The Scottish Ministers may by regulations made under this section empower the Board to enter into contracts with relevant firms for the provision by relevant solicitors connected with those firms of children's legal assistance.

(2) Regulations under this section may prescribe—

(a) the procedures to be followed by the Board in awarding any such contract, and

(b) subject to subsection (3), any terms and conditions which are to be included in any such contract.

(3) Regulations under this section must provide that any contract entered into by virtue of this section must include a provision that, in the event of the termination of the contract, or a breach of it by the relevant firm concerned, the Board may—

(a) withhold payments under the contract, and

(b) require the firm to secure the transfer to a relevant solicitor of—

    (i) any work currently being undertaken by any solicitor connected with them for any client by way of children's legal assistance, and

    (ii) notwithstanding any lien to which any such solicitor might otherwise be entitled, any documents connected with any such work.

(4) Regulations under this section may provide that where the Board has by virtue of this section entered into contracts with any relevant firms for the provision of children's legal assistance in any area, then, unless it seems to the Board to be inappropriate in a particular case, any person seeking such assistance in that area is to be required to instruct a relevant solicitor connected with one of those firms.

(5) Any money due to a firm under a contract made by virtue of this section is to be paid to the firm—

(a) firstly, out of any amount payable by the client in accordance with section 11(2),

(b) secondly, by the Board out of the Fund.

(6) For the purposes of sections 32 and 33, the money paid to a firm, as provided in subsection (5) above, in respect of a contract made by virtue of this section is to be taken to be a payment made in accordance with this Act, and no solicitor connected with such a firm is entitled to any other payment out of the Fund in respect of any work done by the solicitor by virtue of such a contract.

(7) In this section—

"relevant firm" means a firm included in the register maintained under section 28M(1),

"relevant solicitor" means a solicitor included in the register maintained under section 28M(1).".

PART 20

GENERAL

Formal communications

Formal communications

193.—(1) The following are formal communications—

(a) a notice,

(b) a determination,

(c) a direction,

(d) a report,

(e) a statement,

(f) a referral under section 127.

(2) A formal communication must be in writing.

(3) That requirement is satisfied by a formal communication in electronic form which is—

(a) sent by electronic means, and

(b) capable of being reproduced in legible form.

(4) A formal communication sent in accordance with subsection (3) is to be taken to be received on the day it is sent.

Forms

Forms

194.—(1) The Scottish Ministers may determine—

(a) the form of documents produced by virtue of this Act, and

(b) the manner in which those documents are to be conveyed.

(2) The Scottish Ministers may in particular determine that documents may be conveyed by electronic means.

Subordinate legislation

Subordinate legislation

195.—(1) Any power of the Scottish Ministers to make subordinate legislation under this Act is exercisable by statutory instrument.

(2) Any such power includes power to make—

(a) such incidental, supplementary, consequential, transitional, transitory or saving provision as the Scottish Ministers think necessary or expedient,

(b) different provision for different purposes.

(3) Except in any case where subordinate legislation under this Act is subject to the affirmative procedure or the super-affirmative procedure, subordinate legislation under this Act is subject to the negative procedure.

(4) Subsections (2) and (3) do not apply to an order under section 206(2).

Negative procedure

196.—(1) Subsection (2) applies where subordinate legislation under this Act is subject to the negative procedure.

(2) The statutory instrument containing the subordinate legislation is subject to annulment in pursuance of a resolution of the Scottish Parliament.

Affirmative procedure

197.—(1) Subsection (2) applies where subordinate legislation under this Act is subject to the affirmative procedure.

(2) The subordinate legislation must not be made unless a draft of the statutory instrument containing the subordinate legislation has been laid before, and approved by resolution of, the Scottish Parliament.

Super-affirmative procedure

198.—(1) Subsections (2) to (6) apply where subordinate legislation under this Act is subject to the super-affirmative procedure.

(2) The subordinate legislation must not be made unless a draft of the statutory instrument containing the subordinate legislation has been laid before, and approved by resolution of, the Scottish Parliament.

(3) Before laying a draft instrument before the Parliament under subsection (2), the Scottish Ministers must consult—

(a) such persons who are under 21 years of age as they consider appropriate, and

(b) such other persons as they consider appropriate.

(4) For the purposes of such a consultation, the Scottish Ministers must—

(a) lay a copy of the proposed draft instrument before the Parliament,

(b) publish in such a manner as the Scottish Ministers consider appropriate a copy of the proposed draft instrument, and

(c) have regard to any representations about the proposed draft instrument that are made to them within 60 days of the date on which the copy of the proposed draft instrument is laid before the Parliament.

(5) In calculating any period of 60 days for the purposes of subsection (4) (c), no account is to be taken of any time during which the Parliament is dissolved or is in recess for more than 4 days.

(6) When laying a draft instrument before the Parliament under subsection (2), the Scottish Ministers must also lay before the Parliament an explanatory document giving details of—

(a) the consultation carried out under subsection (3),

(b) any representations received as a result of the consultation, and

(c) the changes (if any) made to the proposed draft instrument as a result of those representations.

Interpretation

Meaning of "child"

199.—(1) In this Act, "child" means a person who is under 16 years of age (but subject to subsections (2) to (9)).

(2) In paragraph (o) of section 67(2) and the other provisions of this Act in their application in relation to that paragraph, "child" means a person who is of school age.

(3) Subsection (4) applies where a person becomes 16 years of age—

(a) after section 66 applies in relation to the person, but

(b) before a relevant event.

(4) For the purposes of the application of this Act to the person, references in this Act to a child include references to the person until a relevant event occurs.

(5) A relevant event is—

(a) the making of a compulsory supervision order in relation to the person,

(b) the notification of the person under section 68(3) that the question of whether a compulsory supervision order should be made in respect of the person will not be referred to a children's hearing, or

(c) the discharge of the referral.

(6) Subsection (7) applies if—

(a) a compulsory supervision order is in force in respect of a person on the person's becoming 16 years of age, or

(b) a compulsory supervision order is made in respect of a person on or after the person becomes 16 years of age.

(7) For the purposes of the application of the provisions of this Act relating to that order, references in this Act to a child include references to the person until whichever of the following first occurs—

(a) the order is terminated, or

(b) the person becomes 18 years of age.

(8) Subsection (9) applies where a case is remitted to the Principal Reporter under section 49(7)(b) of the Criminal Procedure (Scotland) Act 1995.

(9) For the purposes of the application of this Act to the person whose case is remitted, references in this Act to a child include references to the person until whichever of the following first occurs—

(a) a children's hearing or the sheriff discharges the referral,

(b) a compulsory supervision order made in respect of the person is terminated, or

(c) the person becomes 18 years of age.

Meaning of "relevant person"

200.—(1) In this Act, "relevant person", in relation to a child, means—

(a) a parent or guardian having parental responsibilities or parental rights in relation to the child under Part 1 of the 1995 Act,

(b) a person in whom parental responsibilities or parental rights are vested by virtue of section 11(2)(b) of the 1995 Act,

(c) a person having parental responsibilities or parental rights by virtue of section 11(12) of the 1995 Act,

(d) a parent having parental responsibility for the child under Part 1 of the Children Act 1989 (c.41) ("the 1989 Act"),

(e) a person having parental responsibility for the child by virtue of—

    (i) section 12(2) of the 1989 Act,

    (ii) section 14C of the 1989 Act, or

    (iii) section 25(3) of the Adoption and Children Act 2002 (c.38),

(f) a person in whom parental responsibilities or parental rights are vested by virtue of a permanence order (as defined in section 80(2) of the Adoption and Children (Scotland) Act 2007 (asp 4)),

(g) any other person specified by order made by the Scottish Ministers.

(2) For the purposes of subsection (1)(a), a parent does not have parental responsibilities or rights merely by virtue of an order under section 11(2)(d) or (e) of the 1995 Act.

(3) An order made under subsection (1)(g) is subject to the affirmative procedure.

Meaning of "relevant local authority"

201.—(1) In this Act, "relevant local authority", in relation to a child, means—

(a) the local authority in whose area the child predominantly resides, or

(b) where the child does not predominantly reside in the area of a particular local authority, the local authority with whose area the child has the closest connection.

(2) For the purposes of subsection (1)(a), no account is to be taken of—

(a) any period of residence in a residential establishment,

(b) any other period of residence, or residence in any other place, prescribed by the Scottish Ministers by regulations.

(3) For the purposes of subsection (1)(b), no account is to be taken of—

(a) any connection with an area that relates to a period of residence in a residential establishment,

(b) any other connection prescribed by the Scottish Ministers by regulations.

Interpretation

[1]**202.**—(1) In this Act, unless the context otherwise requires—

"the 1995 Act" means the Children (Scotland) Act 1995 (c.36),

"affirmative procedure" is to be construed in accordance with section 197,

"CHS" means Children's Hearings Scotland,

"chief social work officer" means the officer appointed under section 3 of the Social Work (Scotland) Act 1968 (c.49) by—

(a) in relation to a compulsory supervision order or an interim compulsory supervision order, the implementation authority,

(b) in relation to a medical examination order or a warrant to secure attendance, the relevant local authority for the child to whom the order or warrant relates,

"child assessment order" means an order mentioned in section 35,

"child protection order" means an order mentioned in section 37,

"compulsory supervision order" has the meaning given by section 83,

"contact order" has the meaning given by section 11(2)(d) of the 1995 Act,

"crime" has the meaning given in section 307(1) of the Criminal Procedure (Scotland) Act 1995 (c.46),

"functions" includes powers and duties; and "confer", in relation to functions, includes impose,

"grounds determination" has the meaning given by section 110(1),

"grounds hearing" has the meaning given by section 90,

"implementation authority"—

(a) in relation to a compulsory supervision order, has the meaning given by section 83(1)(b),

(b) in relation to an interim compulsory supervision order, has the meaning given by section 86(1)(b),

"interim compulsory supervision order" has the meaning given by section 86,

"interim variation", in relation to a compulsory supervision order, has the meaning given by section 140,

"medical examination order" has the meaning given by section 87, "movement restriction condition" has the meaning given by section 84,

"negative procedure" is to be construed in accordance with section 196,

"officer of law" has the meaning given by section 307(1) of the Criminal Procedure (Scotland) Act 1995 (c.46),

"parental responsibilities" has the meaning given by section 1(3) of the 1995 Act,

"parental rights" has the meaning given by section 2(4) of the 1995 Act,

"permanence order" has the meaning given by section 80(2) of the Adoption and Children (Scotland) Act 2007 (asp 4),

"place of safety", in relation to a child, means—

(a) a residential or other establishment provided by a local authority,

(b) a community home within the meaning of section 53 of the Children Act 1989 (c.41),

(c) a police station,

(d) a hospital or surgery, the person or body of persons responsible for the management of which is willing temporarily to receive the child,

(e) the dwelling-house of a suitable person who is so willing, or

(f) any other suitable place the occupier of which is so willing,

"pre-hearing panel" has the meaning given by section 79(2)(a),

"prosecutor" has the meaning given by section 307(1) of the Criminal Procedure (Scotland) Act 1995 (c.46),

"residential establishment" means—

(a) an establishment in Scotland (whether managed by a local authority, a voluntary organisation or any other person) which provides residential accommodation for children for the purposes of this Act, the 1995 Act or the Social Work (Scotland) Act 1968 (c.49),

(b) a home in England or Wales that is—

(i) a community home within the meaning of section 53 of the Children Act 1989 (c.41),

(ii) a voluntary home within the meaning of that Act, or

(iii) a private children's home within the meaning of that Act, or

(c) an establishment in Northern Ireland that is—

(i) a private children's home within the meaning of the Children (Northern Ireland) Order 1995 (S.I. 1995/755),

(ii) an authority home provided under Part VII of that Order, or

(iii) a voluntary home provided under Part VIII of that Order,

"safeguarder" has the meaning given by section 30(1),

"school age" has the meaning given by section 31 of the Education (Scotland) Act 1980 (c.44),

"secure accommodation" means accommodation provided for the purpose of restricting the liberty of children which—

(a) in Scotland, is provided in a residential establishment approved in accordance with regulations made under section 78(2) of the Public Services Reform (Scotland) Act 2010 (asp 8),

(b) in England, is provided in a children's home (within the meaning of the Care Standards Act 2000 (c.14) ("the 2000 Act")) in respect of which a person is registered under Part 2 of that Act, except that before the coming into force of section 107(2) of the Health and

Social Care (Community Health Standards) Act 2003 (c.43), "secure accommodation" means accommodation in relation to England which—

(i) is provided in a children's home (within the meaning of the 2000 Act) in respect of which a person is registered under Part 2 of that Act, and

(ii) is approved by the Secretary of State for the purpose of restricting the liberty of children,

(c) in Wales, is provided in a children's home (within the meaning of the 2000 Act) in respect of which a person is registered under Part 2 of that Act,

"secure accommodation authorisation" has the meaning given by section 85,

"statement of grounds" has the meaning given by section 89(3),

"subordinate legislation" means—

(a) an order,

(b) regulations, or

(c) rules,

"super-affirmative procedure" is to be construed in accordance with section 198,

"warrant to secure attendance" has the meaning given by section 88, and

"working day" means every day except—

(a) Saturday and Sunday,

(b) 25 and 26 December,

(c) 1 and 2 January.

(2) References in this Act to a decision of a children's hearing are references to a decision of a majority of the members of a children's hearing.

(2A) References in this Act to a determination of a pre-hearing panel are references to a determination of a majority of the members of a pre-hearing panel.

(3) References in this Act to varying a compulsory supervision order, an interim compulsory supervision order or a medical examination order include varying the order by adding or removing measures.

NOTE
1. As amended by the Children's Hearings (Scotland) Act 2011 (Modification of Primary Legislation) Order 2013 (SSI 2013/211) Sch.1 para.20(21) (effective June 24, 2013—this being the date on which the 2011 (asp 1) came into force).

General

Consequential amendments and repeals

203.—(1) Schedule 5 contains minor amendments and amendments consequential on the provisions of this Act.

(2) The enactments specified in schedule 6, which include enactments that are spent, are repealed to the extent specified.

Ancillary provision

204.—(1) The Scottish Ministers may by order make such supplementary, incidental or consequential provision as they consider appropriate for the purposes of, in consequence of, or for giving full effect to, any provision of this Act.

(2) An order under subsection (1) may modify any enactment (including this Act).

(3) An order under this section containing provisions which add to, replace or omit any part of the text of an Act is subject to the affirmative procedure.

Transitional provision etc.

205.—(1) The Scottish Ministers may by order make such provision as they consider necessary or expedient for transitory, transitional or saving purposes in connection with the coming into force of any provision of this Act.

(2) An order under subsection (1) may modify any enactment (including this Act).

Short title and commencement

206.—(1) This Act may be cited as the Children's Hearings (Scotland) Act 2011.

(2) The provisions of this Act, other than sections 193 to 202, 204, 205 and this section, come into force on such day as the Scottish Ministers may by order appoint.

(3) An order under subsection (2) may contain transitional, transitory or saving provision in connection with the coming into force of this Act.

SCHEDULE 1

(introduced by section 3)

CHILDREN'S HEARINGS SCOTLAND

Status

1 (1) CHS—
    (a) is not a servant or agent of the Crown, and
    (b) does not enjoy any status, immunity or privilege of the Crown.
    (2) CHS's property is not property of, or property held on behalf of, the Crown.

Membership

2 (1) The members of CHS are to be appointed by the Scottish Ministers.

(2) There are to be no fewer than five and no more than eight members.

(3) The Scottish Ministers may by order amend sub-paragraph (2) so as to substitute for the numbers of members for the time being specified there different numbers of members.

(4) A member holds and vacates office on terms and conditions determined by the Scottish Ministers.

(5) The Scottish Ministers may appoint a person to be a member only if satisfied that the person has knowledge and experience relevant to the functions of CHS and the National Convener.

(6) The Scottish Ministers may appoint a person to be a member only if satisfied that the person, after appointment, will have no financial or other interest that is likely to prejudicially affect the performance of the person's functions as a member of CHS.

(7) The Scottish Ministers may reappoint as a member a person who has ceased to be a member.

Persons disqualified from membership

3 A person is disqualified from appointment, and from holding office, as a member if the person is or becomes—
  (a) a member of the House of Commons,
  (b) a member of the Scottish Parliament, or
  (c) a member of the European Parliament.

Resignation of members

4 A member of CHS may resign office by giving notice in writing to the Scottish Ministers.

Removal of members

5 (1) The Scottish Ministers may revoke the appointment of a member of CHS if—
  (a) the member becomes insolvent,
  (b) the member is incapacitated by physical or mental illness,
  (c) the member has been absent from meetings of CHS for a period longer than 3 months without the permission of CHS,
  (d) the member is otherwise unfit to be a member or unable for any reason to discharge the functions of a member.

(2) For the purposes of sub-paragraph (1)(a) a member becomes insolvent when—
  (a) a voluntary arrangement proposed by the member is approved,
  (b) the member is adjudged bankrupt,
  (c) the member's estate is sequestrated,
  (d) the member's application for a debt payment programme is approved under section 2 of the Debt Arrangement and Attachment (Scotland) Act 2002 (asp 17),
  or
  (e) the member grants a trust deed for creditors.

Remuneration, allowances etc.

6 (1) CHS must pay to its members—
  (a) such remuneration as the Scottish Ministers may determine, and
  (b) such allowances in respect of expenses properly incurred by members in the performance of their functions as may be so determined.

(2) CHS must—
  (a) pay to or in respect of any person who is or has been a member of CHS such pension, allowances or gratuities as the Scottish Ministers may determine, or

(b) make such payments as the Scottish Ministers may determine towards provision for the payment of a pension, allowance or gratuity to or in respect of such a person.

(3) Sub-paragraph (4) applies where—

(a) a person ceases to be a member otherwise than on the expiry of the person's term of office, and

(b) it appears to the Scottish Ministers that there are circumstances which make it right for the person to receive compensation.

(4) CHS must make a payment to the person of such amount as the Scottish Ministers may determine.

Chairing meetings

7 (1) The Scottish Ministers must appoint one of the members of CHS to chair meetings of CHS (the "chairing member").

(2) The chairing member holds and vacates that office on terms and conditions determined by the Scottish Ministers.

(3) If a person is appointed as the chairing member for a period that extends beyond the period of the person's appointment as a member, the person's appointment as a member is taken to have been extended so that it ends on the same day as the period of appointment as chairing member ends.

(4) The chairing member may resign that office by giving notice in writing to the Scottish Ministers.

(5) If the chairing member is for any reason unable to chair a meeting of members, a majority of the members present at the meeting may elect one of those members to chair the meeting.

The National Convener

8 (1) CHS is, with the approval of the Scottish Ministers, to appoint a person as the National Convener (other than the first National Convener).

(2) CHS may, with the approval of the Scottish Ministers, reappoint a person as the National Convener.

(3) CHS must take reasonable steps to involve persons who are under 21 years of age in the process for selection of a person for appointment or reappointment under this paragraph.

(4) The period for which a person is appointed or reappointed under this paragraph is 5 years.

(5) A person appointed or reappointed under this paragraph holds and vacates office on terms and conditions determined by CHS and approved by the Scottish Ministers.

(6) The Scottish Ministers may by regulations prescribe qualifications that must be held by the National Convener.

(7) A person is disqualified from appointment, and from holding office, as the National Convener if the person is or becomes—

(a) a member of the House of Commons,

(b) a member of the Scottish Parliament, or

(c) a member of the European Parliament.

(8) The National Convener may appeal to the Scottish Ministers against dismissal by CHS.

(9) CHS is the respondent in an appeal under sub-paragraph (8).

(10) The Scottish Ministers may by regulations make provision about—

(a) the procedure to be followed in appeals under sub-paragraph (8),

(b) the effect of making such an appeal,

(c) the powers of the Scottish Ministers for disposing of such appeals (including powers to make directions about liability for expenses),

(d) the effect of the exercise of those powers.

Supplementary powers of National Convener

9 The National Convener may do anything that the National Convener considers appropriate for the purposes of or in connection with the functions conferred on the National Convener by virtue of this Act or any other enactment.

Delegation of National Convener's functions

10 (1) The functions of the National Convener conferred by virtue of this Act or any other enactment (other than the functions mentioned in sub-paragraph (2)) may be carried out on the National Convener's behalf by a person who is—

(a) authorised (whether specially or generally) by the National Convener for the purpose, or

(b) a person of a class of person authorised (whether specially or generally) by the National Convener for the purpose.

(2) The functions are—

(a) the function conferred by paragraph 24,

(b) functions conferred by paragraph 1(2) to (6) of schedule 2.

(3) The National Convener may not under sub-paragraph (1) authorise the Principal Reporter, SCRA or a local authority to carry out a function on behalf of the National Convener.

(4) The National Convener may not under sub-paragraph (1) authorise a person employed by SCRA or a local authority to carry out the function conferred on the National Convener by section 8.

(5) If under sub-paragraph (1) the National Convener delegates the function conferred on the National Convener by section 8, the National Convener may not delegate any other function to the same person under that sub-paragraph.

(6) Nothing in sub-paragraph (1) prevents the National Convener from carrying out any function delegated under that sub-paragraph.

(7) The Scottish Ministers may by regulations prescribe the qualifications to be held by a person to whom a function, or a function of a class, specified in the regulations is delegated.

(8) A person to whom a function is delegated under sub-paragraph (1) must comply with a direction given to the person by the National Convener about the carrying out of the function.

(9) CHS may pay to a person to whom a function is delegated under sub-paragraph (1) such expenses and allowances as the Scottish Ministers may determine.

Staff

11 (1) CHS may employ any staff necessary to ensure the carrying out of CHS's functions.

(2) Staff are employed on terms and conditions determined by CHS and approved by the Scottish Ministers.

(3) CHS may—

(a) pay a pension, allowance or gratuity, including by way of compensation for loss of employment, to or in respect of an eligible person,

(b) make payments towards the provision of a pension, allowance or gratuity, including by way of compensation for loss of employment, to or in respect of an eligible person,

(c) provide and maintain schemes (whether contributory or not) for the payment of a pension, allowance or gratuity, including by way of compensation for loss of employment, to or in respect of an eligible person.

(4) CHS may, with the approval of the Scottish Ministers, determine—

(a) who, of the persons who are or have ceased to be employees of CHS, are to be eligible persons, and

(b) the amount that may be paid or provided for.

(5) Sub-paragraphs (6) and (7) apply where—

(a) a person employed by CHS becomes a member of CHS, and

(b) the person was (because the person was an employee of CHS) a participant in a pension scheme established and administered by CHS for the benefit of its employees.

(6) CHS may determine that the person's service as a member of CHS is to be treated for the purposes of the scheme as service as an employee of CHS whether or not any benefits are to be payable to or in respect of the person under paragraph 6.

(7) Any discretion which the scheme confers on CHS as to the benefits payable to or in respect of the person is to be exercised only with the approval of the Scottish Ministers.

Area support teams: establishment and membership

12 (1) The National Convener must establish and maintain a committee (to be known as an area support team) for each area that the National Convener designates for the purposes of this paragraph.

(2) An area designated under sub-paragraph (1) is to consist of one or more local authority areas.

(3) Before establishing an area support team, the National Convener must obtain the consent of each constituent authority.

(4) The National Convener must appoint as members of an area support team—

(a) one person nominated by each constituent authority (if the authority chooses to make a nomination),

(b) such other persons nominated by constituent authorities as the National Convener considers appropriate,

(c) a member of the Children's Panel who lives or works in the area of the area support team, and

(d) sufficient other persons so that the number of members nominated by a local authority is no more than one third of the total number of members.

(5) An area support team may not include the Principal Reporter or a member or employee of SCRA.

(6) An area support team may establish sub-committees consisting of persons who are members of the area support team.

(7) In this paragraph and paragraphs 13 and 14 "constituent authority", in relation to an area support team (or a proposed area support team), means a local authority whose area falls within the area of the area support team.

Transfer of members from CPACs

13 (1) This paragraph applies where the National Convener establishes an area support team under paragraph 12(1).

(2) The National Convener must notify each relevant CPAC member of the National Convener's intention to transfer the member to the area support team.

(3) A notice under sub-paragraph (2) must state that the relevant CPAC member will become a member of the area support team unless the member notifies the National Convener within 28 days of receiving the notice that the person does not wish to become a member of the area support team.

(4) A relevant CPAC member is a person who—

(a) at the time of the establishment of the area support team, is a member of a Children's Panel Advisory Committee whose area falls wholly within the area of the area support team, and

(b) was nominated as such by the Scottish Ministers (or, as the case may be, by the Secretary of State) under paragraph 3 or 4(a) of Schedule 1 to the 1995 Act.

(5) The National Convener must appoint each relevant CPAC member as a member of the area support team unless the member notifies the National Convener in accordance with sub-paragraph (3).

(6) On appointment as a member of the area support team under sub-paragraph (5), a relevant CPAC member ceases to be a member of the Children's Panel Advisory Committee.

(7) In this paragraph—

"area", in relation to a Children's Panel Advisory Committee, means the area of the local authority (or authorities) which formed the Children's Panel Advisory Committee,

"Children's Panel Advisory Committee" includes a joint advisory committee within the meaning of paragraph 8 of Schedule 1 to the 1995 Act.

Area support teams: functions

14 (1) An area support team is to carry out for its area the functions conferred on the National Convener by section 6.

(2) The National Convener may delegate to an area support team to carry out for its area—

(a) a function conferred on the National Convener by paragraph 1(1) of schedule 2,

(b) other functions of the National Convener specified for the purpose by the National Convener.

(3) The National Convener may not specify for the purpose of sub-paragraph (2)(b) the functions conferred on the National Convener by section 8.

(4) Before delegating a function under sub-paragraph (2) to be carried out by an area support team the National Convener must consult each constituent authority.

(5) A function to be carried out by an area support team by virtue of sub-paragraph (1) or (2) may not be delegated by the area support team to a person who is not a member of the area support team.

(6) Nothing in sub-paragraph (1) or (2) prevents the National Convener from carrying out any function mentioned in those sub-paragraphs.

(7) An area support team must comply with a direction given to it by the National Convener about—

(a) the carrying out of the functions mentioned in sub-paragraph (1),
(b) the carrying out of a function delegated to it under sub-paragraph (2).

(8) Before giving a direction to an area support team as mentioned in sub-paragraph (7) the National Convener must consult each constituent authority.

Committees

15 (1) CHS may establish committees.

(2) The members of committees may include persons who are not members of CHS.

(3) A committee must not consist entirely of persons who are not members of CHS.

(4) CHS must pay to a person who is not a member of CHS and who is appointed to a committee such remuneration and allowances as CHS may, with the approval of the Scottish Ministers, determine.

(5) A committee must comply with any directions given to it by CHS.

(6) In this paragraph, only sub-paragraph (4) applies in relation to area support teams.

CHS's supplementary powers

16 (1) CHS may do anything that it considers appropriate for the purposes of or in connection with its functions.

(2) CHS may in particular—

(a) acquire and dispose of land and other property,
(b) enter into contracts,
(c) carry out research relating to the functions conferred on it by virtue of this Act or any other enactment,
(d) publish, or assist in the publication of, materials relating to those functions,
(e) promote, or assist in the promotion of, publicity relating to those functions.

Procedure

17 (1) CHS may determine—

(a) its own procedure (including quorum), and

(b) the procedure (including quorum) of any of its committees.

(2) An area support team may determine—

(a) its own procedure (including quorum), and

(b) the procedure (including quorum) of any of its sub-committees.

Delegation of CHS's functions

18 (1) Any function of CHS (whether conferred by virtue of this Act or any other enactment) may be carried out on its behalf by—

(a) a member of CHS,

(b) a committee of CHS, or

(c) a person employed by CHS.

(2) Nothing in sub-paragraph (1) prevents CHS from carrying out any function delegated under that sub-paragraph.

Financial interests

19 (1) The Scottish Ministers must from time to time satisfy themselves that the members of CHS have no financial or other interest that is likely to prejudicially affect the performance of their functions as members of CHS.

(2) A member must comply with a requirement of the Scottish Ministers to give them any information that the Scottish Ministers consider necessary to enable them to comply with sub-paragraph (1).

Grants

20 (1) The Scottish Ministers may make grants to CHS of amounts that they determine.

(2) A grant is made subject to any conditions specified by the Scottish Ministers (including conditions about repayment).

Accounts

21 (1) CHS must—

(a) keep proper accounts and accounting records,

(b) prepare for each financial year a statement of accounts, and

(c) send a copy of each statement of accounts to the Scottish Ministers by such time as they may direct.

(2) Each statement of accounts must comply with any directions given by the Scottish Ministers as to—

(a) the information to be contained in it,

(b) the manner in which the information is to be presented,

(c) the methods and principles according to which the statement is to be prepared.

(3) The Scottish Ministers must send a copy of each statement of accounts to the Auditor General for Scotland for auditing.

(4) In this paragraph, "financial year" means—

(a) theperiodbeginningonthedateonwhichCHSisestablishedandending—

(i) on 31 March next occurring, or

(ii) if that period is of less than 6 months' duration, on 31 March next occurring after that, and
(b) each subsequent period of a year ending on 31 March.

Provision of accounts and other information to Scottish Ministers

22 (1) The Scottish Ministers may direct CHS to give them accounts or other information specified in the direction relating to CHS's property and activities or proposed activities.
(2) CHS must—
(a) give the Scottish Ministers accounts or any other information that it is directed to give under sub-paragraph (1),
(b) give the Scottish Ministers facilities for the verification of the information given,
(c) permit any person authorised by the Scottish Ministers to inspect and make copies of accounts and any other documents of CHS for the purposes of verifying the information given, and
(d) give the person an explanation, reasonably required by the person, of anything that the person is entitled to inspect.

CHS's annual report

23 (1) CHS must, as soon as is reasonably practicable after the end of each financial year, prepare and submit to the Scottish Ministers a report on the carrying out of its functions during the year.
(2) The report must include a copy of so much of the report made to CHS by the National Convener as relates to the year.
(3) CHS may include in the report any other information that it considers appropriate.
(4) The Scottish Ministers must lay before the Scottish Parliament each report submitted to them.
(5) In this paragraph, "financial year" means—
(a) the period beginning on the date on which CHS is established and ending—
(i) on 31 March next occurring, or
(ii) if that period is of less than 6 months' duration, on 31 March next occurring after that, and
(b) each subsequent period of a year ending on 31 March.

National Convener's annual report

24 (1) The National Convener must, as soon as is reasonably practicable after the end of each financial year, prepare and submit to CHS a report on the carrying out during the year of the functions conferred on the National Convener by virtue of this Act or any other enactment.
(2) The National Convener may include in the report any other information that the National Convener considers appropriate.
(3) In this paragraph, "financial year" means—
(a) the period beginning with the appointment of the first National Convener and ending—
(i) on 31 March next occurring, or

(ii) if that period is of less than 6 months' duration, on 31 March next occurring after that, and

(b) each subsequent period of a year ending on 31 March.

Validity of proceedings and actions

25 The validity of proceedings or actions of CHS (including proceedings or actions of any of its committees) is not affected by—

(a) any vacancy in the membership of CHS or any of its committees,

(b) any defect in the appointment of a member of CHS or any of its committees, or

(c) the disqualification of a person as a member of CHS after appointment.

SCHEDULE 2

(introduced by section 4)

THE CHILDREN'S PANEL

Recruitment and tenure of panel members

1 (1) The National Convener may make arrangements for the recruitment of persons as members of the Children's Panel (a person appointed as a member being referred to in this schedule as a "panel member").

(2) It is for the National Convener to appoint persons as panel members from those recruited under sub-paragraph (1).

(3) The National Convener must reappoint as a panel member a person whose appointment has ceased unless—

(a) the person declines to be reappointed, or

(b) the National Convener is satisfied that sub-paragraph (4) applies.

(4) This sub-paragraph applies if the person is unfit to be a panel member by reason of—

(a) inability,

(b) conduct, or

(c) failure without reasonable excuse to comply with any training requirements imposed by the National Convener.

(5) The period for which a person is appointed or reappointed as a panel member is 3 years.

(6) The National Convener may, with the consent of the Lord President of the Court of Session, remove a panel member during the period mentioned in sub-paragraph (5) if satisfied that sub-paragraph (4) applies.

List of panel members

2 (1) The National Convener must publish a list setting out in relation to each panel member—

(a) the member's name,

(b) the local authority area in which the member resides, and

(c) if the member works, the local authority area in which the member works.

(2) The National Convener must make the list available for public inspection.

Training

3 (1) The National Convener may train, or make arrangements for the training of, panel members and potential panel members.

(2) The National Convener must take reasonable steps to involve persons who are under 25 years of age and in respect of whom a children's hearing has been held in the development and delivery of training under sub-paragraph (1).

(3) The National Convener must, in training (or making arrangements for the training of) panel members under sub-paragraph (1), have regard to the need to provide training on how panel members may best elicit the views of a child to whom a children's hearing relates.

(4) The National Convener may monitor the performance of panel members.

Allowances

4 (1) The National Convener may, with the approval of the Scottish Ministers, determine the allowances to be paid to—

(a) panel members,

(b) potential panel members.

(2) Different determinations may be made for different cases or different classes of case.

(3) The National Convener may pay to panel members and potential panel members allowances determined under sub-paragraph (1).

SCHEDULE 3

(introduced by section 16)

THE SCOTTISH CHILDREN'S REPORTER ADMINISTRATION

Status

1 (1) SCRA—

(a) is not a servant or agent of the Crown, and

(b) does not enjoy any status, immunity or privilege of the Crown.

(2) SCRA's property is not property of, or property held on behalf of, the Crown.

Membership

2 (1) The members of SCRA are to be appointed by the Scottish Ministers.

(2) There are to be no fewer than five and no more than eight members.

(3) The Scottish Ministers may by order amend sub-paragraph (2) so as to substitute for the numbers of members for the time being specified there different numbers of members.

(4) A member holds and vacates office on terms and conditions determined by the Scottish Ministers.

(5) The Scottish Ministers may appoint a person to be a member only if satisfied that the person has knowledge or experience relevant to the functions of SCRA and the Principal Reporter.

(6) The Scottish Ministers may appoint a person to be a member only if satisfied that the person, after appointment, will have no financial or other interest that is likely to prejudicially affect the performance of the person's functions as a member of SCRA.

(7) The Scottish Ministers may reappoint as a member a person who has ceased to be a member.

Persons disqualified from membership

3 A person is disqualified from appointment, and from holding office, as a member if the person is or becomes—
- (a) a member of the House of Commons,
- (b) a member of the Scottish Parliament, or
- (c) a member of the European Parliament.

Resignation of members

4 A member of SCRA may resign office by giving notice in writing to the Scottish Ministers.

Removal of members

5 (1) The Scottish Ministers may revoke the appointment of a member of SCRA if—
- (a) the member becomes insolvent,
- (b) the member is incapacitated by physical or mental illness,
- (c) the member has been absent from meetings of SCRA for a period longer than 3 months without the permission of SCRA,
- (d) the member is otherwise unfit to be a member or unable for any reason to discharge the functions of a member.

(2) For the purposes of sub-paragraph (1)(a) a member becomes insolvent when—
- (a) a voluntary arrangement proposed by the member is approved,
- (b) the member is adjudged bankrupt,
- (c) the member's estate is sequestrated,
- (d) the member's application for a debt payment programme is approved under section 2 of the Debt Arrangement and Attachment (Scotland) Act 2002 (asp 17),

or
- (e) the member grants a trust deed for creditors.

Remuneration, allowances etc.

6 (1) SCRA must pay to its members—
- (a) such remuneration as the Scottish Ministers may determine, and

(b) such allowances in respect of expenses properly incurred by members in the performance of their functions as may be so determined.

(2) SCRA must—

(a) pay to or in respect of any person who is or has been a member of SCRA such pension, allowances or gratuities as the Scottish Ministers may determine, or

(b) make such payments as the Scottish Ministers may determine towards provision for the payment of a pension, allowance or gratuity to or in respect of such a person.

(3) Sub-paragraph (4) applies where—

(a) a person ceases to be a member otherwise than on the expiry of the person's term of office, and

(b) it appears to the Scottish Ministers that there are circumstances which make it right for the person to receive compensation.

(4) SCRA must make a payment to the person of such amount as the Scottish Ministers may determine.

Chairing meetings

7 (1) The Scottish Ministers must appoint one of the members of SCRA to chair meetings of SCRA (the "chairing member").

(2) The chairing member holds and vacates that office on terms and conditions determined by the Scottish Ministers.

(3) If a person is appointed as the chairing member for a period that extends beyond the period of the person's appointment as a member, the person's appointment as a member is taken to have been extended so that it ends on the same day as the period of appointment as chairing member ends.

(4) The chairing member may resign that office by giving notice in writing to the Scottish Ministers.

(5) If the chairing member is for any reason unable to chair a meeting of members, a majority of the members present at the meeting may elect one of those members to chair the meeting.

The Principal Reporter

8 (1) The Principal Reporter is to be appointed by SCRA with the approval of the Scottish Ministers.

(2) SCRA must take reasonable steps to involve persons who are under 21 years of age in the process for selection of a person for appointment under sub-paragraph (1).

(3) The Principal Reporter holds and vacates that office on terms and conditions determined by SCRA and approved by the Scottish Ministers.

(4) The Scottish Ministers may by regulations prescribe qualifications that must be held by the Principal Reporter.

(5) A person is disqualified from appointment, and from holding office, as the Principal Reporter if the person is or becomes—

(a) a member of the House of Commons,

(b) a member of the Scottish Parliament, or

(c) a member of the European Parliament.

(6) The Principal Reporter may appeal to the Scottish Ministers against dismissal by SCRA.

(7) SCRA is the respondent in an appeal under sub-paragraph (6).

(8) The Scottish Ministers may by regulations make provision about—

  (a) the procedure to be followed in appeals under sub-paragraph (6),

  (b) the effect of making such an appeal,

  (c) the powers of the Scottish Ministers for disposing of such appeals (including powers to make directions about liability for expenses),

  (d) the effect of the exercise of those powers.

(9) Nothing in this paragraph affects any appointment in force on the commencement of this paragraph.

Supplementary powers of Principal Reporter

9 The Principal Reporter may do anything that the Principal Reporter considers appropriate for the purposes of or in connection with the functions conferred on the Principal Reporter by virtue of this Act or any other enactment.

Delegation of Principal Reporter's functions

10 (1) The functions of the Principal Reporter conferred by virtue of this Act or any other enactment (other than the duty imposed by paragraph 22) may be carried out on the Principal Reporter's behalf by a person employed by SCRA who is—

  (a) authorised (whether specially or generally) by the Principal Reporter for the purpose, or

  (b) a member of a class of person authorised (whether specially or generally) by the Principal Reporter for the purpose.

(2) Nothing in sub-paragraph (1) prevents the Principal Reporter from carrying out any function delegated under that sub-paragraph.

(3) The Scottish Ministers may by regulations prescribe the qualifications to be held by a person employed by SCRA to whom a function, or a function of a class, specified in the regulations is delegated.

(4) A function of the Principal Reporter may not be delegated to a person who is employed by both SCRA and a local authority unless SCRA consents to the delegation.

(5) The Principal Reporter may give directions about the carrying out of a delegated function.

(6) The persons to whom the function is delegated must comply with the direction.

Staff

11 (1) SCRA may employ any staff necessary to ensure the carrying out of SCRA's functions.

(2) Staff are employed on terms and conditions determined by SCRA and approved by the Scottish Ministers.

(3) SCRA may—

  (a) pay a pension, allowance or gratuity, including by way of compensation for loss of employment, to or in respect of an eligible person,

(b) make payments towards the provision of a pension, allowance or gratuity, including by way of compensation for loss of employment, to or in respect of an eligible person,

(c) provide and maintain schemes (whether contributory or not) for the payment of a pension, allowance or gratuity, including by way of compensation for loss of employment, to or in respect of an eligible person.

(4) SCRA may, with the approval of the Scottish Ministers, determine—

(a) who, of the persons who are or have ceased to be employees of SCRA, are to be eligible persons, and

(b) the amount that may be paid or provided for.

(5) Sub-paragraphs (6) and (7) apply where—

(a) a person employed by SCRA becomes a member of SCRA, and

(b) the person was (because the person was an employee of SCRA) a participant in a pension scheme established and administered by SCRA for the benefit of its employees.

(6) SCRA may determine that the person's service as a member of SCRA is to be treated for the purposes of the scheme as service as an employee of SCRA whether or not any benefits are to be payable to or in respect of the person under paragraph 6.

(7) Any discretion which the scheme confers on SCRA as to the benefits payable to or in respect of the person is to be exercised only with the approval of the Scottish Ministers.

Appeals against dismissal

12 (1) A person employed by SCRA who is of a description or class specified in regulations made by the Scottish Ministers may appeal to the Scottish Ministers against dismissal by SCRA.

(2) SCRA is the respondent in an appeal under this paragraph.

(3) Regulations under sub-paragraph (1) may make provision about—

(a) the procedure for appeals under this paragraph,

(b) the effect of making such an appeal,

(c) the powers of the Scottish Ministers to dispose of such appeals (including powers to make directions about liability for expenses),

(d) the effect of the exercise of those powers.

Committees

13 (1) SCRA may establish committees.

(2) The members of committees may include persons who are not members of SCRA.

(3) A committee must not consist entirely of persons who are not members of SCRA.

(4) SCRA must pay to a person who is not a member of SCRA and who is appointed to a committee such remuneration and allowances as SCRA may, with the approval of the Scottish Ministers, determine.

(5) A committee must comply with any directions given to it by SCRA.

SCRA's supplementary powers

14 (1) SCRA may do anything that it considers appropriate for the purposes of or in connection with its functions.

(2) SCRA may in particular—

(a) acquire and dispose of land and other property,

(b) enter into contracts,

(c) carry out research relating to the functions conferred on it by virtue of this Act or any other enactment,

(d) publish, or assist in the publication of, materials relating to those functions,

(e) promote, or assist in the promotion of, publicity relating to those functions.

Procedure

15 SCRA may determine—

(a) its own procedure (including quorum), and

(b) the procedure (including quorum) of any of its committees.

Delegation of SCRA's functions

16 (1) Any function of SCRA (whether conferred by virtue of this Act or any other enactment) may be carried out on its behalf by—

(a) a member of SCRA,

(b) a committee of SCRA,

(c) a person employed by SCRA,

(d) any other person authorised (whether specially or generally) by it for the purpose.

(2) Nothing in sub-paragraph (1) prevents SCRA from carrying out any function delegated under that sub-paragraph.

Financial interests

17 (1) The Scottish Ministers must from time to time satisfy themselves that the members of SCRA have no financial or other interest that is likely to prejudicially affect the performance of their functions as members of SCRA.

(2) A member must comply with a requirement of the Scottish Ministers to give them any information that the Scottish Ministers consider necessary to enable them to comply with sub-paragraph (1).

Grants

18 (1) The Scottish Ministers may make grants to SCRA of amounts that they determine.

(2) A grant is made subject to any conditions specified by the Scottish Ministers (including conditions about repayment).

Accounts

19 (1) SCRA must—

(a) keep proper accounts and accounting records,

(b) prepare for each financial year a statement of accounts, and

(c) send a copy of each statement of accounts to the Scottish Ministers by such time as they may direct.

(2) Each statement of accounts must comply with any directions given by the Scottish Ministers as to—

(a) the information to be contained in it,

(b) the manner in which the information is to be presented,

(c) the methods and principles according to which the statement is to be prepared.

(3) The Scottish Ministers must send a copy of each statement of accounts to the Auditor General for Scotland for auditing.

(4) In this paragraph, "financial year" means each period of a year ending on 31 March.

Provision of accounts and other information to Scottish Ministers

20 (1) The Scottish Ministers may direct SCRA to give them accounts or other information specified in the direction relating to SCRA's property and activities or proposed activities.

(2) SCRA must—

(a) give the Scottish Ministers accounts or any other information that it is directed to give under sub-paragraph (1),

(b) give the Scottish Ministers facilities for the verification of the information given,

(c) permit any person authorised by the Scottish Ministers to inspect and make copies of accounts and any other documents of SCRA for the purposes of verifying the information given, and

(d) give the person an explanation, reasonably required by the person, of anything that the person is entitled to inspect.

SCRA's annual report

21 (1) SCRA must, as soon as is reasonably practicable after the end of each financial year, prepare and submit to the Scottish Ministers a report on the carrying out of its functions during the year.

(2) The report must include a copy of so much of the report made to SCRA by the Principal Reporter as relates to the year.

(3) SCRA may include in the report any other information that it considers appropriate.

(4) The Scottish Ministers must lay before the Scottish Parliament each report submitted to them.

(5) In this section, "financial year" means each period of a year ending on 31 March.

Principal Reporter's annual report

22 (1) The Principal Reporter must, as soon as is reasonably practicable after the end of each financial year, prepare and submit to SCRA a report on the carrying out during the year of the functions conferred on the Principal Reporter by virtue of this Act or any other enactment.

(2) The Principal Reporter may include in the report any other information that the Principal Reporter considers appropriate.

(3) In this paragraph, "financial year" means each period of a year ending on 31 March.

Validity of proceedings and actions

23 The validity of proceedings or actions of SCRA (including proceedings or actions of any of its committees) is not affected by—

    (a) any vacancy in the membership of SCRA or any of its committees,

    (b) any defect in the appointment of a member of SCRA or any of its committees, or

    (c) the disqualification of a person as a member of SCRA after appointment.

SCHEDULE 4

(introduced by section 24)

TRANSFER OF STAFF AND PROPERTY TO CHS

Interpretation

1 In this schedule—

"recognised" has the meaning given by section 178(3) of the Trade Union and Labour Relations (Consolidation) Act 1992 (c.52),
    "trade union" has the meaning given by section 1 of that Act, and
    "transfer day", in relation to a person, means the day on which a staff transfer order comes into force in relation to the person.

Staff transfer orders

2 (1) The Scottish Ministers may by order (a "staff transfer order") make provision for or in connection with—

    (a) the transfer of persons employed by SCRA to CHS,

    (b) the transfer of persons employed by local authorities from authorities to CHS.

(2) A staff transfer order may in particular—

    (a) prescribe rules by which the transfer of persons, or classes of person, specified in the order can be determined,

    (b) require—

        (i) in relation to persons employed by SCRA, SCRA and CHS acting jointly,

        or

        (ii) in relation to persons employed by a local authority specified in the order, the local authority and CHS acting jointly,

    to make a scheme in relation to the transfer of the persons to whom the order relates.

(3) Sub-paragraphs (4) and (5) apply where—

(a) an order includes a requirement of the sort mentioned in sub-paragraph (2)(b)(i) and SCRA and CHS are unable to comply with the requirement, or

(b) an order includes a requirement of the sort mentioned in sub-paragraph (2)(b)(ii) and the local authority and CHS are unable to comply with the requirement.

(4) The Scottish Ministers may determine the content of the scheme.

(5) The scheme is to be treated as if made in accordance with the requirement imposed by the order.

Schemes for transfer of staff: consultation

3 (1) Sub-paragraph (2) applies where a staff transfer order includes a requirement of the type mentioned in paragraph 2(2)(b)(i).

(2) SCRA must consult the persons mentioned in sub-paragraph (3) about the content of the scheme.

(3) Those persons are—

(a) persons employed by SCRA,

(b) the Principal Reporter,

(c) representatives of any trade union recognised by SCRA.

(4) Sub-paragraph (5) applies where a staff transfer order includes a requirement of the type mentioned in paragraph 2(2)(b)(ii).

(5) The local authority must consult the persons mentioned in sub-paragraph (6) about the content of the scheme.

(6) Those persons are—

(a) persons employed by the local authority,

(b) representatives of any trade union recognised by the local authority.

Effect on existing contracts of employment

4 (1) This paragraph applies where—

(a) a person is to be transferred by virtue of a staff transfer order, and

(b) immediately before the transfer day the person has a contract of employment with the relevant employer.

(2) On and after the transfer day the contract of employment has effect as if originally made between the person and CHS.

(3) On the transfer day the rights, powers, duties and liabilities of the relevant employer under or in connection with the contract of employment of the person are transferred to CHS.

(4) Anything done before the transfer day by or in relation to the relevant employer in respect of the contract of employment or the person is to be treated on and after that day as having been done by or in relation to CHS.

(5) If, before the transfer day, the person gives notice to CHS or the relevant employer that the person objects to becoming a member of staff of CHS—

(a) the contract of employment with the relevant employer is, on the day immediately preceding the day that would, but for the objection, have been the transfer day, terminated, and

(b) the person is not to be treated (whether for the purpose of any enactment or otherwise) as having been dismissed by virtue of the giving of such notice.

(6) Nothing in this schedule prejudices any right of the person to terminate the contract of employment if a substantial detrimental change in the person's working conditions is made.

(7) The person has the right to terminate the contract of employment if—

(a) the identity of the relevant employer changes by virtue of the making of the staff transfer order, and

(b) it is shown that, in all the circumstances, the change is significant and detrimental to the person.

(8) In this paragraph "relevant employer", in relation to a person, means—

(a) where the person has a contract of employment with SCRA, SCRA,

(b) where the person has a contract of employment with a local authority, the local authority.

Transfer of property etc. to CHS

5 (1) The Scottish Ministers may make a transfer scheme.

(2) A transfer scheme is a scheme making provision for or in connection with the transfer to CHS of property, rights, liabilities and obligations of any of the following—

(a) SCRA,

(b) a local authority,

(c) the Scottish Ministers.

(3) A transfer scheme must specify a date (the "transfer date") on which the transfer is to take effect.

(4) A transfer scheme may—

(a) specify different dates in relation to different property, rights, liabilities and obligations,

(b) make different provision in relation to different cases or classes of case.

(5) On the transfer date—

(a) any property or rights to which a transfer scheme applies transfer to and vest in CHS,

(b) any liabilities or obligations to which such a scheme applies become liabilities or obligations of CHS.

(6) A transfer scheme may make provision for the creation of rights, or the imposition of liabilities, in relation to the property, rights, liabilities or obligations transferred by virtue of the scheme.

(7) A certificate issued by the Scottish Ministers that any property, right, liability or obligation has, or has not, been transferred by virtue of a transfer scheme is conclusive evidence of the transfer or the fact that there has not been a transfer.

(8) A transfer scheme may in particular make provision about the continuation of legal proceedings.

(9) A transfer scheme may make provision for CHS to make any payment which—

(a) before a day specified in the scheme could have been made by a person specified in sub-paragraph (2)(a) or (b), but

(b) is not a liability which can become a liability of CHS by virtue of a transfer scheme.

(10) A transfer scheme may make provision for the payment by CHS of compensation in respect of property and rights transferred by virtue of the scheme.

(11) Before making a transfer scheme, the Scottish Ministers must consult—

(a) CHS,

(b) the person mentioned in sub-paragraph (2)(a) or (b) whose property, rights, liabilities and obligations (or any of them) are to be transferred by virtue of the scheme, and

(c) any other person with an interest in the property, rights, liabilities or obligations which are to be so transferred.

SCHEDULE 5

(introduced by section 203(1))

MINOR AND CONSEQUENTIAL AMENDMENTS

Legal Aid (Scotland) Act 1986 (c.47)

1 (1) The Legal Aid (Scotland) Act 1986 is amended as follows.

(2) In section 4 (Scottish Legal Aid Fund)—

(a) in subsection (2)—

(i) in paragraph (aza), after sub-paragraph (ii) insert—
"(iia) children's legal assistance;", and

(ii) after paragraph (aza) insert—
"(azb)any sums payable by the Board under contracts made by virtue of section 33B;", and

(b) in subsection (3), after paragraph (cb) insert—
"(cc) any contribution payable to the Board by any person in pursuance of section 28K of this Act;".

(3) In section 4A (Scottish Legal Aid Board's power to make grants in respect of provision of civil legal aid etc.)—

(a) in subsection (2)—

(i) in paragraph (a) for the words from "aid" to "matters" substitute "aid, advice and assistance in relation to civil matters or children's legal assistance",

(ii) in paragraph (b) after "matters" insert "or children's matters", and

(iii) in paragraph (c) at the end add "or children's matters",

(b) in subsection (13)—

(i) for the words "aid or advice and assistance" substitute "aid, advice and assistance or children's legal aid", and

(ii) at the end add "or children's legal aid", and

(c) in subsection (14), at the end add "and
"children's matters" means matters relating to children's hearings, prehearing panels (as defined in section 79(2)(a) of the 2011 Act) or proceedings under Part 10 or 15 of the 2011 Act".

(4) In subsection (1A) of section 31 (selection of solicitors and counsel)—

(a) after paragraph (a), insert—

"(aa) section 28M(3),",

(b) after paragraph (d), insert—

"(da) regulations made under section 33B(4),", and

(c) in the full-out, after "assistance" insert "or children's legal assistance".

(5) In section 35A (Board's powers to obtain information from solicitors in certain cases)—

(a) after subsection (1) insert—

"(1A) The Board may, for the purpose of determining whether—

(a) a solicitor, an employee of the solicitor or an employee of the solicitor's firm may be committing a criminal offence in connection with children's legal assistance,

(b) a solicitor may be seeking, in relation to children's legal assistance, to recover from the Fund money to which the solicitor is not entitled, as, for example, by performing unnecessary work, or

(c) a solicitor or firm whose name appears on the register maintained under section 28M(1) is or may not be complying with the code of practice under section 28N for the time being in force, require the solicitor or firm to produce such information and documents relating wholly or partly to the provision of children's legal assistance as it may specify, at such time and place as it may specify.", and

(b) in subsection (2), after "(1)" insert "or (1A)".

(6) In section 35B (Board's powers of entry)—

(a) in subsection (1), after paragraph (c) insert "or (ca) a solicitor whose name appears on the register maintained under section 28M(1) may not be complying with the code of practice under section 28N for the time being in force;",

(b) in subsection (2)—

(i) in paragraph (b), at the beginning insert "in the case mentioned in subsection (2A),", and

(ii) after paragraph (b) insert—

"(ba) in the case mentioned in subsection (2B), take possession of any documents which appear to him to relate, wholly or partly, to any children's legal assistance provided in or from those premises;", and

(c) after subsection (2) insert—

"(2A) The case mentioned in subsection (2)(b) is where the warrant is issued in pursuance of—

(a) paragraph (a), (b) or (c) of subsection (1), or

(b) paragraph (d) of subsection (1) where the requirement to produce the documents was made under subsection (1) of section 35A.

(2B) The case mentioned in subsection (2)(ba) is where the warrant is issued in pursuance of—

(a) paragraph (ca) of subsection (1), or

(b) paragraph (d) of subsection (1) where the requirement to produce the documents was made under subsection (1A) of section 35A.".

(7) In section 37(2) (regulations under Act which require to be laid in draft and approved by the Scottish Parliament before being made), after "24(4)" insert ", 28C(3), 28K(2), 28L(1) or (8),".

(8) In section 41 (interpretation)—

(a) after "requires—" insert—

""the 2011 Act" means the Children's Hearings (Scotland) Act 2011 (asp 1);",

(b) after the definition of "the Board" insert—

""children's legal aid" has the meaning given to it in section 28B(2) of this Act;

"children's legal assistance" means—

(a) children's legal aid, and

(b) advice and assistance in relation to children's hearings, pre-hearing panels (as defined in section 79(2)(a) of the 2011 Act) or proceedings under Part 10 or 15 of the 2011 Act;", and

(c) in the definition of "legal aid"—

   (i) after "aid,", where it third occurs, insert "children's legal aid", and

   (ii) the words from "or", where it second occurs, to the end of the definition are repealed.

(9) In section 42 (disposable income and disposable capital: regulations), after subsection (3) insert—

"(4) Regulations under this section may make different provision for—

   (a) children's legal aid and legal aid other than children's legal aid,

   (b) advice and assistance in relation to children's matters and advice and assistance other than advice and assistance in relation to children's matters.

(5) In subsection (4)(b), "children's matters" has the meaning given by section 4A(14).".

Children (Scotland) Act 1995 (c.36)

2 (1) The Children (Scotland) Act 1995 is amended as follows.

(2) In section 12 (restrictions on certain decrees)—

(a) in subsection (1), for "or 54 of this Act" substitute "of this Act or section 62 of the Children's Hearings (Scotland) Act 2011",

(b) in subsection (2)(a), for "or 54 of this Act" substitute "of this Act or section 62 of the Children's Hearings (Scotland) Act 2011".

(3) In section 16 (welfare of child and consideration of views)—

(a) in subsection (1)—

   (i) the words "a children's hearing decide, or" are repealed,

   (ii) the words "their or" are repealed,

(b) in subsection (2), the words "a children's hearing or as the case may be" are repealed,

(c) in subsection (3)—

   (i) for "(4)(a)(i) or (ii) or (b)" substitute "(4)",

   (ii) the words "requirement or", in both places where they occur, are repealed,

   (iii) the words "the children's hearing consider, or as the case may be" are repealed,

(d) for subsection (4) substitute—

"(4) The circumstances to which subsection (2) refers are that the sheriff is considering whether to make, vary or discharge an exclusion order.",

(e) in subsection (5)—
  (i) paragraph (a) is repealed,
  (ii) in paragraph (b), for "Chapters 1 to 3" substitute "Chapter 1 or 3".

(4) In section 17 (duty of local authority to child looked after by them)—

(a) in subsection (6), for paragraph (b) substitute—

"(b) who is subject to a compulsory supervision order or an interim compulsory supervision order and in respect of whom they are the implementation authority (within the meaning of the Children's Hearings (Scotland) Act 2011);",

(b) subsection (6)(c) is repealed,

(c) in subsection (6)(d), for "such responsibilities" substitute "responsibilities as respects the child".

(5) In section 19 (local authority plans for services for children)—

(a) in subsection (2), after paragraph (a) insert—

"(aa) the Children's Hearings (Scotland) Act 2011;",

(b) in subsection (5)—
  (i) in paragraph (c), the words "appointed under section 127 of the Local Government etc. (Scotland) Act 1994" are repealed,
  (ii) for paragraph (d) substitute—

"(d) the National Convener of Children's Hearings Scotland;".

(6) In section 33 (effect of orders etc. made in different parts of the United Kingdom)—

(a) in subsection (1)—
  (i) the words "or to a supervision requirement" are repealed,
  (ii) the words "or, as the case may be, as if it were a supervision requirement" are repealed,

(b) in subsection (2)—
  (i) paragraph (b) is repealed,
  (ii) in the full-out, the words "or requirement" are repealed,

(c) subsection (4) is repealed,

(d) in subsection (5)(b), the words "or to a supervision requirement" are repealed,

(e) in subsection (5)(c), the words "or to a supervision requirement" are repealed.

(7) In section 38(4) (limited disapplication of certain enactments while child being provided with refuge), for "section 83 of this Act" substitute "section 171 of the Children's Hearings (Scotland) Act 2011".

(8) In section 75 (powers in relation to secure accommodation)—

(a) in subsection (1)(b), for "supervision requirement" substitute "compulsory supervision order, interim compulsory supervision order, medical examination order or warrant to secure attendance (all within the meaning of the Children's Hearings (Scotland) Act 2011)",

(b) after subsection (2) insert—

"(2A) In subsection (2), "relevant person" has the meaning given by section 200 of the Children's Hearings (Scotland) Act 2011 and includes a person deemed to be a relevant person by virtue of section 81(3), 160(4)(b) or 164(6) of that Act.", and

(c) for subsection (4) substitute—

"(4) A child may not be kept in secure accommodation by virtue of regulations made under this section for a period exceeding 66 days from the day when the child was first taken to the secure accommodation.".

(9) In section 76(8) (making of child protection order instead of exclusion order)—

    (a) in paragraph (b), for "section 57 of this Act" substitute "Part 5 of the Children's Hearings (Scotland) Act 2011",

    (b) in the full-out—

        (i) for "an order under that section" substitute "a child protection order",

        (ii) after "that" insert "Part".

(10) In section 93(1) (interpretation), in the definition of "children's hearing", for "section 39(3); but does not include a business meeting arranged under section 64, of this Act" substitute "section 5 of the Children's Hearings (Scotland) Act 2011".

(11) In section 93(2)(b) (meaning of "child"), for the definition of "child" substitute—

    ""child" means—

        (i) in relation to section 75, a person under the age of 18 years,

        (ii) in relation to any other section, a person under the age of 16 years;".

Antisocial Behaviour etc. (Scotland) Act 2004 (asp 8)

3 In section 12 of the Antisocial Behaviour etc. (Scotland) Act 2004 (sheriff's power to refer child to children's hearing where antisocial behaviour order made etc.), for subsection (1) substitute—

"(1) This section applies where—

    (a) the sheriff makes an antisocial behaviour order or an interim order in respect of a child, and

    (b) the sheriff considers that a section 67 ground (other than the ground mentioned in section 67(2)(j)) applies in relation to the child.

(1A) The sheriff may require the Principal Reporter to arrange a children's hearing.

(1B) The sheriff must give the Principal Reporter a section 12 statement if—

    (a) the sheriff makes a requirement under subsection (1A), and

    (b) a compulsory supervision order is not in force in relation to the child.

(1C) A section 12 statement is a statement—

    (a) specifying which of the section 67 grounds the sheriff considers applies in relation to the child,

    (b) setting out the reasons why the sheriff considers the ground applies, and

    (c) setting out any other information about the child which appears to the sheriff to be relevant.

(1D) In this section—

"compulsory supervision order" has the meaning given by section 83 of the Children's Hearings (Scotland) Act 2011, "section 67 ground" means a ground mentioned in section 67(2) of that Act.".

SCHEDULE 6

(introduced by section 203(2))

REPEALS

Enactment	Extent of repeal
Rehabilitation of Offenders Act 1974 (c.53)	Section 3. In section 5, in subsection (3), paragraph (b) and the word "and" immediately preceding it; in subsection (5), paragraph (f); and, in subsection (10), the words ", or a supervision requirement under the Children (Scotland) Act 1995,".
Legal Aid (Scotland) Act 1986 (c.47)	Section 29.
Tribunals and Inquiries Act 1992 (c.53)	In Part 2 of Schedule 1, paragraph 61(a) and the title ("Social work") relating to it.
Local Government etc. (Scotland) Act 1994 (c.39)	Sections 127 to 138. Schedule 12.
Children (Scotland) Act 1995 (c.36)	Sections 39 to 74. In section 75(1), paragraph (a) and the word "or" immediately following it. Section 75(5). Sections 75A and 75B. Sections 81 to 85. Section 90. Section 91(3)(a) to (c). Section 92. In section 93, in subsection (1), the definitions of "chief social work officer", "child assessment order", "child protection order", "compulsory measures of supervision", "education authority", "local government area", "place of safety", "the Principal Reporter", "relevant local authority", "supervision requirement" and "working day"; and, in subsection (2)(b), the definition of "relevant person". In section 101(1), in paragraph (a), the words "or under section 87(4) of this Act"; and paragraph (c) and the word "and" immediately preceding it. Section 101(4). In section 105, in subsection (8), the words "44, 70(4), 74, 82, 83"; and subsection (10). Schedule 1. In Schedule 4, paragraph 23(2) and (3).

Vulnerable Witnesses (Scotland) Act 2004 (asp 3)	Section 23.
Antisocial Behaviour etc. (Scotland) Act 2004 (asp 8)	Section 12(2) to (5).
Legal Profession and Legal Aid (Scotland) Act 2007 (asp 5)	Section 72(4) to (6).

APPENDIX TWO

**CHILDREN'S HEARINGS (SCOTLAND) ACT 2011
(RULES OF PROCEDURE IN CHILDREN'S HEARINGS)
RULES 2013**

(SSI 2013/194)

Made: 30 May 2013
Coming into force in accordance with rule 1 (June 24, 2013)

CONTENTS

PART 1

INTRODUCTORY AND GENERAL

PART 2

SELECTION OF CHILDREN'S HEARINGS AND PRE-HEARING PANEL MEMBERS AND DUTIES OF MEMBERS

PART 3

DUTIES AND ROLES OF PERSONS ATTENDING OR PREPARING DOCUMENTS FOR CHILDREN'S HEARINGS AND PREHEARING PANELS

PART 8

SPECIFIC PROVISION FOR ARRANGING A CHILDREN'S HEARING TO BE HELD UNDER SECTION 119 (CHILDREN'S HEARING FOLLOWING DEFERRAL OR PROCEEDINGS UNDER PART 10) OF THE ACT

31. Provision of information to the child, relevant persons and any appointed safeguarder for a children's hearing to which section 119 (children's hearing following deferral or proceedings under Part 10) of the Act applies
32. Information to be given to the members of the children's hearing to which section 119 (children's hearing following deferral or proceedings under Part 10) of the Act applies
33. Provision of information for children's hearing to which section 119 (children's hearing following deferral or proceedings under Part 10) of the Act applies where section 109(7) (determination: power to make interim compulsory supervision order etc.), 115(5) (recall: power to refer other grounds) or 117(5) (new section 67 ground established: sheriff to refer to children's hearing) of the Act also applies.

PART 9

SPECIFIC PROVISION FOR ARRANGING A CHILDREN'S HEARING TO WHICH SECTION 137 (DUTY TO ARRANGE CHILDREN'S HEARING) OF THE ACT APPLIES

34. Provision of information to the child and relevant persons for a children's hearing to which section 137 (duty to arrange children's hearing) of the Act applies
35. Information to be given to the members of the children's hearing to which section 137 (duty to arrange children's hearing) of the Act applies
36. Provision of information for a review hearing where section 136 (duty to initiate review where child transferred) of the Act applies

PART 10

ARRANGING A GROUNDS HEARING WHERE GROUNDS HEARING OR REVIEW HEARING HAS DEFERRED OR APPLICATION MADE TO THE SHERIFF

37. Papers to be sent when new grounds presented after grounds hearing deferred or application made to the sheriff
38. Papers to be sent when new grounds presented after review hearing deferred

PART 11

ARRANGING OTHER CHILDREN'S HEARINGS

39. Arranging a children's hearing under section 45 (review by children's hearing where child in place of safety) or 46 (review by children's hearing where order prevents removal of child) of the Act—2nd working day hearing

PART 12

PRE-HEARING PANELS AND DETERMINATION OF MATTERS WHICH MAY BE REFERRED TO PRE-HEARING PANELS

PART 13

APPOINTMENT OF SAFEGUARDER AND SAFEGUARDERS' REPORTS

PART 14

PROCEDURE AT CHILDREN'S HEARINGS—GENERAL

PART 15

PROCEDURE AT GROUNDS HEARING AND CHILDREN'S HEARINGS
TO
WHICH SECTION 119 (CHILDREN'S HEARING FOLLOWING
DEFERRAL OR PROCEEDINGS UNDER PART 10) OR 137 (DUTY TO
ARRANGE CHILDREN'S HEARING) OF THE ACT APPLIES

59. Procedure at a grounds hearing—grounds put to the child and relevant person
60. Procedure where section 91(1) (grounds accepted: powers of grounds hearing), 119(1) (children's hearing following deferral or proceedings under Part 10), or 138(1) (powers of children's hearing on review) of the Act applies
61. Procedure when proceedings under section 91(2) (grounds accepted: powers of grounds hearing), 119(2) (children's hearing following deferral or proceedings under Part 10) or 138(2) (powers of children's hearing on review) of the Act
62. Procedure where section 91(3) (grounds accepted: powers of grounds hearing), 119(3) (children's hearing following deferral or proceedings under Part 10) or 138(3) (powers of children's hearing on review) of the Act applies
63. Grounds hearing procedures where section 93 (grounds not accepted: application to sheriff or discharge) or 94 (child or relevant person unable to understand grounds) of the Act applies
64. Procedure where section 95 (child fails to attend grounds hearing) of the Act applies
65. Procedure where report required under section 141 (preparation of report in circumstances relating to permanence order or adoption) of the Act
66. Procedure where there is a review of determination that person be deemed a relevant person
67. Breach of duties imposed by sections 144 (implementation of compulsory supervision order: general duties of implementation authority) or 145 (duty where order requires child to reside in certain place) of the Act

PART 16

PROCEDURE WHERE PART 10 OF THESE RULES APPLIES

68. Procedure where rule 37 applies
69. Procedure where rule 38 applies

PART 17

PROCEDURE AT OTHER CHILDREN'S HEARINGS

70. Procedure at a children's hearing held under section 45 (review by children's hearing where child in place of safety) or 46 (review by children's hearing where order prevents removal of child) of the Act
71. Procedure where Reporter receives notice under section 49 (notice of application for variation or termination) of the Act after arranging hearing under section 45 or 46 (review by children's hearing where child in place of safety or order prevents removal of child) of the Act
72. Procedure where hearing held by virtue of section 50 (children's hearing to provide advice to sheriff in relation to application) of the Act

PART 18

GENERAL ISSUES FOR CHILDREN'S HEARINGS

PART 19

PROCEDURE AT A PRE-HEARING PANEL OR A CHILDREN'S HEARING WHERE A NON-DISCLOSURE REQUEST IS MADE

PART 20

NOTIFYING DECISIONS

PART 21

SPECIFIC PROVISION FOR CHILDREN'S HEARINGS ARRANGED
UNDER THE CHILDREN'S HEARINGS (SCOTLAND) ACT 2011
(IMPLEMENTATION OF SECURE ACCOMMODATION
AUTHORISATION) (SCOTLAND) REGULATIONS 2013

PART 22

MISCELLANEOUS

The Scottish Ministers make the following Rules in exercise of the powers conferred by sections 177 and 195 of the Children's Hearings (Scotland) Act 2011 and all other powers enabling them to do so.

In accordance with section 177(4) and 197 of that Act, a draft of this instrument has been laid before and approved by resolution of the Scottish Parliament.

In accordance with paragraph 24(1) and (3) of Schedule 7 to the Tribunals, Courts and Enforcement Act 2007 the Scottish Ministers have consulted the Administrative Justice and Tribunals Council and it has consulted its Scottish Committee.

PART 1

Introductory and General

Citation, commencement and application

1.—(1) These Rules may be cited as the Children's Hearings (Scotland) Act 2011 (Rules of Procedure in Children's Hearings) Rules 2013 and come into force on the same day as section 177 (children's hearings: procedural rules) of the Act.

(2) These Rules shall only apply to proceedings commenced on or after the day on which they come into force.

Interpretation

2.—(1) In these Rules—

"the Act" means the Children's Hearings (Scotland) Act 2011;

"chairing member" means the member of the Children's Panel selected to chair a pre-hearing panel or children's hearing, as the case may be;

"a contact direction" has the same meaning as in section 126(1) (review of contact direction) of the Act;

"National Convener" means the National Convener of Children's Hearings Scotland;

"member of the pre-hearing panel" and "member of the children's hearing" means a member of the Children's Panel selected under section 6 (selection of members of children's hearing) of the Act, in relation to that hearing or pre-hearing, and "member" is to be construed accordingly;

"relevant person" means a relevant person in relation to a child and includes a person deemed to be a relevant person under section 81 (determination of claim that person be deemed a relevant person) or section 160(4)(b) (appeal to sheriff against relevant person determination) of the Act;

"Reporter" means the Principal Reporter or any person carrying out a function on behalf of the Principal Reporter by virtue of paragraph 10(1) (delegation of Principal Reporter's functions) of schedule 3 to the Act;

"section 62 statement" has the same meaning as in section 62(4) (provision of information by court) of the Act.

(2) For the purposes of rule 1(2) of these Rules, proceedings are commenced on the date when any of the following occurs—

(a)   a children's hearing is arranged by the Reporter under section 69(2) of the Act;

(b)   an application is made under Part 5 of the Act; or

(c)   an appeal is made under Part 15 of the Act.

PART 2

Selection of Children's Hearings and Pre-Hearing Panel Members and Duties of Members

Selection of members of children's hearing and pre-hearing panel—supplementary

3.—(1) Where a children's hearing is held in relation to a child, by virtue of the Act or any other enactment, the children's hearing may request that the National Convener select, where practicable, one of the members of that children's hearing to be a member of the next children's hearing to be arranged in relation to that child.

(2) In selecting members of a pre-hearing panel in terms of section 79(2)(a) (referral of certain matters for pre-hearing determination) of the Act the National Convener must ensure that the prehearing panel—

(a)   includes both male and female members of the Children's Panel; and

(b)   so far as practicable, consists only of members of the Children's Panel who live or work in the area of the local authority which is the relevant local authority for the child to whom the pre-hearing panel relates.

Selection of chairing member for pre-hearing panels and children's hearings

4.—(1) Paragraph (2) applies where a pre-hearing panel or children's hearing has been arranged by virtue of the Act or any other enactment and the National Convener or relevant area support team has not selected a chairing member for that pre-hearing panel or children's hearing.

(2) Immediately before beginning the pre-hearing panel or children's hearing, as the case may be, the members of that pre-hearing panel or children's hearing must determine which of their number is to chair the pre-hearing panel or children's hearing, as the case may be.

(3) A member may only be selected to chair a children's hearing if that member has successfully completed the relevant training provided by or on behalf of the National Convener relating to chairing a children's hearing.

Duties of members of the pre-hearing panel or children's hearing relating to documents and information

5.—(1) Any documents which are given to a member of the pre-hearing panel or children's hearing by the Reporter under, or by virtue of, the Act or these Rules must be kept securely in that member's custody and returned to the Reporter at the conclusion of the pre-hearing panel or children's hearing to which those documents relate.

(2) The member must not cause or permit any information which they have obtained by virtue of their involvement in a pre-hearing panel or children's hearing to be disclosed, except as permitted by the Act or these Rules.

Duties of chairing member of a pre-hearing panel or children's hearing

6.—(1) The chairing member of the children's hearing or pre-hearing panel must—
  (a) take reasonable steps to ensure that the child and each relevant person are able to—
     (i) understand the proceedings; and
     (ii) participate in those proceedings;
  (b) where, during the proceedings, the child wishes to express a view, make reasonable arrangements to enable the child to express those views in the manner preferred by the child;
  (c) ensure that a record is made of—
     (i) the decisions or determinations made by the children's hearing or pre-hearing panel, as the case may be; and
     (ii) the reasons for those decisions or determinations; and
  (d) sign and date the record of the decisions or determinations.

(2) Any requirement on the chairing member to inform those attending a children's hearing of the substance of any report, document or information or to explain any matter is subject to any decision of the children's hearing to withhold information under section 178 (children's hearing: disclosure of information) of the Act or by virtue of a non-disclosure request made in accordance with Part 19 of these Rules.

Procedure at children's hearings and pre-hearing panels where not otherwise specified

7.—(1) The procedure at any children's hearing or pre-hearing panel required to be held by virtue of the Act or any other enactment, unless that procedure is provided for under the Act or these Rules, is to be determined by the chairing member.

(2) The children's hearing or pre-hearing panel, if it considers it appropriate to do so, may adjourn the children's hearing or pre-hearing panel, as the case may be—

(a) on the initiative of the children's hearing or pre-hearing panel; or

(b) on the request of any person attending the hearing.

(3) Where a children's hearing or pre-hearing panel has been adjourned it must re-convene on the same day as the adjournment was made.

PART 3

Duties and Roles of Persons Attending or Preparing Documents for Children's Hearings and Pre-Hearing Panels

Requirement to include child's views in documents

8. Where any document is to be given to members of the children's hearing or pre-hearing panel under, or by virtue of, the Act, or these Rules, the document must contain any views expressed by the child which have been given to the person who has prepared that document.

Duties of safeguarder in respect of information and documents

9.—(1) Any documents which are given to a safeguarder by the Reporter under, or by virtue of, the Act or any other enactment must be kept securely in the safeguarder's custody and returned to the Reporter on the termination of the safeguarder's appointment.

(2) The safeguarder must not cause or permit any information which they have obtained by virtue of their appointment as a safeguarder under the Act to be disclosed, except as permitted by virtue of the Act or any other enactment.

Attendance at children's hearings by member of the Administrative Justice and Tribunals Council or the Scottish Committee of that Council or a member of an Area Support Team

10.—(1) Any documents which are given to members of the children's hearing or pre-hearing panel must be given by the Reporter to any of the following persons attending the children's hearing or pre-hearing panel where that person so requests—

(a) a member of the Administrative Justice and Tribunals Council or the Scottish Committee of that Council (acting in that person's capacity as such);

(b) a member of an area support team (acting in that person's capacity as such).

(2) Where documents are given to a person under paragraph (1) those documents must be kept securely in that person's custody and returned to the Reporter at the conclusion of the children's hearing or pre-hearing panel to which they relate.

(3) The person to whom the documents are given under paragraph (1) must not cause or permit any information which they have obtained by virtue of their attendance at a pre-hearing panel or children's hearing to be disclosed, except as permitted by the Act or these Rules.

Role of representative of the child, relevant person or deemed relevant person

11.—(1) Where the child or relevant person, or any person who wishes to be deemed to be a relevant person (each referred to in this rule as "the accompanied person") is accompanied at a children's hearing or pre-hearing panel by a representative that representative may assist the accompanied person to discuss any issues arising for discussion before the children's hearing or pre-hearing panel.

(2) The right of the accompanied person to be represented at the children's hearing or prehearing panel is without prejudice to any right of the accompanied person to legal representation by a solicitor or counsel.

PART 4

General Duties of the Reporter

Record keeping by the Reporter of investigation and determination

12.—(1) This rule applies where section 66(1) (investigation and determination by Principal Reporter) of the Act applies.

(2) The Reporter must keep a record of—

(a) the name and address (if available) of any person providing the notice, information, statement or evidence;

(b) the details of any investigation carried out by the Reporter under section 66 of the Act;

(c) the determination made by the Reporter under section 66(2) of the Act; and

(d) the details of any action taken by the Reporter under sections 68(2), 68(5) (determination under section 66: no referral to children's hearing) or 72(2) (child in place of safety: Principal Reporter's powers) of the Act.

(3) Where the Reporter is required to arrange a children's hearing under section 69(2) (determination under section 66: referral to children's hearing) of the Act the Reporter must notify—

(a) where the information was provided under section 60 (local authority's duty to provide information to Principal Reporter) of the Act, the local authority which provided the information;

(b) where the information was provided under section 61 (constable's duty to provide information to Principal Reporter) of the Act or section 43(5) (arrangements where children arrested) of the Criminal Procedure (Scotland) Act 1995, the chief constable of the Police Service of Scotland.

Record keeping duties of the Reporter in relation to children's hearings

13.—(1) The Reporter must keep a record of the proceedings at each children's hearing and prehearing panel held by virtue of the Act or any other enactment.

(2) The record to be kept by the Reporter must include the information mentioned in paragraph (3) and such other information about the proceedings as the Reporter considers appropriate.

(3) That information is—

(a) the particulars of the place and date of the children's hearing or pre-hearing panel;

(b) the full name and address, date of birth and sex of the child in relation to whom the children's hearing or pre-hearing panel is held;

(c) the full name and address of each relevant person;

(d) which of the persons mentioned in sub-paragraphs (b) and (c) attended the children's hearing or pre-hearing panel;

(e) the full name and address of any representative attending the children's hearing or prehearing panel;

(f) the full name and address of any safeguarder attending the children's hearing or prehearing panel;

(g) the details of any other person attending the children's hearing or pre-hearing panel;

(h) the details of any decision or determination made by the children's hearing or pre-hearing panel or any other course of action taken by the children's hearing or pre-hearing panel;

(i) where the children's hearing to which the record relates is a grounds hearing—

    (i) the details of any section 67 ground which is accepted, or not accepted, or is not understood and by whom;

    (ii) the detail of any direction given by the grounds hearing under section 93(2)(a) (grounds not accepted: application to sheriff or discharge) or 94(2)(a) (child or relevant person unable to understand grounds) of the Act to the Reporter to make an application to the sheriff.

The statement of grounds

14. Where the statement of grounds prepared by the Reporter under section 89 (Principal Reporter's duty to prepare statement of grounds) of the Act includes a ground mentioned in section 67(2)(j) (the child has committed an offence) the facts relating to that ground must have the same degree of specification as is required by section 138(4) (complaints) of, and Schedule 3 (indictments and complaints) to, the Criminal Procedure (Scotland) Act 1995 in a charge in a complaint, and the statement of grounds must also specify the nature of the offence in question.

Duties of Reporters where information to be withheld from a person

15.—(1) Where information is to be withheld from a person under the Act or these Rules the Reporter must ensure that the relevant information is removed from the report or other document or information to be given under the Act, or these Rules, to the person from whom that information is to be withheld.

(2) Where information is withheld under the Act or these Rules the Reporter must inform the persons to whom the report or other document or information has been given under the Act, or these Rules, of the identity of the person from whom the information is being withheld, and what information is being withheld from that person.

Withholding of specified documents and information by the Reporter

16.—(1) This rule applies where a children's hearing or pre-hearing panel is to be held or has been held in relation to a child by virtue of the Act or these Rules and the Reporter is arranging the hearing, notifying persons of the hearing or issuing information or documents for the hearing or is taking any action required as a consequence of the hearing.

(2) Where the Reporter is carrying out the functions referred to in paragraph (1) and considers that disclosing the whereabouts of the child to whom the children's hearing or pre-hearing panel relates, or of any relevant person, would be likely to cause significant harm to the child or any relevant person the Reporter may withhold that information.

(3) Where the address of the child or relevant person is withheld under paragraph (2) the Reporter will give the address of the child or relevant person as that of the Reporter.

Duties of the Reporter where a child is detained under a warrant to secure the attendance of the child

17.—(1) This rule applies where the children's hearing has granted a warrant to secure the attendance of the child at a children's hearing under section 123 (general power to grant warrant to secure attendance) of the Act and the child is being kept in a place of safety under that warrant.

(2) The Reporter must, wherever practicable, arrange the children's hearing to take place on the first working day after the child was first detained in pursuance of the warrant.

Notification and provision of information to a young child

18.—(1) This rule applies where, under the Act or these Rules, the Reporter must—

  (a) notify a child of the date, time and place of a children's hearing or pre-hearing panel to be held in relation to that child; or

  (b) provide a child with any information, confirmation, report or other document in relation to a children's hearing or pre-hearing panel.

(2) The Reporter need not so notify the child or provide the information, confirmation, report or other document where, taking account of the child's age and maturity, the child would not be capable of understanding the notification, information, confirmation, report or other document.

PART 5

Attendance at Hearings

Further provision in relation to the attendance of the child and relevant person at a children's hearing or pre-hearing panel

19.—(1) Paragraph (2) applies where the Reporter has been advised that the child, or relevant person, or an individual who wants to be deemed to be a relevant person, wishes to attend a prehearing panel or children's hearing or part of a children's hearing and—

(a) the child or the relevant person, as the case may be, has been excused from attending that pre-hearing panel, children's hearing or that part of the children's hearing; or

(b) the child, relevant person or individual in question wishes to attend a pre-hearing panel or children's hearing which by virtue of section 80 (determination of matter referred under section 79) of the Act is to determine a matter referred under section 79 (referral of certain matters for pre-hearing determination) of the Act.

(2) The Scottish Children's Reporter Administration must take all reasonable steps to enable the child, relevant person, or the individual in question, as the case may be, to attend the pre-hearing panel, children's hearing or that part of the children's hearing by way of telephone, through video link or by using any other method of communication, if requested to do so by the child, relevant person or individual in question, and if the Reporter is satisfied that the child, relevant person or individual in question has good reason for not attending in person.

Attendance at a children's hearing

20.—(1) The persons mentioned in paragraph (2) are authorised to attend a pre-hearing panel and children's hearing.

(2) Those persons are a constable, prison officer or other person who has in their lawful custody a person who has to attend a pre-hearing panel or children's hearing.

PART 6

Arranging Children's Hearings—General

21. Application of Part

This part does not apply where rule 29 or 36 applies.

Notification of children's hearings—general

22.—(1) Where a children's hearing is to be held in relation to a child by virtue of section 69(2) (determination under section 66: referral to children's hearing) or Parts 9 to 11 (children's hearing; proceedings before sheriff; subsequent children's hearings) or 13 (review of compulsory supervision order) of the Act the Reporter must notify the persons mentioned in paragraph (2) of the date, time and place of the children's hearing, as soon as practicable and no later than 7 days before the intended date of the children's hearing.

(2) Those persons are—

(a) the child;

(b) each relevant person;

(c) any individual other than a relevant person who appears to the Reporter to have or recently have had significant involvement in the upbringing of the child;

(d) any appointed safeguarder;

(e) the chief social work officer of the relevant local authority for the child;

(f) the National Convener.

Other information to be given with notification of a children's hearing to the child and each relevant person

23. The Reporter must when issuing the notice under rule 22(1) to the child and each relevant person also give to the child and each relevant person—
- (a) information on the availability to the child and relevant person of legal advice;
- (b) confirmation of the child's duty to attend the children's hearing under section 73 (child's duty to attend children's hearing) of the Act;
- (c) confirmation of the relevant person's duty to attend the children's hearing under section 74 (relevant person's duty to attend children's hearing) of the Act;
- (d) confirmation of the right of the child and each relevant person to request a pre-hearing panel or children's hearing to determine whether—
  - (i) a particular individual should be deemed to be a relevant person;
  - (ii) the child or relevant person should be excused from all or part of the children's hearing;
  - (iii) it is likely that the children's hearing will consider making a compulsory supervision order including a secure accommodation authorisation in relation to the child;
- (e) information on the means by which the child may express views to the children's hearing;
- (f) confirmation of the right of the child and each relevant person to give any report or other document for the consideration of the children's hearing or pre-hearing panel.

Other information to be given with notification of a children's hearing to certain other persons

24.—(1) Where rule 22 applies, when issuing the notification required under that rule the Reporter must also give to any individual other than a relevant person who appears to the Reporter to have or recently have had significant involvement in the upbringing of the child the information mentioned in paragraph (2).

(2) That information is confirmation of the right of the individual to require a pre-hearing panel or a children's hearing to determine whether the individual should be deemed to be a relevant person.

Information to be sent to the members of the children's hearing

25. Wherever practicable 7 days before, and no later than 3 days before, the intended date of the children's hearing the Reporter must give to the three members of the children's hearing notification of the date, time and place of the hearing.

Provision of information prior to children's hearing

26.—(1) Where the child or any relevant person wish to give to a children's hearing to be held by virtue of section 69(2) (determination under section 66: referral to children's hearing) or Parts 9 to 11 (children's hearing; proceedings before sheriff; subsequent children's hearings), or 13 (review of compulsory supervision order) of the Act any report or other document for the consideration of the children's hearing the child or relevant person, as the case may be, must give a copy of the report or other document to the Reporter, so far as practicable, no later than 4 days before the intended date of the hearing.

(2) Wherever practicable the Reporter must give a copy of any report or other document given under paragraph (1) to the persons mentioned in paragraph (4) (except where that person gave the report or other document to the Reporter) no later than 3 days before the intended date of the hearing.

(3) Where the Reporter obtains any information (including any views of the child given orally to the Reporter) or document which is material to the children's hearing and has not previously been given to the persons mentioned in paragraph (4) the Reporter must give that information or a copy of the document to those persons as soon as possible before the beginning of the children's hearing.

(4) Those persons are—

(a) the child;

(b) each relevant person;

(c) any appointed safeguarder;

(d) the three members of the children's hearing.

PART 7

Specific Provision for Arranging Grounds Hearings

Additional information to be given to the child and each relevant person in relation to a grounds hearing

27.—(1) Where the Reporter is required to arrange a grounds hearing, when notifying the date, time and place of the intended children's hearing under rule 22 the Reporter must give to the persons mentioned in paragraph (2) the information mentioned in paragraph (3).

(2) Those persons are—

(a) the child;

(b) each relevant person; and

(c) any appointed safeguarder (except the information mentioned in paragraph (3)(b)).

(3) That information is—

(a) a copy of the statement of grounds prepared under section 89 (Principal Reporter's duty to prepare statement of grounds) of the Act in relation to the child;

(b) information relating to the retention of the child's DNA and other records kept in connection with the acceptance by the child and relevant person, or the establishment by the sheriff, of an offence specified in an order made by the Scottish Ministers under section 113A(6)(ba) (criminal record certificates) of the Police Act 1997;

(c) a copy of any relevant requirement made by a sheriff under section 156(3)(a) (determination of appeal) of the Act.

(4) Where the Reporter is required to arrange a grounds hearing, no later than 3 days before the intended date of the hearing the Reporter must also give to the persons mentioned in paragraph (5) the information mentioned in paragraph (6).

(5) Those persons are—

(a) the child;

(b) each relevant person; and

(c) any appointed safeguarder (except the information mentioned in paragraph (6)(a)).

(6) That information is—

(a) a copy of any available report or interim report prepared by a safeguarder under section 33(1)(a) (functions of safeguarder) of the Act;

(b) a copy of any report or information provided by the local authority to the Reporter under section 66(4) (investigation and determination by Principal Reporter) or 69(4) (determination under section 66: referral to children's hearing) of the Act;

(c) a copy of any views of the child given to the Reporter by the child or any other person;

(d) a copy of any other report or other document material to the children's hearing's consideration.

(7) This rule does not apply where rule 29 applies.

Information to be given to the members of the grounds hearing

28.—(1) Wherever practicable 7 days before, and no later than 3 days before, the intended date of the grounds hearing the Reporter must give to the three members of the children's hearing a copy of the statement of grounds.

(2) No later than 3 days before the intended date of the grounds hearing the Reporter must give to the three members of the children's hearing—

(a) a copy of any relevant requirement made by a sheriff under section 156(3)(a) (determination of appeal) of the Act;

(b) a copy of any available report or interim report prepared by a safeguarder under section 33(1)(a) (functions of safeguarder) of the Act;

(c) a copy of any report or information provided by the local authority to the Reporter under section 66(4) (investigation and determination by Principal Reporter) or 69(4) (determination under section 66: referral to children's hearing) of the Act;

(d) a copy of any views of the child given to the Reporter by the child or any other person;

(e) a copy of any other report or other document material to the children's hearing's consideration.

(3) This rule does not apply where rule 29 applies.

Provision of information for a grounds hearing where section 69(3) (determination under section 66: referral to children's hearing) of the Act applies or following the making of a child protection order under section 38 (consideration by sheriff: application by local authority only) or 39 (consideration by sheriff: application by local authority or other person) of the Act

29.—(1) This rule applies where—

(a) section 69(3) of the Act applies; or

(b) following receipt of a notice under section 43 (notice of child protection order) of the Act of the making of a child protection order the Reporter is required to arrange a children's hearing under section 69(2) of the Act which is to be held no later than—

(i) where the order contains an authorisation of the type mentioned in section 37(2)(b) (child protection orders) of the Act, the end of the period of 8 working days beginning on the day the child was removed to a place of safety; or

(ii) where the order does not contain such an authorisation, the end of the period of working days beginning on the day the order was made.

(2) As soon as practicable before the beginning of the grounds hearing, the Reporter must notify the persons mentioned in paragraph (3) of the date, time and place of the hearing.

(3) Those persons are—

(a) the child;

(b) each relevant person;

(c) any appointed safeguarder;

(d) any individual other than a relevant person who appears to the Reporter to have or recently have had significant involvement in the upbringing of the child;

(e) the three members of the children's hearing;

(f) the National Convener.

(4) As soon as practicable before the beginning of the hearing, the Reporter must give to the persons mentioned in paragraph (3)(a) to (c) such of the information mentioned in paragraph (5) as is available.

(5) That information is the information mentioned in rules 23, 26, 27 and where applicable rule 30.

(6) As soon as practicable before the beginning of the hearing, the Reporter must give to the persons mentioned in paragraph (3)(e) the information mentioned in paragraph (7) as is available.

(7) That information is—

(a) the information mentioned in rules 26, 28 and where applicable rule 30;

(b) a copy of any relevant child protection order made in relation to the child under section 38 or 39 of the Act.

(8) As soon as practicable before the beginning of the hearing, the Reporter must give to the persons mentioned in paragraph (3)(d) the information mentioned in rule 24.

Arranging a grounds hearing where a compulsory supervision order is already in force in relation to the child

30.—(1) This rule applies where a grounds hearing is to be arranged and a compulsory supervision order is already in force in relation to the child to whom the hearing relates.

(2) No later than 3 days before the intended date of the children's hearing the Reporter must in addition to the information to be given under this Part give to the persons mentioned in paragraph (3) the information mentioned in paragraph (4).

(3) Those persons are—

(a) the child;

(b) each relevant person;

(c) any appointed safeguarder;

(d) the three members of the children's hearing.

(4) That information is—

(a) copies of all decisions and reasons for those decisions made by all pre-hearing panels and children's hearings arranged in relation to the child;

(b) a copy of any notice by the implementation authority under section 131 (duty of implementation authority to require review) of the Act.

(5) This rule does not apply where rule 29 applies.

Specific Provision for Arranging a Children's Hearing to be held Under Section 119 (Children's Hearing Following Deferral or Proceedings Under Part 10) of the Act

Provision of information to the child, relevant persons and any appointed safeguarder for a children's hearing to which section 119 (children's hearing following deferral or proceedings under Part 10) of the Act applies

31.—(1) Where the Reporter is required to arrange a children's hearing to which section 119 of the Act applies, as soon as practicable, and at least 3 days before the intended date of the children's hearing, the Reporter must give to the following persons the information mentioned in paragraph (2)—

(a) the child;

(b) each relevant person;

(c) any appointed safeguarder (except the information mentioned in paragraph (2)(a)).

(2) That information is—

(a) any available report or interim report prepared by the safeguarder under section 33(1)(a) or (c) (functions of safeguarder) of the Act or these Rules;

(b) any report prepared by the local authority;

(c) a copy of any relevant direction by a sheriff under section 108 (determination: ground established), 115 (recall: power to refer other grounds) or 117 (new section 67 ground established: sheriff to refer to children's hearing) of the Act;

(d) a copy of any relevant remit by a court under section 49 (reference or remit to children's hearing) of the Criminal Procedure (Scotland) Act 1995;

(e) a copy of any relevant statement by a sheriff under section 12(1B) (sheriff's power to refer case to children's hearing) of the Antisocial Behaviour etc. (Scotland) Act 2004;

(f) a copy of any relevant requirement made by a sheriff under section 156(3)(a) (determination of appeal) of the Act;

(g) copies of all decisions and reasons for those decisions made by all pre-hearing panels and children's hearings arranged in relation to the child;

(h) any other report, document or information relevant to the matter to be considered by the children's hearing.

(3) This rule does not apply where rule 33 applies.

Information to be given to the members of the children's hearing to which section 119 (children's hearing following deferral or proceedings under Part 10) of the Act applies

32. Where rule 31 applies, wherever practicable 7 days before, and no later than 3 days before, the intended date of the children's hearing the Reporter must give to the three members of the children's hearing—

(a) a copy of the statement of grounds;
(b) any available report or interim report prepared by the appointed safeguarder under section 33(1)(a) or (c) (functions of safeguarder) of the Act or these Rules;
(c) any report prepared by the local authority;
(d) a copy of any relevant direction by a sheriff under section 108 (determination: ground established), 115 (recall: power to refer other grounds) or 117 (new section 67 ground established: sheriff to refer to children's hearing) of the Act;
(e) a copy of any relevant remit by a court under section 49 (reference or remit to children's hearing) of the Criminal Procedure (Scotland) Act 1995;
(f) a copy of any relevant statement by a sheriff under section 12(1B) (sheriff's power to refer case to children's hearing) of the Antisocial Behaviour etc. (Scotland) Act 2004;
(g) a copy of any relevant requirement made by a sheriff under section 156(3)(a) (determination of appeal) of the Act;
(h) copies of all decisions and reasons for those decisions made by all pre-hearing panels and children's hearings arranged in relation to the child;
(i) a copy of any decision of a pre-hearing panel or children's hearing held in relation to the child and the reasons for that decision;
(j) any other report, document or information relevant to the matter to be considered by the children's hearing;
(k) a copy of any relevant child protection order made in relation to the child under section 38 (consideration by sheriff: application by local authority only) or 39 (consideration by sheriff: application by local authority or other person) of the Act.
(2) This rule does not apply where rule 33 applies.

Provision of information for children's hearing to which section 119 (children's hearing following deferral or proceedings under Part 10) of the Act applies where section 109(7) (determination: power to make interim compulsory supervision order etc.), 115(5) (recall: power to refer other grounds) or 117(5) (new section 67 ground established: sheriff to refer to children's hearing) of the Act also applies

33.—(1) This rule applies where section 109(7), 115(5) or 117(5) of the Act applies.

(2) As soon as practicable before the beginning of the children's hearing, the Reporter must notify the persons mentioned in paragraph (3) of the date, time and place of the hearing.

(3) Those persons are—
(a) the child;
(b) each relevant person;
(c) any appointed safeguarder;
(d) any individual other than a relevant person who appears to the Reporter to have or recently have had significant involvement in the upbringing of the child;
(e) the three members of the children's hearing.

(4) As soon as practicable before the beginning of the hearing, the Reporter must give to the persons mentioned in paragraph (3)(a) to (c) such of the information mentioned in rules 23, 26 and 31 as is available.

(5) As soon as practicable before the beginning of the hearing, the Reporter must give to the persons mentioned in paragraph (3)(e) such of the information mentioned in rules 26 and 32 as is available.

(6) As soon as practicable before the beginning of the hearing, the Reporter must give to the persons mentioned in paragraph (3)(d) the information mentioned in rule 24.

PART 9

Specific Provision for Arranging a Children's hearing to which Section 137 (Duty to Arrange Children's Hearing) of the Act Applies

Provision of information to the child and relevant persons for a children's hearing to which section 137 (duty to arrange children's hearing) of the Act applies

34.—(1) Where the Reporter is required to arrange a children's hearing by virtue of section 137(2) of the Act, as soon as practicable and no later than 7 days before the intended date of the children's hearing the Reporter must also give to the persons mentioned in paragraph (2) the information mentioned in paragraph (3).

(2) Those persons are—

(a) the child;

(b) each relevant person;

(c) any appointed safeguarder.

(3) That information is—

(a) a copy of the compulsory supervision order to be reviewed;

(b) copies of all decisions and reasons for those decisions made by all pre-hearing panels and children's hearings arranged in relation to the child;

(c) a copy of any relevant remit by a court under section 49 (reference or remit to children's hearing) of the Criminal Procedure (Scotland) Act 1995;

(d) a copy of any relevant requirement by a sheriff under section 12(1A) (sheriff's power to refer case to children's hearing) of the Antisocial Behaviour etc. (Scotland) Act 2004;

(e) a copy of any relevant requirement made by a sheriff under section 156(3)(a) (determination of appeal) of the Act;

(f) a copy of any notice by the implementation authority under section 131 (duty of implementation authority to require review) of the Act.

(4) No later than 3 days before the intended date of the hearing the Reporter must also give to the persons mentioned in paragraph (5) the information mentioned in paragraph (6).

(5) Those persons are—

(a) the child;

(b) each relevant person;

(c) any appointed safeguarder.

(6) That information is—

(a) a copy of any available report or interim report prepared by an appointed safeguarder under section 33(1)(a) or (c) (functions of safeguarder) of the Act;

(b) a copy of any report or other information provided by the local authority under section 137(4) or (5) (duty to arrange children's hearing) of the Act;

(c) a copy of any views of the child given to the Reporter by the child or any other person;

(d) a copy of any other report or other document material to the children's hearing's consideration.

(7) This rule does not apply where rule 36 applies.

Information to be given to the members of the children's hearing to which section 137 (duty to arrange children's hearing) of the Act applies

35.—(1) Where rule 34 applies no later than 3 days before the intended date of the children's hearing to which section 137 of the Act applies, the Reporter must give to the three members of that children's hearing—

(a) a copy of the compulsory supervision order to be reviewed;

(b) copies of all decisions and reasons for those decisions made by all pre-hearing panels and children's hearings arranged in relation to the child;

(c) a copy of any relevant remit by a court under section 49 (reference or remit to children's hearing) of the Criminal Procedure (Scotland) Act 1995;

(d) a copy of any relevant requirement by a sheriff under section 12(1A) (sheriff's power to refer case to children's hearing) of the Antisocial Behaviour etc. (Scotland) Act 2004;

(e) a copy of any relevant requirement made by a sheriff under section 156(3)(a) (determination of appeal) of the Act;

(f) a copy of any notice by the implementation authority under section 131 (duty of implementation authority to require review) of the Act;

(g) a copy of any available report or interim report prepared by a safeguarder under section 33(1)(a) or (c) (functions of safeguarder) of the Act;

(h) a copy of any report or other information provided by the local authority under section 137(4) or (5) (duty to arrange children's hearing) of the Act;

(i) a copy of any views of the child given to the Reporter by the child or any other person;

(j) a copy of any other report or other document material to the children's hearing's consideration.

(2) This rule does not apply where rule 36 applies.

Provision of information for a review hearing where section 136 (duty to initiate review where child transferred) of the Act applies

36.—(1) This rule applies where section 136 of the Act applies.

(2) As soon as practicable before the beginning of the children's hearing, the Reporter must notify the persons mentioned in paragraph (3) of the date, time and place of the hearing.

(3) Those persons are—
(a) the child;
(b) each relevant person;
(c) any appointed safeguarder;
(d) any individual other than a relevant person who appears to the Reporter to have or recently have had significant involvement in the upbringing of the child;
(e) the three members of the children's hearing;
(f) the National Convener.

(4) As soon as practicable before the beginning of the hearing, the Reporter must give to the persons mentioned in paragraph (3)(a) to (c) such of the information mentioned in rules 23, 26 and 34 as is available.

(5) As soon as practicable before the beginning of the hearing, the Reporter must give to the persons mentioned in paragraph (3)(e) such of the information mentioned in rules 26 and 35 as is available.

(6) As soon as practicable before the beginning of the hearing, the Reporter must give to the persons mentioned in paragraph (3)(d) the information mentioned in rule 24.

PART 10

Arranging a Grounds Hearing Where Grounds Hearing or Review Hearing Has Deferred or Application Made to the Sheriff

Papers to be sent when new grounds presented after grounds hearing deferred or application made to the sheriff

37.—(1) This rule applies where—
(a) a grounds hearing deferred making a decision on whether to make a compulsory supervision order until a subsequent children's hearing under section 91(2) (grounds accepted: powers of grounds hearing) of the Act or directed the Reporter under section 93(2)(a) (grounds not accepted: application to sheriff or discharge) or 94(2)(a) (child or relevant person unable to understand grounds) of the Act to make an application to the sheriff; or
(b) a children's hearing to which section 119 (children's hearing following deferral or proceedings under Part 10) of the Act applies is to be arranged by the Reporter;
and in either case the Reporter is required by virtue of section 69(2) (determination under section 66: referral to children's hearing) of the Act to arrange a further grounds hearing in relation to that child.

(2) In addition to complying with Part 7 of these Rules the Reporter must also comply, so far as practicable, with Part 8.

Papers to be sent when new grounds presented after review hearing deferred

38.—(1) This rule applies where—
(a) the Reporter is required by virtue of section 137(2) (duty to arrange children's hearing) of the Act to arrange a children's hearing in relation to the child; and

(b) the Reporter is required by virtue of section 69(2) (determination under section 66: referral to children's hearing) of the Act to arrange a grounds hearing in relation to that child.

(2) In addition to complying with Part 7 of these Rules the Reporter must also comply, so far as practicable, with Part 9.

PART 11

Arranging other Children's Hearings

Arranging a children's hearing under section 45 (review by children's hearing where child in place of safety) or 46 (review by children's hearing where order prevents removal of child) of the Act—2nd working day hearing

39.—(1) This rule applies where section 45(2) or 46(2) of the Act applies.

(2) As soon as practicable before the beginning of the children's hearing, the Reporter must notify the persons mentioned in paragraph (3) of the date, time and place of the children's hearing.

(3) Those persons are—

(a) the child;

(b) each relevant person;

(c) any individual other than a relevant person who appears to the Reporter to have or recently have had significant involvement in the upbringing of the child;

(d) the person who applied for the child protection order or child assessment order, as the case may be;

(e) the person specified in the child protection order under section 37(2)(a) (child protection orders) of the Act;

(f) any other person prescribed by rules of court for the purposes of section 48 (application for variation or termination) or 49 (notice of application for variation or termination) of the Act;

(g) the three members of the children's hearing;

(h) any appointed safeguarder;

(i) the chief social work officer of the relevant local authority for the child;

(j) the National Convener.

(4) As soon as practicable before the beginning of the hearing, the Reporter must give to the persons mentioned in paragraph (3)(a) to (i) such of the information mentioned in paragraph (5) as is available.

(5) That information is—

(a) a copy of the child protection order;

(b) a copy of the application for the child protection order, or child assessment order, as the case may be;

(c) a copy of any report or other document which is relevant to the children's hearing's consideration.

Arranging a children's hearing under section 50 (children's hearing to provide advice to sheriff in relation to application) of the Act

40.—(1) Where a hearing is to be arranged under section 50 of the Act, as soon as practicable after determining to arrange the hearing the Reporter must notify the persons mentioned in paragraph (2) of the date, time and place of the children's hearing.

(2) Those persons are—

(a) the child;

(b) each relevant person;

(c) any individual other than a relevant person who appears to the Reporter to have or recently have had significant involvement in the upbringing of the child;

(d) the person who applied for the child protection order, or child assessment order, as the case may be;

(e) the person who applied for the child protection order to be varied or terminated;

(f) the person specified in the child protection order under section 37(2)(a) (child protection orders) of the Act;

(g) any other person, to whom the applicant for variation or termination of a child protection order is required to give notice of the making of the application, prescribed by rules of court for the purposes of section 48 (application for variation or termination) or 49 (notice of application for variation or termination) of the Act;

(h) the three members of the children's hearing;

(i) any appointed safeguarder;

(j) the chief social work officer of the relevant local authority for the child;

(k) the National Convener.

(3) As soon as practicable before the beginning of the hearing, the Reporter must give to the persons mentioned in paragraph (2)(a) to (j) such of the information mentioned in paragraph (4) as is available.

(4) That information is—

(a) a copy of the child protection order;

(b) a copy of the application for the child protection order or child assessment order, as the case may be;

(c) a copy of the application under section 48 of the Act for the variation or termination of the child protection order;

(d) any other relevant document or information.

Provision of information for a children's hearing under section 96(2) (children's hearing to consider need for further interim compulsory supervision order)

41.—(1) This rule applies where a children's hearing under section 96(2) of the Act is to be arranged by the Reporter.

(2) Wherever practicable when issuing notice under rule 22 and in all cases no later than 7 days before the intended date of the children's hearing, the Reporter must give to the persons mentioned in paragraph (3) the information mentioned in paragraph (4).

(3) Those persons are—

(a) the child;

(b) each relevant person;

(c) any appointed safeguarder;

(d) the three members of the children's hearing;

(4) That information is—

(a) copies of all decisions and reasons for those decisions made by all pre-hearing panels and children's hearings arranged in relation to the child;

(b) a copy of any interim compulsory supervision order made in relation to the child;

(c) any relevant document or other information for the consideration of the children's hearing.

Arranging a children's hearing under section 126 (review of contact direction) of the Act

42.—(1) Where section 126 of the Act applies, the Reporter must, as soon as practicable and no later than 3 days after the children's hearing mentioned in section 126(1)(a) of the Act, inform those persons mentioned in paragraph (2) of the place, date and time of any children's hearing to be held under section 126(2)(a) or (b) of the Act and the right of those mentioned in paragraph (2)(a) to (g) to attend that hearing.

(2) Those persons are—

(a) the child;

(b) each relevant person;

(c) any person other than a relevant person who appears to the Reporter to have or recently have had significant involvement in the upbringing of the child;

(d) any person who has a contact order regulating contact between the individual and the child;

(e) any person having a right of contact with the child under a permanence order;

(f) any person who requested a children's hearing be held under section 126(2)(b) of the Act;

(g) any appointed safeguarder;

(h) the three members of the children's hearing;

(i) the chief social work officer of the implementation authority or relevant local authority for the child as the case may be;

(j) the National Convener.

(3) Wherever possible when informing the persons mentioned in paragraph 2(a) to (h) and in all cases no later than 3 days prior to the intended date of the children's hearing under section 126 of the Act, the Reporter must give to those persons—

(a) a copy of the contact direction in the relevant order made by the children's hearing mentioned in section 126(1) of the Act and the reasons for that contact direction;

(b) any document or part of any document which is relevant to the children's hearing to be held under section 126 of the Act.

(4) In this rule "relevant order" means—(a) a compulsory supervision order;

(b) an interim compulsory supervision order;

(c) a medical examination order.

Arranging a children's hearing under section 142 (review of determination that person be deemed a relevant person)

43.—(1) This rule applies where a children's hearing under section 142(3) of the Act deferred determining the review under section 142(2) of the Act until a subsequent children's hearing.

(2) Wherever practicable when issuing notice under rule 22 and in all cases as soon as practicable before the beginning of the children's hearing to be held

by virtue of section 142 of the Act, the Reporter must give to the persons mentioned in paragraph (3) any relevant document or other information for the consideration of the children's hearing.

(3) Those persons are—

(a) the child;

(b) any relevant person;

(c) any appointed safeguarder;

(d) the three members of the children's hearing.

Arranging a children's hearing for the purposes of section 49 (reference or remit to children's hearing) of the Criminal Procedure (Scotland) Act 1995

44.—(1) Where a children's hearing is required to provide a report under section 49(1)(b), (3) or (6) of the Criminal Procedure (Scotland) Act 1995, as soon as practicable and no later than 7 days before the intended date of the hearing the Reporter must notify the persons mentioned in paragraph (2) of the date, time and place of the hearing.

(2) Those persons are—

(a) the child;

(b) each relevant person;

(c) any appointed safeguarder;

(d) the three members of the children's hearing;

(e) the chief social work officer of the relevant local authority for t he child;

(f) the National Convener.

(3) As soon as practicable and no later than 3 days before the intended date of the hearing, the Reporter must give to the persons mentioned in paragraph (2)(a) to (c) such of the information mentioned in paragraph (4) as is available.

(4) That information is—

(a) a copy of any relevant remit by a court under section 49 of the Criminal Procedure (Scotland) Act 1995;

(b) copies of all decisions and reasons for those decisions made by all pre-hearing panels and children's hearings arranged in relation to the child;

(c) confirmation of the child's duty to attend the children's hearing under section 73 (child's duty to attend children's hearing) of the Act;

(d) confirmation of the relevant person's duty to attend the children's hearing under section 74 (relevant person's duty to attend children's hearing) of the Act;

(e) information on the means by which the child may express views to the children's hearing;

(f) confirmation of the right of the child and each relevant person to give any report or other document for the consideration of the children's hearing.

(5) As soon as practicable and no later than 3 days before the intended date of the hearing, the Reporter must give to the persons mentioned in paragraph (2)(d) such of the information mentioned in paragraph (4)(a) and (b) as is available.

PART 12

Pre-Hearing Panels and Determination of Matters which may be Referred to
Pre-Hearing Panels

Arranging pre-hearing panel—determination of relevant person status

45.—(1) Where a pre-hearing panel is to be arranged by virtue of section 79(2)(a) or (b) (referral of certain matters for pre-hearing determination) of the Act (whether or not it is also to determine any matter mentioned in section 79(3)), wherever practicable at least 5 days before the intended date of the pre-hearing panel the Reporter must give notice of the pre-hearing panel to the persons mentioned in paragraph (2).

(2) Those persons are—

(a) the child;

(b) each relevant person;

(c) any individual requesting a determination that they be deemed a relevant person under section 79(2)(a) of the Act;

(d) any individual other than a relevant person who appears to the Reporter to have or recently have had significant involvement in the upbringing of the child;

(e) any appointed safeguarder;

(f) the three members of the pre-hearing panel;

(g) the National Convener.

(3) The notice must inform—

(a) the persons mentioned in paragraph (2) of the date, time and place of the pre-hearing panel;

(b) the persons mentioned in paragraph (2)(a) to (e) that they—

(i)   have the right to attend the pre-hearing panel;

(ii) may make representations (orally or in writing) to the pre-hearing panel relating to whether the individual mentioned in paragraph (2) (c) or (d) should be deemed to be a relevant person;

(iii) may give any report or other document relevant to that matter for the consideration of the pre-hearing panel;

(iv) have the right to request that the Reporter takes all reasonable steps to enable the child, each relevant person, or the individual in question, as the case may be, to attend the pre-hearing panel by way of telephone, through video link or by using any other method of communication; and

(c) the individual mentioned in paragraph (2)(c) or (d) that the individual, if deemed a relevant person under section 81(3) (determination of claim that person be deemed a relevant person) of the Act after that determination has been made, may request the prehearing panel to determine any matter mentioned in section 79(3) of the Act.

(4) Where the pre-hearing panel will also determine any other matter referred under section 79(2)(c) of the Act the notice must state that fact and—

(a) inform the individual mentioned in paragraph (2)(c) or (d) that the individual will not be entitled to take part in any discussion on that matter unless they are deemed to be a relevant person; and

(b) inform the persons mentioned in (2)(a), (b) or (e) that they may—

(i)   make representations (orally or in writing) to the pre-hearing panel in relation to any matter to be determined by the panel; and

(ii) give any report or other document relevant to those matters for the consideration of the pre-hearing panel.

Arranging pre-hearing panels to determine matter in section 79(3) (referral of certain matters for pre-hearing determination) of the Act

46.—(1) Where a pre-hearing panel is to be arranged by virtue only of section 79(2)(c) of the Act wherever practicable at least 5 days before the intended date of the pre-hearing panel the Reporter must give notice of the pre-hearing panel to the persons mentioned in paragraph (2).

(2) Those persons are—

(a) the child;

(b) each relevant person;

(c) any appointed safeguarder;

(d) the three members of the pre-hearing panel;

(e) the National Convener.

(3) The notice must inform—

(a) the persons mentioned in paragraph (2) of the date, time and place of the pre-hearing panel;

(b) the persons mentioned in paragraph (2)(a) to (d) of the matters to be determined by the pre-hearing panel; and

(c) the persons mentioned in paragraph (2)(a) to (c) that they—

(i) have the right to attend the pre-hearing panel;

(ii) may make representations (orally or in writing) to the pre-hearing panel;

(iii) may give any report or other document for the consideration of the pre-hearing panel;

(iv) have the right to request that the Reporter takes all reasonable steps to enable the child and each relevant person to attend the pre-hearing panel by way of telephone, through video link or by using any other method of communication.

Provision of information to pre-hearing panel

47.—(1) Where any person mentioned in rule 45(2)(a) to (e) or 46(2)(a) to (c), as the case may be, wishes to make written representations or give any report or other document for the consideration of the pre-hearing panel, as soon as possible and wherever practicable no later than 4 days before the intended date of the pre-hearing panel, that person must give those representations, report or other document to the Reporter.

(2) Subject to the provisions of paragraphs (6) and (7), where the Reporter receives any representations, report or other document under paragraph (1), wherever practicable no later than 3 days before the intended date for the pre-hearing panel the Reporter must give a copy of that information to the persons mentioned in rule 45(2)(a) to (f) or 46(2)(a) to (d), as the case may be, (unless that person gave the information in question to the Reporter).

(3) Where any person mentioned in rule 45(2)(a) to (e) or 46(2)(a) to (c), as the case may be, is unable to attend the pre-hearing panel and wishes to make oral representations for the consideration of the pre-hearing panel that person may make those representations to the Reporter.

(4) The Reporter must make a record of any representations given under paragraph (3) and give a copy of that record to those persons mentioned in rule

45(2)(a) to (f) or 46(2)(a) to (d), as the case may be, as soon as possible before the beginning of the pre-hearing panel.

(5) As soon as possible before the beginning of the pre-hearing panel the Reporter must also give the persons mentioned in rule 45(2)(a) to (f) or 46(2) (a) to (d), as the case may be, any other document, or part of a document, that is relevant to the issues to be determined by the pre-hearing panel and is in the possession of the Reporter.

(6) Where the matter referred to a pre-hearing panel concerns the question of whether a particular person should be deemed to be a relevant person, the obligation under paragraph (2) shall only apply to such material as the Reporter considers relevant to the question of whether that person should be deemed to be a relevant person.

(7) The provisions of Part 19 of these Rules apply to any representations, report or other document received by the Reporter under paragraph (1) as they apply to any document relating to a children's hearing.

Procedure at pre-hearing panel determination of whether to deem an individual to be a relevant person

48.—(1) At the beginning of the pre-hearing panel the chairing member must explain the purpose of the pre-hearing panel.

(2) The pre-hearing panel, despite a referral not having been made under section 79(2) (referral of certain matters for pre-hearing determination) of the Act, must consider whether to deem an individual, who is present at the pre-hearing panel, to be a relevant person on the request of—

    (a) the child;

    (b) any relevant person;

    (c) the individual in question.

(3) Where the pre-hearing panel is to consider whether to deem an individual to be a relevant person under paragraph (2) the provisions of the Act (other than section 81(2) (determination of claim that person be deemed a relevant person)) and these Rules apply as if the matter had been referred under section 79 of the Act.

(4) Where the pre-hearing panel is to determine the matter of whether any individual should be deemed to be a relevant person, the chairing member—

    (a) must invite any of the persons mentioned in paragraph (5), who is in attendance, to give to the pre-hearing panel any representations (orally or in writing) or any other document or information in addition to any given under these Rules that the person wishes to give for the consideration of the pre-hearing panel; and

    (b) may invite any other person that the pre-hearing panel consider appropriate to do so.

(5) Those persons are—

    (a) the child;

    (b) any relevant person;

    (c) any individual in relation to whom the determination is sought.

(6) Each member of the pre-hearing panel must state their determination on that matter under paragraph (2) and the reasons for that determination.

(7) Once each member of the pre-hearing panel has stated their determination on that matter the chairing member must confirm the determination of the pre-hearing panel in respect of the matter and the reasons for that determination.

(8) Where the pre-hearing panel has made a determination under section 81(3) of the Act the chairing member must inform the persons mentioned in paragraph (9) of their right to appeal that determination under section 160 of the Act.

(9) Those persons are—

(a) the child;

(b) each relevant person;

(c) any individual in respect of whom the pre-hearing panel determined that the individual is not to be deemed a relevant person.

Procedure at pre-hearing panel determination of any other matter

49.—(1) Where the pre-hearing panel is to determine any matter of a type mentioned in section 79(3) (referral of certain matters for pre-hearing determination) of the Act, the chairing member—

(a) must invite any of the persons mentioned in rule 48(4)(a) and (b), who is in attendance, to give to the pre-hearing panel any representations (orally or in writing) or any other document or information in addition to any given under these Rules that the person wishes to give for the consideration of the pre-hearing panel; and

(b) may invite any other person that the pre-hearing panel consider appropriate to do so.

(2) Each member of the pre-hearing panel must state their determination on each matter and the reasons for that determination.

(3) Once each member of the pre-hearing panel has stated their determination on each matter the chairing member must confirm the determination of the pre-hearing panel in respect of each matter and the reasons for that determination.

Notice of pre-hearing panel determination

50.—(1) As soon as practicable after the pre-hearing panel the Reporter must give notice of any determination of the pre-hearing panel and the reasons for that determination to the persons mentioned in paragraph (2) as regards—

(a) whether any individual should or should not be deemed to be a relevant person; and

(b) any other matter referred to the pre-hearing panel.

(2) Those persons are—

(a) the child;

(b) each relevant person;

(c) any appointed safeguarder;

(d) the chief social work officer of the relevant local authority for the child.

(3) Where a pre-hearing panel determined that an individual is not to be deemed a relevant person, as soon as practicable after the pre-hearing panel the Reporter must give notice of that determination to the individual in question and the reasons for that determination.

(4) When issuing the notice under paragraph (1) or (3) the Reporter must also give notice of any relevant right of appeal of the recipient of the notice under section 160 (appeal to sheriff against relevant person determination) of the Act.

(5) Where the pre-hearing panel has determined that a child or relevant person is to be excused from attending all or part of the children's hearing, the Reporter must inform the child and relevant person as the case may be, that—

    (a) the child or relevant person has been excused;

    (b) the child or relevant person has the right to attend the hearing; and

    (c) they have the right to request that the Reporter make arrangements to enable the child, or the relevant person, as the case may be, to attend the children's hearing or part of the children's hearing by way of telephone, video link or any other method of communication.

(6) Where the pre-hearing panel has determined that it is likely that a children's hearing will consider making a compulsory supervision order or an interim compulsory supervision order including a secure accommodation authorisation in relation to the child, the Reporter must, as soon as possible after that determination, notify the Scottish Legal Aid Board of that fact and the name and address of the child.

(7) Where the pre-hearing panel has determined that—

    (a) for the purpose of enabling a child or any relevant person to participate effectively in the proceedings before the children's hearing it may be necessary that the child or relevant person be represented by a solicitor or counsel; and

    (b) it is unlikely that the child or relevant person will arrange to be represented by a solicitor or counsel,

the Reporter must, as soon as possible after that determination, notify the Scottish Legal Aid Board of that determination and the reasons for it and the name and address of the child or relevant person.

Provision of information to persons deemed to be relevant persons

51. Where the pre-hearing panel deems a person to be a relevant person under section 81(3) (determination of claim that person be deemed a relevant person) of the Act, as soon as practicable after that determination, the Reporter must give to that person all information given under these Rules which is to be given to each relevant person.

Notification of matter to be determined under section 79 (referral of certain matters for prehearing determination) where not practicable to arrange a pre-hearing panel before the date fixed for the children's hearing

52.—(1) Where section 80(3) (determination of matter referred under section 79) of the Act applies, as soon as practicable, the Reporter must give notice to the persons mentioned in paragraph (2) that the matter to be referred to a pre-hearing panel under section 79(2) of the Act will be referred to the children's hearing.

(2) Those persons are—

    (a) the child;

    (b) each relevant person;

    (c) any individual requesting a determination that they be deemed a relevant person;

    (d) any individual other than a relevant person who appears to the Reporter to have or recently have had significant involvement in the upbringing of the child;

    (e) any appointed safeguarder;

(f) the three members of the children's hearing.

(3) The notice under paragraph (1) must inform—

(a) the persons mentioned in paragraph (2)(a) to (e)—

    (i) of the date, time and place of the children's hearing;

    (ii) of the matters to be determined by the children's hearing by virtue of section 80(3) of the Act;

    (iii) that they have the right to attend that part of the children's hearing;

    (iv) that they have the right to request that the Reporter takes all reasonable steps to enable the child, relevant person, or the person mentioned in paragraph (2)(c) or (d), as the case may be, to attend the children's hearing by way of telephone, through video link or by using any other method of communication;

    (v) that they may make representations (orally or in writing) to the children's hearing relating to any matter referred under section 79 of the Act, except where paragraph (4) applies;

    (vi) that they may give any report or other document relevant to that matter for the consideration of the children's hearing; and

(b) the individual mentioned in paragraph (2)(c) or (d), that the individual, where deemed to be a relevant person under section 81(3) (determination of claim that person be deemed a relevant person) of the Act, may request the children's hearing to determine any matter mentioned in section 79(3) of the Act.

(4) Where the children's hearing will also determine any matter referred under section 79(2)(c) of the Act the notice must inform the individual mentioned in paragraph (2)(c) or (d) that the individual will not be entitled to take part in any discussion on that matter unless they are deemed to be a relevant person.

Provision of information relating to matter referred under section 79 (referral of certain matters for pre-hearing determination) of the Act to the children's hearing

53.—(1) Where any person mentioned in rule 52(2)(a) to (e) wishes to make written representations or give any report or other document for the consideration of the children's hearing, as soon as practicable, and wherever practicable no later than 4 days before the date fixed for the children's hearing that person must give those representations, report or other document to the Reporter.

(2) Where the Reporter receives any representations, reports or other document under paragraph (1), as soon as practicable before the beginning of the children's hearing, the Reporter must give a copy of that information to the persons mentioned in rule 52(2) (unless that person gave the information in question to the Reporter).

(3) Where any person mentioned in rule 52(2)(a) to (e) is unable to attend the children's hearing and wishes to make oral representations for the consideration of the children's hearing that person may make those representations to the Reporter.

(4) The Reporter must make a record of any representations given under paragraph (3) and give a copy of that record to those persons mentioned in rule 52(2) as soon as practicable before the beginning of the children's hearing.

(5) As soon as practicable before the beginning of the children's hearing the Reporter must also give the persons mentioned in rule 52(2) any other

document or part of a document that is relevant to the issues under section 79 of the Act to be determined by the children's hearing and is in the possession of the Reporter.

Children's hearing determining a matter referred under section 79 (referral of certain matters for pre-hearing determination) of the Act

54. Where by virtue of section 80(3) (determination of matter referred under section 79) of the Act the children's hearing is to determine a matter referred under section 79 of the Act—

(a) rules 48(2) to (9) and 49 apply; and

(b) references in those rules to the pre-hearing panel are to be read as references to the children's hearing.

Children's hearings' power to determine whether a person should be deemed to be a relevant person where no referral made under section 79 (referral of certain matters for prehearing determination) of the Act

55.—(1) A children's hearing held in relation to a child by virtue of section 69(2) (determination under section 66: referral to children's hearing) or Part 9 to 11 (children's hearing; proceedings before sheriff; subsequent children's hearings) or 13 (review of compulsory supervision order) of the Act, despite a referral not having been made under section 79 of the Act, must consider whether to deem an individual who is present at the hearing to be a relevant person on the request of—

(a) the child;

(b) any relevant person;

(c) the individual in question.

(2) Where the children's hearing is to consider whether to deem an individual to be a relevant person under paragraph (1) the provisions of the Act (other than section 80 (determination of matter referred under section 79) and these Rules apply as if the matter had been referred under section 79 of the Act.

PART 13

Appointment of Safeguarder and
Safeguarders' Reports

Appointment of safeguarder by pre-hearing panel or children's hearing

56.—(1) Where the pre-hearing panel appoint a safeguarder for the child the Reporter must—

(a) inform the safeguarder of the date, time and place (if known) of the next children's hearing to be held in relation to the child; and

(b) give to the safeguarder the information mentioned in paragraph (3), as soon as practicable before the intended date of the hearing.

(2) Where the children's hearing appoint a safeguarder for the child the Reporter must—

(a) inform the safeguarder of the date, time and place (if known) of the next children's hearing to be held in relation to the child, or the hearing to take place under Part 10 (proceedings before sheriff) of the Act, as the case may be; and

(b) give to the safeguarder the information mentioned in paragraph (3) as soon as practicable and no later than 7 days before the intended date of the hearing.

(3) That information is—

(a) any information given to the three members of the children's hearing under these Rules;

(b) a copy of the pre-hearing panel's or the children's hearing's decision and the reasons for that decision; and

(c) the reasons for the decision by the pre-hearing panel or the children's hearing to appoint a safeguarder.

(4) Where the safeguarder is required to prepare a report under section 33(1)(a) (functions of safeguarder) of the Act, within 35 days of being appointed the safeguarder must prepare and give a report or interim report to the Reporter.

(5) Where an interim report is given to the Reporter under paragraph (4) the safeguarder must also give to the Reporter—

(a) a statement explaining the reasons for the production of an interim report;

(b) details of further investigations or information to be sought by the safeguarder; and

(c) an estimate of how much more time the safeguarder requires to complete the report.

Duty of Reporter on receipt of report from safeguarder

57.—(1) Where the Reporter receives from a safeguarder any report or interim report prepared under section 33(1)(a) or (c) (functions of safeguarder) of the Act, as soon as practicable after receiving that report or interim report the Reporter must arrange a children's hearing to decide whether to make a compulsory supervision order or to review the compulsory supervision order in effect in relation to the child, as the case may be.

(2) Where the Reporter arranges a children's hearing under paragraph (1) and the children's hearing is to make a decision on whether to make a compulsory supervision order the provisions of section 119 (children's hearing following deferral or proceedings under Part 10) of the Act apply to that hearing as if it was arranged by virtue of section 119(2) of the Act.

(3) Where the Reporter arranges a children's hearing under paragraph (1) and the children's hearing is to review the compulsory supervision order in effect in relation to the child section 137 (duty to arrange children's hearing) of the Act applies to that hearing as if it was arranged by virtue of section 137(2) of the Act.

PART 14

Procedure at Children's Hearings—General

Children's hearings procedure—general

58.—(1) At the beginning of a children's hearing the chairing member must—

(a) introduce the members of the children's hearing and explain the purpose of the hearing;

(b) ask whether the child, each relevant person and any appointed safe-guarder has received all relevant information and documents sent under these Rules;

(c) confirm whether the child, each relevant person and any appointed safe-guarder has had the opportunity to review the information and documents sent under these Rules and whether these have been understood by the child and each relevant person.

(2) Where, in response to the chairing member's query under section 121 (confirmation that child given opportunity to express views before hearing) of the Act, the child confirms that the documents provided to the child do not accurately reflect the child's views the chairing member must endeavour to clarify the child's views on the relevant matter.

PART 15

Procedure at Grounds Procedure at Grounds Hearing and Children's Hearings to which Section 119 (Children's Hearing Following Deferral or Proceedings Under Part 10) or 137 (Duty to Arrange Children's Hearing) of the Act Applies

Procedure at a grounds hearing—grounds put to the child and relevant person

59.—(1) When complying with section 90 (grounds to be put to child and relevant person) of the Act, and without prejudice to sections 76 (power to exclude relevant person from children's hearing) and 77 (power to exclude relevant person's representative from children's hearing) of the Act, the chairing member may exclude any relevant person if satisfied that the presence at the hearing of that person is preventing the children's hearing obtaining the acceptance or denial of a section 67 ground specified in the statement of grounds from any person who is required to accept or deny the grounds.

(2) After the exclusion has ended, the chairing member of the children's hearing must explain to the relevant person what has taken place in the relevant person's absence.

(3) Paragraph (4) applies where the child or any relevant person accept a section 67 ground specified in the statement of grounds but do not accept all of the facts relating to that ground narrated in the statement of grounds.

(4) The children's hearing may, where it considers it appropriate to do so, amend the statement of grounds by removing any facts denied or otherwise amending the facts narrated in the statement of grounds.

(5) Where paragraph (4) applies the children's hearing may not amend the section 67 ground specified in the statement of grounds.

(6) Where paragraph (4) applies the children's hearing must be satisfied that any amendments to the facts narrated in the statement of grounds do not call into question the acceptance of a section 67 ground by the child or any relevant person.

Procedure where section 91(1) (grounds accepted: powers of grounds hearing), 119(1) (children's hearing following deferral or proceedings under Part 10), or 138(1) (powers of children's hearing on review) of the Act applies

60.—(1) This rule applies where section 91(1), 119(1) or 138(1) of the Act apply.

(2) The chairing member—

(a) must inform those present at the hearing of the substance of any relevant report or other relevant document;

(b) must take all reasonable steps to obtain the views of the child, each relevant person and any appointed safeguarder in relation to—

(i) any relevant report, document or matter being considered by the hearing; and

(ii) what, if any, measures would be in the best interests of the child;

(c) may invite any other person present at the hearing, as the children's hearing considers appropriate, to express their views on, or provide any other information relevant to, any matter or action being considered by the hearing.

(3) Where the children's hearing has been given an interim report and statement prepared by the safeguarder under these Rules the hearing must consider that interim report and statement.

(4) After considering the interim report and statement the children's hearing may set a further date up to a maximum of 35 days for the provision of the report from the safeguarder and defer making a decision on whether to make a compulsory supervision order until a subsequent children's hearing.

Procedure when proceedings under section 91(2) (grounds accepted: powers of grounds hearing), 119(2) (children's hearing following deferral or proceedings under Part 10) or 138(2) (powers of children's hearing on review) of the Act

61.—(1) Where the children's hearing proceeds under section 91(2), 119(2) or 138(2) of the Act, without prejudice to the powers of the children's hearing in section 92 (powers of grounds hearing on deferral), 120 (powers of children's hearing on deferral under section 119) or 139 (powers of children's hearing on deferral under section 138) of the Act, the children's hearing may—

(a) appoint a safeguarder if one has not already been appointed;

(b) require the Reporter to obtain any report from any person which the children's hearing considers would be relevant to any matter to be determined by the hearing;

(c) set a date for the subsequent children's hearing to be held under section 119 or 139 of the Act, as the case may be;

(d) determine that—

(i) for the purpose of enabling a child or any relevant person to participate effectively in the proceedings before the children's hearing it may be necessary that the child or relevant person be represented by a solicitor or counsel; and

(ii) it is unlikely that the child or relevant person will arrange to be represented by a solicitor or counsel;

(e) require the Reporter, as soon as possible after the determination in subparagraph (d), to notify the Scottish Legal Aid Board of that determination, the reasons for that determination and the name and address of the child or relevant person;

(f) require the Reporter to make arrangements for an interpreter for the child or any relevant person or take any other step with a view to securing participation of the child or any relevant person in the hearing;

(g) give any other direction on any other matter as is necessary to enable the hearing to make a decision on whether to make a compulsory supervision order and if so the measures to be included in that order.

(2) Each member of the children's hearing must—

(a) state their decision on the exercise of the power conferred by section 91(2), 119(2) or 138(2) of the Act, as the case may be, and the reason for that decision;

(b) state their decision on the exercise of the power conferred by section 92(2) or (3), 120(3), (5) or (6), 123 (general power to grant warrant to secure attendance) or 139(3) (powers of children's hearing on deferral under section 138) of the Act as the case may be, and the reasons for that decision;

(c) where the decision is to make an interim compulsory supervision order, interim variation of a compulsory supervision order, medical examination order or to grant a warrant to secure attendance, state the member's decision in relation to any measure to be contained in the order or warrant and the reasons for the inclusion of the proposed measure; and

(d) where any other decision is made to exercise any other power, give any direction or impose any requirement, state their decision on that matter and reasons for that decision.

(3) The chairing member must—

(i) confirm and explain the decision of the children's hearing;

(ii) state the reasons for that decision; and

(iii) subject to sections 73 (child's duty to attend children's hearing), 74 (relevant person's duty to attend children's hearing), 75 (power to proceed in absence of relevant person) and 79 (referral of certain matters for pre-hearing determination) of the Act, inform the child, each relevant person and any safeguarder appointed of the right to appeal the children's hearing's decision to make an interim compulsory supervision order, interim variation of a compulsory supervision order, medical examination order or to grant a warrant to secure the attendance under section 154 (appeal to sheriff against decision of children's hearing) of the Act within 21 days of that decision.

Procedure where section 91(3) (grounds accepted: powers of grounds hearing), 119(3) (children's hearing following deferral or proceedings under Part 10) or 138(3) (powers of children's hearing on review) of the Act applies

62.—(1) This rule applies where the children's hearing is required to proceed under section 91(3), 119(3) or 138(3) of the Act.

(2) Each member of the children's hearing must—

(a) state their decision on whether to make a compulsory supervision order or to terminate, vary or continue the compulsory supervision order, as the case may be, and the reason for that decision; and

(b) where the decision is to make a compulsory supervision order, continue or vary the compulsory supervision order, state the member's decision in relation to any measure to be contained in the order and the reasons for the inclusion of the proposed measure.

(3) The chairing member must—

(a) confirm and explain the decision of the children's hearing;

(b) state the reasons for that decision;

(c) subject to sections 73 (child's duty attend children's hearing), 74 (relevant person's duty to attend children's hearing), 75 (power to proceed in absence of relevant person) and 79 (referral of certain matters for prehearing determination) of the Act, inform the child, each relevant person and any safeguarder appointed of the right to appeal the children's hearing's decision to make a compulsory supervision order, or discharge the referral or terminate, vary or continue the compulsory supervision order under section 154 (appeal to sheriff against decision of children's hearing) of the Act within 21 days of that decision; and

(d) where the decision of the children's hearing is to make a compulsory supervision order, or terminate, vary or continue the compulsory supervision order, subject to sections 73, 74, 75 and 79 of the Act, inform the child, each relevant person and any appointed safeguarder of the right to seek a suspension of the children's hearing's decision under section 158 (compulsory supervision order: suspension pending appeal) of the Act.

Grounds hearing procedures where section 93 (grounds not accepted: application to sheriff or discharge) or 94 (child or relevant person unable to understand grounds) of the Act applies

63.—(1) This rule applies where section 93 or 94 of the Act applies.

(2) Each member of the children's hearing must—

(a) state their decision on whether to proceed under section 93(2)(a) or (b), or 94(2)(a) or (b) of the Act as the case may be, and the reason for that decision;

(b) state any decision on the exercise of the power conferred by section 93(5) or 123 (general power to grant warrant to secure attendance) of the Act and the reasons for that decision;

(c) where the decision is to make an interim compulsory supervision order or grant a warrant to secure attendance state the member's decision in relation to any measure to be contained in the order or warrant and the reasons for the inclusion of the proposed measure.

(3) The chairing member must—

(i) confirm and explain the decision of the children's hearing;

(ii) state the reasons for that decision; and

(iii) subject to sections 73 (child's duty to attend children's hearing), 74 (relevant person's duty to attend children's hearing), 75 (power to proceed in absence of relevant person) and 79 (referral of certain matters for pre-hearing determination) of the Act, inform the child, each relevant person and any safeguarder appointed of the right to appeal the children's hearing's decision to discharge the referral, make an interim compulsory supervision order, or grant a warrant to secure attendance under section 154 (appeal to sheriff against decision of children's hearing) of the Act within 21 days of that decision.

Procedure where section 95 (child fails to attend grounds hearing) of the Act applies

64.—(1) Where section 95(1) of the Act applies each member of the children's hearing must state their decision on whether to require the Reporter under section 95(2) of the Act to arrange another grounds hearing and their reasons for that decision.

(2) The chairing member must—

(a) confirm and explain the decision of the children's hearing; and

(b) state the reasons for that decision;

(3) Where the children's hearing do not require the Reporter to arrange another grounds hearing under section 95(2) of the Act the children's hearing must discharge the referral.

(4) Where paragraph (3) applies, subject to sections 73 (child's duty to attend children's hearing), 74 (relevant person's duty to attend children's hearing), 75 (power to proceed in absence of relevant person) and 79 (referral of certain matters for pre-hearing determination) of the Act, the chairing member must inform each relevant person and any appointed safeguarder of the right to appeal the children's hearing's decision to discharge the referral under section 154 (appeal to sheriff against decision of children's hearing) of the Act within 21 days of that decision.

Procedure where report required under section 141 (preparation of report in circumstances relating to permanence order or adoption) of the Act

65.—(1) Where a children's hearing is required to produce a report under section 141 of the Act, subject to sections 73 (child's duty to attend children's hearing), 74 (relevant person's duty to attend children's hearing), 75 (power to proceed in absence of relevant person) and 79 (referral of certain matters for pre-hearing determination) of the Act, the chairing member must—

(a) explain to the child and each relevant person the purpose of the report to be prepared;

(b) inform the child and each relevant person of the substance of any document or information which is material to the advice to be contained in the report to be prepared by the children's hearing.

(2) Before preparing the report the children's hearing must subject to sections 73, 74, 75 and 79 of the Act—

(a) discuss the case with the child and each relevant person and any safeguarder appointed;

(b) seek the views of the child, each relevant person and the safeguarder on the arrangements which would be in the best interests of the child; and

(c) confirm the advice to be contained in the report.

(3) The chairing member must—

(a) make, or cause to be made, a report of the advice;

(b) sign and date the report; and

(c) give the report to the Reporter at the conclusion of the hearing.

(4) The Reporter must give a copy of the report within 5 days of receiving it under paragraph (3) to—

(a) the child;

(b) each relevant person;

(c) any appointed safeguarder;

(d) the court which requires to come to a decision about an application of the type mentioned in section 131(2)(c) or (e) (duty of implementation authority to require review) of the Act;

(e) the chief social work officer of the implementation authority;

(f) the couple making the application under section 29 (adoption by certain couples) of the Adoption and Children (Scotland) Act 2007 or the person making the application under section 30 (adoption by one person) of that Act, as the case may be.

Procedure where there is a review of determination that person be deemed a relevant person

66.—(1) Where the children's hearing is reviewing whether an individual should continue to be deemed to be a relevant person under section 142(2) (review of determination that person be deemed a relevant person) of the Act the chairing member must inform those present of the purpose of the review.

(2) The chairing member—

(a) must invite the child, each relevant person and any appointed safe-guarder to express their views in relation to whether the individual should continue to be deemed to be a relevant person;

(b) may invite any other person present at the hearing, as the children's hearing considers appropriate, to express their views on that matter.

(3) Where the children's hearing exercises the power under section 142(3) of the Act—

(a) each member of the children's hearing must state their decision and the reasons for that decision;

(b) the chairing member must confirm and explain the decision of the children's hearing on the exercise of that power and the reasons for it;

(c) the chairing member must confirm that the individual will continue to be deemed to be a relevant person.

(4) Where the children's hearing determine the review under section 142(2) of the Act—

(a) each member of the children's hearing must state their determination on the matter and the reasons for that determination;

(b) the chairing member must—

(i) confirm and explain the determination of the children's hearing;

(ii) state the reasons for the determination; and

(iii) subject to sections 73 (child's duty to attend children's hearing), 74 (relevant person's duty to attend children's hearing), 75 (power to proceed in absence of relevant person) and 79 (referral of certain matters for pre-hearing determination) of the Act, inform the child, each relevant person, the individual in relation to whom the determination was made and any safeguarder appointed of the right to appeal the children's hearing's decision under section 160 (appeal to sheriff against relevant person determination) of the Act within 7 days of that determination;

(5) As soon as practicable and no later than 2 working days from the day of the children's hearing the Reporter must give to the persons mentioned in paragraph (6) the information mentioned in paragraph (7).

(6) Those persons are—

(a) the child;

(b) each relevant person;

(c) the individual in relation to whom the determination was made.

(7) That information is—

(a) a copy of the determination of the children's hearing in relation to whether the individual should continue to be deemed to be a relevant person and the reasons for that determination; and

(b) details of the rights of the child, each relevant person and the individual in relation to whom the determination was made, to appeal that decision under section 160 of the Act.

Breach of duties imposed by sections 144 (implementation of compulsory supervision order: general duties of implementation authority) or 145 (duty where order requires child to reside in certain place) of the Act

67.—(1) Where the children's hearing direct the National Convener under section 146(2) (breach of duties imposed by sections 144 and 145) of the Act the chairing member—

(a) must include in the record of the decision of the children's hearing details of the ways in which the implementation authority is in breach of its duty in relation to the child; and

(b) may prepare a report for the National Convener providing such additional information on that matter as the children's hearing considers appropriate.

(2) As soon as practicable after the children's hearing the Reporter must give to the National Convener—

(a) a copy of the children's hearing's decision; and

(b) any report prepared under paragraph (1)(b).

(3) Where it appears to the children's hearing at the further review of the compulsory supervision order to be held by virtue of section 146(5) of the Act that the implementation authority continues to be in breach of its duty and the children's hearing under section 146(6) of the Act directs the National Convener to make an application under section 147 (application for order) of the Act the chairing member—

(a) must include in the record of the decision of the children's hearing details of the ways in which the implementation authority continues to be in breach of its duty in relation to the child; and

(b) may prepare a further report for the National Convener providing such additional information on that matter as the children's hearing considers appropriate.

(4) As soon as practicable after the children's hearing the Reporter must give to the National Convener—

(a) a copy of the children's hearing's decision; and

(b) any report prepared under paragraph (3)(b).

PART 16

Procedure where Part 10 of these Rules Applies

Procedure where rule 37 applies

68.—(1) This rule applies where rule 37 applies.

(2) In relation to the further grounds hearing referred to in rule 37, section 91 (grounds accepted: powers of grounds hearing) of the Act applies as if for subsections (2) and (3) there were substituted—

"(2) The grounds hearing is to be treated as if it were a hearing to which section 119 of the Act applies.".

(3) Where the further grounds hearing proceeds under section 93(2)(a) (grounds not accepted: application to sheriff or discharge) or 94(2)(a) (child or relevant person unable to understand grounds) of the Act, sections 93 (grounds not accepted: application to sheriff or discharge) and 96 (children's hearing to consider need for further interim compulsory supervision order) of the Act apply as if they were modified as follows—

(a) in section 93 of the Act—

(i) after subsection (4) there were inserted—

"(4A) Subsection (5) applies if immediately before the grounds hearing an interim compulsory supervision order was not in force in relation to the child."; and

(ii) after subsection (5) there were inserted—

"(5A) Subsection (5B) applies if immediately before the grounds hearing an interim compulsory supervision order was in force in relation to the child.

(5B) If the children's hearing is satisfied that the nature of the child's circumstances is such that for the protection, guidance, treatment or control of the child it is necessary that a further interim compulsory supervision order be made, the children's hearing may make a further interim compulsory supervision order in relation to the child.".

(iii) in subsection (6) after ""subsection (5)"" there were inserted ""or (5B)"";

(b) in section 96 of the Act in subsection (1)(a) for ""a grounds hearing"" there were substituted ""or 93(5B) a grounds hearing"".

(4) Where the further grounds hearing proceeds under section 93(2)(b) or 94(2)(b) of the Act the children's hearing may proceed, where appropriate, as if the hearing was a hearing to which section 119 (children's hearing following deferral or proceedings under Part 10) applies in relation to any section 67 ground previously accepted or determined by the sheriff to be established under section 108 (determination: ground established) or 117 (new section 67 ground established: sheriff to refer to children's hearing) of the Act.

(5) In paragraph (4) "accepted" has the same meaning as in section 93(7) (grounds not accepted: application to sheriff or discharge) of the Act.

Procedure where rule 38 applies

69.—(1) This rule applies where rule 38 applies.

(2) Where the further grounds hearing proceeds under section 93(2)(a) (grounds not accepted: application to sheriff or discharge) or 94(2)(a) (child or

relevant person unable to understand grounds) of the Act the grounds hearing may continue the compulsory supervision order until the subsequent children's hearing.

(3) Where the further grounds hearing proceeds under section 93(2)(b) or 94(2)(b) of the Act the children's hearing may proceed, where appropriate, to review the compulsory supervision order under section 138 (powers of children's hearing on review) of the Act.

PART 17

Procedure at other Children's Hearings

Procedure at a children's hearing held under section 45 (review by children's hearing where child in place of safety) or 46 (review by children's hearing where order prevents removal of child) of the Act

70.—(1) This rule applies where a children's hearing is held by virtue of section 45 or 46 of the Act.

(2) The chairing member—

(a) must inform those present at the hearing of the substance of any relevant report or other relevant document;

(b) must take all reasonable steps to obtain the views of the child, each relevant person and any appointed safeguarder in relation to—
(i) any report, document or matter being considered by the hearing; and
(ii) what, if any, measures would be in the best interests of the child;

(c) may invite any other person present at the hearing, as the children's hearing considers appropriate, to express their views on, or provide any other information relevant to, any matter or action being considered by the hearing.

(3) Each member of the children's hearing must—

(a) state their decision on whether the conditions for making the child protection order are met and the reasons for that decision; and

(b) where the decision is that the conditions are met state the member's decision in relation to whether the order should be varied and if so the authorisation or requirement to be included in the varied order and the reasons for the inclusion of the proposed authorisation or requirement.

(4) The chairing member must—

(a) confirm and explain the decision of the children's hearing;

(b) state the reasons for that decision; and

(c) where the children's hearing decide to continue the child protection order, subject to sections 73 (child's duty to attend children's hearing), 74 (relevant person's duty to attend children's hearing), 75 (power to proceed in absence of relevant person) and 79 (referral of certain matters for pre-hearing determination) of the Act, inform the child, each relevant person and the other persons in section 48(1) (application for variation or termination) of the Act of the right to make an application to the sheriff under section 48(1) to vary the order or under section 48(2) of the Act to terminate the order, as the case may be.

Procedure where Reporter receives notice under section 49 (notice of application for variation or termination) of the Act after arranging hearing under section 45 or 46 (review by children's hearing where child in place of safety or order prevents removal of child) of the Act

71.—(1) Where the Reporter receives notice under section 49 of the Act of an application to vary or terminate the child protection order, after issuing the notice under rule 39 but before that hearing begins, the Reporter must, as soon as practicable before the beginning of the children's hearing, notify the persons mentioned in paragraph (2)—

(a) that the Reporter has received notice under section 49 of the Act; and

(b) that the hearing will proceed as if it was arranged by virtue of section 50 (children's hearing to provide advice to sheriff in relation to application) of the Act.

(2) Those persons are—

(a) the child in respect of whom the child protection order is made;

(b) each relevant person;

(c) any individual other than a relevant person who appears to the Reporter to have or recently have had significant involvement in the upbringing of the child;

(d) the person who applied for the child protection order or child assessment order, as the case may be;

(e) the person who applied for the child protection order to be varied or terminated;

(f) the person specified in the child protection order under section 37(2)(a) (child protection orders) of the Act;

(g) any other person to whom the applicant for variation or termination of the child protection order is required to give notice of the making of the application under rules of court;

(h) the three members of the children's hearing;

(i) any appointed safeguarder;

(j) the chief social work officer of the relevant local authority for the child;

(k) the National Convener.

Procedure where hearing held by virtue of section 50 (children's hearing to provide advice to sheriff in relation to application) of the Act

72.—(1) This rule applies where a children's hearing is held by virtue of section 50 of the Act.

(2) The chairing member—

(a) must inform those present at the hearing of the substance of any relevant report or other relevant document;

(b) must take all reasonable steps to obtain the views of the child, each relevant person and any appointed safeguarder in relation to—

(i) any report, document or matter being considered by the hearing; and

(ii) what, if any, advice would be in the best interests of the child;

(c) may invite any other person present at the hearing as the children's hearing considers appropriate, to express their views on, or provide any other information relevant to, any matter or advice being considered by the hearing; and

(d) must confirm to the child, each relevant person, the person who applied for the child protection order, the person who applied for the order to be varied or terminated, and any appointed safeguarder the advice to be given to the sheriff to assist the sheriff in the determination of the application under section 48 (application for variation or termination) of the Act.

(3) The chairing member must—

(a) make, or cause to be made, a report of the advice;

(b) sign and date the report; and

(c) give the report to the Reporter at the conclusion of the hearing.

(4) As soon as possible following receipt of the report the Reporter must give a copy of the report to—

(a) the child in respect of whom the child protection order is made;

(b) each relevant person;

(c) any appointed safeguarder;

(d) the sheriff who is to determine the application under section 48 of the Act;

(e) the person who applied for the child protection order, or child assessment order, as the case may be;

(f) the person who applied for the child protection order to be varied or terminated;

(g) the person specified in the child protection order under section 37(2)(a) (child protection orders) of the Act;

(h) any person other than a relevant person who appears to the Reporter to have or recently have had significant involvement in the upbringing of the child;

(i) any other person to whom the applicant for variation or termination of the child protection order is required to give notice of the making of the application under rules of court;

(j) the chief social work officer of the relevant local authority for the child.

Procedure at a children's hearing arranged under section 96(2) (children's hearing to consider need for further interim compulsory supervision order) of the Act

73.—(1) This rule applies where a children's hearing is held by virtue of section 96(2) of the Act.

(2) The chairing member—

(a) must inform those present of the substance of any relevant report or other relevant document;

(b) must take all reasonable steps to obtain the views of the child, each relevant person and any appointed safeguarder in relation to—

    (i) any report, document or matter being considered by the hearing; and

    (ii) what, if any, measures would be in the best interests of the child; and

(c) may invite any other person present at the hearing, as the children's hearing considers appropriate, to express their views on, or provide any other information relevant to, any matter or action being considered by the hearing.

(3) Each member of the children's hearing must—

(a) state their decision on any exercise of the power conferred by section 96(3) of the Act and the reason for that decision;

(b) where the decision is to make a further interim compulsory supervision order state the member's decision and the reasons in relation to any measure to be included in the order.

(4) The chairing member must—

(a) confirm the decision of the children's hearing;

(b) state the reasons for that decision; and

(c) subject to sections 73 (child's duty to attend children's hearing), 74 (relevant person's duty to attend children's hearing), 75 (power to proceed in absence of relevant person) and 79 (referral of certain matters for pre-hearing determination) of the Act, inform the child, each relevant person and any appointed safeguarder of the right to appeal the children's hearing's decision to make an interim compulsory supervision order, under section 154 (appeal to sheriff against decision of children's hearing) of the Act within 21 days of that decision.

Procedure at a children's hearing held under section 126 (review of contact direction) of the Act

74.—(1) This rule applies where a children's hearing is held by virtue of section 126 of the Act.

(2) Where an individual claims that the conditions specified for the purposes of section 126(2)(b) of the Act are satisfied in relation to the individual, the children's hearing must consider that claim before reviewing the contact direction.

(3) Each member of the children's hearing must state whether the member considers that the conditions specified for the purposes of section 126(2)(b) of the Act are satisfied in relation to the individual and the reasons for reaching that view.

(4) The chairing member must confirm whether the children's hearing considers that the conditions specified for the purposes of section 126(2)(b) of the Act are satisfied in relation to the individual and the reason for reaching that view.

(5) After considering, where applicable, whether the conditions specified for the purposes of section 126(2)(b) are satisfied the children's hearing must, where proceeding to review a contact direction, seek views on the contact direction from—

(a) the child;

(b) each relevant person;

(c) any appointed safeguarder;

(d) any individual satisfying the conditions specified in an order under section 126(2)(b) of the Act;

(e) any individual who has a contact order regulating contact between the individual and the child;

(f) any individual who has a permanence order which specifies arrangements for contact between the individual and the child.

(6) Each member of the children's hearings must state their decision in relation to the contact direction and their reasons for that decision.

(7) The chairing member must—

(a) confirm and explain the decision of the children's hearing in relation to the contact direction;

(b) state the reasons for that decision; and

(c) inform any individual of any applicable right of appeal of the children's hearing's decision under section 126(6) of the Act which that individual has under section 161 (appeal to sheriff against decision affecting contact or permanence order) of the Act.

Procedure where advice required under section 49 (reference or remit to children's hearing) of the Criminal Procedure (Scotland) Act 1995

75.—(1) This rule applies where a children's hearing is held following a request to the Reporter under section 49(1)(b), (3) or (6) of the Criminal Procedure (Scotland) Act 1995.

(2) The chairing member—

(a) must inform those present at the hearing of the substance of any relevant report or other relevant document;

(b) must take all reasonable steps to obtain the views of the child, each relevant person and any appointed safeguarder in relation to—

(i) any report, document or matter being considered by the hearing; and

(ii) what, if any, advice or measures would be in the best interests of the child;

(c) may invite any other person present at the hearing, as the children's hearing considers appropriate, to express their views on, or provide any other information relevant to, any matter or advice being considered by the hearing; and

(d) must confirm to the child, each relevant person, and any appointed safeguarder the advice to be given to the court.

(3) The chairing member must—

(a) make, or cause to be made, a report of the advice;

(b) sign and date the report; and

(c) give the report to the Reporter at the conclusion of the hearing.

(4) As soon as possible following receipt of the report the Reporter must give a copy of the report to—

(a) the child;

(b) each relevant person;

(c) any appointed safeguarder;

(d) the court which made the request for advice under section 49 of the Criminal Procedure (Scotland) Act 1995;

(e) the chief social work officer of the relevant local authority for the child.

Procedure where application to suspend the decision of the children's hearing made under section 158 (compulsory supervision order: suspension pending appeal) of the Act

76.—(1) Where the Reporter is required under section 158(2) of the Act to arrange a children's hearing, as soon as practicable the Reporter must give notice of the date, time and place of the children's hearing at which the application for the suspension of the children's hearing's decision will be considered, to the persons mentioned in paragraph (2).

(2) Those persons are—

(a) the child;

(b) any relevant person;

(c) any appointed safeguarder;

(d) the three members of the children's hearing;

(e) the chief social work officer of the implementation authority for the child;

(f) the National Convener.

(3) If the person who applied for the suspension of the children's hearing's decision under section 158 of the Act is required by section 73(2) (child's duty to attend children's hearing) or 74(2) (relevant person's duty to attend children's hearing) of the Act to attend the hearing and fails to do so the children's hearing may, if it considers it appropriate, take no further action in relation to the application.

(4) Before making any decision on the application under section 158 of the Act the children's hearing must invite the child, any relevant person and any appointed safeguarder present at the hearing to make such representations as they wish to make.

(5) Each member of the children's hearing must state their decision on the suspension of the children's hearing's decision under section 158 of the Act, and the reasons for that decision.

(6) The chairing member must confirm the decision of the children's hearing and the reasons for that decision.

Procedure at a children's hearing where a report is required under section 95(2) of the Adoption and Children (Scotland) Act 2007 (duty of children's hearing to prepare report for court)

77.—(1) This rule applies where a children's hearing is required to prepare a report by virtue of section 95(2) of the Adoption and Children (Scotland) Act 2007 [1] (permanence orders — duty of children's hearing to prepare report for court).

(2) The chairing member must explain to the child, any relevant person and any appointed safeguarder the purpose of the report to be prepared.

(3) The report must be prepared when the children's hearing have considered the case of the child and determined whether to make a compulsory supervision order or to vary, or vary and continue, the compulsory supervision order, as the case may be.

(4) Before preparing the report the chairing member must explain to the child, any relevant person and any appointed safeguarder—

(a) that the hearing has determined to make a compulsory supervision order or to vary, or vary and continue, the compulsory supervision order, as the case may be;

(b) the reasons for reaching that determination; and

(c) that the hearing is unable to make a decision to make a compulsory supervision order or to vary, or vary and continue, the compulsory supervision order, pending the decision of the sheriff on the permanence order application or to remit the case under section 96 (application: effect on compulsory supervision order) of the Adoption and Children (Scotland) Act 2007.

(5) The chairing member must—

(a) make, or cause to be made, a report of the advice;

(b) sign and date the report; and

(c) give the report to the Reporter.

(6) The Reporter must, within 5 days of the hearing, give the report to—

(a) the court which requires to come to a decision on the permanence order application;

(b) the child;

(c) any relevant person;

(d) any appointed safeguarder;

(e) the chief social work officer of the implementation authority for the child.

PART 18

General Issues for Children's Hearings

Procedure where a warrant to secure attendance may be granted under section 123 (general power to grant warrant to secure attendance) of the Act

78.—(1) This rule applies where the children's hearing, on the application of the Reporter, is under section 123 of the Act considering granting a warrant to secure the attendance of the child at a children's hearing or a hearing to take place under Part 10 (proceedings before sheriff) of the Act.

(2) The children's hearing must seek the views of the child, each relevant person, and any appointed safeguarder, if present at the hearing.

(3) Where a warrant to secure the attendance of the child is granted, the Reporter must as soon as practicable give to the child, each relevant person and any appointed safeguarder—

(a) a copy of the warrant; and

(b) details of the rights of the child, each relevant person and the safeguarder to appeal the grant of the warrant under section 154 (appeal to sheriff against decision of children's hearing) of the Act.

Procedure where advice sought by children's hearing from National Convener under section 8 (provision of advice to children's hearing) of the Act

79.—(1) This rule applies where a children's hearing seeks advice under section 8 of the Act from the National Convener.

(2) Where a children's hearing defers making a decision or determination on any matter until a subsequent children's hearing and seeks advice from the National Convener under section 8 of the Act the chairing member must—

(a) prepare a request for advice setting out the nature of the advice to be provided and such other details as the children's hearing considers appropriate;

(b) include in the record of the children's hearing decision details of the request for advice and reasons for that request; (c) give that request for advice to the Reporter; and

(d) direct the Reporter to forward to the National Convener the request for advice and a copy of the children's hearing decision and the reasons for that decision.

(3) Where the children's hearing has directed the Reporter to forward a request for advice to the National Convener the Reporter must, as soon as

practicable and within 5 days of receiving the request prepared under paragraph (2), forward it to the National Convener.

(4) The National Convener must respond to any request for advice forwarded under paragraph (3) within 14 days of receiving the request.

(5) The children's hearing must give the advice received from the National Convener under paragraph (4) to all those present at the hearing.

Requirements where compulsory supervision order to be made

80. The children's hearing may not make a compulsory supervision order requiring a child to reside at a place where the child would be under the charge or control of a person who is not a relevant person or vary any compulsory supervision order so that it includes such a requirement unless the children's hearing has—

(a) received and considered a report or information provided by the local authority or implementation authority under section 66(4) (investigation and determination by Principal Reporter), 69(4) (determination under section 66: referral to children's hearing), 137(4) or (5) (duty to arrange children's hearing) of the Act, as the case may be, which provides the local authority's or implementation authority's recommendations on—
   (i) the needs of the child;
   (ii) the suitability to meet those needs of the place or places in which the child is to reside by virtue of the compulsory supervision order;
   (iii) the suitability to meet those needs of the person who is to have charge or control over the child; and
(b) the local authority or implementation authority as the case may be have confirmed that in compiling the report they have carried out the procedures and gathered the information described in regulations 3 and 4 of the Looked After Children (Scotland) Regulations 2009.

Requirements where section 126 (review of contact direction) of the Act applies

81.—(1) This rule applies where—
(a) section 69(2) or (3) of the Act applies;
(b) Parts 9 to 11 or 13 of the Act apply;
(c) following receipt of a notice under section 43 of the Act of the making of a child protection order the Reporter is required to arrange a children's hearing under section 69(2) of the Act which is to be held no later than—
   (i) where the order contains an authorisation of the type mentioned in section 37(2)(b) of the Act, the end of the period of 8 working days beginning on the day the child was removed to a place of safety; or
   (ii) where the order does not contain such an authorisation, the end of the period of 8 working days beginning on the day the order was made.

(2) Where this rule applies and a children's hearing is to be held in relation to a child the Reporter must notify the persons mentioned in paragraph (3) that a children's hearing is to be held in relation to a child, on the date to be specified in the notification, and, when issuing that notification, also give those persons the information mentioned in paragraphs (4) and (5).

(3) Those persons are—

(a) any individual other than a relevant person who appears to the Reporter to have or recently have had significant involvement in the upbringing of the child;

(b) any individual who has a contact order regulating contact between the individual and the child;

(c) any individual who has a permanence order which specifies arrangements for contact between the individual and the child.

(4) That information is confirmation that, where a children's hearing—

(a) makes, continues or varies a compulsory supervision order; or

(b) makes an interim compulsory supervision order, interim variation of a compulsory supervision order or a medical examination order which is to have effect for more than 5 working days,

and the order contains (or is varied so as to contain) a contact direction, the Reporter must arrange a children's hearing under section 126 of the Act for the purposes of reviewing the contact direction if—

(i) a contact order or permanence order mentioned in section 126(3) of the Act is in force; or

(ii) the Reporter is requested to arrange a hearing by an individual who claims to have or recently have had significant involvement in the upbringing of the child.

(5) That information is confirmation that, where a children's hearing is arranged under section 126 of the Act, they will have the right to attend.

Requirements where section 127 (referral where failure to provide education for excluded pupil) of the Act applies

82.—(1) Where the children's hearing requires the National Convener under section 127(2) of the Act to make a referral to the Scottish Ministers, the chairing member—

(a) must include in the record of the decision of the children's hearing details of the ways in which the education authority is in breach of its duty under section 14(3) (education for children unable to attend school etc.) of the Education (Scotland) Act 1980 in relation to the child; and

(b) may make, or cause to be made, a report for the National Convener providing such additional information on that matter as the children's hearing considers appropriate.

(2) As soon as practicable after the children's hearing the Reporter must give to the National Convener—

(a) a copy of the children's hearing's decision and the reasons for the decision; and

(b) any report made under paragraph (1)(b).

Requirements where section 128 (duty to consider applying for parenting order) of the Act applies

83. Where the children's hearing requires the Reporter under section 128(2) of the Act to consider whether to apply under section 102(3) (applications) of the Antisocial Behaviour etc. (Scotland) Act 2004 for a parenting order in respect of a parent of the child, the chairing member—

(a) must include in the record of the decision of the children's hearing details of the reasons why the children's hearing considers that it might be appropriate for a parenting order to be made in respect of that parent of the child; and

(b) may make, or cause to be made a report for the Reporter providing such additional information on that matter as the children's hearing considers appropriate.

PART 19

Procedure at a Pre-Hearing Panel or a Children's Hearing where a Non-Disclosure Request is Made

Non-disclosure requests

84.—(1) In this Part a "non-disclosure request"is a request made by any person that any document or part of a document or information contained in a document relating to a pre-hearing panel or to a children's hearing should be withheld from a specified person falling within the categories specified in section 177(2)(i)(ii) to (iv) of the Act on the grounds that disclosure of that document or part of the document or any information contained in it would be likely to cause significant harm to the child to whom the hearing relates.

(2) The following documents may not be the subject of a non-disclosure request—

(a) the statement of grounds;

(b) a copy of any relevant remit by a court under section 49 of the Criminal Procedure (Scotland) Act 1995;

(c) a copy of any relevant requirement by a sheriff under section 12(1A) or statement under section 12(1B) of the Antisocial Behaviour etc. (Scotland) Act 2004;

(d) any order or warrant to which the child is subject under the Act or these Rules.

(3) A non-disclosure request must—

(a) specify the document or part of the document or information for which non-disclosure is requested and give reasons in each instance for non-disclosure; and

(b) specify the persons to whom the document or part of the document or information is not to be disclosed and give reasons in each instance for non-disclosure.

(4) In this Part reference to "children's hearing"includes pre-hearing panel, where the nondisclosure request relates to documents or information to be considered at a pre-hearing panel.

Determination of a non-disclosure request

85.—(1) The Reporter must refer any non-disclosure request received from any person to a children's hearing for determination.

(2) The Reporter may submit a non-disclosure request to a children's hearing for determination at the Reporter's own initiative.

Procedure following receipt of a non-disclosure request made prior to a children's hearing

86.—(1) A children's hearing must, except in the case of a grounds hearing, consider any nondisclosure request made prior to that hearing at the beginning of the children's hearing.

(2) Where a non-disclosure request has been made prior to a grounds hearing, the non-disclosure request may be determined by the grounds hearing before making a decision on whether to make a compulsory supervision order.

(3) Where the children's hearing requires to consider a request in accordance with paragraph (1) or paragraph (2) it may exclude from the children's hearing the person to whom the documents are requested not to be disclosed where it considers that the presence of that person would prevent proper consideration of the non-disclosure request.

(4) The children's hearing must consider and determine the non-disclosure request.

(5) The person excluded under paragraph (3) must be invited to return to the children's hearing and advised of the children's hearing's determination under paragraph (4).

(6) Where the non-disclosure request is rejected under paragraph (4) the children's hearing must ensure that the document or part of the document or information is given to the excluded person at such time, and in such manner, as it considers appropriate having regard to the best interests of the child to whom the hearing relates.

Procedure following receipt of a non-disclosure request made during a children's hearing

87.—(1) A non-disclosure request may be made during a children's hearing by the child, any relevant person, any appointed safeguarder, the Reporter or the author of any document that is the subject of the non-disclosure request.

(2) Where such a request is made the children's hearing may exclude from the children's hearing the person to whom the documents are requested not to be disclosed where it considers that the presence of that person would prevent proper consideration of the non-disclosure request.

(3) The children's hearing must consider and determine the non-disclosure request.

(4) The person excluded under paragraph (2) must be invited to return to the children's hearing and advised of the children's hearing's determination under paragraph (3).

(5) Where the non-disclosure request is rejected under paragraph (3) the children's hearing must ensure that the document or part of the document or information is given to the excluded person at such time, and in such manner, as it considers appropriate having regard to the best interests of the child to whom the hearing relates.

PART 20

Notifying Decisions

Notifying decision of a children's hearing to the child, relevant person and appointed safeguarder

88.—(1) Where by virtue of the Act or any other enactment a children's hearing has been held in relation to a child the Reporter must give to the persons mentioned in paragraph (2) the information mentioned in paragraph (3) within 5 days of the children's hearing.

(2) Those persons are—

(a) the child;

(b) each relevant person;

(c) any appointed safeguarder.

(3) That information is—

(a) the decision of the children's hearing;

(b) the reasons for that decision;

(c) a copy of any compulsory supervision order, interim compulsory supervision order, medical examination order made, or warrant to secure attendance granted;

(d) a notice of any right to appeal the children's hearing's decision under section 154 (appeal to sheriff against decision of children's hearing) or 160 (appeal to sheriff against relevant person determination) of the Act;

(e) where the child or any relevant person is subject to an order under section 159 (frivolous and vexatious appeals) of the Act, confirmation of the need for that person to seek leave from the sheriff to appeal the decision;

(f) details of any right to seek a suspension of the children's hearing's decision to make, vary, continue or terminate a compulsory supervision order under section 158 (compulsory supervision order: suspension pending appeal) of the Act;

(g) details of the child's and each relevant person's right to seek a review of a compulsory supervision order under, or by virtue of, section 132 (right of child or relevant person to require review) of the Act.

(4) This rule does not apply where rules 66(7), 91, 92, 93 or 96 apply.

Information to be given to the implementation authority and others

89.—(1) Where rule 88 applies within 5 days of the children's hearing the Reporter must give to the persons mentioned in paragraph (2) the information mentioned in rule 88(3)(a) to (c).

(2) Those persons are—

(a) the chief social work officer of the implementation authority where the decision was to make a compulsory supervision order or interim compulsory supervision order and in any other case the chief social work officer of the relevant local authority for the child;

(b) any person who under the compulsory supervision order, interim compulsory supervision order, medical examination order or warrant to secure attendance is responsible for providing any service, support, or accommodation in respect of the child.

(3) Where by virtue of any compulsory supervision order, interim compulsory supervision order or medical examination order the person with whom the child is required to reside is a person other than the implementation authority or a relevant person paragraph (4) applies.

(4) The Reporter must give the information mentioned in rule 88(3)(a) to (c)—

(a) where a social work officer from the implementation authority or relevant local authority for the child, as the case may be, attended the children's hearing resulting in the order in question, and it is reasonably practicable to do so, to that social work officer immediately following the children's hearing;

(b) in any other case, to the chief social work officer of the implementation authority, or relevant local authority for the child, as the case may be, no later than the end of the working day following the conclusion of the children's hearing.

Information to be given to the chief constable and use of that information

90.—(1) Where rule 88 applies and the grounds hearing has proceeded under section 91(3) (grounds accepted: powers of grounds hearing) of the Act or, where rule 68 applies, section 119(3) (children's hearing following deferral or proceedings under Part 10) of the Act, the Reporter must notify the children's hearing's decision to the chief constable of the Police Service of Scotland under section 61 (constable's duty to provide information to Principal Reporter) of the Act or section 43(5) (arrangements where children arrested) of the Criminal Procedure (Scotland) Act 1995.

(2) Where rule 88 applies and the decision of the children's hearing is to make a compulsory supervision order in respect of a person aged 16 years or older, as soon as reasonably practicable, the Reporter must notify the chief constable of the area in which the person resides.

(3) When a child subject to a compulsory supervision order reaches the age of 16 years, the Reporter must, as soon as reasonably practicable, notify the chief constable of the area in which the child resides.

(4) Where section 199(3) and (4) (meaning of "child") of the Act applies to a person, the Reporter must, as soon as reasonably practicable, notify the chief constable of the area in which the person resides of—

(a) the application of section 199(3) and (4) of the Act to that person; and

(b) when a relevant event in section 199(5) of the Act has taken place in relation to that person.

(5) When a person under paragraph (2), (3) or (4) is no longer subject to a compulsory supervision order, the Reporter must, as soon as reasonably practicable, notify the chief constable of the area in which that person resides.

(6) Information disclosed to the chief constable under paragraph (1), (2), (3), (4) or (5) may be used by the chief constable and police forces only for the purpose of—

(a) enabling or assisting them to perform their functions under or by virtue of this Act, the Police Act 1997, or the Protection of Vulnerable Groups (Scotland) Act 2007;

(b) the prevention or detection of crime;

(c) the apprehension or prosecution of offenders; or

(d) the protection of children.

Notifying decision of section 45 or 46 (review of children's hearing where child in place of safety or order prevents removal of child) hearing

91.—(1) The Reporter must as soon as practicable after the hearing held by virtue of section 45 or 46 of the Act give to the persons mentioned in paragraph (2) the information mentioned in paragraph (3).

(2) Those persons are—

(a) the child in respect of whom the child protection order is made;

(b) each relevant person;

(c) any individual other than a relevant person who appears to the Reporter to have or recently have had significant involvement in the upbringing of the child;

(d) the person who applied for the child protection order or child assessment order, as the case may be;

(e) the person specified in the child protection order under section 37(2)(a) (child protection orders) of the Act;

(f) any other person prescribed by rules of court for the purposes of section 48 (application for variation or termination) or 49 (notice of application for variation or termination) of the Act;

(g) any appointed safeguarder.

(3) That information is—

(a) the decision of the children's hearing;

(b) the reasons for that decision;

(c) where the children's hearing's decision was to continue the child protection order, the right of those persons in paragraph (2) to make an application to the sheriff under section 48(1) of the Act to vary the order or under section 48(2) of the Act to terminate the order.

(4) The Reporter must give to the persons mentioned in paragraph (5) the information mentioned in paragraph (3)(a) and (b).

(5) Those persons are—

(a) the chief social work officer of the relevant local authority for the child;

(b) any person who under the child protection order is responsible for providing any service, support, or accommodation in respect of the child.

Notifying decision of section 126 (review of contact direction) hearing

92.—(1) Within 5 days of the children's hearing held under section 126 of the Act the Reporter must give to the persons mentioned in paragraph (2) the information mentioned in paragraph (3).

(2) Those persons are—

(a) the child;

(b) each relevant person;

(c) any appointed safeguarder;

(d) any individual who has a contact order regulating contact between the individual and the child;

(e) any individual who has a permanence order which specifies arrangement for contact between the individual and the child;

(f) any person who requested a children's hearing be held under section 126(2)(b) of the Act.

(3) That information is—

(a) details of the decision of the children's hearing;

(b) the reasons for that decision;

(c) notice of any right to appeal the children's hearing's decision under section 161 (appeal to sheriff against decision affecting contact or permanence order) of the Act;

(d) where the person is subject to an order under section 159 (frivolous and vexatious appeals) of the Act, confirmation of the need for that person to seek leave from the sheriff to appeal the decision.

(4) The Reporter must give to the persons mentioned in paragraph (5) the information mentioned in paragraph (3)(a) and (b).

(5) Those persons are—

(a) the implementation authority where the decision was to make a compulsory supervision order or interim compulsory supervision order and in any other case the relevant local authority for the child;

(b) any person who under the compulsory supervision order, interim compulsory supervision order, medical examination order or warrant to secure attendance is responsible for providing any service, support or accommodation in respect of the child.

Notifying decision of section 158 (compulsory supervision order: suspension pending appeal) hearing

93.—(1) Where a children's hearing has been held by virtue of section 158 of the Act the Reporter must give to the persons mentioned in paragraph (2) the information mentioned in paragraph (3) within 5 days of the children's hearing.

(2) Those persons are—

(a) the child;

(b) each relevant person;

(c) any appointed safeguarder.

(3) That information is—

(a) the decision of the children's hearing;

(b) the reasons for that decision.

PART 21

Specific Provision for Children's Hearings Arranged Under the Children's Hearings (Scotland) Act 2011 (Implementation of Secure Accommodation Authorisation) (Scotland) Regulations 2013

Provision of information for review of secure accommodation authorisation

94.—(1) This rule applies where a children's hearing is to be arranged by virtue of regulation 9 of the Children's Hearings (Scotland) Act 2011 (Implementation of Secure Accommodation Authorisation) (Scotland) Regulations 2013 ("the 2013 Regulations").

(2) As soon as practicable before the beginning of the children's hearing, the Reporter must notify the persons mentioned in paragraph (3) of the date, time and place of the hearing.

(3) Those persons are—

(a) the child;

(b) each relevant person;

(c) the chief social work officer who made the decision under regulation 4 or 7 of the 2013 Regulations;

(d) the head of unit who made the decision under regulation 6 of the 2013 Regulations;

(e) any appointed safeguarder;

(f) any individual other than a relevant person who appears to the Reporter to have or recently have had a significant involvement in the upbringing of the child;

(g) the three members of the children's hearing; and

(h) the National Convener.

(4) The Reporter must, when issuing the notice under paragraph (2), provide those persons mentioned in paragraph (3)(a) to (g) with a copy of—

(a) all decisions and reasons for those decisions made by all pre-hearing panels and children's hearings arranged in relation to the child;

(b) the decision of the chief social work officer made under regulation 5 of the 2013 Regulations; and

(c) the decision of the head of unit made under regulation 6 of the 2013 Regulations.

Procedure where children's hearing to review secure accommodation authorisation

95.—(1) This rule applies where a children's hearing is to be held by virtue of regulation 9 of the Children's Hearings (Scotland) Act 2011 (Implementation of Secure Accommodation Authorisation) (Scotland) Regulations 2013 ("the 2013 Regulations").

(2) The children's hearing must provide the following persons with the opportunity to make representations if they are present at the hearing:—

(a) the child;

(b) each relevant person;

(c) any appointed safeguarder;

(d) the chief social work officer who made the decision under regulation 4 or 7 of the 2013 Regulations; and

(e) the head of unit who made the decision under regulation 6 of the 2013 Regulations.

(3) Each member of the children's hearing must state their decision in relation to the secure accommodation authorisation and the reasons for that decision.

(4) The chairing member must—

(a) confirm and explain the decision of the children's hearing in relation to the secure accommodation authorisation;

(b) state the reasons for that decision; and

(c) inform the child, each relevant person and any safeguarder appointed of any applicable right to appeal the children's hearing's decision under section 154 (appeal to sheriff against decision of children's hearing) of the Act within 21 days of that decision.

Notifying decision of review of secure accommodation authorisation

96.—(1) Within 5 days of the children's hearing held under regulation 9 of the Children's Hearings (Scotland) Act 2011 (Implementation of Secure Accommodation Authorisation) (Scotland) Regulations 2013 ("the 2013 Regulations") the Reporter must give to the persons mentioned in paragraph (2) the information mentioned in paragraph (3).

(2) Those persons are—

(a) the child;

(b) each relevant person;

(c) any appointed safeguarder;
(d) the chief social work officer who made the decision under regulation 4 or 7 of the 2013 Regulations;
(e) the head of unit who made the decision under regulation 6 of the 2013 Regulations.
(3) The information is—
(a) the decision of the children's hearing;
(b) the reasons for that decision;
(c) notice of any right to appeal the children's hearing's decision under section 154 (appeal to sheriff against decision of children's hearing) of the Act.

PART 22

Miscellaneous

Travelling and subsistence expenses

97.—(1) The persons mentioned in paragraph (2) may make a claim, to the relevant local authority for the child, in respect of that person's attendance at a pre-hearing panel or children's hearing.
(2) Those persons are—
(a) the child;
(b) any relevant person;
(c) any person representing the child or any relevant person;
(d) any interpreter acting on behalf of the child or any relevant person;
(e) any individual who claimed to have or recently have had significant involvement in the upbringing of the child;
(f) any individual who has a contact order regulating contact between the individual and the child;
(g) any individual who has a permanence order which specifies arrangements for contact between the individual and the child.
(3) Where a claim is made to the relevant local authority for the child under paragraph (1) the local authority must pay to the claimant travelling expenses and such other expenses and subsistence as have, in the opinion of the local authority, been reasonably incurred by the claimant.
(4) This rule does not apply to a solicitor or counsel representing the child or any relevant person at a pre-hearing panel or children's hearing.

Authentication of documents

98.—(1) Any order, warrant to secure the attendance of a child, notice, report, record or other writing required to be made, granted, given or kept by the children's hearing or pre-hearing panel or chairing member of that hearing under or by virtue of these Rules is sufficiently authenticated if it is signed by the chairing member of the relevant children's hearing or pre-hearing panel.
(2) Any document or notice authorised or required by these Rules to be kept or given by the Reporter is sufficiently authenticated if it is signed by the Reporter.
(3) Any copy of a document to be given to any person by the Reporter may be certified a true copy by the Reporter.

Written communications

99. Section 193 (formal communications) of the Act applies to these Rules and any type of communication made or given under these Rules is also a formal communication and section 193(2) to (4) applies to them.

Service of notification and documents

100. Any notice or other document authorised or required under these Rules to be given by the Reporter to any person may be given by the Reporter or by any police constable.

APPENDIX THREE

ACT OF SEDERUNT
(CHILD CARE AND MAINTENANCE RULES) 1997

(SI 1997/291 (S.19))

Coming into force: 1 April 1997

The Lords of Council and Session, under and by virtue of the powers conferred on them by sections 17, 20, 22, 23, 24 and 28(1) of the Maintenance Orders Act 1950, sections 2(4)(c), 2A(1) and 21(1) of the Maintenance Orders Act 1958, section 32 of the Sheriff Courts (Scotland) Act 1971, section 59 of the Adoption (Scotland) Act 1978 (as modified and applied in relation to parental orders under section 30 of the Human Fertilisation and Embryology Act 1990 and applications for such orders by paragraph 15 of Schedule 1 to the Parental Orders (Human Fertilisation and Embryology) (Scotland) Regulations 1994), section 48 of the Civil Jurisdiction and Judgments Act 1982, sections 27(2), 28(1) and 42(1) of the Family Law Act 1986 and section 91 of the Children (Scotland) Act 1995 and of all other powers enabling them in that behalf, having approved, with modifications, draft rules submitted to them by the Sheriff Court Rules Council in accordance with section 34 of the Sheriff Courts (Scotland) Act 1971, do hereby enact and declare:

ARRANGMENT OF RULES

. . .

CHAPTER 3

CHILDREN'S HEARINGS: APPLICATIONS TO THE SHERIFF

PART I

INTERPRETATION

PART VIIIA

APPLICATIONS FOR REVIEW BY LOCAL AUTHORITY

PART IX

PROCEDURE IN APPEALS BY STATED CASE UNDER PART 15 OF THE 2011 ACT

PART X

APPLICATIONS FOR REVIEW OF GROUNDS DETERMINATION

PART XA

ORDERS UNDER THE CHILDREN'S HEARINGS (SCOTLAND) ACT 2011

PART XI

VULNERABLE WITNESSES (SCOTLAND) ACT 2004

PART XIA

CASES INVOLVING SE'XUAL BEHAVIOUR

. . .

CHAPTER 3

¹CHILDREN'S HEARINGS: APPLICATIONS TO THE SHERIFF

NOTE
1. Heading as substituted by the Act of Sederunt (Children's Hearings (Scotland) Act 2011) (Miscellaneous Amendments) 2013 (SSI 2013/172) art.3(2) (effective June 24, 2013: substitution has effect subject to transitional provisions specified in SSI 2013/172 art.8).

PART I

INTERPRETATION

Interpretation

   13.1.—(1) In this Chapter, unless the context otherwise requires–
[. . .]
"1995 Act" means the Children (Scotland) Act 1995 and (except where the context otherwise requires) references to terms defined in that Act have the same meaning here as given there;
"2011 Act" means the Children's Hearings (Scotland) Act 2011 and (except where the context otherwise requires) references to terms defined in that Act have the same meaning here as given there;
"relevant person" means—
      (aa) a person referred to in section 200(1) of the 2011 Act or
      (bb) a person deemed a relevant person by virtue of section 81(3) or 160(4)(b) of the 2011 Act;
"service" includes citation, intimation or the giving of notice as required in terms of this Chapter.

(2) In this Chapter any reference, however expressed, to disputed grounds shall be construed as a reference to a statement of grounds which forms the subject of an application under section 93(2)(a) or 94(2)(a) of the 2011 Act.

(3) Except as otherwise provided, this Chapter applies to applications to the sheriff (including reviews and appeals) under the 1995 Act or the 2011 Act.

(4) All hearings in respect of applications to the sheriff must be held in private.

NOTE
1. As amended by the Act of Sederunt (Children's Hearings (Scotland) Act 2011) (Miscellaneous Amendments) 2013 (SSI 2013/172) art.3(3) (effective June 24, 2013: amendment has effect subject to transitional provisions specified in SSI 2013/172 art.8).

PART II

GENERAL RULES

PROCEDURE IN RESPECT OF CHILDREN

Application of rules 3.3 to 3.5A

[1]**3.2.**—(1) Rules 3.3 to 3.5 apply where a sheriff is coming to a decision about a matter relating to a child within the meaning of section 27 of the 2011 Act.

(2) Rule 3.5A applies in the circumstances referred to in paragraph (1) and in respect of applications under Part V of this Chapter.

NOTE
1. As substituted by the Act of Sederunt (Children's Hearings (Scotland) Act 2011) (Miscellaneous Amendments) 2013 (SSI 2013/172) art.3(4) (effective June 24, 2013: substitution has effect subject to transitional provisions specified in SSI 2013/172 art.8).

Power to dispense with service on child

[1]**3.3.** Where the sheriff is satisfied, so far as practicable and taking account of the age and maturity of the child, that it would be inappropriate to order service on the child, the sheriff may dispense with service on the child.

NOTE
1. Rules 3.3 and 3.3A as substituted for rule 3.3 by the Act of Sederunt (Children's Hearings (Scotland) Act 2011) (Miscellaneous Amendments) 2013 (SSI 2013/172) art.3(5) (effective June 24, 2013: substitution has effect subject to transitional provisions specified in SSI 2013/172 art.8).

Child to attend hearing

[1]**3.3A.**—(1) This rule applies where an application is made to the sheriff under the 2011 Act, other than where section 103 or 112 of the 2011 Act applies.

(2) A child must attend all hearings, unless the sheriff otherwise directs.

(3) A child may attend a hearing even if the child is excused from doing so.

(4) If the child is not excused from attending the hearing but does not attend the sheriff may grant a warrant to secure attendance in relation to the child.

(5) Paragraph (6) applies if—
(a) the hearing of the application is to be continued to another day; and

(b) the sheriff is satisfied that there is reason to believe that the child will not attend on that day.

(6) The sheriff may grant a warrant to secure attendance in relation to the child.

NOTE
1. Rules 3.3 and 3.3A as substituted for rule 3.3 by the Act of Sederunt (Children's Hearings (Scotland) Act 2011) (Miscellaneous Amendments) 2013 (SSI 2013/172) art.3(5) (effective June 24, 2013: substitution has effect subject to transitional provisions specified in SSI 2013/172 art.8).

Service on Child

[1]**3.4.**—(1) Subject to rule 3.3 and to paragraph (2), after the issue of the first order or warrant to cite, as the case may be, the applicant shall forthwith serve a copy of the application and first order or warrant to cite on the child, together with a notice or citation in–
   (a) Form 26 in respect of an application for a child assessment order under Part III of this Chapter;
   (b) Form 27 in respect of an application to vary or terminate a child protection order in terms of rule 3.33;
   (c) Form 28 in respect of an application for an exclusion order in terms of rules 3.34 to 3.39;
   (d) Form 29 in respect of an application to vary or recall an exclusion order in terms of rule 3.40;
       [. . .]
   (f) subject to subparagraph (g), in Form 31 in respect of an application under section 93(2)(a) or 94(2)(a) of the 2011 Act;
   (g) Form 31A in respect of an application under section 94(2)(a) of the 2011 Act where a procedural hearing has been fixed; and
   (h) Form 31B in respect of an application under section 110(2) of the 2011 Act.

(2) The sheriff may, on application by the applicant or of his own motion, order that a specified part of the application is not served on the child.

NOTE
1. As amended by the Act of Sederunt (Children's Hearings (Scotland) Act 2011) (Miscellaneous Amendments) 2013 (SSI 2013/172) art.3(6) (effective June 24, 2013: amendment has effect subject to transitional provisions specified in SSI 2013/172 art.8).

Procedure for obtaining a child's view

[1]**3.5.**—(1) Subject to section 27(3) of the 2011 Act, the sheriff—
   (a) may order such steps to be taken as he considers appropriate to ascertain the views of that child; and
   (b) shall not come to a decision about a matter relating to a child within the meaning of section 27 of the 2011 Act unless an opportunity has been given for the views of that child to be obtained or heard.

(2) Subject to any order made by the sheriff under paragraph (1)(a) and to any other method as the sheriff in his discretion may permit, the views of the child may be conveyed–
   (a) by the child orally or in writing;
   (b) by an advocate or solicitor acting on behalf of the child;
   (c) by any safeguarder

(ca) by any curator *ad litem*; or

(d) by any other person (either orally or in writing), provided that the sheriff is satisfied that that person is a suitable representative and is duly authorised to represent the child.

(3) Where the views of the child are conveyed orally to the sheriff, the sheriff shall record those views in writing.

(4) The sheriff may direct that any written views given by a child, or any written record of those views, shall–

(a) be sealed in an envelope marked "Views of the child – confidential";

(b) be kept in the court process without being recorded in the inventory of process;

(c) be available to a sheriff only;

(d) not be opened by any person other than a sheriff, and

(e) not form a borrowable part of the process.

NOTE
1. As amended (and heading substituted) by the Act of Sederunt (Children's Hearings (Scotland) Act 2011) (Miscellaneous Amendments) 2013 (SSI 2013/172) art.3(7) (effective June 24, 2013: amendment has effect subject to transitional provisions specified in SSI 2013/172 art.8).

Confidentiality

[1]**3.5A.**—(1) Unless the sheriff otherwise directs, all documents lodged in process are to be available only to the sheriff, the reporter, the safeguarder, the curator *ad litem* and the parties; and such documents must be treated as confidential by all persons involved in, or party to, the proceedings and by the sheriff clerk.

(2) The safeguarder and the curator *ad litem* must—

(a) treat all information obtained in the exercise of their duties as confidential; and

(b) not disclose any such information to any person unless disclosure of such information is necessary for the purpose of their duties.

(3) This rule is subject to rule 3.5.

NOTE
1. As inserted by the Act of Sederunt (Children's Hearings (Scotland) Act 2011) (Miscellaneous Amendments) 2013 (SSI 2013/172) art.3(8) (effective June 24, 2013: insertion has effect subject to transitional provisions specified in SSI 2013/172 art.8).

SAFEGUARDERS

Application

[1]**3.6.** Rules 3.7 to 3.9 apply, as regards a safeguarder, to all applications and proceedings to which this Chapter applies except for an application under section 37 of the 2011 Act for a child protection order.

NOTE
1. As amended by the Act of Sederunt (Children's Hearings (Scotland) Act 2011) (Miscellaneous Amendments) 2013 (SSI 2013/172) art.3(9) (effective June 24, 2013: amendment has effect subject to transitional provisions specified in SSI 2013/172 art.8).

Appointment of safeguarder

[1]**3.7.**—(1) Where a safeguarder has not been appointed for the child, the sheriff—

(a)	shall, as soon as reasonably practicable after the lodging of an application or the commencing of any proceedings, consider whether it is necessary to appoint a safeguarder in the application or proceedings; and

(b)	may at that stage, or at any later stage of the application or proceedings, appoint a safeguarder.

(2)	Where a sheriff appoints a safeguarder, the appointment and the reasons for it must be recorded in an interlocutor.

NOTE

1.	As amended by the Act of Sederunt (Children's Hearings (Scotland) Act 2011) (Miscellaneous Amendments) 2013 (SSI 2013/172) art.3(10) (effective June 24, 2013: amendment has effect subject to transitional provisions specified in SSI 2013/172 art.8).

Rights, powers and duties of safeguarder on appointment

[1]**3.8.** A safeguarder appointed in an application shall–

(a)	have the powers and duties at common law of a curator *ad litem* in respect of the child;

(b)	be entitled to receive from the Principal Reporter copies of the application, all of the productions in the proceedings and any papers which were before the children's hearing;

(c)	subject to rule 3.5(1)(a), determine whether the child wishes to express his views in relation to the application and, if so, where the child so wishes transmit his views to the sheriff;

(d)	make such enquiries so far as relevant to the application as he considers appropriate;

(e)	without delay, and in any event before the hearing on the application, intimate in writing to the sheriff clerk whether or not he intends to become a party to the proceedings; and

(f)	whether or not a party, be entitled to receive from the sheriff clerk all interlocutors subsequent to his or her appointment.

NOTE

1.	As amended by the Act of Sederunt (Children's Hearings (Scotland) Act 2011) (Miscellaneous Amendments) 2013 (SSI 2013/172) art.3(11) (effective June 24, 2013: amendment has effect subject to transitional provisions specified in SSI 2013/172 art.8).

[1]Representation of safeguarder

3.9.—(1) A safeguarder may appear personally in the proceedings or instruct an advocate or solicitor to appear on his behalf.

(2)	Where an advocate or a solicitor is appointed to act as a safeguarder, he shall not act also as advocate or solicitor for the child in the proceedings.

NOTE

1.	Heading as substituted by the Act of Sederunt (Children's Hearings (Scotland) Act 2011) (Miscellaneous Amendments) 2013 (SSI 2013/172) art.3(12) (effective June 24, 2013: substitution has effect subject to transitional provisions specified in SSI 2013/172 art.8).

[1]**3.10.** [. . .]

NOTE

1.	Revoked by the Act of Sederunt (Children's Hearings (Scotland) Act 2011) (Miscellaneous Amendments) 2013 (SSI 2013/172) art.3(13) (effective June 24, 2013: repeal has effect subject to transitional provisions specified in SSI 2013/172 art.8).

FIXING OF FIRST HEARING

Assigning of diet for hearing

[1]**3.11.** Except where otherwise provided in these Rules, after the lodging of any application the sheriff clerk shall forthwith assign a diet for the hearing of the application and shall issue a first order or a warrant to cite in Form 32, Form 32A or Form 33, as the case may be.

NOTE
1. As amended by the Act of Sederunt (Children's Hearings (Scotland) Act 2011) (Miscellaneous Amendments) 2013 (SSI 2013/172) art.3(14) (effective June 24, 2013: amendment has effect subject to transitional provisions specified in SSI 2013/172 art.8).

SERVICE, CITATION AND NOTICE

Service and notice to persons named in application

[1]**3.12.**—(1) Subject to the provisions of rule 3.4 (service on child), after the issue of the first order or warrant to cite, as the case may be, the applicant shall forthwith give notice of the application by serving a copy of the application and the first order or warrant to cite together with a notice or citation, as the case may be, on the persons named in the application or, as the case may be, a person who should receive notice of the application (subject to paragraph (2)) in—

(a) Form 34 in respect of an application for a child assessment order under Part III of this Chapter;

(b) Form 35 in respect of an application to vary or terminate a child protection order in terms of rule 3.33;

(c) Form 36 in respect of an application for an exclusion order in terms of rules 3.34 to 3.39;

(d) Form 37 in respect of an application to vary or recall an exclusion order in terms of rule 3.40;

(f) subject to subparagraph (g), in Form 39 in respect of an application under section 93(2)(a) or 94(2)(a) of the 2011 Act made under Part VII of this Chapter; or

(g) in Form 39A where a procedural hearing has been fixed in respect of an application under section 94(2)(a) of the 2011 Act made under Part VII of this Chapter.

(2) Notice of the application shall be given in the case of a safeguarder or curator *ad litem* by serving a copy of the application and the first order or warrant to cite together with notice in Form 40.

NOTE
1. As amended by the Act of Sederunt (Children's Hearings (Scotland) Act 2011) (Miscellaneous Amendments) 2013 (SSI 2013/172) art.3(15) (effective June 24, 2013: amendment has effect subject to transitional provisions specified in SSI 2013/172 art.8).

Period of notice

3.13.—(1) Subject to paragraph (2), citation or notice authorised or required by this Chapter shall be made not later than forty-eight hours, or in the case of postal citation seventy-two hours, before the date of the diet to which the citation or notice relates.

¹(2) Paragraph (1) shall not apply in relation to citation or notice of the following applications or proceedings–

(a) an appeal referred to in section 157(1), 160(1), 161(1) or 162(3) of the 2011 Act;

(b) a hearing in respect of an exclusion order where an interim order has been granted in terms of rule 3.36;

(c) a hearing on an application to vary or terminate a child protection order;

(d) an application for a child assessment order,

in which cases the period of notice and the method of giving notice shall be as directed by the sheriff.

NOTE
1. As amended by the Act of Sederunt (Children's Hearings (Scotland) Act 2011) (Miscellaneous Amendments) 2013 (SSI 2013/172) art.3(16) (effective June 24, 2013: amendment has effect subject to transitional provisions specified in SSI 2013/172 art.8).

Citation of Witnesses, Parties and Persons Having an Interest

3.14.—(1) The following shall be warrants for citation of witnesses, parties and havers:–

¹(a) the warrant for the hearing on evidence in an application;

(b) an interlocutor fixing a diet for the continued hearing of an application; and

(c) an interlocutor assigning a diet for a hearing of an appeal or application.

(2) In an application or an appeal, witnesses or havers may be cited in Form 41.

(3) The certificate of execution of citation of witnesses and havers shall be in Form 42.

NOTE
1. As amended by the Act of Sederunt (Children's Hearings (Scotland) Act 2011) (Miscellaneous Amendments) 2013 (SSI 2013/172) art.3(17) (effective June 24, 2013: amendment has effect subject to transitional provisions specified in SSI 2013/172 art.8).

Modes of service

3.15.—(1) Service authorised or required by this Chapter shall be made by any mode specified in paragraphs (2) and (3).

(2) It shall be deemed legal service to or on any person if such service is—

(a) delivered to him personally;

(b) left for him at his dwelling-house or place of business with some person resident or employed therein;

(c) where it cannot be delivered to him personally and he has no known dwelling-house or place of business, left for him at any other place at which he may at the time be resident;

(d) where he is the master of, or a seaman or other person employed in, a vessel, left with a person on board or connected with the vessel;

(e) sent by first class recorded delivery post, or the nearest equivalent which the available postal service permits, to his dwelling-house or place of business, or if he has no known dwelling-house or place of business to any other place in which he may at the time be resident;

(f) where the person has the facility to receive facsimile or other electronic transmission, by such facsimile or other electronic transmission; or

(g) where the person has a numbered box at a document exchange, given by leaving at the document exchange.

(3) Where service requires to be made and there is not sufficient time to employ any of the methods specified in paragraph (2), service shall be effected orally or in such other manner as the sheriff directs.

Persons who may effect service

[1]**3.16.**—(1) Subject to paragraphs (2) and (3), service shall be effected—

(a) in the case of any of the modes specified in rule 3.15(2), by a sheriff officer;

(b) in the case of any of the modes specified in rule 3.15(2)(e) to (g), by a solicitor, the sheriff clerk, the Principal Reporter or an officer of the local authority; or

(c) in the case of any mode specified by the sheriff in terms of rule 3.15(3), by such person as the sheriff directs.

(2) In relation to the citation of witnesses, parties and havers in terms of rule 3.14 or service of any application, "officer of the local authority" in paragraph (1)(b) includes any officer of a local authority authorised to conduct proceedings under these Rules in terms of rule 3.21 (representation).

(3) Where required by the sheriff, the sheriff clerk shall cite the Principal Reporter, the authors or compilers of any reports or statements and any other person whom the sheriff may wish to examine under section 155(5) of the 2011 Act (procedure in appeal to sheriff against decision of children's hearing).

NOTE
1. As amended by the Act of Sederunt (Children's Hearings (Scotland) Act 2011) (Miscellaneous Amendments) 2013 (SSI 2013/172) art.3(18) (effective June 24, 2013: amendment has effect subject to transitional provisions specified in SSI 2013/172 art.8).

Production of certificates of execution of service

[1]**3.17.**—(1) The production before the sheriff of–

(a) a certificate of execution of service in Form 43; and

[1](b) additionally in the case of postal service, a receipt of the registered or recorded delivery letter,

shall be sufficient evidence that service was duly made.

(2) It shall be sufficient to lodge the execution of service at the hearing, unless the sheriff otherwise directs or on cause shown.

NOTE
1. As amended by the Act of Sederunt (Children's Hearings (Scotland) Act 2011) (Miscellaneous Amendments) 2013 (SSI 2013/172) art.3(19) (effective June 24, 2013: amendment has effect subject to transitional provisions specified in SSI 2013/172 art.8).

Power to dispense with service

3.18. Subject to rule 3.3, the sheriff may, on cause shown, dispense with service on any person named.

MISCELLANEOUS

Expenses

3.19. No expenses shall be awarded in any proceedings to which this Chapter applies.

Record of proceedings

3.20. Proceedings under this Chapter shall be conducted summarily.

Representation

3.21.—(1) In any proceedings any party may be represented by an advocate or a solicitor or, subject to paragraphs (2) and (3), other representative authorised by the party.

(2) Such other representative must throughout the proceedings satisfy the sheriff that he is a suitable person to represent the party and that he is authorised to do so.

(3) Such other representative may in representing a party do all such things for the preparation and conduct of the proceedings as may be done by an individual on his own behalf.

Applications for evidence by live link

[1]**3.22.**—(1) On cause shown, a party may apply in the form prescribed in paragraph (3) for authority for the whole or part of—
  (a) the evidence of a witness or party; or
  (b) a submission,
to be made through a live link.

(2) In paragraph (1)—
"witness" means a person who has been or may be cited to appear before the sheriff as a witness (including a witness who is outwith Scotland), except in circumstances where such witness is a vulnerable witness within the meaning of section 11(1) of the Vulnerable Witnesses (Scotland) Act 2004;
"submission" means any oral submission which would otherwise be made to the court by the party or such party's representative in person including an oral submission in support of an application;
"live link" means a live television link or such other arrangement as may be specified in the application by which the witness, party or representative, as the case may be, is able to be seen and heard in the proceedings or heard in the proceedings and is able to see and hear or hear the proceedings while at a place which is outside the courtroom.

(3) An application under paragraph (1) shall be made—
  (a) in Form 44A in the case of a witness or party;
  (b) in Form 44B in the case of a submission.

(4) The application shall be lodged with the sheriff clerk prior to the hearing at which the witness is to give evidence or the submission is to be made (except on special cause shown).

(5) The sheriff shall—
  (a) order intimation of the application to be made to the other party or parties to the proceedings in such form as he or she prescribes; and
  (b) hear the application as soon as reasonably practicable.

NOTE
1. As substituted by the Act of Sederunt (Children's Hearings (Scotland) Act 2011) (Miscellaneous Amendments) 2013 (SI 2013/172) art.3(20) (effective June 24, 2013: substitution has effect subject to transitional provisions specified in SSI 2013/172 art.8).

Orders and transfer of cases

3.23.—(1) The sheriff who hears an application under rule 3.22 shall, after hearing the parties and allowing such further procedure as the sheriff thinks fit, make an order granting or refusing the application.

(2) Where the sheriff grants the application, he may–

(a) transfer the case to be heard in whole; or

(b) hear the case himself or such part of it as he shall determine,

in another sheriff court in the same sheriffdom.

Exclusion of certain enactments

3.24. The enactments specified in column (1) of Schedule 3 to this Act of Sederunt (being enactments relating to matters with respect to which this Chapter is made) shall not, to the extent specified in column (3) of that Schedule, apply to an application or appeal.

PART III

CHILD ASSESSMENT ORDERS

Interpretation

[1]**3.25.** In this Part, "application" means an application for a child assessment order in terms of section 35(1) of the 2011 Act.

NOTE

1. As amended by the Act of Sederunt (Children's Hearings (Scotland) Act 2011) (Miscellaneous Amendments) 2013 (SSI 2013/172) art.3(21) (effective June 24, 2013: amendment has effect subject to transitional provisions specified in SSI 2013/172 art.8).

Form of application

3.26. An application shall be made in Form 45.

Orders

3.27.—(1) After hearing parties and allowing such further procedure as he thinks fit, the sheriff shall make an order granting or refusing the application.

(2) Where an order is made granting the application, that order shall be made in Form 46 and shall contain the information specified therein.

[1](3) Where the sheriff, in terms of section 36(3) of the 2011 Act, has decided to make a child protection order pursuant to an application, rules 3.31 to 3.33 shall apply.

NOTE

1. As amended by the Act of Sederunt (Children's Hearings (Scotland) Act 2011) (Miscellaneous Amendments) 2013 (SSI 2013/172) art.3(22) (effective June 24, 2013: amendment has effect subject to transitional provisions specified in SSI 2013/172 art.8).

Intimation

3.28. The local authority shall intimate the grant or refusal of an application to such persons, if any, as the sheriff directs.

PART IV

CHILD PROTECTION ORDERS

Interpretation

[1]**3.29.** In this Part, "application" means, except in rule 3.33, an application for a child protection order in terms of section 37 of the 2011 Act.

NOTE

1. As amended by the Act of Sederunt (Children's Hearings (Scotland) Act 2011) (Miscellaneous Amendments) 2013 (SSI 2013/172) art.3(23) (effective June 24, 2013: amendment has effect subject to transitional provisions specified in SSI 2013/172 art.8).

Form of application

3.30. An application made by a local authority shall be in Form 47 and an application made by any other person shall be in Form 48.

Determination of application

3.31.—(1) On receipt of an application, the sheriff, having considered the grounds of the application and the supporting evidence, shall forthwith grant or refuse it.

[1](2) Where an order is granted, it shall be in Form 49 and it shall contain any directions made under section 40, 41 or 42 of the 2011 Act.

NOTE

1. As amended by the Act of Sederunt (Children's Hearings (Scotland) Act 2011) (Miscellaneous Amendments) 2013 (SSI 2013/172) art.3(24) (June 24, 2013: amendment has effect subject to transitional provisions specified in SSI 2013/172 art.8).

Intimation of making of order

[1]**3.32.** Where an order is granted, the applicant shall forthwith serve a copy of the order on–
  (a) the child, along with a notice in Form 50;
  (b) the persons referred to in section 43(1)(a), (c), (d) and (e) of the 2011 Act, along with a notice in Form 51; and
  (c) such other persons as the sheriff may direct and in such manner as he or she may direct.

NOTE

1. As amended by the Act of Sederunt (Children's Hearings (Scotland) Act 2011) (Miscellaneous Amendments) 2013 (SSI 2013/172) art.3(25) (effective June 24, 2013: amendment has effect subject to transitional provisions specified in SSI 2013/172 art.8).

Application to vary or terminate a child protection order

[1]**3.33.**—(1) An application under section 48 of the 2011 Act for the variation or termination of a child protection order or a direction given under section 58 of the Act or such an order shall be made in Form 52.

(2) A person applying under section 48 of the 2011 Act for the variation or termination of a child protection order shall require to lodge with his application a copy of that order.

(3) Without prejudice to rule 3.5, any person on whom service is made under section 49 of the 2011 Act may appear or be represented at the hearing of the application.

(4) The sheriff, after hearing parties and allowing such further procedure as he thinks fit, shall grant or refuse the application.

(5) Where an order is made granting the application for variation, that order shall be in Form 53.

(6) Where the sheriff so directs, intimation of the granting or refusing of an application shall be given by the applicant to such person as the sheriff shall direct.

NOTE
1. As amended (and heading substituted) by the Act of Sederunt (Children's Hearings (Scotland) Act 2011) (Miscellaneous Amendments) 2013 (SSI 2013/172) art.3(26) (effective June 24, 2013: amendment has effect subject to transitional provisions specified in SSI 2013/172 art.8).

PART V

EXCLUSION ORDERS

Interpretation

[1]**3.34.** In this Part, "application" means, except in rule 3.40, an application by a local authority for an exclusion order in terms of sections 76 to 80 of the 1995 Act; and "ancillary order" and "interim order" shall be construed accordingly.

NOTE
1. As amended by the Act of Sederunt (Children's Hearings (Scotland) Act 2011) (Miscellaneous Amendments) 2013 (SSI 2013/172) art.3(27)(a) (effective June 24, 2013: amendment has effect subject to transitional provisions specified in SSI 2013/172 art.8).

Form of application

3.35. An application shall be made in Form 54.

Hearing following interim order

[1]**3.36.** Where an interim order is granted under subsection (4) of section 76 of the 1995 Act, the hearing under subsection (5) of that section shall take place not later than 3 working days after the granting of the interim order.

NOTE
1. As amended by the Act of Sederunt (Children's Hearings (Scotland) Act 2011) (Miscellaneous Amendments) 2013 (SSI 2013/172) art.3(27)(b) (effective June 24, 2013: amendment has effect subject to transitional provisions specified in SSI 2013/172 art.8).

Orders

3.37.—(1) After hearing parties and allowing such further procedure as he thinks fit, the sheriff shall make an order granting or refusing the application.

(2) Where the sheriff grants an order in terms of paragraph (1), it shall be in Form 55 and shall be served forthwith by the local authority on—

(a) the named person;
(b) the appropriate person;
(c) the relevant child; and
(d) the Principal Reporter.

Certificates of delivery of documents to chief constable

[1]**3.38.**—(1) After the local authority have complied with section 78(4) of the 1995 Act, they shall forthwith lodge in process a certificate of delivery in Form 56.

(2) After a person has complied with section 78(5) of the 1995 Act, he shall lodge in process a certificate of delivery in Form 56.

NOTE
1. As amended by the Act of Sederunt (Children's Hearings (Scotland) Act 2011) (Miscellaneous Amendments) 2013 (SSI 2013/172) art.3(27)(c) (effective June 24, 2013: amendment has effect subject to transitional provisions specified in SSI 2013/172 art.8).

Power to make child protection order in an application for an exclusion order

[1]**3.39.** Where the sheriff, in terms of section 76(8) of the 1995 Act, has decided to make a child protection order under Part 5 of the 2011 Act pursuant to an application, rules 3.31 to 3.33 shall apply.

NOTE
1. As substituted (including heading) by the Act of Sederunt (Children's Hearings (Scotland) Act 2011) (Miscellaneous Amendments) 2013 (SSI 2013/172) art.3(28) (effective June 24, 2013: substitution has effect subject to transitional provisions specified in SSI 2013/172 art.8).

Variation or recall of an exclusion order

3.40.—[1](1) Any application for the variation or recall of an exclusion order and any warrant, interdict, order or direction granted or made under section 77 of the 1995 Act shall be in Form 57.

(2) After hearing parties and allowing such further procedure as he thinks fit, the sheriff shall make an order granting or refusing the application.

(3) Where an order is made granting the application for variation, that order shall be in Form 58.

(4) Intimation of the granting or refusing of an application shall be given by the applicant to such persons as the sheriff shall direct.

NOTE
1. As amended by the Act of Sederunt (Children's Hearings (Scotland) Act 2011) (Miscellaneous Amendments) 2013 (SSI 2013/172) art.3(27)(d) (effective June 24, 2013: amendment has effect subject to transitional provisions specified in SSI 2013/172 art.8).

PART VI
¹[. . .]

¹**3.41.** [. . .]

¹**3.42.** [. . .]

¹**3.43.** [. . .]

PART VII
¹PROCEDURE IN APPLICATIONS UNDER SECTION 93(2)(A) OR 94(2)(A) OF THE 2011 ACT

Interpretation

¹**3.44.** In this Part, "application" means an application under section 93(2)(a) or 94(2)(a) of the 2011 Act.

Lodging of application, etc.

¹**3.45.**—(1) Within a period of 7 days beginning with the date on which the Principal Reporter was directed in terms of section 93(2)(a) or 94(2)(a) of the 2011 Act to make an application to the sheriff, the Principal Reporter shall lodge an application in Form 60 with the sheriff clerk of the sheriff court district in which the child is habitually resident.

(1A) Paragraph (1) is subject to the terms of section 102(2) of the 2011 Act.

(1B) The sheriff may, on cause shown, remit any application to another sheriff court.

(1C) Not later than 28 days after the day on which the application is lodged the sheriff clerk shall fix a hearing on evidence as required under section 101(2) of the 2011 Act.

(2) Where a safeguarder has been appointed by the children's hearing, the Principal Reporter shall intimate such appointment to the sheriff clerk and shall lodge along with the application any report made by the safeguarder.

(3) Paragraphs (4) to (7) apply where an application under paragraph (1) is made by virtue of section 94(2)(a) of the 2011 Act.

(4) The sheriff may fix a procedural hearing to determine whether or not the section 67 grounds in the statement of grounds are accepted by each relevant person.

(5) Such procedural hearing must take place before the expiry of the period of 7 days beginning with the day on which the application is lodged.

(6) The sheriff shall appoint service and intimation of the procedural hearing as the sheriff thinks fit.

(7) Subject to paragraph (9)(a) and (b), subsequent to the procedural hearing the sheriff may discharge the hearing on evidence and determine the application.

(8) Where paragraph (7) applies the sheriff shall make such orders for intimation as the sheriff thinks fit.

(9) Where—
(a) a relevant person does not accept the section 67 grounds in the statement of grounds at the procedural hearing;
(b) section 106(2)(a) or (b) of the 2011 Act applies; or
(c) the sheriff has not fixed a procedural hearing;
a hearing on evidence must take place in accordance with rule 3.47.

NOTE
1. As amended by the Act of Sederunt (Children's Hearings (Scotland) Act 2011) (Miscellaneous Amendments) 2013 (SSI 2013/172) art.3(32) (effective June 24, 2013: amendment has effect subject to transitional provisions specified in SSI 2013/172 art.8).

Withdrawal of application

[1]3.46.—(1) At any stage of the proceedings before the application is determined the Principal Reporter may withdraw the application, either in whole or in part, by lodging a minute to that effect or by motion at the hearing.

(2) The Principal Reporter shall intimate such withdrawal to—
(a) the child, except where service on the child has been dispensed with in terms of rule 3.3;
(b) any relevant person whose whereabouts are known to the Principal Reporter; and
(c) any safeguarder and curator *ad litem*.

(3) In the event of withdrawal in whole in terms of paragraph (1), the sheriff shall dismiss the application and discharge the referral.

NOTE
1. As amended (and heading substituted) by the Act of Sederunt (Children's Hearings (Scotland) Act 2011) (Miscellaneous Amendments) 2013 (SSI 2013/172) art.3(33) (effective June 24, 2013: amendment has effect subject to transitional provisions specified in SSI 2013/172 art.8).

Expeditious determination of application

[1]**3.46A.**—Prior to or at a hearing on evidence under rule 3.47 (or any adjournment or continuation thereof under rule 3.49), the sheriff may order parties to take such steps as the sheriff deems necessary to secure the expeditious determination of the application, including but not limited to—

(a) instructing a single expert;
(b) using affidavits;
(c) restricting the issues for proof;
(d) restricting witnesses;
(e) applying for evidence to be taken by live link in accordance with rule 3.22.

NOTE
1. As inserted by the Act of Sederunt (Children's Hearings (Scotland) Act 2011) (Miscellaneous Amendments) 2013 (SSI 2013/172) art.3(34) (effective June 24, 2013: insertion has effect subject to transitional provisions specified in SSI 2013/172 art.8).

Hearing on evidence

[1]**3.47.**—(A1) If, at a hearing on evidence (or any adjournment or continuation thereof under rule 3.49), the section 67 grounds (or as they may be amended) are no longer in dispute, the sheriff may determine the application without hearing evidence.

(1) In the case of every section 67 ground, the sheriff shall, in relation to any ground which is in dispute, hear evidence tendered by or on behalf of the Principal Reporter, including evidence given pursuant to an application granted under rule 3.23.

(2) At the close of the evidence led by the Principal Reporter in a case where it is disputed that the ground set out in section 67(2)(j) of the 2011 Act applies, the sheriff shall consider whether sufficient evidence has been led to establish that ground and shall give all the parties an opportunity to be heard on the question of sufficiency of evidence.

(3) Where the sheriff is not satisfied that sufficient evidence has been led as mentioned in paragraph (2), he shall make a determination to that effect.

(4) Paragraph (4A) applies where—

(a) paragraph (2) applies and the sheriff is satisfied that sufficient evidence has been led;
(b) any other section 67 ground is in dispute.

(4A) The child, the relevant person and any safeguarder may give evidence and may, with the approval of the sheriff, call witnesses with regard to the ground in question.

(5) Where the sheriff excuses the child from attending all or part of the hearing in accordance with section 103(3) of the 2011 Act, the following persons shall be permitted to remain during the absence of the child—

(a) any safeguarder appointed in relation to the child;
(b) any curator *ad litem* appointed in relation to the child;
(c) any relevant person;
(d) the child's representative.

(6) Subject to paragraph (7), the sheriff may exclude any person, including the relevant person, while any child is giving evidence if the sheriff is satisfied that this is necessary in the interests of the child and that—

(a) he must do so in order to obtain the evidence of the child; or

(b) the presence of the person or persons in question is causing, or is likely to cause, significant distress to the child.

(7) Where the relevant person is not legally represented at the hearing and has been excluded under paragraph (6), the sheriff shall inform that relevant person of the substance of any evidence given by the child and shall give that relevant person an opportunity to respond by leading evidence or otherwise.

(8) Where evidence has been heard in part and a safeguarder thereafter becomes a party to proceedings, the sheriff may order the evidence to be reheard in whole or in part.

NOTE
1. As amended (and heading substituted) by the Act of Sederunt (Children's Hearings (Scotland) Act 2011) (Miscellaneous Amendments) 2013 (SSI 2013/172) art.3(35) (effective June 24, 2013: amendment has effect subject to transitional provisions specified in SSI 2013/172 art.8).

Amendment of the statement of grounds

[1]**3.48.** The sheriff may at any time, on the application of any party or of his own motion, allow amendment of any statement of grounds.

NOTE
1. As amended (and heading substituted) by the Act of Sederunt (Children's Hearings (Scotland) Act 2011) (Miscellaneous Amendments) 2013 (SSI 2013/172) art.3(36) (effective June 24, 2013: amendment has effect subject to transitional provisions specified in SSI 2013/172 art.8).

Adjournment for inquiry, etc.

[1]**3.49.** The sheriff on the motion of any party or on his own motion may continue the hearing fixed under rule 3.45(1B) in order to allow time for further inquiry into any application, in consequence of the amendment of any statement under rule 3.48, or for any other necessary cause, for such reasonable time as he may in the circumstances consider necessary.

NOTE
1. As amended by the Act of Sederunt (Children's Hearings (Scotland) Act 2011) (Miscellaneous Amendments) 2013 (SSI 2013/172) art.3(37) (effective June 24, 2013: amendment has effect subject to transitional provisions specified in SSI 2013/172 art.8).

Power of sheriff in making findings as to offences

[1]**3.50.** Where in a statement of grounds it is alleged that an offence has been committed by or against any child, the sheriff may determine that any other offence established by the facts has been committed.

NOTE
1. As amended by the Act of Sederunt (Children's Hearings (Scotland) Act 2011) (Miscellaneous Amendments) 2013 (SSI 2013/172) art.3(38) (effective June 24, 2013: amendment has effect subject to transitional provisions specified in SSI 2013/172 art.8).

Decision of sheriff

[1]**3.51.**—(1) Subject to rule 3.47(3), the sheriff shall give his decision orally at the conclusion of the hearing.

(2) The sheriff clerk shall forthwith send a copy of the interlocutor containing that decision to—

(a) the child, except where service on the child has been dispensed with in terms of rule 3.3;

(b)　any relevant person whose whereabouts are known;

(c)　any safeguarder and curator *ad litem*;

(d)　the Principal Reporter; and

(e)　such other persons as the sheriff may direct.

(3)　The sheriff may, when giving his decision in terms of paragraph (1) or within 7 days thereafter, issue a note of the reasons for his decision and the sheriff clerk shall forthwith send a copy of such a note to the persons referred to in paragraph (2).

NOTE

1.　As amended by the Act of Sederunt (Children's Hearings (Scotland) Act 2011) (Miscellaneous Amendments) 2013 (SSI 2013/172) art.3(39) (effective June 24, 2013: amendment has effect subject to transitional provisions specified in SSI 2013/172 art.8).

[1]**3.52.**—(1)　Subject to paragraph (3) a warrant granted under the 2011 Act may be signed by the sheriff or the sheriff clerk.

(2)　A warrant signed by the sheriff clerk shall be treated for all purposes as if it had been signed by the sheriff.

(3)　A warrant to secure attendance must be signed by the sheriff.

NOTE

1.　As substituted by the Act of Sederunt (Children's Hearings (Scotland) Act 2011) (Miscellaneous Amendments) 2013 (SSI 2013/172) art.3(40) (effective June 24, 2013: substitution has effect subject to transitional provisions specified in SSI 2013/172 art.8).

PART VIII

[1]PROCEDURE IN APPEALS TO THE SHERIFF AGAINST DECISIONS OF CHILDREN'S HEARINGS

NOTE

1.　Heading as substituted by the Act of Sederunt (Children's Hearings (Scotland) Act 2011) (Miscellaneous Amendments) 2013 (SSI 2013/172) art.3(41) (effective June 24, 2013: amendment has effect subject to transitional provisions specified in SSI 2013/172 art.8).

Form of appeal

[1]**3.53.**—(1)　This Part applies to appeals to the sheriff under sections 154(1), 160(1), 161(1) and 162(3) of the 2011 Act.

(1A)　An appeal to the sheriff under the sections of the 2011 Act prescribed in paragraph (1B) must be—

(a)　made in the form prescribed in paragraph (1B);

(b)　accompanied by a copy of the decision complained of and any document relevant to it that was before the children's hearing; and

(c)　lodged with the sheriff clerk of the sheriff court district in which the child is habitually resident or, on cause shown, such other court as the sheriff may direct.

(1B)　The prescribed sections and form of appeal are—

(a)　in the case of an appeal under section 154(1) (appeal to sheriff against decision of children's hearing), in Form 61;

(b)　in the case of an appeal under section 160(1) (appeal to sheriff against relevant person determination), in Form 62;

(c)　in the case of an appeal under section 161(1) (appeal to sheriff against decision affecting contact or permanence order), in Form 63;

(d) in the case of an appeal under section 162(3) (appeal to sheriff against decision to implement secure accommodation authorisation), in Form 63A. (2) Subject to paragraph (3), the appeal shall be signed by the appellant or his representative.

(3) An appeal by a child may be signed on his behalf by any safeguarder.

(4) Where leave to appeal is required by virtue of section 159(2) of the 2011 Act, such application for leave shall be—

(a) made by letter addressed to the sheriff clerk setting out the grounds on which the application is made;

(b) accompanied by a copy of the decision referred to in section 159(2) of the 2011 Act;

(c) lodged with the sheriff clerk with the relevant form of appeal.

(5) On receipt of such application the sheriff clerk shall forthwith fix a hearing and intimate the application and the date of the hearing to the other parties to the proceedings.

(6) Where leave to appeal is granted, the appeal will proceed in accordance with rule 3.54.

NOTE

1. As amended by the Act of Sederunt (Children's Hearings (Scotland) Act 2011) (Miscellaneous Amendments) 2013 (SSI 2013/172) art.3(42) (effective June 24, 2013: amendment has effect subject to transitional provisions specified in SSI 2013/172 art.8).

Appointment and intimation of first diet

[1]**3.54.**—(1) On the lodging of the appeal, the sheriff clerk shall forthwith assign a date for the hearing and shall at the same time intimate to the appellant or his representative and, together with a copy of the appeal, to—

(a) the Principal Reporter;

(b) subject to the provisions of paragraph (4), the child (if not the appellant);

(c) any relevant person (if not the appellant);

(d) any safeguarder;

(e) any other person the sheriff considers necessary, including those referred to in section 155(5)(c) and (e) of the 2011 Act; and

(f) in the case of appeals under section 162(3), the chief social work officer of the relevant local authority for the child.

(2) The sheriff clerk shall endorse on the appeal a certificate of execution of intimation under paragraph (1).

(3) Intimation to a child in terms of paragraph (1)(b) shall be in Form 64.

(4) The sheriff may dispense with intimation to a child in terms of paragraph (1)(b) where he considers that such dispensation is appropriate.

(5) The date assigned for the hearing under paragraph (1) shall be within the time limits prescribed in, or by virtue of, the 2011 Act and in any event, no later than 28 days after the lodging of the appeal.

NOTE

1. As amended by the Act of Sederunt (Children's Hearings (Scotland) Act 2011) (Miscellaneous Amendments) 2013 (SSI 2013/172) art.3(43) (effective June 24, 2013: amendment has effect subject to transitional provisions specified in SSI 2013/172 art.8).

Answers

[1]**3.55.**—(1) Subject to paragraph (1A), if any person on whom service of the appeal has been made wishes to lodge answers to the appeal, he or she must do so not later than 7 days before the diet fixed for the hearing of the appeal.

(1A) Paragraph (1) does not apply to those appeals referred to in section 157(1), 160(1), 161(1) or 162(3) of the 2011 Act.

(2) Any person who has lodged answers shall forthwith intimate a copy thereof to any other person on whom service has been made under rule 3.54(1).

NOTE
1. As amended by the Act of Sederunt (Children's Hearings (Scotland) Act 2011) (Miscellaneous Amendments) 2013 (SSI 2013/172) art.3(44) (effective June 24, 2013: amendment has effect subject to transitional provisions specified in SSI 2013/172 art.8).

Procedure at hearing of appeal

[1]**3.56.**—(1) Before proceeding to examine the Principal Reporter and the authors or compilers of any reports or statements, the sheriff shall hear the appellant or his representative and any party to the appeal.

(2) On receipt of any further report required by the sheriff under or by virtue of the 2011 Act, the sheriff shall direct the Principal Reporter to send a copy of the report to every party to the appeal.

(3) At any appeal the sheriff may hear evidence—
(a) where a ground of the appeal is an alleged irregularity in the conduct of a hearing, as to that irregularity;
(b) in any other circumstances where he considers it appropriate to do so.

(4) Where the nature of the appeal or of any evidence is such that the sheriff is satisfied that it is in the interests of the child that he should not be present at any stage of the appeal, the sheriff may exclude the child from the hearing during that stage and, in that event, any safeguarder appointed and any relevant person or representative of the child shall be permitted to remain during the absence of the child.

(5) Subject to paragraph (6), the sheriff may exclude any relevant person, or that person and any representative of his, or any such representative from any part or parts of the hearing for so long as he considers it is necessary in the interests of any child, where he is satisfied that—
(a) he must do so in order to obtain the views of the child in relation to the hearing; or
(b) the presence of the person or persons in question is causing, or is likely to cause, significant distress to the child.

(6) Where any relevant person has been excluded under paragraph (5) the sheriff shall, after that exclusion has ended, explain to him the substance of what has taken place in his absence and shall give him an opportunity to respond to any evidence given by the child by leading evidence or otherwise.

(7) Where an appeal has been heard in part and a safeguarder thereafter becomes a party to the appeal, the sheriff may order the hearing of the appeal to commence of new.

NOTE
1. As amended by the Act of Sederunt (Children's Hearings (Scotland) Act 2011) (Miscellaneous Amendments) 2013 (SSI 2013/172) art.3(45) (effective June 24, 2013: amendment has effect subject to transitional provisions specified in SSI 2013/172 art.8).

Adjournment or continuation of appeals

[1]**3.57.**—(1) The sheriff may, on the motion of any party or on his own motion, adjourn or continue the hearing of the appeal for such reasonable time and for such purpose as may in the circumstances be appropriate.

(2) In the event of such adjournment or continuation the sheriff may make such order as the sheriff deems necessary to secure the expeditious determination of the appeal.

NOTE
1. As amended (and heading substituted) by the Act of Sederunt (Children's Hearings (Scotland) Act 2011) (Miscellaneous Amendments) 2013 (SSI 2013/172) art.3(46) (effective June 24, 2013: amendment has effect subject to transitional provisions specified in SSI 2013/172 art.8).

Decision of sheriff in appeals

[1]**3.58.**—(1) The sheriff shall give his decision orally either at the conclusion of the appeal or on such day as he shall appoint, subject to the provisions of, or by virtue of, the 2011 Act.

(2) The sheriff may issue a note of the reasons for his decision, and shall require to do so where he takes any of the steps referred to in section 156(2) or (3) of the 2011 Act.

(3) Any note in terms of paragraph (2) shall be issued at the time the sheriff gives his decision or within 7 days thereafter.

(4) The sheriff clerk shall forthwith send a copy of the interlocutor containing the decision of the sheriff, and where appropriate of the note referred to in paragraph (2), to the Principal Reporter, to the appellant (and to the child or any relevant person, if not the appellant), any safeguarder and such other persons as the sheriff may direct, and shall also return to the Principal Reporter any documents lodged with the sheriff clerk.

(5) Where section 159 of the 2011 Act applies the sheriff clerk shall send a copy of the interlocutor containing the decision of the sheriff to the Scottish Legal Aid Board.

NOTE
1. As amended by the Act of Sederunt (Children's Hearings (Scotland) Act 2011) (Miscellaneous Amendments) 2013 (SSI 2013/172) art.3(47) (effective June 24, 2013: amendment has effect subject to transitional provisions specified in SSI 2013/172 art.8).

[1]PART VIIIA

PART VIIIA APPLICATIONS FOR REVIEW BY LOCAL AUTHORITY

NOTE
1. As inserted by the Act of Sederunt (Children's Hearings (Scotland) Act 2011) (Miscellaneous Amendments) 2013 (SSI 2013/172) art.3(48) (effective June 24, 2013: insertion has effect subject to transitional provisions specified in SSI 2013/172 art.8).

Review applications by local authority

[1]**3.58A.**—(1) This Part of Chapter 3 applies to applications to the sheriff for a review under section 166(2) of the 2011 Act.

(2) An application shall be made in Form 64A and must contain—
  (a) the name and address of the local authority;
  (b) the name of the child in respect of whom the duty was imposed and the child's representative (if any);

(c) the name and address of any relevant person in relation to the child and such person's representative (if any);

(d) the name and address of any safeguarder;

(e) the name and address of any curator *ad litem*;

(f) the name and address of any other party to the application;

(g) the name and address of any other local authority with an interest;

(h) the date and determination made and the place of the sheriff court which made the determination, or alternatively the date and decision made by the children's hearing;

(i) the grounds for the making of the application;

(j) any reports, affidavits and productions upon which the applicant intends to rely.

NOTE
1. As inserted by the Act of Sederunt (Children's Hearings (Scotland) Act 2011) (Miscellaneous Amendments) 2013 (SSI 2013/172) art.3(48) (effective June 24, 2013: insertion has effect subject to transitional provisions specified in SSI 2013/172 art.8).

Hearing on application

[1]**3.58B.**—(1) After lodging the application in terms of rule 3.58A, the sheriff clerk shall assign a date for hearing the application and shall issue a warrant to cite in Form 64B, which shall require any party to lodge answers if so advised within such time as the sheriff shall appoint.

(2) Subject to the provisions of rule 3.3 (power to dispense with service on child), after the issue of the warrant to cite, the applicant shall forthwith give notice of the application by serving a copy and the warrant on the persons referred to in rule 3.58A.

(3) At the hearing the sheriff may determine the application or allow such further procedure as the sheriff thinks fit.

(4) The provisions of rule 3.51 shall apply to any order made under this Part.

NOTE
1. As inserted by the Act of Sederunt (Children's Hearings (Scotland) Act 2011) (Miscellaneous Amendments) 2013 (SSI 2013/172) art.3(48) (effective June 24, 2013: insertion has effect subject to transitional provisions specified in SSI 2013/172 art.8).

PART IX

[1]PROCEDURE IN APPEALS BY STATED CASE UNDER PART 15 OF THE 2011 ACT

NOTE
1. Heading as substituted by the Act of Sederunt (Children's Hearings (Scotland) Act 2011) (Miscellaneous Amendments) 2013 (SSI 2013/172) art.3(49) (effective June 24, 2013: insertion has effect subject to transitional provisions specified in SSI 2013/172 art.8).

Appeals

[2]**3.59.**—(A1) This Part applies to appeals by stated case under section 163(1), 164(1), 165(1) and 167(1) of the 2011 Act.

[1](1) An application to the sheriff to state a case for the purposes of an appeal to the sheriff principal to which this Part applies shall specify the point of law upon which the appeal is to proceed or the procedural irregularity, as the case may be.

[1](2) The appellant shall, at the same time as lodging the application for a stated case, intimate the lodging of an appeal from the decision of the sheriff to—

  (a) the Principal Reporter;

  (b) the child (if not the appellant), except where service on the child has been dispensed with in terms of rule 3.3;

  (c) any relevant person (if not the appellant);

  (d) any safeguarder;

  (e) any other party to proceedings.

(3) The sheriff shall, within 21 days of the lodging of the application for a stated case, issue a draft stated case—

  (a) containing findings in fact and law or, where appropriate, a narrative of the proceedings before him;

  (b) containing appropriate questions of law or setting out the procedural irregularity concerned; and

  (c) containing a note stating the reasons for his decisions in law,

and the sheriff clerk shall send a copy of the draft stated case to the appellant and to parties referred to in paragraph (2).

(4) Within 7 days of the issue of the draft stated case—

  (a) the appellant or a party referred to in paragraph (2) may lodge with the sheriff clerk a note of any adjustments which he seeks to make;

  (b) the appellant or such a party may state any point of law or procedural irregularity which he wishes to raise in the appeal; and

  (c) the note of adjustment and, where appropriate, point of law or procedural irregularity shall be intimated to the appellant and the other such parties.

(5) The sheriff may, on the motion of the appellant or a party referred to in paragraph (2) or of his own accord, and shall where he proposes to reject any proposed adjustment, allow a hearing on adjustments and may provide for such further procedure under this rule prior to the hearing of the appeal as he thinks fit.

(6) The sheriff shall, within 14 days after—

  (a) the latest date on which a note of adjustments has been or may be lodged; or

  (b) where there has been a hearing on adjustments, that hearing,

and after considering such note and any representations made to him at the hearing, state and sign the case.

(7) The stated case signed by the sheriff shall include—

  (a) questions of law, framed by him, arising from the points of law stated by the parties and such other questions of law as he may consider appropriate;

  (b) any adjustments, proposed under paragraph (4), which are rejected by him;

  (c) a note of the procedural irregularity averred by the parties and any questions of law or other issue which he considers arise therefrom,

as the case may be.

(8) After the sheriff has signed the stated case, the sheriff clerk shall—

  (a) place before the sheriff principal all documents and productions in the appeal together with the stated case; and

(b) send to the appellant and the parties referred to in paragraph (2) a copy of the stated case together with a written note of the date, time and place of the hearing of the appeal.

(9) In the hearing of an appeal, a party referred to in paragraph (2) shall not be allowed to raise questions of law or procedural irregularities of which notice has not been given except on cause shown and subject to such conditions as the sheriff principal may consider appropriate.

(10) The sheriff may, on an application by any party or of his own motion, reduce any of the periods mentioned in paragraph (3), (4) or (6) to such period or periods as he considers reasonable.

(11) Where the sheriff is temporarily absent from duty for any reason, the sheriff principal may extend any period specified in paragraph (3) or (6) for such period or periods as he considers reasonable.

NOTES
1. As amended by the Act of Sederunt (Child Care and Maintenance Rules) (Amendment No.2) 1998 (SI 1998/2130) art.2(2) (effective September 1, 1998).
2. As amended by the Act of Sederunt (Children's Hearings (Scotland) Act 2011) (Miscellaneous Amendments) 2013 (SSI 2013/172) art.3(50) (effective June 24, 2013: amendment has effect subject to transitional provisions specified in SSI 2013/172 art.8).

Lodging reports and information in appeals

[1]**3.60.** Where, in an appeal–
(a) it appears to the sheriff that any report or information lodged under section 155(2) of the 2011 Act is relevant to any issue which is likely to arise in the stated case; and
(b) the report or information has been returned to the Principal Reporter,
the sheriff may require the Principal Reporter to lodge the report or information with the sheriff clerk.

NOTE
1. As amended (and heading substituted) by the Act of Sederunt (Children's Hearings (Scotland) Act 2011) (Miscellaneous Amendments) 2013 (SSI 2013/172) art.3(51) (effective June 24, 2013: amendment has effect subject to transitional provisions specified in SSI 2013/172 art.8).

Hearing

3.61.—(1) The sheriff principal, on hearing the appeal, may either pronounce his decision or reserve judgement.

(2) Where judgement is so reserved, the sheriff principal shall within 28 days give his decision in writing which shall be intimated by the sheriff clerk to the parties.

Leave of the sheriff principal to appeal to the Court of Session

[1]**3.61A.**—(1) This rule applies to applications for leave to appeal under section 163(2), 164(2) or 165(2) of the 2011 Act.

(2) An application shall be made by letter addressed to the sheriff clerk, which must—
(a) state the point of law or procedural irregularity upon which the appeal is to proceed;

(b) be lodged with the sheriff clerk before the expiry of the period of 7 days beginning with the day on which the determination or decision appealed against was made.

(3) On receipt of such application the sheriff clerk shall—

(a) forthwith fix a hearing which should take place no later than 14 days from the date of receipt of the application;

(b) intimate the application and the date of the hearing to the other parties to the proceedings.

(4) Where leave to appeal is granted, the appeal shall be lodged in accordance with the timescales prescribed in the relevant section of the 2011 Act.

NOTE
1. As inserted by the Act of Sederunt (Children's Hearings (Scotland) Act 2011) (Miscellaneous Amendments) 2013 (SSI 2013/172) art.3(52) (effective June 24, 2013: insertion has effect subject to transitional provisions specified in SSI 2013/172 art.8).

PART X

¹APPLICATIONS FOR REVIEW OF GROUNDS DETERMINATION

NOTE
1. Heading as substituted by the Act of Sederunt (Children's Hearings (Scotland) Act 2011) (Miscellaneous Amendments) 2013 (SSI 2013/172) art.3(53) (effective June 24, 2013: substitution has effect subject to transitional provisions specified in SSI 2013/172 art.8).

Application

¹**3.62.**—(1) An application under section 110 of the 2011 Act for a review of a grounds determination made in terms of section 108 of the 2011 Act (determination that grounds for referral established) shall contain—

(a) the name and address of the applicant and his or her representative (if any);

(b) the name and address (if known) of the person who is the subject of the grounds determination (even if that person is no longer a child), if not the applicant;

(c) the name and address of the safeguarder (if any);

(d) the name and address of the curator *ad litem* (if any);

(e) the name and address of any person who is, or was at the time the grounds determination was made, a relevant person in relation to the child, if not the applicant;

(f) the date and grounds determination made and the place of the sheriff court which made the grounds determination;

(g) the grounds for the making of the application;

(h) specification of the nature of evidence in terms of section 111(3) of the 2011 Act not considered by the sheriff who made the grounds determination;

(i) the explanation for the failure to lead such evidence on the original application; and

(j) any reports, affidavits and productions upon which the applicant intends to rely.

(2) Where the applicant does not wish to disclose the address or whereabouts of the child or any other person to persons receiving notice of the application, the applicant shall set out his or her reasons for this.

NOTE
1. As substituted by the Act of Sederunt (Children's Hearings (Scotland) Act 2011) (Miscellaneous Amendments) 2013 (SSI 2013/172) art.3(54) (effective June 24, 2013: substitution has effect subject to transitional provisions specified in SSI 2013/172 art.8).

Hearing on application

[1]**3.63.**—(1) Where an application has been lodged in terms of rule 3.62, the sheriff clerk shall—
   (a) assign a diet for hearing the application;
   (b) issue a warrant to cite in Form 65 requiring the Principal Reporter to lodge answers if so advised within such time as the sheriff shall appoint.

(2) Subject to the provisions of rule 3.4 (service on child), after the issue of the warrant to cite, the applicant shall forthwith give notice of the application by serving a copy and the warrant on the persons named in rule 3.62 and such other persons as the sheriff directs.

(3) After hearing parties and having considered the terms of section 111(3) of the 2011 Act and allowing such further procedure as the sheriff thinks fit to secure the expeditious determination of the application, the sheriff shall make an order as appropriate.

(4) The provisions of rule 3.51 shall apply to any order made under paragraph (3).

NOTE
1. As amended by the Act of Sederunt (Children's Hearings (Scotland) Act 2011) (Miscellaneous Amendments) 2013 (SSI 2013/172) art.3(55) (effective June 24, 2013: amendment has effect subject to transitional provisions specified in SSI 2013/172 art.8).

[1]**3.64. [. . .]**

NOTE
1. Revoked by the Act of Sederunt (Children's Hearings (Scotland) Act 2011) (Miscellaneous Amendments) 2013 (SSI 2013/172) art.3(56) (June 24, 2013: repeal has effect subject to transitional provisions specified in SSI 2013/172 art.8).

[1]PART XA

PART XA ORDERS UNDER THE CHILDREN'S HEARINGS (SCOTLAND) ACT 2011

NOTE
1. As inserted by the Act of Sederunt (Children's Hearings (Scotland) Act 2011) (Miscellaneous Amendments) 2013 (SSI 2013/172) art.3(57) (effective June 24, 2013: insertion has effect subject to transitional provisions specified in SSI 2013/172 art.8).

Interim compulsory supervision order

[1]**3.64A.**—(1) Where a sheriff makes an interim compulsory supervision order under section 100, 109 or 156(3)(d) of the 2011 Act, such order shall be in Form 65A and, subject to rule 3.3, shall be intimated forthwith to the child by the Principal Reporter in Form 65B.

(2) An application for the extension or extension and variation of an interim compulsory supervision order shall be made to the sheriff in Form 65C.

(3) An application for the further extension or further extension and variation of an interim compulsory supervision order shall be made to the sheriff in Form 65D.

(4) Subject to rule 3.3, an application under paragraph (2) or (3) must be intimated forthwith by the applicant to the child and each relevant person and such other persons as the sheriff determines and in such manner as the sheriff determines.

(5) Where the sheriff grants an application under paragraph (2) or (3), the interlocutor shall state the terms of such extension or extension and variation and subject to rule 3.3, shall be intimated forthwith to the child by the Principal Reporter in Form 65B.

(6) Subject to paragraphs (1) and (5), where the sheriff—

(a) makes an interim compulsory supervision order under paragraph (1); or

(b) grants an application under paragraph (2) or (3),

the Principal Reporter shall intimate the order forthwith to the implementation authority and to such other persons as the sheriff determines in Form 65E.

NOTE

1. As inserted by the Act of Sederunt (Children's Hearings (Scotland) Act 2011) (Miscellaneous Amendments) 2013 (SSI 2013/172) art.3(57) (effective June 24, 2013: insertion has effect subject to transitional provisions specified in SSI 2013/172 art.8).

Compulsory supervision order

[1]**3.64B.** Where a sheriff varies or continues a compulsory supervision order, the interlocutor shall state the terms of such variation or continuation and shall be intimated forthwith by the sheriff clerk to the parties and the relevant implementation authority.

NOTE

1. As inserted by the Act of Sederunt (Children's Hearings (Scotland) Act 2011) (Miscellaneous Amendments) 2013 (SSI 2013/172) art.3(57) (effective June 24, 2013: insertion has effect subject to transitional provisions specified in SSI 2013/172 art.8).

Medical examination order

[1]**3.64C.** Where a sheriff varies or continues a medical examination order, the interlocutor shall state the terms of such variation or continuation and shall be intimated forthwith by the sheriff clerk to the parties and the relevant local authority or establishment.

NOTE

1. As inserted by the Act of Sederunt (Children's Hearings (Scotland) Act 2011) (Miscellaneous Amendments) 2013 (SSI 2013/172) art.3(57) (effective June 24, 2013: insertion has effect subject to transitional provisions specified in SSI 2013/172 art.8).

[1]PART XI

VULNERABLE WITNESSES (SCOTLAND) ACT 2004

NOTE

1. As inserted by the Act of Sederunt (Child Care and Maintenance Rules) Amendment (Vulnerable Witnesses (Scotland) Act 2004) 2005 (SSI 2005/190) rule 2(3) (effective April 1, 2005).

Interpretation

[1]**3.65.** In this Part–

"the Act of 2004" means the Vulnerable Witnesses (Scotland) Act 2004;

"child witness notice" has the meaning given in section 12(2) of the Act of 2004;

"review application" means an application for review of arrangements for vulnerable witnesses pursuant to section 13 of the Act of 2004.

"vulnerable witness application" has the meaning given in section 12(6)(a) of the Act of 2004.

NOTE
1. As inserted by the Act of Sederunt (Child Care and Maintenance Rules) Amendment (Vulnerable Witnesses (Scotland) Act 2004) 2005 (SSI 2005/190) rule 2(3) (effective April 1, 2005) and further amended by the Act of Sederunt (Child Care and Maintenance Rules) Amendment (Vulnerable Witnesses (Scotland) Act 2004) 2006 (SSI 2006/75) rule 2(2) (effective April 1, 2006) and the Act of Sederunt (Children's Hearings (Scotland) Act 2011) (Miscellaneous Amendments) 2013 (SSI 2013/172) art.3(58) (effective June 24, 2013: amendment has effect subject to transitional provisions specified in SSI 2013/172 art.8).

Extent of application of this Part

[1]**3.66.** This Part of Chapter 3 shall apply to proceedings where an application is made to the sheriff under section 93(2)(a), 94(2)(a) or 110 of the 2011 Act or an appeal is made under Part 15 of the 2011 Act.

NOTE
1. As inserted by the Act of Sederunt (Child Care and Maintenance Rules) Amendment (Vulnerable Witnesses (Scotland) Act 2004) 2005 (SSI 2005/190) rule 2(3) (effective April 1, 2005) and further substituted by the Act of Sederunt (Children's Hearings (Scotland) Act 2011) (Miscellaneous Amendments) 2013 (SSI 2013/172) art.3(59) (effective June 24, 2013: substitution has effect subject to transitional provisions specified in SSI 2013/172 art.8).

Child Witness Notice

[1]**3.67.** A child witness notice lodged in accordance with section 12(2) of the Act of 2004 shall be in Form 75.

NOTE
1. As inserted by the Act of Sederunt (Child Care and Maintenance Rules) Amendment (Vulnerable Witnesses (Scotland) Act 2004) 2005 (SSI 2005/190) rule 2(3) (effective April 1, 2005).

[1]**3.68.**—(1) The party lodging a child witness notice shall intimate a copy of the child witness notice to all other parties to the proceedings and to any safeguarder and complete a certificate of intimation.

(2) A certificate of intimation referred to in this rule shall be in Form 76 and shall be lodged together with the child witness notice.

NOTE
1. As inserted by the Act of Sederunt (Child Care and Maintenance Rules) Amendment (Vulnerable Witnesses (Scotland) Act 2004) 2005 (SSI 2005/190) rule 2(3) (effective April 1, 2005) and further amended by the Act of Sederunt (Children's Hearings (Scotland) Act 2011) (Miscellaneous Amendments) 2013 (SSI 2013/172) art.3(63)(a) (effective June 24, 2013: amendment has effect subject to transitional provisions specified in SSI 2013/172 art.8).

[1]**3.69.**—(1) On receipt of a child witness notice, a sheriff may—
(a) make an order under section 12(1) of the Act of 2004 without holding a hearing;
(b) require of any of the parties further information before making any further order;

(c) fix a date for a hearing of the child witness notice and grant warrant to cite witnesses and havers.

(2) The sheriff may, subject to any statutory time limits, make an order altering the date of the proof or other hearing at which the child is to give evidence and make such provision for intimation of such alteration to all parties concerned as he deems appropriate.

(3) An order fixing a hearing for a child witness notice shall be intimated by the sheriff clerk—

(a) on the day the order is made; and

(b) in such manner as may be prescribed by the sheriff,

to all parties to the proceedings and such other persons as are named in the order where such parties or persons are not present at the time the order is made.

NOTE

1. As inserted by the Act of Sederunt (Child Care and Maintenance Rules) Amendment (Vulnerable Witnesses (Scotland) Act 2004) 2005 (SSI 2005/190) rule 2(3) (effective April 1, 2005).

[1]Vulnerable Witness Application

NOTE

1. As inserted by the Act of Sederunt (Child Care and Maintenance Rules) Amendment (Vulnerable Witnesses (Scotland) Act 2004) 2006 (SSI 2006/75) rule 2(3) (effective April 1, 2006).

[1]**3.69A.** A vulnerable witness application made in accordance with section 12(6)(a) of the Act of 2004 shall be in Form 76A.

NOTE

1. As inserted by the Act of Sederunt (Child Care and Maintenance Rules) Amendment (Vulnerable Witnesses (Scotland) Act 2004) 2006 (SSI 2006/75) rule 2(3) (effective April 1, 2006).

[1]**3.69B.**—(1) The party making a vulnerable witness application shall intimate a copy of the vulnerable witness application to all other parties to the proceedings and to any safeguarder and complete a certificate of intimation.

(2) A certificate of intimation referred to in this rule shall be in Form 76B and shall be lodged together with the vulnerable witness application.

NOTE

1. As inserted by the Act of Sederunt (Child Care and Maintenance Rules) Amendment (Vulnerable Witnesses (Scotland) Act 2004) 2006 (SSI 2006/75) rule 2(3) (effective April 1, 2006) and further amended by the Act of Sederunt (Children's Hearings (Scotland) Act 2011) (Miscellaneous Amendments) 2013 (SSI 2013/172) art.3(63)(b) (effective June 24, 2013: amendment has effect subject to transitional provisions specified in SSI 2013/172 art.8).

[1]**3.69C.**—(1) On receipt of a vulnerable witness application a sheriff may–

(a) make an order under section 12(6) of the Act of 2004 without holding a hearing;

(b) require of any of the parties further information before making any further order; or

(c) fix a date for a hearing of the vulnerable witness application and grant warrant to cite witnesses and havers.

(2) The sheriff may, subject to any statutory time limits, make an order altering the date of the proof or other hearing at which the vulnerable witness

is to give evidence and make such provision for intimation of such alteration to all parties concerned as he deems appropriate.

(3) An order fixing a hearing for a vulnerable witness application shall be intimated by the sheriff clerk—

(a) on the day the order is made; and

(b) in such manner as may be prescribed by the sheriff,

to all parties to the proceedings and such other persons as are named in the order where such parties or persons are not present at the time the order is made.

NOTE

1. As inserted by the Act of Sederunt (Child Care and Maintenance Rules) Amendment (Vulnerable Witnesses (Scotland) Act 2004) 2006 (SSI 2006/75) rule 2(3) (effective April 1, 2006).

[1]Review of arrangements for vulnerable witnesses

NOTE

1. As inserted by the Act of Sederunt (Child Care and Maintenance Rules) Amendment (Vulnerable Witnesses (Scotland) Act 2004) 2005 (SSI 2005/190) rule 2(3) (effective April 1, 2005).

[1]**3.70.**—(1) A review application shall be in Form 77.

(2) Where the review application is made during the sheriff's hearing of the case, the sheriff may dispense with the requirements of paragraph (1).

NOTE

1. As inserted by the Act of Sederunt (Child Care and Maintenance Rules) Amendment (Vulnerable Witnesses (Scotland) Act 2004) 2005 (SSI 2005/190) rule 2(3) (effective April 1, 2005).

[1]**3.71.**—(1) Where a review application is in Form 77, the applicant shall intimate a copy of the review application to all other parties to the proceedings and to any safeguarder and complete a certificate of intimation.

(2) A certificate of intimation referred to in this rule shall be in Form 78 and shall be lodged together with the review application.

NOTE

1. As inserted by the Act of Sederunt (Child Care and Maintenance Rules) Amendment (Vulnerable Witnesses (Scotland) Act 2004) 2005 (SSI 2005/190) rule 2(3) (effective April 1, 2005) and further amended by the Act of Sederunt (Children's Hearings (Scotland) Act 2011) (Miscellaneous Amendments) 2013 (SSI 2013/172) art.3(63)(c) (effective June 24, 2013: repeal has effect subject to transitional provisions specified in SSI 2013/172 art.8).

[1]**3.72.**—(1) On receipt of a review application, a sheriff may–

(a) if he is satisfied that he may properly do so, make an order under section 13(2) of the Act of 2004 without holding a hearing or, if he is not so satisfied, make such an order after giving the parties an opportunity to be heard;

(b) require of any of the parties further information before making any further order;

(c) fix a date for a hearing of the review application and grant warrant to cite witnesses and havers.

[2](2) The sheriff may, subject to any statutory time limits, make an order altering the date of the proof or other hearing at which the witness is to give evidence and make such provision for intimation of such alteration to all parties concerned as he deems appropriate.

(3) An order fixing a hearing for a review application shall be intimated by the sheriff clerk–

(a) on the day the order is made; and

(b) in such manner as may be prescribed by the sheriff,

to all parties to the proceedings and such other persons as are named in the order where such parties or persons are not present at the time the order is made.

NOTES

1. As inserted by the Act of Sederunt (Child Care and Maintenance Rules) Amendment (Vulnerable Witnesses (Scotland) Act 2004) 2005/190 (Scottish SI) rule 2(3) (April 1, 2005)

2. As amended by the Act of Sederunt (Child Care and Maintenance Rules) Amendment (Vulnerable Witnesses (Scotland) Act 2004) 2006 (SSI 2006/75) rule 2(4) (effective April 1, 2006).

[1]Determination of Special Measures

NOTE

1. As inserted by the Act of Sederunt (Child Care and Maintenance Rules) Amendment (Vulnerable Witnesses (Scotland) Act 2004) 2005 (SSI 2005/190) rule 2(3) (effective April 1, 2005).

[1]**3.73.** When making an order under section 12(1), 12(6) or 13(2) of the Act of 2004 a sheriff may, in light thereof, make such further orders as he deems appropriate in all the circumstances.

NOTE

1. As inserted by the Act of Sederunt (Child Care and Maintenance Rules) Amendment (Vulnerable Witnesses (Scotland) Act 2004) 2005 (SSI 2005/190) rule 2(3) (effective April 1, 2005) and further amended by the Act of Sederunt (Child Care and Maintenance Rules) Amendment (Vulnerable Witnesses (Scotland) Act 2004) 2006 (SSI 2006/75) rule 2(5) (effective April 1, 2006).

[1]Intimation of an Order Under Section 12(1) or 13(2)

NOTE

1. As inserted by the Act of Sederunt (Child Care and Maintenance Rules) Amendment (Vulnerable Witnesses (Scotland) Act 2004) 2005 (SSI 2005/190) rule 2(3) (effective April 1, 2005).

[1]**3.74.** An order under section 12(1), 12(6) or 13(2) of the Act of 2004 shall be intimated by the sheriff clerk—

(a) on the day the order is made; and

(b) in such manner as may be prescribed by the sheriff,

to all parties to the proceedings and such other persons as are named in the order where such parties or persons are not present at the time the order is made.

NOTE

1. As inserted by the Act of Sederunt (Child Care and Maintenance Rules) Amendment (Vulnerable Witnesses (Scotland) Act 2004) 2005 (SSI 2005/190) rule 2(3) (effective April 1, 2005) and further amended by the Act of Sederunt (Child Care and Maintenance Rules) Amendment (Vulnerable Witnesses (Scotland) Act 2004) 2006 (SSI 2006/75) rule 2(5) (effective April 1, 2006).

[1]Lodging Audio and Audio-Visual Recordings and Documents

NOTE

1. Heading as inserted by the Act of Sederunt (Child Care and Maintenance Rules) Amendment (Vulnerable Witnesses (Scotland) Act 2004) 2005 (SSI 2005/190) rule 2(3) (effective April 1, 2005) and as substituted by the Act of Sederunt (Children's Hearings (Scotland) Act 2011)

(Miscellaneous Amendments) 2013 (SSI 2013/172) art.3(60)(c) (effective June 24, 2013: substitution has effect subject to transitional provisions specified in SSI 2013/172 art.8).

[1]**3.75.**—(1) Where evidence is taken on commission pursuant to an order made under section 12(1), 12(6) or 13(2) of the Act of 2004 the commissioner shall lodge any audio or audio-visual recording of the commission and relevant documents with the sheriff clerk.

(2) On any audio or audio-visual recording and any documents being lodged the sheriff clerk shall—
  (a) note—
    (i)   the documents lodged;
    (ii) by whom they were lodged; and
    (iii) the date on which they were lodged, and
  (b) intimate what he has noted to all parties concerned.

NOTE
1. As inserted by the Act of Sederunt (Child Care and Maintenance Rules) Amendment (Vulnerable Witnesses (Scotland) Act 2004) 2005 (SSI 2005/190) rule 2(3) (effective April 1, 2005) and further amended by the Act of Sederunt (Child Care and Maintenance Rules) Amendment (Vulnerable Witnesses (Scotland) Act 2004) 2006 (SSI 2006/75) rule 2(5) (effective April 1, 2006) and by the Act of Sederunt (Children's Hearings (Scotland) Act 2011) (Miscellaneous Amendments) 2013 (SSI 2013/172) art.3(60) (effective June 24, 2013: substitution has effect subject to transitional provisions specified in SSI 2013/172 art.8).

[1]Custody of Audio or Audio-Visual Recordings and Documents

NOTE
1. Heading as inserted by the Act of Sederunt (Child Care and Maintenance Rules) Amendment (Vulnerable Witnesses (Scotland) Act 2004) 2005 (SSI 2005/190) rule 2(3) (effective April 1, 2005) and further substituted by the Act of Sederunt (Children's Hearings (Scotland) Act 2011) (Miscellaneous Amendments) 2013 (SSI 2013/172) art.3(61)(c) (effective June 24, 2013: substitution has effect subject to transitional provisions specified in SSI 2013/172 art.8).

[1]**3.76.**—(1) The audio or audio-visual recording and documents referred to in rule 3.75 shall, subject to paragraph (2), be kept in the custody of the sheriff clerk.

(2) Where the audio or audio-visual recording of the evidence of a witness is in the custody of the sheriff clerk under this rule and where intimation has been given to that effect under rule 3.75(2), the name and address of that witness and the record of his evidence shall be treated as being in the knowledge of the parties; and no party shall be required, notwithstanding any enactment to the contrary—
  (a) to include the name of that witness in any list of witnesses; or
  (b) to include the record of his evidence in any list of productions.

NOTE
1. As inserted by the Act of Sederunt (Child Care and Maintenance Rules) Amendment (Vulnerable Witnesses (Scotland) Act 2004) 2005 (SSI 2005/190) rule 2(3) (effective April 1, 2005) and further amended by the Act of Sederunt (Children's Hearings (Scotland) Act 2011) (Miscellaneous Amendments) 2013 (SSI 2013/172) art.3(61) (effective June 24, 2013: amendment has effect subject to transitional provisions specified in SSI 2013/172 art.8).

[1]Part XIA

Part XIA Cases Involving Sexual Behaviour

Note

1. A new rule 3.76A is inserted and existing rules 3.77–3.81 are moved into a new Part XIA by the Act of Sederunt (Children's Hearings (Scotland) Act 2011) (Miscellaneous Amendments) 2013 (SSI 2013/172) art.3(62) (effective June 24, 2013: amendment has effect subject to transitional provisions specified in SSI 2013/172 art.8).

Interpretation and application of this Part

[1]**3.76A.**—(1) This Part of Chapter 3 applies to proceedings where—

(a) an application is made to the sheriff under section 93(2)(a), 94(2)(a) or 110 of the 2011 Act or an appeal is made under Part 15 of the 2011 Act; and

(b) the section 67 ground involves sexual behaviour engaged in by any person.

(2) In the case of relevant appeals the provisions of sections 173 to 175 of the 2011 Act shall be deemed to apply as they apply to applications.

(3) The evidence referred to in section 173(2) of the 2011 Act may be in writing or take the form of an audio or audio-visual recording.

(4) In this Part an "admission application" means an application to the sheriff for an order as to evidence pursuant to section 175(1) of the 2011 Act.

Note

1. A new rule 3.76A is inserted and existing rules 3.77–3.81 are moved into a new Part XIA by the Act of Sederunt (Children's Hearings (Scotland) Act 2011) (Miscellaneous Amendments) 2013 (SSI 2013/172) art.3(62) (effective June 24, 2013: amendment has effect subject to transitional provisions specified in SSI 2013/172 art.8).

[1]Application for Admission of Restricted Evidence

Note

1. A new rule 3.76A is inserted and existing rules 3.77–3.81 are moved into a new Part XIA by the Act of Sederunt (Children's Hearings (Scotland) Act 2011) (Miscellaneous Amendments) 2013 (SSI 2013/172) art.3(62) (effective June 24, 2013: amendment has effect subject to transitional provisions specified in SSI 2013/172 art.8).

[1]**3.77.**—(1) An admission application shall be in Form 79.

(2) Where an admission application is made during the sheriff's hearing of the case, the sheriff may dispense with the requirements of paragraph (1).

Note

1. A new rule 3.76A is inserted and existing rules 3.77–3.81 are moved into a new Part XIA by the Act of Sederunt (Children's Hearings (Scotland) Act 2011) (Miscellaneous Amendments) 2013 (SSI 2013/172) art.3(62) (effective June 24, 2013: amendment has effect subject to transitional provisions specified in SSI 2013/172 art.8).

[1]**3.78.**—[2](1) Where an admission application is made under rule 3.77, the applicant shall intimate a copy of the admission application to all other parties to the proceedings and to any safeguarder and complete a certificate of intimation.

(2) A certificate of intimation referred to in this rule shall be in Form 80 and shall be lodged together with the admission application.

Notes

1. A new rule 3.76A is inserted and existing rules 3.77–3.81 are moved into a new Part XIA by the Act of Sederunt (Children's Hearings (Scotland) Act 2011) (Miscellaneous Amendments) 2013

(SSI 2013/172) art.3(62) (effective June 24, 2013: amendment has effect subject to transitional provisions specified in SSI 2013/172 art.8).
2. As amended by the Act of Sederunt (Children's Hearings (Scotland) Act 2011) (Miscellaneous Amendments) 2013 (SSI 2013/172) art.3(63)(d) and (64) and (effective June 24, 2013: amendment has effect subject to transitional provisions specified in SSI 2013/172 art.8).

[1]**3.79.**—(1) On receipt of an admission application, a sheriff may–

[2](a) grant the admission application in whole or in part;

(b) require of any of the parties further information before making any further order;

(c) fix a date for a hearing of the admission application and grant warrant to cite witnesses and havers.

(2) The sheriff may, subject to any statutory time limits, make an order altering the date of the proof or other hearing to which the admission application relates and make such provision for intimation of such alteration to all parties concerned as he deems appropriate.

(3) An order fixing a hearing for an admission application shall be intimated by the sheriff clerk–

(a) on the day the order is made; and

(b) in such manner as may be prescribed by the sheriff,

to all parties to the proceedings and such other persons as are named in the order where such parties or persons are not present at the time the order is made.

NOTES
1. A new rule 3.76A is inserted and existing rules 3.77–3.81 are moved into a new Part XIA by the Act of Sederunt (Children's Hearings (Scotland) Act 2011) (Miscellaneous Amendments) 2013 (SSI 2013/172) art.3(62) (effective June 24, 2013: amendment has effect subject to transitional provisions specified in SSI 2013/172 art.8).
2. As substituted by the Act of Sederunt (Children's Hearings (Scotland) Act 2011) (Miscellaneous Amendments) 2013 (SSI 2013/172) art.3(65) (effective June 24, 2013: substitution has effect subject to transitional provisions specified in SSI 2013/172 art.8).

[1]**3.80.**—(1) When making an order pursuant to rule 3.79(1)(a) a sheriff may, in light thereof, make such further orders as he deems appropriate in all the circumstances.

NOTE
1. A new rule 3.76A is inserted and existing rules 3.77–3.81 are moved into a new Part XIA by the Act of Sederunt (Children's Hearings (Scotland) Act 2011) (Miscellaneous Amendments) 2013 (SSI 2013/172) art.3(62) (effective June 24, 2013: amendment has effect subject to transitional provisions specified in SSI 2013/172 art.8).

[1]**3.81.**—(1) An order made pursuant to rule 3.79(1)(a) shall be intimated by the sheriff clerk–

(a) on the day the order is made; and

(b) in such manner as may be prescribed by the sheriff,

to all parties to the proceedings and such other persons as are named in the order where such parties or persons are not present at the time the order is made.

NOTE
1. A new rule 3.76A is inserted and existing rules 3.77–3.81 are moved into a new Part XIA by the Act of Sederunt (Children's Hearings (Scotland) Act 2011) (Miscellaneous Amendments) 2013 (SSI 2013/172) art.3(62) (effective June 24, 2013: amendment has effect subject to transitional provisions specified in SSI 2013/172 art.8).

[1]Lodging restricted evidence

Note

1. A new rule 3.76A is inserted and existing rules 3.77–3.81 are moved into a new Part XIA by the Act of Sederunt (Children's Hearings (Scotland) Act 2011) (Miscellaneous Amendments) 2013 (SSI 2013/172) art.3(62) (effective June 24, 2013: amendment has effect subject to transitional provisions specified in SSI 2013/172 art.8).

[1]**3.81A.**—(1) Where the sheriff makes an order under section 175(1) or (c) of the 2011 Act, the applicant shall lodge any relevant recording and documents with the sheriff clerk.

(2) On the recording and documents being lodged the sheriff clerk shall—

(a) note—

(i) the evidence lodged;

(ii) by whom they were lodged;

(iii) the date on which they were lodged; and

(b) intimate what he or she has noted to all parties concerned.

(3) The recording and documents referred to in paragraph (1) shall, subject to paragraph (4), be kept in the custody of the sheriff clerk.

(4) Where the recording of the evidence of a witness is in the custody of the sheriff clerk under this rule and where intimation has been given to that effect under paragraph (2), the name and address of that witness and the record of his or her evidence shall be treated as being in the knowledge of the parties; and no party shall be required, notwithstanding any enactment to the contrary—

(a) to include the name of that witness in any list of witnesses; or

(b) to include the record of his or her evidence in any list of productions.

Note

1. A new rule 3.76A is inserted and existing rules 3.77–3.81 are moved into a new Part XIA by the Act of Sederunt (Children's Hearings (Scotland) Act 2011) (Miscellaneous Amendments) 2013 (SSI 2013/172) art.3(62) (effective June 24, 2013: amendment has effect subject to transitional provisions specified in SSI 2013/172 art.8).

INDEX